WESTMINSTER:
A BIOGRAPHY

WESTMINSTER: A BIOGRAPHY

From Earliest Times to the Present

Robert Shepherd

 The National Archives

B L O O M S B U R Y
LONDON • NEW DELHI • NEW YORK • SYDNEY

Bloomsbury Academic

An imprint of Bloomsbury Publishing Plc

50 Bedford Square	175 Fifth Avenue
London	New York
WC1B 3DP	NY 10010
UK	USA

www.bloomsbury.com

First published 2012

Reprinted 2012

British Library Cataloguing-in-Publication Data
A catalogue record for this book is available from the British Library.

ISBN: HB: 978-0-8264-2380-1

Typeset by Fakenham Prepress Solutions, Fakenham, Norfolk NR21 8NN
Printed and bound in Great Britain

CONTENTS

Author's Note ix
List of Maps and Plans xi
Maps and Plans xiv

PART ONE BEGINNINGS 1

1 'That terrible place' 3

2 The Confessor and his marvel 11

3 'Two nations in the womb' 19

4 Norman rule and resistance 25

PART TWO MAKING THE ROYAL CAPITAL 35

5 An unlikely founding father 37

6 Seat of government 45

7 'The most glorious work in England' 51

8 Parliament 63

9 Edward I and the Stone of Destiny 69

10 From Charing Cross to St Stephen's 77

11 Chaucer's Westminster 83

12 Raising the roof 91

13 Sanctity and sanctuary 97

PART THREE **REVOLUTIONARIES** 105

14 A new era 107

15 Whitehall Palace 115

16 End of the old order 123

17 The shape of things to come 131

18 A tale of two sisters 135

19 Holy terror 143

20 Scandal and splendour 151

21 Killing the king 157

22 Republicans and restorers 169

23 Flight and fire 179

PART FOUR **NEW POLITICAL CAPITAL** 189

24 Cockpit of power 191

25 Number 10 and the prime minister 201

26 Georgian icons 207

27 Mobs and scribblers 215

28 Pitt's village 227

29 From bad debts to high hopes 233

30 Village at war 237

31 Assassination 243

32 Royal farce 249

33 Reform 255

34 Fire! 261

PART FIVE GLOBAL ICONS 265

35 Victorian phoenix 267

36 Golden age 275

37 Dynamite 287

38 Pomp and circumstance 293

39 War and peace 303

40 Bitter fruit 311

41 Finest hour 321

42 Masters and modernisers 329

43 New wine in old bottles 341

Notes 353
Bibliography 385
Index 393

AUTHOR'S NOTE

This book is about the heart of Westminster, a cockpit of power for a thousand years. Westminster is a political capital, a ceremonial stage and a spiritual centre. Its heart largely corresponds to the area occupied by the medieval town. It is less than a mile in length, from north to south, and no more than half a mile in width, from east to west. It is home to Westminster Abbey, the Palace of Westminster, Whitehall and Downing Street, and is bordered by Trafalgar Square to the north, the Thames to the east, Millbank to the south and St James's Park to the west.

Maps of the area at various dates, together with plans of the Palace of Westminster, Westminster Abbey and the old Whitehall Palace, are grouped together at the start of the book for ease of reference.

I am especially indebted in researching and writing this book to the librarians and staff of the London Library, the City of Westminster and the Royal Borough of Kensington and Chelsea, for their courteous and efficient assistance.

I should like to thank Richard Mortimer, Keeper of the Muniments at Westminster Abbey, and his colleagues at the Abbey's Library and Museum, for their advice and help with research. I should also like to thank Duncan Jeffery, Assistant Receiver General (Communications) and Laura King, Press and Communications Officer, for allowing me access to Westminster Abbey. I am grateful to Dr Simon Thurley and Simon Hurst for answering my queries.

I should also like to thank the following for their assistance with the maps and plans: Dr Mark Collins, Estates Archivist and Historian, Parliamentary Estates Directorate; Christine Reynolds, Assistant Keeper of the Muniments, at Westminster Abbey; Rory Lalwan, Senior Archives Assistant, and his colleagues at the City of Westminster Archives Centre; and Laura Simpson and Hester Vaizey at the National Archives, Kew.

I am grateful to the following for permission to reproduce the maps and plans: The British Museum for Civitas Londinium (The Agas Map of London), c.1560; The National Archives for A Survey & Ground Plot of the Royal Palace of White Hall, by Fisher, engraved and published by George Vertue, 1747; John Rocque's Map of London, 1745/6; Plan of the Cities of London and Westminster, by Richard

Horwood; Westminster City Archives for Parts of the Parishes of St Martin, St Margaret and St John, *c.*1900, the Strand Board of Works; The Parliamentary Estate for plans of the Medieval Palace of Westminster in the Eighteenth Century and The Palace of Westminster, Principal Floor Plan (nineteenth century); The Dean and Chapter of Westminster for the plan of Westminster Abbey; and the Ordnance Survey for the street plan of modern Westminster.

My editors, Ben Hayes, who commissioned this book, and Claire Lipscomb, who provided encouragement and advice, and their colleagues at Continuum deserve special thanks. I also owe a debt of gratitude to Jonathan Pegg and Shaheeda Sabir for all their support.

I should also like to thank everybody with whom I have worked at BBC Westminster for their friendship and support, and all those at the Houses of Parliament, in Downing Street, across Whitehall and at Westminster Abbey, who have allowed me access on many occasions, made me welcome and in the process taught me a great deal about Westminster's past.

While every effort has been made to trace the owners of copyright, the author and publisher will be happy to rectify any errors or omissions in further editions.

Robert Shepherd, London, 2012

LIST OF MAPS AND PLANS

1 Westminster, from the Abbey to Charing Cross, *c.*1560, in Elizabeth I's reign (p.xiv): From Civitatis Londinium. Source: Crace Collection, XVII.3, The British Library; © The Trustees of the British Museum.

2 Whitehall Palace in 1680, during Charles II's reign (p.xv): From A Survey and Ground Plot of the Royal Palace of Whitehall with the Lodgings and Apartments belonging to the their Majesties, AD 1680, by Inigo Fisher, engraved by George Vertue, 1747. Source: The National Archives, London, Englamd (MPE1/325). © Crown copyright and database right 2012.

3 Westminster, 1746, with its first bridge and new Bridge Street and Parliament Street (p.xvi): From Plan of the Cities of London and Westminster and the Borough of Southwark, by John Rocque. Image reproduced courtesy of The National Archives, London, England (MR1/874).

4 Westminster, 1746, showing its growth south of the Abbey (p.xvii): From Plan of the Cities of London and Westminster and the Borough of Southwark, by John Rocque. Image reproduced courtesy of The National Archives, London England (MR1/874).

5 Westminster in the 1790s, when Pitt the Younger was Prime Minister (p.xviii): London and surrounding area surveyed by R. Horwood, Image reproduced courtesy of The National Archives, London, England (MR1/683).

6 The old Palace of Westminster at the end of the eighteenth century (p.xix): Source: Medieval Palace: Parliamentary Estates Directorate (Plowman Craven); © Parliamentary Copyright.

7 The Palace of Westminster's Principal Floor, built in the nineteenth century (p.xx): Source: The Principal Floor Plan, Parliamentary Estates Directorate (J. Rix); © Parliamentary Copyright.

8 Westminster in 1900, before King Street and nearby streets were demolished (p.xxi): From Parts of the Parishes of St Margaret, St Martin and St John, by Arthur Ventris, Surveyor and Engineer to the Board of Works for the Strand District, c.1900. Source: City of Westminster Archives Centre; © City of Westminster Archives Centre.

9 Westminster Abbey (p.xxii): Line drawing of Westminster Abbey. Source: The Muniment Room & Library, Westminster Abbey; © Dean and Chapter of Westminster.

10 Modern Westminster, street plan (p.xxiii): From: Ordnance Survey. Source: Contains Ordnance Survey data © Crown copyright and database right 2012.

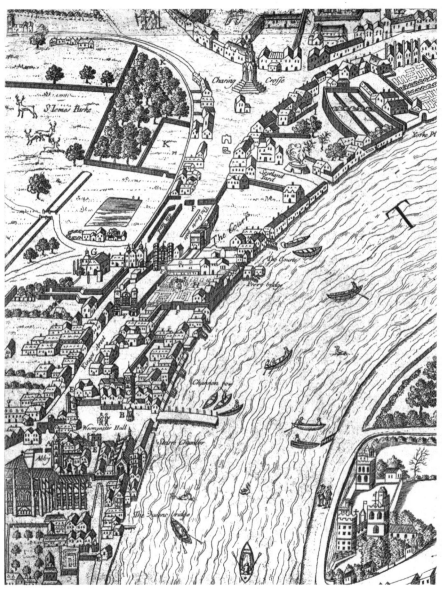

FIGURE 1 Westminster, from the Abbey to Charing Cross, *c.*1560, in Elizabeth I's reign

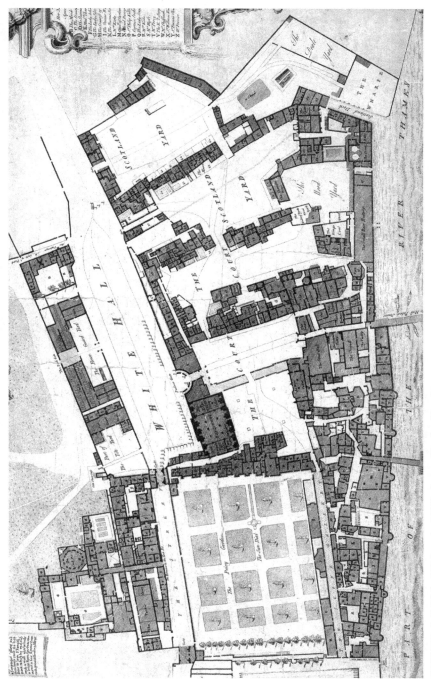

FIGURE 2 Whitehall Palace in 1680, during Charles II's reign

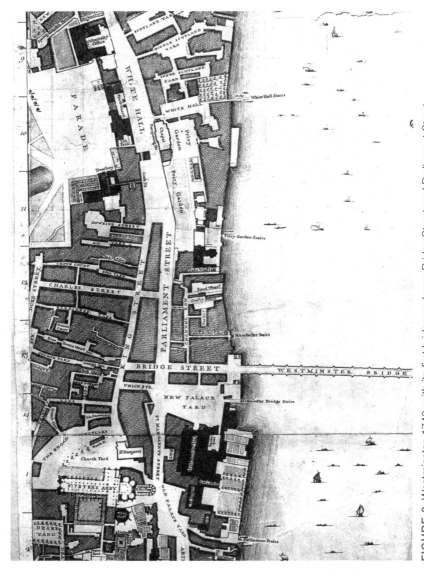

FIGURE 3 Westminster, 1746, with its first bridge and new Bridge Street and Parliament Street

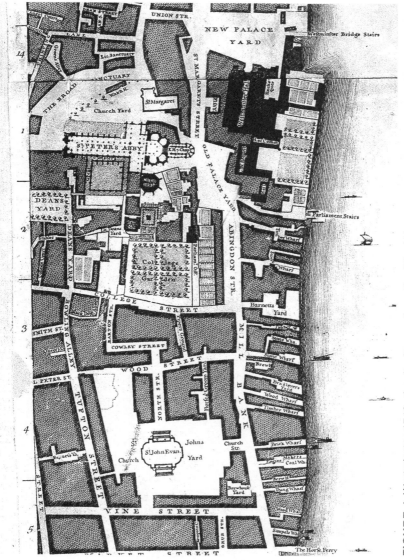

FIGURE 4 Westminster, 1746, showing its growth south of the Abbey

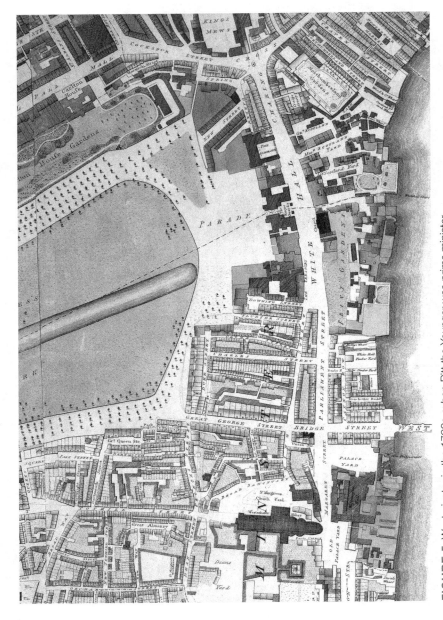

FIGURE 5 Westminster in the 1790s, when Pitt the Younger was prime minister

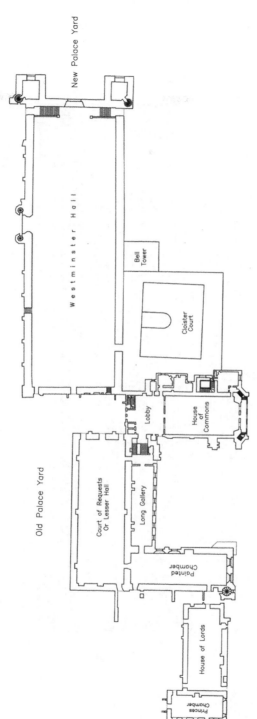

FIGURE 6 The old Palace of Westminster at the end of the eighteenth century

New Palace Yard

Westminster Hall

Bell Tower

Cloister Court

Old Palace Yard

Lobby

House of Commons

Court of Requests Or Lesser Hall

Long Gallery

Painted Chamber

House of Lords

Princes Chamber

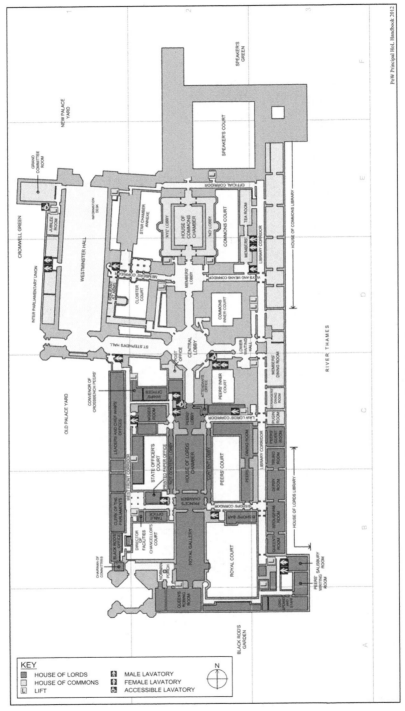

FIGURE 7 The Palace of Westminster's Principal Floor, built in the nineteenth century

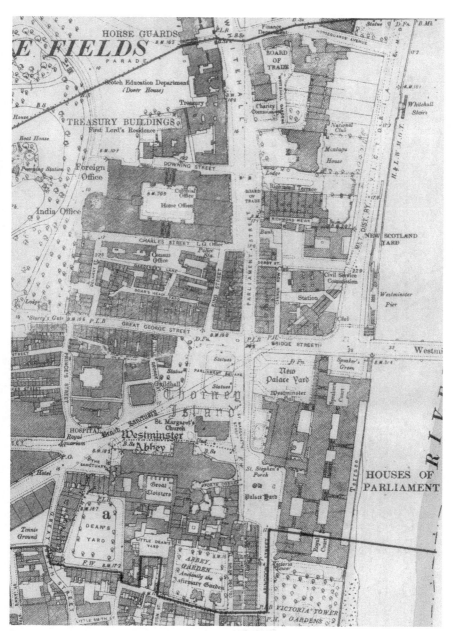

FIGURE 8 Westminster in 1900, before ancient King Street and nearby streets were demolished. 'Thorney Island' is also marked by St Margaret's Church.

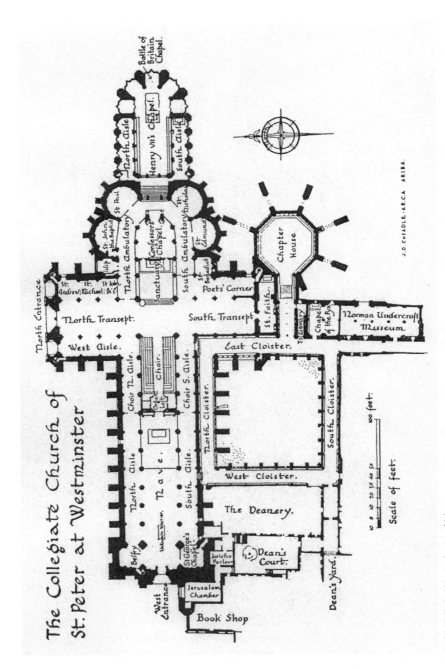

The Collegiate Church of St. Peter at Westminster

J.O. CHEADLE · A.R.C.A · A.R.I.B.A.

Battle of Britain Chapel.

North Aisle

Henry VII's Chapel.

South Aisle

St Paul

St John the Baptist

St John the Evangelist

St Nicholas

Confessor's Chapel.

North Ambulatory

Sanctuary

South Ambulatory

St Edmund

St Benedict

St. Andrew. St. Michael. St John Ev'l.

North Entrance

North Transept.

Poet's Corner

South Transept

Chapter House

St Faith.

Library

Chapel of the Pyx

Norman Undercroft Museum

West Aisle.

East Cloister.

North Cloister.

Choir N. Aisle.

Choir.

Choir S. Aisle.

South Cloister.

Organ Loft.

Nave.

North Aisle

South Aisle

West Cloister.

The Deanery.

Belfry

Unknown Warrior

St George's Chapel

Jericho Parlour

Dean's Court.

Dean's Yard.

West Entrance

Jerusalem Chamber

Book Shop

100 feet.

10 0 10 20 30 40 50

Scale of feet.

FIGURE 9   Westminster Abbey

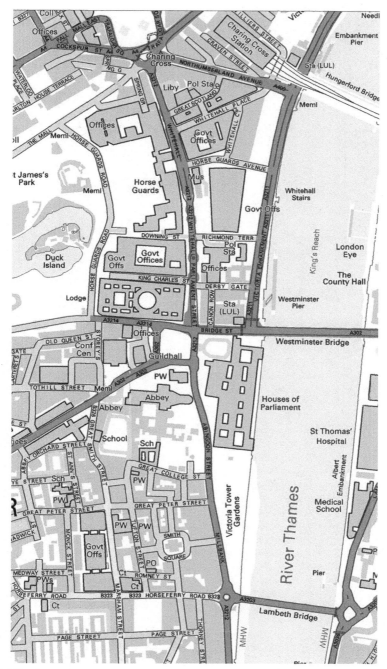

FIGURE 10 Modern Westminster, street plan

PART ONE

BEGINNINGS

1 'THAT TERRIBLE PLACE'

Westminster has always been concerned with its image. A charter, dated AD 785, states, chillingly, '*in loco terribili, quod dicitur aet Westmunster*' – '[in] that terrible place which is known as Westminster'. These words, written on a small, stiff vellum sheet measuring about 6½ inches by 8½ inches and closely packed with neat lines of small script, were once thought to be the earliest written reference to Westminster. However, the charter is a much later forgery that was sanctioned in the 1150s by Osbert of Clare, a prior at Westminster Abbey. Prior Osbert must rank as one of Westminster's earliest known 'spin doctors'.

With today's widespread cynicism about politics, many may be tempted to agree that Westminster is indeed a 'terrible place'. But why would Osbert, whose purpose in life was to laud his beloved Abbey, describe Westminster in this way? Some have assumed that he was describing the geographical location of early Westminster as 'terrible', in the sense of being desolate. However, Arthur Stanley, an eminent Victorian Dean of Westminster, suggests that although the site of Westminster was originally 'marsh within marsh and forest within forest', it 'presented several points of attraction'. With fresh water, dry land and plenty of fish to eat, it was not all that inhospitable.[1]

The most likely explanation is that Osbert used the word 'terrible' in a very different sense to its usual meaning today. He wanted to show that Westminster had a long-established reputation for holy terror, by which he meant religious awe. His choice of language, or 'spin', as it would be called in modern Westminster, reflects the monks' sensitivities about the Abbey's antiquity and its rivalry with other great, religious houses. Osbert's motives were to win a legal dispute with St Albans Abbey over a contested piece of land in Hertfordshire, and to bestow upon Westminster a spiritual reputation that stretched back to earliest times.

The key to Westminster's character lies in its origins, its myths and its rivalries. Its story begins between 8,000 and 9,000 years ago when rising sea levels, after the last Ice Age, separated Britain from continental Europe. The landscape eventually began to assume its present contours. The Thames was wider and shallower than today's embanked river, with gravel and sand bars dotted across its clay-covered flood plain. Between about 6,500 and 5,000 years ago, one such bar gradually evolved into a small island, or eyot, on the west bank of the Thames as it meandered northwards on its journey to the sea.

Many histories of London and Westminster state that this island was formed as a result of another ancient river, the Tyburn, flowing into the Thames at this point. The Tyburn's route can be traced from its source in modern-day Hampstead as it passes beneath Marylebone and Mayfair, across Piccadilly and Green Park, and finally through Pimlico, where it joins the Thames near Vauxhall Bridge. However, the notion that the Tyburn diverged near the present Buckingham Palace and a second stream flowed through Westminster to meet the Thames near the Abbey, is unproven. An erroneous nineteenth-century map seems to have caused the trouble. This common mistake is dismissed magisterially in the recent volume on the City of Westminster in the Victoria History of the Counties of England series: 'there is no evidence that the medieval watercourses around the abbey site were linked to the Tyburn'.[2]

These 'medieval watercourses' were probably natural springs and streams. The main one was known as 'Longditch', and arose to the north of ancient Westminster, near the present Pall Mall or possibly in the eponymous Spring Gardens, to the west of Whitehall, near Trafalgar Square. Longditch ran southwards, between modern-day Whitehall and St James's Park, along Storey's Gate and across Tothill Street before passing round the south of the Abbey precincts and heading into the Thames. North of the Abbey and the Palace of Westminster, another stream (known as the Clowson in the Middle Ages and later as the King's Ditch) ran across the present Whitehall and into the Thames: whether it was linked to Longditch is unclear. Other streams arose in what is now St James's Park.[3]

The small island created by the Thames and the local streams that flowed into it was 'overgrown with thorns, and environed with water', according to John Stow, the sixteenth-century historian of London. He was explaining the origins of the island's name of Thorney, derived from Anglo-Saxon (the '-ey' denoting an island). Thorney's natural advantages were better described by Dean Stanley, whose worrying fondness for spending long nights digging among the royal coffins in the Abbey's vaults, made him something of an expert on the local topography: 'the gravel soil and the close, fine sand, still dug up under the floor of the Abbey and in St Margaret's churchyard was necessarily healthy; and in the centre of the thickets, there bubbled up at least one spring, perhaps two'. Stanley identified one spring in the churchyard and another in Dean's Yard. The latter 'was the vivifying centre of all that has grown up around' and continued supplying fresh water in the late nineteenth century through a 'well-worn pump'.[4]

Westminster Abbey occupies the crown of the old Thorney Island; Parliament Square stands on a plateau. To the east, the island slopes down to the shore of the Thames where the Houses of Parliament and the entrance to Westminster under-ground station now stand. Elsewhere, its northern shore lies across the present

Parliament Street, its western shore is by Storey's Gate and Great Smith Street, and its southern shore runs across Millbank. Some 4,000 years ago, the crown of the island was about ten feet above the shore line. Thorney was attractive to settlers, offering close supplies of timber for building and fuel; reeds and rushes for thatch and fodder, and meat from wildlife in the nearby marshes, rivers and woods.

By the mid-Bronze Age, 3,500 years ago, the island was farmed by communities in the area and was partly cleared for cultivation. The earliest surviving structure in the area was unearthed in 1983 north of Thorney, on a site in Richmond Terrace, between Whitehall and the Embankment. Carbon-dating showed that an alder wood platform and post were installed about 2,500 years ago. There is evidence of an Iron Age woodland beneath New Palace Yard and of arable cultivation beneath Storey's Gate. Celtic items found in the Thames near Westminster, including a bronze parade helmet by Waterloo Bridge and a shield at Battersea, suggest that offerings were being made to the gods along this stretch of the river about 2,000 years ago, by which time a rise in the river level had submerged the sites of today's underground station, Westminster Hall and the Houses of Parliament. In Roman times, Thorney's dimensions were about 500 yards by 320.[5]

Thorney offered a solid base for ferrying people and goods across the Thames or further along the river. Intrepid traders and travellers picked their way through the marshy terrain by following lines of stakes along an ancient trackway on the route of present-day Tothill Street. 'Tot' or 'Toot' is said to have been derived from 'Teut', the old British name for the god of travelling merchants and wayfarers, and the source of our 'Tuesday'. The god was represented by sacred stones set upon high ground, hence 'Tot-hills'. An ancient lease names a local field as the 'Toothill', signifying the highest local point, where a beacon might also have been lit and an observation post manned. Originally, the hill was probably another gravel bar in the Thames flood plain. Although it was long since flattened by urban development, it also lent its name to Tothill Fields, the marshy common land to the south of Westminster.

The Thames may have been fordable at Thorney, as a sand bar extends from the ancient island into the river. Before the Embankment was built in the 1860s, which made the river narrower and deeper, a boy from Westminster School claimed to have waded across at low tide. By the time of the main Roman invasion in AD 43, the dominant tribe in southern England, the Catuvellauni, were using Thorney as a river crossing to transport foodstuffs, metals and slaves from their stronghold at Verulanium (near St Albans) to Europe via the port of Richborough in east Kent, in return for luxuries. It became a main artery of Roman Britain and was later known as Watling Street. An architectural historian of the Abbey, W. R. Lethaby, claimed that, 'there is much evidence to show that the great Roman road, later called the Watling Street, passed close by a river ford'.[6]

The river crossing, whether by ferry or ford, was made slightly upstream from where Westminster Bridge stands, between the present-day Houses of

Parliament on the west bank and the Albert Embankment on the east bank, where St Thomas's Hospital stands. Before the hospital was built in the early 1870s, this area was known as Stangate and had long been the site of a ferry. The eighteenth century antiquary, William Stukeley, called it 'Stanega Ferry', and nineteenth century historians supported the idea that it stood on the Roman route: 'from Lambeth to Fisher's Gate on the Sussex coast, the word *Gate* is added to the names of nearly all the places through which the Roman road passes'.[7]

Thorney's destiny was changed after AD 50 by the Romans' decision to build a new town downstream, where the river's depth and narrowness allowed sea-going vessels to berth and a bridge to be built. Londinium became a magnet for traders and travellers, and Thorney was put under cultivation to supply the booming town. However, a significant Roman settlement was established on the site of the present abbey. A second century sculpture of a child was discovered in Great College Street, remnants of fine Gaulish ware were found on a Romano-British rubbish pit near Number 10 Downing Street, and a Roman boat was found at Storey's Gate, by the old Longditch. The insistence of the Abbey's medieval monks that a Roman Temple of Apollo had been the first building on Thorney probably owed more to their rivalry with St Paul's Cathedral than to historical accuracy. John Flete elaborated this idea in the fifteenth century by suggesting that in AD 184 a British king, Lucius, a convert to Christianity, built the first church, although during Diocletian's rule it became a pagan Temple of Apollo. However, there never was a British 'King Lucius'.[8]

The founders of the first church on Thorney were probably Anglo-Saxon traders. From the AD 600s until about AD 850, Anglo-Saxon London, or *Lundenwic*, lay between the old Roman capital and Thorney. This vibrant trading centre straddled the area now occupied by Aldwych and the Strand. During the late eighth century, some traders moved to its western outskirts and lived in a substantial timber hall immediately to the north of Thorney on what is now Treasury Green, by Number 10 Downing Street. A new hall seems to have replaced the first one during the ninth century.[9]

These settlers may have founded a small wooden church, or minster, on Thorney. Being located to the west of *Lundenwic*, it was called the 'west minster'. There was a tradition that the land was originally granted by Offa, the powerful Anglo-Saxon king of Mercia, in the eighth century. However, Anglo-Saxon prosperity attracted Viking raiders from the AD 830s and the minster was severely damaged and eventually deserted. Only the West Saxon dynasty survived and eventually repulsed the Danish occupation. At sometime around AD 959 a new monastery church of St Peter's was founded on Thorney by Dunstan (*c.*909–88), who was related to the Wessex kings, enjoyed their patronage as abbot of Glastonbury (*c.*943), and encouraged a monastic revival as Bishop of Worcester (957–9) and London (959), and Archbishop of Canterbury (959–88).

The precise date of Westminster Abbey's foundation is disputed, but it was possibly in AD 959, that Edgar, the Wessex ruler of England, gave Dunstan the site on Thorney Island and permission to establish a Benedictine monastery. In all, Dunstan spent more than £200 buying land for the monastery, including five hides (600 acres) at Westminster. But the king, to the monks' great irritation, sold Dunstan land that might have previously belonged to the church before being absorbed into the royal demesne. The earliest authentic mention of Westminster occurs in a document dated 993.[10]

Dunstan recruited twelve Benedictine monks from Glastonbury. The black-robed monks were to become important figures in the Westminster village that grew around the Abbey and were a familiar sight there for nearly 600 years. Another of Dunstan's legacies has outlasted the monks. In AD 973, he established the *Ordo* for Edgar's coronation at Bath as King of England in a ceremony that epitomized Dunstan's belief in church and state working together. His *Ordo* remains the basis for the English coronation ritual to this day.

But soon after Edgar's coronation, another series of Danish raids began and in 1016 the Dane Cnut became King of England. Cnut possibly built the first royal palace at Westminster. He lives on in English folklore as 'King Canute' who stupidly ordered the tide to stop coming in. An early account of this incident was given by Henry, Archdeacon of Huntingdon, in about 1130. According to Henry, when the tide came in and soaked Cnut, the king cried: 'Let all the world know the power of kings is empty and worthless, and there is no king worthy of the name save Him by whose will heaven, earth, and sea obey eternal laws'. Far from portraying Cnut as a fool, Henry describes the incident as one of the king's 'magnificent deeds'. For the remainder of his reign, Cnut 'never wore the golden crown, but placed it on the image of the crucified Lord, in eternal praise of God the great king'. But Henry's depiction of Cnut as a pious and humble king was, perhaps, an early instance of what we now call political 'spin'.[11]

The idea that Henry of Huntingdon put a spin on his account of Cnut's reign raises an intriguing possibility. Henry's account was written about a century after the event. It seems likely, according to Diana Greenway, who edited and translated Henry's history, that some of his accounts were drawn from English stories or ballads. It is plausible that some of these spoken sources voiced popular dissent, since Cnut had continued to impose an unpopular, land tax ('Danegeld') to fund his standing army. Today's popular version that ridicules Cnut may therefore be closer to the early folk stories and ballads than it is to Henry of Huntingdon's later obsequious account.[12]

We are unlikely ever to know for certain if Cnut's confrontation with the waves occurred or where it happened; but there are good reasons for thinking that, if it happened, the location was Thorney. By the mid-eleventh century, the Thames had become tidal there and it was also a period of major flooding. The incident was first located at Thorney by the Anglo-Norman poet, Geffrie Gaimark, whose *L'Estoire des Engleis* appeared in the 1130s at about the same time as Henry of Huntingdon's account and, presumably, drew on the same popular sources. Gaimark was later echoed by the chroniclers Fabyan and Knyghton who, according to Dean Stanley, located the dramatic incident 'on the banks of the Thames as it ran by the Palace of Westminster at flowing tide, and the waves cast forth some part of their water towards him, and came up to his thighs'. The sixteenth-century historian, John Norden also locates Cnut's soaking near a royal palace. He adds that, 'in the time of Edward the Confessor, a palace at Westminster was destroyed by fire, which had been inhabited by Canute about the year 1035'.[13]

Norden's comments assume added significance following the recent discovery of evidence for a palace at Thorney in the early eleventh century. A timber structure found beneath Parliament Square, on the east of the central island and under the road opposite New Palace Yard, may have been a timber bridge across a wide, walled ditch built *c.*950–1050 and probably in the early eleventh century. This walled ditch, bordering the Palace and Abbey precincts, and what appears to have been a bridge entering the palace, almost certainly pre-date the reign of Edward the Confessor. The circumstantial evidence is persuasive that Cnut was the first king to build his palace at Westminster. Royal palaces in Europe were traditionally built adjacent to a monastery, and it made sense for a Danish king to establish a base on the Thames.[14]

The Abbey on Thorney also served as a temporary prison for the infant sons of Edmund 'Ironside', Cnut's Wessex rival for the crown, who had been assassinated in 1016; but the young princes were soon shipped abroad. Cnut became a benefactor to the Abbey and donated relics that supposedly included an arm of St Cyriacus, covered in gold and silver, which could be seen in the Abbey as late as the fourteenth century.

The inspiration behind Cnut's close interest in the Abbey was Wulnoth, a monk celebrated for 'his great wisdom and fine elocution'. Cnut is said to have procured Wulnoth's appointment as abbot early in his reign, in about 1020. Widmore suggests that because of this 'interest at court the monastery was preserved from any molestation in those troublesome times'. The Abbey was 'so near the King's Palace', Widmore ventures, that it was 'no wonder that the king and his courtiers were acquainted with the church and the abbot, and became benefactors to the place'.[15]

Events after Cnut's sudden death in 1035 were to demonstrate Westminster's new-found importance. A bitter wrangle over the succession ensued between his young sons. Harold 'Harefoot' had been born to Cnut's first wife Aelfigu of Northampton while Harthacnut was the son of the second wife Emma of Normandy, the widow of Ethelred II, known as 'Ethelred the Unready'. A partition of England failed, and after only two years, 'Harefoot' ruled all England as King Harold I. When he died in March 1040, he became the first English king to be buried in the Abbey. Harold's claim to the throne had been disputed, and either he or his advisers probably thought that his legitimacy as monarch would be enhanced by making Westminster Abbey his final resting place.

A grisly incident on one mid-summer's day in 1040 indicates the Abbey's symbolic significance. Gathered at Harold's grave was a high-powered posse, including the Archbishop of York, Aelfir Puttoc; Godwin, Earl of Wessex; the royal officials, Stir and Eadric; and the executioner, Thrond. In public view, they dug up the dead king's decomposing body, removed it from the Abbey and disposed of it in the nearby marshes. This macabre, public disinterment was performed on the orders of Harthacnut, Harold's half-brother and successor, in an attempt to undermine Harold's legitimacy as monarch. Harold's body was found in a ditch by a local fisherman and re-buried in the cemetery for Danish settlers, where St Clement Danes now stands in the Strand.

Harthacnut's reign was brief. He died in 1042, aged only about 23, after suddenly collapsing at a wedding feast in Lambeth, across the river from Westminster. The Danes had ruled England for fewer than 30 years. Harthacnut was succeeded by his half-brother Edward, the son of Ethelred II and Emma. Edward, known to history as 'the Confessor' to distinguish him from his murdered uncle, Edward the Martyr, was to make Westminster the ceremonial capital of England.[16]

2 THE CONFESSOR AND HIS MARVEL

Westminster was a secluded suburb during the early years of Edward the Confessor's reign. After Cnut's palace burned down, the monastery was 'insignificant in buildings and numbers, for under the Abbot only a small community of monks served Christ. Moreover, the endowments of the faithful were slender, and provided no more than their daily bread'. This sketch from *Vita Aedwardi Regis*, a life of King Edward, by a visiting monk from St Bertin's monastery in Flanders, scarcely suggests that Westminster was about to become Edward's capital, but its proximity to London was important:

> … it both lay hard by the famous and rich town and also was a delightful spot, surrounded with fertile lands and green fields and near the main channel of the river, which bore abundant merchandise of wares of every kind for sale from the whole world to the town on its banks.[1]

Edward was the first monarch to make Westminster his main residence. In addition to its favourable location and natural advantages, its monastery church was dedicated to St Peter, whom Edward worshipped with special devotion. Although Edward had been crowned in Winchester, the Wessex capital, its bishop was alleged to have had an affair with Edward's mother, Emma. Edward's re-building of Westminster's palace and abbey expressed his grand design to turn England into a Norman-style kingdom, achieve imperial status and become the equal of any European ruler. His ambition was rooted in his Norman inheritance. His mother was the daughter of Richard I, Count of Normandy, and was described as 'the gem of the Normans' by the chronicler, Henry of Huntingdon. During the Danish invasions of England and Cnut's reign, Edward took exile in Normandy and developed a thoroughly Norman outlook.

For most of Edward's 23-year reign, Westminster's monastery grounds and the nearby fields became a vast building site. Boatmen and carters delivered huge supplies of stone and wood. Scaffolders created great traceries of wooden poles and planks. Carriers heaved and hoisted load after load of lime, stone, water and wood into place. Carpenters and masons chiselled, hammered and sawed, as, day-by-day, inch-by-inch, they turned the king's far-sighted vision for a new-look Westminster into reality.

Edward re-built Cnut's palace to the east of the Abbey, on land lying near the Thames. In common with domestic buildings of the period, Edward's palace included a hall and a private chamber. Tradition holds that Edward later died in his private chamber, subsequently known as 'St Edward's Chamber' and, after a twelfth-century makeover, as 'the Painted Chamber'. Westminster is depicted in the Bayeux tapestry, embroidered after Edward's death, probably in the 1070s. Edward is portrayed sitting on a throne, but the beguiling representation of his palace and his nearby abbey owes more to the embroiderers' creativity than their accuracy. A craftsman is shown standing on a ladder that stretches from a palace window to the Abbey roof, where he puts a weather-cock in place with one hand while clinging to the palace roof with the other. However, Edward's palace stood more than 100 yards from the Abbey.

Edward's palace fronted onto the eastern side of present-day Old Palace Yard, between the modern Houses of Parliament and College Green, through which traffic thunders along Abingdon Street. The site of the main hall, sometimes known as the Lesser Hall or White Hall, lay in front of the present House of Lords, and extended lengthways on a north-south axis from today's St Stephen's Porch. The present-day equestrian statue of Richard the Lionheart stands on the site of the hall, towards its south-west corner. The rest of Edward's palace extended eastwards towards the Thames, on the site now occupied by the House of Lords.

Although medieval courtiers led itinerant lives as they followed their peripatetic monarchs round the kingdom, they became as much a part of Westminster life as the monks. Edward seems to have brought a small household with him from Normandy. A close adviser, Robert Champart, Abbot of Jumièges, moved to England in 1044 to become Bishop of London and, in 1051, Archbishop of Canterbury. The king's family was also prominent at court: notably Edith, his queen; Emma, his mother; three younger brothers-in-law; nephews, great-nephews and nieces, and other young princes and nobles. Other kinsmen courtiers were Robert fitzWimarch, who may have been his major-domo, and Osbern, his chaplain. Edward's private chamber, the hall and courtyard were staffed by 'stallers' (place-men), such as Esgar, Steward of the King's Hall, Regenbald, Chancellor, and Godwin, the Queen's Steward.[2] Archbishops, bishops, abbots and earls attended great councils at Edward's palace, accompanied by their retinues, who swelled the demand for hospitality and shelter.

Edward's chamberlain, Hugolin, looked after the royal treasure. He emerges as something of an iron chancellor in a legend depicted in the Abbey on the fifteenth-century screen of the Confessor's shrine. While Edward was resting at the end of a day, Hugolin opened the royal chest to pay the servants; but when the chamberlain became involved with other business, a dish-washer from the palace kitchen, noticing that the king was asleep, stole some of the royal treasure. However, Edward had only been pretending to sleep, and when the thief tried his luck for a third time, the king suddenly warned the startled thief to flee before Hugolin returned. 'He will not leave you even a halfpenny', Edward cried. Later, the king told an angry Hugolin that: 'The thief hath more need of it than we have – enough treasure hath King Edward!'[3]

Hugolin's loyalty to Edward probably cost him his life. Flete, the fifteenth-century Westminster monk and historian, describes Hugolin as the 'principal chamberlain', who was, 'among all the magnates of this realm, Edward's most loyal knight'. Hugolin was first buried in the cloister of the Abbey, but, after Henry III's later re-building of the Abbey, was moved to a tomb in the Chapter House. His epitaph mentions 'the famous Hugolin with the broken crown of his head', suggesting that he was killed, or executed, defending Edward's endowments to the Abbey, or perhaps the king's policies or reputation.[4]

The Abbey's shrine to the Confessor also depicts one of the biggest tax cuts in English history, when Edward abolished the hated 'Danegeld' in 1051. The king supposedly entered his treasury one day and saw a demon dancing on the casks containing the gold raised by 'Danegeld'. He immediately scrapped the hated tax.

Edward's biggest project was his re-building of St Peter's, Westminster. It was to be a marvel of its age, an awe-inspiring, revolutionary synthesis of European and English influences constructed on a scale to rival the great imperial churches of Germany. Edward was motivated, according to the *Vita Aedwardi Regis*, by his decision 'to have his burial place there'. He committed ten per cent of 'all his royal revenues', and 'there was no weighing of the costs, past or future, so long as it proved worthy of, and acceptable to, God and St Peter'.[5]

A decade or so after Edward's death, Sulcard, a Westminster monk, challenged the earlier account of how the re-building was financed. Sulcard claimed that it was funded by money originally earmarked for a promised pilgrimage by Edward to St Peter's in Rome on his accession to the throne. However, Edward was dissuaded from leaving the country by English land-owning magnates, who feared the worst if their new monarch went abroad. The king stayed put and instead used the savings to re-build St Peter's, Westminster. In the twelfth century, Sulcard's story was elaborated by Osbert of Clare, who suggested that Pope Leo IX had absolved Edward of the sin of breaking his vow, on condition that he spent the proposed cost of his pilgrimage on the poor and a church dedicated to St Peter. However, the cost of Edward's grand project was immensely more expensive than that of a pilgrimage and demanded a sizeable flow of funds for about 50 years, until the monastic buildings were completed circa 1100.

Edward had been inspired by Europe's great monastic revival during his 25-year exile, and its new style of architecture known as Romanesque, or Norman. As a member of Normandy's royal household, he had been impressed by plans to develop a multi-purpose, royal complex at Fécamp, where an abbey and a favoured palace shared a common enclosure. He was aware of the political and religious support that the French monarchy derived from its close relationship with the Abbey of St Denis, the royal burial church outside Paris, and he was influenced by the awesome sense of majesty evoked by the great churches built in the Holy Roman Empire. Building a vast, new abbey in a continental style near his palace at Westminster would put him on a par with his European and imperial counterparts.[6]

The new abbey may have been commissioned as early as 1044, the year in which Edward summoned Robert Champart from Jumièges to London. Work was probably under way by 1050. Today, there remain only tantalizing traces of the men who built it – the craftsman shown in the Bayeux tapestry and three names in the records: Teinfrith, a church-wright or master mason; Godwyn Greatsyd ('fat purse'), a mason, who also donated land; and Leofsi Duddesunu, probably another mason.[7]

The length of the new Abbey, at 322 feet, exceeded that of any English church and was of a similar scale to the huge churches of Mainz and Speyer on the Rhine. Its ground-plan covered about the same area as the present-day Abbey (before the addition of Henry VII's Chapel). It was not as tall as today and its masonry was a green-grey, soft sandstone, carted to the site from mines in Reigate and Godstone.

Edward's Abbey was the first cross-shaped church in England, and its massive stone pillars and leaded roof contrasted with the wooden beams and rafters of existing Saxon churches. The Bayeux tapestry shows the eastern section beyond the crossing comprising two bays, each with a window, while the western nave is shown with five bays complete. Archaeological evidence shows that the whole nave had a dozen bays. As glass was not often used in windows until the twelfth century, the Abbey might originally have used shutters or oiled cloth. The transepts, or arms, of the church extended from the crossing to the north and south, and each had two-storey chapels on their eastern side reached by spiral stairs from vaulted ground floors.

The interior of the Abbey was richly decorated with sculptures and carvings in a naïve Romanesque style. According to *La Estoire de Seint Aedward le Rei*, written in Norman French, probably by a monk at Westminster, about 200 years later: 'The pillars and entablature / Are rich without and within, / At the bases and capitals / The work rises grand and royal, / Sculptured are the stones / And storied the windows'. A stone capital that might have adorned the cloister is preserved in the Abbey Museum. It dates from 1120 or 1140 and its carved decoration showing the Judgement of Solomon suggests that the Abbey's interior was impressive.[8]

A central, two-storey tower with cupola and conspicuous stair turrets rose above the crossing of the new church. Twin towers were added at the western end of the Abbey, in an extra bay, probably in about 1100, although the author of *La Estoire* in the thirteenth century assumes that they were built in Edward's time.

The early Norman twin towers were a striking feature until the re-building of the Abbey in the thirteenth century. Only their lower stages survive, invisibly, within the present Abbey's eighteenth-century, western towers.

A remarkable remnant of Edward's Romanesque church survives to the south of the Abbey. The battered oak door of a non-descript storeroom, off a shadowy vestibule between the east cloister and the Chapter House, has been identified in dendrochronology tests as dating from the 1050s, and is therefore England's oldest surviving door. It was made from five huge planks of an English oak that grew between 924 and 1030, probably on the Abbey's estates in Essex, and was felled between 1032 and 1064. This research shatters the legend that the scraps of skin visible beneath the ironwork on the inner face of the door are human. They were said to be the flayed hide of either a Dane, or of a fourteenth century robber who broke into the King's Treasury. However, the hide has been confirmed as that of a cow.

The door has lost its original decoration, most of its ironwork, and its elegant curved top. Its size (6 feet, 6 inches by 4 feet), and the double-sided form, suggest that it originally occupied an important position. According to the Abbey's consultant archaeologist Warwick Rodwell the ancient door may later have protected the room where Edward the Confessor's body and relics were kept during Henry III's re-building.[9]

When the new church was functioning in about 1065, building began on the new monastery that Edward planned to the south. In the words of *La Estoire*: 'He makes there a cloister and a chapter house in front / Towards the east, vaulted and round, / Where his ordained ministers / May hold their secret chapter'. The cloisters, chapter-house, refectory, dormitory and latrines, and the infirmary with its chapel, were completed during the decades after Edward's death. Significant parts of these buildings survive and evoke monastic life some 900 years ago. The present Great Cloister occupies much the same position as its eleventh-century predecessor. In its south-east corner, the eleventh century, tunnel-vaulted Dark Cloister and its adjoining passage to the Little Cloister and Abbey garden, used to be thronged with monks at fixed times as they headed for the Abbey, or returned to the dormitory, latrines and refectory.[10]

The museum and the neighbouring Pyx Chamber, or Chapel of the Pyx, off the east side of the Great Cloister, date from 1066–75. They occupy the undercroft of the old dormitory. The circular piers, undecorated capitals, groin vaults and some of the plain traverse arches were part of the original, Romanesque monastery. Above the south side of the Great Cloister, the remains of the refectory wall can be seen. The monastery's rich decoration is revealed on the refectory's west wall, in a section of red and white chequer design glazed tiles and stonework.[11]

Edward recruited Benedictine monks for his new abbey, many coming from Crediton, Devon, on the removal of its see to Exeter. Such was the scale of the Confessor's transformation that by 1086 there were about 80 monks, roughly a six-fold increase, plus many lay servants. Edward's new abbey ranked seventh in order of income among England's 50 monasteries.[12]

The Abbey was initially shared by monks and parishioners, with the latter group sitting on the northern side of the aisle to hear mass. However, as Westminster developed, and the population grew, the increased numbers attending the Abbey evidently disturbed the Benedictines as they observed their religious duties. This conflict was resolved by building a smaller church, St Margaret's, near the Abbey's main, north door, on the same side of the Abbey where the villagers had prayed. An ancient document reveals the monks' irritation towards their fellow worshippers by explaining that St Margaret's was built 'for the greater honour and peace of the monks as of the parishioners'. It marked the start of a tradition of exclusivity by the Abbey superiors that outlasted the Benedictines.[13]

St Margaret's first recorded reference dates from the time of Abbot Herbert (1121–36). Its patron saint, Margaret of Antioch, was a popular saint in Anglo-Saxon times and there is a Westminster tradition that a chapel of St Margaret had existed on the northern side of the Saxon abbey, but was demolished when Edward's new church was built. The supposed existence of this chapel is recalled in a thirteenth century carving of St Margaret and the dragon in the Abbey's north transept, in a spandrel at the nearest point to the parish church.

By late 1065, the main body of Edward's abbey was largely complete. Edward was aged about 60, but his health was faltering. 'At midwinter', reports the *Anglo-Saxon Chronicle*, 'King Edward came to Westminster, and had the minster there consecrated, which he had himself built, to the honour of God and St Peter, and all God's saints'. Courtiers came to Westminster, 'from the whole of Britain', attracted by the consecration and were probably also encouraged to attend by the king's poor health.[14]

In keeping with tradition, Edward wore his crown on Christmas Day, held court in his palace, attended a service in the Abbey and dined at a state banquet with his bishops and nobles. But that night he was suddenly taken ill, probably with a stroke, and retired to his chamber. On Tuesday 27 December he grew rapidly worse. The Abbey was consecrated in his absence on Wednesday 28, the festival of the Holy Innocents. Queen Edith presided at the ceremony, and as Dean Stanley recounts: 'the walls of Westminster Abbey, then white and fresh from the workmen's tools, received from Stigand [the Archbishop of Canterbury] their first consecration – the first which, according to the legend of St Peter's visit, had ever been given to the spot by mortal hands'.[15]

That evening, Edward sank into a deep stupor. Three days later, he appeared to rally briefly, only to become delirious. Gathered at his deathbed were Queen Edith, who sat on the floor, warming his feet in her lap, and, standing close by, Harold Godwinson, the queen's brother, Robert fitzWimarch, the keeper of the palace, and Archbishop Stigand. During his ranting, the king claimed that his earls, abbots, bishops and other clergy had become servants of the devil, and warned of forthcoming disasters. According to the *Vita Aedwardi*, the queen realized the scandalous state of the English church and was convinced of the truthfulness of Edward's dire prophecy. Stigand emerges from this account as one of the main culprits. The Archbishop is said to have whispered in the ear of Harold, whom he supported as Edward's successor, that the king was out of his mind.

As Edward approached death, he became calmer. He committed the protection of his wife, his kingdom and his foreign servants to Harold, and his body to burial in the Abbey, as he had planned. He died in his chamber in his palace, probably after another stroke, on Wednesday 4 or Thursday 5 January 1066. As his body lay in the palace, his face blushed like a rose, his white beard seemed lilywhite and his thin stretched-out fingers were paler than ever.[16]

Crowds flocked from neighbouring villages to witness Edward's funeral in the newly hallowed Abbey on Friday 6 January, the feast of Epiphany. This remarkable event is depicted in the Bayeux tapestry, in which the hand of God is portrayed in the sky above the Abbey pointing down to indicate where the king should be laid to rest. Edward's body is shown, wrapped in a woollen shroud, with only the face showing, while a prelate gives his blessing. A simple procession accompanies the body to the Abbey. Inside the main church, the corpse, now completely shrouded, is carried head first on an open bier by eight pall-bearers shouldering poles (four men in front, four behind). The bier is accompanied on either side by an acolyte with bells, and behind follows a group of clergy, and four choristers singing the anthem.

Edward was buried in a stone sarcophagus sunk in the pavement before the high altar to St Peter, as was fitting for the founding father of the great, Romanesque Abbey. On a couple of occasions his remains were moved, but the exact site of Edward's original tomb was finally confirmed in 2005 during high frequency radar tests that showed the underlying archaeology. The results revealed that Edward was first buried about ten feet behind the modern Abbey's high altar, and eight feet beneath the present-day shrine to him erected by Henry III during his re-building of the Abbey in the thirteenth century. Having moved the high altar several yards to the west, Henry III erected the shrine to the Confessor, that still stands today, directly above the spot where Edward was first laid to rest more than 940 years ago.[17]

3 'TWO NATIONS IN THE WOMB'

Edward the Confessor's death plunged England into a leadership crisis. The childless monarch had promised his kingdom to his cousin, William, Duke of Normandy, but on his deathbed entrusted it to his brother-in-law, Harold Godwinson, England's most powerful magnate who, as ruler of Wessex, had opposed the growing Norman influence during Edward's reign. Edward was buried in Westminster Abbey on the morning of the feast of Epiphany, 6 January 1066. That afternoon, Godwinson was crowned Harold II, almost certainly in the Abbey.

However, within ten months of his coronation, Harold II was dead, killed in battle with William and his invading army at Hastings. The defeat of England's last Saxon king ushered in an era of bloody Norman oppression. William's conquest of England was brilliantly stage-managed. Having subdued southern England and London in December 1066, he 'made it one of his first cares to give thanks for his success at King Edward's tomb, at Westminster' – the 'better to ingratiate himself with the English', as William of Malmesbury, the twelfth-century historian, observed. In addition to visiting the Abbey and offering 50 marks of silver and rich palls for the altar and Edward's tomb, William confirmed his plan to hold his coronation there on Christmas Day.[1]

William sought to establish his claim as Edward's rightful successor by being crowned on a spot directly above the Confessor's grave. But he also wanted to ensure that security was tight and the Norman cavalry standing guard outside the Abbey were understandably twitchy. 'Two nations were indeed in the womb' in Dean Stanley's words, as English abbots, bishops magnates, monks, townspeople and villagers gathered uneasily with Norman clergy, courtiers and soldiers in the Abbey.[2]

'Christus vincit! Christus regnat! Christus imperat!' was the jubilant cry as the coronation procession began. Known as the *Laudes Regiae*, the accompanying chant was an innovation imported from Normandy, William's dukedom. In Westminster Abbey, William was hailed as 'the great and peace giving King, crowned by God, life and victory'. This divine sanction of William's claim to the English throne was symbolized during the ceremony by the act of unction. As the contemporary Norman chronicler, William of Jumièges noted, William was accepted by England's magnates, crowned and also 'anointed with holy oil by bishops of the kingdom'.[3]

William ensured that his coronation was easily visible to the congregation. A raised dais, or stage, was built before the high altar at the main crossing of the church, beneath the central tower. It was important that he was seen to have been 'elected' king by the conquered English and conquering Normans alike. Viewing points were also reached from the turret staircases that led to the upper chapels in the north and south transepts. William stood before the high altar, accompanied on either side by a Norman and an Anglo-Saxon prelate: Geoffrey, Bishop of Coutances, and Ealdred, the Archbishop of York, who held the golden crown. When the moment arrived for the new king to be publicly acclaimed, Geoffrey, Bishop of Coutances, addressed the Normans in the Abbey in French, asking them: 'If the king presented please you, declare it to us, for it is fitting this be done by your free choice'. In response, came a roar of approval. Ealdred then repeated the question for the Anglo-Saxons, who began shouting their approval.[4]

However, when the jittery Norman horse-guards outside heard this sudden cacophony, some of it in a strange language, they feared that a riot had begun in the Abbey. In a panic, William's soldiers set fire to the Abbey gates and thatched houses nearby. Inside the Abbey, word quickly spread of the fires outside. As the great throng scrambled to leave, rushing for the doors and fleeing into the wintry precincts, some were trampled by the Norman cavalry.

William stayed in the Abbey, trembling from head to foot. After a brief suspension, the remainder of the ceremony was hurried through against the noise of the hubbub outside. In a change to Saxon precedent, William swore the oath after, and not before, he had been anointed, thus taking the oath as God's chosen successor. This change was designed 'to reinforce the sanctity of the king's oath', according to Roy Strong, the expert on coronation ritual. Before Ealdred placed the crown on the king's head, William swore in his harsh tones, 'that he would rule this people as well as any king before him best did'. After his oath, William was invested by the bishops with symbolic regalia, and was enthroned.[5]

But why did Ealdred, Archbishop of York, officiate at William's coronation and the crowning, in 1068, of William's queen, Matilda? The Archbishop of Canterbury, Stigand, might have been expected to officiate, but he was identified with Harold's regime, having stiffened Godwinson's resolve to become king. Stigand was also out of favour in Rome. In 1067, William's Italian-born religious adviser and respected theologian, Lanfranc, visited the Vatican. The pope was soon denouncing pre-Conquest apostasy in England and spoke of a 'source of evil' – a clear reference to Stigand.

Stigand's weakness increased Ealdred's influence. On one occasion, according to Westminster tradition, Ealdred came to London to remonstrate with the king about a plundering expedition by the new Norman rulers in Yorkshire. Finding William in the Abbey, the archbishop attacked him publicly. The king fell at his feet, trembling. William's aides tried to push Ealdred away, 'but he persisted, and would not leave the place without a full apology'. After Ealdred's death in 1069, and Stigand's sacking by a papal legate in 1070, the appointment of William's trusted adviser, Lanfranc, as Archbishop of Canterbury speeded the Norman settlement.[6]

Westminster Abbey was especially vulnerable, as it was closely identified with the defeated Anglo-Saxons. Edward the Confessor was buried there and Harold had been crowned there. Although William confirmed its estates, he lavished patronage on his newly founded abbey at Battle, in Sussex. He made no new grants to Westminster, failed to fund the unfinished Abbey's building programme and required its estates to support between 15 and 25 expensive knights. The abbot was made a tenant-in-chief of the king and thus clearly subordinate to the crown's secular authority.

Yet the process of 'Normanization', whereby all prelates were 'sifted to the branne', never eradicated Westminster Abbey's Anglo-Saxon tradition. Edward the Confessor's tomb became a focus of this tradition. According to Westminster legend, an early demonstration of the supernatural powers supposedly associated with the Confessor occurred in 1074, during a synod held at the Abbey by Archbishop Lanfranc. This synod was ostensibly called to examine the qualifications and conduct of the clergy, but in reality it was designed to make room for Norman appointees by ejecting bishops and abbots who were deemed to be of insufficient learning.

The synod's unintended climax came when Wulfstan, Bishop of Worcester, was charged with being 'a most illiterate and foolish man, and unfit for the station he held; a very idiot, unacquainted with the French language, and incapable either to instruct the church or counsel the king'. Lanfranc demanded that he surrender his pastoral staff and ring. However, Wulfstan refused to give his staff of office to the archbishop and insisted that he would, 'make that resignation to King Edward, who conferred it on me'. He then left the synod, walked straight into the church, stood before the tomb of the Confessor and addressed Edward in his native Saxon tongue. After placing his staff upon the stone tomb, Wulfstan returned to the synod, where he sat among the monks in an ordinary habit.

When the synod became aware of Wulfstan's action, a messenger was sent to retrieve his staff. However, the staff could not be moved, and neither King William nor Archbishop Lanfranc could disengage it from the stone. One version of the legend has Wulfstan turning to William and saying, in the few Norman words that he could command: 'A better than thou gave it to me – take it if thou canst'. Later, when Wulfstan finally returned to the tomb, the staff readily submitted to his touch. After this miracle, Wulfstan was allowed to retain his episcopal dignity. This story was widely believed. In the early thirteenth century, King John cited it to a papal envoy as proof that English kings had the right to nominate bishops. However, the envoy is said to have retorted with a sneer that John was more like the Conqueror than the Confessor.

The Bayeux tapestry survives as testimony to the fierce propaganda war that raged during the 1070s. Its filmic, frame-by-frame narrative seeks to legitimize William's conquest. In a riveting scene after Harold's coronation, a group of people are depicted looking up at the sky, awestruck at the sight of a large, fiery star high above them. This brilliant stellar object was Halley's Comet, visible between late April and early June 1066. Such heavenly phenomena were regarded as bad omens. The message was clear: hapless Harold was doomed.

However, Westminster's resistance to William's Normanization of the church brought the first written version of a foundation legend that stressed the Abbey's Anglo-Saxon roots and its close link with Rome. The story told by Sulcard, a Westminster monk during the Conqueror's reign, was added to and embellished by later monks and historians until the fifteenth century. Its portrayal of seventh century Thorney is entrancing, but its narrative is spurious.[7]

The fable links the Abbey's foundation with Augustine's mission from Rome, begun in 597. It tells what supposedly happened when Mellitus, the first bishop of London and a friend of St Augustine, was about to consecrate the first church on Thorney. The story begins on the eve of the new church's consecration, one stormy Sunday night. A local fisherman, Edric, was casting his nets from the shore of the island into the Thames, when his attention was suddenly attracted by a bright light on the far bank. Edric crossed the river in his boat and found 'a venerable personage, in foreign attire'. This elderly stranger was looking for someone to ferry him across the wide, 'dark stream' to Thorney, that was 'flooded round by the heavy rains'. He promised to reward Edric for his trouble, and the fisherman duly took him across.[8]

As soon as they landed on Thorney the stranger proceeded to the church, creating, on his way, two natural springs with his staff. Suddenly, the night sky lit up in 'celestial splendour', illuminating the building so brightly that there was no 'darkness or shadow'.

> The apostle then consecrated the fabric amidst a company of the heavenly host, and a chorus of celestial voices; and whilst the most fragrant odours spread around, the wonders of the scene were augmented by angels, who were seen ascending and descending in the same manner as in Jacob's vision, recorded in the Scriptures.[9]

Edric remained in his boat during the ceremony, awestruck by the spectacle. When the elderly stranger returned to the boat, he revealed that he was St Peter.

He commanded Edric to tell Mellitus all that he had seen and to refrain from a second consecration. The fisherman, plucking up his courage, requested his promised reward. At this, St Peter, 'bidding him cast his nets into the water, repaid his services by a miraculous draught of salmon'. The apostle assured Edric that 'neither he nor any of his brethren should at any time want a supply of that kind of food', provided that they never fished again on Sundays and made an offering of every tenth fish to the use of the newly-consecrated Church'. St Peter then disappeared.[10]

The next morning, when Bishop Mellitus and Sebert, King of the East Saxons (604–616/7), arrived at the church at the appointed hour, they were met at the door church by Edric. The fisherman held a salmon that he presented, 'from St. Peter in a gentle manner to the Bishop'. He showed them the incontrovertible evidence of what had taken place: 'the twelve crosses on the church, the walls within and without moistened with holy water, the letters of the Greek alphabet written twice over distinctly on the sand' of the now sacred island, 'the traces of the oil, and, (chiefest of miracles) the droppings of the angelic candles'. Mellitus professed himself entirely convinced and left the church, 'satisfied that the dedication had been performed sufficiently, better, and in a more saintly fashion than a hundred such as he could have done'. In commemoration Mellitus supposedly ordered that the name of the place should be changed from Thorney to Westminster, after the new church that was known as the West Minster (*occidentale monasterium*).[11]

The idea of the tithe of salmon and the notion that St Peter consecrated the church in order to exclude it from the Bishop of London's jurisdiction were introduced by Osbert of Clare in 1141 in his Life of Edward the Confessor. The rivalry between the Abbey and London lingers today, as the Bishop continues to require permission from the Dean and Chapter of Westminster to enter the Abbey precincts. A fourteenth century version of the fable was probably written by William of Sudbury, another Westminster monk, for King Richard II. In turn, John Flete drew on this version for his fifteenth-century history.

Flete testifies to the fable's success in guaranteeing the Westminster monks their supply of salmon from a lengthy stretch of the Thames between Staines upstream and Gravesend downstream. In 1231, they won legal backing for their claim, when they took Martin, Rector of Rotherhithe, to court over salmon caught in his parish, arguing that St Peter had given them the tithe of all salmon taken from the Thames. In the event, the Rector was allowed to keep half and the monks took half. Flete concluded that an increasing scarcity of salmon in the river reflected divine judgement on fishermen who failed to comply with St Peter's bequest. The custom of the tithe fish was observed as late as 1382. The Abbey's annual ceremony was described by Dean Stanley:

> ... one of the fishermen, as representative of Edric, took his place beside the Prior, and brought in a salmon for St Peter. It was carried in state through the

middle of the Refectory. The Prior and the whole fraternity rose as it passed up to the high table, and then the fisherman received ale and bread from the cellarer in return for the fish's tail.

Although it is difficult today to believe that large quantities of salmon were caught in the river, 'Thames salmon' with asparagus remained a customary dish until Charles I's reign.[12]

Westminster Abbey is properly named 'the Collegiate church of St Peter', probably in recollection of St Peter's in Rome, the mother church of St Augustine's mission to England. The name exemplified its claim to be a 'little Rome', directly linked to the Holy See and therefore free from interference by the Bishop of London. Papal backing was given to the threat that anyone who infringed the Abbey's charters would be specially condemned by St Peter, who holds the keys to heaven.

The Abbey's immediate neighbourhood was steeped in references to the saint. 'The soil of St. Peter', was a recognized legal phrase. The 'Cock' public house that stood in Tothill Street took its name from the saint's symbol, and workmen building Henry III's new abbey in the mid-thirteenth century were paid their wages in this hostelry. A black marble image of St Peter, and some marble steps, were said to have been seen during an inspection in about 1780 at the bottom of an ancient well in the Long Ditch area, between present-day Tothill Street and Great George Street.

The most enduring reminder of the Abbey's foundation fable is the supposed tomb of King Sebert, beneath the oak Sedilia in the Abbey's south ambulatory by the Confessor's chapel. But there is a gruesome twist to Sebert's story. The medieval monks wrongly assumed that the lead coffins unearthed in the original church belonged to its founders, and that they were King Sebert and his wife, Ethelgoda. During the Abbey's thirteenth-century re-building, the remains were deposited at the entrance to the Chapter House, but in 1307, they were removed to the Choir. The right arm of one of the corpses had apparently not decayed and skin still clung to the bone.

However, the Abbey's foundation fable is not supported by historical evidence. Bede's *Ecclesiastical History of the English People*, published c.731, does not mention Thorney, although he refers to Ethelbert's founding of St Paul's and records the founding of many other monasteries. Furthermore, the charters of King Edgar, St Dunstan and Edward the Confessor that supposedly suggest a foundation at Thorney in Sebert's time, are spurious. Yet the fable and its assertion of Anglo-Saxon rights resonated during the Middle Ages. The idea of 'two nations in the womb', one Norman, the other Anglo-Saxon, never disappeared. As late as 1555, the foundation fable was cited by the last Abbot of Westminster, Feckenham, when he appeared before the House of Commons, as justification for the Abbey's inviolable right of sanctuary for poor offenders.

4 NORMAN RULE AND RESISTANCE

Westminster can be a misleading place. New Palace Yard, despite its name, is more than 900 years old. Overlooked by Big Ben's clock tower, the courtyard serves as a backdrop in snaps taken of tourists standing with the policemen who guard its entrance on Parliament Square. Its name derives from the 'new palace', built by William the Conqueror's son, William II, that was dominated by Westminster Hall. The courtyard was originally a nondescript, marshy outer yard, and, although it was walled by the late thirteenth century, remained open to the public for much of its history. Its name distinguishes it from Old Palace Yard, originally part of Edward the Confessor's palace, which also dates from the eleventh century.

The Normans' determination to impose their rule on England made a lasting impact at Westminster: ceremonially, physically and politically. Although the Conqueror spent much of his reign abroad, when in England he asserted his authority at crown-wearing ceremonies. According to the *Anglo-Saxon Chronicle*, 'three times a year he wore his crown, as often as he was in England … and then there were with him all the powerful men from all over England, archbishops and bishops, abbots and earls, thegns and knights'. On these occasions the celebratory *Laudes Regiae* was sung at a solemn mass, followed by a great feast.[1]

The crown-wearing ceremonies were held during Easters at Winchester and Windsor; Christmases at Gloucester and Westminster; and Whitsuns at Westminster. At his Gloucester crown-wearing in 1085, the ageing and overweight king, anxious about the threat of another Danish invasion, commissioned the *Domesday Book*. In addition to confirming the Norman takeover, this property survey provided fleeting glimpses of a treasurer, Henry, 'the first properly identifiable civil servant', according to Peter Hennessy, the historian of Whitehall.[2]

Within a fortnight of the Conqueror's death in September 1087, William's second son and chosen successor, William 'Rufus', was crowned William II in Westminster Abbey by Archbishop Lanfranc. 'Rufus' was a nickname awarded posthumously, suggesting red hair or a ruddy complexion. The hastily arranged ceremony prevented the Conqueror's estranged first son, Robert Curthose, obtaining the crown. During his reign, William II struggled to subdue the Welsh and outwit the machinations of England's barons. These exertions cost much blood and treasure and brought dire hardship. Henry of Huntingdon, who witnessed these events in childhood, accused William II of 'not shaving but skinning the English peoples with taxation and the worst exactions'.[3]

Large amounts of the treasure garnered by William II were spent 'upon the Tower of London, and the makynge of Westminster Hall', according to Robert Fabyan, the sixteenth century historian. It was customary for magnates of the time to build a great hall in which to feast and impress, but the massive scale of William II's Great Hall at 240 feet by 68, was unrivalled in England and, probably, in Europe. Westminster Hall is the profane twin of Edward the Confessor's grandiose Abbey. These vast buildings, built close together within 33 years of each other, were designed to strike awe into the king's subjects. This intention was captured by Matthew Paris, the medieval historian, when recounting William II's boastful comment on holding court in his Great Hall for the first time in 1099: 'Having entered to inspect it, with a large military retinue, some persons remarked that "it was too large, and larger than it should have been;" the King replied, that "it was not half so large as it should have been, and that it was only a bed-chamber in comparison with the building which he intended to make"'.[4]

Westminster Hall was the Norman equivalent of a state broadcasting station and the internet.[5] Its huge size enabled large numbers to witness court ceremonies, royal pronouncements and, from the late twelfth century, when the royal law courts began sitting there, legal cases and verdicts. No sooner was a ceremony finished, a writ issued or a judgement made, than the word spread through the Hall, outside to Westminster, London and to the country beyond. The numbers using the hall were swelled by its other function as an indoor market. It was the heart of Westminster life for about 700 years, a social networking site, where all manner of people jostled together and 'tuned in' to the latest news: courtiers, innkeepers, lawyers, ministers, monks, MPs, printers, pick-pockets, prostitutes, traders, valets and many more.

The Great Hall's construction took only about two years. The Isle of Thorney again became a bustling building site swarming with workmen. Blocks of stone from Caen and Reigate, and great logs of timber, were hauled ashore, where they were cut, dressed, drilled or planed, and then carted, dragged, hoisted or lifted into place. As the Hall rapidly took shape, plasterers and painters created a richly detailed and brightly decorated interior. The Hall was built parallel to the river, on a north-south axis, on a spit of gravel between the Abbey and the Thames; but its proximity to the river made it vulnerable to flooding and it has been repeatedly inundated.

Originally, the Hall might have been entered by doors on either side. The main door, in the northern wall fronting New Palace Yard, might have been added later.

The king's throne rested on a dais at the southern end, where a large flight of stone steps now stands. The Norman walls remain around the lower part of the Hall, although they have been re-faced. They were built 40 feet high and 6 feet 8 inches thick. The Hall is not symmetrical: its south wall is not square with the side walls and its side windows are not directly opposite one another. The roof was probably shaped like today's, but was most likely supported by two rows of columns, probably wooden. The columns probably created a triforium arcade and wall passage around the hall. The tops of the wall buttresses that supported the Hall can be seen on the west side, alongside Parliament Square and St Margaret's Church.

An impression of the Great Hall's decorative, Norman stonework can be gleaned from the eight surviving stone capitals on display in the Jewel Tower. They were discovered in the walls by the nineteenth-century restorers, having been re-used as wall core by Richard II's fourteenth-century workmen. Most were badly damaged, but these remaining examples show carved animals, plants and people. One of them is among the earliest 'story-telling' capitals in England, showing a soldier attacking a tower and providing details of the construction of an early Norman castle.

Smoke curled upwards through the Great Hall from a central hearth, or hearths, to the rafters and escaped through the roof. Each corner of the Hall had a door: the one in the south-west probably led to the kitchens, near the current site of St Stephen's entrance to the House of Commons. The flattened, earthen floor was about four feet below the present level, and had an open gully that carried kitchen waste to the river, but the smell became too much for Henry III and in 1259 a conduit was built.[6]

After the Whitsuntide crown-wearing ceremony in Westminster Abbey in 1099, at which Edgar, King of Scotland, was accorded the honour of bearing the sword, William II hosted a great royal banquet for the first time in his new Great Hall. This feast was celebrated some 40 years later by the poet, Geoffrye Gaimar, in his *Lestoire des Engles*. Some 300 ushers guided the barons, bishops and other senior courtiers to their places and marshalled the servants who brought the food and drink from the kitchen, while guarding the silver vessels and keeping the food from the greedy.[7]

William II's retinue was unlike his father's. Whereas the Conqueror's courtiers were hale and hearty, with short hair and sensible shoes, his son's were long-haired, had small beards, and wore eye-catching, luxurious clothes and shoes with long, curling points. Echoes of the gossip about William's courtiers resonate in chronicles of the time. He emerges as a boorish dandy, who was short (his mother was only about four feet tall) with a protruding belly. He dressed in short tunics, and wore his hair long and parted in the middle.

Homosexuality was supposedly rife in William II's court. 'Nor did they exercise their unspeakable debauchery in secret', rages a splenetic Henry of Huntingdon, 'but unashamedly in the light of day'.[8] Eadmer, the biographer of Anselm, the

Archbishop of Canterbury, and no friend of the king, reports that by 1094 the young male courtiers grew their hair like girls and minced around. According to William of Malmesbury, the court was followed by a band of effeminates and prostitutes, who indulged the courtiers' lechery. By implication, William was gay. He never married and apparently left no bastards, but his favourite, Ranulf Flambard, chief judge and tax collector whom William allowed to buy the bishopric of Durham, was heterosexual. The much-loathed Flambard was described by Henry of Huntingdon as a perverter of justice and a despoiler. William II's friends terrorized any part of the country through which the king passed and, according to Henry of Huntingdon, 'robbed and subverted everything, even going unpunished when they committed rape … ' At Westminster, William irritated the monkish chroniclers by his soldier's disdain for religion and his exploitation of the church. He sold bishoprics and kept abbacies vacant for long periods in order to pocket their revenues.[9]

However, an apparent act of generosity by William – perhaps confirming the Abbey's earlier benefactions – led to his commemoration on a capital in its old Norman cloister that showed the king attended by Gilbert Crispin, Westminster's Norman Abbot, and a monk. This sculpture was later incorporated, apparently as just another piece of stone, in the palace gate built by Richard III in 1484 and pulled down in 1706. It was unearthed in 1807, when taverns and houses were demolished on the site of present-day Parliament Square.

One of many fads to sweep through the hot-house atmosphere at Westminster was prompted by a bizarre, courtly jest in the Great Hall during the Whitsuntide feast of 1099, or possibly 1100. Walter Giffard, Earl of Buckingham, wanted 30 of his valets to be dubbed knights by the king, but was kept waiting for the ceremony. In jest, he had his own head and those of his men shaved. When they were finally presented, the king burst out laughing at the sight, but the new fashion instantly caught on and soon more than 300 of those present in the Great Hall had shaven heads.[10]

Within three months of his Whitsuntide court in 1100, William II was dead. Aged only about 40, he was shot through the heart by an arrow while hunting in the New Forest. Although apparently an accident, the king might have been assassinated, possibly by the French, whom he was planning to attack.[11]

For the second time within 35 years, the death of a childless king prompted a leadership crisis in England. The Conqueror's eldest son, Robert Curthose, who was returning from a triumphant First Crusade, was again pre-empted by a younger brother. The Conqueror's youngest son, Henry, who was in his early thirties, had been among William II's hunting party. Immediately after the king's death, his black-haired, broad-chested younger brother galloped from the New Forest to Winchester, where he won the support of a rump of barons and control of the royal treasure. Without further delay, he rushed to Westminster, probably making the 70-mile journey in a day.

On Sunday 5 August 1100, only three days after William II's death, Henry I was crowned King of England in the Abbey. Such was the urgency that Maurice, Bishop of London, officiated, since neither archbishop was available at this short notice: Canterbury was in exile and York was too far away to comply with Henry's urgent deadline. The hasty ceremony set a precedent. It was the result of political expediency, but its impact was profound. Anxious to reduce support among the Norman barony for Robert, and aware of the deep alienation that William II had created throughout England, Henry sought to mend fences. The oath sworn by the candidate for coronation was transformed into a political manifesto and written down for the first time. The final draft must have been completed at Westminster by Henry and his adviser, Robert of Meulan, on the eve of the coronation, ready to be issued as a charter immediately after the ceremony, then copied by scribes and dispatched to shire courts and bishoprics across the kingdom.[12]

Henry promised to restore 'the law of King Edward together with such emendations to it as my father made with the counsel of his barons'. Henry's recognition of the validity of Anglo-Saxon laws and liberties was enormously significant. It spawned the first treatises on English law, the *Leges Henricus primi* and its companion, the *Quadripartitus*, and prompted the issue of a royal writ requiring shire and hundred courts to meet 'as they were wont to do in the time of King Edward, and not otherwise'. Henry's oath was taken up by subsequent generations as a key guarantee of the rights of free Englishmen and women and became a precedent for the Magna Carta.[13]

Henry was a pragmatic ruler. He strengthened his hold on the crown, pleasing the Anglo-Saxons and the Scots by proposing marriage to Matilda, the daughter of Malcolm III of Scotland and Queen Margaret, granddaughter of Edmund Ironside and a descendant of the West Saxon kings. At Westminster Abbey, on 11 November 1100, Anselm, Archbishop of Canterbury, performed the royal wedding and crowned Matilda queen. Following a papal condemnation in 1099 over the royal investiture of prelates, Henry was at odds with Anselm, but he allowed him to preside over a great synod in Westminster Abbey in 1102. When Anselm later disrupted Henry's efforts to regain control of Normandy by threatening excommunication, the king compromised and, at a council of magnates and prelates at his Westminster palace in August 1107, relinquished his right to invest prelates with pastoral staff and ring.

The old rivalry between the archbishops of Canterbury and York was never far below the surface. When Anselm tried to assume the leading role at the Westminster synod in 1102, Gerard, Archbishop of York, fought for equal status. As monks from Canterbury were preparing to make Anselm's seat higher than anyone else's, Gerard, 'openly cursing', kicked it over and refused to sit down until his seat was made as high as the other archbishop's.[14]

Henry I concentrated on creating an efficient, centralized state and was the founding genius of the systematic use of favours, honours, rewards and sanctions that continues to pervade Westminster and oil the wheels of government. The king 'would rather contend by counsel than the sword' wrote William of Malmesbury: 'he conquered without bloodshed if he could, and if not, with as little as possible'. By fathering a large progeny (including more than twenty bastards), he had sons to champion his cause and daughters who could be married off as tools of diplomacy. The magnificent Whitsuntide court at Westminster on 13 June 1109 was attended by envoys of imposing physique and splendid attire sent to Westminster by Heinrich, the future Holy Roman Emperor, who was in his mid-twenties. Heinrich sought the hand of Matilda, Henry's seven year-old daughter and eldest child. Contracts were signed and oaths sworn pledging both parties to the future union.

However, the alliance with the Emperor came at a price. Matilda's dowry amounted to a massive 10,000 silver marks, prompting Henry I to levy an extra three shillings on every hide in England. As the *Anglo-Saxon Chronicle* noted: 'this was a very severe year in the country because of taxes that the king took for the marriage of his daughter'. This increase in taxes and the payment of the dowry may have triggered reform of the royal accounts. In 1111, the existence of the exchequer court (*scaccarium*), dealing with royal receipts and spending, is recognized for the first time in a writ.[15]

The Exchequer, as the court became known, was initially based at Winchester, although its officials accompanied Henry as he toured his kingdom. It took its name from a four-cornered board, five feet by ten, surrounded by a small ledge, or border, and covered by a chequered cloth (hence 'exchequer') similar to a chess board with 'columns drawn for thousands, hundreds, scores and tens of pounds, for shillings, and for pence'. The king's officials sat at this table, with its chequered cloth serving as an accounting device, and calculated the royal finances. Wooden 'tally sticks' served as receipts for money, with carefully graded notches indicating the amounts, and the Exchequer's annual audits were recorded on cylindrical parchments known as 'pipe rolls'. The chance survival of the pipe roll for 1130 reveals the extent of Henry I's patronage and his creation of a system of itinerant royal judges to administer the king's justice across the country.[16]

Henry I died at Rouen in December 1135, having succumbed once too often to his appetite for lampreys. After his death, a remarkable document, the *Constituto domus Regis* (the Establishment of the King's Household), was compiled, presumably as a guide for future monarchs, listing the organization and fixed allowances of all Henry's staff, including even the tent-keepers and ushers. Henry's chief household officers – the Chancellor, Master-butler, Master-chamberlain and Treasurer – were the administrative nucleus of the Anglo-Norman state and the forerunners of modern Whitehall.

Despite Henry's efforts to bequeath good governance, his kingdom was plunged into civil war after his death. His only legitimate son, William, had drowned at sea in 1120. Henry's court had sworn to uphold the succession of his recently widowed daughter, Empress Matilda, and, if she were to have one, of a legitimate son. Eventually, in 1133, her marriage to Geoffrey Plantagenet, the teenage heir to the Count of Anjou, produced a son, the future Henry II. However, on Henry I's death, Matilda and Geoffrey overestimated their strength, and, while they dallied in Normandy, Stephen, the late king's nephew, made straight for England, where he won support. The Archbishop of Canterbury overcame his scruples and crowned Stephen king in Westminster Abbey on Sunday 22 December 1135. The coronation gave Stephen an enormous advantage: whatever the rights and wrongs, he was the anointed king whom the Empress Matilda was seeking to overthrow.

The decisive moment in the ensuing civil war came in 1141. In February, Stephen was captured at the battle of Lincoln and, by the spring, preparations were being made for the Empress Matilda's coronation at Westminster. She had persuaded Londoners to admit her to their city but treated them in a high-handed manner. By contrast, Stephen was prepared to recognize the city as a commune, able to choose its own officials and raising its own taxes. As a result, Londoners rallied to the king's cause, rang their bells as a call to arms, and marched en masse to Westminster, where Matilda and her followers were preparing to enjoy a pre-coronation banquet.

As soon as Matilda received warning of the London mob, she and her followers took to their horses. As they fled Westminster, 'a mob of citizens, great beyond expression or calculation, entered their abandoned lodgings' and plundered them. The invasion of Westminster and Matilda's flight were salutary: the London mob remained a constant threat on Westminster's horizon. Any ruler who ignored the mob did so at his or her peril.

Westminster Abbey's resistance to the monarch was more subtle, but its power was real. The medieval Church enjoyed enormous wealth: religious houses were better placed than most landowners to defend their privileges and resist the Norman plunder. The *Domesday Book* showed that England's 35 monasteries received annual revenues of £11,066 in total, equivalent to one-sixth of national income. Westminster was one of the wealthier abbeys with an income of £584, and only six others received more, including Glastonbury (£828), Ely (£768) and Bury St Edmund's (£639).[17]

Key weapons in the Church's armoury were the monastic *scriptoria*, where armies of scribes toiled for long hours writing and copying books, charters, writs and other texts. These scribes had enjoyed a near monopoly until the Norman conquest, often writing the charters from which their own religious communities benefited. Although the Normans created a royal *scriptorium*, it was not until the middle of the twelfth century that royal scribes were writing most royal charters.

From 1083, Westminster Abbey had flourished for about 30 years under the leadership of Gilbert Crispin, an Abbot of great ability and learning who had served as Lanfranc's chaplain. The Abbey's re-building progressed, with cloisters and a dormitory completed, and, possibly, a refectory. Gilbert displayed immense skill in the conflict between the papacy and monarchs. He also trod a careful path between the sensitivities of a largely Anglo-Saxon community and the danger for the Abbey of being seen as a focus of anti-Norman sentiment.

On Gilbert's death, Osbert of Clare was elected Prior and became acting head, but in 1121 he was overlooked when Henry I appointed Herbert, the almoner, as the new Abbot. The Abbey's fortunes had begun to falter during Gilbert's declining years, and under Herbert the buildings fell into disrepair. Osbert complained, and although he had some effect, he was stripped of his office and banished to Ely for an unknown period. However, by 1134, Osbert was reinstated and continued as prior after King Stephen appointed his illegitimate son, Gervase of Blois, as successor to Abbot Herbert in 1138.

Westminster Abbey was Osbert's great passion. He devoted his life to defending its privileges and promoting its interests. He set up a team of scribes who embellished existing documents and produced a stream of forgeries, all designed to enhance the Abbey's rights and improve its status. His scribes, who lived and worked to the south of the Abbey on the site now occupied by Westminster School, traded claim and counter-claim with their monastic rivals about their respective churches' antiquity, holy relics, patronage, privileges and wealth.

According to the Abbey's historian, Widmore, the blame for the forgeries should be pinned on the Normans, who 'made it as it were necessary, by disregarding the old Saxon Charters of Land and Privileges, and reducing the Monks to the hard condition of either losing what belonged to them or defending it by forged instruments in Latin'. A former dean, John Armitage Robinson, suggested that the monks sometimes re-worked 'Saxon documents that were unintelligible to the Normans into impressive Latin charters', and gave their interpretation of privileges granted before the Conquest.[18]

Analysis of the hand-writing suggests that a scribe, who worked under Osbert's supervision in 1139 and again after 1154, was responsible for drafting faked documents supposedly issued by King Edgar, Archbishop Dunstan, Edward the Confessor, William the Conqueror, King Stephen and Archbishop Theobald. Other forgeries perpetrated at the Abbey were falsely attributed to King Offa, Henry I and Pope Paschal II.[19]

The charter, dated AD 785, that describes Westminster as a 'terrible place' purports to record Offa's grant of land at Aldenham, Hertfordshire, 'to St Peter, and to the needy people of God', who lived in Westminster. It contains some convincing details of a substantial grant of property, amounting to ten hides (roughly equivalent to 1,200 acres). In return, the abbot of Westminster, Ordbriht gave the king an armlet worth 100 mancuses (equivalent to 3,000 pence, or £12. 10s.). It is impossible to put a firm date on this deal, but Aldenham was one of Westminster's early possessions, and the rights to this property were long disputed between the Abbots of Westminster and St Albans. A later forgery, concerning the same land, was attributed to King Edgar in the tenth century and was probably drafted by the Westminster monks as evidence.[20]

Osbert also became convinced that the Abbey was failing to exploit one of its greatest assets: the legacy of King Edward the Confessor. The Normans had been nervous that any cult of the Confessor might become the focus of Anglo-Saxon resistance, but Osbert was convinced that the Abbey was missing a golden opportunity. The Confessor's canonization would give Westminster its own saint and transform Edward's tomb into a shrine for pilgrims. Osbert began preaching the cult of the Confessor after attending Edward's anniversary mass and being cured of a fever, which he regarded as evidence of the Confessor's miraculous powers. He re-wrote an old biographical record of the Confessor as a saint's life. His *Vita Aedwardi regis* became the centrepiece of his campaign for the Confessor's canonization. When the papal envoy, Alberic, held a church council at Westminster in 1138, Osbert presented him with his Life of Edward.

The biography included a vivid description of the opening of the Confessor's tomb in 1102, an event that Osbert might have witnessed as a pupil at Westminster. According to Osbert, the exhumation occurred during Edward's 'translation', which suggests that the Confessor's tomb was moved, perhaps to a new shrine. Osbert describes the opening of Edward's tomb in the presence of Abbot Gilbert Crispin, Bishop Gundulf of Rochester, and other 'men of note': 'So firm and bright was the flesh, so perfect all the garments, that their soundness told that God in truth was magnified in Edward, setting forth in his flesh an image of the resurrection of the saints'. When Bishop Gundulf sought to pluck a beard hair from the dead king, he was admonished by Gilbert and desisted.[21]

Osbert later led a delegation to Rome to press the case for Edward's canonization with Pope Innocent II. Although the pope deferred by requesting more evidence of Edward's saintliness, he responded to Osbert's reports on the Abbey's plight. The Abbey's privileges were confirmed, and Abbot Gervase was ordered to restore all the lands, revenues, churches and tithes that had been granted away without the consent of the monastery. However, Gervase was also told to suppress murmurers and disorderly monks. Osbert's complaints had angered Gervase, and he was sacked again.

Undeterred, Osbert assembled more supporting evidence, including charters supposedly issued by Edward. Osbert hoped to convince the pope of the Abbey's wealth in the Confessor's day and to show how poor it had become since: 'through the violence of tyrants'. Although he claimed to have found Edward's charters among the Abbey muniments, he and his scribes had almost certainly forged them.[22]

Osbert disappears from the records and may have died in 1158, but it is possible that he lived to see his hopes fulfilled. On 7 February 1161, a new pope, Alexander III, canonized Edward the Confessor as reward for Henry II's support during a papal schism. It seems fitting that Westminster's saint was canonized for political reasons. The shrine of the Confessor became a destination for pilgrims and remains a draw for devout Christians and tourists. In 2003, President George

W. Bush and his wife, Laura, prayed at the shrine. The cult of the Confessor originated when the Abbey was at its most vulnerable after the Norman conquest. Its success was largely the work of one of the Abbey's most redoubtable characters, Osbert of Clare, whose qualifications as the patron saint of Westminster spin doctors are unrivalled.

PART TWO

MAKING THE ROYAL CAPITAL

5 AN UNLIKELY FOUNDING FATHER

enry II was the French-speaking head of the vast Angevin Empire that stretched from the Pyrenees to the Scottish borders; yet this dynamic, fidgety, short-tempered king became the unlikely founding father of Westminster as the seat of government. At Christmas 1153, a dozen years after Henry's mother, Empress Matilda, fled the London mob, her 20-year-old son returned to Westminster. In a deal that ended the bloody dispute over the English crown: he was confirmed as King Stephen's successor.

On Sunday 19 December 1154, Henry and his wife, Eleanor of Aquitaine, were 'crowned and consecrated with becoming pomp and splendour' in Westminster Abbey. The new king and queen made a handsome couple. According to the historian, Alison Weir, Henry was of medium height with a strong chest and short reddish hair, and Eleanor was a legendary beauty, probably with auburn hair. After the ceremony, they rode through the streets to cries of 'Waes Hael!' and 'Vivat Rex!' from crowds of onlookers.[1]

Westminster Palace was described at the time by Fitzstephen, a clerk and biographer of Thomas Becket, as 'an incomparable structure, guarded by a wall and bulwarks'. The route between Westminster and the City, along what is now Whitehall, the Strand and Fleet Street 'was a continued suburb, mingled with large and beautiful gardens and orchards belonging to the citizens'. At Westminster, King Street linked Whitehall to the precinct gates of the Abbey and Palace, on the site of Parliament Square. To the west of the Abbey, Tothill Street ran along the line of the modern street of the same name. The old village of Westminster was clustered round the gates of the Abbey and Palace gates. The Thames was, in effect, a second main street along Westminster's east border, where the number of landing stages (confusingly called 'bridges'), wharves and water-gates increased as Westminster grew.[2]

Westminster's growth was fuelled by Henry II's strengthening of the Crown's power. However, the king's ambition set him on a collision course with the church. His mistake was not to foresee that after Thomas Becket, his Chancellor and close aide, was confirmed as Archbishop of Canterbury at Westminster Abbey in May 1162, he would champion the church as fiercely as he had once promoted the Crown. When the king sought to reduce the power of ecclesiastical courts in October 1163, Becket sprang to the defence, countering that 'the clergy by reason of their orders and distinctive office, have Christ alone as king'.[3]

Within a fortnight of their clash, Henry and Becket met at a midnight ceremony in the Abbey for the transfer of the remains of the recently sanctified King Edward the Confessor to a new shrine. Becket and the new abbot, Laurence, opened the Confessor's grave before the high altar. The Confessor's body was said to have been perfectly preserved, with his long, white, curling beard still visible. The ring of St John was removed as a relic, and the king's vestments were taken and made into copes.

However, the deteriorating relationship with Henry prompted Becket to flee into exile. In his absence, the Archbishop of York crowned Henry's heir, after the king adopted the French tradition of holding the coronation of the eldest son during the monarch's lifetime. The feud between Canterbury and York simmered for years. In 1175, matters came to a head in 'the celebrated contest' between Richard, Archbishop of Canterbury, and Roger, Archbishop of York, in St Catherine's Chapel, Westminster Abbey, during a church council attended by a papal legate. Richard of Canterbury occupied the seat to the legate's right, but Roger of York felt that his prior consecration entitled him to sit in that place. In the words of the chroniclers: 'in springs Roger of York, and, finding Canterbury so seated, fairly sits him down on Canterbury's lap – a baby too big to be danced thereon; yea, Canterbury's servants dandled this large child with a witness, who plucked him from thence, and buffeted him to purpose'. Roger later alleged that he had been seized by the Bishop of Ely, 'thrown on his face, trampled down, beat with fists and sticks, and severely bruised'. After the scuffle, Roger rushed, with torn cope, into the main part of the Abbey where he denounced Richard and the Bishop of Ely to the king. Henry ordered his overwrought archbishops to keep the peace.[4]

A year or so after this episcopal fracas, Henry II's treasurer, Richard FitzNigel, sat at a turret window overlooking the Thames, north of a wharf known as Endehithe, roughly on the site of modern-day Horse Guards Avenue. He was writing *Dialogus de Scaccario* (Dialogue of the Exchequer): the first treatise on the work of a government department in England, following the transfer of the Court of the Exchequer and most of the king's treasure from Winchester to Westminster. This seemingly prosaic piece of re-organisation was overshadowed by Becket's return and shocking murder in Canterbury Cathedral; but the Exchequer's move signalled Westminster's emergence as the seat of government.

Henry II substantially improved Westminster Palace, making it his most important residence. By 1190 a building to accommodate the Exchequer had been completed, but this was only one of many new additions. A second storey was added to the old Lesser Hall; and extra apartments were built nearer the river – the king's wardrobe, the cloister, a kitchen and the king's (or painted) chamber. The year 1184 marks the first mention of St Stephen's Chapel; and another chapel, St John's, existed by 1186–7. A river wall and dock were built at the north end of New Palace Yard in about 1179–80, and a water gate and bridge there are first mentioned in 1184. Timber precinct walls and a gate were built between New Palace Yard and Green Yard, an inner court, located between the Palace and St Margaret's Church.[5]

The growing importance of the Palace prompted more officials to move into the area, as the historian of medieval Westminster, Gervase Rosser, has shown. The site of Treasury Green, near the present Number 10 Downing Street, was drained by ditches from about 1160. Remnants of buildings that fronted onto King Street date from the end of the twelfth century. In about 1195, FitzNigel's kinsman, William of Ely, moved into the area at about the time that he became the king's treasurer. Other courtly newcomers to Westminster included the Mauduit family, hereditary chamberlains of the Crown, and landowners in Winchester, who bought in Long Ditch, near Tothill Street.[6]

The Abbey later acquired the royal Treasurers' property, on the site of present-day Horse Guards Avenue, but in 1224 the monks sold it, including a chapel, houses, and a court and stable, to Hubert de Burgh, Henry III's chief minister and regent. In about 1240, after de Burgh departed on a pilgrimage to the Holy Land, his substantial property was bought by the Archbishop of York, Walter de Gray, who gave it to the see of York in perpetuity. York House, or York Place, remained the Westminster residence of the Archbishops of York for about 300 years.

Henry II made Westminster Hall the headquarters of the English legal system. Since the days of King Alfred, the monarch, wherever he happened to be holding court, had settled legal disputes with his advisers and officials. But in 1178 Henry ordered that five judges should hear cases in one place while he was away. Two years later, Ranulf de Glanvil, a senior official, explained in his *Treatise on the Laws and Customs of England*, that a *capitalis curia*, or chief court, was based in the Palace of Westminster, in addition to the court that accompanied the king on his travels. The new chief court met regularly and had a permanent nucleus of judges. During the next century or so, the English common law, based on custom, precedent and judicial decisions, was forged by judges who heard cases in Westminster Hall, debated them in their nearby offices and lived in houses rented from the Abbey.

Henry II bequeathed Westminster systems of administration and law that survived – just – the tumultuous reigns of his sons, Richard I and John. The contrasting images of 'Coeur de Lion' and 'the fouler presence' (his successor King John), became the stuff of legend. Richard's memory is celebrated outside the modern Palace of Westminster in the form of an imposing, bronze, equestrian statue that stands 30-feet high on the site of the old Lesser Hall. The sculpture is the only such commemoration of an English monarch in the precincts of the Houses of Parliament.

England's enduring Lionheart myth is extraordinary. Richard's parents were French, he was brought up in France and he spoke no English. He became king on Henry II's death in 1189 only because of the death of his older brother; spent only six months of his ten-year reign in England; and bled his kingdom dry fighting his wars. However, he was tall, elegant, had red-gold hair and was a good swordsman. He made an immediate impact on his arrival in England after his father's death, when he, and his strikingly attractive mother, Queen Eleanor, rode through London, its streets hung with tapestries and garlands, and spread with rushes. From St Paul's, a procession escorted them to Westminster.

Richard I's coronation on Sunday 3 September 1189 was designed to herald a new age. It is also the first such occasion for which there is a detailed account, by Roger of Howden, a royal official and circuit judge. Richard's coronation procession from the Palace to the Abbey was led by 'the bishops and abbots and many clerks vested in silken copes, with the cross, torch-bearers, censers and holy water going before them', who led the king, 'to the high altar of the church of Westminster with an ordered procession and triumphal chanting: and the whole way by which they went, from the door of the king's chamber to the altar, was covered with woollen cloths'.

Kneeling before the altar, Richard swore his coronation oath, promising to 'keep peace, honour and duty towards God and holy church … exercise right justice and equity among people committed to his charge … annul any evil laws and customs that might have been introduced into the realm, and make good laws and keep them without fraud or evil intent'. After the oath came the anointment, and the moment when Duke Richard became Richard I, King of England:

> Then they stripped him altogether, except his shirt and breeches, and his shirt was torn apart at the shoulders. Then they shod him with buskins [short boots] worked with gold. Then Baldwin, Archbishop of Canterbury, poured the holy oil on his head, and with prayers appointed for this purpose, anointed him king in three places, to wit, his head, his breast, and his arms, which signifies glory, courage and knowledge …

After his anointment, Richard was clothed in the royal vestments and taken to the altar, where he vowed to honour his oath. 'Then he himself took the crown from the altar, and gave it to the Archbishop, and the Archbishop set it on his head, and two earls held it up on account of its weight'. After mass, the coronation procession left the Abbey and returned to the king's chamber, with Richard, 'crowned and carrying the sceptre in his right hand and the rod in his left'.[7]

The Lionheart myth evokes the idea of a new dawn that is ultimately doomed. The date of Richard's coronation was regarded as ill-fated by astrologers, while the appearance of a bat in the Abbey during the coronation service, circling round the king's throne was seen as another bad omen. However, real events were more ominous. As the newly crowned king and his guests enjoyed their gargantuan feast in the Palace, a race riot flared up outside. A royal proclamation issued the day before the coronation had barred Jews from attending. When leaders of London's Jewish community arrived at the Palace gates with gifts for the new king, the crowd would not allow them in and 'committed great outrages on their persons'. The violence spread to the City and continued through the night as Jews were killed or robbed, and their houses plundered or burnt down. The next day, some of the rioters were arrested and three were hanged. Although Richard issued orders to every shire that Jews should be allowed to live in peace, a wave of savage anti-Semitism spread across his kingdom.[8]

In December 1189, just two months after his coronation, Richard I left England for Normandy. He spent six months in his French territories, before departing in early July 1190 with the French king, Philip, at the head of the Third Crusade. His prowess as a brilliant commander and military tactician in the Middle East is commemorated in his portrayal outside the Houses of Parliament as a warrior king. He came to epitomise chivalrous values after being taken hostage in late 1192 on his way back from the Middle East, and being sold to the Emperor, Henry VI. His mother, Eleanor, held court that Christmas at Westminster oblivious of Richard's fate. It was from Westminster a year later that she departed for Germany to seek his release. Her entourage passed along the 'Royal Street' (present-day Whitehall), turned right at St Catherine's hermitage in the small village of Charing (present-day Trafalgar Square) and headed along the Strand towards St Paul's Cathedral, where she collected the final tranche of silver for Richard's ransom.

Richard finally set foot on English soil again in March 1194. He and Eleanor made a state entry into London and, after a thanksgiving service at St Pauls, 'were hailed by joy along the Strand' as they rode to Westminster. But by the summer, Richard had left for Normandy, never to return. His departure was later described by the historians of the Palace, Edward Brayley and John Britton: 'King Richard the First, being at dinner at Westminster, in the Hall which is called the *Little Hall* [or 'lesser hall] he received tidings that King Philip of France had entered Normandy, whereupon he swore that he would never turn away his face until he had met him and fought with him'. Richard supposedly 'directed an opening to be made in the wall … immediately made his way through it, and proceeded to Portsmouth'. A chronicle written some decades after Richard's death claimed that the wall remained unrepaired.[9]

Richard's early death in 1199, followed by the disastrous reign of his brother, made the Lionheart's reputation. The unique tribute to him outside the Palace of Westminster is testimony to his myth, and the patronage of another royal who died early: Prince Albert, the Royal Consort. The sculptor of Richard I's statue, Baron Carlo Marochetti, a native of Turin who came to England in 1848, was a particular favourite of Prince Albert. His clay model for the statue was shown at the Great Exhibition of 1851 before being moved to New Palace Yard. Sir Charles Barry, the architect of the new Palace of Westminster, thought that it was inappropriate to his neo-Gothic design. The casting of the bronze statue in 1856 provoked fresh debate on where it should be placed. Marochetti favoured Old Palace Yard, others argued for New Palace Yard, and one critic suggested sarcastically that it would be more appropriate near the Horse Guards.

Marochetti finally got his way. His statue was erected in Old Palace Yard by public subscription in October 1860. *The Times* claimed that it ranked 'with the few great statues of that class in Europe', but Francis Turner Palgrave, a senior Whitehall official, critic and poet, dismissed it as, 'an essentially vulgar and low-class work precisely on the grounds that call forth the wonder of uncultivated spectators'. Eighty years later, during World War II, the statue's sword was bent by an exploding bomb, but was later repaired.[10]

In contrast with the heroic Lionheart, his brother and successor, King John, has been cast as pantomime villain. 'Foul as it is, hell itself is defiled by the fouler presence of John', was the damning verdict of Matthew Paris, the thirteenth-century chronicler. John reportedly failed to act with dignity during his coronation at Westminster Abbey in May 1199, apparently laughing, allowing the sword to fall from his hand, and hurrying away without receiving the Holy Sacrament. His capture of Richard's preferred heir Prince Arthur of Brittany, in 1202, and the young Prince's disappearance and presumed murder, left a damning stain on John's reputation. His loss of the Angevin Empire in France and his legacy of civil war guaranteed him a bad press. No wonder that the Archbishop of Canterbury, Hubert Walter, who presided at John's coronation was later anxious to explain himself to history, claiming that he had 'scrupulously gone through the forms of election on that day; and that foreseeing the King's violent career, he had wished to place every lawful check on his despotic passions'.[11]

Amidst the drama of King John's reign, the mundane business of managing the Palace continued. In October 1205, 'the sum of £10 was directed to the King's Treasurer, Robert de Leveland for the repair of the king's houses at Westminster, by the view and testimony of lawful men'. In January 1214, 'the treasurer and chamberlains of the Exchequer were commanded by writ to deliver to the abbot and convent of Holy Cross at Waltham the tin lavatory ("stagneum lavatorium") which was constructed in the king's house at Westminster in the time of his father [Henry II], and was afterwards removed'.

After one of John's infrequent visits in 1207, 'the barons of the Exchequer were ordered to account with Robert De Leveland for what he had expended for the laying *fine sand* in the king's houses at Westminster, when the King slept there on Friday, Saturday and Sunday next before the feast of All Saints'. John spent a couple of Christmases at Westminster late in his reign. A wardrobe account reports that in May 1213, 'a payment of sixpence was made to Roger Aquarius for a bath for the king's use at Westminster, on the eve of the preceding Christmas'. And the same account in December lists a payment by the king, at Westminster, of three marks for three barrels of honey.[12]

The chroniclers' emphasis on John's flaws was encouraged by courtiers who were anxious to dissociate themselves from a reign that culminated in the barons' revolt. At the time of John's sudden death in October 1216, Westminster and much of southern England were under French occupation. Despite the promise given by Louis, the Dauphin, to establish 'good laws' and restore 'lost heritages', his supporters raided Westminster's royal treasury and took what loot they could carry. Although the monks denied the raiders access to the Abbey, Louis managed to steal the royal regalia.[13]

The barons' revolt resulted in the *Magna Carta,* widely regarded as a seminal statement of basic liberties and parliamentary government. Yet the principle that royal power should be observed within certain limits was scarcely revolutionary: the precedent was Henry I's coronation oath, more than a century earlier. *Magna Carta* was re-drafted after John's death and further changes were made by a great council at Westminster in the autumn of 1217. The definitive version was finally issued in 1225.

As Westminster was occupied by the barons and their French allies when the nine-year-old Henry III succeeded to the throne, royalist supporters hurriedly arranged for the king to be crowned elsewhere. Henry's coronation was held at Gloucester on 28 October 1216, the only occasion since 1066 when a coronation of an English monarch was held somewhere other than at Westminster Abbey. The Bishop of Winchester, Peter des Roches, presided instead of the Archbishop of Canterbury, Stephen Langton, who was suspended for having failed to excommunicate the barons. There was no act of unction for fear of infringing the rights of Canterbury, and, instead of a crown, a lady's chaplet or garland was placed on the young Henry's head – perhaps because King John had lost his crown in the Wash estuary shortly before his death. It took more than three years before Henry, by then aged 13, was given a second coronation at Westminster Abbey on Whit Sunday, 1220, when he was crowned by Archbishop Langton. The feasting and celebrations exceeded those of Richard I's coronation.

6 SEAT OF GOVERNMENT

enry III's long reign, from 1216 to 1272, spanned the middle of the thirteenth century. His extravagance and his costly campaign to regain Anjou and Normandy taxed his subjects beyond endurance; but he made a huge impact at Westminster. He built the modern abbey, and during his reign several key components of English government developed: the office of Chancellor of the Exchequer, the Privy Council and Parliament. As a result of his reforms, a legal system took shape in Westminster Hall that later spread to America and gave the world the rule of law.

Henry III spent more time and money at Westminster than his predecessors. Urgent repairs to the Palace were needed after the occupation by rebels and the French. The City of London was made to pay as punishment for backing the revolt. In 1217, 'the mayor and sheriffs of London were commanded to pay 100s [shillings] out of the farm of that city, for the repair of the king's houses at Westminster'. In the following year, 'the treasurer and chamberlains were directed to pay Odo, the goldsmith who became keeper of the works at the king's palace, ten marks to repair the quay, and to make other repairs'. Other commissions included, 'the repair of the king's hall and houses' (10 pounds in 1221 and a further 20 pounds the following month); 'the construction of a wall at the king's gate' (20 pounds in 1223); and 'the repair of the quay, the windows of Westminster Hall, and the performance of other works' (20 pounds in 1223).

The size of some payments shows that new building work was under way. A writ issued in 1221, commanded the Treasurer and Chamberlains of the Exchequer 'to pay William of Pontefract £33.6s.8d. for timber purchased for the king's houses on this spot'. In 1223, payments of 30 pounds and a further 100 shillings, were to be made for building work on the Palace. In 1224, 'the Barons of the Exchequer were commanded to allow the Sheriff of Kent £6.9s.10d, which he had expended in the purchase of stone for the building of the king's wall at Westminster'.

Henry's presence at the Palace during much of 1222 and 1223 is confirmed by the purchase of rushes 'for the king's two chambers', 'six casks of Gascon wine', and a payment of £150 in expenses incurred when the king was ill. Henry also had a 'great gibbet' made after rioting Londoners had razed to the ground the house of the Abbot's bailiff and neighbouring buildings in their fury at the bailiff's alleged cheating over a wrestling bout in St Giles's Fields. Three rioters were hanged and many more had hands and feet amputated. By insisting on pledges of military service from 60 citizens and forcing Londoners to pay 'many thousand marks', Henry appeared to act 'on the ungenerous principle of increasing the prosperity of Westminster at the expense of the inhabitants of London'.[1]

Henry III's financial demands drove his reform of government and Westminster's development as the capital. New rooms for the Exchequer were built at the north-west end of Westminster Hall, fronting onto the site of New Palace Yard. In 1228 Henry 'ordered his treasurer and chamberlains to pay to a certain painter 20s. for painting the great Exchequer chamber'. However, the Exchequer soon came under threat. By 1231, the king's finances sank into an ever deeper mess, exacerbated by heavy spending on unsuccessful military campaigns in France and Wales. Henry began taking more notice of Peter des Roches, the Bishop of Winchester, whose nephew Peter de Rivallis became treasurer of the king's household in 1232, and treasurer of the Exchequer in 1233.[2]

However, de Rivallis's attempt to reform royal finances by replacing the Exchequer as the main financial department with the itinerant royal chamber exacerbated the crisis. Bitter opposition to de Rivallis and his uncle surfaced at the King's Council at Westminster Palace in February 1234. The meeting had to be dissolved, 'in consequence of the expostulations of some of the bishops, who, in warning him [Henry] against evil counsellors, said that "their measures would prove as ruinous to himself as they had been to his father"'. At a further meeting, the bishops threatened the king and his ministers with excommunication unless there was a change of regime.[3]

In the spring of 1234, with the country in revolt and no money to fight a civil war, Henry ordered des Roches from court and dismissed de Rivallis. When de Rivallis was tried at Westminster, he took care to remind everyone of his clerical status by arriving bareheaded and showing his tonsure, although he also took the precaution of wearing a dagger. In the end, de Rivallis retreated to the sanctuary of Winchester Cathedral.

Despite the Exchequer's brief demise, its importance and its professionalism increased. An official known as the Chancellor of the Exchequer first appeared as head of its secretarial department during Henry III's reign. The Exchequer's permanent presence off Westminster Hall put it at the heart of government and helped to boost the Palace's importance over other royal residences. The Exchequer became a place where members of the council, judges, sheriffs, bailiffs and others could meet to discuss their business. Exchequer clerks, who were servants of its officials, lived in nearby streets, usually as tenants of the Abbey.[4]

Henry also recognized a growing distinction within the King's Council between his close advisers and the wider body of barons and clerics, by introducing an oath for 12 members of his inner circle. The inner, or sworn council became known informally as the 'privy council' and was to become, under the Tudors, the main engine of government. Today's Privy Council is much larger and its role is mainly symbolic, but its members swear an oath of confidentiality based on a Tudor update of the original one.[5]

While these changes were afoot, the King's Council sanctioned a very traditional form of diplomacy. In February 1235, two ambassadors of Frederick, the Holy Roman Emperor, arrived demanding that Henry's 21-year-old sister, Isabella, should marry their master. The king's councillors considered this demand for three days before giving their unanimous consent. The princess was brought from safe custody in the Tower of London to meet the envoys, whose delighted reaction at this wedding by proxy was graphically captured by Matthew Paris:

> when they had for a while delighted themselves with beholding the virgin, and judged her to be all things worthy of the imperial bed, confirmed by oath the emperor's proposal of matrimony, presenting to her, on the part of their master, the wedding-ring. And when they had placed it on her finger, they declared her to be the empress of the Roman empire, exclaiming together, "Vivat Imperatrix, vivat!"

The Archbishop of Cologne and the Duke of Louvain, 'with a noble train', arrived to escort the bride to Germany. After a great feast at Westminster, Isabella and the emperor's envoys were 'accompanied to Dartford by the king and a large concourse of earls, barons and other nobles'.[6]

In the same year, negotiations began for Henry, in his mid-twenties, to marry Eleanor, the 12-year-old daughter of the Count of Provence. Queen Eleanor's coronation, in 1236, is one of the first for which details were noted, because of rivalries at court. 'Great disputes arose about the services of the officers of the king's household, and about the rights belonging to their offices', according to the Red Book of the Exchequer. Although Simon de Montfort 'held water for the King to wash before dinner', Roger de Bigod, Earl of Norfolk, had contested this honour. A notable absentee was Hugh de Albini, the hereditary Chief Butler, who had been 'excommunicated by the Archbishop of Canterbury for refusing to let the Primate hunt in his Sussex forest'. A Court of Claims was subsequently set up before each coronation to adjudicate on such courtly rivalries.[7]

At Eleanor's coronation feast, the citizens of London enjoyed their right of serving as butlers. Matthew Paris describes them heading towards Westminster Hall

> dressed in silk garments, with mantles worked in gold, and with costly changes of raiment, mounted on valuable horses, glittering with new bits and saddles, and riding in troops arranged in order. They carried with them three hundred and sixty gold and silver cups, preceded by the king's trumpeters and with

horns sounding, so that such a wonderful novelty struck all who beheld it with astonishment.

Inside the Great Hall, the Londoners 'poured the wine abundantly into precious cups'. The sheer scale of the festivities left Matthew Paris struggling for words:

> But how shall I describe the dainties of the table, and the abundance of divers liquors; the quantity of game, the variety of fish, the multitude of jesters, and the attention of waiters? Whatever the world pours forth of pleasure and glory was there especially displayed'.[8]

The scene in Westminster Hall was dramatically transformed a month later. After torrential rain, the heavy flow of water downstream met the incoming tide. As Matthew Paris reported: the river 'overflowed into the great Palace at Westminster, and spreading itself, so covered the area that the middle of the Hall might be passed in boats, and persons rode through it on horseback to their chambers'.[9]

A fascinating glimpse of life at Westminster at this time can be gleaned from a judicial inquiry into a murder committed close by the Palace. The murder victim, Henry Clement, a clerk and messenger of the Justiciar of Ireland, had foolishly boasted that he was responsible for the killing of the respected courtier, Richard Marshal, Earl of Pembroke, in Ireland. Clement was staying in the house of Master David, a surgeon, opposite the Palace's main gate, in a paved street between the Abbey and Palace. The surgeon's house was typical of the period, with a hall, from which inside stairs led up to an upper room, and an adjacent lodging occupied by Alice, who was either David's landlady or tenant. At the back was a courtyard, with a smaller dwelling that was probably a stable with a room above. The town was so crowded that one of the witnesses to Clement's murder was sleeping in the courtyard of the surgeon's house, two others (a messenger and his servant) were asleep in the hall, while across the street some of the king's servants were encamped in tents outside the palace gate.

The latter were woken by the neighing of horses and clattering of hooves as about 16 men, some of them armed, rode up to the surgeon's house, dismounted by the light of a blazing torch, broke down the door and rushed upstairs. The surgeon was wounded and Clement was killed in what was probably a revenge killing by Marshal's supporters. Most of the gang escaped, but the likely leader, William Marisco, was later arrested, tried and executed at the Tower of London in 1242.[10]

Despite a costly military fiasco in Gascony in 1242–3, rebellion in Wales and the risk of conflict with the Scots, Henry commissioned further expensive work on his palace. The sheriff of Kent was commanded, 'with all possible speed to purchase, and cause to be conveyed to Westminster, 100 barge loads of grey stone'. The Treasurer and Chamberlains were ordered to pay £1,949.13s.5d to Edward, Keeper of the King's Works in succession to his father, Odo, for the work he 'had expended in the erection of a new chamber near to our Hall at Westminster, and of our Conduit, and in other works there'. Other works included a two-storey chamber, 'long and of good size', built to accommodate the knights of the royal household, and a porch that enabled Henry to descend from his horse 'with fitting dignity'.[11]

During the 1250s, Henry III commissioned a new High Table, or Bench, and a throne made of dark Purbeck Marble to replace the old wooden High Table that stood on a dais at the southern end of Westminster Hall and symbolised royal authority. The new Table measured about 12 feet in length, by 3 feet in width, and 3 feet in height. Before a coronation ceremony in the Abbey, a new king or queen took possession of their kingdom at this Table and was presented with the crown, sceptres and other regalia symbolizing royal power. Its accompanying throne stood between gilt-copper leopards against the south wall. The Table disappeared almost 400 years later after the execution of Charles I, but fragments were unearthed in 2006 beneath the flight of steps near where it once stood at the south end of Westminster Hall.

The King's (or Queen's) High Table (or Bench) gave its name to the court of the King's or Queen's Bench, the senior criminal court. The king or queen – or in his or her absence, the Lord Chancellor – sat at the south end of the Great Hall and presided over criminal cases. From 1234, professional judges sat in the Court of King's Bench. A separate court of Common Pleas was set up after Magna Carta for disputes that did not directly involve the king or queen. During the fourteenth century, the Chancery emerged as a separate court for redress of grievances not covered by common law or Acts of Parliament. By the sixteenth century the King's Bench and Chancery were established in opposite corners at the south end of the Great Hall.

Westminster Hall became a great legal bazaar. Lawyers and their clients created a constant hubbub as they scurried and swarmed about the place, clutching their documents, consulting one another, contesting their case and haggling over their fees. The courts were good for trade: hostelries and stalls sprang up around Westminster Hall, providing every imaginable service and distraction. Legal business, with its accompanying circus, was a major feature of life in Westminster Hall until the nineteenth century.

The Great Hall and other parts of the Palace also hosted Henry's regular acts of charity. Inspired by the Confessor's example, the king marked the main feast days by feeding the hungry. In 1244, an estimated 10,000 poor descended on Westminster Palace in a single day. The old and sick crammed into the Great and Lesser Halls for their hand-outs of food; crowds of children were fed in the Queen's Chamber; and the rest were nourished in the richly decorated King's Chamber. Henry's devotion to the Confessor also inspired the grand project for which he will always be remembered: re-building Westminster Abbey.[12]

7 'THE MOST GLORIOUS WORK IN ENGLAND'

E ven today, when buildings tower high into the sky, the magnificent sight of Westminster's thirteenth-century Abbey soaring majestically heavenwards is awe-inspiring. Inside, the overwhelming impression of great height is accentuated by the building's narrowness. The Abbey is three times taller than it is wide and, with a maximum interior height of 102 feet, has the highest Gothic vault in England. These exceptional proportions were designed to create an acute sense of humility and wonder. Ever since the present Abbey took shape it has reinforced Osbert of Clare's earlier portrayal of Westminster as an awesome, 'terrible place'.

Much of Westminster Abbey as we know it today was created by Henry III. He was inspired by his religious devotion to the canonized King Edward the Confessor, and spurred on by political ambition to emulate his brother-in-law, Louis IX of France. Henry envisaged Westminster as a French-style, political centre for England, complete with a new shrine to its royal saint, and a great, new Abbey modelled on the Gothic-style, high-rise, northern French cathedrals.[1]

At the age of 13, on the eve of his second coronation at Westminster, Henry had laid the foundation stone of a new Lady Chapel at the eastern end of the Confessor's abbey, on the site now occupied by Henry VII's Chapel. The first offering laid upon the altar of the Lady Chapel was the spurs worn by the king at his coronation. Henry's close interest in the Abbey was further encouraged by an historic church ruling in 1222 that confirmed Westminster's special status, freeing it from the jurisdiction of the Bishop of London and Archbishop of Canterbury, and affiliating it directly to Rome. New Abbots visited the Vatican for confirmation by the pope, who sometimes also gave them diplomatic missions. As a result, Westminster Abbots were open to new influences, as the re-built abbey was to demonstrate.[2]

In the summer of 1245, despite the cost of dispatching troops to crush a Welsh rebellion, Henry III commissioned the re-building of the Abbey. Demolition of the east end of Edward the Confessor's Romanesque church began in July, during the week of the Abbey's feast commemorating St Peter. The following year,

Henry's will expressed his wish to be buried at Westminster, making him the first monarch since the Confessor to opt for the Abbey as his final resting place and strengthening the sense of a royal presence at Westminster, regardless of the living monarch's actual whereabouts.[3]

It took 24 years before Henry III's new abbey was consecrated, and even then the building was unfinished. During its construction, its precincts became a bustling, noisy building site. The number of workmen fluctuated between about 100 in winter and more than 400 in summer. In addition to carpenters, glaziers, lime-burners, marblers, masons, painters, plumbers, polishers, scaffolders, stone-cutters and tillers, the supply chain involved many others, some of whom never came near the Abbey: quarrymen and woodmen, financiers and merchants, jewellers and weavers, sailors and waggoners. Great loads of building material were carried by land and water to Westminster: Kentish ragstone; Caen and Reigate freestone; Purbeck marble; Derbyshire lead; timber from Berkshire, Essex and Kent; chalk and sand; willow osiers for the scaffolding; and cloth and jewels for decoration and ornamentation.[4]

The itinerant craftsmen tended to keep their own company. The masons' chief lodge was located against the north side of the Abbey's nave (facing present-day Parliament Square). Some workmen settled in Westminster because the Palace, and the growing number of houses, inns and shops offered the chance of employment when work on the new church went slack. The re-building of the abbey was initially directed by the king's master mason, Henry of Reyns: so called because he had worked in Rheims, home of the French coronation cathedral. The new abbey was influenced by Rheims and other French cathedrals, notably Amiens and Saint-Chapelle in Paris, and by the English Gothic tradition.[5]

Henry of Reyns was granted the use of two houses in Westminster in 1246, presumably for drawing detailed plans and designs for the masonry. By about 1253, when he left – perhaps he died young, as he disappears from the records – the new Chapter House, its vestibule and a northern section of the cloisters were finished. The project continued under the direction of John of Gloucester. Some changes were made to the original plans, possibly influenced by Henry III's visits to Chartres Cathedral and Parisian churches on his way home from Gascony in late 1254. By 1259, the transepts, apse and crossing were completed. John of Gloucester was followed as master mason by Robert of Beverley, whose good relations with the Abbey eventually earned him a supply of wine until his death in 1285. By 1261, the cost of the work had reached an estimated £29,345.19s.8d., with a further £260 outstanding.[6]

Funding Henry's grand project required all the king's ingenuity. He created a separate exchequer – with the Archdeacon of Westminster and Edward of Westminster as treasurers – to handle money that he appropriated for the new abbey. The king also turned impresario. In 1245, he developed Westminster's long-standing annual fair by granting the Abbot of Westminster two annual fairs of three days each: one in January on the anniversary of St Edward's burial; and the other, in October, on the anniversary of the translation of the Confessor's remains to the shrine in the old abbey. Sales duties levied at the fair were earmarked for the abbey's re-building. The fairs were held in the cramped confines of St Margaret's churchyard, between narrow lanes of shops and tenements, in defiance of papal and royal decrees banning such events in churchyards. An order by Henry that the fairs should move to Tothill Fields, to the south of the abbey, was ignored, probably because this site was marshy.[7]

Henry's rivalry with Louis IX, and his desire that his new abbey should emulate the French royal church of St Denys, prompted him to launch a spectacular propaganda coup in October 1247, during the feast that marked the translation of St Edward's remains to the Confessor's shrine in the old abbey. The king believed that he had obtained from the Holy Land one of the greatest relics of all time: a phial containing drops of Christ's blood. Henry planned to deliver this blood relic personally to Westminster Abbey in a carefully orchestrated and theatrically staged ceremony attended by the ecclesiastical and lay magnates. The king was at pains to ensure that Matthew Paris was on hand to record the great event, much as today a film-crew or photographer is on hand. The chronicler came cheap, as his reward was dinner in the Abbey's new refectory.[8]

The ceremony began at St Paul's, where Henry, having spent the previous day keeping vigil and fasting on bread and water, received a vase containing the blood relic. He made the journey to Westminster wearing 'a poor cloak without a hood' and walking slowly along the dirty and uneven road, carrying the vase before him with both hands while keeping his eyes either fixed on the treasure or looking up to heaven. A cloth cover was held above his head on four spears, while two attendants supported his arms to prevent him being overcome by fatigue. At Westminster, people packed the remaining parts of the old abbey, eager to witness the spectacle. The voices of the bishops of Norwich and Lincoln could be heard above the hubbub, preaching that the blood relic was superior even to Louis IX's holy cross.[9]

As the building costs mounted, Henry extended October's St Edward's fair to 15 days in 1248, banned all other fairs held at the same time and forced London's shops to close for the duration, causing 'great trouble and paines to the citizens'. London shopkeepers had little choice but to hire stalls for St Edward's Fair, and Londoners had no choice but to shop in Westminster, where the crowds were often 'turmoiled too pitifullie in mire and dirt, through occasion of raine'.[10]

Henry's fleecing of Londoners risked provoking its mob. When their resentment turned to mounting anger in 1250, the king summoned Londoners and their families, 'even to the boys of twelve years old', to Westminster, where they crammed into the Great Hall. There, according to Matthew Paris, 'the king, humbly, as if about to shed tears, entreated each one of the citizens … to disavow all kind of anger, malevolence, and rancour towards him'. He confessed to having, 'in many ways injured them, taking away their goods ...' His histrionic display worked. The Londoners accepted his apology, but 'no restitution was made of what had been taken from them'.[11]

The transformation of Westminster during Henry III's long reign was magnificently apparent on 13 October 1269, the feast day of St Edward the Confessor, when the new abbey was consecrated. It was the anniversary of the Confessor's canonization and translation of his remains in 1163 to the shrine created by Henry III's grandfather. The ageing king was anxious to celebrate his achievement in rebuilding the abbey and erecting a new shrine to the Confessor. He had spent £41,248 on the building and more than £5,000 on the shrine – vast sums in those days – and was prompted by his memory of 'the grandest ceremony of the kind that England had ever seen,' in which he, in his early boyhood, had played a part: the translation of the remains of St Thomas of Canterbury.[12]

The king's immediate family gathered together for what was to be the last time. Henry was accompanied by his wife, Eleanor of Provence; his brother, Richard of Cornwall; his heir, the future Edward I, who was about to leave on crusade; Edward's wife, Eleanor of Castile; and his second son, Edmund. Henry and many of his nobles 'clothed in white garments, had passed the preceding night in the abbey church, watching and praying, and performing acts of charity'. After the consecration, the Confessor's coffin was removed from its old tomb. The king and his brother carried it on their shoulders, in view of the whole church. The king's sons, Edward and Edmund, and other senior courtiers, 'with as many other nobles as could come near to touch it', helped support the coffin as it moved slowly to the new shrine.[13]

However, the day was marred by another Westminster tradition: a dispute over precedence. The bishops remained in their stalls, instead of joining the procession behind the Confessor's body, because they refused to follow the Archbishop of York, whose insistence on carrying his cross was seen as a challenge to the rights of the Archbishop of Canterbury. Another quarrel, between the citizens of London and Winchester over their respective roles provoked some of the former to leave early. Fortunately, another Westminster tradition was observed afterwards, when 'the king magnificently feasted a great multitude of the assembled company, of all ranks, in his Palace'.[14]

As Henry III's health deteriorated, he spent more time at Westminster. During the autumn of 1272, his final days were disturbed by the cries of Londoners in Westminster Hall protesting over the disputed election of a Mayor. Peace came when a settlement was reached on 11 November. Five days later, the king died. He was 65 years old and had reigned for 56 years. Henry was given a magnificent funeral in his rebuilt abbey. Afterwards, oaths of homage were sworn to his absent successor, Edward I, and Henry's great seal was ceremonially broken in sight of the congregation. But Henry III's final resting place near his shrine to the Confessor was not yet built. His body was first buried, in full regalia, in the coffin where the Confessor's remains had lain till 1269, 'and still, as Henry might suppose, sanctified by their odour'. Miracles were said to have occurred at his burial site, and a cult developed, but only for a short time.[15]

Although, sainthood eluded Henry III, the re-built abbey is an inspirational legacy. It comprises the eastern part of the main building: the chancel (with the shrine to St Edward the Confessor and sanctuary), the crossing, the choir and the eastern end of the nave. It also comprises the Abbey's north and south transepts; the chapel of St Faith; and – beyond the main building – the north-east quarter of the great cloister, adjoining the nave and south transept; and the Chapter House and its vestibule.

In design, Henry III's abbey is a synthesis of French and English Gothic. Its height and proportions, and the design of its apse and its tracery – especially in the rose windows in the transepts – are French; while the thick walls and complex ornamentation are English. 'So completely was the whole work identified with Henry III', noted Dean Stanley, 'that when, in the reigns of Richard II and Henry V, the Nave was completed, the earlier style – contrary to the almost universal custom of the medieval builders – was continued, as if by a process of antiquarian restoration'.[16]

However, since the Reformation, it has been impossible to enjoy fully Henry's aesthetic achievement. 'We tread on the wreck of the most glorious work in England,' observed James Peller Malcolm, in the early nineteenth century, 'venerable through age, costly in its materials and invaluable for its workmanship. What must have been the glories of this holy place soon after the completion of the church! An admirer of the arts must view it with deepest regret.'[17]

Medieval worshippers were more fortunate. For more than 250 years, the interior of Henry's abbey was a blaze of colour, decorated with a brilliance that glittered in the light of numerous candles, and which, to the modern eye, would seem garish. The Abbey's arches, roof bosses and surfaces were illuminated by a dazzling display of blues, gilts, greens and reds in an array of different patterns. The vivid spectacle was enhanced by rich tapestries, some of which hung round the choir until 1644. Stained glass windows cast coloured beams of light through the church.[18]

The centre-piece of Henry's rebuilt abbey, the ornate shrine of St Edward the Confessor, was, in Dean Stanley's pen-portrait, 'of gold, adorned with precious stones, and placed in an exalted situation'. In keeping with tradition, the Confessor's shrine was constructed to the east of the altar. However, Henry's earlier addition of the Lady Chapel at the east end meant moving the high altar westward to its present, central position. 'A mound of earth, the last funeral "tumulus" in England', according to Stanley, 'was raised between the altar and the Lady Chapel, 'and on its summit was raised the tomb in which the body of the Confessor was to be laid'. The shrine was visible from the far western end of the nave for about 200 years until the present screen, or reredos, was installed during the reign of Henry VI.[19]

On each side of the shrine were golden statues, one of the Confessor, and the other of St John in the guise of the mysterious pilgrim, standing on the two spiralling marble pillars that now support the shrine's western end. The base of the shrine is polished stone and glass inlaid in Purbeck marble. It incorporates seven recesses – three each on its northern and southern sides, and one on its eastern side – in which pilgrims could kneel and pray. Stanley suggests that these recesses were intended for the victims of the glandular disease, scrofula, 'who came to ensconce themselves there for the sake of receiving from the sacred corpse within the deliverance from the "King's Evil", which the living sovereign was believed to communicate by his touch'. This medieval notion that people could be cured of scrofula by the sovereign's touch prompted a later visitor to the Abbey, Joseph Addison, the eighteenth century politician and writer, to report in the *Spectator*: 'We were then shown Edward the Confessor's tomb, upon which Sir Roger [Addison's fictional character, Sir Roger de Coverley] acquainted us that he was the first who touched for the evil'.[20]

But the shrine seen by Addison – and by visitors today – is an inferior reconstruction. Henry's original was stripped of its gold and jewels following an order in 1536 to remove images, relics and shrines from England's cathedrals and churches. By January 1540, when the Abbey was dissolved, the Confessor's shrine had been demolished to its base and St Edward's body secretly buried elsewhere in the Abbey. The shrine's repair was begun in 1556, after the Catholic Queen Mary I had restored the Abbey and its monks, and the Confessor's body was re-interred. But the work, supervised by Abbot John de Feckenham, was botched: the base was rebuilt with stonework and plaster, and painted and gilded in imitation of the original, Italianate work. The golden and bejewelled ark above the shrine, shown in a sketch by Matthew Paris, was replaced by a two-tier, wooden cover, which was supposedly improved in the 1960s.[21]

Complementing the Confessor's shrine, artistically and spiritually, was the Westminster Retable, an exquisitely painted panel that stood at the back of the high altar, facing the congregation. This carved altar-piece, measuring 10 feet by 3 feet, is the Abbey's greatest treasure and represents 'the finest late thirteenth century panel painting remaining from northern Europe'. It was commissioned by Henry III for the Abbey's consecration. Although the identity of its artist is unknown, the retable is Britain's oldest surviving oil painting. The discovery of traces of ultramarine pigment, extracted from lapis lazuli imported in the thirteenth century from Afghanistan, offers a rare glimpse of the global trade in expensive goods some 750 years ago.

The impact of the original Westminster Retable must have been stunning. It gave the appearance of being a solid gold altarpiece decorated with jewels and paintings, an effect achieved by using copper alloy, silver foil, pieces of glass and gold leaf to imitate jewels, porphyry and enamel. Its five main compartments depicted standing figures. The original portrayal of Christ in the centre panel can still be seen. He blesses with his right hand, while holding in his left hand a tiny globe, symbolizing him as saviour of the world. Although the globe is only 1.6 inches across, its detail includes trees, animals and birds, the waters of the earth and a sun and moon. Christ is flanked by the Virgin Mary holding a palm and St John the Evangelist holding a palm and a book. The best preserved figure is St Peter, to whom the Abbey is dedicated. He stands in the far left compartment, beneath a canopy, holding the key of Heaven. The figure on the far right is missing and was perhaps St Paul or St Edward the Confessor. The eight star-shaped medallions in the two compartments on either side of the central panel depicted Christ's miracles, but only three on the left are identifiable: the raising of Jairus's daughter, the healing of the blind man and the feeding of the five thousand.[22]

The Westminster Retable survived the destruction of church iconography during the Reformation by chance, probably because it was a large piece of wood that could be put to practical use. From the start of the seventeenth century it was used as the roof of a cupboard that housed the Abbey's funeral effigies. Its existence was first recorded in 1725 and was finally salvaged and moved to the Abbey in 1827. By the mid-nineteenth century it had been moved to a glass case and was admired as 'a very wonderful work of art' by Sir George Gilbert Scott, the Victorian architect and surveyor of the Abbey. Conservation work began in the 1990s, and the restored retable can be viewed in the Abbey Museum.[23]

The brilliant use of polished stone, glass and marble in the Abbey achieves its most compelling effect in the geometrically patterned pavement in front of the main altar. This extravagant and intriguing, multi-coloured, square mosaic – each side measures 24 feet 10 inches – appears to have been an integral part of Henry III's abbey; yet it was only incorporated after the re-building had begun, following the election, in 1258, of a new Abbot of Westminster, Richard of Ware. The following year, he journeyed to Italy for his confirmation by Pope Alexander IV, who happened to be staying at his summer retreat of Anagni. In the local cathedral, Richard of Ware saw the stunning mosaic pavements made by craftsmen known as the Cosmati: after Cosmatus, the name of one of their leading families. On his return to Westminster, Abbot Ware apparently persuaded Henry III to commission a mosaic, or Cosmati, shrine for the Confessor.[24]

Following a further visit to the Vatican in 1266 or 1267, the Abbot returned with Cosmati craftsmen, and stones such as porphyry, jasper and Thasos marble. The pavement was created in 1268, as its contemporary inscription shows. In 1269, Abbot Ware received £50 from the king in part-payment for the cost of the pavement, but was never paid in full. Although John Flete, the fifteenth-century Westminster monk, suggested that the Abbot was left out of pocket, the pavement was probably a gift to the Abbey by Pope Alexander's successor Clement IV reflecting Westminster's special relationship with Rome.[25]

The Cosmati pavement is one of Britain's greatest medieval treasures and mysteries. Its abstract, geometric design, with its intriguing, interlinked pattern of multi-coloured hexagons, roundels, spirals and squares, is probably intended to symbolize the divinely ordered pattern of the universe. It also originally contained a mysteriously worded brass inscription in Latin, of which only eleven letters remain. Before the words were finally obliterated, they were noted by Flete, but instead of offering explanation they present a baffling, ancient riddle.[26]

The inscription's first sentence gives the pavement's provenance: 'In AD 1212 with 60 less four [i.e. in 1268], King Henry III, the City [i.e. Rome], Odoricus [the craftsman] and the Abbot [Richard of Ware] set in place these porphyry stones'. Odoricus almost certainly refers to Petrus Oderisius, the Cosmati craftsman who probably worked on the Confessor's original shrine and the pavement, and who also worked on the tomb of Pope Clement IV.[27] Another part of the inscription was set within an inner, diagonal square and ran around four outer roundels. The inscribed words begin: 'If the reader wittingly reflects upon all that is laid down, / he will discover here the end of the *primum mobile* ...'. To the literate medieval mind, these lines reflect their understanding of the universe, based on the work of the Greek astronomer, Ptolemy. The '*primum mobile*' (first moved), had been set in motion by God and provided the motive power of the other spheres of the universe. The rest of the verse was supposedly a formula for calculating the end of the universe. For medieval Christians, this cataclysmic event would accompany the second coming of Christ and Day of Last Judgement. It was Henry III's hope, according to the historian, David Carpenter, that people 'would throng to the Abbey, absorb the awesome message of the pavement, and then gain comfort from the sight of the Confessor's shrine rising beyond it in its marbled, golden and jewelled splendour'. The abstract, geometric pavement served as a focus for contemplation by the Abbey's clergy on the divine nature of the universe, its birth and death, and its eventual return to eternity. Fittingly, Abbot Ware's remains lie beneath the stones he brought to Westminster.[28]

The pavement also served the monarch's purpose. At the symbolic climax of the coronation service, monarchs sat directly above its central roundel while they were anointed with holy oil. Their earthly power was legitimized as part of the divine order of the universe. Henry III's commissioning of the pavement can be seen as a reassertion of the divine right of kings and a riposte to Simon de Montfort and other rebellious barons.[29]

In the 1250s, Matthew Paris wrote that Henry III was building a 'Chapter House beyond compare'. Paris's impression of this architectural gem stands the test of time. The Chapter House is the work of Henry of Reyns, the king's first master builder on his grand project. Remarkably, the original floor tiles remain, having been re-laid during the chamber's nineteenth-century restoration. Among the exquisite medieval patterns is a Latin inscription: *Ut rosa flos florum, sic est domus ista domorum* – 'As the rose is the flower of flowers, so this house is the house of houses'.[30]

The beauty of the Chapter House is exceptional, but its purpose was functional.

Its role was defined by Abbot Ware, a stern upholder of order, in the customary book he commissioned in 1266, setting down the monastery's practices and rules:

> It is the 'Little House' in which the Convent meets to consult for its welfare. It is well called the *Capitulum* (Chapter House), because it is the *caput litium* (the head of strifes), for there strifes are ended. It is the workshop of the Holy Spirit, in which the sons of God are gathered together. It is the house of confession, the house of obedience, mercy and forgiveness, the house of unity, peace, and tranquility, where the brethren make satisfaction for their faults.

For almost 300 years, the Abbey's monks assembled there at about nine o' clock each morning, after early mass in the main church. The setting was designed to inspire a sense of awe and divine order. 'They marched in double file through the vestibule, of which the floor still bears traces of their feet', notes Dean Stanley. As they entered, they bowed to a great crucifix that probably faced them, above the seats at the east end of the chamber, where the Abbot, the three priors and the sub-prior sat.[31]

The monks sat on stone benches round the walls of the Chapter House. They observed strict rules – for instance, signalling to one another across the chamber was forbidden. These assemblies began with the allocation of the day's tasks among the monks, before moving to the monastery's business and welfare. In addition to catechizing and reading, it was an opportunity for monks to raise complaints against one another and to confess their own wrongdoings. Those who were guilty acknowledged their faults at the step before the Abbot's stall. The scenes, as Stanley remarks,

> recall a rough school rather than a grave ecclesiastical community. The younger monks were flogged elsewhere. But the others stripped, wholly or from the waist upwards, or in their shirts, girt close round them, were scourged in public here, with rods of single or double thickness, by the 'mature brothers', who formed the Council of the Abbot ... the criminal himself sitting on a three-legged bench – probably before the central pillar, which was used as a judgement seat or whipping post.

The younger monks and novices were reprimanded and punished in the cloisters. According to Stanley, 'If flogging was deemed insufficient, the only further punishment was expulsion'.[32]

Abbot Ware's disciplinary code was imposed in a sublime setting. Sir George Gilbert Scott, the renowned architect who restored the Chapter House to its former glory during 1866–73, observed that 'a more elegant interior could scarcely be found'. The chapter house at Westminster is one of England's earliest, following those of Worcester and Lincoln. 'The chapter house in England', notes the Victorian expert, the Rev. Mackenzie Walcott, 'was almost essentially a national peculiarity, unlike the alleys or oblong rooms which take their place on the Continent'. The diameter of Henry of Reyns's octagonal chamber is about 18 feet, the height to the crown of the vaulting is about 54 feet, and the slender, central pillar of Purbeck marble, is about 35 feet high. Huge windows, almost 40 feet tall and 20 feet wide, fill the space on six of the eight walls. Above the entrance is a smaller seventh window. The eighth, north west, wall is hard against the Abbey's south transept and is decorated by blank tracery in the style of the six windows.[33]

Three tiers of stone steps round the chamber provided seating for 80 monks. On the east wall an extra, fourth tier afforded the abbot, his three priors and the sub-prior, additional dignity. The walls also contain 37 shallow recesses below the window sills. Each recess is decorated by stone arcading, with round, trefoil arches. The five deeper recesses on the east wall further emphasized the status of the abbot and his senior brothers. On the opposite, west wall, above the entrance are two English Gothic sculptures, representing the Annunciation: the statue of the Virgin Mary is of Reigate stone; that of the Archangel Gabriel of Caen stone. These figures and the stonework were once richly coloured and the walls painted.[34]

The floor of the Chapter House remains 'probably the most perfect and one of the finest' medieval tile pavements, as Scott described it in 1861. Its intriguing designs were made with light-coloured clay inlaid in darker clay, then fired and glazed. The tiles run 'in parallel strips, from east to west, the patterns changing in each strip, though repeated on corresponding sides.' The duplicate strips display Henry III's arms: a shield bearing the three lions of England, flanked by mythical beasts (wyverns at each side and centaurs at the base). Other tiles show various human figures (archer, bishop, horseman, king, queen), while a recurring geometrical design represents the rose window in the north transept of the new abbey. Ancient Abbey legends are recalled by a smiling fish (the salmon granted to the local fisherman by St Peter) and by the Confessor giving a ring to a pilgrim who turned out to be St John. Some tiles were replaced in the nineteenth century – they are darker and retain their glazing – but most of the original floor has survived.[35]

The Chapter House of an abbey or cathedral rarely excites much interest, but many people know Westminster's Chapter House as the setting of a crucial part of the plot of Dan Brown's blockbuster novel, *The Da Vinci Code*, published in 2003. However, when the film adaptation of this bestseller was being shot two years later, the Abbey's Dean and Chapter refused to allow filming inside either the main church or the Chapter House. The scene was shot in Lincoln Cathedral's Chapter House, with murals painted on a special layer over the wall to make it look like Westminster's.[36]

Beneath the Chapter House lies an octagonal undercroft, or 'crypt'. Although the east side of the undercroft was equipped with an altar and a piscina and recess for washing and storing vessels for the mass, it was used as a treasury: the thick, central stone column is hollowed out and probably served as a locker for valuables. The undercroft seemed to offer complete security with its low, heavily barred windows and exceptionally thick walls, but Henry III's son, Edward I, was to discover to his great cost that there was no guarantee of safety.[37]

8 PARLIAMENT

I n November 1236, Henry III adjourned a legal case in the court of the King's Bench for consideration by the 'parliament', due to meet at Westminster the following January. The record of Henry's decision in the court's rolls marks the first official use of the term, 'parliament'. At this time, 'parliament' meant an event rather than an institution. On this occasion, the event was a meeting of the King's Great Council, whose members included officers of the royal household, government officials, barons and senior clerics. In January 1237, the Council heard legal cases, passed legislation, re-issued the *Magna Carta* and granted the king a tax on moveable goods in return for concessions on the extent of the royal demesne.

After 1237, these meetings of the Great Council were increasingly described as parliaments. Henry III's incorrigible profligacy and constant shortage of funds gave this body a keener political edge than the old 'witans' of the Anglo-Saxon kings or councils of his Norman predecessors. The written record of the parliament held at Westminster in January 1242, when Henry was refused supplies for a military expedition in Europe, is 'the first authorized account of a parliamentary debate,' according to the historian, F. M. Powicke.[1]

The parliament held in the refectory of Westminster Abbey in November 1244 humiliated Henry: 'the King most urgently, not to say shamelessly, demanded pecuniary aid from them,' reported Matthew Paris, 'but as they had been so often injured and deceived, they unanimously, and as it were with one mouth, refused it to his face'. Henry was left 'eagerly gaping after money', before a deal was struck three months later.[2]

Yet Henry kept demanding more money, and parliament kept resisting. In desperation, he sold off his royal plate and jewels to fund an expedition to restore order to Gascony, led by his brother-in-law, Simon de Montfort, Earl of Leicester. Henry's plan for a crusade to the Middle East forced cuts in royal household budgets and met opposition when parliament met at Westminster. In desperation, he took the extraordinary step in 1253 of proclaiming his sincerity to senior clerics and magnates in Westminster Hall, offering to submit to excommunication if he disobeyed the charters that defined his obligations and power. Fortunately for Henry, this oath was later annulled by the pope.[3]

Westminster was changed forever when the conflict between king and parliament became inextricably intertwined with a bitter, personal clash between Henry III and the opportunistic de Montfort. Henry's political insensitivity had so inflamed the barons and clergy in parliament that de Montfort could plausibly don the mantle of reformer. He had been brought up in France before coming to England in 1230 in his early twenties to claim his inheritance to the earldom of Leicester. From 1234, he attended the King's Great Council and in January 1238, long before he turned rebel, secretly married Henry's sister Eleanor, widow of the Earl of Pembroke, at Westminster. This confirmed his growing influence: Henry gave his sister away at a private ceremony 'in the king's small chapel, which is in a corner of his chamber'.[4]

The king confirmed the earldom of Leicester to de Montfort in the spring of 1239, but the new earl had run up debts and his money problems soon sparked a public falling-out between them. His failure to consult the King before naming him as security for his debts provoked Henry to upbraid him, when he and Eleanor arrived for a royal service at Westminster Abbey. Henry barred him from the service and ordered the couple's ejection from the home he had lent them at the late Bishop of Winchester's palace at Southwark. Although de Montfort later served as the king's lieutenant in Gascony, in 1252 he was tried in Westminster Hall on charges of brutality. He never forgave Henry this humiliation.[5]

Parliament repeatedly refused to meet the crippling cost of the campaign in Gascony, and was dismayed in 1257 when Henry crassly presented his younger son, Edmund, 'dressed in the Apulian fashion', before them, implying that another expedition, this time to Sicily was a *fait accompli*. The king's request for taxation, 'made the ears of all tingle, and struck fear to their hearts, especially as they knew this tyranny took its rise from the pope'. Even the heavens seemed to have turned against Henry, as bad weather brought starvation and 'mortal fevers,'[6] while a revolt by Llywelyn ap Gruffud, Prince of Wales, escalated.[7]

The crisis came to a head at Westminster Palace in the spring of 1258 when the barons demanded radical reforms. Their patience finally snapped when Henry requested further aid against Llywelyn. An armed group stormed into the parliament, led by de Montfort and his fellow earls: Gloucester, Norfolk (the Earl Marshal), and Richmond (Peter of Savoy, the queen's uncle). After an angry row, Henry submitted to their demand for a ruling commission to be set up. Parliament was adjourned until June, when it re-convened in Oxford, on neutral ground. This 'Mad Parliament', as it was later nicknamed by royalists, vested power in a council of 15 barons and bishops, and appointed Hugh Bigod to the revived post of justiciar, or chief minister. Four knights from every county were also ordered to report grievances against royal and local officials.[8]

The king was bitter about his treatment. One July afternoon in 1258, he left Westminster Palace for a boat excursion and dinner on the Thames, but was suddenly caught in a thunderstorm. Frightened for his safety, he ordered an immediate landing and was put ashore at the bishop of Durham's palace, off the Strand, where de Montfort happened to be staying. When de Montfort heard of the king's unexpected arrival, he went to see him.

'What do you fear? The storm has now passed over', Montfort asked. 'I fear thunder and lightning beyond measure', replied Henry, with a severe look, 'but, by God's head, I fear you more than all the thunder and lightning in the world'.[9]

The barons' demands for the redress of grievances against royal and local officials became law at the parliament of October 1259. The provisions were read aloud, in the king's presence, to a public meeting in Westminster Hall, where Boniface, Archbishop of Canterbury and the other bishops, dressed in full canonicals, declared any opponents of the new settlement excommunicated. In the same year, the king surrendered his family's historic claims to Normandy and Anjou in return for cash from the French king, Louis IX. A new Great Seal omitting any mention of his family's ancient claims was presented to Henry who ordered that the old one incorporating his lost territories be destroyed and the fragments distributed among the poor.[10]

Henry briefly recovered power by exploiting fears among his barons that their stand-off with the king might result in civil war. But his *annus horribilis* in 1263 revealed his weakness. Negotiations with de Montfort failed, the king fell ill, and part of the palace burnt down – 'the king's little hall at Westminster, with manie other houses thereunto adjoining, was consumed with fire, by negligence of one of the king's servants'. On top of all this, the London mob descended on Westminster and attacked the homes of the king's supporters and a royal mansion, 'which they nearly pulled down, scarcely leaving one stone upon another, and taking away all the posts, tiles and stones that were of use for any building'.[11]

A messy power struggle ensued. Henry retreated to the Tower of London, but an autumn parliament at Westminster did not fully trust de Montfort. Henry's ploy in asking Louis IX, to arbitrate, prompted de Montfort to use force and his victory at the Battle of Lewes in May 1264, left Henry without real power and only 'the shadow of a name'. The next month's parliament in Westminster Hall was a landmark. In addition to the barons and senior clergy, 'four knights, as representatives of each of certain counties, were required to attend'. For the first time, the key elements of a summons to later parliaments were evident: the knights represented their shires, they were coming to attend a parliament and their brief was 'to discuss the affairs of the king and kingdom'. De Montfort's parliament created a council of nine, headed by a ruling triumvirate of himself, the bishop of Chichester, and Gilbert de Clare, the new Earl of Gloucester.[12]

De Montfort's 'model' parliament held at Westminster between January and March 1265 was the House of Commons 'in embryo', but his inclusion of citizens and burgesses reflected his weakening support among the barons. As Brayley and Britton note,

> knights were summoned as representatives of the counties, and citizens and burgesses for cities and boroughs, as well as of four members for each of the cinque ports. For the cities and boroughs two members only were in general summoned, but the city of London was represented by four citizens; most probably in return for the strenuous support which they had given the barons.

Although the grievances of the knights and burgesses were redressed, de Montfort's powers were increased and a leading opponent, Robert de Ferrers, Earl of Derby, was imprisoned.[13]

However, there was growing resentment at the enrichment of de Montfort's sons. In March, Henry, 'who was still held under control' by de Montfort, assigned Edward's houses at Westminster to one of de Montfort's sons, 'for his own residence'. This resentment cost Montfort dear. The desertion of the Earl of Gloucester deprived him of his last ally in the Welsh marches, where Prince Edward launched the royalist fight-back. On 2 August 1265, de Montfort was killed in battle with Edward's forces at Evesham.[14]

Although sporadic fighting continued, Henry III wore his crown at the feast of St Edward at Westminster in October 1265, in celebration of victory. By early 1267, when he crushed a resistance in the Isle of Ely, he was so hard up that he pawned the 'gold, precious stones, jewels, and other valuables' deposited in the Confessor's shrine. In the spring, Westminster suffered sudden invasion when the Earl of Gloucester rebelled. According to Thomas Wykes, an Augustinian canon, 'insurgents ... attacked the king's Palace at Westminster ... and breaking with clubs and levers the doors and windows carried them into Southwark, where they constructed a kind of barrier for their defence'.[15]

With the eventual collapse of Gloucester's revolt, the civil war ended. From the 1260s, no general tax was levied in England without the consent of representatives. Between 1268 and 1270, knights were probably summoned to two parliaments and burgesses to at least one. Both groups were represented in Edward I's first parliament in 1275. De Montfort's innovation had outlived him and eventually evolved into the modern House of Commons.[16]

Today, the armorial shields of de Montfort and other barons in the wall arcades of the Quire aisles of Westminster Abbey are reminders of their revolt. After seizing power the barons allowed work to continue on the Abbey but tried to give it a less royalist emphasis by installing their shields. De Montfort's shield, with its rampant, forked-tailed lion on a red background, on the wall of the third bay of the North Quire aisle, is Westminster's only contemporary memorial of an early founder of parliamentary government.[17]

De Montfort's great rival, Edward I, realized that parliament was necessary to bolster his royal authority. He summoned 46 parliaments during the 33 years between his coronation and his death in 1307. His first parliament met in Westminster Hall on 19 May 1275 and was the first at which the Commons – burgesses and knights, representing the towns and shires – were lawfully present. Although the burgesses and knights sat together with the barons and clergy, rather than separately, the Commons was specifically stated to have given its consent in 1275 to the first statute of Westminster. Many grievances that had arisen during the king's absence on a crusade were dealt with in the statute's 51 clauses, from bail and cattle-rustling, to shipwrecks, tolls and wardships. Other grievances were tackled in two later statutes of Westminster: in 1285, a mass of law and custom was replaced by fairer measures, and in 1290, landowners' feudal rights in property sales were protected.[18]

The Commons also gave their consent in 1275 to a statute that granted the king the customs on wool and leather: the first occasion on which these duties received legal sanction. Edward used the money to raise an army against Llywelyn who had refused to do him homage. The Welsh prince submitted in late 1277 and spent Christmas with the king at Westminster. Five years later, Llywelyn was killed during another revolt in Wales, but he is shown in the oldest surviving painting of parliament at work, seated to the king's left, on a lower seat.[19]

This first picture of Edward I's parliament in session dates from some years after Edward's reign and may not be entirely accurate, but it is the best illustration of a medieval parliament. Alexander, King of Scotland, was summoned because of his English fiefs in Cumberland and Westmorland and sits to Edward's right, on a lower seat. On Alexander's right, one rung lower still, sits the Archbishop of Canterbury. On Llywelyn's left, also one rung lower, sits the Archbishop of York. A woolsack at the head of the assembly seats the Chancellor, the two Chief Justices and the Baron of the Exchequer. Two other woolsacks in the centre of the assembly are each occupied by four judges. The abbots and bishops sit in two rows of benches along one side, to the king's right. Facing them across the assembly, and to the king's left, are two rows of barons. At the far end of the assembly, opposite the king, is a 'cross bench' occupied by some of the Commons. No women are shown, but the Abbesses of Shaftesbury, Barking, St Mary, Winchester and Wilton were summoned to attend parliament during Edward I's reign.[20]

The tempo of life in medieval Westminster changed dramatically whenever the king was in residence. In the 1280s, 570 retainers, ranging from knights to kitchen boys, were entitled to receive the household robes. The monarch's arrival transformed Westminster into a rumbustious capital. Its inns, lodging-houses and stables were packed, and its narrow lanes and streets crammed – even more so when a parliament had been called. At the heart of the royal household was the department of the wardrobe, the main spending department of central government. It was staffed by clerics who paid and supplied the army and navy, and drew up the household accounts. The king's instructions, in the form of letters authenticated with the privy seal and chancery writs, were conveyed by a corps of between ten and 17 official messengers on horseback and many part-time, unmounted couriers.[21]

Edward's great innovation was to open parliament to the people in 1275. Previously, only judges and ministers could refer business to parliament, but by allowing his subjects to petition it directly with their grievances, Edward created a popular institution that the English came to regard as their own. The massive response to Edward's initiative generated a huge workload and, in turn, prompted reform. Parliament's oldest surviving records, the parliamentary rolls, date from 1290, when Gilbert Rothbury was appointed Clerk of the King's Council and became the first known Clerk of Parliament.[22]

During the early 1300s, four-fifths of the parliamentary roll was occupied by the hearing of petitions, many of which were delegated to committees. By adjudicating petitions, parliament was modifying statute law and curbing the king's power. The green baize bag that hangs from a hook on the back of the Speaker's chair for the receipt of petitions is a reminder of parliament's early popularity as a dispenser of justice to all who sought it. Today, presenting a petition or adding one's name to Number 10's e-petitions are ways of putting an issue on the political agenda.

The intense resentment caused by the cost of the king's wars in Wales, Gascony and Scotland prompted further parliamentary reform. In 1294, knights of the shire were summoned with full powers to act on behalf of their communities. In 1295, one pair of knights was summoned from each county, together with burgesses and citizens, to do what should be ordained by common counsel. This assembly became known later as 'the Model Parliament'.[23] In the same year, writs summoning the clergy contained the telling phrase 'what touches all should be approved by all'. None of this could prevent a major crisis in 1297 when the king's demands for military service and heavier taxes were resisted. But finally, as the historian, Michael Prestwich has noted, it became 'an established principle' that taxes should be negotiated with the community of the realm, i.e. in parliament.[24]

No records exist of exactly where parliament met in the palace, except for great occasions in Westminster Hall such as the promulgation of the second statute of Westminster in 1285. Most discussions were probably held in smaller rooms, such as the Painted Chamber. But from 1292, the Palace was rendered unsuitable by the re-building of St Stephen's Chapel and work on the Painted Chamber, and in 1298 a major fire further restricted the available accommodation. Parliament met at various venues, including the Archbishop of York's house at Westminster in 1293 and 1305, and in 1299, having begun at Westminster, moved to Stepney. In January 1307, while Edward was based in the north during his war against the Scots, he summoned his last parliament to Carlisle. But wherever parliament met, it had changed fundamentally during Edward's reign.[25]

9 EDWARD I AND THE STONE OF DESTINY

Scotland is hard-wired into Westminster's history. The oak Coronation Chair on which monarchs are crowned in Westminster Abbey was commissioned by Edward I after his invasion of Scotland in 1296 as a curious form of trophy cabinet for the looted Stone of Scone, or Stone of Destiny. Yet Scotland had already made an indelible imprint on Westminster long before Edward looted the Scots' symbol of royal authority.

The Scots' most enduring trace is 'Scotland Yard', now the common name for the Metropolitan Police and, specifically, for its head-quarters. The first 'Scotland Yard' took its name from Great Scotland Yard, now a side-street off Whitehall, where, in 1829, the newly created Metropolitan Police was based. Great Scotland Yard is so-called because it was originally the site of a property owned by the Scottish royal family.

According to legend, the tenth century Scottish king, Kenneth II, was granted a house on this plot when he visited Thorney to pay homage to King Edgar. By the twelfth century, Scottish royalty were making occasional visits to Westminster. Malcolm IV passed through in 1159 *en route* to Europe, and in June 1170 William I, the Lion King, attended the coronation of Henry II's son. During the thirteenth century, Scotland Yard became 'the residence of the Scottish kings when they attended the English Parliament as barons of the realm'. Alexander III performed homage to Edward I at Westminster in October 1278 for his English lands, having received a guarantee that this would not impinge on Scottish independence.[1]

The Elizabethan historian John Stow wrote of 'a large plot of ground enclosed with brick, and is called Scotland, where great buildings hath been for the receipt of the kings of Scotland, and other estates of that country'. Scotland Yard was described elsewhere as a 'palace with large pleasure grounds extending to the river'. The last member of the Scottish royal family who lived at Scotland Yard was Margaret, Queen of Scots, Henry VIII's older sister, 'who had her abiding there when she came to England after the death of her husband' James IV at the battle of Flodden. On arriving in London on 3 May 1516 Margaret was greeted with month-long celebrations, including jousts, but she returned to Scotland after a year, and in 1519, the southern part of Scotland Yard was merged with York Place, Cardinal Wolsey's grand power-base. During Elizabeth I's reign, Scotland Yard fell into ruin. After the union of the English and Scottish crowns in 1603, when James VI of Scotland succeeded to the English throne as James I, 'the raison d'être' of the palace had ceased to exist. It was partly demolished and the site housed government offices and storage yards.[2]

Edward I's idea of closer union between England and Scotland had been to assert his feudal claim as lord superior of Scotland. Edward and his queen, Eleanor of Castile, personified medieval, courtly ideals. Eleanor had accompanied her husband on his crusade in 1270, and the couple made a sensational impact on their return to England after Henry III's death. Edward was an imposing 6 feet 2 inches in height, had fought for his religion in the Holy Land and was returning to be crowned with his devoted queen, the daughter of the King of Castile. Their journey through London to Westminster prompted ecstatic celebrations: 'The exterior of the houses were hung with the richest silks and tapestry, the conduits flowed with the choicest wines, and gold and silver were profusely scattered among the population by the more affluent citizens'.[3]

On 19 August 1274, Edward and Eleanor became the first English king and queen to be crowned together. Theirs was also 'the first Coronation in the Abbey as it now appears, bearing the fresh marks of his father's munificence'. Edward's mother, Eleanor of Provence, was present, as was Alexander III of Scotland, Henry's son-in-law. The procession to the banquet in Westminster Hall was unusually splendid, and as Knighton reports: 'The King of Scotland was accompanied by one hundred knights on horseback, who as soon as they had dismounted, turned their steeds loose for anyone to catch'.[4]

However, Alexander's untimely death in 1286 set in train the events that were to culminate in Edward's invasion of Scotland. After settling the disputed Scottish succession in favour of John de Balliol in 1292, Edward insisted on John appearing before the English Parliament at Westminster and conceding Edward's claim as Scottish overlord. However, Scottish nobles defied Edward by declining to serve in his invasion of France, and in February 1296 they signed a treaty with the French. The following month, Edward invaded Scotland.[5]

After victory at Dunbar, Edward declared himself King of Scotland. He sought to end Scottish claims to independence by removing the royal regalia and official records, and seizing the coronation stone from Scone Abbey, near Perth. The Stone of Scone, or Stone of Destiny, as it became known, was a rectangular slab of sandstone measuring 27 inches by 17 inches by 10½ inches. It had been used in the inauguration ceremonies of Scottish kings since ancient times and its removal was a deep insult to the Scots.[6]

Edward I brought the Stone of Destiny to Westminster Abbey to prove that his conquest of Scotland was complete and to ensure that the Scots would have no other king but the English king. He commissioned his goldsmith, Adam, to make an expensive bronze chair into which the stone was to be installed: but in August 1297 the work fell victim to spending cuts caused by the cost of Edward's wars. Instead, Walter of Durham, a painter at the Palace since Henry III's time and whose skills included woodwork, was commissioned to make an oak chair that incorporated the stone.

The chair was made in about 1300, but it was not decorated until around 1330, possibly as an act of celebration by the abbot and monks of Westminster at the failure of Edward III's plan to return the stone to Scotland. The use of gilding, coloured glass and painted enamels covered with clear glass, must have created a dazzling impression. On the back were gilded depictions of trellises of oak and vine leaves with birds, a grotesque, a knight on horseback and a green man. The back's interior portrayed a seated man, probably Edward the Confessor, but the bottom part of the chair, with its four lions, was added as recently as 1727.[7]

Walter of Durham's handiwork survives as the Coronation Chair in which English kings and queens have been crowned since at least the late fourteenth century. However, it seems that this was not always the intention. A fourteenth-century note at the Abbey about the Chair shows the following phrase crossed out: 'in order that the kings of England and Scotland might sit on it on the day of their Coronation'. Instead, the Chair was placed next to the altar in St Edward's chapel, where it may have been used by the priest officiating at the coronation or by the king when he removed his regalia.[8]

The earliest documented use of Walter of Durham's Chair at a coronation is in 1399 during Henry IV's ceremony, although contemporary illustrations show Edward II being crowned in what looks like the chair in February 1308, and Richard II sitting in the Chair with his coronation regalia after he was crowned in July 1377. Battered and scarred by numerous initials carved into its wood by visitors and boys at Westminster School, the Coronation Chair is a remarkable link with Westminster during the Anglo-Scottish war 700 hundred years ago.[9]

The build-up to war brought the first of many state trials in Westminster Hall when Sir Thomas de Turberville, an English knight, was charged with spying for the French, whom he hoped would encourage the Scots to rebel. On 8 October 1295, he was brought to his trial from the Tower of London 'secured on the back of a sorry mount by a rope under its belly', with his hands tied in front of him. He was escorted by six 'tormentors', dressed like devils, and the hangman. In the packed and noisy Westminster Hall, he was tried for treason and sentenced to a traitor's death by the chief justice of the King's Bench seated on a dais in the Hall. Sir Thomas was dragged to the gallows on an ox-hide drawn by six horses, with his tormentors insulting and beating him, before he was hanged and left to rot 'as long as anything of him should remain'.[10]

Edward I's pre-occupation with his Scottish war created a political vacuum at the heart of Westminster. Added disruption was caused, according to Stow,

London's historian, by a severe fire in March 1298 that, 'being driven with the wind', spread from the Palace to the Abbey. Such was the damage to the palace that Edward moved into the archbishop of York's palace in present-day Whitehall. For long periods during 1300, 1301 and 1303, Edward abandoned Westminster altogether while waging war in Scotland. Westminster's abbot, Walter of Wenlock, also spent little time in the capital, instead staying in his other manors, with the result that a lax regime developed – some monks mixed with criminals and outlaws, while others met prostitutes in the Palace garden.[11]

This laxity at the Abbey was risky, because its treasury contained the king's jewellery, crowns and regalia, gold and silver plate, cups of state, valuable coins, ceremonial swords and other precious items. The treasury was thought to be impregnable. It was located in a small crypt beneath the Chapter House and served as a strong-room for Edward's most valuable items. According to Paul Doherty, the historian, the keys to its strong-door were held only by senior royal officials. Despite evidence of pilfering and a theft of silver plate from the refectory, the failure of attempted break-ins in 1296 and 1302 created a false sense of security.[12]

The identity of the thief who stole the silver plate was only discovered after he committed a much bigger robbery. He was Richard of Pudlicote, who had come to Westminster Hall to sue the king for financial loss after being arrested in Flanders as surety for Edward's war debts. Having stolen the silver plate, Pudlicote hatched a plot to rob the king's treasury. In April 1303, a month after Edward left for Scotland, Pudlicote and his accomplices broke in through one of the crypt's six windows. They removed an array of brooches, rings, stones, gold coins and silver goods, hiding many items in St Margaret's churchyard.

Although no alarm was raised at first, some of the loot was found in the churchyard and some turned up further afield. Edward first heard of the robbery in Scotland and ordered an urgent inquiry. John of Droxford, 'keeper of the King's wardrobe, accompanied by those appointed to make the inquiry', surrounded the Abbey with troops, 'found the chests and coffers broken open' in the treasury, and carried out a thorough search of the monastery. Stolen treasure was discovered in the house of the sacrist Adam of Warfield and other loot was retrieved elsewhere in the monastery. Pudlicote was found with £2,200 worth in his possession, and other items were discovered under the beds of the keeper of the palace, John Skenche, and of his lieutenant, William of the Palace. Some of the treasure was never found.[13]

Pudlicote was part of an inside job. Although he led the break-in, his fellow ringleaders were Warfield and William of the Palace, who drank together and consorted with prostitutes. These three were aided and abetted by at least ten monks and other Abbey servants and workers; various riff-raff from the under-world at Westminster; and unscrupulous dealers and goldsmiths in the city of London. Without Warfield and some of the monks, the robbery would have been impossible. They held the keys to the gates of the Abbey close, and they must have let in the thieves. William of the Palace also played a crucial part because, as deputy keeper, he controlled access to the palace and its grounds. He was also acting keeper of the Fleet prison, where other gang members had 'met in a certain house within the close of the prison' before the robbery.[14]

Abbot Wenlock and all 48 monks at Westminster were indicted and sent to the Tower of London 'on the charge of stealing to the value of £100,000'. In March 1304, William of the Palace and four other lay suspects 'were sentenced to be dragged through the city and hanged on elms at Smithfield'. However, Skenche, who was William's boss, was restored to his office as keeper of the palace. Twelve monks were held in prison for two years without trial, 'but at length, on Lady Day 1305, the King, who had come to the church at Westminster to return thanks for his victory over the Scots, gave orders for their discharge'.[15]

Pudlicote was sentenced to death in November 1305. He was humiliated and ridiculed as he was brought from the Tower of London in a wheelbarrow to Westminster, where he was hanged, probably on the Abbot's gallows in Tothill Lane. A grisly legend held that Pudlicote was also flayed, and that the skin found beneath ironwork on the ancient door off the vestibule near the Abbey's Chapter House might have been his. However, scientific tests have disproved this myth. The Abbey was never used again as the king's main treasury. Instead, the royal treasures were transferred to the Tower of London.[16]

Pudlicote's execution came only months after the show trial in Westminster Hall of Sir William Wallace, the Scottish military commander and resistance leader. He was brought for trial from the city to Westminster on horseback early in the morning of 23 August 1305. A laurel crown was placed on his head, mocking his claim that one day he would wear a crown at Westminster. Wallace denied the charge of treason on the grounds that he had never taken an oath to Edward, but having been declared an outlaw he was allowed no defence. The verdict was given on the same day. He was dragged on a hurdle to Smithfield and hanged, drawn and quartered. His head was displayed on London Bridge and his quarters at Newcastle, Berwick, Stirling and Perth, but his grim fate made him a martyr.[17]

The defiant coronation of Robert Bruce at Scone the following year, provoked Edward I's fury. However, the 66-year-old English king was ailing and his 22-year-old son, Edward, Prince of Wales, was put in charge of the invasion force. Three hundred heirs to military tenancies were summoned to Westminster in late May, where these sons of earls, barons and knights were kitted out from the royal wardrobe in 'purple, silk, fine linen, and girdles embroidered with gold, according to their respective rank'.

The palace was unable to accommodate all the conscripts and, while most of them de-camped to London, the king insisted that Prince Edward and 'the noblest of young men' should stay in the Abbey. However, 'so great was the clang of the trumpets and pipes, and the noise of acclamations, that the convent could not hear the service of the choir'. The next day, there was even greater commotion in the Abbey when the Prince returned triumphantly after being knighted by his father: 'There was then such pressure about the high altar that two knights died, and several fainted away'. Once the crowd had been moved away from the altar, the prince knighted his military companions.[18]

Prince Edward led his army into Scotland in August 1306, but it was not until the following summer that his ageing father advanced towards the border. On 7 July 1307, the 68-year-old monarch died at Burgh by Sands, between Carlisle and the Solway Firth, having enjoined the prince, 'that every time the Scots should rebel against him, he would summon his people and carry against them the bones of his father; for he believed most firmly that, as long as his bones should be carried against the Scots, those Scots would never be victorious'.[19]

Despite Edward I's wish, and the continued Scottish revolt, the king was buried at Westminster Abbey in a large, undecorated Purbeck marble tomb-chest, with no effigy. A large wooden canopy above Edward's tomb was destroyed in 1774 when fighting broke out during the night-time funeral of William Pulteney, the Earl of Bath, a leading Whig politician. But why was Edward I's tomb left undecorated? The suggestion, advanced by Dean Stanley, is that the unfinished tomb honours Edward I's pact with his son, that 'his flesh should be boiled, his bones carried at the head of the English army until Scotland was subdued, and his heart sent to the Holy Land, which he had vainly tried in his youth to regain from the Saracens'. By leaving Edward's tomb unfinished, it would have been easier, at some later date, to open it and remove his bones and heart, thereby honouring his last wish. This idea is strengthened by the gruesome ritual, authorized by royal warrants and performed every two years until 1399, of opening Edward I's tomb and renewing the wax on the cloth around his body.[20]

The curiosity roused by these warrants prompted antiquarians in 1774 – the year of the funeral riot – to re-open the tomb. Edward I's tall, well-preserved body was found in a marble coffin, wrapped in a large, waxed linen cloth, beneath which were the royal robes: a red silk damask tunic with gold tissue, and a mantle of crimson velvet, with a piece of rich cloth of gold laid over them. On his head was a gilt crown. A sceptre had been placed in his right hand, and in his left was a rod bearing a dove and oak leaves in green and white enamel. This macabre event descended into farce: one of the respected antiquaries at the tomb was required to undergo 'a search for the embezzlement of a finger of the great Plantagenet'. The scene of the tomb opening was later satirized by Thomas Rowlandson in his cartoon, 'Death and the Antiquaries'. William Combe's accompanying verse mocked the antiquaries: 'A curious wish their fancies tickled / To know how Royal Folk were pickled'.[21]

William Blake, the artist and poet, was present at the opening of Edward's coffin and sketched the corpse. He was at that time an apprentice engraver in his mid-teens who had the task of making drawings of the royal tombs. As Peter Ackroyd has shown, Blake's experiences in Westminster Abbey influenced his later art. He had several visions and once saw 'the aisles and galleries of the old cathedral suddenly filled with a great procession of monks and priests, choristers and censer-bearers, and his entranced ear heard the chant of plain-song and chorale, while the vaulted roof trembled to the sound of organ music'.[22]

Edwardus Primus Scotorum Malleus hic est, reads the inscription on Edward's tomb: 'Here is Edward I, hammer of the Scots'. The Anglo-Scottish wars periodically pre-occupied his son and grandson for another 30 years. The shattering English defeat at Bannockburn, combined with Edward II's extravagance, and the rumours about the sexual nature of his friendships with his favourites, Piers Gaveston and Hugh Despenser, led to his downfall. The leaders of the coup, Roger Mortimer, first earl of March, and his lover, Edward's queen, Isabella, shrewdly involved Parliament by issuing writs for it to meet under the authority of the Great Seal, taken from Edward II on his capture.[23]

Parliament was subjected to a skilful public relations exercise when it met at Westminster in January 1327. The London mob, having been won over by Mortimer, bayed outside for Edward II to go while the teenaged Prince Edward was presented as the new king. Doubts about the legality of removing the monarch dissolved when the imprisoned king cracked under immense pressure and surrendered the throne. In Westminster Hall on 24 January, Lords, Commons and the London mob heard the Archbishop of Canterbury, Walter Reynolds, announce the king's deposition and Edward III's accession. This supremely unctuous occasion was epitomized by the theme of his sermon: *'Vox populi, Vox Dei'.*[24]

When Edward III headed to Berwick in May 1333 to launch his campaign against the Scots, his court followed. For the next five years, the king and his court were based in the north. Their prolonged absence prompted the Westminster community to petition Edward in 1337, arguing that it could not pay its taxes because of the loss of rent and trade. The claim was upheld by a royal inquiry.[25]

War with France, the following year, revived Westminster. The great Anglo-French dynastic conflict, later known as 'the Hundred Years' War', shifted England's centre of political gravity back to the south. In 1339, Parliament was summoned to meet at Westminster. All 31 Parliaments during the rest of Edward III's reign met there, compared with 13 of the previous 29 parliaments. The Exchequer and the Court of Common Pleas also returned. State openings of parliament were held in the Palace's Painted Chamber, when 'the state of the king' (later to become the King's, or Queen's, Speech) was delivered by the chancellor, the chief justice or the archbishop of Canterbury.[26]

10 FROM CHARING CROSS TO ST STEPHEN'S

I n December 1290, close by the King's Mews – the site of Trafalgar Square – the funeral cortege of Edward I's beloved wife, Eleanor of Castile, took its final, overnight rest before her burial in the Abbey. After Queen Eleanor died of a fever at Harby, near Lincoln, her grief-stricken husband commemorated her by erecting a cross at each of the 12 resting places on her last journey to Westminster. The original crosses were probably wooden, but between 1291 and 1294 Edward replaced them with ornate, stone crosses.

The 'Eleanor Cross' at Charing, a hamlet at the north end of Westminster, notorious for its prostitutes, was reputedly 'more elegant than the others'. It was made of Caen stone, 'beautifully wrought with many figures' and steps of Corfe marble. Although the original thirteenth-century cross was destroyed in 1647 on the orders of the puritan parliament, a spire-shaped, substitute cross was erected in the mid-1860s, several hundred yards to the east of the original site, during the construction of Charing Cross Station. Its designer was Edward Barry, architect of the Charing Cross Hotel and son of Sir Charles Barry, architect of the present Palace of Westminster. Today, this medieval-style Eleanor Cross rises some 70 feet in the station forecourt and evokes an emotional episode in Westminster's history.[1]

Edward's decision to place Eleanor's tomb near that of his father confirmed the creation of a royal mausoleum at the Abbey. Edward's stylish conversion had begun with the construction of a majestic, Italianate tomb for Henry III in the most honoured position in the Abbey, close by Edward the Confessor's shrine. The tomb was finished by 1280, and, like the shrine, was the work of the Cosmati craftsmen. The king delayed the transfer of his father's body from the Confessor's old coffin, hoping that a cult would develop to rival that of the late French king, Louis IX. However, he was disappointed, and finally, on the night of 11 May 1290, Henry III's body was taken with little ceremony from its temporary resting place near the high altar and laid in its new tomb. Eighteen months later, Henry's remains were disturbed again when, in keeping with his final wish as ruler of Gascony, his heart was given to the nuns of Fontevrault.

Topping Henry's magnificent tomb is a fine, crowned effigy in gilded bronze, commissioned in 1291 by Edward from the London goldsmith and bronze caster, William Torel, who set up a temporary workshop in the Abbot's cemetery. The effigy of Queen Eleanor, also by Torel, is even finer than that of Henry III. The gilt-bronze top of the tomb, and the crossed pillows beneath her crowned head, are covered with the castle of Castile and the lion of Leon, emblems of her Spanish origins. In a curious twist, the documented career of Torel ends with the treasury robbery in 1303, when he bought two gold rings from one of the chief suspects.

The glory of the royal mausoleum at the Abbey was complemented by the splendour of the royal palace. One of the Palace's gems was the King's Chamber: a magnificent long, narrow room that had been a state bedroom and audience chamber since the days of Edward the Confessor. The King's Chamber, which was on the first floor of an imposing two-storey building that was 80 feet in length, 26 feet in width and 31 feet in height, was located off the Lesser Hall, near the south end, furthest from the Great Hall. It ran on an east-west axis, parallel with, and about 35 yards to the south of, St Stephen's Chapel (the site of St Stephen's Hall in the present Palace). From 1259 until Tudor times, state openings of parliament were held in this chamber, when members assembled to learn why the monarch had summoned them.[2]

The King's Chamber was also known as St Edward's Chamber, because it was thought that the Confessor died there. Later, it was more usually referred to as the Painted Chamber because of the beautiful wall paintings commissioned by Henry III and Edward I. Almost nothing original remains of its murals, but the room was one of the glories of medieval Europe for about 200 years: from Henry III's reign until the fifteenth century, when the wall paintings fell into disrepair and were covered up. Fortunately, conservationists in the early nineteenth-century re-discovered the murals and made watercolour copies before the old Palace burnt down in 1834.[3]

Henry began re-building the King's Chamber during the 1220s in a style appropriate to a grand, royal capital. Surviving records show his close interest in the work. In 1236, he ordered his treasurer 'to have the king's great chamber at Westminster painted of a good green colour, in the manner of a curtain', and the following year sanctioned payment to Odo, 'keeper of our works at Westminster, for the making of pictures in our chamber there'. After the original decoration was destroyed by fire in 1263, Henry set about replacing the murals. Even the civil war with Simon de Montfort could not deter him: in 1265 he ordered his treasurer to pay 'to the painters of the king's chamber seven pounds and ten shillings, for the pictures made in the said chamber, in the chapel behind his bed'.[4]

The state bed, symbolizing a medieval king's authority, was the chamber's main focus. Enclosed by green curtains, it stood against the north side wall, towards the east end, and its posts were decorated with Henry's favoured gold stars on a green ground. On the wall directly above the bed, and enclosed within its wooden canopy, a great mural showed the Confessor's Coronation on a panel more than 10 feet in length and 6 feet in height.[5]

Edward I extended the chamber's Old Testament murals and favoured scenes featuring Judas Maccabeus, whose military exploits were associated at Edward's court with the Arthurian legend. In 1292, a 'Master Walter' spent three shillings on materials for work in the chamber, including white lead, ochre, oil, varnish, verdigris, vermilion, plaster, thread and tools. The result was a chamber brilliantly decorated with ultramarine and vermilion backgrounds, on which black, blues, crimsons, gold, greens, purples and white were inlaid.[6]

The colours of the murals dazzled in the light from seven large, arched windows: three in the north wall, two in the south wall, and two in the east end wall overlooking the river. The floor's glazed tiles were similar to those in the Abbey's Chapter House. The ceiling was 'embellished with gilded and painted tracery', decorated with ornamental paterae in the wood panelling and studded with coloured bosses. Two fragments of the ceiling's painted panels, depicting a seraph and a prophet, were preserved because the bosses were placed over them, and can be viewed in the British Museum. By the time that work stopped during 1297, because of the financial crisis caused by Edward's military campaigns, the chamber's splendour rivalled that of the Abbey's. Twenty-five years later, two Irish friars Simon Simeon and Hugo the Illuminator passed through Westminster on a pilgrimage to Jerusalem, and marvelled at 'that well-known Chamber, on whose walls all the histories of the Wars of the whole Bible are painted beyond description ... to the admiration of the beholders, and with the greatest regal magnificence'.[7]

Edward I's grand vision of re-building St Stephen's Chapel was finally realized by his grandson, Edward III, in August 1348, only months before the Black Death swept through Westminster. The original St Stephen's had been in existence since at least 1206, when King John granted the chapelship to the Clerk of his Exchequer, Baldwin de London, and was probably used by domestic staff. Henry III made improvements, but it was his son, Edward I, who created an aesthetic master-piece that transformed the look of Westminster, and became a template for the magnificent chapels at Eton, and King's College, Cambridge: both of which survive. Edward I's ambition was stimulated by the visually stunning, Gothic-style, two-tiered Sainte-Chapelle, built in the late 1240s by Louis IX at his palace on the Ile de la Cité in Paris. The English king commissioned Michael of Canterbury, the mason who made the penultimate 'Eleanor Cross' at Cheapside in the City, to realize his dream for a new St Stephen's. Work began in April 1292 and proceeded apace until the financial crisis of 1297.[8]

When St Stephen's was completed 50 years later by Edward III, the slender, two-storey building rose elegantly above the higgledy-piggledy old palace. Its design and corner turrets accentuated its height, creating one of Westminster's most distinctive landmarks for almost 500 years. The building was beautifully proportioned, measuring about 90 feet in length, 38 feet in width and 100 feet in height. Its walls were made of free-stone, the piers of Caen stone, and the friezes and carved parts were sculpted in white stone from the Rotherham area.

The upper chapel, sometimes called the King's Chapel in contemporary records, was dedicated to St Stephen and was about 42 feet in height. The altar, columns, doorways and two rows of seats round the chapel, were made of Purbeck marble; 12 stone statues, each at least 6 feet in height, stood on brackets. The lower chapel, St Mary's, was intended for servants and workers at the Palace, and was about 20 feet in height. It introduced architectural styles new to England, but fire halted work in 1298.[9]

St Stephen's charter of endowment, dated 20 August 1348, created a collegiate chapel of one dean and 12 secular canons, with as many vicars and other servants. On 1 January 1353, Edward III allowed the canons free passage through Westminster Hall, both day and night; and granted them land to the north of the chapel (between the river and Westminster Hall) on which their houses were built in a row, parallel with the hall's east wall. St Stephen's canons have long since gone, and their houses later became the site of the Speaker's rooms, but their trace remains in Canon Row, built on the site of their garden.[10]

In the shadow of St Stephen's north wall, nestling in spaces between the buttresses, was one of the Palace's four wells, and, next to it, a bathroom. The bath was commodious, measuring 12 feet by 6 feet, and 5 feet in depth. Close by was St Stephen's Cloister, probably built after 1394. This four-sided cloister stood immediately to the north of the chapel, between the canons' houses and Westminster Hall. It was re-built in the early sixteenth century, and after the 1834 fire parts of it were incorporated in the present Palace of Westminster.[11]

During 1346–7, while the finishing touches were added to the chapel building, the English won famous victories over the French at Crecy and Calais. Military prowess brought control of the Channel but offered no protection against the Black Death. This fearful plague arrived in Dorset from the continent in August 1348, the very month that Edward III endowed St Stephen's, and reached Westminster in the winter of 1348–9, eventually killing nearly half the population of England. William Ramsey, who had become the master-mason at St Stephen's in 1337 died in the spring of 1349. His glorious epitaph was the upper storey of the west porch built in a new, perpendicular style that influenced English architecture.[12]

In March 1350, while death and devastation stalked his realm, Edward III issued the first writ authorizing Hugh de St Albans, his master of the painters, 'to take and choose out, in such places as he should see fit … as many painters and other workmen as should be wanted for executing those works'. Listed among the painters' supplies in the account books are gold foil, oil, silver, vermilion, verdigris, red and white lead and ochre; and, for their brushes, 'hogs' hair', 'squirrels' tails', and the feathers of peacocks and swans.[13]

However, the severe shortage of craftsmen after the Black Death hampered progress. The impatient king resorted to forced labour. In June 1363, Edward III granted sweeping powers to a royal official, William de Walsyngham, 'to take so many painters in our City of London as may be sufficient' for work on St Stephen's Chapel, and to bring them to the palace, 'for our works, at our wages, there to remain as long as may be requisite: and to arrest all who shall oppose or prove rebellious in the matter, and commit them to our prisons'. This imperious instruction solved the immediate problem at St Stephen's, but it betokened an era of labour scarcity and rebelliousness that was ultimately to undermine feudal authority.[14]

England's best artists and craftsmen, recruited by fair means and foul – some from as far afield as Lincolnshire and Warwickshire – created beautiful stained glass windows; gilded and painted every inch of the walls from top to bottom with motifs, including royal lions and fleurs-de-lys; gave the wooden roof a blue background covered with patterned gold and silver stars; installed beautiful furniture and fittings, including crucifixes and chalices encrusted with pearls, rubies and sapphires; and portrayed chivalric, legendary and religious themes around the chapel.[15]

The dazzling splendour of St Stephens's interior rivalled any other medieval building. Painted figures around the walls consisted of 46 angels, each 5 feet in height, with wings of peacock feathers; 20 youths, about 3 feet in height, at the same level as the angels; 32 knights in their armour, with their arms emblazoned on their shields and their banners and names underneath; and another 20 youths, similar to those by the angels, at the same level as the knights. Under the windows were another 80 paintings, many of them containing 10 or 12 figures and featuring historical subjects from the scriptures and legends of the saints, including the marriage of Canaan, the martyrdom of St Eustace and the destruction of Job's children. Recesses and walls were decorated with other religious works, and also portraits and paintings of Edward III, Queen Philippa and their daughters and sons.[16]

It had taken the three Edwards 71 years to re-build and decorate St Stephen's Chapel. The magnificent result remained largely true to Edward I's original vision. It leaves echoes in the name and dimensions of St Stephen's Hall, but the only remnants of its former glory are the vault and carved bosses in St Mary's Chapel. Yet, the impact of St Stephen's was huge: its artistic splendour enhanced the status of the Palace as the seat of government; its design influenced English architecture; and its dimensions shaped the House of Commons.

11 CHAUCER'S WESTMINSTER

Geoffrey Chaucer, the greatest English medieval writer, frequented Westminster intermittently from the mid-1360s, when he was a young official in the royal household, until his death, as a renowned poet, almost 40 years later. In his masterpiece, *The Canterbury Tales*, the character of the 'gentil Pardoner of Rouncival' refers to the priory of St Mary Roncesvalles at the north end of medieval Westminster, where modern Whitehall, Northumberland Avenue and the Strand now meet. Chaucer fought in the Hundred Years' War and went on diplomatic missions, but between times attended the royal court and witnessed royal funerals at the Abbey. In his thirties, he became comptroller of the staple port of London; but after resigning, served during the autumn of 1386 as a knight of the shire in what has become known as the 'Wonderful Parliament'. Later, he was Clerk of the King's Works for two years, and, in the years before his death, rented a house in the Abbey precincts.

Chaucer's Westminster was recovering fast from the devastating Black Death, and was further boosted in 1353 when parliament made it one of only ten English staple towns. These commercial centres enabled the trade in wool – England's main export – and other commodities to be regulated; and facilitated the collection of customs duties. Westminster's wool staple expanded rapidly on the site of modern Bridge Street: between Parliament Square and Westminster Bridge. A new hall, offices and warehouses were built, with a weigh-house and landing stage; and a mayor, constables and court of the staple were appointed. Between 1405 and 1423, Richard ('Dick') Whittington was the mayor of the wool staple. An influx of foreign merchants pushed up rents to the great benefit of Westminster Abbey, a major landlord in the town.[1]

Chaucer knew two of Westminster's most important craftsmen: Henry Yevele and Hugh Herland. More than 600 years later their legacy provides a tangible link with the poet's capital. Master mason Yevele, and master carpenter Herland, were senior craftsmen at the Palace. As such, they attended the funeral of Edward III's queen, Philippa, in Westminster Abbey in 1369; as did Chaucer. The three men's paths probably crossed on other occasions before 1389, the year in which Chaucer became Clerk of the King's Works, and the two craftsmen became his professional colleagues.

One of Yevele's and Herland's earliest collaborations was the Jewel Tower, built during 1365–6, and now a familiar Westminster landmark opposite the Houses of Parliament, across Old Palace Yard. Yevele was paid one shilling a day, and Herland, then assistant to his father, William, received 8d a day. The L-shaped, three-storey tower, with its white Kentish-stone walls, round-arched windows and moat, was commissioned by Edward III as a new King's Privy Wardrobe: a safe repository where his precious stones and gold and silver ware could be weighed and assayed.[2]

Edward's main Privy Wardrobe at the Tower of London was busy with storage and supplies for the French wars, and he wanted a safer treasury than the one that had been robbed beneath the Chapter House. His solution was a tower, surrounded by a moat and a walled garden, sited well away from busy Westminster Hall, and tucked in a corner of Old Palace Yard. Although it was near the royal apartments, much of it was built on land owned by the Abbey. It took the monks six years to acquire other land in compensation, and, even then, they had to buy it themselves. No wonder that Abbot Litlyngton built a sturdy precinct wall.[3]

The ground floor of the Jewel Tower housed an office for William Sleaford, Clerk of the King's Works at the Palace. A fine roof-vault is divided into two bays, and the carved roof bosses feature grotesque heads above a triple rose, intertwined birds and four grimacing, open-mouthed faces. A smaller room is cross-vaulted, with a recess in its east wall for a garderobe, or latrine, that discharged into the adjacent moat. Similar recesses in the higher floors also housed latrines.[4]

Another of Yevele's buildings dominated the Westminster skyline for more than 300 years. In 1367, the master mason completed a square, high clock tower, with a low pyramid roof, on the north side of New Palace Yard, opposite Westminster Hall. The clock tower was built using similar materials to those in the Jewel Tower. Judges in Westminster Hall regulated court sittings by the hourly chimes of its four-ton bell, known as 'Great Tom of Westminster'. However, in 1698, parliament failed to pay for the tower's repair and Sir Christopher Wren reluctantly demolished it. 'Great Tom' became the hour bell of St Paul's Cathedral and, remarkably, after two re-castings, still rings out.[5]

Evocative remnants of Chaucer's time survive at the Abbey, where two outstanding abbots, Simon Langham (1349–62) and Nicholas Litlyngton (1362–86), created a building boom. The design and work was in the hands of John Palterton, the Abbey's master mason from 1352 until Yevele took over in the late 1380s. Langham personified the close ties between church and state. While serving as Abbot, he also became the King's Treasurer, and was later Lord Chancellor. He also became Bishop of Ely, Archbishop of Canterbury (the only Westminster abbot ever to do so) and cardinal at the papal court at Avignon.

Langham's greatest architectural legacy is the Great Cloister where he helped fund the re-building and completed the south walk in Perpendicular style.[6]

Litlyngton had supervised the Abbey's works as Prior and inherited Langham's burning ambition to revive Henry III's plan for the nave. Although he raised, and also personally donated large sums, the Crown had to stump up about a quarter of the £25,000 cost. The western part of the nave faithfully copies the thirteenth-century, French Gothic style, although it took more than a century before Henry III's vision was realized. Litlyngton also commissioned a beautifully illuminated Missal for the high altar, at a personal cost of £34.4s.7d. Now known as the Litlyngton Missal, it bears his monogram and arms.[7]

The Abbot's House – now the Deanery – was described by Lethaby as the most complete remaining medieval house in London. The Abbot's state dining-room was completed by Palterton in 1375. The ceiling is supported by corbels, decorated with angels holding shields, some of them with Litlyngton's arms. Tall windows have stone tracery decorated with dagger motifs, echoing those in the Great Cloister. In the sixteenth century, the hall of the Abbot's House was taken over by the local grammar school, later to become the fee-paying Westminster School. Elizabeth I attended performances of Latin plays in 1564 and 1565 in what had become College Hall. The long tables of chestnut wood along each side were taken from the wreck of a vessel in the Spanish Armada.[8]

The Abbot's state room became known as the Jerusalem Chamber, probably because of the tapestries, or pictures, of the history of Jerusalem on its walls. The Chamber juts out beyond the Abbey's west front, at the foot of the south-west tower, but is partly hidden behind the present-day Abbey Bookshop. Its interior measures 36 feet by 18 feet and has a superb painted oak roof decorated with Litlyngton's mitre and initials, 'NL', alternating with 'R' for Richard II. It was there that parts of the King James Bible were written in 1611, and the New English edition of the New Testament was written in 1961.

Litlyngton's legacy south of the Abbey powerfully evokes the medieval monastery. Its most impressive surviving features are the Abbot's House, the Great Cloister (which Litlyngton completed), and parts of the monks' infirmary. He also commissioned the range of offices along the east side of Dean's Yard, including a cellarer's department (now Number 20, housing the Chapter Office); a guest house (Number 19); a tower, known as the Blackstole Tower, after the 'black stool' (where loaves for outsiders were distributed); and a hospice for the Treasurer and Monk Bailiff (now Number 18).[9]

Litlyngton's bell tower, malthouse, dam and water-mill no longer survive. The Abbey Gatehouse, built in about 1370 on the approach to the Abbey's west door, was one of Westminster's most distinctive landmarks. It stood on the site now occupied by a red granite column: a memorial to Westminster scholars who fell in the Crimean War. The Gatehouse was paid for by William Warfield, the Abbey cellarer, who leased its two shops, one on either side. The building had two gateways beneath pointed, shallow arches, and its upper-storey housed a gaol. During the Peasants' Revolt in 1381, the rioters set the prisoners free. Eventually falling into disrepair, the Gatehouse was demolished in the late eighteenth century.[10]

Chaucer's monk in *The Canterbury Tales* eschewed St Benedict's frugal strictures, relished 'fat swan' as his favourite roast, and was a 'lord full fat'. Recent comparisons of skeletons from monastic and secular cemeteries in London by Philippa Patrick, an archaeological researcher, show that monks 'were almost five times as likely to develop some form of obesity-related joint disease as their secular counterparts.[11]

Westminster's monks lived off 'the fat of the land'. On feast days, according to Barbara Harvey, the historian of the medieval Abbey, the monks tucked into a forerunner of 'spotted dick' known as 'principal pudding': a fatty concoction spotted with currants, and made of suet (animal fat), eggs and breadcrumbs. The Benedictine ban on meat was eased by various ruses such as allowing offal and entrails to be eaten as 'umble pie', cooked in ale. Butter was used liberally, and milky dishes and cheese were regular fare. Outside Lent, a monk ate about five eggs a day. On about 60 or 70 major annual feast days and anniversaries, special dishes of game, venison, small birds and freshwater fish were served. On some feast days, a rich cheese flan was followed in the evening by 'dowcet': a custardy dish of milk, cream, eggs, sugar and currants.[12]

Many monks took comparatively little exercise and servants were hired for manual work. Depending on the time of year, daily services began with Matins at midnight, after which the monks returned to bed until Lauds at about 5 a.m. For the rest of the day about one third of the monks observed a further series of religious duties, interspersed with more reading and the copying of manuscripts in the north cloister that caught the sun. About 30 or so of the monks were involved in managing and running the Abbey. After the morning chapter meeting, attended by all the monks, there was some physical work until dinner at 11 or 11:30 a.m, and then more services at mid-day, early afternoon, and Vespers at 4:30 p.m. The monks might enjoy a gentle game of bowls, just across the Mill Ditch in what is now Tufton Street. Archery butts set up in the Infirmary Garden in 1462 provided a more decorous activity than another pastime: visiting prostitutes. In 1447 a brothel called the Maydenshed was frequented by monks. Supper was served at about 6 p.m. After the last service of the day at 7 p.m., the monks might drink in the refectory until bedtime, and some crept down later for more night-time drinking.[13]

The Abbey had its own bakery, brewery and granary, and farm land inside the precincts and beyond. The abbot's mill was in what is now Millbank, near the junction with Great College Street where the monastery's southern wall ran alongside the bank of the Mill Ditch. The monks used to cross the Mill Ditch by an old timber bridge to reach the Abbey's kitchen garden (on the site of Barton

Street and Cowley Street); orchard (on the site of Abbey Orchard Street); and vineyard (between what is now Great Peter Street and Horseferry Road). Further afield to the north, their convent garden occupied what is now Covent Garden. In the monastery grounds, the infirmary garden (now the College Garden) supplied herbs and dandelions to treat the sick, and contained beehives, damson trees and a fishpond.[14]

The Abbey was, by medieval standards, a big business. By the twelfth century, it owned about two-thirds of the medieval village around it and the Palace. Its local estate stretched from Chelsea in the west almost to the city walls of London in the east. Profiting from the property boom after 1350, the Abbey bought inns, and tenements for rent, to meet the growing demand from craftsmen and shopkeepers who moved into the area. It also encouraged the endowment of land in return for prayers for the souls of the dead: purgatory was quite a money-spinner. Around the country, by 1100, the Abbey owned about 60 estates covering some 60,000 acres; but by the time of its dissolution, 440 years later, it owned almost twice as many estates.[15]

The abbot took a large slice of the Abbey's income: 32 per cent at the end of the thirteenth century and 23 per cent a century later, according to Harvey. The abbots attended parliaments and sat on official commissions. They were also sometimes summoned to the king's council and sent on diplomatic missions. Otherwise, the abbots 'flitted about' between the abbey's properties in the country, 'with a monk or two in their train to act as seneschal [steward of his lands] and chaplain'. The Abbot's manor house at Neate, in what is now Pimlico, was a favourite retreat where they sometimes entertained monarchs.[16]

However, the monks' well-ordered routine was upset by their political neighbours. Edward III's need to raise taxes for his rapacious war machine explains the increased frequency of parliaments and the emergence of the Commons as a separate body. In 1340, it was established that the Lords could only impose taxes on their own number, whereas the Commons could bring communities' grievances to the king's notice through petitions to parliament, and grant or deny taxation on behalf of their communities.[17]

The Commons began meeting separately from the king and Lords in 1341. At first, the burgesses and knights of the shire remained in the Painted Chamber after the state opening of parliament, while the king and Lords withdrew to the Lesser Hall; but in 1352, the Commons moved to the Abbey's Chapter House. Unfortunately, the MPs damaged the beautiful building, and this probably explains why, in about 1380, the monks moved the MPs to the refectory. Although their carousing upset the monks, the arrival of about 270 members of the Commons and 100 lords for a convivial, noisy few weeks was welcomed in local hostelries and shops.[18]

Parliament's growing voice also changed the language of government. Few burgesses or knights of the shire naturally spoke Latin and Norman French, the languages in which legal and official business was conducted, and in 1362 parliament enforced the use of English in law courts. A year later, Simon Langham's opening speech as Lord Chancellor gave a lead in making English the official language of parliament. This parliamentary recognition of the English vernacular led to the official downgrading of Latin and Norman French. William Langland in *The Vision of Piers Plowman*, and Chaucer in *The Canterbury Tales*, produced poems in English that rank among the classics of European literature. However, it was too much to hope that MPs might emulate their eloquence. 'Some members slumbered and slept and said very little', wrote an early pioneer of the parliamentary sketch in 1400. 'Some mumbled and stammered and did not know what they meant to say ... Some were so pompous and dull-witted that they got hopelessly muddled before they reached the close of their speeches'.[19]

As the ageing Edward III lost his grip, and after the Prince of Wales – the 'Black Prince' – died in 1376, the Commons flexed their muscle. During a record-breaking ten-week session, in what became known as the 'Good Parliament', MPs captured the mood of the country: 'a great murmur and grudge began to spring against certain persons about the king', reported the chronicler, Fabyan. The knights of the shire led the attack against senior courtiers, among them William Latimer, the Chamberlain, who was accused, among other misdemeanours, of helping wool exporters evade the regulations of the wool staple; and against Alice Perrers, a malign influence on the king, who 'had long time misused her for his concubine'.[20]

These charges heralded two major innovations: the first use of impeachment – a trial by the Lords at the instigation of the Commons – established parliament's power to hold ministers and officials to account; and by choosing Sir Peter de la Mare, a knight of the shire for Herefordshire, to represent the views of MPs in their joint meeting with the Lords, the Commons gained its first Speaker. When the Lords tried to exclude some MPs, he insisted that the whole Commons should attend.[21]

However, the political initiative soon returned to the court when the king's younger son John of Gaunt emerged as the new power behind the throne. Latimer was pardoned, and de la Mare imprisoned and replaced in 1377 by Sir Thomas Hungerford, the first officially recorded holder of the title of Speaker. As Chief Steward of Gaunt's estates, Hungerford owed his political advancement to Gaunt and was his mouth-piece in the Commons. The 'Bad Parliament', as it became known, compounded its error by imposing the flat-rate poll tax, the trigger for the bloody Peasants' Revolt in 1381.[22]

The Speaker was the Commons' spokesman to the king, but his appointment required royal approval. The king inevitably expected the Speaker to keep an eye on MPs. The first known 'protestation' by a Speaker, disclaiming personal responsibility for criticisms expressed by MPs, was made by Sir James Pickering in 1378. Three years later, Sir Richard Waldegrave tried to resign, apparently because of his reluctance to voice MPs' criticisms of the government. The invidious position of these early Speakers, when criticism of the government might be regarded as treason, is recalled today by the feigned reluctance of a newly elected Speaker to take the chair.

Edward III's 50 year reign ended in June 1377. When his body was brought to the Abbey in a solemn funeral procession, a life-size wooden effigy of him lay on the carriage, splendidly dressed in robes from the Great Wardrobe. The effigy's painted, life-like head – with a mask (probably Edward's death mask), beard, wig and crown – lay on a gold pillow, beneath a canopy fringed with silk. In its hands were the orb and sceptre. Funeral effigies had developed sometime after Henry III's death in 1272. Their purpose was to represent the deceased monarch on his or her journey to appear before the King of Kings. After Edward's funeral, his effigy was kept at the Abbey, where his carved, wooden figure can still be seen in the Museum.[23]

12 RAISING THE ROOF

leven days after the funeral of Edward III, his ten-year-old grandson, Richard II, was crowned at Westminster. The contrast between the plainly-dressed boy who entered the Abbey, and the newly crowned king who returned to his Palace in brilliant robes, was awe-inspiring. Remarkably, a glimpse of this splendid transformation survives in a wooden-panel portrait that hangs in the Abbey on a pillar at the west end of the nave.

The portrait was probably painted some time after Richard's coronation, but it is the oldest known, surviving, contemporary portrait of an English monarch. The Christ-like appearance of his face was intended to convey the divine nature of the boy-king's earthly power. Richard is depicted sitting in the oak Coronation Chair, holding an orb and sceptre and wearing a gilt crown. He is dressed in a green vest, patterned with golden motifs and the letter R; a crimson robe lined with ermine; and an ermine cape, vermilion socks and gilt shoes.[1]

Surviving manuscripts give more detail about his coronation than is known about any earlier ceremonies. The *Liber Regalis*, probably written and illustrated for the coronation of Richard's queen, Anne of Bohemia, in 1382, describes 'the order according to which a king must be crowned and anointed', and the words and clothes deemed appropriate for the occasion. It was based on Richard's coronation and its main elements have been followed ever since.[2]

Two highly political changes had been made at Richard II's coronation. In 1327, Edward III had made an additional pledge: to uphold the laws that the 'commonalty', or people, chose. It had been forced on him by the barons in reaction to Edward I's broken promises and the shenanigans at Edward II's coronation, when his favourite, Piers Gaveston, had ostentatiously flaunted himself in purple velvet embroidered with pearls, and presumptuously assumed an important role. Richard II's advisers, realizing that it was impossible to drop the additional pledge, inserted the weasel words, '*juste et rationabiliter*'. The king was thus bound only to uphold 'just and reasonable' laws passed by parliament: a brilliant and cynical piece of drafting.[3]

The order of the ceremony was also changed. The awkward problem of legiti-mizing Edward III, after his father's forced abdication, had been overcome by emphasizing the Anglo-Saxon tradition of election. Edward became the lawful king *after* receiving the acclaim of the barons and the people; but 50 years later, Richard II took the oath *before* being presented to the congregation for their acclamation. This ploy cast the relationship between king and people in a new light. The old order had stressed the would-be king's status as ruler *de facto,* and dependent on popular acclaim to become *de jure.* The new order transformed people's acclamation into a show of allegiance to a king who was already their ruler *de jure.*[4]

The theatricality of Richard II's coronation was enhanced by a strange debut. The boy-king had fainted after the long service, and as he was carried out, a knight appeared at the Abbey's north door, wearing the king's mail and armour, and riding the king's 'best but one' charger. This splendid figure was the King's Champion, Sir John Dymoke. His right to perform the duty was inherited through the Marmion family, reputedly champions of the dukes of Normandy, and had been settled in the court of claims. The champion's role was to take on anyone who challenged the king's right to be crowned and to prove, in combat if necessary, that the new king was the lawful monarch.[5]

However, the authorities took no chances. Dymoke was advised to withdraw from the Abbey precincts and wait until the coronation feast in Westminster Hall, where his challenge would be seen as part of the celebrations. As a further precaution, senior stewards and officials 'rode mounted on noble chargers into the hall … to allay debates and dissensions that might arise there'. The Dymoke (later Dymock) family provided the King's Champion at subsequent coronations. The challenge was last enacted at the coronation of George IV in 1821, but Edward VII restored the Champion as a banner-bearer in 1902.[6]

In January 1392, the 15-year-old king married Anne of Bohemia, who was the same age; but little more than two years later she fell victim to the plague. Richard's anguish exploded into 'a frenzy of rage' at her funeral in the Abbey when Richard FitzAlan, Earl of Arundel, a long-standing enemy, arrived conspicuously late and added insult to injury by asking permission to leave early. The furious king seized a baton from one of the attendants and struck Arundel such a blow that he 'fell to the ground, with blood streaming out all over the floorstones'. Removing the bloodstains from the sacred pavement, delayed the end of the service until 'night came on'.[7]

The queen's effigy accompanied her coffin. The carved and painted wooden head, probably based on Anne's death-mask, can be seen in the Abbey Museum. Richard commissioned joint gilt-bronze tomb effigies of Anne and himself: the first such joint monument in the Abbey. At Richard's request, his bronze effigy was shown holding the right hand of the queen's. In a macabre twist some centuries later, visitors used to insert their hands through a hole in the tomb's wooden casing. In 1766, a boy from Westminster School removed the king's jawbone, but eventually it was returned by his descendants.[8]

Richard's and Anne's Purbeck marble tomb, was one of many projects on which the prolific mason Henry Yevele worked. He had probably been collaborating with the carpenter Hugh Herland on Edward III's tomb in the mid-1380s, when Richard II decided to transform Westminster Hall into a statement of his own supreme power and as the seat of government and the law. It had been in constant use for 300 years and, despite occasional repairs, was dilapidated and scruffy.[9]

Westminster Hall and its adjacent buildings were known as the Great Palace, as distinct from the Privy Palace with its private apartments. The Exchequer was located in a building off the Great Hall, reached by a staircase in the north-west corner; the Chancery was housed in the south-west corner; the Court of Common Pleas was located by the west wall, towards the north end; and the Court of the King's Bench occupied the south-east corner. Each court's oak bar surround, trestle table, judges' raised bench and benches for clerks and litigants, were all easily dismantled and moved for feasts and other public occasions.[10]

Richard began his grand project by commissioning 13 statues of English kings from the Confessor to himself. Six of them, with gilded crowns and robes painted emerald green and crimson, were placed on the inside wall at the south end of Westminster Hall. More than 600 years later, these majestic figures, although lacking their original paint, provided an imposing backdrop when President Obama addressed parliamentarians in the Hall below.[11]

The decision to re-roof Westminster Hall was taken in 1393 and work began the following year. In 1395 the Gloucestershire masons, Richard Washbourne and John Swalwe, were engaged 'to heighten the entire walls of the Hall to the extent of two feet of assize, with Reigate ashlar and Caen stones ... according to the purport of a form and model devised by Master Henry Zeneley (Yevele), and delivered to the said masons by Watkin (Walter) Walton, his warden'. A horizontal stone frieze was then added below the windows along the side walls, decorated with carvings of Richard's personal emblem – the chained white hart – and the royal crest and helmet of the Plantagenet kings. This frieze incorporated 26 great stone corbels, or blocks, on which the massive roof timbers rest. Above the frieze, the Norman windows were replaced by windows of two lights and perpendicular-style tracery. Large windows were installed at each end. Yevele's north façade, with its window, two towers and a central pinnacle 28 feet in height, was finished in 1401.[12]

Westminster Hall's magnificent hammer-beam roof with its vast, unsupported 68-foot span, is the work of Yevele, Herland and Walton. An estimated 660 tons of oak timber was supplied. The great beams, prepared near Farnham in Surrey, were taken to the Thames by carts – some pulled by teams of 16 horses – and shipped downstream to Westminster. The hammer posts each weighed about 3.5 tons and measured almost 21 feet in length, while the collar beams were over 40 feet. It required astonishing effort and skill to lift the massive timbers to such a great height and align their interlocking joints. The lead on the roof added another 176 tons to the huge weight bearing down on the walls. On the ridge of the roof, two great lanterns, or turrets, were constructed to let smoke out, and air and light in.[13]

Exactly how the force of the roof's great weight is supported is still debated; but its intricate web of hammer posts and beams, arched braces and ribs, cross-beams and rafters, is an aesthetic delight. In an ingenious flourish, the hammer beams are decorated by angels, apparently in flight, carved out of the solid wood, with only the wings added. The angels' shields display the royal arms of the period: the fleur-de-lys of France, quartered with the three leopards of England. Richard II's great legacy has been authoritatively described as 'probably the finest timber-framed building in Europe'.[14]

Ironically, the first major meeting held beneath the new roof, in September 1399, heard the announcement of the king's abdication. Richard had been high-handed with parliament, accusing the Commons, in January 1397, of causing 'great offence' when they submitted a petition that criticized the royal household's extravagance. When parliament met that September, members assembled in a temporary shed 'betwixt the clocke Tower, and the gate of the olde great hall' because of the building work in Westminster Hall. According to Stow, the shed was 'open on both sides, and at both endes, that all men might see and heare what was both sayd and done': a feature that made more menacing the presence outside of 200 of the king's archers. The Speaker, Sir John Bussy, was in Richard's pay and took the lead in seeing that the Earl of Arundel was found guilty of treason. For good measure, Richard sought to force the 1397 parliament to bind its successors by requiring the Lords and Commons to swear an oath on the shrine of St Edward the Confessor that they would uphold its decisions or suffer the fate of traitors.[15]

By December 1398, work on Westminster Hall was sufficiently advanced for Richard to celebrate Christmas in exuberant fashion beneath its stupendous roof. Wearing a specially commissioned golden robe, embellished with jewels and pearls, Richard enjoyed the daily jousting and tilting, and relished the great feasts at which 28 oxen, 300 sheep and countless fowl were eaten. However, the king soon met his nemesis. Henry Bolingbroke, Duke of Hereford and heir to the extensive duchy of Lancaster, was also a rival for the throne as he was next in line if Richard remained childless. Richard had exiled him over a dispute at court and, after the death of Henry's father in March 1399, reneged on a promise to let Henry claim his inheritance. Having given his rival cause to rebel, Richard also gave Henry his opportunity by embarking for Ireland in May. Henry invaded England, won support, and by the end of August, Richard was his prisoner.[16]

Richard's fate was sealed when parliament met in his magnificently renovated Westminster Hall in September 1399: 'they had hung and trimmed [the hall] sumptuously,' Stow noted, 'and had caused to be set up a royall chaire, in purpose to choose a newe king, neere to which the prelates were sat, and on the other side sate the Lords, and after, the Commons, in order'. The Archbishop of York read Richard's renunciation of the throne, obtained under duress. The Archbishop of

Canterbury then 'demanded of the States and People then present, whether, for their own interest and the welfare of the realm, they would admit the cession so made?' Lords and Commons agreed, and 'amidst reiterated shouts of approbation, a final sentence of deposition was solemnly pronounced against the late king'.

Henry Bolingbroke, Duke of Lancaster and grandson of Edward III, hesitated in his seat for a moment, before rising, making the sign of the cross on his forehead and chest, and claiming the crown. His actions had been justified, he argued, because the 'realm was in point of being undone for default of governance and undoing of the good laws'. Henry's claim was accepted and, after a few minutes in silent prayer, he was placed in the royal seat by the two archbishops, to cheers of acclaim. The business of this one-day parliament concluded with a Proclamation that a new parliament was to meet on 6 October; and that a week later, on St Edward's day, Henry IV was to be crowned in Westminster Abbey.[17]

Yet Henry IV's coup was never fully accepted. During a dinner party of the deposed king's supporters at the Abbot's House in December 1399, six conspirators supposedly withdrew into a secret chamber in order to swear their loyalty to Richard. According to Dean Stanley, this chamber existed 'behind the wall of the present Library of the Deanery, and which was opened, after an interval of many years in 1864'. The plot earned the then Abbot, William Colchester, his reputation as 'the grand conspirator' in Shakespeare's King Richard II.[18]

Little more than 13 years later, the Jerusalem Chamber, in the Abbot's House, was the scene of Henry IV's death: an occasion dramatized by Shakespeare in Henry IV Part II. The king had been praying at St Edward the Confessor's shrine, on the eve of his long-planned crusade to the Holy Land, when he fell ill and was hurriedly carried into the nearby Chamber. According to the chronicler, Fabyan, Henry IV asked if the room had a name and was shocked to learn that it was Jerusalem: 'for now I know that I shall die in this chamber, according to the prophecy of me before said, that I should die in Jerusalem'. In Shakespeare's version, Henry had been moved to a nearby room, and he utters the following request, now always linked with the Chamber: 'But bear me to that chamber; there I'll lie; / In that Jerusalem shall Harry die'.[19]

13 SANCTITY AND SANCTUARY

The idea of a recluse, or anchorite – usually a senior monk or nun – living a solitary life in a tiny cell, is extraordinary to the modern mind; but the Abbey's anchorite was an important part of life in medieval Westminster. He had special sanctity and was regarded as something of an oracle. St Margaret's Church had a female recluse. However, interceding with the saints for the souls of the dead did not liberate a woman from her traditional role: in 1538–40, 'my lady Ancresse' received a small sum for washing clothes.[1]

Insulting an anchorite's sanctity brought divine retribution, according to a Westminster legend. William Ushborne, a keeper of the Palace, anxious to get his hands on the valuable lead from a dead anchorite's coffin, persuaded a plumber to dig it up. Although the plumber collapsed and died, Ushborne ignored the bad omen and unlawfully appropriated common wasteland between the Palace and Abbey precincts, where College Green now stands. He created a pond in which he kept fresh fish for his table. One day, enjoying a supper with neighbours, he took a few mouthfuls of fish and suddenly screamed: 'Look – look – here is come a fellow who is going to choke me'. Ushborne died on the spot before he could be given the final eucharist.[2]

The Abbey's anchorite was also regarded as an oracle. During the Peasants' Revolt against the poll tax in 1381, as mobs rampaged through the streets, Richard II left the safety of the Tower 'to visit Saint Edward's shrine, and to see if the Commons [of London] had done any mischiefs there'. After inspecting the damage caused by the rioters the King made confession to the anchorite, John Murymouth.[3]

Murymouth's successor, in about 1393, was John London, a former keeper of the Confessor's shrine. He was probably the recluse to whom a distraught Henry V made confession after the death of his father in March 1413: 'After he [Henry] had spent the day in wailing and groaning', a royal chaplain noted, 'the weeping prince' took advantage of the night-time darkness and 'secretly visited a certain recluse of holy life at Westminster and laying bare to him the secret sins of his whole life, was washed in the laver of true repentance'.[4]

When John London died in 1428, his fellow monks went into shock. An anonymous account suggests how news of the anchorite's death spread:

> After the singing of Mattins … Brother Innocent, my neighbour on the right, sang the news in my ear when we turned to the Altar for the *Gloria*: 'Dead is our holy Ankret; he is dead; he died at midnight; the Abbot confessed him; he is dead'. I for my part in like manner transmitted the news to Brother Franciscus.

The news presented the monks with a daunting problem. ' "And who – if any – will succeed him?" and at this question we hung our heads and dropped our eyes, and murmured, "Nay, if one were worthy; but these vows are too much for me" '. In the event, Humphrey of Lambhythe, the sub-prior offered himself to the Abbot for 'this living sacrifice'. All of Westminster packed the Abbey for his consecration: 'the women chattered, the men talked loudly, the girls looked at the Brothers as they passed, and whispered and laughed … And all alike craned their necks to see the man who was going to be shut up in a narrow cell for the rest of his days'.[5]

The whereabouts of the anchorite's cell, demolished after Henry VIII's dissolution of the monasteries, remained a mystery for many years. However, in 1878, an old doorway was found after the removal of a stone tablet in St Benedict's Chapel, and during the 1930s cleaning work revealed a window near the doorway. Lawrence Tanner, Keeper of the Abbey Muniments, recalled that according to medieval records, the anchorite made offerings at St Benedict's altar. The doorway probably led to the anchorite's cell, 'from the interior of which he could have seen through the window the altar of St Benedict's Chapel'.[6]

The doorway to the anchorite's cell is identifiable inside the Abbey by the carved bust of St Benedict above it, in commemoration of Westminster's monks. The cell itself was located against the walls of the Abbey, near its east door which opens on to the private path once used by monarchs between the Palace and the Abbey. It is now used by judges each autumn as they walk in their wigs and gowns from the Abbey to Westminster Hall to celebrate the new legal year with the Lord Chancellor.[7]

One of England's most famous Lord Chancellors, Sir Thomas More, in his history of Richard III, has a character vilify the many taking sanctuary in the Abbey as 'a rabble of thieves, murderers and malicious, heinous traitors'. Sanctuary was as much part of life in medieval Westminster as the recluse, and has left its trace in the names of The Sanctuary, outside the Abbey's west door; and Broad Sanctuary and Little Sanctuary, between Parliament Square and Victoria Street.[8]

The Abbey's sanctuary had its own church in what is now the Little Sanctuary, with a nearby 60-foot belfry tower re-built by Edward III in the 1370s. Its three great bells were usually rung for special occasions, funerals and memorial services: 'Of those bells, men said that their ringing soured all the drink in the town'. After the church's demolition in about 1750, the area became a market.

When this closed in 1912 and work began on Middlesex Guildhall (now occupied by the Supreme Court), the belfry tower's timber foundations were unearthed.[9]

The sanctuary at Westminster offered protection from the law for all manner of crimes, including murder and treason. This extraordinary right of asylum in the Abbey precincts for anyone who wanted to 'take Westminster', as it was said, derived from two sources: the Abbey's special sanctity as a saint's shrine; and its legal status as a 'chartered' sanctuary where the monarch waived his judicial powers in favour of the lord of the manor. The abbot thus held the franchise, or 'liberty' of Westminster, and could offer more or less permanent refuge, whereas most of England's 30 other monastic sanctuaries provided only limited protection for 40 days at most.[10]

In addition to sheltering many innocent fugitives, as the historian, Gervase Rosser notes, the sanctuary also harboured William Burgh, a horse thief, who trapped his victims on the main routes to Westminster. When the Abbot of Westminster led a church procession: 'Before him went all the Sanctuary men, with cross keys upon their garments', including three murderers. And when prisoners were escorted through Westminster to the Gatehouse gaol near the Abbey's west door, a great detour was made round the sanctuary, along a winding street that became known as Thieving Lane, in order to prevent 'untoward emancipations'.[11]

The desecration of the Abbey's sanctuary in 1378 came as a dreadful shock. Two squires, Robert Hawley and John Shakell, had got on the wrong side of John of Gaunt, the most powerful figure at the court – Richard II was his young nephew. Hawley and Shakell had been imprisoned in the Tower of London, but escaped and took sanctuary at Westminster. Abbot Litlyngton's refusal to surrender the fugitives brought a savage response when a posse of 50 soldiers invaded the sanctuary. Shakell was arrested, but Hawley fled inside the choir of the Abbey. Although High Mass was being celebrated, the soldiers burst in and hacked at him as he tried to flee. He died in front of the Prior's Choir, and a sacrist was also killed.

Hawley was regarded as a martyr to the injured rights of the Abbey and was buried in the south transept near St Benedict's Chapel, where his grave is marked by a stone with the indent of a lost brass of a man in armour. The perpetrators of the sacrilege were excommunicated by Archbishop Sudbury, and the Abbey was shut for four months before being re-consecrated. Abbot Litlyngton attended parliament at Gloucester (MPs had been meeting in the Chapter House at Westminster before Hawley's murder), and defended his abbey's liberties, but the rights of sanctuary were reduced.[12]

Within three years, the Abbey suffered a second violent invasion. In mid-June 1381, Westminster experienced its first, but not its last, poll tax riot. The mob supporting Wat Tyler's Peasants' Revolt broke into the Abbey, where Richard Imworth, the Steward of the Marshalsea prison at Southwark, had taken refuge.

In desperation, Imworth clung to the pillars of St Edward the Confessor's shrine, but the mob dragged him away and beheaded him.[13]

The deepening crisis of Richard II's reign and the long shadows cast into the fifteenth century by Henry IV's coup, culminating in the bloody Wars of the Roses, made Westminster Abbey a welcome haven for political fugitives. In 1388, the king defended the Abbey's right of sanctuary against his enemies at court when a parson, William De Chesterton, took refuge there after criticising Thomas Arundel, the Archbishop of Canterbury and Lord Chancellor.

Not all would-be fugitives made it to the Abbey's haven. Sir Robert Tresilian, Chief Justice of the King's Bench, and one of Richard II's supporters, met a grisly end after being found guilty of treason while in hiding. He was spotted in Westminster as he watched events from a roof, and dragged to parliament. Tresilian sought sanctuary at the Abbey, but Richard's opponents denied him the right and the judge was forcibly taken to the scaffold, stripped, hanged and had his throat cut.[14]

Chaucer had been a colleague of Tresilian's while serving as a justice of the peace. The poet wisely kept away from London and Westminster, but it has been suggested that after Richard was deposed in 1399, Chaucer might have become a political fugitive in the precincts of Westminster Abbey, where Abbot Colchester was up to his neck in a conspiracy to restore Richard to the throne. According to Terry Jones and his colleagues, Chaucer signed a 53-year lease on a tenement in the Abbey precincts in December 1399, only a week after Colchester and his fellow conspirators had dined in the Abbot's House. Jones's team argue plausibly that by moving to the Abbey, Chaucer was 'nailing his colours to the mast of Richard II's sinking ship'.[15]

Did Chaucer move into the Abbey's precincts because it gave him the option of taking sanctuary? He had loyally served Edward III and Richard II, and was closely identified with Richard's cause. Chaucer had also aimed scurrilous gibes at church and churchmen in *The Canterbury Tales* and other poems, which was unlikely to endear him to the ruthless Archbishop, Arundel. Although Henry IV re-affirmed his annuity and pledged a further grant, Chaucer received only partial payment and by 1400 was no longer collecting his money personally. In June, the poet disappears from the record, and at some point before 28 September 1401, his house was let to another tenant. Chaucer may have died from natural causes, but the absence of any reference to the death or funeral of such a well-known figure is puzzling.

Was Chaucer murdered and the crime hushed up? His bones were buried at some unspecified time in the floor of the Abbey's south transept, at the entrance of Saint Benedict's Chapel. His sixteenth-century tomb may not contain a body at all, and its inscription stating that he died on 25 October 1400 is unreliable. Chaucer's contemporary and fellow poet Thomas Hoccleve who worked at the privy seal office in the Palace, later implied that Chaucer died suddenly. Chaucer had been mugged before, and perhaps was attacked and killed on his way home one dark night. Arundel and Henry IV were capable of arranging such a murder. Perhaps, as Terry Jones and his colleagues surmise, Chaucer died in 1402, after being taken captive and held where other dissidents were detained, in the Archbishop's prison at Saltwood Castle in Kent. The murderous rivalries of the time demand an open verdict on Chaucer's death.[16]

Perhaps the Abbey's most tragic fugitive was Elizabeth Woodville, queen of Edward IV (1461–70 and 1471–83), who twice took sanctuary at Westminster during the Wars of the Roses. She first sought refuge there after her husband was deposed and forced into exile. Elizabeth left the Tower of London by darkness of night on 1 October 1470, with her three daughters, all aged under five, took a barge to Westminster and moved into the Sanctuary. Lady Scrope was paid £10 by the government to attend the queen, probably to keep tabs on her.[17]

On 1 November 1470, Elizabeth gave birth to her first son, the future Edward V. The prince was baptized in the Abbot's House, with Abbot Millyng, the Prior and Lady Scrope as godparents. The following April 1471, when her husband triumphantly returned, Elizabeth left the sanctuary. The £520 donated to the Abbey by the king and queen paid for more roofing work on the nave.[18]

Twelve years later, Elizabeth returned after Edward IV's death in April 1483. Her hopes of an early coronation for the 12-year-old Edward V had been dashed when he was taken into custody by his surviving, 30-year-old uncle, Richard, Duke of Gloucester (the future Richard III), who acted as his protector. Realizing the threat to her son's succession, Elizabeth fled the Palace under cover of night, 'probably through the postern-gate, into the "Abbot's Place"'. She took sanctuary in the Abbot's House with her younger son, Richard, Duke of York, and her five surviving daughters.[19]

News of the queen's flight into sanctuary so perturbed the Archbishop of York and Lord Chancellor, Thomas Rotheram, that he left his bed in York Place (in what is now Whitehall) and dashed to the Abbey. He found Elizabeth, 'sat alone, on the rushes, all desolate and dismayed', and all about her, 'much heaviness, rumble, haste, and business; carriage and conveyance of her stuff into the Sanctuary; chests, coffers, packers, fradels [bundles], trussed all on men's backs'. Amidst all this confusion, Rotheram presented her with the Great Seal, and, apparently, promised that he would crown her younger son, Richard, if Edward V was set aside. He left at dawn, 'by which time he might, in his chamber see, all the Thames full of boats of the Duke of Gloucester's servants watching that no man should pass to the Sanctuary'. Rotheram soon regretted his action and tactlessly sought the Seal's return; but it was too late, and he was sacked as Lord Chancellor.[20]

Gloucester maintained his re-assuring pretence about Edward V, prompting the council to nominate him as Lord Protector and set a date for the young king's coronation in June. The pressure on Elizabeth to entrust her younger son, Richard, to his uncle's care became intense. On 16 June 1483, the sanctuary was surrounded by soldiers while, inside, the elderly Archbishop of Canterbury, Thomas Bourchier, who had crowned Edward IV and Elizabeth, led a deputation from the council and tried to wheedle his way round her: by handing over Richard, the boys would be together and the king would be happier as he awaited his coronation; and anyway Richard was too young to have committed any offences that might justify his claiming sanctuary. Elizabeth furiously retorted that it was 'a goodly gloss, by which that place that may defend a thief may not save an innocent'. When the Archbishop pledged his body and soul for the prince's safety, the queen relented. Kissing her son goodbye, she uttered the fateful words: 'for God knoweth when we shall kiss one another again'.[21]

With both princes in his control, the Protector launched his coup. Edward V's coronation was postponed. Then doubts were cast on the princes' legitimacy and the legality of their parents' marriage. Next, Elizabeth's brother, her son by her first marriage, and her cousin, were executed. On 26 June, in a symbolic usurpation, the Protector attended Westminster Hall, accompanied by his followers, and sat in the royal chair in the Court of the King's Bench. On 13 July, Gloucester achieved his ambition when the hapless Archbishop Bourchier reluctantly crowned him Richard III in Westminster Abbey. All the bell-ringing and cheering were heard next door in the Abbot's House by the deposed queen.[22]

Elizabeth remained in sanctuary with her daughters. With no sign of the princes' whereabouts, the princesses became potential figureheads for revolt. The discovery of a plot to smuggle them abroad prompted Richard III to blockade the Abbey: 'the solemn Church of Westminster and all the adjacent region was changed after the form of a camp or fortress'.[23] In late 1483, rumours of the princes' deaths undermined a revolt intended to restore them. After parliament confirmed Richard III's kingship in January 1484, Elizabeth realized that she could not live in sanctuary indefinitely. On 1 March, she agreed terms with Richard III for her own and her daughters' safekeeping and left the Abbot's House.

However, Elizabeth was soon back, but not as a fugitive. In 1486, after Richard III had been killed at Bosworth Field and her eldest daughter, Elizabeth of York, had married Henry VII, the dowager queen took out a 40-year lease on the Abbot's House. The following year she withdrew to Bermondsey Abbey, where she died in 1492.[24]

The fate of Edward IV's and Elizabeth's two young sons, 'the princes in the Tower' of popular legend, remains a great mystery. The popular legend that they were murdered in the Tower on the orders of Richard III is given credibility by the contents of an urn, which stands on a white marble monument, in the north aisle of Henry VII's Chapel in Westminster Abbey. Inside the urn are the bones of children found by workmen in 1674 under a staircase at the Tower of London. Charles II was convinced, as the epitaph states, 'by the most certain indications', that the remains were those of Edward V and Richard. At his command, these bones were laid to rest in the Abbey, in the sarcophagus designed by Sir Christopher Wren.[25]

However, speculation persisted, and in 1933 the urn was opened and its bones examined. Lawrence Tanner, who was present, reports that the ages and relationship of the children, and signs that at least one of them had met a violent end, were not inconsistent with the popular legend. The verdict is best summed up as 'not proven'. But huge advances have been made since the 1930s in the science and techniques of autopsies, not least in DNA profiling, and further analysis of the bones is long overdue.[26]

There is speculation that the younger boy, Richard, might have survived. The historian, David Baldwin, suggests the possibility that Edward died from natural causes and Richard was released and taken to St John's Abbey, Colchester, where he worked as a bricklayer. Richard might also have been re-united with his mother, Elizabeth, but kept his identity secret for fear of reprisals by the Tudors. Perhaps he was the Latin-speaking bricklayer called Richard Plantagenet, who died in Kent in 1550, 65 years after Henry VII's accession.[27]

The right of sanctuary became an irritant to Tudor monarchs, although Henry VII's uncle, Owen Tudor, had taken refuge at Westminster and later became a monk there. Henry VII wanted the abuse of sanctuary curtailed, and in 1487 Pope Innocent VIII introduced some limited restrictions on the rights of sanctuarymen. Following Henry VIII's break with Rome, treason was removed from the list of offences for which sanctuary could be claimed. With the abolition of chartered sanctuaries, Westminster became one of only eight 'sanctuary towns' that could offer asylum for a reduced list of crimes. During the reigns of Edward VI and Mary I, the crimes of arson, rape, sacrilege and treason were briefly restored to the list.[28]

After the monastery was finally dissolved early in Elizabeth I's reign, the Abbey offered immunity only from civil action. Its legal privileges were finally abolished by James I in 1624.[29] Nothing better demonstrates the contrast between medieval religious sensibilities and modern judicial power than the decision to locate the Supreme Court, now the pinnacle of the English criminal justice system, on the spot where the Abbey's Sanctuary once offered refuge from over-mighty rulers.

PART THREE

REVOLUTIONARIES

14 A NEW ERA

On 30 September 1476, a business deal was agreed at Westminster Abbey. William Caxton, a merchant and diplomat in his fifties, recently returned from Bruges, paid Abbot John Eastney a year's rent of ten shillings for a shop near the Abbey. This seemingly routine contract marked the start of a new era at Westminster, with rising prosperity increasing the population of St Margaret's parish from 2,000 in Chaucer's day to 3,000 by the end of Caxton's.

While in Europe, Caxton had realised that Johannes Gutenberg's perfection of movable-type printing created huge commercial opportunities. Caxton learned how printing worked and while in Bruges published the first book printed in English: a translation from French of Raoul Lefevre's, *History of Troy*. The wooden hand-operated machine that Caxton brought to Westminster a couple of years later was the first printing press in England. The demand for relatively cheap, printed books was such that by 1500, his Westminster press had published about 200 or so titles; while across Europe more books had been produced in under 50 years than in the previous millennium.[1]

Although Caxton put Westminster in the vanguard of technological and social change, he saw himself as a businessman, not a revolutionary. He probably heard from his brother, Richard, who had become a monk at Westminster, that the Abbey was a good place to set up a business, as it offered legal protection and marketing opportunities. The precise whereabouts of Caxton's first shop was forgotten over the years. His advertisement bidding customers 'to come to Westminster to the Almonry at the sign of the Red Pale', suggests that he ran his business from what is now the corner of Victoria Street and Great Smith Street, by the modern Department for Business. However, he only moved his printing press there six years after setting up his business, and continued to rent his shop by the Abbey.[2]

The location of his original shop was finally identified from the Abbey's records by Lawrence Tanner. It lay to the south, 'in a house adjoining or close to the Chapter House'. Situated by the path between the Abbey and Palace, the shop was ideally placed to attract a literate clientele of courtiers, lawyers, monks, officials and politicians as they walked between the two.[3]

Caxton's earliest surviving document from his Westminster press, dated 13 December 1476, could scarcely have been less revolutionary in its intent. It was an indulgence, absolving recipients of their sins, written in Latin. On 18 November 1477, he published the *Sayings of the Philosophers*, an English translation from French, commonly regarded as the first book printed in England; but his first edition of Chaucer's *The Canterbury Tales* was probably issued earlier and appealed to a wider market. Caxton's dedications in his books to members of the royal family, including those to Edward, Prince of Wales, in *History of Jason*, 1477, and to Edward IV in Cicero's *Old Age*, 1481, impressed courtiers and enhanced his reputation. However, the death of Edward IV in 1483, followed by the disappearance of Edward V and the execution of the Earl Rivers, brother of Edward IV's widow, Elizabeth Woodville, robbed Caxton of patrons.[4]

After Richard III's coup, Caxton was loyal to Elizabeth, but he was, above all, a practical businessman. In January 1484, parliament encouraged the fledgling print industry by providing for the protection and residence of foreign printers and booksellers. This measure helped skilled immigrants such as Caxton's foreman Wynkyn de Worde who probably hailed from Alsace. Later that year, Caxton began ingratiating himself with the usurper's regime when he presented *The Order of Chivalry* to 'my redoubted, natural and most dread sovereign lord King Richard'.[5]

Caxton was an active churchman at St Margaret's, Westminster, which from the 1480s was being re-built in the elegant perpendicular style; though the white stone-cladding was not added until the eighteenth century. While pages of print flowed from Caxton's press, he and his fellow parishioners continued the annual tradition of celebrating St Margaret's day on 20 July. On the eve of the festival, a bonfire was kept burning all night before the door of the church. Inside, the high altar was hung with rich cloths of gold and silk, often loaned by keepers of the palace and other royal residences. The day itself began with mass, at which choristers from the Lady Chapel of Westminster Abbey, or possibly from the King's Chapel, sang. After the service, a procession of virgins, accompanied by a minstrel band, wended its way through the parish, in honour of St Margaret's chastity. The festival's climax was a play re-enacting St Margaret's encounter with the dragon: as she was being devoured, her protestation of her faith caused the beast to explode. The tradition of 'hocking' was also relished. On the second Monday after Easter Sunday, women were captured and bound with ropes until they paid a small toll to be released. The next day, the roles were reversed as the women bound the men.[6]

Caxton had a set-back after Richard III's defeat at Bosworth, and it took him more than three years to win Henry VII's patronage; finally succeeding through the offices of the Earl of Oxford, for whom he published *The Four Sons of Aymon*. Caxton also published the statutes of Henry's first three parliaments held in 1485, 1487 and 1489–90; and an increasing number of religious books. The *Sarum*

Missal, which he had printed in Paris, was the most profitable service book in pre-Reformation England and was used by every mass-saying priest, church or chapel. The churchwarden's accounts of St Margaret's indicate that Caxton died in about March 1492 and was buried in the churchyard. His memorial, a stained glass window, was destroyed in World War II, and he is now commemorated by a tablet beside the window by the east door. Caxton's impact on Westminster lasted for many decades in its printing houses and bookshops. His international legacy is the English printed word and its revolutionary role in promoting debate and inquiry.[7]

St Margaret's close neighbour, Henry VII's Chapel, was built between 1502 and 1509, making it the first major addition to the Abbey since Henry III's re-building 250 years earlier. Henry VII's Chapel was described as *miraculum orbis*, 'a wonder of the world', by John Leland, the sixteenth century poet and antiquary. Some 300 years later, its late English perpendicular style of architecture inspired the winning design for a new Palace of Westminster by Sir Charles Barry and Augustus Welby Pugin.[8]

The chapel's exuberant design asserted the first Tudor monarch's claim to be ranked alongside the Abbey's most revered, royal founders: Edward the Confessor and Henry III. It was the culmination of Henry Tudor's determination to assert his legitimate claim to the throne, a process that began with his crowning on Bosworth Field: etched in the national memory because of Shakespeare's drama-tization of the scene.

The victorious 28-year-old's right to the throne was distinctly tenuous, and the more doubts that surround a new king's legitimacy, the more likely it is that he would favour ostentatious display. Henry VII was no different from previous usurpers. Henry IV arranged his coronation, in 1399, on the symbolic date of 13 October, St Edward the Confessor's feast day. Arriving late, he let it be known that he had heard three Masses and spent hours with his confessor, and was probably crowned with an imperial-style, arched, or closed, crown.[9]

In 1483, Richard III was escorted to Westminster by his personal army of 6,000 northern supporters and made his offerings at the shrine of the Confessor while 'the monks sang Te Deum with a faint courage'. At his coronation, he and Queen Anne presented a striking sight as they sat on a specially raised platform: 'stripped from the waist upwards, to be anointed – the dukes around the King, the bishops and ladies around the Queen'.[10]

Henry VII was the latest usurper anxious to establish his legitimacy, despite being the son of Edmund Tudor, first earl of Richmond (half-brother of Henry VI through their mother, Catherine of Valois), and Margaret Beaufort (great-great-granddaughter of Edward III through John of Gaunt's liaison with Katherine Swynford). No expense was spared on the coronation. Cardinal Archbishop Thomas Bourchier was dragged out for a third time 'to consecrate the doubtful claims of a new dynasty'.[11]

Writs summoning Henry's first parliament were issued before the coronation, and parliament duly confirmed Henry's title as king only eight days after the ceremony in the Abbey; but more was needed. The Commons through their Speaker, Thomas Lovell, petitioned the king to honour the oath he had sworn before usurping Richard by marrying 'that illustrious lady Elizabeth, daughter of King Edward IV' and so render possible 'the propagation of offspring from the stock of kings'. Henry's marriage to Elizabeth of York in Westminster Abbey in January 1486 personified the new peace between the warring houses of Lancaster and York. The new dynasty's unifying emblem, the Tudor rose, was promoted as aggressively as any modern party's new logo and has lasted a lot longer.[12]

Henry VII's hopes of founding a new, unifying dynasty were soon improved by the birth of an heir, Arthur, in September 1486, followed by Margaret in November 1489 and the future Henry VIII in June 1491. However, plots by defeated Yorkists and uprisings remained a threat, supported variously by the French, Scots and disaffected members of Ireland's ruling elite. The most unsettling conspiracy involved Perkin Warbeck (real name, Pierrechon de Werbecque), a precocious, French-born impostor. Warbeck claimed that he was Richard, Duke of York, one of the missing 'princes in the Tower' and, as the surviving son of Edward IV, the rightful heir to the throne.

The deep sense of insecurity among Henry's courtiers allowed an improbable impostor such as Warbeck to create panic at Westminster. The Lord Chamberlain of the King's Household, Sir William Stanley, was implicated in the plot, found guilty of treason and beheaded. Warbeck tried invading Kent and the Scottish borders, and then supported a Cornish tax revolt before surrendering. He briefly escaped custody at Westminster in 1498, but afterwards 'was set for a whole day in the stocks upon a scaffold before the entrance to Westminster Hall, where he read his confession, written with his own hand, "not without innumerable reproaches, mocks, and scornings"'. After allegedly plotting while in the Tower, Warbeck and his fellow conspirators were tried in the Lesser Hall of Westminster Palace. Warbeck was hanged at Tyburn aged 25, in November 1499.[13]

Warbeck's threat changed the royal routine at Westminster. Medieval kings had eaten, dressed, bathed and relieved themselves in public as the constant focus of court life, but after Sir William Stanley's treachery in the mid-1490s, Henry introduced a privy chamber of essential body-servants and granted them exclusive access to his private lodgings. This elite corps was recruited from relatively humble origins as they were less likely to indulge in courtly intrigue. Access to the monarch brought increasing power to the Tudor privy chamber. The most intimate duties fell to the 'Groom of the Stool', who was charged with seeing that 'the house of easement be sweet and clear'. This post had lost its lavatorial function by the seventeenth century, when its true origin was disguised by the title of 'Groom of the Stole'. Despite the subsequent demise of this office, Westminster careers can still be advanced by a readiness, metaphorically, to perform the same service.[14]

Henry VII was adept at presentational ploys, now described as 'public relations' and 'branding'. Royal events such as the three-year-old Prince Henry's creation as Duke of York in 1494, and the arrival of 15-year-old Catherine of Aragon in 1501 to marry Arthur, Prince of Wales, were celebrated with spectacular tournaments and entertainments. Before the latter occasion, the Palace roofs were repaired, and new glass was installed in the great windows at both ends of Westminster Hall, featuring the arms of England and roundels painted with the Tudor emblems of red roses and portcullises. The Hall's great north door was renewed, its porch lavishly painted and gilded with portcullises, flowers, roses and stars, with a carving above of two lions supporting a great red rose adorned with an imperial crown.[15]

Henry relished crown-wearings, revived the tradition of touching for the king's evil and became a patron of the arts, entertainment and sport. His prolific placement of the unifying emblem of the Tudor rose on buildings, royal charters and his servants' liveries, widely proclaimed his right to rule. The crown imperial was stamped on coins and emblazoned above a portcullis – the badge of his mother's family, the Beauforts – on crimson and gold copes for the Abbey.[16]

Nowhere else is Henry VII's desire to establish his royal legitimacy demonstrated more vividly than in the beautiful chapel that bears his name, at the east end of Westminster Abbey. Initially, he planned to exploit a religious cult associated with his murdered uncle, Henry VI, and create a shrine at Windsor, in a new chapel being built for his own burial. However, Henry VII reckoned without the Westminster monks, who contested the plan. The Privy Council heard eye-witness accounts of Henry VI's visits to the Confessor's shrine at Westminster from officials and workers, including the Abbot's falconer and barber, a clerk, priest, weaver, and scriveners. They testified that Henry VI had indicated where he wanted to be buried in the Abbey; and his master-mason, John Thirske, marked the grave's outline on the pavement using an iron pike. Their evidence was confirmed in the 1920s when some linoleum was removed from the Abbey floor and Thirske's long, wavering scratch was revealed.[17]

As a result of the monks' intervention, Henry built his new Lady Chapel – now generally known as Henry VII's Chapel – at Westminster instead of Windsor. Demolition of Henry III's old Lady Chapel and the surrounding buildings, including the White Rose tavern, began in October 1502. The work disturbed the coffin of Anne Mowbray, the wife of Richard, Duke of York, the younger of the princes in the Tower. Anne was aged only eight or nine when she died in 1481, only three years after her marriage. Her remains were re-discovered in 1964, when her small lead coffin was unearthed in the City. She was re-buried in a small chapel at the east end of Henry VII's Chapel.[18]

At 2.45 p.m. on 24 January 1503, in Henry VII's presence, the foundation stone of the new chapel was laid on the king's behalf by John Islip, Abbot of Westminster. The building is probably the work of the king's master mason, Robert Janyns. Its gates, walls and windows, and Henry VII's chantry inside the chapel, are festooned with the king's arms, badges, and emblems: Tudor roses; fleurs-de-lys; Welsh dragons; greyhounds for Richmond; and portcullises for Beaufort.[19]

The extravagant exterior of Henry VII's Chapel is an exhilarating example of late English perpendicular architecture. The walls consist almost entirely of glass bay windows set in complex patterns of stone panelling, including 14 tall, octagonal turrets. Horizontal bands of carved emblems run round the entire building. Janyns enhanced his spell-binding symmetry with four sets of bow windows along each side and, around the east end, central V-projections in the five sets of windows.[20]

Above the lower storey, the turrets are decorated with niches that housed statues of Old and New Testament figures until about 1720, when they were removed, apparently for fear that they might fall on those attending parliament, or possibly because Protestant clerics objected to them. The turrets are crowned with rounded domes, embellished with crockets. Flying buttresses soar from each turret and span to the clerestory. In a delightful touch, carved animals are shown at play along the top bars. The chapel's *tour de force* is the interior design of its roof, high above the nave and chancel. The awe-inspiring fan vault, with its huge, hanging stone pendants, is the finest example anywhere of this very English style. The intricate patterns of fans, arches, lacework and tracery are embellished by the ubiquitous fleurs-de-lys, portcullises and Tudor rose emblems.[21]

The stained glass windows were destroyed by puritans during the 1640s, but the unrivalled collection of early Tudor statues set in niches below the windows survived. Of the original 107 statues of religious figures 95 remain, including St Wilgeforte or Uncumber, a virgin with a beard, to whom women prayed to get rid of their husbands. In the nave, the original, ornate wooden stalls in the three western bays are among the best examples of English gothic church furniture. More stalls were added when George I re-founded the Order of the Bath in 1725, at the prompting of Sir Robert Walpole, who desired the revival of Henry IV's chivalric honour in order to win support in parliament. The Order is now usually awarded to officers in the armed forces and retired civil servants.[22]

In the chapel's chancel stands the magnificent tomb of the first Tudor king and his queen, Elizabeth of York, behind a bronze screen bearing Henry's emblems. The black marble tomb chest, decorated with copper gilt angels, putti and roundels, and adorned by gilt bronze effigies of the king and queen lying side by side, was created by Pietro Torrigiano, a Florentine sculptor. He brought Renaissance art to Westminster while working in the Abbey precinct between 1511 and the early 1520s.[23]

Elizabeth died less than three weeks after the foundation stone of Henry VII's Lady Chapel had been laid. During her funeral procession and service, her effigy lay on top of her coffin, clothed in her robes of state, with her crown on its painted head. At Henry's funeral at the Abbey in May 1509, his effigy lay on his coffin, on cushions of gold, dressed in his robes of state, with his crown on its head, and a ball and sceptre in its hands. Their effigies' carved, wooden heads are displayed in the Abbey's museum, together with the full-length effigy of Catherine of Valois, Henry V's widow and grandmother of Henry VII by her second marriage to Owen Tudor. Catherine had died in 1437 at the age of 36 and was buried in the Abbey's old Lady Chapel. When this building was demolished to make way for Henry VII's Chapel, her remains were put in a wooden coffin near Henry V's tomb, where they awaited re-burial for almost 300 years. Samuel Pepys saw her remains by special favour in February 1669. After kissing the corpse's mouth, he reflected: 'that this was my birthday thirty-six years old that I did first kiss a Queen'.[24]

The burial vaults of Henry VII's Chapel served as a royal mausoleum for 250 years. However, Henry's requirement that the monks should offer prayers and observe rituals for his and his family's souls was swept away within 30 years by his successor's religious revolution. Henry VII had founded a powerful dynasty, but it allowed his successor to become a ruthless despot.

15 WHITEHALL PALACE

n April 1512, a 'great part of this Palace at Westminster was once againe burnt'. The blaze, in the fourth year of Henry VIII's reign, had a greater impact than previous fires. Starting in the kitchens, it destroyed the privy Palace that housed the royal family's lodgings and serving quarters. The 20-year old king and his court were forced to move out. Monarchs had dwelt in the Palace for about 450 years, but no king or queen ever lived there again.[1]

When attending parliamentary sessions, after the fire, the king stayed at Lambeth Palace, the Archbishop of Canterbury's residence. Although Lambeth was across the river, it offered better accommodation than York Place, the residence of the Archbishop of York, only a quarter of a mile to the north of Westminster Hall. However, in 1514, a new Archbishop of York, Thomas Wolsey, began transforming York Place into a grander palace. He was in his early forties, and had been royal chaplain and Henry VIII's almoner. Wolsey's formidable ability and drive had propelled him from his modest origins as the son of an Ipswich butcher to high rank in church and state. A cardinal's hat was ceremonially bestowed on him in Westminster Abbey in the autumn of 1515; by Christmas he was also Lord Chancellor.[2]

Each morning, Cardinal Wolsey's procession ostentatiously made its stately way from York Place, along King Street, to the Palace. The cardinal was 'apparelled all in red' in the best cloth, according to his gentleman-usher, George Cavendish, with 'fine sables about his neck'. Wolsey rode a mule: an incongruous symbol of Christian humility, as the animal was draped in crimson velvet and had gilt stirrups. Wolsey's escort was led by noblemen and gentlemen carrying the great seal of England, the cardinal's hat, two great crosses of silver, another two great pillars of silver, and 'his pursuivant-at-arms with a great mace of silver gilt'. Also accompanying him were four footmen holding gilt pole-axes and his cross-bearers on horses draped in 'fine scarlet'.[3]

After alighting outside Westminster Hall, the cardinal entered and headed to his right, towards the Chancery court on the west side. He held to his nose a hollowed-out orange with a sponge inside, doused in 'vinegar and other confections against the pestilent airs'. At the bar of the Chancery, he might stop and chat with judges and court officials before he began hearing cases for the first part of the morning. At eleven o'clock, Wolsey would leave the Chancery in great pomp, sniffing his perfumed orange again as he made his way through the throng in Westminster Hall to the Star Chamber.[4]

The name, 'Star Chamber', retains a chilling ring. The court gained its fearsome reputation after Wolsey ruthlessly turned it into a political weapon. Originally known as the 'Chambre des Estoyers', or 'Estoilles', and dating from at least Edward III's reign, its name probably derives from the gilded stars that had once adorned the courtroom ceiling. Today, the 'Star Chamber' is Westminster vernacular for the bruising meetings at which ministers make last-ditch pleas against Treasury cuts to their spending plans.

Wolsey presided over the Star Chamber as Lord Chancellor and sat with his fellow King's Councillors (sometimes numbering as many as 40) who became both judges and prosecutors. 'It was a strange matter to see,' observed Stow 70 years later, 'a man not trayned up in the laws, to sit in the seate of judgement, to pronounce the lawe'. However, Wolsey was undeterred by his lack of legal training, and his determination to rein in overmighty subjects and ensure equal access to the law, had popular appeal. However, in May 1516, he argued that not even judges should regard themselves as being above the law. His chilling doctrine held that strong monarchy was the fount of all authority and legitimized Tudor despotism.[5]

Cardinal Wolsey wanted a residence worthy of his power. Only the best craftsmen would do. Henry Redman, his master mason, soon succeeded Henry Vertue as the King's Master Mason. Wolsey also employed the king's glazier, sergeant plumber and chief joiner. By the winter of 1517–18, the cardinal had built a new chamber to the south-west of the fifteenth-century great hall. Remarkably, the undercroft beneath Wolsey's great hall survives to this day beneath the present Ministry of Defence and is commonly known as Henry VIII's wine cellar. It has a fine Tudor brick-vaulted roof, about 23 yards in length, 10 yards in width and 6.5 yards in height. Its five bays are supported by four octagonal, central piers; its east wall is the last remnant of the archbishop's fifteenth-century palace.[6]

Wolsey substantially expanded the property to the north and south. He built a long gallery along the banks of the Thames, linking the existing buildings to new development further south. These acquisitions, and reclamation of land from the river, enabled Wolsey to expand the gardens; but politics thwarted his grand plan. Although he began a second phase of major works in 1527, completing a new hall, chapel and lodgings, two years later the cardinal fell victim to Henry's impatience at the delay in securing a divorce from Catherine of Aragon.[7]

Catherine's previous marriage to Henry's elder brother, Arthur, had been a diplomatic arrangement, and on his death, she was effectively passed to Henry. When Queen Catherine failed to produce a male heir, the king became desperate for an annulment. Wolsey sought to expedite the divorce, but his efforts were delayed by papal and European politics. He was also increasingly unpopular, having been first minister for more than a decade, and became a victim of a whispering campaign by Anne Boleyn, daughter of a courtier and sister of the king's mistress, who was inveigling herself with the king.[8]

Events came to a head in Westminster Hall on 9 October 1529. While Wolsey was presiding as usual in Chancery, he was indicted in King's Bench on an absurd charge of *praemunire*: acting on papal, as opposed to royal, authority in affairs of state. Wolsey surrendered the great seal on 18 October. The next day, he was subjected to the same ruthless treatment that he had inflicted on others when he appeared in the Star Chamber and was replaced as chief minister. On 22 October, Wolsey pleaded guilty and forfeited his property to Henry. He left York Place for the last time by river, embarking at his unfinished landing stage, with only one cross borne before him.[9]

Two days after Wolsey's departure, Henry VIII disembarked at the same spot to inspect the vacant property. He was accompanied by Anne Boleyn; her mother, Lady Elizabeth; and Henry Norris, the King's Groom of the Stool. According to Simon Thurley, the architectural historian, the great hall, with its steep, pitched roof and windowed gable ends, was the largest building; alongside was a chapel and nearby a banqueting house. The grounds included gardens and extensive kitchens and lodgings for the cardinal's army of servants.[10]

The king visited again on 27 October, and then returned on 2 November and stayed for the parliamentary session until 17 December. Wolsey was denounced at the opening of Parliament by the new Lord Chancellor, Thomas More. By February 1530, an ambassador reported that the king was spending all his time at York Place with Anne, leaving Catherine alone at Richmond Palace. Wolsey was finally broken by his implication in a plot to deny papal approval for Henry's marriage to Anne Boleyn. He died little more than a year after his eviction from York Place.[11]

Henry's take-over of York Place gave him the opportunity to prove his status as a major European monarch. He spent Christmas 1529 at Greenwich Palace planning a grandiose, new palace by extending and improving Wolsey's former residence. Although York Place was not formally vested in the Crown until early 1530, Henry ordered the removal of a fine, new gallery from Wolsey's Esher home and had it brought, stone by stone, to Westminster.[12]

Henry's new palace was soon nicknamed 'Whitehall', distinguishing it from its predecessor and from its ancient, royal neighbour, Westminster Palace. Shakespeare, in his play, *Henry VIII*, has a gentleman say:

You must no more call it York Place; that's past:
For since the Cardinal fell, that title's lost;
'Tis now the King's and called Whitehall.[13]

The name, 'Whitehall', may be explained by Henry's eager pillaging of materials from other royal palaces for material. A demolition man, Ralf Williams, received 6d. a day 'for the devising and making of engines for the overthrowing of the walls of the king's olde palace of Westminster' plus £4 to take down 'a Toure of stone and bricke at the king's place within his paleis'. More than 3,000 cartloads of 'olde stone, bricks and chaulke' were hauled up King Street to provide rubble for the walls of Whitehall Palace.[14]

The light hue of the stones removed from the old palace might have prompted the new palace's name. Alternatively, the name might derive from medieval common usage, since 'White Hall' quite often denoted the main hall of a mansion or palace. But whatever its origin, Whitehall stuck as the name by which the new palace was known and also came to denote Westminster's northern quarter.[15]

The building of Whitehall Palace epitomized the rise of modern tyranny. Nobody was allowed to stand in Henry's way. Better-off tenants in tenements on King Street were bought out, but poorer tenants were simply thrown out. The hospital and chapel of St Mary Rounceval were demolished. Henry also bought 185 acres of land to the west of King Street from Eton College for his hunting park: its remnants are Green Park and St James's Park.

By September 1531, more than 900 craftsmen and labourers were employed on a building site that sprawled across the north end of Westminster. The start and end of each working day was signalled by loud blasts on six horns – a single horn had been sufficient for the workmen refurbishing the old palace in 1308. However, as Simon Thurley points out, Henry often countermanded the evening horns. Work sometimes went on all night by candle light. Men bailed out water-logged foundations at midnight; others carried on working despite the rain beneath canvas tents; and paint and plaster were hurriedly applied and dried by charcoal braziers. Henry's impatience resulted in jerry building and extra costs in overtime, compensation for injuries and surgeons' fees.[16]

At Easter 1532, as the Palace took shape, the royal court was in uproar over Henry's choice of Anne Boleyn as his next queen. Criticism of the match by his sister, Princess Mary, provoked a fracas in the Abbey's Sanctuary in which a principal gentleman of Mary's husband, the Duke of Suffolk, was killed. Afterwards, Mary and her husband retreated to their house in Oxfordshire.[17]

By January 1533, Anne was pregnant and married Henry, probably before dawn on the 25th. The secret ceremony was held in an upper chamber of the Holbein Gate, a new Gatehouse that straddled the busy King Street and also served as a private bridge, allowing royals and courtiers to cross without having to leave Henry's extensive new palace. Hans Holbein, the painter, whose name became associated with the gatehouse, might have used one of its rooms as a lodging or workshop. No record of the wedding exists and few witnesses attended.[18]

Henry urgently sought to legitimize the marriage. Parliament was recalled and a bill introduced that struck at the heart of papal authority in England by restricting the right to make appeals to Rome. The bill was the work of Thomas Cromwell, Wolsey's former protégé and the son of a Putney blacksmith, cloth merchant and innkeeper. Cromwell's emergence as Henry's key adviser in his dispute with Rome had been rewarded, in 1532, by his appointment as Master of the Jewels and Clerk of the Hanaper (a department of Chancery), and, the following year, as Chancellor of the Exchequer. Cromwell had no truck with critics, such as Sir George Throckmorton, who was told: 'to live at home, serve God, and meddle little'.[19]

Cromwell's Act in Restraint of Appeals became law in April 1533. It declared the realm of England to be an empire, 'governed by one supreme head and king'. By banning appeals to the pope, it made the king the undisputed, final, legal authority. On 23 May, Thomas Cranmer, an ally of the Boleyn family, whose skilful advocacy of the king's divorce had been rewarded with the archbishopric of Canterbury, duly declared Henry's marriage to Catherine illegal. Five days later Cranmer pronounced Henry's marriage to Anne lawful.

Anne's coronation on Whit Sunday, 1 June 1533, was designed to confirm her rightful status. Henry also turned it into a test of loyalty, although the only senior figure who refused to attend was Sir Thomas More, who had already resigned over the church's loss of independence. Henry celebrated the coronation with an extravaganza, emphasizing his supremacy and Anne's legitimacy as queen, which entered Westminster folklore. The display began on Thursday 29 May, when Anne left Greenwich Palace by water. As her flotilla headed upstream to the Tower, cannons boomed out from ships at Limehouse and other moorings.

Two days later, Anne made her way in the traditional procession through the City to Westminster. Dressed in white, she wore a gold coronet, with her dark hair falling loose to her waist. Her procession was the first of its type to pass through the Holbein Gate on its way to Westminster Hall. The seating and statues set in the interior and exterior walls were gilded, and the windows re-glazed. Inside, the vast Hall was 'well and richly hung with cloth of Arras' tapestries', and decorated with 'a marvelous rich cupboard of plate'. Outside, the great north front was painted the colour of Caen stone, and the gateway though which Anne entered was elaborately decorated with angels, fleurs-de-lys, roses, heraldic beasts, portcullises, the arms of Saint Edward and of England: all painted in a blaze of gold, green, jasper, red, vermilion and white.[20]

At Anne's grand reception in Westminster Hall, 'spice-plates and wine' were served. Afterwards, she withdrew 'into White Hall for that night', and was escorted there by water. The following morning, Whit Sunday, shortly after eight o'clock, Anne returned to Westminster Hall, where the lords and ladies, archbishops and bishops, the barons of the Cinque Ports, the Mayor of the City and aldermen, all assembled in their coronation robes. They were joined by 12 mitred abbots in their full pontificals, and the Abbot of Westminster in his regalia, with his monks in their best copes.[21]

From the Hall, Anne walked in the traditional procession in her robes of purple velvet and ermine, with her gold coronet on her head, along the 700-yard railed route carpeted with 'blue ray cloth' laid from the dais of the King's Bench to the Abbey's high altar. Archbishop Cranmer presided, and Mass was celebrated by Westminster's newly elected Abbot Boston (born William Benson), a placeman of Thomas Cromwell's, and the first outsider to hold the post for 300 years. Henry watched from behind a lattice-work screen: keeping the tradition that the king observed the proceedings in secret.[22]

After the ceremony in the Abbey, the queen's procession returned to Westminster Hall for the traditional feast. Anne presided at the top table, with Cranmer to her right. Henry watched from 'the kinges closett', a specially-built box which he shared with the French and Venetian ambassadors. Four other tables extended lengthways along the hall, at which dignitaries sat. Before the feast began, 'the Duke of Suffolk (High Constable that day, and Steward of the fest) [entered] on horseback, and marvellously trapped in apparel with richesse'. Accompanying him, also on horseback, was Lord William Howard, deputizing for his brother, the Duke of Norfolk, as Marshal of England. Other nobles served as butler, carver, cupbearer and so on, and 'did their service in such humble sort and fashion, as it was a wonder to see the pain and diligence of them'. According to this contemporary report: 'And thus all things nobly and triumphantly done at her Coronation her Grace returned to White Hall, with great joy and solemnity'.[23]

The main entry to Whitehall Palace by land was through the Court Gate on the east side of King Street (where Horse Guards Avenue now meets Whitehall). The Court Gate led into a large courtyard, with a great hall opposite, from which the chapel and royal living quarters were reached. Anne's private suite replaced the former archbishop's rooms, while Henry took the newer parts of Wolsey's house and had additional rooms built. The Privy Gallery was the spine of the Palace. Its outer walls were painted with black and white antique work; its interior was decorated with linen-fold panelling; and its floor was covered with rush mats. The gallery linked the river-front, the residential areas and Holbein Gate.[24]

Holbein Gate stood on what is now the busy dual carriageway of Whitehall, outside Dover House, to the south of Horse Guards. It was one of Westminster's main landmarks for about 250 years. The gate's main archway allowed coaches to pass along King Street, while pedestrians used a smaller archway on its eastern side. Built in English Gothic style, with flint and stone chequer-work, the gatehouse had octagonal turrets at each corner, and was decorated with Tudor rose and portcullis badges. Terracotta roundels contained busts of Roman emperors, an endorsement of the idea that every king is an emperor within his own kingdom: the basis of Henry's supreme authority over church and state.[25]

Henry designated the western part of Whitehall Palace as his recreation centre. Parkside, as it was known, was also planned round a gallery, this one leading from King Street to a new building, the Cockpit. Designed for cockfighting, it was square, with battlements and an octagonal tower, and inside was rather like a theatre with a ring of seats. It stood between what is now Downing Street and Horse Guards Parade. A Tudor garden wall was discovered beneath Number 11 Downing Street, and part of the palace precinct wall was found beneath other buildings on the northern side of the street. Henry's upper gallery survives as 'Cockpit Passage'. Beginning inside what is now the Cabinet Office (Number 70, Whitehall), it runs parallel to present-day Downing Street and links with the passage to Number 10.[26]

Henry's enthusiasm for tennis has left its mark inside the front entrance of Number 70, Whitehall, where part of the Great Close Tennis Court, dating from 1532–3, can be seen. Its remnants include a 30 feet stretch of the west wall; a three-light mullioned window nearly 16 feet in height; and the north-west turret, 45 feet in height, with its flint and stone chequered top: one of four turrets that stood at each corner of the court and measured over 80 feet in height. A stretch of wall from the Great Open Tennis Court also remains to the north of the surviving turret. Henry's two other tennis courts – again, one 'open' to the sky, the other covered, or 'close' – were sited off the south side of Cockpit Passage. Windows permitted views of the play, and the present walls incorporate the restored, arched entrance to the 'close' court, windows and a fireplace.[27]

Henry built a tiltyard for jousting and military displays on the site now occupied by Horse Guards. The king watched from a window in the Tiltyard Gallery, an extension of the Privy Gallery to the west of the Holbein Gate. The gallery lay at the south end of the tiltyard and Henry looked northwards to the far end, where competitors entered through a gate from the stables. The tilt barrier ran along the centre of the yard and prevented competitors crashing head-on. It was about 320 feet in length, allowing about 80 feet at either end for the mounting blocks and weapons. The tiltyard was only about 80 feet in width, including the spectators' area. Its inaugural tournament was part of the celebrations held on the day after Anne Boleyn's coronation when 'there were great justs at the tilt done by eighteen Lords and knights'. The tradition of military display before the monarch continues nearby on Horse Guards Parade, where the annual ceremony of 'Trooping the Colour' is held.[28]

In 1536, Parliament passed an Act that designated Henry VIII's new palace at Whitehall 'the King's Palace at Westminster' and gave it extensive grounds. This statute legalized Henry's great land grab of almost the whole northern quarter of Westminster. It confirmed that his new palace

shall include all the street or way leading from Charing Cross to the Sanctuary gate at Westminster, and also all the houses, buildings, lands, and tenements, on both sides of the said street, unto Westminster Hall, from the Thames on the east part to the Park wall on the west part.

When these boundaries are translated to a modern street plan, they extend from near Northumberland Avenue in the north to the Cenotaph and beyond in the south; and from the old Thames shoreline beneath the Ministry of Defence in the east and into Downing Street and Horse Guards Parade in the west. Although very little survives of Whitehall Palace's fabric, it left an indelible imprint on Westminster's lay-out.[29]

16 END OF THE OLD ORDER

Westminster saw its old world turned upside down by Henry's break with Rome. By April 1534, people were required to swear an oath of succession as decreed in a new statute which excluded Catherine of Aragon's daughter, Mary, from succeeding to the throne, in favour of Anne Boleyn's daughter, Elizabeth. In November, a second statute, the Act of Supremacy, imposed the most sweeping extension of the treason law since 1352 by making it treasonable to say anything rebellious against the royal family; to deny their titles; or to call the king a heretic, tyrant, infidel or usurper.

During the spring and summer of 1535, Westminster Hall hosted notorious show trials of the kind now associated with Hitler's Germany or Stalin's Russia. Thomas Cromwell tolerated no opposition as he surveyed England's religious houses and valued their property ready for their dissolution. John Houghton, prior of the London Charterhouse, and John Fisher, the frail Bishop of Rochester, were tried, found guilty of treason and executed.

On 1 July 1535, Thomas More, the most respected Englishman in Europe, was brought to trial in the Great Hall at the court of the King's Bench, where as Lord Chancellor he had presided in pomp. When he arrived by river from the Tower, he looked drawn and his clothes were threadbare. The charge of treason meant that More was denied counsel or the right to call witnesses of his own. His own silence in court was described by one of the judges, the attorney-general Sir Christopher Hales, as 'a sure token and demonstration of a corrupt and perverse nature, maligning and repyning against the statute'. The solicitor-general, Richard Rich, testified that More had rejected the king's title as supreme head of the Church of England. The jury, who feared gaol or worse if they found More innocent, took only 15 minutes to decide his guilt.[1]

After sentence was passed, More broke his silence to deliver his final words in Westminster Hall. In a defiant assault on Henry's new order, More advocated learning from wiser counsels across time and space:

For of the aforesaide holy Bisshopps I have, for every Bisshopp of yours, above one hundred; And for one Councell or Parliament of yours (God knoweth what maner of one), I have all the councels made these thousande yeres. And for this one kingdome, I have all other christian Realmes.

More was led to Westminster stairs and taken to the Tower where he was beheaded.[2]

Dissolution of the monasteries sparked an extraordinarily public dispute between the queen and Henry's chief minister over public spending. Anne wanted the money to go to educational charities, as had been the tradition when monasteries were closed; Cromwell had more urgent priorities, such as repairing the king's strained finances and restoring England's defences. Huge sums (about two-thirds of the Crown's known revenues) also disappeared into the king's secret funds. Anne tried to undermine Cromwell by orchestrating a remarkably outspoken attack on him. At the Palm Sunday service in the royal chapel, attended by the King's Council and Court, John Skip, the queen's almoner, used his sermon to castigate Cromwell as a latter-day 'Haaman', an evil and murderous chief minister in the Old Testament.[3]

Cromwell decided that Anne had to go. Her loss of a male child by miscarriage had revived the king's anxiety about his lack of an heir, and Cromwell exploited Henry's insecurity by cooking up charges of adultery against Anne and implicating his main rival at court, Henry Norris, the Groom of the Stool, Keeper of the Privy Purse and Chief Gentleman of the Privy Chamber. The trial of Norris and three other courtiers in Westminster Hall in May 1536 was rigged. They were denied their own counsel and access to the evidence. Cromwell also made sure that the jury was packed against them. The limit of Henry's mercy was to reduce the sentence of hanging, drawing and quartering to that of beheading. On 19 May, Anne, who was not yet 30 years old, was also beheaded on Tower Green.[4]

Only 11 days after Anne's execution, Henry married his third wife, Jane Seymour, who had been a lady-in-waiting to Anne at Whitehall Palace. Jane's coronation was scrapped when Westminster was hit by the plague, but her legitimacy as queen was not in doubt after Catherine's death, Anne's execution and Henry's disinheritance of his daughters, Mary and Elizabeth, in a new Act of Succession. Jane's future as queen seemed assured after the birth of the future Edward VI in October 1537, but she died at Hampton Court 12 days later.

Cromwell's rule of terror provoked unrest in Lincolnshire in 1536 and fuelled unrest across the north of England, known as the 'pilgrimage of grace'. A special war council was set up, drawn from the nobility, as it was thought politic for Cromwell not to be directly involved. In June 1539, Cromwell's anti-papal propaganda reached its hubristic climax in a spectacular, mock naval battle on the river at Westminster. Two barges, with 'one for the Bishop of Rome and his cardinalles, one for the Kinges Grace', were rowed to and fro, passing three times between the landing stages at the old Palace and Whitehall Palace, firing blanks at one another, until 'at last the Pope and his cardinalles were overcome, and all his men cast over the borde into the Thames'.[5]

A year later, Thomas Cromwell was gone. Nemesis came in the shape of the king's fourth wife, Anne of Cleves, a German princess. Her marriage to Henry in January 1540 had been part of Cromwell's diplomacy. The king had been impressed by Holbein's flattering portrait, but was bitterly disappointed when he saw Anne in the flesh and became frustrated by his inability to consummate the marriage. 'For Godde's sake, devyse for the relefe of the King', pleaded Sir Thomas Wriothesley, with Cromwell, 'for if he remain in this gref and trouble, we shal al one day smart for it'.[6]

Cromwell had constantly battled with his aristocratic rivals on the King's Council, who regarded him as an upstart. On Saturday 10 June 1540, his enemies launched their coup. As the King's Councillors left parliament for dinner at Whitehall Palace, Cromwell's bonnet was blown off by the wind, but the others failed to observe the polite custom of doffing their own hats. At dinner, Cromwell was studiously ignored. When he later joined his colleagues in the council chamber, he found the others already sitting down. 'You were in a great hurry, gentlemen, to get seated', he commented, but was again ignored. As he was about to take his usual seat, the Duke of Norfolk suddenly told him: 'Cromwell, do not sit there; that is no place for thee. Traitors do not sit amongst gentlemen'. 'I am not a traitor', replied Cromwell. But at this point, the captain of the guard entered, took him by the arm and arrested him. When Cromwell demanded to talk with Henry, he was reminded that as a result of his law the king should speak to no one accused of treason.[7]

As Cromwell was led away, he was further humiliated. Norfolk ordered the captain to stop. Declaring that, 'traitors must not wear the Garter', Norfolk took the bejewelled medallion of St George and the dragon from round Cromwell's neck, while the Earl of Southampton tore the Garter insignia from his clothes. The noblemen's vengeful stripping of the Garter emblems that Cromwell had worn with such pride revealed the resentment felt among aristocrats towards an upwardly mobile reformer. Cromwell was led away by the captain and six halberdiers.[8]

A month after Cromwell's arrest, the annulment of Henry's marriage to Anne of Cleves was ratified by the convocations of Canterbury and York, meeting in Westminster's Chapter House. A fortnight later, Henry married Catherine Howard. Cromwell fell victim to the same ruthless methods that he had deployed when a Bill of Attainder was passed indicting him of heresy, treason and other crimes. He was beheaded in July 1540.

The senior nobles who had ousted Cromwell ruled through the old, informal Privy Council by reforming it into an effective executive body, on the lines of the war council that had dealt with the northern rising. The reformed Privy Council numbered about 20 and included senior office-holders and powerful magnates.

It was given a clerk and a minute-book and developed into the engine-room of government under the Tudors and Stuarts.[9]

Henry's expansion of Whitehall Palace symbolized the subordination of Church to Crown. In the early 1530s, parishioners of St Margaret's who lived north of the new Palace had suddenly discovered that their way to church was blocked by the king's building work. As a result, they had to pass through Whitehall Palace's Court Gate whenever they wanted to attend St Margaret's, including when they took their dead for burial. However, Henry feared infection from the dead and in 1534 ordered people living to the north of his new Palace to become parishioners of St Martin's in the Fields.[10]

The old order at Westminster was dealt a final hammer-blow in January 1540, when Henry's stooge, Abbot Boston, surrendered the Abbey. The king pocketed its net annual income of about £2,800 and became the largest local landowner, while also acquiring extensive property elsewhere. The Confessor's shrine was defiled: its relics, jewels and gold images were removed; its gold feretory around the coffin was melted down for the king's treasury; and the body of the saint was removed and buried in an obscure part of the Abbey. The monastery's refectory was pulled down, the lead was taken from the roof of St Catherine's Chapel, and other buildings were cleared away or put to alternative use.[11]

However the Abbey's role as the coronation church and royal mausoleum ensured its survival, unlike other great abbeys that fell into decay. On 17 December 1540, the Abbey became the cathedral church of the new diocese of Westminster. Thomas Thirlby, a loyal official of the king and Dean of the Chapel Royal, was consecrated in Henry VII's Chapel as the first Bishop of Westminster. Abbot Boston became the first Dean and reverted to his birth name, William Benson.[12]

Within two years, Westminster Abbey – as it was still commonly known – was re-founded as the Collegiate Church of St Peter's, with the intention of creating a community of scholars at its heart. The newly constituted Abbey supported 12 'petty canons', a grammar school with a well-paid master, 40 scholars, and a choral foundation of 12 singing men and ten choristers. Four former monks took posts as petty canons, four more were granted university studentships, and others received pensions. In addition, the new foundation was committed to fund ten 'regius' professors and 20 students at Oxford and Cambridge. Westminster's close links with Henry's new colleges of Christ Church, Oxford, and Trinity, Cambridge, were later formalized.[13]

In contrast to the deterioration of the Abbey's fabric after dissolution, Henry lavished £28,676 on Whitehall Palace during 1541–8. Simon Thurley's thorough research reveals the extent of the transformation. Along the riverside, the king built an impressive stone waterfront of more than 512 feet in length. He extended the Palace's waterfront into the Thames by between 50 feet and 100 feet and reclaimed more than 4,000 square yards of the foreshore. The new waterfront provided the foundation for a timber-framed gallery, 400 feet in length. At the gallery's north end was the Privy Kitchen, built on arches above the river, with a sump through which kitchen waste fell and was flushed by the tides. At its south end, a large house built for Princess Mary, gave splendid views of the Thames from its many windows.[14]

Henry's purchase of extra land to the south of his Palace enabled him to relocate its gardens. The orchard was replanted further south, while its old site became the great garden, later 'the privy garden'. It had a gallery along its east wall overlooking flower beds that were divided by low rails and decorated by poles bearing models of heraldic beasts. The original privy garden, 'whiche was before applied to lascivious and courtly pastimes', as John Foxe, the protestant zealot, primly noted, had been re-located to the north of the Privy Gallery. It became a cobbled courtyard, with an open cloister round its sides, painted with flowers and royal arms. In March 1548, an outdoor pulpit was set up in the centre, and the courtyard became known as 'the Preaching Place'. Foxe's *Book of Martyrs* shows Bishop Latimer preaching to a crowded courtyard while Edward VI listens from a first floor window. The courtyard later hosted wrestling for Queen Elizabeth's entertainment.[15]

Henry built a second gatehouse on King Street, about 110 yards south of the Holbein Gate. The King Street Gate provided another bridge for courtiers to the Parkside buildings. It had circular towers and its outer walls were adorned with busts, pediments and the signs of the zodiac. Together with the Holbein Gate, it formed part of the processional route from Whitehall Palace to the old Palace and Abbey.[16]

Inside the Palace walls, the main public room was the Great Hall, across a courtyard from the Court Gate entrance. It was there that courtiers, officials and servants dined, and great feasts and entertainments took place. Two other main rooms were reached from the Great Hall, through a courtyard to the south. The Great Chamber (sometimes known as the guard, or watching, chamber), hosted events and entertainments, notably court masques and revels, sometimes accompanied by the king's musicians. In the nearby Presence Chamber, ambassadors were received, peers created and senior courtiers dined.[17]

When the king was in residence, these public rooms were the heart of the Palace for courtiers, officials and servants, who gathered there to gossip, eat or sleep. A vital moment in the day came when the king passed through the public areas in formal procession on his way to hear mass in the Chapel Royal. His route was lined by courtiers, ambassadors and others; some simply hoping to be recognized, others seeking favours or redress of grievances.[18]

By the 1540s, Whitehall Palace was becoming the main seat of government, and some of the king's private rooms were less private. The newly created Privy Council met in the Council Chamber near Henry's private quarters, allowing its members access to the King's Privy Gallery. In 1537, the commissioning of a fresco by Holbein for the king's Privy Chamber reflected the room's changing role.

The painting was a group portrait of Henry and his queen, Jane Seymour, with Henry VII and Elizabeth of York, and was intended to leave visiting ambassadors, courtiers and officials in no doubt about Henry's dynastic and imperial status, and his supreme power as head of Church and State. Although Holbein's fresco was destroyed in the disastrous fire of 1698, copies of his portrait of the King created an iconic image of Henry's swaggering self-confidence as he stands resolute, his physique emphasizing power, his clothes and emblems signifying authority, his left hand poised by his dagger suggesting controlled menace, while his calm, uncompromising gaze looks the viewer straight in the eye.[19]

Henry created new, secret rooms, beyond his bedchamber. They included two in Holbein Gate: a study and an upper library; the latter containing maps, a globe, looking glasses, terracotta statues, a javelin, armour and other personal items. The king's most trusted confidant during his last years was Sir Anthony Denny, who became Groom of the Stool in 1546 after six years as deputy. The Groom of the Stool's team looked after the king's personal latrine, or close-stool: a well-upholstered, wooden box with a hole in the top and a pewter pot inside. Whenever Henry relieved himself, he was attended by the Groom or a subordinate, a dubious honour when Henry suffered acute constipation in later years.[20]

A good idea of the Palace's interior can be gleaned from a group portrait, *The Family of Henry VIII*, painted by an unknown artist in 1545. It is set in a columned room, or gallery, on the ground floor and shows Henry with Jane Seymour (who was dead by then) and his children, Edward, Mary and Elizabeth. The canopy of the king's chair is a piece of intricate embroidery suspended from the ceiling, which itself is divided into squares, each with a royal badge. The columns and carved panelling display finely detailed grotesque-work, highlighted with paint and goldleaf.[21]

A man seen through an open archway to the right is the king's trusted fool, Will Somer, in his green outfit with a purse. His head is being scratched by his pet monkey, perched on his shoulder, wearing clothes and a cap. The woman through the left archway is probably Princess Mary's fool, Jane. Aspects of the Palace can be glimpsed behind the two fools: the great or Privy Garden, to the south, with its low rails and heraldic beasts on poles; a gabled house, possibly Princess Mary's lodgings, or a banqueting house, its wall painted with grotesque patterns; the clock-house near Westminster Hall; a turret of the great tennis-play; and part of the north transept of Westminster Abbey.[22]

Inside the Palace, as Thurley describes it, tapestries hung from the walls, and inventories itemized 167 paintings, 35 maps and 14 mirrors, mostly made of steel. The king's rooms were hung with silks: 'cloth of gold' (damask or velvet silks with gilt yarns) in the king's and queen's bedchambers; cut-velvet and silk wall-hangings elsewhere. The windows had curtains or shutters. Tiles, bricks or flagstones covered the ground floor. On the upper floors, the boards were usually covered with mats, or plaster of Paris, carpets being reserved for important occasions. The seating was mostly forms and stools. The king sat, elevated, on decorated seats of authority, covered in cloth of gold, with balls of gilt and silver, and a canopy, dais, footstool, cushion and rug. Henry's carved and gilded bed of walnut was enlarged in 1542 to measure 7 feet 6 inches by 7 feet wide.[23]

The running of Henry's Palace provided work for hundreds of servants. About 800 people had to be catered for every day whenever the king and his court stayed there. Some 600 were entitled to eat in its great hall, where two meals a day were served, at midday and 4pm, while another 230 of the kitchen staff and domestic servants ate elsewhere. Many local people found seasonal work at Whitehall. There were a number of departments, including the wardrobe, a jewel-house and a laundry. There was a great kitchen supplied by a cellar, bakehouse and pantry; and a boiling-house, buttery, pitcher-house, poultry, spicery and woodyard.[24]

Whitehall Palace generated extra business for Westminster as more people were drawn there during the 'season', especially as the increasingly immobile king, incapacitated by a leg ulcer and his huge bulk, stayed longer at Whitehall. As a 23-year-old, Henry had been 6 feet 3 inches tall, with a 35-inch waist and 42-inch chest; but before he turned 50 in 1541, his waist had ballooned to 54 inches and his chest to 58 inches. In July 1546, Sir Anthony Denny took delivery of 'two chaires called trammes for the kings maiesty to sitt in to be carried to and fro in his galleries and chambers'.[25]

By the autumn, Henry was hardly seen in public; the state of his legs worsened and he became grossly obese. During January 1547, he was bed-bound, and began drifting in and out of consciousness. Near the end, unable to move or speak, he managed to squeeze Archbishop Cranmer's hand as a sign that he had faith in Christ. At about two o'clock in the morning of Friday 28 January, Henry VIII died. His death was kept secret for three days. The last parliament of Henry's continued to meet, unaware of his demise, while behind the scenes his senior officials plotted. As Henry's successor, Prince Edward, was only nine years old, power would reside with whoever emerged as the leader of the ruling council. 'Remember what you promised me in the gallery at Westminster', Sir William Paget, the king's secretary, later wrote to the victorious Duke of Somerset, 'before the breath was out of the body of the King that dead is'. When parliament met on Monday 31 January, an emotional Lord Chancellor, Wriothesley, announced Henry VIII's death. The king's will was read and the names of the new ruling council announced.[26]

17 THE SHAPE OF THINGS TO COME

'We shape our buildings and afterwards our buildings shape us', Winston Churchill told MPs during the Second World War when he proposed that the blitzed Chamber of the Commons should be re-built in its 'old form'. The Commons' Chamber had already been re-built once before in its 'old form'; after the old palace burnt down in 1834. The story of the Chamber's appearance and distinctive character, and the reasons for parliament's importance, date from the European reformation and England's break with Rome, when Westminster was in thrall to holy terror and martyrdom.[1]

The accession of the nine-year-old Edward VI in 1547 heralded a Protestant revolution. Although Henry VIII had broken with Rome, he regarded himself and his English church as Catholic; but Edward was brought up as a Protestant, largely through the influence of Henry's sixth wife, Katherine Parr. The young king's uncle, Edward Seymour, the Duke of Somerset, was the great power in the land as Lord Protector, Governor of the King's Person, Lord Treasurer and Earl Marshal. 'Protector Somerset' dominated the ruling council, working with a group of advisers who included Sir William Paget, formerly Henry's secretary, and William Cecil, the future Lord Burghley. Together with Archbishop Cranmer, they launched a Protestant revolution.[2]

Edward VI's coronation procession in February 1547 was a striking sight as the pale and slender king, with fair, reddish-hair and grey eyes passed beneath the triumphal arches of the Holbein and King Street gates in Whitehall. He wore a silver gown, embroidered with gold silk, and matching doublet, boots and belt, and a cap of white velvet all inlaid with silver tracery and clusters of diamonds, pearls and rubies. The ceremony was shortened, and its content revised by the Privy Council on the pretext of the king's 'tender age'; but Cranmer and his allies were determined to entrench the Protestant revolution by changing the coronation oath. Cranmer insisted that as Edward's authority derived from God, the oath affirmed the king's supremacy and was not the terms on which he might be held to account. Roy Strong notes that 'any hint of election' was eliminated, while according to the historian, Dale Hoak, Cranmer's revision gave the king the right to decide on what constituted law and liberty.[3]

Somerset and the ruling council decided that it was better politically and legally to impose their Protestant revolution through Acts of Parliament instead of by royal prerogative. Henry VIII had thought it politically helpful after 1533 to have his reforms passed by parliament, and after 1547 further reforms were driven by a ruling council who sat in parliament. This system of having a monarch rule through a council of men in parliament became the template for English parliamentary government. Protector Somerset's new model marked a turning point in the role of parliament and was continued by Somerset's secretary, William Cecil, who later became Elizabeth I's senior adviser. No longer were Acts of Parliament merely declaratory, or definitions of the law as it was thought to exist; instead, they became new laws in their own right. In the Act of Uniformity in 1549, parliament authorized church doctrine and liturgy for the first time and outlawed the use of Latin during mass.

Somerset's Protestant zeal had a baleful effect on English churches, draining them of their colour and destroying their medieval heritage of art and popular culture. Candles and shrines were banned; stained-glass windows were smashed and re-glazed with plain glass; frescoes and murals disappeared beneath whitewash; and church-ales, maypoles, mystery plays, pageants and processions were eliminated. The parishioners of St Margaret's whitewashed their church walls, removed its imagery, rood and tabernacles, and took down its altar table, but they baulked at Somerset's plan to demolish it completely and use the stone for his new palace on the Strand.[4]

Somerset's workmen had knocked down the church of St Mary-le-Strand and several bishops' houses, and had also taken 20 tons of Caen stone from Westminster's old monastery, but they met their match at St Margaret's. According to Peter Heylyn, a seventeenth-century clergyman and historian: 'the workmen had no sooner advanced their scaffolds, when the parishioners gathered together in great multitudes, with bows and arrows, staves and clubs, and other such offensive weapons, which so terrified the workmen that they ran away in great amazement, and never could be brought again upon that employment'.[5]

However, the Protestant purge gathered pace with the appointment of Richard Cox, Edward VI's Protestant tutor, as dean of Westminster, in October 1549. Within a matter of months, Cox carried out the king's and council's orders that 'all manner of garnishments and apparel of silver and gold, such as altar-cloths, copes, etc., should be taken away … . and to deface and carry out of the library at Westminster all books of superstition, such as missals, breviaries, processionals, etc'.[6]

Somerset's decision, in December 1547, to close the remaining chantry chapels shaped British politics in a way that he could never have foreseen. Foremost among the chapels was the Collegiate Chapel of St Stephen's in Westminster

Palace. The suppression of a royal chapel sent a clear message that there were to be no exemptions in cleansing the church of Catholic imagery and worship. In addition, it was decided to accommodate the House of Commons in St Stephen's chapel, thereby relegating a magnificent, royal house of prayer into a political talking shop.[7]

Bringing MPs into the Palace, where the House of Lords already met, also accorded with the view among Somerset's advisers that parliament's duty, under their direction, was to enact the Protestant revolution. The Commons were in no mood to resist. Around this time, they sent one of their number, an MP named Stone, to the Tower for speaking ill of Somerset; a shameful act but also an important precedent, as it was the first time that the Commons had punished one of their members.[8]

The Commons seem to have begun meeting in St Stephen's in November 1548. Accounts for 1549–50, prepared by Lawrence Bradshaw, Surveyor of the King's Works, gives a sum of £344.16s.10.5d for 'sondry charges made & done in & upon the Parlyament house at Westminster some tyme Saynt Stephen's Chappell'. Bradshaw also had a warrant for £100 in August 1549 from the revenues of the Duchy of Lancaster, 'towards the reparation of the Parliament Hows, and of the Hows to kepe the Registres of the Kings Majestie'.[9]

After Somerset fell victim to a coup, his rival, Northumberland, was ill at ease with parliament and preferred, if possible, to govern without it. During 1551, events worked in his favour: the 'great sweat' (a fever epidemic) prompted the court to leave Whitehall; and in the autumn, Somerset's arrest and trial at Westminster Hall raised fears of riots. When the verdict on Somerset was finally announced in December, the great crowd gathered outside thought, mistakenly, that he had been cleared. According to Stow, they 'made such a shriek, casting up of caps … that their cry was heard to the Long Acre beyond Charing Cross, which made the Lords astonished'. Parliament met on 23 January 1552, the day after Somerset's execution on Tower Hill.[10]

The Speaker's chair was placed on the altar steps at the east end of the former chapel, nearest to the Thames. Today, four brass studs at the east end of St Stephen's Hall mark the spot where the chair stood. The Chamber itself was only 57 feet 6 inches in length and a mere 32 feet 10 inches wide. At the west end of the building, a great screen divided it from the adjoining Commons' lobby that measured 28 feet by 30 feet. The Chamber and lobby were linked by a door in the centre of the screen. When MPs left the Chamber through this door, they bowed their heads to the Speaker, either in reverence to the former altar, or perhaps simply to avoid their hats being knocked off. Whatever the reason, MPs still bow as they leave in what has become a sign of respect to the Speaker.[11]

Along the side walls were several raised tiers of carved, wooden stalls where the dean, canons and vicars had once prayed and sung, facing one another across the narrow body of their chapel. Here, the MPs now sat, addressing speeches to each other across the floor of their new Chamber. As early as 1571, the existence of what is now called 'the government frontbench', was detected by an MP, John Vowell, who wrote that, 'upon the lower row, next the Speaker, sit all such of the Queen's Privy Council and head offices as be knights and burgesses of the House, but after, everyone sitteth as he cometh'. Those MPs who generally supported the government tended to gather together and sit in the same tier of stalls, whereas those who opposed the government tended to sit on the opposite tier. The 'government benches' and 'opposition benches', as they became known, thus faced one another across the Chamber, and this arrangement may have encouraged England's adversarial politics.[12]

The original wall paintings disappeared behind panelling, whitewash or tapestries; and the soaring, painted vault vanished behind a false ceiling. The monks' carved stalls were eventually replaced by benches covered with green serge; the royal coat of arms took the place of Biblical stories on the walls behind the Speaker's Chair; and in 1673, the sundial set high in one of the windows was finally superseded by a clock.[13]

St Stephen's was never ideal as a debating Chamber. MPs' complaints about their discomfort became a familiar refrain, but the intimacy of St Stephen's, with its tiered seating, created an appropriately theatrical setting for the dramatic events that unfolded there during its long history. When the Palace of Westminster was re-built after 1834, the site of the old Chamber became St Stephen's Hall. The re-built Commons' Chamber in the new Palace of Westminster was re-located but largely retained the lay-out inherited from St Stephen's Chapel. The present Chamber, re-built after the Blitz, retains the intimacy and theatricality of its sixteenth-century predecessor: qualities inadvertently bestowed on the Commons by the unlikely figure of Protector Somerset.

18 A TALE OF TWO SISTERS

Duwhich uring the brief Edwardian Protestant revolution, Westminster Abbey was stripped of its recently bestowed cathedral status and subsumed into the see of London, under Nicholas Ridley, the Protestant reformer, whom Edward had designated Bishop of London. Although the Abbey's status as a cathedral was re-asserted by parliament in 1552, the first and last Bishop of Westminster, Thirlby, was packed off to Norwich. Thirlby's changes to some of Westminster's leases in order to fund repairs at St Paul's, its ancient rival, prompted the revival of the saying: 'robbing Peter to pay Paul'.[1]

By the spring of 1553, Edward was ill with tuberculosis of the lungs. After some final visits to the park at Westminster, he was taken by royal barge to Greenwich where he died in July, aged 15. His funeral at Westminster Abbey marked the first occasion in which the burial service of the English Prayer Book was used for an English monarch.[2]

The king's advisers had tried, before Edward's death, to entrench their Protestant revolution by drafting a 'Devise for the succession' that excluded his half-sisters, Mary, who was Catholic, and Elizabeth, Henry's daughter by Anne Boleyn. The 'Devise' nominated Lady Jane Grey, Edward's 15-year-old Protestant cousin, as successor. The impression that Jane was merely a political pawn was strengthened when Somerset's successor, the Duke of Northumberland, arranged a marriage between his son and the reluctant Jane and then tried to limit the succession to 'Jane and her heirs male'.[3]

Mary, a mature, 37-year-old, showed that she possessed a monarch's courage by proclaiming herself queen. She won growing support among the country gentry, forcing Northumberland to back down, and prompting the ruling council to desert him. The hapless Jane, who had stayed at the Tower since her proclamation as queen, was taken prisoner. She had reigned for only nine days.

On 1 October 1553, Mary Tudor came by river to Westminster Hall for her coronation. She insisted on being anointed with oil from Europe to avoid being tainted by the oil used for Edward VI, her Protestant half-brother; and a chair blessed by Pope Julius III replaced the coronation chair that had been used since at least 1399. Mary was crowned by an opponent of Edward VI's – the Bishop of Winchester and new Lord Chancellor, Stephen Gardiner. The Archbishop of Canterbury, Cranmer, and the Bishop of London, Ridley, were under arrest for their support of Jane Grey; while the Archbishop of York, Holgate, who was a Protestant reformer, was about to be sent to the Tower. Mary's dull coronation feast ended with an unruly crowd scrambling for left-overs and souvenirs; and there was no tournament.[4]

The queen was childless. Unless she produced an heir, she was likely to be succeeded by her 20-year-old half-sister, Elizabeth, daughter of the marriage that had caused England's break with Rome. The marriage between Mary's mother, Catherine, and Henry VIII, was declared legal: confirming Mary's legitimacy as queen, while rendering Anne Boleyn's marriage unlawful and Elizabeth a bastard.[5]

Parliament dutifully passed the Act of Repeal, reinstating mass, clerical celibacy and Catholic ritual. This had been expected, but Mary's sudden plan to marry Philip II of Spain came as a shock, provoking fears of foreign and religious domination and sparking a bloody revolt. An all-night watch was mounted at Whitehall in early 1554, as Sir Thomas Wyatt, a soldier in his thirties, led about 3,000 rebels towards Westminster. There was panic at the Palace. 'So being all armed', one of the royal guards recalled, 'we came up into the Chamber of Presence, with our poleaxes in our hands. Wherewith the Ladies were very fearful. Some lamenting, crying, and wringing their hands, said: "Alas, there is some great mischief toward! We shall all be destroyed this night! What a sight is this! To see the Queen's Chamber full of armed men. The like was never seen, nor heard of!"'[6]

As Wyatt's rebels left their overnight camp at Knightsbridge, they were watched and harried by the Earl of Pembroke, the queen's shrewd commander. After clashing at Charing Cross with troops led by the 74-year-old Lord Chamberlain, Sir John Gage, Wyatt pressed on eastward for the City; but some rebels headed down King Street and fired arrows through the open Court Gate. After the gates were shut, the royal guards fled into the Palace. The assault on Whitehall excited fears in the Palace that Pembroke had joined the revolt. In the panic, 'divers timorous and cold hearted soldiers came to the queen, crying, "All is lost! Away! Away! A barge! A barge!"' However, Mary held her nerve. After being assured that Pembroke was still 'in the Field', she urged her aides to pray. 'I warrant you', she told them, 'we shall hear better news anon. For my lord will not deceive me, I know well. If he would, God will not'.[7]

The mayhem inside the Palace was witnessed by Edward Underhill, a fervent Protestant known as the 'hot gospeller', who had been banned as a heretic from keeping watch. Underhill urged Sir Richard Southwell, who was guarding the rear of Whitehall with 500 men, to 'command the gates to be opened that we may go to the Queen's enemies'. Mary agreed on condition that they did not leave her sight. 'So the gate was opened, and we marched before the Gallery window: where she spake unto us; requiring us, "As we were Gentlemen, in whom she only trusted, that we would not go from that place"'.[8]

About an hour later, news reached the Palace that Wyatt had surrendered. As news spread, the bells of St Margaret's pealed in celebration. The next day, three of the rebels were executed and buried in the churchyard. However, Henry Machyn, the diarist, recorded a show of royal clemency in the Whitehall tiltyard, when several hundred rebels with halters round their necks ready for hanging knelt before the queen and were pardoned. Mary was less tolerant of her main rival, Lady Jane Grey, who was beheaded five days after the revolt.[9]

By the autumn of 1554, the queen's new husband, Philip of Spain, was cutting a dash at Westminster. One Sunday afternoon, Philip and a favourite, Lord Fitzwalter, both in their late twenties, 'and divers Spaniards did ride in divers colours, the King in red, and some [in] yellow, some in green, some in white, some in blue, and with targets and canes in their hands ... and trumpets in the same colours, and drums made of kettles, and banners in the same colours'. Philip, the showman, held spectacular tournaments. On Lady Day in 1555, 'ther was as [great] justs as you have seen at the tylt at Westminster', when the challengers were an unnamed Spaniard and Sir George Howard; Philip entered with, 'a great retinue all in blue, and trimmed with yellow', and their helmets bearing 'great plumes of blue and yellow feather'.[10]

Philip had brought with him a 3,000-strong entourage: almost as many retainers as there were parishioners in St Margaret's. Funerals at the Abbey were held 'after the fashion of Spain'. Local people resented losing work to the newcomers, and a 'great fray' began 'at Charyng crosse' at eight o'clock 'be-twyn the Spaneardes and Englysmen'. On another occasion, 'debauched' Spaniards fired their pistols in the Abbey, when the Dean's men found them in the cloister. Richly dressed Spanish courtiers became targets for thieves. Among those hanged at Charing Cross for robbing Spaniards in the Abbey, was John Tooley, who declared his hatred for popery as he was carted to the gallows. His corpse was later dug up, tried, excommunicated and burnt beside the gallows as a heretic.[11]

Mary's counter-reformation was gaining momentum. In November, Cardinal Reginald Pole, the papal legate, returned to England. Both Houses of Parliament were summoned to Whitehall Palace, where, according to John Strype, the historian, Pole 'harangued' them, 'persuading them to be reconciled to the Church of Rome and offering the Pope's benediction and absolution, which they accepted'. During the cardinal's speech, 'the Queen sat highest, richly apparel, and her Belly laid out, that all men might see she was with child'. Mary hoped that the prospect of a Catholic heir might persuade MPs to sanction Philip's coronation as king. In Strype's account, 'some thought that the Queen, for that cause, did lay out her belly the more'. Unfortunately, for Mary and Philip, the pregnancy appears to have been imaginary.[12]

Philip was as brazen as Mary. His escort from Holbein Gate to attend 'high mass' at the Abbey, comprised 600 Spanish courtiers, dressed in their court costumes of white velvet, striped with red. They were accompanied by the knights of the garter, six of whom later escorted Cardinal Pole, in his full pontificals, from Lambeth Palace across the Thames to the old palace, where a 'yet grander ceremony' was held in Westminster Hall, attended by Mary, Philip and both Houses of Parliament.[13]

These grand displays were part of an increasingly bloody battle for Westminster's soul. At St Margaret's on Easter day, 1555, a priest from the Abbey, John Cheltham, was about to administer the sacrament according to Catholic rites, when a man rushed forward in protest, drew his wood-knife and 'hyt the prest on the hed and struck hym a grett blowe'. The attacker, William Flower, a convert to Protestantism, was held in the Abbey Gatehouse. Ten days later his hand was amputated before he was burned at the stake in the churchyard of St Margaret's. After Flower's sacrilege, a service was held to purify the church, presided over by Edmund Bonner, the Bishop of London. The service was followed by a great feast of half a veal, four green geese, three capons, a dozen rabbits, a dozen pigeons, a sirloin of beef and two gallons of wine.[14]

About 300 Protestants, including Archbishop Cranmer and Bishops Latimer and Ridley, were burnt at the stake during the last three and a half years of Mary's reign. Despite doubts among some courtiers, the queen failed to call a halt. The 'Marian Martyrs' were immortalized by the Protestant propagandist, John Foxe. At the Abbey, the clergy gradually converted, one-by-one, to Catholicism, although not without ructions: the Chapter Book recorded that over dinner, 'Hugh Price breaks John Wood's head with a pot'. The annual St Peter's Day fair was revived, with 'a goodly procession' followed by Mass, while St Margaret's celebrated holy days again.[15]

The re-foundation of Westminster Abbey as a monastery church in November 1556 was the jewel in the crown of Mary's counter-reformation. The black, hooded habits of the Benedictine order were issued to the new Abbot, John Howman from Feckenham, and 13 monks. Abbot Feckenham was 'a short man, of a round visage, fresh colour, affable, and pleasant', who had served as Mary's chaplain. On 22 November, Feckenham led his fellow Benedictines to the Abbey 'in procession after the old fashion in their monks' weeds, in cowls of black serge, with two vergers carrying two silver rods in their hands'. Mary later attended evensong there. On the anniversary of the Confessor's death, his shrine 'was again set up, and the Altar with divers jewels that the Queen sent hither'.[16]

But only two years after the Abbey's re-foundation, the queen died. During the afternoon of 17 November 1558 'all the churches in London dyd ryng' in celebration of Elizabeth's accession as queen. At Westminster, the Abbey's bells rang out on every 17 November for more than 300 years, as Elizabeth's accession day came to be regarded as Foundation Day of the modern Abbey.[17]

The accession of a vivacious auburn-haired, dark-eyed, 25-year-old queen heralded a new era; but the sectarian conflict was suppressed, not healed. After spending Christmas at Whitehall Palace, Elizabeth prepared for her coronation procession from the City by embarking for the Tower in her barge on a flood-tide, 'towed by a long galley rowed by 40 men in their shirts, with a band of music'. Elizabeth's readiness to dispense with protocol and personalize the pageantry won people's hearts. A sceptical onlooker, the Mantuan envoy, Il Shifanoya was dismayed by Elizabeth's enthusiastic response to well-wishers outside the Abbey: 'She returned very cheerfully, with a most smiling countenance for every one, giving them all a thousand greetings, so that in my opinion she exceeded the bounds of gravity and decorum'.[18]

The new queen revived the coronation tournament. During her long reign, she was a keen spectator at the Whitehall tiltyard, where she enjoyed the exploits of her champions, notably Sir Henry Lee; her courtiers, including the soldier and poet, Sir Philip Sidney; and her favourites, Dudley and the Earl of Essex. In 1561, 'at great cost', according to Machyn, Elizabeth paved 'from the end of the Tyltt rond abowt the sydes, and closyd in the tylt'. The queen also 'commanded the bear, the bull and the ape to be bayted in the Tiltyard'. Her birthday was celebrated by annual exercises, a forerunner of the annual Trooping of the Colour. The popularity of the tiltyard also attracted prostitutes. The royal jester, Archie Armstrong, caused a scandal when he was found in the judge's seat with a woman and 'his points undone'.[19]

During tournaments, a large platform and stair were erected for presentations and speeches outside the Tiltyard Gallery, below the royal window where the monarch sat. The gallery's interior was described by Lupold von Wedel, a foreign visitor in 1585: 'the ceiling is gilt, and the floor is ornamented with mats. There were fine paintings on the walls'. From this 'sumptuous Gallery', Stow noted in his 1603 survey, 'the Princes with their Nobility use to stand or sit, and at Windowes to behold all triumphant joustings, and other military exercises'. According to the historian, Alan Young, 'the gallery was divided by hangings and tapestries into different "rooms"'.[20]

The Queen's Champion, Sir Henry Lee, became responsible in 1580 for organizing the royal tournaments as master of the armoury. By adding to his role of Champion those of director, producer and main script-writer, he combined the jousting with music, narrative and verse. Annual tilts to celebrate Elizabeth's accession became a popular festival in praise of the queen. When Lee retired ten years later, the royal choir sang John Dowland's arrangement of the Elizabethan lyric, *My golden locks, time hath to silver turned*, with its evocative line, *My helmet now shall make a hive for bees*.[21]

Elizabeth was a good talent-spotter. William Cecil was in his late thirties when he became her principal secretary. His grandfather had thrown in his lot with Henry Tudor before Bosworth and his father had served in Henry VIII's Privy Chamber. Cecil first impressed as secretary to Protector Somerset and later served on the Privy Council and became an MP. As Elizabeth's secretary of state, Cecil saw all official correspondence and used his power to become chief minister, a position he later combined with being Lord Treasurer. He was ennobled as Lord Burghley in 1571.

Elizabeth and Cecil together dominated English politics for more than 30 years and created a new, Anglican settlement. The queen made clear her intentions from the outset. She walked out of her first Christmas morning mass in the chapel royal at Whitehall Palace, after Bishop Oglethorpe defiantly held up the host for adoration, despite her order to lower it; and when she was greeted at the Abbey by Abbot Feckenham, in full pontificals, and the monks, each carrying a lighted torch, she remarked dismissively: 'Away with those torches, for we see very well'.[22]

On 8 May 1559, Elizabeth gave the royal assent to the Acts of Supremacy and Uniformity. The ban on Catholic worship had been strongly opposed in the House of Lords by Catholics, the bishops and Abbot Feckenham. A staged debate at the Abbey between Catholic and Protestant clerics, attended by MPs and peers, turned into a 'pitched battle'. The Uniformity Bill finally squeaked through after the Catholic bishops of Lincoln and Winchester were sent to the Tower for their 'disorders, stubbornesse and self-will'. However, Elizabeth's Anglican settlement sought to accommodate a broad swath of religious opinion. Whereas Henry VIII had been supreme head of the Church of England, Elizabeth was its supreme governor: a concession to those who held that only Christ was head of the church.[23]

Nonetheless, Catholic Westminster Abbey was dissolved. The last known survivor of its Benedictine monks, Robert Buckley (Dom Sigebert), remained a link with the old faith of medieval England until his death in 1610. Yet, Elizabeth respected Westminster's ancient exemption from the authority of Canterbury and London – a proud right that dated from 1222 – by granting the Collegiate Church of St Peter in Westminster (the Abbey's, formal, Anglican title) privileged status as a Royal Peculiar, placing the Abbey under the personal and sole jurisdiction of the sovereign. On 21 May 1560, under the terms of Elizabeth's royal charter, the queen's personal appointee as dean, William Bill, and a chapter of prebendaries (later canons), took possession of the Abbey.

The status of Royal Peculiar has been jealously guarded. It was a custom that a new archbishop of Canterbury, or a new bishop of London, on his first visit, had to sign a document in the Jerusalem Chamber, recognizing the Abbey's 'peculiar' status, before he was admitted into the church. When George Bradley, Dean at the turn of the twentieth century, bade his dinner guest, Bishop Creighton, farewell at the Dean's Yard gate, he commented: 'Now I return you to your diocese'. In practice, being a Royal Peculiar has given the Abbey's Dean and Chapter great independence for 450 years, as the sovereign's role has been limited to decisions on the Abbey's constitution and government.[24]

The wider impact of the Abbey's status as a Royal Peculiar was profound. The Abbot had controlled St Margaret's Church and parish since 1189, when Pope Clement III confirmed that the church was outside the diocese of London. The Abbot had also run the 'vill' or town as his own back yard and owned much of it. In 1560, all his property – including the unwelcome windfall of the Gatehouse gaol – was passed to the new Dean and Chapter. However, Cecil, the power behind the throne, shamelessly pulled the strings of power at Westminster. In 1561, on Cecil's recommendation, Gabriel Goodman succeeded the short-lived Dean Bill. Goodman remained city boss at Westminster for 40 years, surviving local government reform in 1585 to emerge as head of the new court of burgesses. Goodman is immortalized by a magnificent memorial in St Benedict's chapel in the Abbey and is mainly remembered for encouraging the development of the College of St Peter, better known as Westminster School.[25]

The queen, herself a keen scholar, and Cecil, also took a close interest in the school. Their involvement helped Goodman secure places for Westminster boys at Christ Church, Oxford and Trinity College, Cambridge. Elizabeth and her Privy Council attended the boys' performances of plays by Plautus and Terence in College Hall, the state dining-room of the Abbot's House. Among the pupils influenced by the emphasis on classical drama and verse was Ben Jonson, the future playwright and poet.[26]

Cecil's appointment as High Steward of Westminster illustrates his grip on power: the High Steward was appointed by the Dean and Chapter, and the Dean was a royal appointment. For more than 50 years from 1561, Cecil and his son, Robert, combined the positions of High Steward and Chief Minister. From 1585, either the Dean or his deputy, the High Steward, appointed the Court of Burgesses and presided at its meetings. While the loyal Dean Goodman's writ ran in the parish of St Margaret's, the Cecils had most influence in the parishes of St Martin's and St Clement's. Cecil's direct descendant, the third Marquis of Salisbury, was the last High Steward in 1900 while Prime Minister.[27]

Cecil added Westminster to the parliamentary constituencies that he controlled as the queen's business manager. Some seats were directly in Cecil's gift, but he influenced many other seats through his contacts and through his power over matters of inheritance and property as Master of the Court of Wards. He dangled the prospect of jobs and sinecures in front of MPs, used the services of advisers and writers, and appointed the Speaker. Speakers Bell (1572–6) and Puckering (1584–6, 1586–7) owed their seats to Cecil and supported his campaign against Mary, Queen of Scots, and her claim on the succession as the grand-daughter of Henry VIII's sister, Margaret.

The unresolved question of the succession smouldered during Elizabeth's 44-year reign, but periodically erupted into a full-blown crisis. The queen regarded the succession as one of many 'matters of state' that were off-limits for parliament, but she was sufficiently astute to keep open her option of marriage. Her fondness for her handsome favourite, Lord Robert Dudley, set tongues wagging at court, especially after his wife died in mysterious circumstances; but although Elizabeth and Dudley lived close to one another at Whitehall Palace, speculation about their marriage never became anything more than that.

Elizabeth's financial vulnerability prompted parliament to renew their pressure over the succession. Royal finances were dramatically squeezed throughout the sixteenth century, as prices increased fourfold while Crown revenues only doubled. When Elizabeth sought to raise an extra £250,000 in October 1566, MPs again raised the question of her marriage and the succession. Elizabeth was furious and shouted at her Councillors when they advised her to give way. The deadlock lasted almost a fortnight until a deputation of MPs and peers was allowed to petition the queen at Whitehall Palace. Elizabeth re-asserted her authority by dismissing parliament and not summoning another for four years. In the Commons, Peter Wentworth later had the temerity to suggest that unless MPs could speak freely, parliament would become 'a very schoole of flattery and dissimulacion and soe a fitt place to serve the Devil'. Wentworth's reward for repeatedly demanding free speech was repeated imprisonment in the Tower, where he died in 1597.[28]

Attempts to control the printed word involved savage sanctions. The printing press and the succession crisis between them spawned a new political weapon – the pamphlet. In 1564, John Hales, an MP and former supporter of Somerset's Protestant revolution, published a book arguing that the Grey family had the superior claim to the succession. Supporters of Mary Queen of Scots replied in kind. A pamphlet war ensued and the words 'puritan' and 'papist' became terms of sectarian abuse.

Hales's punishment was gaol, but he got off lightly compared with John Stubbe, a Protestant writer and lawyer. In 1579, Stubbe attacked Elizabeth's proposed marriage with the 24-year-old Catholic, Francis, Duke of Anjou, who seemed to sweep the 46-year-old queen off her feet. Stubbe's book was banned, and he was arrested, together with his publisher, Hugh Singleton, and an MP, William Page, who tried to distribute copies. Elizabeth wanted them hanged, but they were sentenced to have their right hands cut off.

Although the elderly Singleton was pardoned, Stubbe and Page were dealt with in the yard outside Westminster Hall. It took three blows to chop off Stubbe's hand. He cried out, 'God save the Queen,' fainted and was carried away. When Page's hand was cut off, he said, 'I have left there a true Englishman's hand'. The crowd watched in shocked silence. Parliament passed a law against 'seditious words and rumours uttered against the Queen's Most Excellent Majesty', but the battle over free speech had only just begun.[29]

19 HOLY TERROR

Pope Pius V's excommunication of Elizabeth I in early 1570 was a fateful moment for English Catholics. Before this papal bull, they risked becoming martyrs; afterwards, they were seen as traitors, potential or actual. The pope's intervention raised the spectre of Elizabeth's being assassinated or overthrown with holy blessing, and created a climate of fear similar to that experienced in modern times at the height of the Cold War or during terrorist campaigns.

The threat to Elizabeth was real. The Spanish Ambassador, Guerau De Spes, was encouraged by the pope's ruling and was optimistic about prospects for an invasion: 'As things are going here and in Ireland, it looks as if the enterprise might be effected in both islands at the same time, as in Ireland most of the nation will rise as soon as they see your Majesty's standard borne by ships on their coast'. Although an invasion failed to materialize on this occasion, a plot was discovered that led to a treason trial in Westminster Hall.[1]

Early on the morning of 16 January 1572, Thomas Howard, Duke of Norfolk, a Catholic and England's most senior aristocrat, disembarked at Westminster Palace, accompanied by Sir Owen Hopton, Lieutenant of the Tower, and was escorted by more than 100 halberdiers through the Star Chamber to the Lord Treasurer's room. There Howard awaited his call to stand trial for high treason. Shortly after eight o'clock, he was led into Westminster Hall, where a 'scaffold' (a temporary stage) had been erected near the court of Chancery, in the south-west corner. Seated on the scaffold were his judges: 26 fellow peers, presided over by the Earl of Shrewsbury, Lord High Steward of England. The Great Hall was packed by a great crowd, all standing.

Howard was out of his depth during the intrigues that flourished after the Catholic Mary, Queen of Scots, fled to England. Mary's presence was unsettling for Elizabeth, because Catholics believed that Mary, as the grand-daughter of Margaret Tudor, had a better claim to the throne than Elizabeth, whom they regarded as illegitimate. Howard had been implicated in the Northern Rising of 1569, a revolt led by Catholic aristocrats, and two years later was accused of being involved in a plot against Elizabeth. The plot's organizer, Roberto Ridolfi, an Italian banker and fervent Catholic, envisaged a Spanish invasion, Elizabeth's removal and the installation of Mary as queen with Howard as her consort. However, Elizabeth could not bring herself to execute Mary. Instead, Howard was subjected to a show trial.

At his trial, Howard stood 'a long half pace from the bar' guarded by two officers who had brought him from the Tower. Nearby, the Chamberlain of the Tower stood with an axe while Howard, 'with a haughty look, and oft biting his lip, surveyed the lords on each side him'. Later that evening, after it had turned dark outside, Howard was found guilty. The edge of the axe was turned towards him, signifying that he was to be executed.[2]

The Ridolfi Plot intensified the risks run by Catholic émigré priests, such as Edward Campion, who arrived in 1580 and travelled the country incognito. While avoiding arrest, Campion enraged the government by launching a series of publicity coups: preaching in Smithfield and challenging his critics to debate religion. Elizabeth's response was to make an example of Jesuits: 'to the terror of others'. A proclamation ordered their arrest and parliament made it treasonable to convert people to 'the Romish religion'.[3]

Campion was eventually caught in 1581, tortured during 'three long visits to the rack-house' and brought to Westminster Hall charged with plotting against Elizabeth. Despite his eloquence, he and his fellow defendants were found guilty. After the sentence of hanging, drawing and quartering was announced, the spectators in the packed Hall were astonished to hear Campion singing God's praise in the Te Deum. Campion's reply to the Lord Chief Justice's question, asking if the condemned men had anything to say, captured the English Catholics' dilemma: 'if our Religion do make us Traitors, we are worthy to be condemned; but otherwise are and have been as true subjects as the Queen had'. An MP and Catholic convert, William Parry, who dared to criticise the anti-Jesuit legislation and might have been a spy, was found guilty of treason. He was executed outside Westminster Hall in March 1585, where he was disembowelled while alive and 'gave a great groan'.[4]

Mary, Queen of Scots, eventually fell victim to Sir Francis Walsingham, Elizabeth's wily principal secretary and spymaster. A portrait of Walsingham shows a neatly-bearded, ruff-wearing knight in his early 50s, but he emerges as a one-man prototype of the modern Joint Intelligence Committee and the heads of MI5 and MI6. His spies discovered a plot against Elizabeth dreamed up by Anthony Babington, a 24-year-old Derbyshire Catholic gentleman and former page to Mary. Walsingham covertly set up a secret postal system between the plotters and Mary, with the person handling the correspondence in his pay. Without this deception the plot would probably never have gone as far as it did, but it enabled Walsingham to intercept Mary's supportive letters and entrap her.

Babington and 13 others were tried in Westminster Hall and executed in September 1586. Mary's trial began with a two-day hearing at Fotheringhay Castle, Northamptonshire, and was concluded in the Star Chamber at Westminster

Palace. Elizabeth was reluctant to sign the death warrant, but she was persuaded to summon parliament, which duly petitioned for Mary's execution. Elizabeth signed the warrant in February 1587.

Although the imminent threat of a Spanish attack was temporarily lifted by Sir Francis Drake's 'Cingeing of the king of Spaines Beard', the long-dreaded invasion force materialized the following year. The repulse of the 130-ship Spanish Armada, as it was harried along the Channel, disrupted by English fire-ships and buffeted by storms, was celebrated in England as evidence of God's support: as the inscription on a victory medal declared, *Flavit Deus et Dissipati Sunt*, 'God blew with His wind and they were scattered'.[5]

The victorious Lord Admiral, Charles, Lord Howard of Effingham, cousin of the queen and one of her closest male companions, commissioned ten gold-trimmed tapestries, each about 27 feet by 15 feet, to commemorate the fleet's triumph. The huge Armada tapestries were later bought by Elizabeth's successor, James I. From about the 1650s, they were hung at Westminster Palace in the House of Lords where their mythologized images of warring galleons and cavorting sea monsters covered the walls of the Chamber from the floor to the ceiling. After the tapestries were burnt in the fire that destroyed the Palace in 1834, Prince Albert, as chairman of the Fine Arts Commission of the new palace, commissioned six paintings to recreate their glory. Although only one painting had been finished by the time of Albert's death, the project was completed in 2010, by the artist, Anthony Oakshett and his team. The paintings can now be seen in the Prince's Chamber in the House of Lords.[6]

The Armada cast a long shadow: for English Protestants, it remained proof of the constant threat of invasion; for English Catholics, it kindled a flame of hope. In 1592, Guy Fawkes, a Catholic in his early twenties, left England to fight as a Spanish mercenary in the Netherlands. Eleven years later, he visited Spain in the hope of encouraging another invasion, but his subsequent disappointment provoked him to join the most desperate plot in Westminster's long history of holy terror.

Rumours of a plot to assassinate Elizabeth in November 1602 forced the queen to change her usual route from Richmond Palace to Whitehall for her Accession Day celebrations and travel entirely by water. As a rule, she alighted at Chelsea and dined with her cousin, Charles Howard, before completing her journey by coach: 'All the way from Chelsea to Whitehall was full of people to see her', as Bishop Goodman recalled. However, by the end of her reign Elizabeth preferred to travel at 'dark night': 'she did desire to be seen and to be magnified; but in her old age she had not only great wrinkles, but she had a goggle throat, with a great gullet hanging out, as her grandfather Henry VII is painted withal'. Soon afterwards, the 69-year-old queen spoke movingly to MPs, assembled in the Presence Chamber at Whitehall Palace, of her royal burden: 'to be a King and wear a crown is a thing more glorious to them that see it, than it is pleasant to them that bear it'.[7]

The 44-year reign of the last Tudor monarch ended on 24 March 1603. At Elizabeth's funeral 'Westminster was surcharged with multitudes of all sorts of people in their streets, houses, windows, leads and gutters', reported John Stow. When they saw her effigy 'lying upon the coffin set forth in Royall robes, having a crown upon the head thereof and a ball and scepter in either hand, there was such a general sighing, groaning and weeping as the like they that hath not beene seene or knowne in the memory of man'. Elizabeth is buried beneath a white marble monument, erected by James I, in the north aisle of Henry VII's chapel, and is united in death with her half-sister Mary I, whose coffin rests under hers.[8]

James VI of Scotland, son of Mary, Queen of Scots, was proclaimed King of England at ten o'clock in the morning, only hours after Elizabeth's death, by a small, hunch-backed courtier at Whitehall's Court Gate. He was Robert Cecil, who had followed his father, Lord Burghley, as Elizabeth's chief minister, and had already been in secret communication with James, who as a Protestant would uphold Elizabeth's religious settlement. The proclamation justified James's 'undoubted right' to the English crown as he was descended from Henry VII's daughter, Margaret Tudor, the sister of Henry VIII. However, there was no mention of Margaret Tudor's marriage to James IV of Scotland; neither was there any reference to James's mother, Mary Queen of Scots; nor to his father Henry Lord Darnley, who was also a grandchild of Margaret Tudor. Instead, as Jenny Wormald the historian has noted, the proclamation referred to the marriage of Henry VII and Elizabeth of York. Their marriage had ended the 'bloody and Civil Warres ... to the joy unspeakable of this Kingdome'. By invoking the Tudor myth, the message was clear: James I would end the crippling uncertainty over the succession and remove the threat of invasion or civil war.[9]

Cecil's proclamation addressed an English audience. Politicians at Westminster welcomed a personal union of the two crowns in as much as it entrenched the Protestant settlement and strengthened national security. However, this very English unionism was at odds with James I's ambition of a union of equals. In 1604, his proposal for a full union with Scotland provoked a fierce backlash at Westminster, where MPs feared the loss of England's identity.

In November 1605, however, parliament's impassioned debates over the union were eclipsed by the dramatic discovery of a well-advanced plot to assassinate the King and the entire ruling establishment at the state opening of parliament. The Gunpowder Plot almost succeeded because of the anonymity afforded by Westminster's overcrowded alleyways and streets. About 7,000 people lived in St Margaret's parish, a warren of boarding houses, inns, market-stalls, shops, stables, stores and tenements, some of which were jammed hard against the walls of the ancient buildings. On the riverfront, busy landing stages handled a constant flow of cargo boats and ferries.

The would-be assassins feared James I's accession for the same reasons that the court and parliament welcomed it: the king had fathered three heirs and offered stability. However, James's notion of stability was open to interpretation. He gave Cecil the impression of being disinclined to persecute Catholics and ready to tolerate their private worship; whereas, according to Thomas Percy, an intermediary for the Earl of Northumberland, who favoured Catholic toleration, James had promised to give protection to Catholics and allow them to hold public office.[10]

James initially raised Catholic hopes by ending fines on recusants and appointing Northumberland and Henry Howard, to his council. However, in July 1603, two Catholic plots were discovered; and, within a year, James had sought common ground with puritans, had priests expelled, and re-introduced fines on recusants. In his first King's Speech to parliament, he rejected physical persecution of Catholics, but warned against any 'growing' of their religion and urged the Anglican bishops 'to win souls to God', i.e. seek converts. As any lingering hope of Catholic salvation by invasion withered when England and Spain sought peace, a small band of desperate Catholics decided that their only option was a bloody coup.[11]

The Gunpowder Plot was devised in early 1604 by Robert Catesby, his cousin, Thomas Winter, and a friend, John Wright. They were in their thirties and had previously sought Spanish intervention: now, the charismatic Catesby urged, it was time 'to blow up the parliament howse with gunpowder'. Winter feared that if their plot failed, English Catholicism might be destroyed by the backlash, but Catesby insisted that the plight of Catholics, 'required so sharp a remedy'.[12]

During the spring of 1604, Winter visited Flanders, where he was again fobbed off by the Spaniards; but he sought out Guy Fawkes, who knew about explosives, and persuaded him to return to England. In London, Winter and Fawkes met Catesby and Thomas Percy, who had been appointed to the King's Body Guard by Northumberland, the Captain of the Gentlemen Pensioners. Percy's privileged access at Westminster was central to the plan. In June, he subleased a small lodging next to the House of Lords, off an alleyway along the southern wall of the Palace that ran between Parliament Stairs and Old Palace Yard. The lodging belonged to Thomas Whinniard, Keeper of the King's Wardrobe, and afforded a direct route to the House of Lords. Its keys were handed to Fawkes who posed as Percy's servant under the pseudonym of John Johnson.[13]

The end of the parliamentary session in July gave the plotters seven months to prepare before the next session, due to start in February 1605. A new recruit, Robert Keyes, was put in charge of Catesby's house in Lambeth, where gunpowder and firewood were stored before being ferried across the Thames. However, the threat of the plague caused the next session of parliament to be postponed for eight months, until October. In March, Percy leased a ground-floor vault close to Whinniard's lodging and directly below the first-floor Chamber of the House of Lords. The vault had been part of the medieval palace kitchen and was used as a store for coal, firewood and general clutter.

By the end of July, Fawkes and Keyes had ferried the gunpowder in small barrels across the river and stored it in 36 large barrels known as hogsheads. However, persistent fears of the plague prompted a further postponement of parliament's return until 5 November 1605. During October, three more recruits joined, bringing the number to 13, including Catesby's cousin, the reluctant Francis Tresham.[14]

Finally, all was set. During the state opening in the House of Lords, Fawkes was to light the fuse of an estimated 18 hundredweight of gunpowder. The King, seated in the middle of the Chamber, directly above the vault, would be killed outright, as, probably, would everybody else: the queen, the princes, the Privy Council, MPs, Lords, most bishops and senior judges. Fawkes was to escape by boat across the river and flee abroad. While he briefed foreign courts, his fellow plotters were to exploit the political vacuum at Westminster by launching a Catholic uprising in their native midlands and declaring the nine-year-old Princess Elizabeth queen.[15]

That was the plan; but on the night of 26 October, Lord Monteagle, an ambitious, 30- year-old courtier, rushed into Whitehall with an anonymous letter warning him not to attend the state opening of parliament. Monteagle found the first minster, Robert Cecil, now Earl of Salisbury, at supper with several Privy Councillors. Salisbury had already been warned by his spy network that some mischief was afoot and initiated secret inquiries into the letter's cryptic warning that 'they shall receive a terrible blow this Parliament, yet they shall not see who hurts them'. The identity of the letter-writer is a mystery. Monteagle's brother-in-law, Tresham, a late and doubtful recruit to the plot, probably spilled the beans. The historian Antonia Fraser suggests that Tresham might have mentioned the plot in conversation with his brother-in-law, Monteagle, who had more to gain from revealing it.[16]

Fawkes was unaware of any betrayal and on 30 October checked that the gunpowder was in place. Two days later, Salisbury saw James at Whitehall Palace and showed him the letter. On Saturday 2 November, the Privy Council decided that the Houses of Parliament should be searched on the eve of the state opening. The next day, Catesby, Percy and Winter decided to go ahead. On the Monday morning, Percy visited Syon House, Northumberland's riverside mansion near Isleworth, and felt assured by the earl's apparently calm demeanour that the Privy Council knew nothing about any plot. Percy was mistaken, but his visit implicated the earl, who was later stripped of office and imprisoned in the Tower for 15 years.[17]

A search of the Houses of Parliament was made on the Monday afternoon led by the Great Chamberlain, Thomas Howard, Earl of Suffolk, accompanied by Monteagle. After examining the Chamber of the Lords they went to the ground-floor vault. Although they noticed a large pile of firewood, a servant told them that it belonged to his master, Thomas Percy, who leased the nearby lodging. Suffolk took the servant at his word, but later described him as 'a very tall and desperate fellow'. Monteagle was also puzzled that Percy had leased a lodging in the Palace.[18]

Suffolk's report roused the suspicions of the king and Salisbury. Late that night Sir Thomas Knyvett, a member of the King's Privy Chamber, led a second search party. In the vault below the House of Lords, the party encountered the man who claimed to be Percy's servant wearing a cloak and hat, and booted and spurred ready for a journey, despite the late hour. Edmund Doubleday, a local burgess and vestryman at St Margaret's, struggled to arrest him, while another local man, Peter Heywood, seized his lantern.[19] After his arrest, Fawkes continued to insist that he was John Johnson. However, a 9-inch match was found in his pocket, and barrels of gunpowder were found beneath the pile of firewood. By four o'clock in the morning, some of the council gathered in the king's bedchamber in Whitehall Palace, where the defiant Fawkes was brought. Refusing to name his accomplices, he regretted only that the plot had failed: 'God would have concealed it, but the devil was the discoverer'.[20]

Rumours soon spread across Westminster. The first bonfires were lit in Westminster and the City rejoiced that the king was safe. The bells of St Margaret's rang out the next day in relief, 'at the tyme the Parliament House should have been blown up'. Parliament met briefly in the afternoon. The only mention of the plot in the *Commons Journal* is a handwritten note by the clerk, Ralph Ewens, in the left-hand margin:

> This last Night the Upper House of Parliament was searched by Sir Tho. Knevett; and one Johnson, Servant to Mr. Thomas Percye, was there appre-hended; who had placed Thirty-six Barrels of Gunpowder in the Vault under the House, with a Purpose to blow King, and the whole Company, when they should there assemble. Afterwards divers other Gentlemen were discovered to be of the Plot.

His note was later framed and is displayed in the 'Noes' voting lobby of the Commons.[21]

MPs joined the Lords in their Chamber, where the king spoke of,

> the Cruelty of the Plot itself, wherein cannot be enough admired the horrible and fearful Cruelty of their Device, which was not only for the Destruction of My Person, nor of My Wife and Posterity only, but of the whole Body of the State in general; wherein should neither have been spared, or Distinction made, of Young nor of Old, of great nor of small, of Man nor of Woman.[22]

Fawkes's refusal to disclose details of the plot ended on the rack at the Tower. Catesby, Percy and other plotters were tracked down and killed, but Winter and two others were also brought to the Tower. On 27 January 1606, eight plotters were ferried upstream to a crowded Westminster Hall, where the better-off spectators paid as much as ten shillings for a seat. The king observed the day-long trial secretly from a concealed room in the Hall; and Queen Anne, and Prince Henry also watched without being seen. The plotters were found guilty of high treason and sentenced to be hanged, drawn and quartered.[23]

Four of the plotters were executed on Thursday 30 January near St Paul's; the remaining four, Winter, Fawkes, Robert Keyes and Ambrose Rookwood, were executed the next day in Old Palace Yard, close to the scene of their planned outrage. Winter was hanged first, and while still alive was taken down, castrated, and disembowelled; his heart was cut out and, finally, he was beheaded. Fawkes waited as the others died in excruciating pain. Weakened by torture, he had to be lifted on to the scaffold, 'but yet with much ado by the help of the hangman went high enough to break his neck with the fall'.[24]

The Gunpowder Plot was a disaster for English Catholics. They had to wait until 1829 before they could take part in politics and public life. Salisbury, ever the pragmatic politician, exploited the sense of relief after the plot's discovery by persuading MPs to sanction extra government subsidies. But the familiar rhyme, 'Remember, remember the fifth of November', echoes the fear that has haunted Westminster since 1605. On the eve of each subsequent state opening of parliament, the vaults of the Houses of Parliament have been searched by a contingent of The King's (or Queen's) Body Guard – a corps of the Yeomen of the Guard – in their distinctive red and gold Tudor-style uniforms, armed with swords and lanterns. Henry VII originally formed this special corps from the archers who gave him personal protection at the Battle of Bosworth, and they are England's oldest surviving military unit. Today, before each state opening of parliament, in addition to the traditional search of the vaults, police conduct a massive security operation.[25]

20 SCANDAL AND SPLENDOUR

The elegant Banqueting House, standing roughly half-way between Trafalgar Square and Parliament Square, adorns modern Whitehall. This classical, stately building is the last remaining large-scale structure of Whitehall Palace; although it was built in a very different style from the rest of the great Tudor pile. The Banqueting House provides an evocative link with the self-indulgent opulence of James I's court, and the dramatic power struggle between Crown and Parliament that came to dominate Westminster during the seventeenth century.

In addition to the Banqueting House, the legacy of England's first Stuart king includes the Authorized, or King James, Bible, and one of the world's most iconic flags, the Union Jack. The publication of the King James Bible in 1611 reflected James's commitment to learning. Some of the scholars who translated the scriptures worked in Westminster Abbey's Jerusalem Chamber. James also erected white marble monuments in opposite aisles of Henry VII's chapel on the tombs of Elizabeth I, and his mother, Mary Queen of Scots. In 1612 he had brought Mary's remains from Peterborough Cathedral, near her place of execution, and re-interred them at the Abbey.

James's ambition for a full union between England and Scotland failed because of fierce opposition from MPs at Westminster. Nonetheless, he assumed the title of King of Great Britain; announced that he would introduce a single currency; and persuaded parliament to accept free trade between the kingdoms, and adopt a British flag. The flag's design combined the crosses of St George and St Andrew and became known as the 'Union Jack'. The origin of its popular name is debated, but 'jack' is the term for a flag flown on a ship's bow and also a short version of 'Jacobus', the Latin for James.

Friction between Crown and Parliament was exacerbated by the Scots' dominance of the king's entourage: James's favourite since adolescence, Esme Stuart, Duke of Lennox, was appointed Steward of the Household; and Thomas Erskine, who replaced Sir Walter Raleigh as Captain of the Yeomen of the Guard, later became Groom of the Stool. Violent clashes between Englishmen and Scots close to James culminated in 1612 in the murder of John Turner, a fencing master, in revenge for having accidentally put out the eye of Lord Sanquhar, a Scottish baron. James made an example of Sanquhar, who was hanged in a silken halter (in deference to his rank) on a gibbet outside the 'great gate of Westminster Hall' in June 1612. Another Scot, James Hay, was among the court's sleazier spendthrifts. Hay rose from service in the king's bedchamber to become a diplomat and was elevated as the Earl of Carlisle. He invented the 'ante-supper', a banquet of sumptuous food merely to be looked at, and on Twelfth Night, 1621, gave a feast of 1,600 dishes that employed 100 cooks for eight days at a cost of over £3,300.[1]

The court's profligacy was politically disastrous, at a time when the Crown's revenue was being eroded by inflation. Salisbury, who ran the government from the Council Chamber in Whitehall Palace in his capacity as Secretary of State and Lord Treasurer, was appalled by the scale of the government's ballooning debt. He tried to negotiate a compromise with parliament, or 'Great Contract', to reduce the deficit and grant the king a reliable income without the need for regular parliamentary votes. In a vain attempt to win MPs' support, Salisbury took great care over the parliamentary pageantry for Prince Henry's creation as Prince of Wales, but MPs baulked at losing any of their power over supply. Amid much acrimony, James dissolved his first parliament.[2]

Cash for honours helped Salisbury plug the hole in the king's finances. Sales of the new hereditary rank of baronet attracted 88 buyers in 1611. Twenty-six baronetcies were created for well-off Catholic families, keen to display their loyalty after the disastrous Gunpowder Plot. From 1615 peerages were sold for an average going rate of about £10,000. At the start of James's reign, there were 59 peers, a number that had hardly grown for 300 years; but he created an extra 62.[3]

Distrust between the king and parliament deepened after Salisbury's death in 1612. Two years later, the 'Addled Parliament' failed to resolve the conflict with the king, who wanted to increase the use of 'impositions', i.e. taxes levied without regular parliamentary approval. 'The House of Commons is a body without a head', James raged: 'The members give their opinions in a disorderly manner. At their meetings nothing is heard but cries, shouts and confusion'. In 1621, James forbade parliament from debating his son Charles's planned marriage to the king of Spain's daughter, the Infanta Maria Anna; but the MPs reacted by drawing up a 'protestation', asserting their right to debate urgent matters. In response, James ordered the *Commons Journal* to be brought to the Council Chamber, tore out the offending pages and dissolved parliament yet again. In the event, the marriage negotiations failed, and Charles married Henrietta Maria of France.[4]

James was in no position to occupy the moral high ground. The rottenness at court was revealed in the sensational murder trials of Robert Carr, Earl of Somerset, and his wife, Frances, in Westminster Hall in 1615. The victim was Sir Thomas Overbury, who had been the mentor and intimate friend of Robert

Carr, one of the king's favourites. The Somersets' trial revealed the bitter rivalry at court between Overbury's faction and another led by Henry Howard, Earl of Northampton. Howard wanted to recruit Carr into his faction by marrying him to his great-niece, Frances. Overbury was determined to stop the marriage but was arrested after refusing an ambassadorship: a ploy designed to remove him from the country. He died in the Tower, apparently from poisoning, and Carr and Frances, who had married, were charged with his murder.[5]

Westminster Hall was packed by 'a world of people' for the murder trial of the earl and countess in May 1616. A lawyer paid the huge sum of £10 for seats for himself and his family for two days. The Lord High Steward presided at the south end of the hall; one level below sat the 21 peers summoned to try the Somersets; and below them were the judges in their scarlet robes. Dressed in black, the pale and trembling Frances cut a dramatic figure as she confessed to the crime 'with a low voice but wonderful fearful'. Her husband pleaded not guilty. Although the Somersets were condemned to death, they were pardoned by James.[6]

James's court was cast in an even worse light by the trial and execution of Sir Walter Raleigh, the adventurer and courtier, at Westminster in 1618. Raleigh had fallen out with Salisbury and opposed the Stuart succession: in 1603 he was found guilty of conspiring against James. He was sentenced to death, but his harsh treatment made him a popular hero and he was reprieved. He spent a dozen years in the Tower but reinvented himself as a writer, notably with *The History of the World*, that portrayed the wickedness of kings.[7]

On his eventual release in March 1616, Raleigh organized a hare-brained voyage to the Americas in search of El Dorado that ended in disaster. His reckless exploits were seen as a threat to the king's hopes for a Spanish alliance. On his return, he was summoned before the Privy Council, where he was accused of planning to foment war between England and Spain, abandoning his men and betraying James. Raleigh appeared before the King's Bench, where he was told that he was to be executed in keeping with the earlier sentence in 1603. His plea that the king's sanctioning of his expedition meant that the earlier sentence had been lifted was rejected by the Lord Chief Justice.[8]

James ordered that Raleigh's execution should be carried out as early as possible the next morning in Old Palace Yard, in order to prevent an appeal. Raleigh spent his last night in Westminster's medieval Gatehouse gaol outside the west door of the Abbey. Raleigh's last visitor was his wife, Bess. It was probably after she left that Raleigh recalled a poem that he wrote before they married, and added two lines that made a moving epitaph:

Even such is time, that takes in trust
Our youth, our joys, our all we have,
And pays us but with earth and dust;
Who, in the dark and silent grave,

When we have wandered all our ways,
Shuts up the story of our days,
But from this earth, this grave, this dust,
My God shall raise me up, I trust.[9]

At about 8 a.m., Raleigh was escorted by 60 armed guards from the Gatehouse to a packed Old Palace Yard, where he made the scaffold his stage. He addressed the crowd for three-quarters of an hour, denying the allegations of treachery and disloyalty made against him. According to an eye-witness, he 'died with such high spirits as if he were going to a wedding. I do not think that there was ever such a spectacle in the time of the Romans'. His head was put in a red leather bag and taken by his wife. Raleigh's body was buried in the chancel of St Margaret's church, just yards from where he was executed. His biographer, Raleigh Trevelyan, suggests that the burial at Westminster may have been in deliberate defiance of the king.[10]

Within a year of Raleigh's execution, James commissioned the new Banqueting House at Whitehall Palace; one of England's most sublime buildings. The king's earlier banqueting house, built in 1606, had burned down in 1619 after cleaners dropped a candle and failed to raise the alarm. James had never liked its heavily colonnaded interior, and turned for something better to his Surveyor of the King's Works, Inigo Jones.[11]

Jones was an architectural revolutionary and brilliant stage designer. He first made an impact at court in 1605 at the simultaneous celebration of Twelfth Night and the investiture of the future Charles I as Duke of York. The highlight of the festivities was *The Masque of Blackness*, performed in Elizabeth I's timber and canvas banqueting house. Jones designed the costumes, stage sets and the machinery for extravagant special effects. He and the librettist, Ben Jonson, rejuvenated the medieval masque, creating an exotic mixture of ball, fancy dress party, opera and theatre, all performed for, and in honour of, the monarch.[12]

The Masque of Blackness caused a sensation when James's Danish wife, Queen Anne, and her ladies appeared with their faces and hands blacked-up. In the great crush of hangers-on who crowded the palace, tables heaped with food for a banquet were overturned; jewels, purses and other valuable items were lost; and one woman was caught making love on top of the terrace. One of the most exotic moments at a Twelfth Night party occurred during Jonson's *The Vision of Delight* in 1617, when Pocahontas, the visiting Algonquian Indian princess, saw James I's handsome, 25-year-old favourite, the future Duke of Buckingham, dance the part of the 'primer bailarín'.[13]

Inigo Jones had been inspired by the work of the Renaissance architect, Andrea Palladio and, seizing the moment, in 1619 applied his study of Palladio's neo-classical style to create a bold, revolutionary design for the new Banqueting House. One of his keenest supporters, Queen Anne, did not live to see the first stone laid, but by 1622, Jones's Banqueting House had risen, phoenix-like, on Whitehall. The elegant new building reflected the king's inclinations: artistic, ceremonial and convivial. Jones's well-proportioned design, with two storeys resting on a raised basement, and with seven bays of large windows, creates a sense of spaciousness. As Thurley notes, Jones originally incorporated three subtly different colours in the exterior facing: brownish, Oxfordshire stone for the raised basement; tobacco-coloured, Northamptonshire for the main walls; and white Portland to highlight the pillars and decorative carving, but since the early nineteenth century the entire building has been clad in Portland stone.[14]

The new Banqueting House was mainly used for formal court and state occasions, although it also hosted Maundy ceremonies and touching for the King's Evil. Monarchs and their courtiers entered the ground floor through a door at the south end, linked to the Palace's main Privy Gallery. This was the route used by James and his intimates when they wanted to enjoy a debauched evening in the raised basement, where Jones built an arched, brick 'grotto' for the king's pleasure. The public entrance was through a door at the north end.[15]

Inside the Banqueting House, people were greeted by the breathtaking sight of Jones's magnificent saloon: a great space in the shape of a double cube, 55 feet by 55 feet by 100 feet. Its geometric proportions reflected classical design, but Jones innovated by adding a gallery cantilevered round three sides: its height echoing the division between the two storeys outside. The bays and pillars superimposed on the interior walls also matched the outside; but unlike today, the saloon was decorated with huge, wall tapestries and the first-floor windows were left blank. Jones's Roman-style niche for the throne was removed after a few years and replaced by the English monarch's traditional raised dais and canopy.[16]

High above the splendid saloon is a beautiful ceiling that was one of Jones's most daring innovations. The flat roof allowed him to dispense with the Jacobean pattern of interlocking squares, lozenges and stars; and create, instead, large panels in the ceiling, the largest four of which measure 28 feet by 20 feet. In a stroke of genius, Jones invited Peter Paul Rubens, the great Flemish artist, to paint canvases for the panels and give the geometric design an exuberant, baroque, counterpoint. Rubens was undaunted by the challenge when first approached in 1621, but he was heavily committed and it was another eight years before the artist eventually viewed the building, discussed the specifications with Charles I and agreed a contract.[17]

Rubens took immense care while painting each canvas to ensure that its perspective worked for the viewer in the hall beneath. The central canvas above the dais at the throne end, 'The Peaceful Reign of James I', portrays James as the British King Solomon, about to be crowned with the laurels of victory as he points towards Peace and Plenty, represented by female figures. The theme of all-conquering magnanimity is reinforced in the oval canvases on either side: Temperance tramples on intemperance, and Apollo bestows liberality.[18]

The artist designed the large oval canvas in the centre of the ceiling, 'James I Being Carried to Heaven', for visitors to see as they entered the hall; not by the monarch from the throne. The late king is shown resting his foot on an imperial globe as he is raised towards heaven by Justice. On either side, long decorative panels feature genii and putti with animals and a garland. Above the public entrance at the north end of the hall, the large, main canvas shows the 'Union of the Crowns'. It was designed for the monarch to view from the throne and depicts Minerva holding two crowns over a naked infant, representing the future Charles I, under James's gaze. The oval to the right shows 'Hercules Crushing Discord', alluding to the Stuarts' conflict with Catholic and Puritan MPs. In the oval to the left, Minerva spears Ignorance, as her owl flies above bearing an olive wreath'.[19]

The Banqueting House began as a celebration of James I's reign, but it became a commemoration. After the installation of Rubens's paintings, masques were no longer held there for fear of damage from the torch smoke. The Banqueting House also highlighted the difference between James and his predecessor, Elizabeth. She cultivated her image as the people's queen; whereas James intended his showpiece to impress courtiers, dignitaries and foreign royals. Although the building's design was revolutionary, its political impact was reactionary.

21 KILLING THE KING

Until the 1640s, nobody was famous for being in parliament, but Charles I's disastrous reign transformed MPs into national heroes. John Hampden was a relatively obscure MP from a Calvinist family in Buckinghamshire until Charles made the mistake of selecting him as the subject of a test case on the legality of 'ship money', the infamous levy that enabled the king to rule without parliament. John Pym was a humourless estate manager and puritan, whose sense of inner certainty and attention to detail saw him emerge as parliament's leader. William Lenthall, an undistinguished Oxfordshire lawyer, plucked up his courage as Speaker and put his duty to the Commons before that to the king. These men are sanctified in the modern Houses of Parliament in two icons that glorify parliament's heroic past: Lenthall is honoured in one of Charles West Cope's frescoes on the English Civil War; and Hampden, Pym and their allies are revered in John Seymour Lucas's oil painting, *The Flight of the Five Members, 1642*.

Events conspired against Charles after he succeeded his father, James, in 1625. He married the Catholic French princess, Henrietta Maria, after elaborate negotiations, during which a reluctant Dean of Westminster, John Williams, was ordered to entertain the French with a choral concert in the Abbey with the composer, Orlando Gibbons, at the organ, followed by dinner in the Jerusalem Chamber. A delay in Henrietta Maria's arrival led Charles to postpone his first parliament; a recurrence of the plague forced it to take refuge at Oxford; and the adjournment of the law courts at Westminster Hall left the streets 'empty of People, and overgrown with Grass'.[1]

In the following February, the continued fear of contagion forced the cancellation of Charles's Coronation procession. The king's great day was marred by mishaps. On his way to the ceremony, the royal barge collided with the pier at parliament Stairs; at the Abbey, the congregation hesitated when the Archbishop presented the new king, until Lord Arundel prompted half-hearted cries of, 'God Save King Charles!'; and during the afternoon, earth tremors shook Westminster, creating fears of further disasters.[2]

Had Charles been capable of making the political weather, he might have made a better fist of a difficult legacy. He was at first unable to govern without parliament because of his urgent need of money. But he was infuriated in 1629, when MPs attacked high church beliefs and held the Speaker down in his chair to prevent him doing as Charles wished by closing the debate. The king responded by arresting the MPs and issuing a proclamation that, as Lord Clarendon later noted, 'was commonly understood to inhibit all men to speak of another Parliament'.[3]

Despite the absence of MPs during the 1630s, Westminster was kept busy by well-to-do English and European tourists, who hoped to catch a glimpse of the king, enjoy a walk in Whitehall's gardens, attend a royal tournament or visit the Abbey. The burgeoning tourist trade was satirized by John Donne: 'The man that keeps the Abbey tombs, / And for his price doth, with whoever comes, / Of all our Harries and our Edwards talk'.[4]

Westminster was a bustling, modern seat of government, although it was still run by the Dean and Chapter of the Abbey as if it were a medieval manor. St Margaret's parish was teeming with about 16,000 inhabitants. Its alleys and streets were crammed with jerry-built housing, while aristocrats had townhouses in Canon Row, near the old palace, and along the Strand. Inns and taverns were packed into Tothill Street and King Street, where the Sun Tavern occupied a prime site opposite New Palace Yard, and was owned by Thomas Larkin, the king's master locksmith. The 285 alehouses licensed in St Margaret's and St Martin's in 1634 were frequented by servants, workmen and the less well-off.[5]

Even the walls of Whitehall Palace afforded no protection from the smoke and stench of Westminster's chimneys, brewhouses, fish-stalls and brickworks. The nearby streets were rife with disorder and vagrancy. King Street, outside the main gate, was clogged by stalls and packed with hucksters and shoppers. Their cries and chatter rose to a rowdy crescendo whenever criminals were led past, sometimes whipped as they went, on their way to the Fleet prison. The well-to-do often travelled by water – royals and aristocrats in their own barges, others in richly-decorated wherries – but the demand for hackney coaches and sedan chairs was growing. A pleasure garden north of Whitehall's tiltyard, at Spring Gardens, attracted aristocrats and the gentry. The demand for luxury goods from the royal family, courtiers and aristocrats, supported craftsmen and retailers.[6]

Charles's grandiose plan to re-build Whitehall Palace was never realized, although he re-developed Scotland Yard and added other buildings, including a room for his artistic treasures; an elaborate clock house; and a new masque house, where Jeffery Hudson, Henrietta Maria's dwarf, played Tom Thumb in Inigo Jones's production of Ben Jonson's *Fortunate Isles*. Charles's passion for art had been fired while courting the Spanish Infanta in Madrid. He returned with works by Titian and Durer, and later paid £18,000 to the bankrupt Gonzagas of Mantua in return for a fabulous haul of 400 items, including Raphaels, Correggios and Giulio Romanos. His appointment of Anthony Van Dyck, as 'principalle Paynter in Ordinary to their Majesties' in 1632, produced a series of brilliant portraits, timeless in their sensitivity, yet evoking a self-assured elite blithely unaware of impending disaster. The inventory drawn up after his death listed 1,200 items. Charles's lasting legacy in Whitehall is the Rubens ceiling in the Banqueting House.[7]

Despite parliament's absence during the 1630s, the battle between church and state raged at the Abbey. Dean John Williams, a politically ambitious Welshman, and William Laud, whom Charles appointed Bishop of London in 1628, were old adversaries. Laud appointed his chaplain, Peter Heylyn, to the Abbey Chapter to spy out any closet puritanism. Laud managed to drag Williams before the Star Chamber in 1637, when he was fined the then colossal sum of £10,000, and sent to the Tower. In the same year, John Bastwick, Henry Burton and William Prynne were put in the pillory in New Palace Yard, for publishing attacks on the established church. Bastwick and Burton had their ears cropped, and Prynne's previously cropped ears were brutally shorn. Prynne also had his nose slit and the initials 'SL' for seditious libel, branded on his cheeks: he claimed that they stood for 'Stigma of Laud'. The following year, John Lilburne, the future leader of the republican Leveller movement, was punished for publishing anti-episcopal pamphlets by being tied to a 'cart's arse' and whipped with a knotted rope all the way to the pillory.[8]

MPs returned to Westminster in April 1640 laden with a backlog of grievances after parliament's 11-year break. Among the new intake was Oliver Cromwell, whose election for Cambridge reflected the puritans' growing strength; a development resented by courtier MPs, such as Sir Philip Warwick, who, in his memoirs, sneered at Cromwell's 'plain cloth suit, which seemed to have been made by an ill country tailor'.[9]

Charles's failure to end a revolt in Scotland caused by his attempt to curb the Presbyterian kirk had forced him to recall parliament and seek funds for a new Scottish campaign. The Crown's financial crisis grew worse when the narrowness of the judges' ruling against Hampden made 'ship money' virtually impossible to collect. The Commons' reluctance to finance the Scottish campaign confirmed the king's suspicions that his critics were collaborating with the Scots, and on 5 May he dissolved 'the Short Parliament', as it became known.

Yet, within six months Charles made a humiliating climb-down after a Spanish subsidy failed to materialize and the Scots occupied Newcastle. The MPs who assembled at Westminster on 3 November 1640 later became known as 'the Long Parliament'; a tag that testifies to the Crown's demise. Pym and his colleagues ruthlessly exploited Charles' weakness. The king's power to dissolve parliament was removed and Charles agreed to summon parliament every three years. The dreaded Star Chamber was abolished, unleashing a flood of political pamphlets, including the first reports of parliament; a breach of parliamentary privilege that MPs ignored. Archbishop Laud was impeached and Charles' high-church reforms were dropped. Williams was freed and, on returning to the Abbey, heard the incorrigible Heylyn preach against the puritans.[10]

The king's chief minister, Thomas Wentworth, Earl of Strafford, was impeached and in March 1641 was tried in Westminster Hall. The king and queen watched secretly from a close box. Charles' plea in the House of Lords to spare Strafford was rejected. As a mob rampaged through Whitehall Palace, Charles signed Strafford's death warrant: a loss of nerve for which he never forgave himself.

Many MPs regarded Charles as a closet Catholic. News of the slaughter of hundreds of Ulster Protestants left them in no mood to entrust him with control of the army in Ireland. Instead, Cromwell persuaded MPs that the Earl of Essex, who took parliament's side, should command the Irish force. Hampden said of Cromwell: 'That sloven whom you see before you hath no ornament in his speech; that sloven, I say, if we should ever come to a breach with the king (which God forbid!) – in such a case, I say, that sloven will be the greatest man in England'.[11]

In the mounting crisis, Pym summoned London's trained bands of men to guard parliament. The tension increased on 22 November 1641, when MPs provocatively voted for the 'grand remonstrance', blaming Charles' failures on popish advisers and demanding that the king should appoint councillors whom they trusted. Public demonstrations became more violent. In December, when MPs debated the Militia Bill, effectively giving parliament control of the army, apprentice boys in Westminster Hall jostled the Lieutenant of the Tower, Colonel Lunsford.

On the 27 December, crowds picketed parliament in support of Pym's bill to remove voting rights from bishops in the Lords. The protestors prevented bishops and Catholic peers from entering parliament; and jostled Dean Williams (who was also Bishop of Lincoln and Archbishop of York elect), who had his clothes torn and needed protection to return to the deanery. Lilburne was wounded by musket fire in New Palace Yard while protesting against the bishops with sword in hand. In the melee, David Hide, a disbanded army officer, drew his sword and said he would 'cut the throat of those round-headed dogs that bawled against bishops'. The origin of the term, 'roundhead', has also been attributed to Henrietta Maria's query about Pym at Strafford's trial when she asked who the round-headed man was. Whatever the origins, 'roundhead', referring to the cropped hair worn by some puritans, and 'cavalier' (from the Spanish, *caballero*), implying catholicism and foreignness, became terms of abuse.[12]

On 3 January 1642, as rowdiness and rumours swirled round Westminster Palace, the Attorney-General, Sir Edward Herbert, on the orders of the king, made a statement in the Lords accusing five MPs – Pym, Hampden, Sir Arthur Hesilrige, Denzil Holles and William Strode – and a peer, Viscount Mandeville (Edward Montagu, later Earl of Manchester), of high treason. However, Charles' plan immediately went awry. Baron Digby was supposed to follow the statement by demanding the immediate arrest of those accused, but he panicked and stayed silent. In the Commons, news that the king's men were sealing the trunks, doors, and papers of the five named members provoked protests and led MPs to delay their response to the king's demand to hand them over.

Charles almost lost his nerve, but, steeled by the queen's contemptuous outburst against him, he made a fateful mistake. The next afternoon, 4 January 1642, as the five named MPs sat in the Commons' Chamber, Charles left Whitehall for St Stephen's 'with his pensioners [yeomen guards], and followed by about two hundred courtiers, and soldiers of fortune, most of them armed with swords and pistols'. The five MPs had been tipped off and, when they learned of the king's approach, had fled. Incredibly, Charles had failed to guard the river and they escaped by boat.[13]

Shortly before 3 o'clock, the king led his troops through Westminster Hall to its south-east corner and up the stairs to the members' lobby. As the Commons Journal recorded the following day: 'a great Multitude of Men, armed in a warlike Manner with Halberds, Swords, and Pistols [who] came up to the very Door of this House, and placed themselves there, and in other Places and Passages near to the House, to the great Terror and Disturbance of the Members thereof'. The king, accompanied by his nephew, Charles Lewis, Elector Palatine of the Rhine, entered the Chamber, leaving the door open so that MPs could see his troops outside 'making much of their pistols'.[14]

Members stood and bowed as the king removed his hat. He then walked towards the Speaker's chair: 'Mr Speaker, I must for a time make bold with your chair'. Speaker Lenthall made way for him. Charles asked, 'Is Mr Pym here?' but there was no response. When he asked the Speaker if the five named members were present, Lenthall, showing exceptional courage, knelt and replied: 'May it please your majesty, I have neither eyes to see, nor tongue to speak in this place but as the House is pleased to direct me, whose servant I am here; and humbly beg your majesty's pardon that I cannot give any other answer than this to what your majesty is pleased to demand of me'. Charles surveyed the benches 'a pretty while', before declaring ruefully that, 'all my birds have flown'. He then left the chair and walked out, barely controlling his anger, amid cries of 'Privilege! Privilege!'[15]

The next day, Charles went to the Guildhall to demand the surrender of the five members, but he was mobbed in the streets with cries of 'privileges of Parliament!' At Whitehall, he could not leave his private apartments without hearing the angry, jeering crowds outside. On 10 January 1642, the king left Westminster for the safety of Windsor.

The day after Charles' inglorious exit, the five fugitive MPs returned by barge and were greeted as heroes. 'King Pym' ruled, as parliament asserted its supremacy over a runaway monarch. In Kent, the hangman's burning of a royalist petition provoked Richard Lovelace, a courtier, poet and former officer in Charles' army, to march on London with several hundred followers to present their royalist petition to parliament. Lovelace's defiance earned him 'seven weeks' custody' in Westminster's Gatehouse prison, near the Abbey. There he supposedly wrote *To*

Althea from Prison, that begins, 'Stone walls do not a prison make / Nor iron bars a cage'.

After Charles' flight Whitehall Palace was compared with 'the decay'd buildings of ruin'd Troy', in a pamphlet entitled, *A deep sigh breath'd through the lodgings at Whitehall*. There was 'no racket nor balling in the Tenis Court, no throng nor rumbling of Coaches before the Court Gates' at Whitehall. In 1643, a gun platform was built by the Banqueting House and Holbein Gate to defend Westminster from the royalists.[16]

As England descended into civil war parliament began purging Westminster. Sir Robert Harley's Commons committee for the Demolition of Monuments of Superstition and Idolatry chalked up many victims, notably Edward I's Eleanor Cross at Charing. The chapel in Whitehall Palace, and St Margaret's Church, were stripped of the brass on their monuments and tombs; paintings were defaced or removed; screens torn down; stained glass smashed, and walls plastered. The Abbey's biggest loss was the destruction of Torrigiano's renaissance high altar in Henry VII's chapel. The altar's copper screen and other metal work in the chapel, were broken up, or melted down; ceremonial copes worn by the dean and canons were sold; college plate was melted down; and tapestries depicting the history of Edward the Confessor were moved to parliament.[17]

Royalists suspected that soldiers billeted at the Abbey burned the altar rails, destroyed the organ, pawned the pipes for ale and sat round the communion table eating, drinking, singing and smoking. According to one story, two MPs who made an inventory of the royal regalia in the Abbey's Chamber of the Pyx could not resist putting them on and fooling about. Although the source of this accusation was Heylyn, the regalia were certainly shown no respect when they were later broken up and sold by Oliver Cromwell's regime. After the Restoration, the three swords of Temporal Justice, Spiritual Justice and Mercy were recovered. The only other surviving items are the twelfth-century gold anointing spoon, and the Black Prince's Ruby worn by Henry V at Agincourt. This ruby, now set in the Imperial State crown, symbolizes royal continuity.[18]

Pym's death in late 1643, at the age of 59, robbed parliament of its leading figure; but Oliver Cromwell, then in his mid-40s, steadily took Pym's place. In stature, Cromwell 'was of a good size'. In the Commons he spoke with 'his sword struck close to his side, his countenance swollen and reddish, his voice sharp and untenable, and his eloquence full of fervour'. His genius lay in combining political skill with military prowess. He was instrumental in passing the self-denying ordinance that banned MPs and peers from commanding troops – Cromwell being one of the exceptions – and created a New Model Army. Cromwell won a crushing victory at Naseby in June 1645. The following year, Charles surrendered.[19]

Cromwell emerged as the leader of the army because he championed it in parliament and held it together in late 1647 when the Levellers, led by Lilburne, won support and mutiny threatened. The revolutionary moment came in 1648 when Charles' escape to the Isle of Wight prompted uprisings. This 'second civil war' was ruthlessly curtailed by the army; but the episode convinced Cromwell that peace depended on removing the king. Abdication seemed to be the preferred option; but Cromwell was determined to settle the matter once and for all, believing that he was acting according to God's will, discerned by reading the Bible.

In December 1648 about 7,000 troops occupied Westminster, replacing the city's volunteers who had guarded parliament. Cromwell's son-in-law, Henry Ireton, was among half-a-dozen officers and MPs, including Speaker Lenthall, who drew up a list of about 80 to 90 critics. On the 6th, Colonel Pride, a brewer by trade, put a guard round the Commons and stood on the stairs leading to the Commons' entrance, blocking entry to members on the army's list. 'Pride's purge' created the 'Rump Parliament', effectively under army control.[20]

England's military coup sent political shockwaves across Europe. Cromwell feared the risk of a counter-revolution, and Charles' refusal to abdicate made a trial inevitable. When the Lords rejected the ordinance for the trial, MPs voted to abolish the upper house. The Commons set up a High Court of Justice, comprising 135 named commissioners, to try the king for having traitorously levied war 'against the present parliament and the people there represented'.[21]

The commissioners first met in the Painted Chamber on 8 January 1649 to prepare for the trial, but barely half of them ever turned up. The next day in Westminster Hall, the usual hubbub of shoppers and traders was interrupted by loud drums and the blast of six trumpeters as the Serjeant at Arms rode into the hall carrying the mace, escorted by two troops of horse, for the proclamation of the king's trial for high treason.[22]

Charles' trial was held at the southern end of the Great Hall: the spot where the king was tried is marked by a plaque in the stone steps that now occupy the area. The court was sited close to the passageways along which the king was led to and from court under close guard, and was separated from the public by a high wooden partition and railing across the hall, although galleries on either side of the court were open to the public. The presiding judge, John Bradshaw, was said to have worn a beaver hat lined with steel plates in order to avoid assassination. Sharpshooters were posted outside on the leads in case of an attempted rescue of the king.[23]

On the ice-cold morning of Monday 20 January 1649, Charles was carried across the park from St James's to Whitehall Palace in a sedan chair, guarded by foot soldiers. From Whitehall a covered barge brought him upstream to the landing stage of the late Sir Robert Cotton, in whose four-storey house within the Palace precincts the king stayed while being tried. The trial began at about 2 p.m. The commissioners, including Cromwell and Ireton, took their place on tiered benches, covered in red baize, at the southern end of the Hall. Bradshaw sat in a raised chair at a desk in the front row.

The king was escorted into the Hall under guard and walked to the red velvet chair in the dock. His tall black hat, cloak and clothes served to highlight his blue ribbon and George medal, and the silver star of the Garter. Close by sat the three prosecuting lawyers. When the senior counsel, Cooke, prepared to read the charge, Charles asked him to stop, tapping him on the arm with his silver cane; but the top fell off and he had to pick it up himself. At Bradshaw's direction, Cooke recited the charge: the king had 'traitorously and maliciously levied war against the present parliament and people therein represented', and was 'a tyrant, traitor and murderer, and a public and implacable enemy to the Commonwealth of England'.[24]

In a strong voice, untroubled by his usual speech impediment, Charles asked, 'I would know by what power I am called hither', dismissing the Commons' right to establish the court and challenging the judges' authority to try their lawful king. When Bradshaw adjourned the hearing, the king left, to cries from the soldiers of 'Justice! Justice!' Some spectators joined in, but others shouted: 'God save the King'. Reports of the proceedings were printed in six regular, licensed newspapers and the public appetite was such that three new titles appeared. The king's words were not censored, and pamphlets circulating in the capital attacked his trial.

Before the hearing resumed on Monday 22nd, the commissioners agreed that if Charles refused to answer the charge his silence would be taken as a plea of guilty. When the king later persistently disputed the court's legality, Bradshaw called him a 'delinquent', lost his temper and threatened that the next session would be the last one. The continued deadlock on Tuesday 23rd prompted the commissioners to adjourn to the Painted Chamber where they heard witnesses against the king.

On the afternoon of Saturday 27th, the commissioners returned to the Hall to pass sentence. Bradshaw, clothed in red for this solemn and unique occasion, prevented Charles from making a speech, but when the judge claimed that the charge had been brought 'in the name of the people of England', a woman's voice called out from the gallery: 'Not half, not a quarter of the people of England. Oliver Cromwell is a traitor'. Lady Fairfax, wife of parliament's brilliant commander, was voicing her husband's displeasure at the trial.

Finally, a clerk read out the sentence of 'death by the severinge of his head from his body'. The commissioners then stood up to indicate their agreement, and Charles left the court to another chorus from the soldiers: 'Execution! Justice! Execution!

The king's death warrant was signed by fewer than half of the commissioners. Most of the 59 commissioners who signed the document probably did so willingly; but Cromwell had to persuade about 20 of them to sign, allegedly cajoling Henry Marten by scrawling ink on his cheek, and by entering the Commons Chamber on Monday 29th, demanding signatures from any commissioners who had slipped past him. The warrant was issued later that day and ordered three colonels – Hacker, Hunks and Phayre – to ensure that the king was beheaded the next day: 'In the open streete before Whitehall'.[25]

Security was the overriding concern in selecting the site outside the Banqueting House for the king's execution. This location was much easier to guard than Tower Hill or Tyburn where executions were traditionally held. Whitehall Palace also served as the army's headquarters. At this late stage, the execution was still opposed at the highest level of the army. Fairfax summoned a council of war on Monday 29th, but failed to persuade his fellow officers to postpone the beheading. His friends urged him to rescue the king the next day, assuring him of the support of 20,000 men, but Fairfax was not prepared to imperil the lives of others.

While the scaffold was being erected in Whitehall, the king was held at St James's Palace. The next day, Charles rose before dawn and asked his aide, Thomas Herbert, for two shirts as he wanted to avoid shivering in the bitter cold and seeming afraid. At about ten o'clock on Tuesday 30 January, a dull, freezing morning, the king emerged from St James's Palace wearing a long black coat over grey stockings and, it is said, a rich red silk waistcoat.

An escort of foot soldiers immediately gathered round Charles and his attendants: Colonel Tomlinson, in charge of the guard, William Juxon, the Bishop of London, and Herbert. The king set a brisk pace and, beneath a grey sky, the procession marched, with drums beating, through the bare, frosty park. Charles entered Whitehall for the last time by the open, wooden staircase that led from the park between the Tiltyard and a group of houses and galleries in the area known as The Cockpit (behind present-day Number 10 Downing Street). As Charles passed, the Earl of Pembroke, an old courtier, watched from his window with the Earl of Salisbury. Neither earl was later inclined to let sentiment temper ambition: after the king's execution, they accepted a republican regime, and when the Lords was abolished they sought election to the Commons.

As Charles was escorted along the Tiltyard Gallery, he passed paintings of his father and mother; portraits by Van Dyck; the allegory of Peace and War painted for him by Rubens; and the full-length portrait of the emperor Charles V by Titian, that he had brought back from Spain. Crossing the street by Holbein Gate and walking along the Privy Gallery, he may have glimpsed through the windows the black-draped scaffold against the front of the Banqueting House and the troops and crowd in the street below. At about 10.30 a.m., he was taken to a room on the south side of the Privy Gallery, overlooking the garden, with Westminster Hall and the Abbey beyond.

Although the scaffold was ready, the king had to endure a delay of several hours while a bill was rushed through the Commons forbidding anyone being proclaimed king after Charles' execution. Close by, Fairfax made a last attempt to persuade senior officers to stop the execution, Whether Fairfax met Cromwell is not known; but it was too late. By midday, 200 cavalry stood guard in King Street and soldiers packed neighbouring streets.

Shortly before 2 p.m., the Commons passed the bill forbidding anyone succeeding Charles. When the final knock on the door came, Charles, accompanied by Juxon, followed Colonel Hacker. All the way, they walked between two lines of soldiers, standing shoulder to shoulder. Behind the soldiers, crowds of people struggled to catch a glimpse of the monarch, some calling out prayers or blessings. The most poignant moment came when Charles was led through the Banqueting House and the weak winter light filtered through the partly boarded and bricked up windows, rendering the Rubens' ceiling barely visible.

Charles walked up the stair tower at the building's northern end, and stepped through a temporary doorway made in a window. The crowds, packed in the street below and at any window, balcony or roof that afforded a view, suddenly saw the small figure of the king emerge onto the scaffold, accompanied by Bishop Juxon. Waiting on the black-draped platform were Colonels Tomlinson and Hacker; several soldiers on guard; and short-hand writers with note books and ink horns. The executioner and his assistant each wore a mask, wig and false beard, anxious to avoid being identified as regicides. The historian C. V. Wedgwood believes that the king was beheaded by the official executioner, Richard Brandon, assisted by a soldier. The chains and manacles attached to the scaffold in case the king tried to resist were not needed.

As the proximity of the mounted troops drawn up beneath the scaffold prevented the king's last words carrying to the crowds below, he addressed those gathered on the platform, glancing as he spoke at notes taken from his pocket. He saw his execution as atonement for his sacrifice of Strafford: 'An unjust sentence that I suffered to take effect, is punished now by an unjust sentence on me'. Defending monarchical rule against republicanism, he declared: 'I am the Martyr of the people'.

Charles told the executioner that after a brief prayer, he would signal when he was ready. With Juxon's help, he pushed his hair beneath a white satin cap, took off his George (the Garter medal insignia) and handed it to the bishop, saying cryptically: 'Remember'. He stood for a moment, praying silently with his hands and eyes raised to Heaven, then removed his cloak and lay down, putting his neck on the block. As the executioner made sure that there was no loose hair to impede the blow of the axe, Charles said: 'stay for the sign'.

Everyone fell silent. Moments later, the king stretched out his hands; the executioner raised his axe. The Archbishop of Armagh James Ussher watching from Wallingford House (where Admiralty House now stands) fainted at the sight. Then, with a single blow, the king's head was severed. At this instant, as an eye-witness, Patrick Henry, recalled, 'there was such a grone by the thousands then present, as I never heard before and desire I may never hear again'. Henry was, at the time, a seventeen-year-old Oxford student and Old Boy of Westminster School, where prayers were said publicly for the king before the execution.

Charles' severed head was immediately held high as proof of his death. Within half an hour, the crowds had been dispersed by the cavalry, but not before some soldiers and spectators had dipped their handkerchiefs in the king's blood, scraped blood-stained earth from beneath the scaffold and torn pieces off the blood-soaked drape. The growth of a popular cult to a martyred king was the parliamentarians' worst fear; and so, instead of burying Charles at Westminster Abbey, a royal shrine and magnet for pilgrims and political demonstrators, his remains were taken away. In 1813 all doubt about the precise location of his final resting place was ended when workmen discovered his coffin in Henry VIII's vault, in St George's Chapel, Windsor.

The parliamentarians censored any depiction in England of the king's execution, but the shock felt across Europe created a foreign market for images of the beheading. At Whitehall, le Sueur's bronze equestrian statue of the king was taken from the Palace garden and sold to a brazier called Rivers in Seven Dials for melting down. However, Rivers was 'either a royalist or a sly boots' and buried it; while doing a brisk trade in brass-handled cutlery passed off as mementoes. After the Restoration, the statue was unearthed and, in 1674, was set up in its present position at the top of Whitehall, where it is honoured during the annual commemoration of Charles' execution.[26]

Each year, on the Sunday nearest to 30 January, the 'King's Army' of the English Civil War society commemorates the anniversary of Charles I's execution by re-tracing his final route from St James's Palace, through Horse Guards to the Banqueting House. The re-enactors lay a wreath at the site of the scaffold in Whitehall, where the king was beheaded; hold a memorial service, and present their awards and commissions to their officers. Afterwards, they march to the top of Whitehall, past the bronze equestrian statue of Charles, where a wreath has already been laid, and finally return along the Mall to St James's.

The horror of Charles I's public beheading resonates more than 360 years later, but it is difficult to grasp the sheer disbelief felt at the time. As God's chosen ruler, the monarch was the inviolable source of all political authority; but the swing of an axe in Whitehall demolished the divine right of kings and heralded modern politics.

22 REPUBLICANS AND RESTORERS

The chief adversaries in the clash between Crown and Parliament defiantly face one another outside the Houses of Parliament. Charles I's bust gazes from its niche on the wall of St Margaret's church, across the busy street towards a small green alongside Westminster Hall, where Cromwell's bronze statue glares back. Cromwell is depicted in the military garb of leather tunic and thigh boots with spurs; his right hand on his sword and his left holding a bible.

Cromwell's statue was commissioned in 1895, after decades of controversy, by Lord Rosebery, the prime minister, over tea with the sculptor, Hamo Thornycoft, at Number 10. The ensuing row over erecting a monument to a dictator, regicide and butcher of the Irish contributed to the fall of Rosebery's government. The statue's low-lying site prompted Lord Salisbury, the Conservative leader, to quip that a ditch was the perfect place for it. Yet, for many others Cromwell personifies English radicalism. Isaac Foot, a Liberal politician, founded the Cromwell Association in 1937, and passed his enthusiasm to his son, Michael; Labour's leader in the 1980s.[1]

Cromwell led England on a voyage into the unknown. He had acted on what he believed was God's will when deposing Charles I, but divine guidance was less forthcoming on how to govern without a king. Replacing the royal insignia on coats of arms, coins, maces and seals, and designating England a Commonwealth instead of a kingdom, was relatively straightforward; the task of creating workable political institutions was the devil's own job.

Cromwell's immediate priority in 1649 was survival. A new, 41-man, council of state wielded executive power; but the army's ranks were radicalized by lack of pay and the shelving of plans for a new parliament elected on a wider franchise. Cromwell crushed the Levellers' mutiny and was then away from Westminster for more than two years, eliminating resistance in Ireland and Scotland; but after his victory at Worcester in September 1651, and the resultant flight of Prince Charles, the heir to the throne, Cromwell received a hero's welcome. Some 4,000 defeated royalists were brought to a prison camp on Tothill Fields, south of the Abbey, but holding them on marshy ground was disastrous: about 1,200 died, and survivors were sold as slaves to merchants trading with Africa.

The republican victory inspired John Milton, the poet and polemicist, to eulogize Cromwell as 'our chief of men.' Milton is easily Westminster's most eloquent spin doctor. He was appointed 'Latin secretary' (Latin was diplomacy's *lingua franca*) in 1649, having defended the king's execution in his tract, *Tenure of Kings and Magistrates*. Milton and his family were provided with an apartment at the Scotland Yard and were allowed to choose hangings from the Palace when Charles I's art treasures were sold. But in 1652 after the loss of his sight and his wife's death, Milton was evicted and for some years lived by St James's Park in Petty France, where he began dictating *Paradise Lost*.[2]

During a chance meeting in St James's Park in November 1652, Cromwell and Bulstrode Whitelocke, a member of the council and MP, were bemoaning the corruption and idleness of the Rump Parliament, when Cromwell wondered aloud: 'what if a man should take upon him to be king?' Cromwell's patience with the Rump snapped the following April when MPs ignored his demand to dissolve parliament. When news of their defiance reached Cromwell at his lodgings in The Cockpit, at the rear of present-day Number 10 Downing Street, he arranged for troops to follow him to the Commons.[3]

Cromwell listened to the debate with mounting fury until the Rump was about to vote, and then launched a withering assault. Telling MPs that they had 'grown intolerably odious to the whole nation', he declared: 'You have sat here too long for any good you have been doing, Depart, I say, and let us have done with you. In the name of God, go!' When an MP dared to object, an enraged Cromwell called in the troops, and about 40 musketeers rushed into the Chamber of the House of Commons. Moving to the table of the House, Cromwell ordered that the Commons mace, the symbol of its authority, be taken away, asking: 'What shall we do with this bauble?' Finally, he 'ordered the guard to see the House clear'd of all the members', seized the records of the House, 'and having commanded the doors to be locked up, went away to Whitehall'.[4]

Cromwell's dictatorial action and disrespect for 'this bauble' was subsequently to enshrine the Mace's revered status as the symbol of the Commons' authority. Maces had originally been used as weapons. The bodyguard of Serjeants at Arms formed by Edward I in 1279 had the royal arms stamped on their maces as proof that they had royal authority. In 1415, MPs successfully petitioned Henry V to appoint Nicholas Maudit as the first Serjeant at Arms specifically designated to the Commons; and over time, the Serjeant's Mace became the symbol of authority handed down by the monarch to the Commons: without the Mace, the Commons has no authority. The mace that Cromwell ordered to be removed was a replacement for one that he had ordered to be destroyed in 1649. It was this substitute, known as Maundy's 'bauble' after its maker Thomas Maundy that Cromwell ordered to be taken away.

Cromwell replaced the Rump Parliament with 140 nominated members in a new constituent assembly. When the assembly moved to the Commons Chamber and called itself a parliament, critics lampooned it as 'the Barebones Parliament', after one of its members, a leather seller and preacher, who gloried in the name of Praisegod Barbon. However, the Barebones, or Nominated Parliament, lasted only five months before its moderates voted for dissolution, and a troop of musketeers again cleared parliament.

Cromwell's response was to become king in all but name. In December 1653, he was invested in Westminster Hall as Lord Protector for life, with the power to prorogue and dissolve parliament. The protectorate's first parliament met in September 1654, but Cromwell dissolved it the following January when MPs tried to limit his power over the militia. State control of the press followed in 1655, when newspapers were banned with the exception of the state-controlled *Mercurius Politicus* and *Public Intelligencer*.

Cromwell ascended to full kingly power two years later, buoyed on a wave of public fear after a 'wicked design to take away the Lord Protector's life, and to fire Whitehall'. John Thurloe, secretary of state, news controller and spymaster, reported that two men had been arrested in Whitehall Palace after planting a bomb 'of combustible stuff' under a seat in the chapel. Had the bomb ignited, Cromwell and most others inside the palace would have been blown up or burned alive. The two suspects, Miles Sindercombe and John Cecil, were arrested the next day.[5]

The mastermind was Edward Sexby – sometime London apprentice, Cromwellian soldier, radical campaigner, military governor, cashiered army captain, and secret agent – who believed that the republic could only be restored by killing Cromwell. Sexby based himself abroad, mixed with other émigré plotters, and recruited Sindercombe, another radical ex-soldier. Sindercombe in turn brought in Cecil, a former trooper, and two other accomplices. The bomb plot was an act of desperation, as Sindercombe had previously tried to shoot Cromwell on at least four occasions. He avoided a traitor's death by poisoning himself in the Tower. Sexby was later captured while secretly visiting England and died in the Tower, but not before publishing *Killing Noe Murder*, in which Cromwell was accused of being as tyrannical as Caligula and Nero.[6]

A coronation in all but name in June 1657 ended England's republican experiment. The ancient Coronation Chair, complete with the Stone of Destiny, was taken from Westminster Abbey for the only time in its history and brought to Westminster Hall for Cromwell's second investiture as Lord Protector. Cromwell arrived by river, alighting at Westminster stairs. The procession into the hall mimicked a coronation, and the Speaker, Sir Thomas Widdrington, who presided, used language similar to the archbishop's. Sir Thomas helped Cromwell don a mock-royal purple robe, girded him with sword, and handed him bible and sceptre, before administering a monarch's traditional coronation oath. Finally,

Cromwell sat in the Coronation Chair, sceptre in hand, to the accompaniment of trumpet fanfares, heralds' proclamations of obedience and cries of 'God save the Lord Protector!'[7]

On Cromwell's death 15 months later, his body was buried in Henry VII's Chapel, as befitted 'royalty'. However, the placing of a crown on the head of Cromwell's effigy when it was later carried through the streets provoked fury.[8] Cromwell's son Richard succeeded as Lord Protector, but the generals ignored him and recalled the Rump Parliament. The younger Cromwell was left powerless inside Whitehall Palace and resigned in May 1659.

Into this political vacuum stepped General George Monck, who had served in the royalist, parliamentary and Commonwealth armies. Monck was 'a very dull man'. according to Samuel Pepys, a 27-year-old clerk at the Exchequer, but he acted decisively to prevent a coup by army radicals, leading his troops south from Coldstream and occupying Westminster in February 1660. The Rump was held in such contempt that, as Pepys noted: 'Boys, do now shout "kiss my parliament" instead of "kiss my arse"'. In May, a newly elected Convention Parliament voted to restore the Stuart monarchy. Monck was the first man to greet Charles when he landed at Dover and was rewarded with the Garter and the dukedom of Albemarle. His 'Coldstreamers' were the only Commonwealth regiment to survive the Restoration, and became the Coldstream Guards.[9]

Oliver Cromwell's effigy was hung from a Whitehall window by a mob and, on Charles II's return, was put on a post and burned. After the Restoration Cromwell's body and those of other regicides were disinterred from the Abbey, hanged at Tyburn and buried in a pit: although there is some debate about the identities of the corpses. Their decapitated skulls were impaled on pikes and displayed above the south end of Westminster Hall, where Charles I had been tried. The skull said to have been Cromwell's remained there for nearly 20 years until it was blown down in a storm – to the horror of an unfortunate sentry below – only yards from where Cromwell's statue now stands.[10]

On 29 May 1660, Charles II's 29th birthday, the king returned to Westminster, escorted by 'above 20,000 horse and foote, brandishing their swords and shouting with unexpressable joy'. Charles was a charismatic, handsome man, more than six feet tall, and soon adopted the shoulder-length wig of curled hair that became a trademark of Restoration England. After arriving at Whitehall Palace at about seven o'clock, he was greeted by senior peers and MPs. At Westminster Abbey, bishops and clergy gathered in King Henry VII's Chapel and sang the *Te Deum* in gratitude for Charles's safe delivery.[11]

Charles's coronation was held on St George's Day, 1661. The crown jewels and regalia at his ceremony were replacements for those destroyed in 1649. They cost £31,000, a massive sum in those days, and continue in use to this day. Pepys watched the procession from a scaffold inside the north end of the Abbey, but could not see the ceremony. Although he heard the great shout of approval when Charles was crowned, he left before the end as he had to relieve himself having waited inside the Abbey since four o'clock in the morning. However, Pepys enjoyed the spectacle of the coronation feast, complete with the Champion's appearance and, refreshed by food from the peers' table, enjoyed ogling the ladies and listening to the music.[12]

Pepys and his wife lived in Axe Yard, a cul-de-sac of about 25 houses off King Street, by the Axe tavern, immediately south of present-day Downing Street. It was only a brief walk across the main street to Whitehall Palace, where Pepys attended official and ministerial meetings and picked up backstairs gossip from courtiers and staff, especially William Chiffinch, who succeeded his older brother Tom as the king's personal aide in 1666. Pepys frequently walked the short distance to New Palace Yard and Westminster Hall, where he picked up news and women.[13]

Politics, gossip and scandal were keenly debated in Miles's coffee house, beneath the sign of a Turk's Head in New Palace Yard; and Man's, near Charing Cross. Both coffee houses thrived by quenching the thirst for the newly fashionable drinks from the Americas and Asia, and satisfying the appetite for news in the days before regular deliveries of news-sheets and letters. Westminster's coffee house gossips also received a regular, albeit unofficial flow, of inside information about the court, some of it probably from Pepys. Charles's chief minister, Edward Hyde, the Earl of Clarendon, condemned the coffee houses, 'with their calumnies and scandals', but attempts to close them down in 1666 and 1675 failed.[14]

By 1660, Pepys was clerk to George Downing, an ambitious teller of the exchequer in his mid-thirties. Downing, the nephew of John Winthrop, one of the founders of Massachusetts, had been educated at Harvard College and, after returning to England, had married well and served as a Cromwellian soldier, spy and MP. He earned a knighthood by quickly changing sides when the monarchy was restored. His success in extraditing three regicides from Europe brought him a baronetcy, but blackened his reputation as he had been chaplain in the regiment of one of the victims, John Okey. Downing went on to transform the Exchequer into a modern Treasury.[15]

Downing had begun acquiring property to the west of Whitehall Palace during the Commonwealth. In February 1664 his claim to the lease on a site immediately north of Axe Yard was granted. The land was occupied by the Cockpit lodgings and Hampden House, a residence built by Elizabeth Hampden on the site of the old Axe brewery and an inn known as 'Le Pecocke.' She had inherited the lease from her aunt, the widow of Sir Thomas Knyvet: the man who had surprised Guy Fawkes beneath the House of Lords in 1605. The Hampden family delayed demolition of this house, but in 1682 Downing was able to re-develop the site and built 15 houses in a new cul-de-sac. It became known as Downing Street at the end adjoining King Street, and as Downing Square, by the current site of Numbers 10 and 11.[16]

Charles II stayed at Whitehall for the first two years of his reign and was often seen feeding the fowl or walking his dogs in St James's Park. The park was being landscaped, and Pepys watched the work there in October 1660 after dinner at the Leg Tavern in King Street. A couple of days later at Charing Cross, Pepys saw the regicide Major-General Harrison hanged, drawn and quartered. The following Sunday 14th, Pepys visited Whitehall chapel where he noticed the king laugh at a badly-sung anthem, and observed Charles's younger brother, James, Duke of York, flirting with Barbara Palmer, who was already expecting her first child by Charles.[17]

Barbara was an attractive 19-year-old with dark hair and blue eyes, who was said to have slept with the king on his first night at Whitehall Palace. She was born Barbara Villiers, a cousin of the Duke of Buckingham. At the age of 15 she was the Earl of Chesterfield's mistress and later married a lawyer, Roger Palmer. By 1660, the Palmers were living in King Street in a house that backed on to the Palace orchard. Barbara bore Charles a child every year between 1661 and 1665. As the first publicly accepted king's mistress since medieval times, she fought to win quasi-royal status for her sons. Charles elevated her husband to an earldom in late 1661, making her the Countess of Castlemaine (later, the Duchess of Cleveland) and guaranteeing her male offspring noble rank. Barbara's first son, Charles, was created Duke of Southampton in 1675, following the precedent of the king's first recognized bastard son, James, born to Lucy Walter in 1649, who had become Duke of Monmouth in 1663.[18]

Castlemaine enticed Charles with the 15-year-old Frances Stuart, the queen's maid-of honour. Pepys regarded 'La Belle Stuart' as the greatest beauty he ever saw. Charles became infatuated with Frances but was only allowed to fondle her. To his 'great fury' she eloped in 1667 with Charles Stuart, Duke of Richmond and Lennox. That summer, Frances was portrayed as Britannia on medals commemorating the end of the second Anglo-Dutch war, but the following year she caught smallpox and was scarred. Her beauty was re-captured after her death in the effigy that she ordered as her memorial and which survives in the Abbey museum, dressed in her coronation robes of 1701. Alongside perches her companion of 40 years, a small grey African parrot, reputedly the oldest stuffed bird in England.[19]

Charles's love of the theatre and his roving eye led to affairs with at least two actresses, Moll Davis and Nell Gwyn. A glimpse of Charles's complicated love life is provided by John Evelyn. After a visit to Whitehall in March 1671, he accompanied the king to St James's Park and entered the royal garden between what is now the Mall and the backs of the houses in Pall Mall where Nell Gwyn lived. Evelyn witnessed 'a very familiar discourse' between the king and 'Mrs Nellie', as she looked out of her garden on a terrace and Charles stood below on 'the greene Walke'. Evelyn's displeasure grew as Charles then walked to the duchess of Cleveland's, 'another Lady of Pleasure and curse of our nation'.[20]

By 1671, Charles's main mistress at court was Louise de Kéroualle, the daughter of a Breton count, who had served in the household of Charles's sister and become a maid of honour to the queen. In 1673, Louise became Duchess of Portsmouth. Her quarters in Whitehall palace were constantly enlarged and improved until they finally comprised some 40 lavishly decorated rooms. In the closing years of the reign, Louise often deputized for Charles while he stayed away from Whitehall.[21]

Charles's fondness for women was matched by his susceptibility to new fashions and louche cronies. When word spread in November 1663 that the king and his brother, James, intended to wear 'perriwigs'. Pepys immediately adopted the new look and was ribbed by James on his next visit to Whitehall. Extravagant wigs epitomized the Restoration court, where nothing was done by halves. Restoration wits such as the Duke of Buckingham, the Earls of Bristol, Dorset and Rochester, Sir Charles Berkeley (later the Earl of Falmouth) and Sir Charles Sedley, cut their teeth in the King's Chamber, where they opportunistically ridiculed their rivals. Their main target was Clarendon, for being both chief minister and a stuffy lawyer.[22]

Clarendon was at the peak of his power in the early years of Charles' reign, especially after the king's brother, James, married his daughter Anne Hyde, who was pregnant by him, in October 1660. Clarendon is credited with the 'Clarendon Code' – principally the Corporation and Uniformity Acts – that restored the Anglican supremacy by barring Catholics and Protestant non-conformists from municipal office and universities. Although he gave his name to these measures, he wanted to moderate them but was prevented by the staunchly Anglican, 'Cavalier Parliament', elected in 1661.

Clarendon survived efforts to undermine him by rivals egged on by Castlemaine, who remarked that she hoped to see his head on a stake outside Westminster, but he was finally undone by a series of disasters: the plague in 1665–7, the Great Fire of London in 1666, agricultural depression, corruption at court and naval humiliation by the Dutch in 1667. The crises left the government short of money and prompted Clarendon to suggest a forced loan; but raising the spectre of ship money was fatal. Charles was easily persuaded to dismiss him, having long resented him as an interfering busybody. When Clarendon left Whitehall Palace, he suffered the indignity of seeing Castlemaine with Lord Arlington, his strongest rival, and Baptist May, keeper of the King's Privy Purse, looking 'out of her open window with great gaiety and triumph.'[23]

Clarendon's sacking marked a sea-change at Westminster. The king had accepted the argument of Arlington and his allies that unless Clarendon went, parliament would be unmanageable. Clarendon's failure led to the formation of a more effective court party by Arlington and Thomas Clifford, later Lord Clifford. An embryonic Cabinet, together with nascent political parties, began to emerge as politicians sought a *modus operandi*.[24]

The term 'cabanett councell' had been coined by Francis Bacon during James I's reign to describe an inner group among the king's advisers. Although Charles

I had appointed a small committee, or 'cabinet council', of key privy councillors to deal with important matters, a more formal Cabinet Council was finally established during the 1660s and 1670s. Big decisions were made by the king with a small inner group; government business was processed by the Privy Council; and the busy Treasury and Admiralty were run by boards of commissioners. Membership of the inner circle depended 'on a willingness to serve the Crown and a capacity to be of service'. The capacity to be of service meant building up the court party largely through patronage, sinecures and family influence.

As big decisions invariably involved foreign policy, the king's inner group comprised the Privy Council's Foreign Committee, and included major office-holders who had to be consulted or at least informed: the Lord Chancellor, the Lord Treasurer, both Secretaries of State, the Lord Admiral and a few other trusted courtiers. It became known as the Cabinet Council and usually met on Mondays. However, Charles II's penchant for secret dealing created cliques at court who knew more of his actions on certain matters than some members of his Cabinet Council.[25]

The most notorious of Charles's cliques was the group of five ministers who signed the Treaty of Dover with Louis XIV of France in 1670, and whose initials happened to spell 'cabal': Clifford, the Lord Treasurer; Arlington; the Duke of Buckingham; Lord Ashley (the future Earl of Shaftesbury), the Chancellor of the Exchequer; and the Earl of Lauderdale, the Governor of Scotland. However, only the Catholic sympathizers, Arlington, Clifford, and the Catholic James, Duke of York, knew of a secret version, under which, in return for Louis's sending troops in the event of a revolt and the offer of a subsidy, Charles promised to convert to Catholicism and work to make England Catholic again. Any leak of the religious terms of the treaty would have caused a political explosion.[26]

Charles's motives were suspected when, in 1672, he introduced a Declaration of Indulgence that suspended the penal laws against Protestant non-conformists and Catholics. The strongly Anglican parliament forced Charles to withdraw the Declaration, and passed a Test Act that required anyone holding public office to take Anglican communion.

The Test Act's biggest scalp was the king's Catholic brother, James, Duke of York – the lawful heir to the throne – who resigned as Lord Admiral, and failed to take the Anglican sacrament at Easter 1673. The prospect of Queen Catherine's bearing an heir had all but vanished after a series of miscarriages. James's two daughters, Mary and Anne, were being raised as Protestants, but their mother's death in 1671, and James's second marriage in the autumn of 1673 to the Catholic Mary Beatrice d'Este increased the likelihood of a Catholic monarchy, as any surviving son was likely to inherit the throne.

Lord Shaftesbury, now the Lord Chancellor, became anxious at the prospect of a Catholic succession and began scheming to prevent a Catholic royal family. Using his office as Lord Chancellor to rig the parliamentary timetable, he allowed MPs time to draft an extraordinary address to Charles, urging that James's marriage not be consummated. He also revived the idea of persuading the king to divorce, and tried, together with other ministers, to persuade Charles to send James away from court. Unsurprisingly, James was furious, and in November 1673 Shaftesbury was sacked. Westminster politics was dominated by personalities and factions; but the distinction between the court party and the country party, who generally opposed Catholic toleration, the French alliance and the king's excessive power, was polarized by the debate over excluding James from the throne.

The 'exclusion crisis' began in St James's Park on the morning of 13 August 1678, as Charles took his usual walk. He was approached by an acquaintance, Sir Christopher Kirby, who warned of a 'popish plot' to assassinate him and raise a Catholic revolt. Charles headed straight back to Whitehall and alerted his chief minister, Thomas Osborne, the Earl of Danby. Danby cross-examined Kirby and his source, Israel Tonge, a rabidly anti-Catholic preacher, who, it transpired, was a willing conduit for the real source.

Tonge's informant was Titus Oates, a Catholic convert and former Anglican priest in his late twenties, whose troubled past had disposed him to peddle lies and harbour grudges. Oates swore his evidence before the Westminster magistrate, Sir Edmund Berry Godfrey, and was cross-examined by the Privy Council in the presence of a sceptical king. Encouraged by all the attention, Oates wove an intricate web of deceit and implicated Edward Coleman, James's secretary, who was known to be Whitehall's strongest supporter of a Catholic restoration. The bogus 'popish plot' induced panic and the mysterious murder of Godfrey, the magistrate, gave it credence.

Shaftesbury emerged as the senior opposition politician. Charles dissolved parliament in January 1679, but when a new parliament was elected Shaftesbury reckoned that more than 60 per cent of MPs supported his opposition. In response, the king appointed Shaftesbury to his Privy Council, but inside Whitehall Shaftesbury continued calling for James's exclusion. The Commons voted for an exclusion bill introduced by Shaftesbury's ally, William, Lord Russell; but in response Charles dissolved the first Exclusion Parliament in July 1679.

Charles's reluctance to call another parliament prompted Shaftesbury and his allies to campaign for exclusion in mass petitions and in the courts. A monster petition signed by 20,000 people in Westminster and Southwark demanded a recall of parliament, but Charles dug his heels in. When a new parliament met in October 1680, Shaftesbury called for a committee to be set up to investigate the 'popish plot' and strongly supported a new exclusion bill, although predictably it was defeated in the lords. On 23 December, he called for exclusion and urged that no taxes be voted until 'the King shall satisfie the People, that what we give is not to make us Slaves and Papists'. The second Exclusion Parliament lasted fewer than three months.[27]

Another parliament was called within a couple of months, but Charles summoned MPs and peers to Oxford, the old royalist stronghold, far away from the radical influence of London. However, the gulf between the exclusionists and the king remained unbridgeable. Shaftesbury's suggestion that Charles's eldest son, the Duke of Monmouth, should be his successor outraged Charles, and after the Commons introduced yet another Exclusion Bill, the king dissolved parliament. The third Exclusion Parliament lasted only a week and was the last occasion on which parliament met outside Westminster.

Charles could afford to do without parliament after 1681 because of a new secret financial deal with Louis XIV. Without parliament, the exclusionists lost their main platform. Shaftesbury was accused of high treason and held in the Tower for four months until the courts rejected the charge. He fled to Amsterdam and died there in 1683. The discovery in 1684 of the 'Rye House plot', an attempt to assassinate Charles and James as they returned from the Newmarket races, enabled Charles to arrest many of his exclusionist opponents, who became known as Whigs.

'Instead of Cavalier and Roundhead, now they are called Tories and Wiggs' [sic], a diarist noted in October 1681. John Dryden, the playwright, poet and Old Boy of Westminster school, satirised the new party politics in *Absalom and Achitophel*, published to coincide with Shaftesbury's trial for treason: 'Wit and fool are consequents of Whig and Tory; and every man is a knave or an ass to the contrary side'.[28]

The tit-for-tat in pejorative nicknames had a sectarian edge and reflected English fears of uprisings in Ireland and Scotland. 'Tory' was the abusive term hurled at supporters of the status quo by exclusionists. According to North, an eighteenth-century lawyer, the exclusionists suspected James of favouring Irishmen and began calling their opponents, '*Irish*, and so *wild Irish*, thence *Bogtrotters*', until 'the Word *Tory* was entertained, which signified the most despicable Savages among the Wild Irish'. As the *Oxford English Dictionary* explains: 'Tory' derives from the Irish word *toraidhe*, or *toraighe*, meaning 'pursuer'. By 1646, it is used in official reports to describe the dispossessed Irish who had become outlaws and survived by plundering and killing English settlers.

'Whig', was the equally abusive term hurled at exclusionists by supporters of the status quo. It was probably derived from 'Whiggamore', after the 'whiggamore raid' in 1648 by western Presbyterian supporters of the Scottish National Covenant who marched on Edinburgh. In 1679, in Scotland, 'The Whiggs horse and foot fell in pell, mell, upon the Dragoons', but in London the nickname was applied to exclusionists: 'After the breaking out of the popish plot severall of our scholars were tried and at length discovered to be whiggs'.[29] 'Tory' and 'Whig' began as terms of abuse, but they became the names of the two main Westminster parties.

23 FLIGHT AND FIRE

Two remnants of late seventeenth-century Whitehall are reminders of Britain's epoch-changing revolution. The large metal wind vane above the north end of the Banqueting House was hurriedly erected by blacksmiths in the autumn of 1688 for an anxious king seeking early warning of a shift in the wind that would lead to an invasion from Europe. Nearby, off Horse Guards Avenue, by the Ministry of Defence, are Queen Mary's Steps; part of a riverside extension to Whitehall Palace commissioned in 1691 by a queen who confidently looked forward to the future with her Dutch husband. In the three years between these dates, a political revolution had swept through Westminster.

The events leading to Westminster's revolution began in the bitterly cold winter of 1685. In January, John Evelyn witnessed Charles II 'sitting and toying with his concubines', while a French boy sang love songs and about 20 courtiers gambled round a large table. However, 'six days after was all in dust'. Charles died on 6 February, and was succeeded by his 51-year-old brother, James, Duke of York, who became James II of England and James VII of Scotland. Little more than a week afterwards, Evelyn lamented that James 'to the great griefe of his subjects, did now the first time go to Masse publicly'. However, James's failure to father a legitimate son after 11 years of marriage to Mary of Modena, suggested that any Catholic restoration would be short-lived, as next in line to the throne was Mary, James's Protestant elder daughter from his first marriage. She was the wife of her cousin, William, the Protestant Prince of Orange and ruler of the Dutch Republic.[1]

By May 1685, the divergence between James and his subjects was becoming clear. The new, Tory-dominated Parliament met for the state opening only days after Titus Oates, instigator of the 'popish plot', had been paraded round Westminster Hall 'with a Paper on his Head declaring his Offence' and thrown in the pillory outside, where he was pelted with eggs and rubbish. Yet, at Whitehall Palace, work began on Sir Christopher Wren's design for a new Roman Catholic chapel, symbolizing James's insensitivity.[2]

James's early dominance was bolstered by his defeat of two uprisings led by Protestant dukes. Under Monmouth's threat, James doubled the size of his standing army in England to 20,000; never to reduce it. Although Louis XIV's attack on the basic rights of nearly two million French Protestants in the autumn utterly changed the political mood, James was impervious to the impact of this 'dismal tragedy'. In his fury at MPs' refusal to support his standing army or dispense with the Test Act for Catholic officers, James prorogued Parliament. It never met again while he was in England.

The news of Mary of Modena's pregnancy in late 1687 was a political bombshell. Suddenly, a Catholic dynasty was a probability. By the following spring, William of Orange's anxious English supporters wanted to know his intentions. William's main concern was building up a coalition against the Catholic French monarch, and knowing that, at best, all he could hope from James was neutrality, he replied, according to the historian Bishop Gilbert Burnet, that, 'if he was invited by some men of the best interest ... to come and rescue the nation and the religion ... he could be ready by the end of September to come over'. William began preparing a fleet, although he did not rule out negotiations with James.

In England, the man 'in whose hands the conduct of the whole design was chiefly deposited, by the prince's [William's] own order' was Henry Sidney. As Burnet explained, Sidney had 'entered into such particular confidence with the prince', while ambassador to the Dutch Republic, that William trusted him implicitly. During 1688, Sidney approached leading members of the English estab-lishment, including Danby, the Earl of Devonshire, and also Henry Compton, Bishop of London. Among his most crucial recruits were 'three chief officers of the army, Trelawny, Kirk and Churchill'.[3]

Events during the summer of 1688 forced the pace. The birth of a son to Mary of Modena at St James's Palace on 10 June filled Anglican churchmen and politi-cians with dread. Instead of the traditional ecstatic celebrations on the birth of a male heir to the throne, Burnet claimed that the rejoicings 'were very cold and forced'. It was even alleged that the pregnancy had been bogus and a baby had been smuggled into the queen's bed chamber in a warming-pan.[4]

In contrast to the muted response to the Prince's birth, the acquittal in Westminster Hall on 29 June of seven Anglican bishops, including Archbishop Sancroft, prompted heart-felt public rejoicing. The bishops had been charged with seditious libel after protesting against the king's order that the Anglican clergy should read James's 1687 Declaration of Indulgence from the pulpit. While bonfires were lit and bells were rung in celebration at the bishops' acquittal, the English conspirators – Sidney, Danby, Devonshire, Shrewsbury, Lumley, Russell and Compton – drafted a formal invitation to William. The 'Immortal Seven' as they would later be mythologized, claimed that 'there are nineteen parts of twenty of the people throughout the Kingdom, who are desirous of change', and promised William that 'we who subscribe to this will not fail to attend upon your highness upon your landing'.

By the end of July, William had decided to invade. Sidney arrived in the Netherlands in mid-August with a manifesto for William's invasion, but the

Prince was unimpressed: 'by the conclusion I throw myself entirely at the mercy of Parliament'. Persistent westerly winds prevented the Dutch fleet sailing. At Westminster, an anxious king looked at his wind vane, dreading an easterly wind, while most of his subjects were desperately hoping for one. The English myth of a 'Protestant wind', dating from the defeat of the Spanish Armada a century earlier, was revived.

This myth was evoked in *Lilliburlero*, a catchy ballad that was wildly popular in the autumn of 1688, and included the line, 'Ho by my shoul 'tis a protestant wind'. *Lilliburlero* had been written the previous year as a satire on James's appointment of the Catholic earl of Tyrconnel as lord deputy of Ireland, but its mockery of Catholics and the Irish caught on as a protest against James's drafting of Irish reinforcements into England. Thomas Wharton, the Whig politician who wrote the lyrics, boasted that *Lilliburlero* had 'sung a deluded Prince [James] out of three kingdoms'.

On James's fifty-second birthday, Sunday 14 October, the capital's wind vanes indicated that an easterly had picked up. Within weeks, a massive fleet of 49 warships and 200 transports, stretching for almost 19 miles, was sailing along the English Channel to the cheers of crowds gathered along the cliff tops. William finally landed at Torbay on the highly symbolic date of 5 November.

Within weeks of landing, William's propagandists were publishing two gazettes a week. Soon an early satirical comic, *The Roman Post Boy*, appeared with bawdy and insulting jokes about Catholics and Irish. 'Every thing (till now concealed) flies abroad in publique print, & is cried about the Streetes', observed Evelyn.[5]

Despite his earlier reservations, William pledged that he would 'concur in everything' that a 'free and lawful Parliament shall determine', although he later regretted his promise. William was portrayed as 'robust and healthy' with 'wonderful proportions of features', 'benign', 'affable' and 'of ... sweet temper'. In reality, he was a painfully thin asthmatic who stood only five feet five inches tall, had a slightly deformed back and crooked nose, and was renowned for being irritable and sullen.

James was devastated by the defections of the Duke of Grafton, one of Charles II's illegitimate sons; Prince George of Denmark, his son-in-law; and John Churchill. On 26 November, the king also discovered that Princess Anne, his younger daughter, together with Churchill's wife, Sarah, had fled Whitehall to join the Williamites. The following day, in a desperate bid to save his crown, James summoned a Great Council at Whitehall, at which about 40 peers advised him to call parliament, dismiss Catholics from office and negotiate with William. But it was too late. Although William harboured hopes of a settlement, his Whig supporters were set on scuppering any deal with James.[6]

As anti-Catholic riots swept the country, James became worried for his own and his family's safety. He wanted his queen and baby son to leave Westminster and take refuge in France; but his admiral, Dartmouth, refused to ferry them across the Channel. Dartmouth's advice was prescient: 'can the Prince's being sent to France have other prospect than the entailing a perpetual warre upon your nation and posterity, and giving France a temptation to molest, invade, nay hazard the conquest of England which I hope in God never to see'.[7]

In desperation, James turned to the Comte de Lauzun, a disgraced favourite of Louis XIV. At about two o'clock on the morning of 10 December, the queen, disguised as an Italian laundress and carrying the Prince, left Whitehall Palace by the backstairs, accompanied by de Lauzun and two nurses. The escape party took a boat to Lambeth before making their way to Gravesend, where they embarked for Calais.[8]

'It looks like a Revolution', Evelyn noted after James's Irish troops lost skirmishes at Reading and Windsor. James, deciding to flee Whitehall, burned the writs summoning a new parliament. In the early hours of the 11 December, he left his bed chamber, slipped out by the backstairs and departed by coach from Whitehall, heading south. According to some accounts, he took a boat across the Thames from Westminster Palace, while others say that he was rowed across from the horse ferry, beyond Millbank. Midway across, James threw the heavy metal Great Seal of England into the wintry river to prevent William forming a legal government.[9]

'No sooner was the king's withdrawing known', reported the *English Courant*, 'but the Mobile [mob] consulted to wreak their vengeance on Papists and Popery'. On the night after James's flight, the London sky was more brightly lit than at any time since the Great Fire of 1666. The city was gripped by the 'Irish Fear' as rumours spread of marauding Irish soldiers. Within half an hour about 100,000 men were in the streets and it took several hours before people realised it was a false alarm'.[10]

In the king's absence and amidst growing violence, a provisional government was set up at London's Guildhall by peers who had originally been summoned by James to discuss a settlement. The next day, 12 December, they moved to the Council Chamber of Whitehall Palace and invited James's Privy Council to join them. Outside, the mob grew more threatening. Extra guards were posted at St James's and at Whitehall: 300 foot guards were drawn up outside the Banqueting House and 'three pieces of cannon before the Gate'.[11]

Then came news that James was still in England. His plan to sail for France from a quiet backwater on the Isle of Sheppey had been thwarted by local fishermen. In the general anti-Catholic hysteria, they mistook him for a local Jesuit and detained him. James was eventually recognized, and the provisional government at Whitehall dispatched the earl of Feversham, James's French-born army commander, with a detachment of guards to bring James back safely. As he entered the capital, the king was cheered by Londoners, who hoped that his return indicated that a peaceful settlement had been agreed.

However, William would not discuss a settlement, and intimated to a delegation of senior peers that James might not be safe in London. When the peers suggested that the king should be advised to withdraw, William insisted that they, not he, should tell James. By nominating three peers, Halifax, Shrewsbury and Delamere as his messengers, William shrewdly implicated senior English politicians in James's final flight.

On the night of 17 December, in pouring rain, three battalions of Dutch foot guards and some cavalry, led by William's commander, General Solms, established their base at St James's Palace. They then marched on Whitehall Palace, their matches lit ready for action, arriving at about 11 o'clock. James had assumed that their arrival in the vicinity presaged William's readiness to discuss a settlement, but Solms produced William's orders to remove James from the capital. After some discussion, James told his sentries to withdraw and William's guards took their posts round the Palace. At about one o'clock, Halifax, Shrewsbury and Delamere arrived. Finally, James agreed to go.

At 11 o'clock on the morning of the 18th, the king left his apartment at Whitehall Palace by the back stairs and boarded the royal barge. Escorted by a small flotilla of barges and about a hundred Dutch guards, James was taken downstream to his chosen destination of Rochester. Within a week, he fled to France, set up court at St Germain-el-Laye and became, in effect, Louis XIV's pawn.[12]

Five hours after James's departure from Whitehall, Prince William of Orange rode into the capital to a crescendo of church bells and exuberant crowds waving oranges impaled on sticks. 'All the world go to see the Prince at St James's where there is a great Courte', Evelyn wrote. 'He is very stately, serious, & reserved'. William was preoccupied with the challenge ahead. Settling the English constitutional crisis and establishing control of Ireland and Scotland, distracted him for two years from the European theatre of war.[13]

'There were many peculiarities in the spectacle', Dean Stanley, observed somewhat sniffily of the 'double Coronation' of William III and Mary II in April 1689: 'The tall queen and the short king walked side by side'. Mary's height of almost six feet was accentuated by her statuesque physique; while William's shortness was exaggerated by his thin build. The odd couple were joint sovereigns; not sovereign and consort. They were crowned by Henry Compton, Bishop of London, since Archbishop Sancroft refused to swear allegiance to William: an episcopal rift that fuelled scurrilous rumours of a boxing match in the Abbey between the prelates. A second Coronation Chair was provided for Mary, into which she 'was lifted like her husband, girt with the sword, and invested with symbols of sovereignty'. When Princess Anne, who was standing near, remarked cattily: 'Madam, I pity your fatigue', Mary retorted tartly: 'A crown, sister, is not so heavy as it seems'. The novelty of Mary's equal status ensured that the direct line of succession to a monarch's child was upheld – James's baby son having been dismissed as a fake.[14]

At first, the Commons and Lords were deadlocked on whether the throne was vacant. When the Lords finally agreed that James had vacated the throne, bonfires were lit 'at many noblemen's doores' and church bells were rung in celebration.

Compromise became the order of the day, encouraged by George Savile, Marquess of Halifax, who was Speaker of the Lords in the Convention Parliament. Halifax's influential pamphlet, *The Character of a Trimmer*, written in 1685 as an attack on extreme Tories, but not published until 1688, eulogized moderation as an English virtue. 'Trimmer' Halifax likened his approach to steadying a boat against those at the extremes, who risked weighing down on one side or the other and capsizing it. In which direction the boat should be steered was less clear, but the 'Trimmer' founded a long tradition in British politics. His twentieth-century heirs included the Conservatives Harold Macmillan, whose credo was entitled *The Middle Way*; and 'Rab' Butler, who called his memoirs *The Art of the Possible*.

At the Banqueting House on the morning of 13 February 1689, Ash Wednesday, William and Mary attended a ceremony with members of the Convention Parliament. Halifax, speaking for both houses, formally invited them to accept the crown. Their confirmation was signalled at Court Gate by trumpeters who gave three blasts; the last of which prompted a great cheer from the huge crowd outside. The shift from a traditional monarchy to a constitutional one based on parliamentary government was enshrined in the new coronation oath in which William and Mary swore to govern 'according to the Statutes in Parliament agreed on' and to maintain the Protestant church.[15]

The 26 year-old queen's jubilation the following week when she moved into Whitehall Palace shocked courtiers. 'Mary came to Whitehall, laughing and jolly as to a wedding, as to seem quite transported', wrote Evelyn.

> She rose early the next morning, and in her undress, as it was reported, before her women were up, went about from room to room, to see the convenience of Whitehall; lay in the same bed and apartment where the late Queen lay, and within a night or two sat down to play at basset, as the Queen, her predecessor, used to do.

Princess Anne's confidante, Sarah Churchill, later Duchess of Marlborough, struck by Mary's lack of feeling or respect for her father, observed: 'and if she felt no tenderness, I thought that she should still have looked grave, or even pensively sad, at so melancholy a reverse of his fortune'.[16]

William's asthma made it impossible for him to spend long in smoky Westminster, so he bought Kensington Palace and had it re-built by Wren. Although Whitehall Palace remained the seat of government and hosted ceremonies and entertainments, in 1691 a fire in the royal lodgings 'burnt violently for several hours' and destroyed much of the southern part of the Palace. A riverside terrace garden was built for Mary, but all that remains is the flight of curved stone steps that once led down to the Thames.[17]

William's coup is celebrated as a 'Bloodless' or 'Glorious Revolution', but it took years of bloody warfare to complete. In January 1690, William prorogued parliament in order to forestall mounting opposition, especially to his handling of James's French-backed invasion of Ireland. William told the Lords of his regret that people were 'burthened with heavy Taxes', but had resolved 'to go thither in person'. William's need to fund his Irish, Scottish and European wars enabled MPs to increase their power. As early as October 1689, MPs responded to William's request for extra funds during 1690–1 by attaching strings to how it was spent. Dissatisfied with the mishandling of naval finance, the Commons appropriated, or earmarked, £400,000 from a new land tax specifically for the navy and itemised how it was to be spent: £200,000 for the speedy payment of sailors, £100,000 for victualling and £100,000 for stores. Appropriation of supply gave parliament the power to influence specific policies.[18]

The crown's annual income during James II's reign had never exceeded £3 million, but as Tim Harris, the historian of the revolution, has shown, by 1696 annual military spending reached £8.1 million. The war machine's voracious appetite for money was met by floating long-term, funded loans. The government's guarantee on these loans, during 1692–3, was the origin of the national debt, resulting in the creation of the Bank of England in 1694. The interest on these loans had to be guaranteed by parliamentary grants of taxation.[19] As a result, William accepted the Triennial Act in 1694, requiring that parliament should meet at least every three years and that no parliament should last more than three years. The Civil List Act in 1697 provided a regular income for the king to meet the costs of his household and government, while parliament took responsibility for all defence spending. Parliament had made itself indispensable.[20]

The Crown responded by seeking new ways of managing parliament. Influential MPs and peers with good debating skills and family connections were recruited as the king's advisers. The Cabinet also became more important because of William's frequent absences abroad. The king took all the major decisions, but when he left for Ireland in the summer of 1690 he created a nine-man Cabinet to advise Mary. Despite William's brief reliance on ad hoc meetings of advisers, known as the 'Whig Junto' during 1694–5, he later revived the Cabinet. Smaller groups of ministers were set up to consider specific issues, while the Cabinet generally met in the king's presence on Sundays at a royal palace. The Cabinet usually included the Lord Chancellor, Lord President, Lord Privy Seal, two Secretaries of State, household officers such as the Lord Steward and Lord Chamberlain, and other important figures such as the Archbishop of Canterbury.[21]

Mary's tragic death from smallpox in December 1694, at the age of 32, left William inconsolable for a month. He was deeply attached to his wife, despite his long affair with Elizabeth Villiers, and rumours of homosexual liaisons with his favourites, Bentinck and Keppel (created the Earls of Portland and Albemarle respectively). Mary's remains lay in state for almost two weeks at Whitehall Palace, where the walls were covered with black cloth and purple velvet. Despite bitterly cold weather that froze the Thames solid, the streets were crowded with people waiting to pay their respects.[22]

Mary's funeral on 5 March 1695, 'was long remembered', according to Macaulay, 'as the saddest and most august that Westminster had ever seen'. On a dark, snowy day, the monarch's hearse, with crown and sceptre on her coffin of purple and gold, passed from Whitehall to the Abbey along a gravelled path, between railings lined with black cloth. Both Houses of Parliament with their maces followed the hearse for the first time, 'the Lords robed in scarlet and ermine, the Commons in long black mantles'. As mourners entered the Abbey, they were overwhelmed by the sight of the nave, choir and transept 'in a blaze with innumerable waxlights', and by the majestic sound of the solemn funeral anthem specially composed by Henry Purcell, a former organist at the Abbey.[23]

Mary's coffin lay beneath a catafalque designed by Wren while Archbishop Tenison preached the sermon. During the service, a robin that had flown into the Abbey perched poignantly on her hearse, while 'the distant booming of cannon was heard every minute from the batteries of the Tower'. Mary's remains were laid to rest with other Stuarts in the vault beneath Henry VII's Chapel. Life-like wax effigies of Mary and William stood in the Abbey for many years and these, and Mary's Coronation chair, are displayed in the Abbey Museum.[24]

Within three years of Mary's funeral, most of Whitehall Palace was destroyed in a catastrophic blaze. The fire began on 4 January 1698 in top floor lodgings when linen sheets being dried on a charcoal brazier caught fire. In no time the flames spread to the roof timbers and smoke was billowing into the sky. In a desperate bid to make firebreaks, explosives were detonated but the burning debris started new fires. Lodgers and staff scrambled to rescue their possessions and the Palace's treasures, while looters scaled the walls and made off with what they could. Several people were killed and many injured.

By the time that the fire was extinguished the following day, the state rooms and royal apartments were reduced to rubble. King Street acted as a firebreak, and the recreational part of the Palace and the Holbein and King's Gates survived. Celia Fiennes, the inveterate traveller, observed that the Banqueting House was 'the only thing left of the vast building which by accident or carelessness, if not designe, has laid it in ashes'. The scale of devastation and the sense of malaise were evoked by Ned Ward, alias *The London Spy*:

> After we had taken a survey of the ruins, & spent some melancholy thoughts upon the tatter'd object that lay in the dust before us, we walk'd thro' several out-courts, till we came to Scotland Yard, where gentlemen soldiers lay basking in the sun, like so many lazy swine upon a warm dunghill.[25]

The fire ended more than 600 years of history. Monarchs had kept a main residence at the heart of Westminster since the eleventh century, but after the fire of 1698, they never lived there again. In less than a decade after James II's flight, Westminster's physical and political landscapes had changed fundamentally. Yet, the upheavals of revolution and war created a new constitutional settlement and laid the robust financial foundations on which Britain built a global empire.

PART FOUR

NEW POLITICAL
CAPITAL

24 COCKPIT OF POWER

The cockpit of power in Britain is the maze of offices and corridors lying behind the front doors of Number 10 Downing Street and the Cabinet Office, on nearby Whitehall. The site was once occupied by the royal Cockpit and its adjoining buildings. For the past 300 years and more, the decisions made in the tight cluster of buildings wedged between Downing Street, Horse Guards Parade and Whitehall, have determined the country's destiny and shaped people's lives. Although this cramped site only became the seat of government by accident after 1698, when most of Whitehall Palace was destroyed by fire, its story is central to the early eighteenth century changes in British politics.

King William and his successor and sister-in-law, Queen Anne, hoped to rebuild the eastern half of Whitehall Palace, but the ambitious plans commissioned from Sir Christopher Wren came to nothing. More modest work on the existing palaces at Kensington, Hampton Court and St James's took immediate priority, and the Banqueting House was converted into a chapel for William. However, the costs of the continental wars against the French during both William's and Anne's reigns precluded heavy spending at home.

Although Whitehall Palace was never re-built, Henry VIII's residential and governmental palace left an indelible imprint. After the fire, the court retreated to St James's Palace across the park, but the pressing need to carry on the work of government necessitated an urgent solution. The surviving, western part of Whitehall Palace bordering the park, where Henry had his cockpit and tennis courts, was hurriedly converted. Wren set up a council chamber and offices for the Treasury and council of Trade, and provided the king with an apartment.[1]

Keeping the government based in Westminster was highly significant. The physical separation between the royal residence across the park and the government's offices in Whitehall reflected, and reinforced, the new political reality. The monarch remained head of government, but by 1698 the government depended on parliament to fund its debt, meet military and other costs, and pass legislation. Managing parliament was essential and ministers needed to stay at Westminster.

Nobody came to understand better how to manage parliament than Robert Walpole, a politician who was first elected in 1701. Born into the prosperous north Norfolk gentry, educated at Eton and Cambridge, the short and stocky 25-year-old Walpole succeeded his late father, a Whig, as MP for Castle Rising. The following year, he won his grandfather's former seat of King's Lynn. Walpole immediately began honing his parliamentary skills and developed close relationships with other young Whigs, including his influential Norfolk neighbour, Charles, Viscount Townshend. Walpole's reputation as a rising star was confirmed in 1703 by his election to the prestigious Kit-Cat Club, a Whig dining club, whose members were immortalized by one of its number, Sir Godfrey Kneller, portraitist to William and his successors: Anne, from 1702, and George I, from 1714.

Walpole's career was shaped by factional infighting as a succession crisis and renewed continental war destabilized politics. After the death of Anne's only surviving son and heir, the Duke of Gloucester, in 1700, parliament passed the Act of Settlement the following year. This provided for a Protestant succession on Anne's eventual demise by offering the crown to Sophia, Electress of Hanover, granddaughter of James I. However, when the deposed king, James II, died the following year, Louis XIV provocatively recognised his son, James Stuart, as heir to the British thrones, thereby raising the Jacobite spectre (so called because the Latin form of the name James is *Jacobus*). The ensuing European war gave Walpole his first opportunity to shine in government, and during the rest of his long career he exploited the Jacobite bogey shamelessly. Walpole presented himself as a bulwark of stability (an image strengthened by his widening girth), while smearing his Tory opponents as crypto-Jacobites, just as during the Cold War the left were portrayed as crypto-communists.

Having shone as a Whig debater in the Commons, Walpole was appointed to the Admiralty council in 1705. Within three years, he was promoted to Secretary at War and impressed Anne's 'duumvirate': Sidney, Earl of Godolphin, First Lord of the Treasury; and John Churchill, Duke of Marlborough, her military commander. Although Anne was afflicted by gout when she became queen in her late thirties and had to be carried to the Abbey for her coronation in a 'Chaire of Crimson velvet with a low back, by which meanes her mantle and Robe was cast over it', she revelled in court life, and revived 'touching for the king's evil' (although she was the last monarch to perform the ceremony). An active head of government, she appointed and consulted ministers, and presided at twice-weekly cabinet meetings.[2]

Anne regularly attended debates in the Lords and is depicted there, seated on the throne, in one of the paintings of both houses in session in about 1710 by Peter Tillemans, Kneller's Flemish-born associate. The Armada tapestries, visible in the painting of the upper chamber, appear highly appropriate for a queen who gloried in Marlborough's brilliant victories during 1704–9. Tillemans's companion piece of the Commons shows Wren's recently constructed galleries, supported by slender columns, 15 feet above the wood-panelled chamber and extending along both sides. A new gallery at the west end is not shown. The galleries provided extra seating to accommodate 45 Scottish MPs after the Act of Union in 1707 created the unitary state of Great Britain, entrenching the Glorious Revolution and securing England's northern security. Wren also lowered the ceiling, and installed three round-arched windows at the east end, behind the Speaker's chair.[3]

Anne relied increasingly on the Whigs to secure parliamentary support for the union and military spending. As the party divide widened, the Tories accused the Whigs of prolonging the war to benefit their wealthy city cronies. In early 1710, Tory anger finally erupted over the impeachment of Dr Henry Sacheverell, an high Anglican preacher. The trial, in Westminster Hall, was largely orchestrated by Walpole. Sacheverell's alleged crime was a thinly veiled attack on the Whigs in sermons at St Paul's, but what riled the Whigs was that the printed version sold 40,000 copies.

Sacheverell's trial lasted almost a month and was more popular than the theatre. Each day Anne was carried in her chair across the park to watch from a private box. Walpole accused the preacher of attacking the 1688 revolution, undermining the new settlement and preparing the ground for a Jacobite restoration. However, the government's unpopularity fuelled riots across London, in which dissenting chapels were burnt and the Bank of England threatened. Although Sacheverell was found guilty, his lenient punishment – a limited preaching ban and public burning of his offending sermons – was seen as a moral victory.[4]

Within months, the Tories won a general election and Anne brought the Tory political fixer and former Cabinet minister, Robert Harley, back into her government, first as Chancellor of the Exchequer and in 1711 as First Lord of the Treasury, creating him Earl of Oxford. Harley built a governing party in parliament, but his hopes of establishing a stable, cross-party government were dashed by a growing partisan gulf as Walpole, having left the government, led the Whig attack on the conduct of the war. Walpole became a target for the Tories, and MPs accepted evidence suggesting that he had taken a bribe while war secretary to help a banker friend win army contracts. He was disqualified as an MP and thrown into the Tower for six months, but his imprisonment transformed him into a Whig martyr and national figure.

Walpole's rise to fame was boosted by a boom in newspapers and pamphlets after the repeal of the Licensing Act, a form of press censorship, in 1695. He later came to hate the press but, after his release from the Tower, pamphleteering gave him a platform until he returned to the Commons in 1713. The highly partisan nature of debate in parliament and in the capital's coffee houses, fuelled an insatiable appetite for news and comment. The result was a frenzied newsprint boom and a golden age of journalism, whose star writers were Joseph Addison, Richard Steele and Jonathan Swift.

Like Walpole, Addison and Steele won preferment through the Whigs' Kit-Cat club. In 1706, Addison joined the government in his mid-thirties as an under-secretary, and became responsible for running the *London Gazette*, the official government newspaper. The following year he secured the post of Gazetteer for Steele, his Irish-born, former contemporary at the Charterhouse school in London. Steele became a forerunner of today's Whitehall press secretaries and spin doctors. He was based in the Cockpit in Whitehall, working in the offices of the secretaries of state, where he could draw on ambassadors' dispatches and ministerial meetings. However, the job's limitations and his frustration at being passed over for ministerial office led him to launch his own paper, the *Tatler*, in April 1709. Among the writers whom he recruited was his fellow Irishman, Jonathan Swift.

Swift, a clergyman at St Patrick's Cathedral, Dublin, had first befriended Addison while visiting London with the Lord Lieutenant of Ireland from 1707 to 1709. However, by 1710, the political tide had turned against the Whigs and Swift, once more in London, was impressed that Harley the Tory Chancellor agreed to improve support for the Irish clergy. Swift found Harley and his fellow Tory St John congenial and began contributing to the Tory paper, the *Examiner*. By early 1711, he was one of the Tory inner circle, attending Harley's Saturday Club dinners, and was, in effect, Tory chief writer. Later that year, his pamphlet, *The Conduct of the Allies*, attacking the Whigs for prolonging war to benefit a wealthy city clique, sold 11,000 copies in three months.[5]

Swift's friends, Addison and Steele, no longer in office after the Whig election defeat in 1710, replaced the *Tatler* with a new venture that became one of the most celebrated newspapers in the English language. *The Spectator* was launched on Thursday, 11 March 1711 and published six days a week. 'My publisher tells me that there are already Three thousand of them distributed every day', Addison boasted in the tenth edition. Betraying a media magnate's cocky assumptions on readership figures, he declared, 'I may reckon about Threescore thousand [60,000] Disciples in London and Westminster'. However, he could justifiably lay 'ambitious' claim to having 'brought Philosophy out of the Closets and Libraries, Schools and Colleges, to dwell in Clubs and Assemblies, at Tea-Tables and in Coffee-Houses'.[6]

Addison and Steele hit on the device of appearing non-partisan by writing as an eponymous, detached observer. 'I never espoused any Party with Violence', declared Mr Spectator (alias Addison) in the first issue, 'and am resolved to observe an exact Neutrality between the Whigs and the Tories, unless I shall be forced to declare myself by the Hostilities of either Side'. The next day, Steele adopted the guise to introduce Mr Spectator's fellow club members: notably Sir Roger de Coverley, a bluff Tory squire up from Worcestershire, and Sir Andrew Freeport, a self-made Whig merchant in the city. These partisan caricatures enabled Addison and Steele to portray Tory and Whig views without being identified with them, although their paper's general stance was liberal Whig.[7]

Mr Spectator was also the vehicle for his authors' beautifully written and sharply observed essays on life in general and literature in particular. 'I very often walk by myself in Westminster Abbey', Addison wrote on 30 March 1711, 'Where the gloominess of the place, and the use to which it is applied, with the solemnity of the building, and the condition of the people who lie in it, are apt to fill the mind with a kind of melancholy, or rather thoughtfulness, that is not disagreeable'. Having surveyed 'this great magazine of mortality', where 'innumerable multitudes of people lay confused together under the pavement of that ancient cathedral', Addison gave a critique of its epitaphs, from the 'extravagant' to the 'modest'. His thoughts lead to a sober reflection on Westminster itself:

> when I see kings lying by those who deposed them, when I consider rival wits placed side by side, or the holy men that divided the world with their contests and disputes, I reflect with sorrow and astonishment on the little competitions, factions and debates of mankind.[8]

The *Spectator*'s first run ended in December 1712, after 555 issues. Steele launched two more anti-Tory papers during 1713, the *Guardian* in March (with contributions from Addison) and the *Englishman* in October. He was elected to parliament, where he joined Addison, but their friendship eventually fell victim to their divided loyalties – Steele backed Townshend's and Walpole's Whig faction, but Addison served as Secretary of State (1717–18) in the government of their rivals, Charles Spencer, Earl of Sunderland, and James, Earl of Stanhope. Shortly before Addison's death in 1719, Steele's criticism of his friend's patrons provoked an exchange of personal insults between the two writers.

Addison's body lay in state in the Abbey's Jerusalem Chamber as a mark of public esteem, and was buried beneath the north aisle of King Henry VII's Chapel. His night-time funeral in the Abbey explains these lines by Thomas Tickell, his disciple and aide in government: 'How silent did his old companions tread, / By midnight lamps, the mansions of the dead'. Addison's final estrangement from Steele is especially poignant, as it revealed his own susceptibility to 'the little competitions, factions and debates of mankind'.

Steele's partisanship had previously ended his friendship with Swift, who was increasingly close to the Tories. In late 1713, Steele alleged in a pamphlet entitled *The Crisis*, that on Queen Anne's death, the Catholic Pretender, James Stuart, might be installed as king. *The Crisis* sold a staggering 40,000 copies and provoked Swift, by then Dean of St Patrick's, Dublin, to accuse Steele of sedition. Harley's Tory government took up the charge, and despite a brilliant defence by Walpole – re-elected after his release from the Tower – Steele was expelled from parliament.[9]

In the event, there was no crisis on Anne's death in August 1714. The succession passed smoothly to George I, Elector of Hanover, whose mother, Sophia, the previous heir to the throne, had died only weeks earlier. Anne's posthumous effigy in the Abbey Museum shows a full face and ample physique similar to that of her sister, Mary. A more evocative memorial is her stone statue, standing on a pedestal, in Queen Anne's Gate. It dates from at least 1708, and once stood in a corner of what was then Queen Square.

The old square occupied what is now the western half of Queen Anne's Gate. Its fine houses were built circa 1704–5 and re-capture a sense of the Westminster that Addison knew. The eastern end of Queen Anne's Gate was originally Park Street, first developed in 1686 but later largely re-built. Further east, Queen Street (now Old Queen Street) was developed along an old lane. Number 24, Old Queen Street was built circa 1690–1700. During the twentieth century, it housed the Conservative Research Department between 1929 and 1979. The Cockpit Steps, leading down to Birdcage Walk, are a 1960s re-build of seventeenth-century steps named after a nearby, but long since demolished, successor to the Cockpit at Whitehall Palace. In May 1798, the prime minister of the day, William Pitt the Younger, and his friends, Henry Addington and Dudley Ryder, bustled up the steps and took a carriage from Queen Street to Wimbledon for the premier's duel with George Tierney, a radical MP, whom Pitt had slighted during a debate. Fortunately, neither man fired his pistol accurately.[10]

The last Stuart queen is also remembered at Westminster in the nickname, 'Queen Anne's Footstool', given to St John's in Smith Square, one of the finest examples of English baroque architecture. St John's four ornate, columned corner towers, each topped with a stone pineapple, give it the appearance of an upturned footstool. Legend has it that when the architect, Thomas Archer, consulted Queen Anne about its design, she kicked over her footstool and snapped, 'Like that!' Charles Dickens in *Our Mutual Friend*, suggests that it resembles, 'some petrified monster, frightful and gigantic, on its back with its legs in the air'. Another legend suggests that the towers were added as an after-thought to stabilize the building against subsidence; but although its marshy site between the Abbey and the horse ferry prolonged its completion, Archer's towers were part of his original design.[11]

St John's was commissioned as a result of the Fifty Churches Act, passed in 1711 in response to London's rapidly expanding population. It took 15 years to build and was finally completed in 1728. After fire-bombing during the Second World War, St John's was restored and became a leading concert venue. The early Georgian streets between Smith Square and the Abbey re-capture a sense of Walpole's Westminster. This quarter retains something of the 'still place' described by Sybil in Benjamin Disraeli's 1845 novel, although the 'deadly repose' portrayed by Dickens is sometimes disturbed by modern traffic.

In the days of Dickens and Disraeli, these streets were home to artisans, but during the twentieth century many houses became handy billets for MPs. R. A. Butler, the Conservative politician, lived at Number 3, one of several original houses built by John Mackreth in 1726 on the north side of Smith Square, at its junction with Lord North Street. In 1955, Butler was filmed leaving this house as Chancellor to deliver his budget. Number 8, also an original house, was home to

Oswald Mosley, who left the Labour Party and in 1932 set up the British Union of Fascists. Mackreth also built Lord North Street, where the historical aura is enhanced by original railings, torch extinguishers and fading wartime signs to air raid shelters. Harold Wilson, the Labour prime minister, lived here during the early 1970s, between his two spells at Number 10.

Opposite the top of Lord North Street, Cowley Street and its continuation, Barton Street, have fine early Georgian houses. Both streets were developed from 1722 by Barton Booth, an actor-manager, whose country house was at Cowley in Middlesex. Barton Booth appeared in Addison's 1713 hit, *Cato*, that opened sensationally in Drury Lane to cheers and jeers from rival gangs of Tories and Whigs. The following year, Booth successfully lobbied George I's new Whig government for Steele to be appointed governor of the Theatre Royal. The best preserved houses in Cowley Street are Numbers 13–19. During the 1920s, Number 15 was home to William Wedgwood Benn, the Liberal MP who switched allegiance to the Labour Party and served in the Cabinet, and whose son, Tony Benn, followed him as a Labour MP and Cabinet minister. 'The Salutation' public house stood on the corner of Cowley Street and Barton Street from the 1720s until its conversion in about 1890; in a curious twist of fate, it later became home to Lord Reith, the fiercely self-righteous first Director-General of the BBC. In Barton Street, Number 2 bears a tablet of 1722 inscribed with the charming wish: 'Peace on thy house passer by'. While living at No 14, T. E. Lawrence, better known as 'Lawrence of Arabia', wrote *Seven Pillars of Wisdom*. Barton Street joins Great College Street, that runs along the route of the old Abbey's mill stream and is bordered by the Abbey garden wall of 1374–6.[12]

Property development seemed a safer investment than the stock exchange after the first international speculative boom and financial crash in 1720. The crisis might have sunk the Whig government, but it was skilfully managed by Walpole. The origins of this boom and bust lay in the attempts by the British and French governments to reduce the cost of financing the huge state debts incurred during almost a quarter of a century of warfare. Joint-stock companies were encouraged to take over the national debt in return for trading monopolies and began issuing shares in what were, as Peter Jay has noted, 'debt-for-equity swaps'. The prospect of huge profits being made by companies with government-backed monopolies sent shares in France's Mississippi Company and Britain's South Sea Company soaring. In the first six months of 1720, British government ministers helped talk up the price of South Sea shares from £128 to £1,050.

However, when the French tried to dampen speculation in the summer of 1720 the public lost confidence and the bubble burst. Among the many investors who lost a fortune was Sir Isaac Newton, the discoverer of gravity, pioneering mathematician and philosopher, and who, as warden of the Mint, fixed the value of the pound against gold, the basis of the later gold standard. Walpole's part in screening ministers and courtiers from charges of corruption over the South Sea

Bubble crisis earned him the nickname of 'Skreen-Master General'. Walpole had made his presence essential to the government's survival.[13]

On 3 April 1721, Walpole replaced Sunderland as First Lord of the Treasury, although it was not until Sunderland's death a year later that the Townshend-Walpole duumvirate could take full control. Although they knew there was no imminent Jacobite threat, they ruthlessly exploited memories of the invasion in 1715 by the Pretender, James Stuart, and ordered troops to assemble in Hyde Park. Walpole also hoped to make an example of a leader of the alleged plot, Francis Atterbury, Bishop of Rochester and former Dean of Westminster. Instead of risking a treason trial, Walpole had parliament pass a bill that enabled Walpole to strip Atterbury of his bishopric and banish him. Walpole's cunning and ruthlessness strengthened his position in the government, increased his support among Whigs and re-assured the king.

From the mid-1720s, Walpole began to emerge as the dominant partner in the duumvirate, but his cool relationship with the Prince of Wales, the future George II, posed a threat. Walpole responded by cultivating the Prince's wife, Caroline – who talked politics with her husband – instead of befriending the Prince's mistress, Henrietta Howard, as his rivals had. His judgement was proved right in 1727 when George I died and, contrary to expectations, he continued in office under George II. As Walpole coarsely quipped, his main rival, Spencer Compton, 'took the wrong sow by the ear ... I took the right'.[14]

George II's accession is better remembered for a more uplifting reason. At his coronation on 10 October 1727, the Abbey echoed, for the first time, to George Frideric Handel's noble and stirring anthem, 'Zadok the Priest'. Handel had arrived in London, where he settled, in 1710 soon after his appointment as Kapellmeister to the Elector of Hanover, the future George I, and quickly won acclaim for his music. His stirring anthem has been performed at every coronation since, although it was mistakenly sung in the wrong place on the first occasion in the general confusion that marred George II's ceremony.[15]

It is 'extraordinary', as Roy Strong observes, that the roots of Handel's anthem 'lie as far back as the last quarter of the tenth century'. Aspects of Edgar's coronation as English King in 973 AD became part of future coronations, including the solemn bestowal of unction, accompanied by prayers and followed by an anthem that began: 'Zadok the Priest and Nathan the Prophet anointed Solomon King; and they blew the trumpets, and piped the pipes, and rejoiced with great joy, so that the earth rent with the sound of them ...'. Handel transformed this tenth century anthem into a glorious, musical masterpiece.[16]

Ancient ritual and modern science were lauded in the Abbey during 1727. The funeral of Sir Isaac Newton on 28 March, attracted a massive crowd, numbering 30,000 on one estimate.[17] Voltaire (François-Marie Arouet), the French writer and philosopher, who spent more than two years in London, was hugely impressed by the reverence shown Newton 'in his lifetime', and the 'respect paid to him after his death; the greatest men in the nation disputing who should have the honour of holding up his pall'. Newton's body lay in state for a day in the Jerusalem Chamber, before his pall was borne into the Abbey by the Lord Chancellor, two dukes and three earls, and was followed by members of the Royal Society. His burial place is marked by a black marble gravestone in the nave. It lies in front of his baroque monument standing against the choir screen, to the north of the entrance to the choir.[18]

Today, many of the crowds flocking to Westminster know of Newton's burial in the Abbey from Dan Brown's *The Da Vinci Code*. The designer of the Newton's monument, William Kent and his constructor, J. Michael Rysbrack, were at pains to include references to Newton's many fields of expertise. Newton is shown reclining on a sarcophagus, his intelligent-looking features probably taken from a death mask. Above his figure is a globe, showing the constellations and the course of the 1680 comet, as determined by Newton. The monument was completed in 1731. William Kent knew Walpole, having designed fine interiors and furniture for Houghton Hall, the prime minister's magnificent mansion in Norfolk. At Westminster too, Walpole and Kent made a lasting impact on the cockpit of power.

25 NUMBER 10 AND THE PRIME MINISTER

No other country has anything quite like Number 10 Downing Street. The official residence of Britain's head of government is an apparently modest terrace house in a nondescript cul-de-sac. Even more quirkily, the inscription on Number 10's polished brass letter-box reads 'First Lord of the Treasury', not 'Prime Minister'.

Number 10's quirkiness dates back almost three centuries to the day when Britain's first prime minister moved in. 'Yesterday', reported the *London Daily Post* on 23 September 1735, 'the Right Hon. Sir Robert Walpole, with his Lady and family removed from their House in St. James's Square, to his new House adjoining the Treasury in St. James's Park'. The house, the largest in a terrace of fifteen, had been a gift from George II. However, Walpole was anxious to avoid the cost of renovating the jerry-built property and also prevent accusations of being in the king's pocket. On Walpole's insistence, the Treasury picked up the bill and the house became the official residence of the First Lord of the Treasury, not Walpole's own.

Walpole's sensitivity is understandable. Among the many insults hurled at him were the terms 'Premier' or 'Prime Minister'. In the early eighteenth century, these terms were generally used to describe the sole minister of a despot. Calling a British minister a 'premier', or 'prime minister' thus implied that the minister was guilty of being a creature of the monarch, or of getting above himself. In 1741, Sir Samuel Sandys, a leading Whig critic, demanded Walpole's removal because 'According to our constitution, we can have no sole and prime minister'. Sandys complained that Walpole had 'assumed the sole direction of all public affairs' and 'monopolized all the favours of the crown, and engrossed the sole disposal of all places, pensions, titles, and ribbons, as well as of all preferments, civil, military, or ecclesiastical'. However, Walpole was at pains to dismiss the idea of his being a 'prime minister' as a fantasy of his enemies: 'having first conferred upon me a kind of mock dignity, and styled me the prime minister, they … impute to me an unpardonable abuse of that chimerical authority, which only they have thought necessary to bestow'.[1]

Despite Walpole's vigorous repudiation of the title, he is generally regarded as the first British prime minister. After his appointment as First Lord of the Treasury in 1721, he initially shared power in the ministry with Townshend, but from 1727 he was the strongest Cabinet minister, and during the first dozen years of George II's reign he was trusted by the king and queen. Walpole's longevity in office enabled him to bring more of his own supporters into Government. Above all, he was remarkably skilful as first Lord of the Treasury at the crucial task of managing parliament, especially getting money bills through. Nowhere was Walpole's ascendancy more evident than in his development of Downing Street as his power base at the heart of government.

Although Downing Street was Walpole's temporary home, he wanted visiting diplomats and politicians to feel as they entered that they were about to meet a leader who was the equal of any foreign chief minister or royal ruler. He made the house a showcase for more than a hundred items from his highly valued art collection and left an indelible stamp on the building. One of the main designers was William Kent, likeable and multi-talented, who, together with his patron Lord Burlington revived Inigo Jones's Palladianism. Kent had designed the interiors of Walpole's re-built neo-classical Norfolk mansion Houghton Hall; in Downing Street, his elegant rooms were the perfect setting for Walpole to display more than a hundred of his paintings, including works by Canaletto, Castiglione, Claude, Rubens, Teniers and van Dyck.

The palatial impression created by Walpole behind Downing Street's unprepossessing terrace façade was only possible because the new residence was a merger of the terrace house with a much grander town house at the back. The larger house had been built by Charles II in 1673 on the site of the old Cockpit lodgings, and was L-shaped, with its longer arm stretching alongside the nearby park (now Horse Guards Parade). It was intended for the Duke of Buckingham, but he fell from favour and it was occupied by Elizabeth Villiers (Charles II's daughter by Lady Castlemaine). She married Lord Lichfield, and when they eventually left, William III's master of the horse, Lord Overkirk, moved in. The Overkirks, in turn, were followed by George I's adviser, Count Bothmar, before the residence became Walpole's. The shape of the grand house at the rear of Number 10 can be seen from Horse Guards Parade.[2]

The two houses were first linked on their Whitehall side, with the remainder of the space between them becoming a courtyard. Today, the main linking walkway runs from Number 10's entrance hall, with its distinctive black and white chequer-patterned marble floor, through a second, smaller hall, and along a corridor dating from the early 1780s (with windows onto the courtyard), towards the back of the building. Curiously, the ground floor at the front of Number 10 becomes the first floor at the rear, because the ground slopes down from Downing Street towards Horse Guards Parade.

At the back of the building, the largest first-floor corner room (furthest from

Whitehall) became Walpole's levee room and study, where the Cabinet met. It continues to meet there today, beneath a portrait of Walpole on the wall above the original fireplace. I experienced his baleful gaze while seated at the Cabinet table recording an interview with Gordon Brown, the then prime minister, for BBC Radio 4's *The Prime Ministers*. 'When you're sitting in the chair of the Prime Minister', Brown told Nick Robinson, the BBC's Political Editor, 'Walpole is behind you, and you've got no sense that he's there. If you're sitting on the other side, as I used to do as Chancellor, you look up at him and see this rather foreboding figure'. The room's historical aura is overpowering. 'You look around this cabinet room', Brown reflected, and 'you've got a sense of what's been happening for not just years, but centuries'.[3]

The Cabinet room was extended at its east (Whitehall) end in 1796, and two pairs of Corinthian pillars were installed to support the interior wall on the floors above. A French window at its west end leads onto Bothmar's old terrace, from which a double flight of stairs leads down into the garden. Originally, the adjoining rooms at the back of the house were used as Walpole's dressing room and as a parlour, but they are now offices.[4]

On the floor above was Walpole's drawing room (above the Cabinet room), a dining room and Lady Walpole's bedroom (on the Whitehall side). The Walpoles had led separate lives for many years, and his mistress, Maria (Molly) Skerrett often stayed with him in the house, even when his children were there. Today, the Walpoles' living quarters are palatial drawing rooms, known as the white (above the cabinet room), terracotta and pillared rooms. They retain 1730s' door-cases, cornices and white marble fireplaces, but were stylishly renovated in the late 1980s by Quinlan Terry. The terracotta room has a tiny figure of a busy thatcher in the frieze above the door-case, Terry's *jeu d'esprit* alluding to the then prime minister, Margaret Thatcher.[5]

Along the Whitehall side of the building, beyond the pillared room, are two elegant, wood-panelled rooms, added in the mid-1820s by Sir John Soane: the small dining room and the state dining room. The latter became the venue of the presidential-style prime minister's televised press conferences, introduced by Tony Blair in 2002. Number 10's sizeable corps of media and press handlers work in offices on the floor below, including the bow-windowed room that fronts Number 10, on its Whitehall side.

Number 10's front door is a history lesson in itself. Walpole, as a devotee of grand houses and the trappings of power, might have been expected to retain the grander house's entrance from the park as the front door of his new official residence. However, he was immensely practical. Although he owed his office as First Lord of Treasury to the king, his usefulness to the Crown and his power depended on managing parliament. The entrance from the park was therefore closed in preference to the entrance on Downing Street that gave a direct and faster route to the Houses of Parliament.

The house was not at first known as Number 10 because houses then were rarely numbered. The systematic numbering of houses only developed after the 'Paving Acts', starting in 1762, tidied up the clutter of street signs. Westminster pioneered this reform, its bill having been hastened through the Commons after an accident to Speaker Onslow's carriage as it passed through the narrow entrance to Craig Court, a small street on the east side of Whitehall, near present-day Trafalgar Square.[6] Even then, houses were often re-numbered if new plots were developed in a street, or if a street was re-configured (present-day Downing Street is the result of a merger with old Downing Square). It is sometimes said that Number 10 was originally Number 5 Downing Street, apparently because the 1931 Survey of London contains a map that identifies the building on the current site of Number 10 as 'number 5'. However, the numbering is merely the key to a map showing plots of Crown property.[7]

Walpole's new residence put him at the centre of power. It gave better access to parliament and crucially, as the *London Daily Post* noted, was 'adjoining the Treasury'. By the 1730s, the Treasury was the dominant department of state. As Peter Hennessy notes in his study of Whitehall, by the mid-eighteenth century it accounted for 'some 14,000 of the 17,000 people employed in government departments'; although, most of the Treasury's officials were based round the country, collecting duties and taxes: not in Whitehall. The Treasury's headquarters had moved to the site of the old Cockpit after the 1698 fire destroyed Whitehall Palace, but by 1732 the Board of Works reported that the building was in a 'ruinous and dangerous condition'. A year later William Kent was commissioned to design a new building on the same site, between Walpole's new residence and the remnants of the old Tudor palace on Whitehall's west side.[8]

Although the final building was less ambitious than Kent had planned, its impressive north-facing, stone front, with seven bays and ionic portico, can still be clearly seen from Horse Guards Parade, standing to the left of Number 10. Today, Kent's Treasury Block is part of the Cabinet Office and hosts official meetings. Its fine board room retains many of Kent's original features. It is about 30 feet square and 25 feet high, and contains the large, carved table where board members sat, and an impressive chair of state, bearing the royal monogram. Seated on this beautifully carved and gilded chair, with its lion's-paw feet, dolphin's head arm-ends and crimson velvet upholstery, the king presided over ministerial meetings of the Treasury board and read the King's Speech on the day before parliament met. George III was the last king to do both.[9]

Kent's Treasury Block was completed two years after Walpole first crossed his new front doorstep in Downing Street. Kent also drew many detailed designs for a new Houses of Parliament. His plans were never commissioned, but the idea of a Palladian Palace of Westminster remains an intriguing 'what if?'

In a scurrilous cartoon of the period, a vast, bare bottom is shown, with breeches lowered, straddling the entrance to a passageway: to the Treasury according to some; to St James's Palace say others. Although the identity of the bare-bottomed man was not revealed, everybody knew that it was Walpole. The cartoon's caption reads: 'whosoever went out, or whosoever came in, passed beneath, and with idolatrous reverence lift up their eyes and kissed the cheeks of the postern'. Another man is shown about to pass below the bare bottom, along the path of preferment, while pushing a hoop inscribed: 'Wealth, Pride, Vanity, Folly, Luxury, Want, Dependence, Servility, Venality, Corruption and Prostitution'.[10]

The cartoon hit home because Sir Robert Walpole, as first Lord of the Treasury, transformed the often highly personal ruse of royal patronage into a systematic instrument of power. Walpole, as Kenneth Baker, an aficionado of political cartoons, has observed, 'gave out the jobs, the sinecures, the captaincies, the peerages, he got the MPs their seats, and it was known as the "Robinocracy" – government by Robin, for Robin, by Robin'. The satirists had a field day: 'That statesman has the strongest hold / Whose tool of politics is gold', observed John Gay, in his *Fables*, published during 1727–8.[11]

Walpole made a personal fortune during his long ministerial career and looked after his family. In 1738, his 21 year-old son, Horace, just down from Cambridge, was awarded the lifelong sinecure offices of Usher of the Exchequer, Comptroller of the Pipe and Clerk of the Escheats. 'We all of times corrupt have heard', Gay observed, 'When paultry minions were preferr'd; / When all great offices, by dozens, / Were filled by brothers, sons, and cozens'. Walpole's defence against the charge of nepotism was brazen: 'I know not whether any man can accuse me of doing what he would not have done in the same circumstances. It will not surely be expected that I should obstruct his majesty's favours when offered to my family'.[12]

Gay's attacks on Walpole were sharpened by having lost all his money in the South Sea Bubble. In his 1728 smash hit, *The Beggar's Opera*, the characters Peachum and Macheath represent both Jonathan Wild, a notorious highwayman, and Walpole, who had let the South Sea directors go unpunished. The ruling elite's corruption is mocked in the lament sung by the chorus, joined by Macheath and Matt the Mint, to the tune of the Whig anthem, *Lilliburlero*: 'The Modes of the Court so common are grown, / That a true Friend can hardly be met, / Friendship for Interest is but a loan, / Which they let out for what they can get'.

None the less Walpole had the brass neck to attend the opera's first night. Gay died in 1732, aged 47, and was buried in Westminster Abbey, where the epitaph he composed for himself reads: 'Life's a jest; and all things show it. / I thought so once; but now I know it'.

'Every man has his price' is a phrase commonly associated with Walpole and it could serve as his unofficial epitaph. Although there is no proof that he used these precise words, he reportedly acknowledged that, 'with respect to bribery, the price must be higher or lower generally in proportion to the virtue of the man who is to be bribed'. Walpole's success in getting government business through parliament prompted one MP to describe his supporters as 'disciplined troops regularly paid'.[13]

However, patronage and the purchase of parliamentary seats from landowners in 'rotten boroughs' were the most effective means open to Walpole in managing parliament. His shameless pragmatism enabled him to show, as the historian John Cannon observed, 'that this parliamentary system does not lead necessarily to anarchy and confusion and disillusion'. Walpole lacked the strong party machine that sustains modern prime ministers, although they also continue to dish out honours, offices and peerages. The overall stability created by Walpole, using fair means and foul, prompted his French contemporaries, Voltaire and Montesquieu, to laud England's constitution.[14]

26 GEORGIAN ICONS

After Big Ben, the Houses of Parliament and Number 10, Westminster is best known to the world by the Abbey's two towers, Horse Guards and Westminster Bridge. The Abbey's towers and Horse Guards were part of the Georgian building boom that included Number 10's re-modelling and Kent's Treasury Building. Today's bridge is the Victorian successor to the first, Georgian bridge that was nearing completion in 1746 when the celebrated Venetian artist, Giovanni Antonio Canal, commonly known as Canaletto, arrived in London. Canaletto came to London to be near his English clientele, whose grand tours were disrupted by the War of the Austrian Succession.

One of Canaletto's most brilliant Westminster paintings shows the procession of the Order of the Bath leaving the Abbey in 1749, beneath the two recently completed towers that soar high above the west door. Henry III had planned to erect the tall towers when he rebuilt the Abbey, but he ran out of money and only the lower stages were built. Two hundred and fifty years later, Henry VII's priority was a new chapel at its east end, and the west towers stayed unfinished. Another 200 years later, the king's surveyor, Sir Christopher Wren, then in his eighties, advised the Dean and Chapter that three projects were required for 'a proper completing of what is left imperfect': the erection of a 'lofty spire' above the central crossing, 'the making of the North Front more magnificent', and 'the finishing of the two Western Towers'. The 'lofty spire' remains an aspiration; the north front was finally improved in the late 1800s; but work began on the towers in 1735, the year that Walpole moved into Downing Street.

The Abbey's towers were completed by Wren's protégé Nicholas Hawksmoor in the Gothic style appropriate to the medieval Abbey, in 1745, the year of the doomed Jacobite invasion by Charles Stuart, the Young Pretender. Hawksmoor, a brilliant exponent of the classical style, probably derived his Gothic design from the towers at Beverley Minster, where he oversaw repairs. However, he also incorporated his trademark baroque features, enriching the overall Gothic effect. After his death in 1736, the construction was supervised by John James, who also re-built and heightened the tower of nearby St Margaret's church during 1735–7 in similar, Gothic style. Today, the Abbey's pinnacled towers offer a splendidly uplifting sight: enhanced since the 1990s by cleaning and restoration; the painting of the heraldic carving; and the installation of statues of saints, the virtues and twentieth century martyrs in the front's niches.[1]

In contrast to the Abbey's towers, the Horse Guards Building on the western side of Whitehall is unashamedly classical. Horse Guards is probably best known as the pale stone backdrop in tourist snapshots of the mounted horse guards on duty in Whitehall. Its central cupola adds an exotic flourish to the skyline, while the clock's simple round of chimes ringing out the quarter hour have, for centuries, punctuated the rituals of ministerial meetings in nearby Downing Street and across Whitehall.

The symmetrical Horse Guards Building, with its central block and adjoining wings, was the last hurrah of the architect, William Kent. It was finally built during the 1750s on the site of Henry VIII's old tiltyard. A guard house had been hurriedly put up here during the civil war and was later replaced by a barracks for Charles II's personal protection corps of Horse Guards and Foot Guards. Charles's rickety old building is shown in Canaletto's splendid panorama of Horse Guards, Whitehall and Downing Street, viewed from St James's Park in the late spring of 1747. In an amusing detail, men urinate against the park wall at the back of Downing Street.

Kent's design for the new Horse Guards Building was completed by a pupil, and its construction was overseen by Kent's assistant, John Vardy. Kent's influence is greater on the new building's western side, facing Horse Guards Parade; Vardy's on the Whitehall side. In the middle of Kent's three-storey central block, is one archway for a carriage and two archways for pedestrians to pass between Whitehall and Horse Guards Parade. The carriage archway had been a feature of Charles's building and was retained by Kent. On the ceiling above the central arch, the carved initials 'SMF' and 'StMW' stand for St Martin's in the Fields and St Margaret's, Westminster, and indicate that the parish boundary between the two churches runs through the building.

To the south, Dover House was built during the mid-1750s by James Paine and replaced lodgings and a small open tennis court. During the 1770s, it was home to the French Ambassador, the Marquis de Noailles, until Britain and France went to war in 1778 during the American War of Independence. Its fine Ionic portico and slim columns on Whitehall, and its three-storey Palladian façade overlooking Horse Guards Parade, are largely the work of Henry Holland in the 1780s, when the house was substantially modified for the young Prince Frederick, Duke of York.

From 1792 it was known as Melbourne House after the prince swapped houses with Viscount Melbourne, and during the early nineteenth century was home to his son and daughter-in-law, William and Caroline Lamb. The Melbourne family was host to a louche Whig set, and Caroline's affairs included a notorious relationship with the poet, Lord Byron. She died at Melbourne House in early

1828, three years after Byron's death in Greece. Byron's body had lain in state for two days in a house in nearby Great George Street, but he had been denied burial at the Abbey because of his notoriety. William Lamb succeeded to the title of Viscount Melbourne, and became prime minister in 1834. The building's current name dates from a later resident politician, who was created Lord Dover in 1831 and died there two years later, aged only 37.

By comparison with Dover House, the brick building on the northern side of the Horse Guards Building is rather drab. It was built on the old tiltyard site, as the Paymaster-General's office in the early 1730s. It is now occupied by parliamentary counsel, the lawyers who advise ministers on drafting the ceaseless flow of new laws that issue from Whitehall. The rear, stone facade looking onto Horse Guards Parade is more attractive but is not original. It dates from the 1760s and belonged to a house in nearby Great George Street, from where it was salvaged in the early twentieth century.

The final set of government buildings on the west wide of Whitehall, to the north of the old tiltyard, is the Admiralty complex: its development in the eighteenth century marking Britain's emergence as the world's greatest sea power. Admiralty House, lying back from the main road, was built in the late 1780s by the Admiralty's surveyor, Samuel Pepys Cockerell (grandson of the diarist's nephew and heir), to provide separate accommodation for the First Lord of the Admiralty. More recently, Admiralty House has provided a home and office for prime ministers during refurbishments of Number 10.

The Old Admiralty, next door, is the oldest government office building and is shown in Canaletto's panorama. This large brickwork pile was built during 1723–6 by Thomas Ripley, Comptroller to the Office of Works and former carpenter and coffee-shop owner. The site's link with the Admiralty goes back a century, when Wallingford House stood here. This property was acquired in 1622 by Charles I's favourite the Duke of Buckingham three years after his appointment as Lord High Admiral. Buckingham set up a Council of the Sea that later became the Board of the Admiralty. After his assassination in 1628, his body lay in state in his house. Today, Ripley's Old Admiralty is shielded by Robert Adam's more attractive colonnaded Admiralty Screen on Whitehall. Erected in 1760–1 during street widening, Adam's classical gem is enhanced by symbolic sea horses above the pillars of its central arch and ships' prows portrayed in its end pediments.[2]

Westminster's greatest Georgian icon was its first bridge over the Thames, although as the historian, Richard Walker has shown, its commissioning caused a furore; its funding was controversial; and its construction was marred by mishaps. Westminster had only two ferries to carry people and goods across the river – one to Lambeth Palace and another to Stangate (where St Thomas's Hospital now stands) – while its medieval streets were clogged with carts, cabs and carriages. King Street, the old main road leading from the Abbey to Whitehall and the north, was, in Daniel Defoe's words, 'a long, dark, dirty and very inconvenient Passage'.[3]

Plans for a bridge at Westminster had been blocked since 1664 by an alliance of City businessmen and Thames watermen. However, dreadful traffic jams and gangs of thieves in Westminster's narrow approach roads revived calls for a bridge. In the 1720s, MPs vetoed the recommendation of a Commons Select Committee for a bridge, but by 1734 supporters of a bridge were meeting at the Horn Tavern in New Palace Yard. Maps of the river were drawn by Charles Labelye, an engineer and mathematician of French protestant origin; while surveys for the approach roads were prepared by Thomas Lediard, a magistrate and former diplomat who lived in Smith Square.[4]

Westminster's petition for a bridge was presented to parliament in February 1736. However, a high spring tide intruded on the debate, flooding the Palace's cellars and ground floor, and 'the Judges etc. were oblig'd to be carry'd out' of Westminster Hall. Of five possible sites for a bridge, MPs opted for the middle one at New Palace Yard; an option that entailed heavy clearance costs for removing houses and shops but delivered MPs to the door of the Houses of Parliament. By the summer, an unwieldy, 175-strong commission of dignitaries and politicians were meeting in the Jerusalem Chamber to oversee the bridge's construction. In July, opposition to the project turned violent when a package left near the Court of Chancery at Westminster Hall exploded. As the hall filled with smoke, 'the judges started from the benches, the lawyers were all running over one another's backs to make their escape, some losing part of their gowns, others their periwigs, in the scuffle'. The perpetrator, Rev. Robert Nixon, objected to the damage that a bridge would inflict on trade in the City and Southwark. He was fined, made to walk through the Great Hall with a paper on his forehead admitting his offence, and gaoled for five years.[5]

The cost of the bridge caused much controversy. Although five state lotteries were held between 1736 and 1741, none of them raised sufficient funds and much of the estimated cost of £389,500 was finally borne by the taxpayer. This financial mess provoked the author, Henry Fielding, an opponent of lotteries, to quip that the new crossing should be called the 'Bridge of Fools', because of the country's folly in building it for Westminster. The bridge was finally commissioned in May 1738 to cross the river from the Woolstaple, a few yards from New Palace Yard. Initially, the engineer Labelye made good progress. The first piles were driven in during September and the first stone was laid by the Earl of Pembroke in January 1739. Each of the 14 supporting stone piers was built inside a massive, wooden, water-tight container sunk into the river bed, rather like a dry dock.[6]

Politics threatened to intrude later in 1739, when the prime minister, Robert Walpole, bowed to the demands of the war party after Captain Robert Jenkins had reportedly shown MPs a piece of gristle, supposedly his ear that had been cut off by a Spanish officer. The fear among the boat crews bringing Portland stone to Westminster of being press-ganged for the Royal Navy, threatened to disrupt supplies. In the event, war was less of a threat to Labelye's bridge than acts of god, mishap and sabotage. From Boxing Day 1739 until well into February, the Thames froze solid. Crowds flocked on to the ice to enjoy the temporary coffee houses and stalls, in scenes reminiscent of the popular 'Frost Fairs' on the river during the bitterly cold winters in the late seventeenth century. However, the damage from ice and sightseers took until mid-March to repair. Another freeze the following winter caused further delay.[7]

By the spring of 1745 the bridge's white Portland and green Purbeck stone arches were sparkling above the river. Canaletto's painting of the following year: *The City seen through an Arch of Westminster Bridge*, has a builder's bucket hanging from it. The last stone, except for the balustrade and pavement, was finally laid on 25 October 1746, in time for a magnificent river pageant to mark the swearing-in of the Lord Mayor of London before the barons of the Exchequer at Westminster. The magnificent spectacle of the mayoral state barge, and the barges of the City livery companies, being rowed through the arches of the new bridge by uniformed watermen is the subject of Canaletto's *Lord Mayor's Day*. However, Canaletto sacrificed accuracy for effect by adding statues and other details to the bridge. Except for a plume of chimney smoke on Millbank, near St John's, Smith Square, Westminster is shown in a distinctly Italian light with little sign of its usual smoky haze.[8]

Although people began using the bridge before the final touches were completed, it was discovered in 1747 that one of its stone piers was sinking. The repairs took more than three years and feature in several Canaletto works. Two earthquakes, in February and March 1750, severely tested the bridge. In Westminster Hall, people were terrified that the roof would fall in, while at the Abbey chunks of masonry came crashing down from the recently built western towers. During the second tremor, Horace Walpole was woken in nearby St James's by 'a violent vibration and great roaring ... heard all the windows in the neighbourhood flung up ... and found people running into the streets ... [and] two old houses flung down, several chimneys, and much china-ware'.[9]

The following November, Labelye's stone bridge opened with a late night ceremony in which local worthies walked across, a band played 'God Save the King' and gun salutes were fired. Festivities continued the next day, as boats crammed the river and crowds packed the bridge, walking to and fro. The bridge survived for little more than a century, but the new road plan devised in 1740 by Thomas Lediard and completed by his son, survives.[10]

Lediard's ambitious plan for broad, straight thoroughfares, enabled politicians and local worthies on the bridge's commission to demolish a swath of thief-infested slums off dingy King Street. By the mid-1750s, Bridge Street had obliterated the ancient Woolstaple, while Parliament Street sliced through the old privy garden and bowling green. Today's familiar street lay-out was completed by James Mallors, a builder, who created Great George Street in the 1750s, linking the bridge and St James's Park by extending the line of Bridge Street through another cluster of higgledy-piggledy alleys. To the south, Dirty Lane, the ancient route from Old Palace Yard to the Horse Ferry was straightened, widened and re-named as Abingdon Street. The palladian-style villa fronting onto Old Palace Yard was built in the mid-1750s for the Clerk of Parliaments and his assistant. The remnants of Abingdon Street's eighteenth-century houses were demolished in the 1960s to make way for an underground car park and a stretch of grass known as College Green.[11]

Lediard's civic-minded idea for a public, open space in Whitehall by the Thames in place of the Palace's gutted ruins had little appeal for Westminster's bigwigs. Similarly, a design for a new palace went no further than the drawing board. The site was irresistible for Britain's landholding elite, who now dominated court and parliament, and wanted to build convenient, and suitably grand, town houses. The family names of the new Whitehall residences signalled the change from a royal palace complex to a grandees' quarter – Cadogan, Carringon, Fife, Gwydyr, Montagu, Pelham, Pembroke and Richmond. Canaletto's painting of 1747, *Whitehall and the Privy Garden*, looks north from the window of the Duke of Richmond's dining room and captures the transition. It shows the stables of Richmond House and the back of Montagu House, while the old privy garden and Holbein Gate are both intact. The latter was demolished 12 years later as an obstruction to traffic.[12]

This changing Westminster scene was familiar to several young writers who lodged in Downing Street. Tobias Smollett, the writer, tried to set up a surgeon's practice in a room in the row of houses opposite Number 10 in the 1740s. Horace Walpole, who had lived in Number 10 with his father, later took lodgings almost opposite. In November 1762, the young James Boswell, the future friend and biographer of Samuel Johnson, became a lodger in the 'healthful' and 'genteel street' after arriving from Scotland. His landlord, Mr Terrie, was chamber-keeper to the Office of Trade and Plantations in nearby Whitehall.[13]

The following March, Boswell and a friend heard William Pitt the Elder speak in the Commons: 'and then indeed I heard oratory. The ease, the fluency, the grace with which he spoke was amazingly fine'. Three days later, Boswell found alternative evening entertainment with a prostitute in St James's Park; and in May he picked up 'a strong, jolly young damsel at the bottom of Haymarket' and had sex on Westminster Bridge. 'The whim of doing it there with the Thames rolling below amused me much'. The following month, he took a prostitute into Whitehall's privy garden, but 'the wretch picked my pocket of my handkerchief'. A few weeks later, Boswell left Downing Street for chambers in the Temple.[14]

The demolition of Holbein Gate, followed by the destruction of Whitehall, or Court, Gate in 1765, symbolized the passing of old Westminster. At the Abbey, the last funeral effigy to be added to the collection was that of Katherine, Duchess of Buckingham, who died in 1743, the same year as the Battle of Dettingen in Germany, where George II became the last British monarch to lead his troops into battle. Katherine, who was not only a duchess, but presumed herself to be an illegitimate daughter of James II, was anxious for recognition of her rank and had, in Horace Walpole's words, 'made a funeral for her husband as splendid as that of the great Marlborough'. After her young son died, she wrote to Sarah, Duchess of Marlborough, asking to borrow the hearse that had carried the duke's corpse. When Sarah refused, Katherine retorted that according to the undertaker: 'I may have a finer for twenty pounds'. Katherine commissioned her own effigy, dressed in robes worn at Queen Anne's coronation, and kept it at Buckingham House. Almost 20 years after her death, the building was bought by George III and eventually became Buckingham Palace.[15]

When King George II died in November 1760, his funeral was held at night, as was then fashionable. Horace Walpole watched the procession pass through 'a line of foot-guards, every seventh man bearing a torch, the horse-guards lining the outside, their officers with drawn sabres and crape sashes on horseback, the drums muffled, the fifes, the bells tolling, and minute guns'. The Abbey's interior was 'so illuminated that one saw it to greater advantage than by day; the tombs, the long aisles and fretted roof, all appearing distinctly, and with the happiest chiaro scuro'. However, the prime minister, the 'burlesque' Duke of Newcastle, disrupted the solemnity with 'a fit of crying the moment he came into the chapel'. The duke needed smelling salts from the archbishop, 'but in two minutes his curiosity got the better of his hypocrisy and he ran about the chapel with a looking glass to spy who was or was not there'.[16]

George II became the last British monarch to be buried in Westminster Abbey: in the spacious, new vault that he had commissioned for himself and his family, beneath the nave of Henry VII's chapel. His remains lie in a large yellow and black marble sarcophagus, together with those of his wife, Caroline of Ansbach, for whose funeral in 1737 Handel specially composed his anthem, 'The ways of Zion do mourn'. George had not wanted to be separated from his wife in death and their coffins were placed together with one side of each coffin removed. According to Dean Stanley, when the royal vault was later opened, in 1871, the two planks were seen leaning against the wall.[17]

Stanley, who had a morbid fascination with the royal tombs, regularly went at dead of night with a group of workmen to open up the vaults. The historian, James Froude, accompanied the Dean on one occasion: 'I have had my hand in the coffin of Mary, Queen of Scots, which had been broken by another falling on it. It was the weirdest scene – the flaring torches, the banners waving from the draught of air, and the dean's keen eager face seen in profile had the very strangest effect. He asked me to return with him the next night, but my nerves had quite enough of it'.[18]

George II was succeeded by his 23-year-old grandson, George III, the son of Prince Frederick, who had died nine years earlier. The coronation was held in 1761, and Horace Walpole was on hand to witness the events:

The multitudes, balconies, guards, and processions made Palace-yard the liveliest spectacle in the world … [Westminster] hall was the most glorious. The blaze of lights, the richness and variety of habits, the ceremonial, the benches of peers, and peeresses, frequent and full, was as awful as a pageant can be.[19]

Yet the awestruck Walpole could also find amusement in the antics of the prime minister who once again behaved in an unseemly fashion. 'Of all the incidents of the day', Walpole noted, 'the most diverting was what happened to the Queen. She had a retiring-chamber, with all conveniences, prepared behind the altar. She went thither – in the most convenient what found she, but – the Duke of Newcastle!' Queen Charlotte had discovered the prime minister using her private toilet. Walpole was unimpressed by the confusion that delayed the day's ceremonies. His disappointment was shared by Thomas Gray, the poet, who observed that after the ceremony in the Abbey, 'it was so dark that the people without doors saw scarce anything of the procession.'[20]

George III's coronation was the last one attended by the Dukes of Aquitaine and Normandy. With them went any vestige of the English monarch's claim on France. According to a rumour reported by the philosopher, David Hume, an unanticipated visitor from France was Charles Stuart ('Bonnie Prince Charlie'), the Young Pretender. He had supposedly come to London under the name of Mr. Brown and told somebody in the Abbey who recognized him that he was there 'out of curiosity'. He claimed, less credibly, not to envy the new king. Those looking for omens at a coronation wondered what the fall of the largest jewel from the Crown might portend. Twenty years later they could knowingly point to the loss of America.[21]

27 MOBS AND SCRIBBLERS

The mob and the press were feared by Britain's ruling class at Westminster in the eighteenth century because they were much less easy to control than elections or parliament. No government was defeated at a general election during the whole of this period. For one thing, there were fewer elections after 1715. The Septennial Act, passed on the pretext of the Jacobite uprising, more than doubled the maximum life of a parliament and helped entrench the Whigs in power.

Also, only about 300,000 people (approximately 5 per cent of adults) were entitled to vote, and they had to do so in public. As a result, many seats were in the pockets of landed magnates or the Crown through patronage. Seats were traded as if they were property and were sometimes bestowed on precociously young politicians: among prime ministers Walpole became an MP at the age of 24, North at 22, Pitt (the younger) at 21 and Grey at 22. Politics at Westminster often focused on the leading Whig personalities and their factions who jostled for office; while ministers generally sought to avoid antagonizing those MPs whose priority was promoting local interests.[1]

Governments managed parliament through family connections and patronage. At no time between 1689 and 1815 did the number of MPs drawn from outside the gentry or nobility ever exceed 100 (less than one fifth of the total). Sixty per cent of all MPs between 1734 and 1832 were drawn from only 922 families, and more than 17 per cent were sons of peers. Patronage and privilege were reinforced by a savage penal code. As Ian Gilmour, the politician and writer noted, parliament increased the number of offences carrying the death penalty by more than one a year between the Restoration and 1820.[2]

The Whig strangle-hold on power meant that government arrogance and incompetence went largely unpunished. Instead, people's anger, frustration and protest erupted in print, on the stage and sometimes on the streets. Newspapers discovered that they could sell copies by criticizing the government, and cartoonists found a ready market by poking fun at politicians. Walpole railed against the newspapers, as has every prime minister since, but what angered him most was the nightly ridicule heaped on him on the London stage. He took his revenge in the 1737 Licensing Act, giving the Lord Chamberlain, an officer of the royal household, the power to censor plays; a power that lasted until 1968.

Press reporting of parliament was regarded by Walpole as especially intrusive. In the seventeenth century, MPs had wanted, with good reason, their debates to be kept secret from the monarch. Having triumphed over the Crown, parliament then wanted its debates kept secret from the people; but by the start of the eighteenth century licensing the press had broken down. News-sheets, produced by scriveners working in the courts in Westminster Hall, began reporting parliament, based on intelligence from messengers and officials, and gossip in the Great Hall. John Dyer, the first 'news-writer' reporting parliament in the 1690s was repeatedly seized by the Serjeant-at-Arms and brought to the bar of the house, where he confessed, asked forgiveness, paid his fees and was released, ready to start all over again.[3]

Although newsletter writers were banned by a Commons resolution in 1703, Abel Boyer, a French pamphleteer, ingeniously evaded the ban in his new monthly, *The Political State of Britain* by reporting parliament in the guise of a letter to a friend abroad and disguising the names of speakers. Despite being fined and briefly imprisoned, Boyer carried on and his monthly lasted till 1737, eight years after his death. By this time, two rival monthlies, Edward Cave's the *Gentleman's Magazine* and Thomas Astley's the *London Magazine*, were cautiously reporting parliament.[4]

Cave's sales rose to 15,000 copies a month. Some politicians collaborated by giving Cave their speeches in advance, but in 1738 he pushed his luck too far by publishing a speech before it had been delivered. MPs reasserted their traditional opposition to reporting in a debate that was itself reported unofficially. 'I have read some debates of this House, Sir,' Walpole reportedly complained, 'in which I have been made to speak the very reverse of what I meant. I have read others of them wherein all the wit, the learning, and the argument has been thrown into one side, and on the other nothing but what was low, mean, and ridiculous'. MPs duly re-asserted the ban on all reporting of parliament by passing the following resolution: 'That it is an high indignity to, and a notorious breach of Privilege of, this House, for any News-Writer, in Letters or other Papers ... to give therein any Account of the debates, or other Proceedings of this House ... and that this House will proceed with the utmost severity against such offenders'.[5]

The press fought back. The *London Magazine* pretended they were publishing the debates of a political club, while Cave disguised them as 'Debates in the Senate of Magna Lilliputia', in which Sir Robert Walpole became Sir Rubs Waleup, and so on. One of Cave's parliamentary reporters for five years from 1738 was Samuel Johnson. Many years later, at a London dinner attended by Johnson, a guest remarked that a speech by the elder Pitt in 1742 surpassed any by the most eloquent speakers in history. To general astonishment, Johnson declared: 'That speech I wrote in a garret in Exeter Street'. As he explained, he 'never was in the gallery of the House of Commons but once'. Instead, he relied on Cave and his team, who paid the doorkeepers for a seat and took notes. 'I composed the speeches in the form they now have in the parliamentary debates,' Johnson confessed, before adding, 'I took care that the Whig dogs should not have the best of it'. Johnson also told his friend James Boswell that he stopped writing parliamentary reports when he realized that they were thought genuine, 'for he would not be accessory to the propagation of falsehood'. In his *Life of Johnson*, Boswell dismissed the Doctor's less reputable successors as 'obscure scribblers'.[6]

However, not even Walpole could insulate himself entirely from public unrest. His plans in 1733 to impose a general excise duty while cutting land tax sparked widespread protests. His plan would have benefited landowners most and created more government office-holders across the country. In the end, Walpole backed down, but on the April night when he told MPs of his retreat, a huge crowd gathered in the Commons lobby and the adjoining Court of Requests. Walpole refused to leave by a back way and, despite being escorted by 50 constables and friends, was mobbed and jostled. After reaching a nearby coffee house he left by an exit unknown to the mob.[7]

Walpole claimed that there had been a plot to assassinate him, implying that it was those Jacobites again, and rallied Whig MPs in caucus at the Cockpit. However, his authority never fully recovered. He had built his reputation on keeping Britain at peace, and when the country was dragged into the War of Jenkins's Ear, his standing slumped. At the 1741 election, despite all the Whig fixing, Walpole secured only a small Commons majority. Less than a year later, on 11 February 1742, he resigned.

'The greatest men in England have fallen into the error that to be master in the Cabinet is to be master of the nation', observed the Earl of Egmont in 1751. 'The general voice of the whole people were against and he fell by it'. Egmont was describing an exceptional moment in eighteenth-century politics. Reporting of Westminster remained heavily censored. In 1747, Cave was arrested, brought before the bar of the House of Lords, reprimanded and fined for reporting the trial in Westminster Hall of Lord Lovat, the Jacobite conspirator who became the last man in England to be publicly beheaded.[8]

It was another five years before the *Gentleman's Magazine* guardedly resumed reporting parliament. Reporters sat in the strangers' gallery – a term that oozes disdain – pretending to be ordinary members of the public, but their reporting was easily disrupted by MPs on the government benches who ordered the clearance of the strangers' gallery whenever they expected an effective speech by an independent or opposition MP. This ploy helped to earn the 'Unreported Parliament' of 1768–74 its tag, but MPs' attempts to stop newspapers publishing anything other than sketchy reports provoked a violent clash.[9]

John Wilkes, who lived and set up a press in Great George Street, did most to open up parliament. He was an unlikely hero. He won his first seat through patronage and then held it by buying votes. A member of the notoriously licentious Hellfire Club, he was caricatured by William Hogarth as a demagogue with a hideous squint. However, Wilkes's brilliant pen propelled him to fame. *North Briton,* the paper he launched in 1762, took its satirical title from *Briton,* a cheerleader for the government led by Bute, a Scottish earl.

When *North Briton* No. 45 denounced the King's Speech, George III's new ministry under George Grenville prosecuted it for seditious libel. Wilkes and his associates were arrested under a general warrant issued against unnamed persons, but Wilkes was then set free on the spurious grounds of parliamentary privilege. At the news of his release, shouts of 'Wilkes and Liberty!' from the crowds in Westminster Hall rang through the old Palace. The scenes outside were witnessed by Boswell, who saw Wilkes 'followed to his house in Great George Street by an immense mob who saluted him with loud huzzas while he stood bowing from his window'.[10]

Ministers were determined to silence Wilkes by fair means or foul. Their campaign gave rise to an extraordinary occasion in the House of Lords in November 1763, when Wilkes's *Essay on Woman,* an obscene parody of Pope's *Essay on Man,* printed privately for his fellow rakes in the Hellfire Club, was read to a predictably packed Chamber. The Commons declared that the *North Briton* was a seditious libel and that Wilkes could not claim parliamentary privilege after all. Wilkes fled to France, was expelled from the Commons and, after failing to attend his trial, was outlawed. However, the *North Briton* case eventually brought a victory for liberty when judges rejected the use of general warrants.

Yet, Westminster had not heard the last of Wilkes. He returned to England to contest the 1768 general election and, despite losing in the City of London, won Middlesex (in effect, greater London north of the Thames). Although he was imprisoned for seditious libel and expelled from parliament, he was re-elected and became a popular hero. The government, in some desperation, put up as their candidate, Colonel Henry Luttrell. Despite losing, Luttrell was awarded the seat anyway. However, this blatant chicanery galvanized the opposition. The Wilkes affair dominated politics. In January 1770 it dented the government's majority and prompted the prime minister, the Duke of Grafton, to resign.

Grafton was the seventh prime minister during the first ten years of George III's reign, a tally that reflected the intense rivalry among leading Whigs and their difficulty in coping with the assertive young king. Yet George was clearly pained by the rapid turnover in premiers. 'Whatever you may think', he pleaded when asking Frederick, Lord North, to form a government, 'do not take any decision unless it is the one of instantly accepting without a further conversation with Me'. North accepted but always denied that he was 'prime minister', because the term retained a pejorative sting.[11]

North had a tough time in the press, whose sales had been boosted by the Wilkes drama in Middlesex. North's round face, full cheeks and bulging eyes, were mercilessly caricatured. Horace Walpole called him the 'blind trumpeter' and another contemporary described him as a 'great heavy booby-looking seeming changeling'. A scurrilous cartoon showed him presiding over a Privy Council meeting in a bog house, wiping his bottom with his proposals on corruption and government reform. North was remarkably relaxed about these attacks, but the controversy over reporting parliament was much trickier.[12]

By 1771, the press were flouting the ban on reporting, by carrying extensive coverage of parliamentary debates. In February, Colonel George Onslow, known as 'Little Cocking George', a nephew of a recent, long-serving Speaker, Arthur Onslow, insisted that the printers of the *Middlesex Journal* and the *Gazetteer*, John Wheble and Roger Thompson, be brought to the Bar. MPs on the government benches supported Onslow, but the printers failed to attend and their arrest was ordered. Wilkes, who was banned from being an MP until the next election, seized his opportunity to embarrass the government. When MPs brought similar charges against other London printers, John Miller of the *London Evening Post*, joined Wheble and Thompson in defying parliament. The Serjeant-at-Arms sent a Commons messenger to arrest Miller in the City on 15 March, but the messenger was arrested and sent for trial by three City magistrates: Wilkes, the Lord Mayor, Brass Crosby, and Alderman Richard Oliver.[13]

As Wilkes hoped, the crisis escalated into a head-on clash between London and Westminster. On 25 March, a huge crowd escorted Brass Crosby and Oliver from the Mansion House to parliament, to appear before MPs at the bar of the House. As MPs debated what should be done, the Chamber was penetrated by the menacing shouts and deep hum of the mob outside. Oliver was committed to the Tower, and Crosby, who was ill with gout, had to return to learn his fate. Two days later, a larger and more tumultuous crowd accompanied the Lord Mayor from the Mansion House. Respectable merchants, shopkeepers and tradesmen travelled in a line of carriages that extended from St Paul's to Charing Cross, but there was also a large unruly element. As the crowd massed in Old Palace Yard, MPs had great difficulty forcing their way into the house. Every carriage was stopped. MPs who backed the Lord Mayor were cheered while those against him were mobbed. Constables trying to keep order had their staves wrested from them and used by the crowd.[14]

North was pulled from his carriage, which was wrecked, his hat was torn to shreds and he was struck on the head by a constable's baton. As the crowd mobbed him, he cried, 'Gentlemen, gentlemen, is this liberty? Do you call this liberty?' 'Yes' replied one of his assailants, 'and great liberty, too'. North only escaped with his life into Westminster Hall because of the timely help of Sir William Meredith, an MP who was one of the City's greatest champions. The shock of being mobbed reduced North to tears.

The mob's threatening protest at the doors of parliament delayed the debate until eight o'clock in the evening. MPs on the government benches sat with their clothes torn and dishevelled. Some of the crowd forced their way into the passages near the Chamber, and menacing shouts could be heard. A large force of horse and foot were ready near St Stephen's, but the sheriffs, accompanied by MPs sympathetic to the protest, such as Edmund Burke, Lord John Cavendish and Sir George Savile, agreed to go outside and calm the mob. Most of the crowd dispersed after being assured that the Lord Mayor wanted them to leave.

The Commons finally voted to commit the Lord Mayor to the Tower. Crosby left the Houses of Parliament at 12:30 a.m. and was taken in his own coach, accompanied by the deputy Serjeant-at-Arms. A huge crowd had waited in Whitehall, where they took the horses from the carriage and drew it as far as Temple Bar. There they tried to pull the deputy Serjeant-at-Arms from the coach, but Crosby pacified them. The crowd brought Crosby to the Mansion House, but he then drove quietly and unobserved in a hackney coach to the Tower. Although Crosby and Oliver had been sent to the Tower, they were released after four months. North quietly backed down. After the printers' riots, reporting of parliament was established. A few years later, the Lords threatened to enforce the ban but thought better of taking on Wilkes, who had become Lord Mayor of London.[15]

Although the ban on parliamentary reporting was no longer enforced, taking notes was banned and MPs periodically had the strangers' gallery cleared. One journalist rose to these challenges better than most. William Woodfall, editor of the *Morning Chronicle*, a Whig paper launched in 1769, memorized what MPs said and was the first to report debates the day after they took place. 'Memory Woodfall' became a familiar figure in the strangers' gallery, leaning forward with both hands clasped on his stick, his eyes closed, listening intently. His only refreshment was hard-boiled eggs. He used to peel off the shell in his hat, but one night a rival substituted a raw egg and its contents spilt over Woodfall's clothes.[16]

After 1789, James Perry took over the *Morning Chronicle* and devised a system in which reporters took it in turns to do a stint in the gallery and then write up the notes in the office. Perry's take-over was partly funded by John Bellamy, who had been appointed parliament's housekeeper in 1773. Bellamy helped Perry get seats for his reporters and saw that their 'copy' was promptly dispatched. He also ran a wine business while making a fortune from a kitchen and tavern that provided MPs with a chop, steak or pie, and glass of port or sherry from the wood. 'Bellamy's', as it became known, also supplied refreshments for reporters near the strangers' gallery: 'On a landing at the top of the stairs on a small table, they could have the most excellent cold beef and beetroot salad for three shillings and sixpence'.[17]

North's predictable victory in the 1774 general election inspired the *London Magazine* to print a satirical cartoon, 'The Colossus of the North', in similar vein to Walpole's portrayal as a giant outside the Treasury. A gigantic North stands outside Westminster Hall on two pillars, one marked 'Tyranny' and the other 'Venality'. He straddles a 'Corruption's Stream' of MPs who were re-elected through bribery and patronage. In his right hand, North clutches papers marked Places, Pensions and Lottery Tickets (the latter items were often given as bribes). Nearby, Britannia holds a placard declaring: 'Those that should have been my Rescuers have been my Destroyers'. She looks towards Wilkes, who sweeps at the flow of MPs with a broom and proclaims: 'I'll stem the stream'.[18]

The flaming torch held aloft by North in his left hand is labelled 'America'. On 16 December 1773, less than a year before North's election victory, American colonists had boarded ships in Boston harbour and emptied tea chests into the sea – 'The Boston Tea Party'. At Westminster, North had responded defiantly to this attack on tea duty: 'Let it go forth to the world that the parliament of Great Britain will protect their subjects and their property'.[19]

Within 18 months Britain was at war in America. As the British campaign went from bad to worse, crowds gathered in Downing Street and booed North, putting him off his work. Discontent with the war fuelled demands for political reform at home. In the Commons, the Government was defeated on John Dunning's resolution: 'that the influence of the Crown has increased, is increasing and ought to be diminished'. Two months later, dissatisfaction spread to the streets, triggered by North's retreat in the face of violent unrest when he tried to apply the 1778 Catholic Relief Act in Scotland. The Act had been introduced to recruit Catholic troops for the American war, but North's retreat encouraged Lord George Gordon, an MP and younger son of a Scottish duke, to take up the fight in England.

Gordon was a garrulous maverick who wore his long red hair 'without curl or powder, in the precise form of antient puritans', according to a contemporary quoted by the historian, John Paul de Castro. Gordon's Protestant Association was set up to mobilize support for repeal of the 1778 Act. Notices were put up telling people about his petition to parliament and where they could sign copies. Gordon's mixture of reactionary views and revolutionary fervour chimed with a public who felt frustrated at being ignored by Westminster. The disastrous American war intensified public disillusion.[20]

Gordon's petition attracted a staggering 100,000 signatures. The stupendous force of the pent-up resentment unleashed by Gordon became apparent on Friday 2 June 1780, when a crowd of 60,000 gathered at St George's Fields (now the site of Waterloo Station), to support Gordon as he delivered the mass petition to parliament. At noon, under a baking sun, the great crowd marched forth, six to nine abreast, singing hymns, their blue banners held aloft and many wearing blue cockades. The main contingent made for the City before heading to Westminster along the Strand and Whitehall. Two smaller contingents crossed the river by Blackfriars and Westminster Bridges. Others joined, including thieves on the make and trouble-makers.

The shocking events that followed were Britain's worst civil unrest since the Monmouth rebellion of 1685. They became deeply etched in folk memory.

Sixty-one years later, Charles Dickens, the former parliamentary reporter turned novelist, wrote *Barnaby Rudge*, with the sub-title, '*A Tale of the Riots of 'Eighty*'.

On that hot June day in 1780, customers of Alice's coffee house near the Houses of Parliament watched as Gordon's supporters poured into Old Palace Yard 'like a tide'. As the marchers halted, there was 'an uniform elevation of voices in three repeated cheers'. According to Frederick Reynolds, the future dramatist, and then a pupil at Westminster School:

> many thousands of disorderly persons occupied every avenue to the House of Parliament, the whole of Westminster Bridge, and extended nearly to the northern end of Parliament Street, the greatest part of it however was composed of persons decently dressed, who appeared to be incited to extravagance by a species of fanatical phrenzy [sic]. They talked of dying in the good cause.

Many crowded into Westminster Hall, forcing the courts to adjourn, while others took control of the passages leading to the Commons.[21]

Outside, carriages bringing MPs and Lords to parliament were driven back by the mob to cries of 'No popery!' The slogan was chalked on the carriages' panels, and blue cockades were put on the horses' heads. The prime minister, Lord North, was recognized in a carriage driven furiously past Horse Guards. Protesters rushed at the horses and surrounded the vehicle. The carriage door was forced open and North lost his hat, but the guards hurriedly rode up and dispersed the crowd. Several coaches were demolished. The wheels were wrenched off the Bishop of Lincoln's coach, and he was seized by the throat till blood oozed from his mouth, before being saved by a local lawyer who took him to his house. After borrowing a curled wig, round hat and green coat, the Bishop left incognito and escaped. Several Lords were injured, some robbed and others arrived dishevelled, wigless and badly shaken.[22]

In the Commons, Lord George Gordon, presented his petition for repeal of the Catholic Relief Act and claimed 120,000 signatures. The menacing scenes immediately outside the Chamber, where protesters packed the lobby, were re-captured by Dickens, with his intimate knowledge of the Houses of Parliament, and portrayed by 'Phiz' (Hablot K. Browne) in an accompanying illustration. Whenever an MP arrived with 'dress disordered and hair disheveled', the crowd 'yelled and screamed in triumph'. As the door to the Chamber was cautiously opened to admit late arrivals, the protesters 'grew more wild and savage, like beasts at the sight of prey, and made a rush against the portal which strained its locks and bolts in their staples, and shook the very beams'.

Gordon appeared periodically on one of the 'short, steep and narrow' flights of stairs leading to the strangers' gallery to address his supporters in the packed lobby, and was heard by the Commons chaplain, Rev Thomas Bowen, telling them,

'Lord North calls you a mob'. In the Lords, the debate on the Duke of Richmond's call for annual elections and manhood suffrage was disrupted by 'frequent interruptions from the thundering of the mob at the doors and the shouting without'. Lord Mansfield, 'quivered on the woolsack like an aspen', adjourned the House early and fled with other peers to make their escape by boat.[23]

Shortly after nine o'clock, a party of Horse and Foot Guards headed for the Houses of Parliament. They were surrounded by the mob, and when they brandished their swords were pelted with stones and faggots stolen from a nearby bakery. However, they succeeded in drawing the crowd away from the lobby of the Commons.[24]

By Saturday the riots seemed to have fizzled out, but that night violence flared again. For two terrifying days, the Irish were attacked, Catholic chapels burnt down and businesses looted as the unrest spread. On Tuesday 6 June, George Crabbe, the young Suffolk poet, visited Westminster and found the Horse and Foot Guards out in force, lining the middle of the streets, clearing the way for MPs and peers to reach parliament safely. At first they were driven back by demonstrators who 'boldly paraded the streets with colours and music'. Lord Sandwich was dragged from his coach at the corner of Bridge Street and Parliament Street and was lucky not to be torn limb from limb before escaping into a coffee house. Finally, the Horse broke through and 'after the cavalry had passed through them, the mob lay in the most ludicrous manner one over another, like a pack of cards'. Later, Justice Hyde sought to quell the mob in New Palace Yard by reading the riot act. In the Commons, a subdued Gordon backed measures to quell the riots.[25]

In the early hours of Wednesday 7th, rioters rushed to Whitehall and into the cul-de-sac of Downing Street with lighted torches and bundles of faggots. They planned to attack Number 10, but were confronted by Lieutenant David Howell with a detachment of 20 cavalry. As the lieutenant later recalled: 'I was obliged to charge through them, when three men were cut by the Dragoons under my command, but I believe no lives lost'.[26]

That evening, despite the worst riots in living memory, North gave dinner at Number 10. Among the guests were Sir John Macpherson, a future governor-general of India, and North's private secretary, William Brummell, whose son (later known as 'Beau') had been born in Downing Street and whose second birthday it happened to be. Macpherson later recalled: 'dinner had scarcely been removed', when the cul-de-sac 'became thronged with people', who seemed determined 'to proceed to acts of outrage'. North asked what was being done to defend Number 10 and was assured that there were 'twenty or more grenadiers, well-armed, stationed above stairs … ready on the first order to fire into the mob'. The prime minister wisely ordered that the crowd should be told of the grenadiers' presence in order to prevent bloodshed.[27]

Although more people poured into Downing Street, no attempt was made to force Number 10's front-door. As the evening wore on, the crowd gradually calmed down and began to disperse. But in the City, rioters attacked the Bank of England. Prisons, businesses and shops were ablaze, while soldiers fired on rioters and used their swords.[28] Inside Number 10, as Macpherson recalled, North and his guests

> sat down again quietly at the table and finished our wine. Night was coming on, and the capital presenting a scene of tumult of conflagration in many quarters. Lord North, accompanied by us all, mounted to the top of the house, where we beheld London blazing in seven places, and could hear the platoons firing regularly in various directions.

Displaying great sang-froid, North nodded at St John, one of his heavily armed dinner guests, and joked: 'I am not half so much afraid of the mob as of Jack St John's pistol'.[29]

The turning point came the next morning, when large numbers of troops moved into position on London and Blackfriars Bridges, while a smaller force secured the approaches to Westminster Bridge. The troops killed an estimated 285 rioters, while another 173 were taken to hospital. The estimated death toll of the riots was between 800 and 1,000. Gordon was tried in Westminster Hall. His trial began on a cold, wet, February day, but a great crowd gathered outside and the court was packed. Gordon was acquitted of having planned to levy war against the king, and resumed his political career.[30]

The Gordon riots were a failure. Their only effect was to bolster North's weak Government. A year later, North was brought down by military defeat abroad. News of Britain's surrender to American forces at Yorktown reached London on Sunday 25 November 1781. Sir Nathaniel Wraxall, the diarist and MP, noted North's reaction when Lord George Germain, Secretary of State for America, accompanied by Lord Stormont, the Secretary of State, and Lord Thurlow, Lord Chancellor, delivered the appalling news to North at Number 10:

> The First Minister's firmness, and even his presence of mind, which had withstood the riots of June 1780, gave way for a short time under this awful disaster. I asked Lord George [Germain] afterwards how he [North] took the communication when made to him. "As he would have taken a ball in his breast", replied Lord George. For he opened his arms, exclaiming wildly, as he paced up and down the apartment during a few minutes, "O God! it is all over!" Words which he repeated many times under emotions of the deepest consternation and distress.[31]

Defeat at Yorktown cost North his Commons' majority. His departure from office on 20 March 1782 showed that the king had to take heed of parliament's wishes when choosing a prime minister. As for North, he is remembered as the prime minister who lost America; but Edward Gibbon, the historian, MP and sometime lodger in Dean's Yard, Westminster, intended no irony when he dedicated his great work, *The History of the Decline and Fall of the Roman Empire* to his friend, North, whom he greatly respected.

28 PITT'S VILLAGE

William Pitt, the Younger, was Britain's most phenomenal prime minister. Only 24-years-old when he moved into Number 10, he lived there longer than any other prime minister. He was shaped by the Westminster village; shaping it in turn. Although his great rival, Charles James Fox, served as Westminster's MP for more than 25 years and was portrayed as 'The Westminster Watchman' for his defence of people's freedoms, Pitt dominated the political capital where Britain's destiny was determined.

Born in 1759, Pitt the Younger was the son of a prime minister, and the scion of two very political families. He grew up seeing his father, William Pitt (Pitt the Elder), the Earl of Chatham, feted as a national hero for defeating the French and establishing British supremacy in North America, India and the Caribbean. In 1763, his uncle, George Grenville, became only the second prime minister to live in Downing Street. Two years later, Grenville was bitterly attacked by the elder Pitt, his brother-in-law, for passing the Stamp Act, a measure that provoked riots and sowed the seeds of American revolt.

Pitt's meteoric rise to power reflected a political maturity beyond his years. His father schooled him to be a statesman and nothing else, bestowing on him a mastery of oratory that enabled him to command parliament, but leaving him painfully awkward outside a small circle of male cronies. In 1778, the 18-year-old Pitt saw his ageing father collapse in the Lords while attacking the doomed war against the Americans, and he began to assume the old statesman's mantle. Pitt's arrival in the Commons in January 1781 aged only 21 was not exceptional; his future rival, Charles James Fox, whose father, Henry, had been a rival of Pitt's father, had become an MP at 19. But Pitt's maiden speech was exceptional, prompting Burke to remark, 'He is not a chip off the old block; he is the old block itself'.[1]

Pitt was completely at home in the Commons, having watched its debates since childhood. The Chamber had the ambience of one of the less decorous gentlemen's clubs. To the surprise of Carl Moritz, a Prussian visitor, members 'enter the House in greatcoats, boots and spurs!' He also observed that MPs kept their hats on and wore no special clothing. Pitt's friend, William Wilberforce, the slavery abolitionist, later recalled that a miserly MP called Elwes (probably the inspiration for Dickens's character, Scrooge), lost his wig in the Chamber as another MP, Bankes, standing up to leave, unknowingly whisked it off with his dress-sword. Bankes left the Chamber wondering what caused the roar of laughter, unaware of the wig dangling from his sword and the hapless Elwes chasing behind.[2]

It was not unusual, according to Moritz, to see an MP 'stretched out on one of the benches while the rest are in debate. One may be cracking nuts, another eating an orange or whatever fruit may be in season; they are constantly going in and out …'. MPs brought in refreshments from the lobby. A young woman orange seller called Mullins was stationed there, according to Joseph Pearson, the principal door-keeper, 'with a basket of oranges on one hand, and hard biscuits on the other, chiefly for the use of my friend Charley Fox, who seems more relieved by a biscuit in a hot debate, than I am by a bumper of brandy'.[3]

Although women who provided refreshments were welcome, other women were barely tolerated. Until the early 1780s there are occasional references to women sitting in the strangers' gallery listening to the debates, as in January 1743 when 'some gentlewomen' were unable 'to hold their water' and urinated on a couple of members seated below. The references get fewer by the 1760s, and within about 20 years, women were excluded from the gallery. Lady Wallace, and the wife of Richard Brinsley Sheridan, are said to have dressed as men to sit in the gallery, but less intrepid women who wanted to watch debates were restricted to sneaking a view from above the Chamber by peering through 'pigeon-holes' in the ventilator shaft that passed through an upper storey in St Stephen's chapel.[4]

Pitt enjoyed the masculine world of the Commons with its culture of heavy drinking. During a major debate early in his premiership, he was so drunk that he had to retire briefly behind the Speaker's chair while Fox was speaking. Wilberforce saw Pitt go to 'Solomon's porch', an old entry to the chapel, and 'holding the door open, while he yielded to his malady, and turning his ear towards the House, that, if possible, he might not lose a single sentence that Fox uttered'. Pitt and Henry Dundas, his friend, used to joke, while sitting in the House together after a good dinner, as follows: Pitt – 'I can't see the Speaker, Hal; can you?' Dundas – 'Not see the Speaker, Billy! – I see two!'[5]

Pitt stood out from the crowd with his angular six-foot frame, auburn hair, and a nose, according to the painter, George Romney, 'Turned up at all mankind'.[6] He used to breeze through Westminster Hall, along the passageway leading to the Commons and through the lobby as though he owned the place. 'From the instant that Pitt entered the doorway [of the commons]', noted the Sir Nathaniel Wraxall,

he advanced up the floor with a quick and firm step, his head erect and thrown back, looking neither to the right nor to the left, not favouring with a nod or a glance any of the individuals seated on either side, among which many who possessed £5,000 a year would have been gratified by even so slight a mark of attention. It was not thus that Lord North or Fox treated parliament …[7]

Pitt's youthful air of confidence set him apart from older politicians, who were discredited by the disastrous loss of the American colonies. His rival, Fox was also free of blame for the American fiasco and in March 1782, at the age of 33, became Britain's first Foreign Secretary, when a departmental re-organization created the Foreign Office. Pitt and Fox were formidable politicians, but in every other respect were opposites. Moritz, who watched the young Foreign Secretary in the Commons, described him as 'dark, small, thickset, generally ill-groomed'. Fox was a charismatic, reckless, romantic figure who gambled at Newmarket races and Brooks's club, drank till all hours, had affairs with women and generated such deep loyalty among his political friends that they became known as Foxites. Fox's louche way of life and his belief that the Crown posed the greatest threat to the country led to a mutual antipathy between him and George III.[8]

In contrast to Fox, Pitt contrived to show his independence without damaging his career. He began by rashly turning down a junior government office and then urged reform on MPs, many of whom owed their seats to the corrupt system that he attacked. Yet such was Pitt's evident talent and exceptional, political pedigree that in July 1782, aged 23, he became the youngest ever Chancellor of the Exchequer. It was as Chancellor that Pitt first moved into Number 10; the prime minister, the Earl of Shelburne, preferring to stay at his house in Berkeley Square.

When Pitt entered Number 10, the front door looked much as is does today. Its hallmark seven-petal fanlight, lion's head door-knocker, letter-box, exterior lantern and supporting swirls of ironwork, all date from the mid-1770s. Once inside, Pitt crossed the entrance hall's black and white chequer-patterned marble floor, also dating from the mid-1770s. As he walked along a new corridor towards the back of the house, he passed on his right a recently closed courtyard. Number 10's east side had also been re-built and a vaulted kitchen installed, but, to Pitt's dismay, the repairs cost the country twice the estimated £5,500.[9]

Pitt's first stay at Number 10 lasted only eight months. After the Shelburne Government was brought down by the 'baneful alliance' of Fox and North, George III tried to persuade Pitt to become prime minister. As Pitt lacked a majority in the Commons he declined, but in December 1783 the king controversially forced the issue by organizing the Fox-North coalition's defeat in the Lords. Instead of returning to Number 10 straightaway, Pitt stayed at his brother's house in Berkeley Square while trying to form his 'mince pie administration', so-called because it was not expected to last much beyond Christmas.

Although Pitt suffered a series of defeats in the Commons in January 1784, he exploited his power of patronage, while cunningly showing his probity by declining the newly vacant sinecure of Clerk of the Pells, worth £3,000 a year, for himself. Instead, he handed the post to Colonel Barre MP, a hero of the capture of Quebec, thereby saving the public purse the cost of a pension that the MP had been controversially granted. During February, Pitt faced a new challenge when independent MPs met at Westminster's St Alban's Tavern and called on him and Fox to form a coalition. However, Pitt, sensing that his support was growing, refused to be pinned down. 'He beheld the prize for which they were contending nearly attained and secured,' noted the diarist, Wraxall. 'His insatiable ambition impelled him to govern alone'.[10]

Any possibility of a Pitt-Fox coalition was finally extinguished on 28 February, when Pitt's carriage was attacked by Fox's supporters as Pitt headed home up St James's Street after receiving the Freedom of the City. The boisterous mob escorting Pitt were thwarted when they attempted a detour to Fox's home in St James's Place, but their plan brought them closer to Brooks's club, where Fox often gambled. Outside the club, a Foxite mob assaulted Pitt's carriage and forced open the door. Although the carriage was wrecked, Pitt was somehow rescued and managed to reach White's, a safer club up the street. The real victim of the fracas was Fox, whose reputation was further damaged, while public sympathy lay with Pitt. Wits at Brooks's exacted some revenge by penning sarcastic verses about Pitt. These began appearing in the *Morning Herald* later that year under the title, *Criticisms of the Rolliad* (after *The Iliad*), and included the pithy gibe about the prime minister's youthfulness: 'A sight to make surrounding nations stare; / A kingdom trusted to a schoolboy's care'.

With the tide of opinion running strongly in Pitt's favour, the king willingly granted his prime minister's wish for an early election. Pitt gained about 70 seats, giving him a commanding three-figure majority, but the 1784 election is most remembered for the sensational contest in the City and Liberties of Westminster. Fox's fight to defy Pitt and the king by holding the seat he had narrowly won in 1780 became the stuff of political legend; although Fox pragmatically reserved a place in the new parliament by also having himself returned for the safe seat of Tain Burghs in the Orkneys.[11]

The Westminster constituency extended far beyond the old medieval village and comprised much of what is now London's west end. The outcome of the poll was unusually unpredictable, because patronage held less sway in the largest seat in the land numerically. About one in four men (approximately 12,000 in total) were entitled to vote by dint of paying a local 'scot and lot' property tax. Among them were artisans, courtiers, professionals, servants, shopkeepers and traders. Polling was held in public in Covent Garden and lasted for forty days: in Pitt's view, 'forty days poll, forty days riot, forty days confusion'.[12]

Westminster elected two MPs, and as Admiral Lord Hood, a naval hero and supporter of Pitt's, was sure to top the poll, the real fight was for the second seat. At times, there were violent fights, such was the bitterness between Fox's supporters and those of Sir Cecil Wray, the second government candidate. Both sides obtained support with canvassing from aristocratic ladies: Wray enlisting the

Countess of Salisbury; Fox recruiting the Duchesses of Portland and Devonshire. Georgiana Devonshire, a 26-year-old society beauty, campaigned tirelessly in Foxite blue and buff, leaving her coach to walk the streets and visit voters in their homes. Allegations about her unconventional campaigning first appeared in the pro-government *Morning Post* on 31 March: 'We hear the D— of D— grants *favours* to those who promise their votes and interest to Mr Fox'. Within days, a lewd cartoon, showing Georgiana embracing a tradesman, became widely available in clubs, coffee houses and taverns. For a while, Georgiana withdrew from the campaign, to the relief of her mother, Countess Spencer. When she later returned, she chatted with the crowds and visited shops where she and her friends overpaid, hinting at more if the owners voted for Fox. The insults continued, and her coach was followed by rowdy sailors, who sang: 'I had rather kiss my Moll than she; / With all her paint and finery; / What's a Duchess more than woman? / We've sounder flesh on Portsmouth Common!'[13]

Fox's support grew during the final weeks and by the close of poll he was in second place. However, Wray, the defeated candidate, demanded a scrutiny of the result and the high bailiff declined to declare Hood and Fox elected. Fox was furious and had to take his seat on the opposition front bench as MP for Tain Burghs when the Commons met. The row rumbled on for ten months until Fox was finally declared MP for Westminster.

The hullaballoo of Westminster's 1784 election campaign had barely died down when a fresh commotion occurred, outside the Abbey, on the fine spring morning of Wednesday 26 May. A long delay in opening the Abbey's doors for the first in a series of concerts to commemorate the twenty-fifth anniversary of Handel's death, created a great crush. The frightening scene was witnessed by Charles Burney, a music critic:

> such a crowd of ladies and gentlemen were assembled together as became very formidable and terrific to each other, particularly the female parts of the expectants; for some of these being in full dress, and every instant more incommoded and alarmed, by the violence of those who pressed forward, in order to get near the door, screamed; others fainted; and all were dismayed and apprehensive of fatal consequences …

Eventually, the crowd was admitted, and 'except for dishevelled hair, and torn garments, no real mischief seems to have happened'. The concert opened with Handel's coronation anthem, 'Zadok the Priest', 'And from the moment that the first sound of this celebrated and well-known composition, was heard, to the final close, every hearer seemed afraid of breathing, lest it should obstruct the stream of harmony in its passage to the ear'.[14]

The grandest concert in the series of five took place at the Abbey three days later, when George III and an audience of 4,500 heard 525 performers render

Handel's 'Messiah'. The concerts made a huge impact. The king's attendance on three occasions gave them a political impact that the organizers from the Concerts of Ancient Music never intended, having originally scheduled them for April. However, by the time they were held, the king's defeat of the Fox-North coalition, his support for Pitt, and the continuing row over the Westminster election had put the clash between Crown and Parliament centre-stage. The king had a strong incentive to seek favourable publicity. By making a show as patron of Handel, George III out-manoeuvred Fox. As the historian William Weber has noted, the concerts came to be seen as a celebration of the end of the political crisis and an expression of hope for a harmonious new order.[15]

29 FROM BAD DEBTS TO HIGH HOPES

opes for harmony after Pitt's resounding election victory in 1784 were first undermined by the legacy of the American war, and then shattered by shock-waves from the French revolution. Pitt was confronted by a mountain of government debt and a lack of international confidence. As a result of the American war, the national debt had soared to almost £250 million – more than £15 billion in today's prices, equivalent at the time to one and a half times Britain's total annual output (the same ratio between debt and output as in 2011–12, if the state bail-out of banks is included).[1]

Pitt's response was ingenious: cutting duties and boosting trade, while cracking down on smugglers and increasing revenue. In 1784, he slashed tea duty from an average 119 per cent to a uniform 25 per cent, compensating for the initial loss of revenue by increasing window tax and introducing a shop tax. His tax hikes provoked riots in London and caused a mob to besiege Downing Street, but Pitt stood firm. He forced down the price of tea, helped by tea merchants, and thus made smuggling unprofitable and turned Britons into tea drinkers. Duties on wines, spirits and tobacco were reduced, the power of customs officers increased, and a commercial treaty with France negotiated by Pitt's envoy, William Eden.

The national debt was tackled by creating a sinking fund that grew through compound interest. By 1792, national debt had fallen by a third and a confident Pitt persuaded the king to sack Thurlow, the Lord Chancellor, for having criticized the sinking fund. Thurlow's dismissal marks the start of Cabinet collective responsibility, a convention that has since underpinned Cabinet government. As public finances improved and trade boomed, Pitt dropped his hated shop tax, slashed the number of separate duties and cut taxes.[2]

Although sovereign debt crises in the early twenty-first century give Pitt's experience contemporary resonance, most aspects of life in his day were very different. In September 1786, before modern anaesthetics were available, Pitt had to have a cyst cut out from his cheek. The excruciating operation was conducted at Number 10 by John Hunter, Surgeon Extraordinary to George III. Beforehand,

Pitt asked how long it would take and was told six minutes. As Hunter set to work, the prime minister distracted his mind by looking out of a window at the back of Number 10 and concentrating on the Horse Guards' clock. After the operation was over, Pitt addressed only one remark to Hunter: 'You have exceeded your time half a minute'.[3]

Personal tragedy struck only a matter of days after Pitt's operation, when his sister, Harriot, who had married his friend, Edward Eliot, died at Number 10 following the birth of their child. Pitt was deeply affected; not only had he lost a sister of whom he was especially fond, he had depended on Harriot for contact with people other than his small circle of male cronies, and she had also kept an eye on his personal finances. For a while, Jane, Duchess of Gordon, took it upon herself to become Pitt's hostess, but her pushiness and use of coarse language caused them to drift apart.

Pitt's lack of interest in women was mocked in cartoons and in this gibe from the wits at Brooks's: "Tis true, we oft abuse him, / Because he bends to no man; / But slander's self dares not accuse him / Of stiffness to a woman'. Some years later, Pitt allowed a dalliance with Eleanor Eden, daughter of his friend, Lord Auckland, to lead to speculation about a possible marriage, but he brusquely scotched any such idea, citing 'an insurmountable obstacle'. One theory is that he feared passing on a strain of madness in the Pitt family and wanted to spare Eleanor any such risk. It is more likely that Pitt had homosexual inclinations, but in his day any admission or evidence of such feelings would have destroyed his all-consuming ambition. He had reached the top of politics young and, as he subordinated everything in his life to the business of governing, he remained asexual.[4]

Among Pitt's contemporaries, only the charismatic Charles James Fox might have thwarted Pitt's overwhelming ambition; but Fox failed to seize his opportunities. In 1786, opposition attacks on Warren Hastings, the former Governor-General of India, reached a crescendo. Fox, assuming that Pitt would defend Hastings, opened a Commons debate on Hastings's alleged bad treatment of an Indian prince. However, the prime minister sprang a huge surprise on friend and foe alike by unexpectedly supporting the charge against Hastings. It was a brilliant coup, as Pitt's biographer, William Hague, has shown, wrong-footing Fox while confirming Pitt's reputation for integrity.[5]

Hastings's trial in Westminster Hall in February 1788, following his impeachment for murder and extortion, promised to revive the high political drama of earlier state trials, although the ancient Hall was no longer the bustling, edgy, vibrant heart of Westminster. The law courts at its south end – Chancery and the King's Bench – were protected from noisy shoppers and menacing mobs by a Gothic screen erected in 1739 and further extended in height in 1755, within touching distance of the carved angels on the great beams above. After 1770, fewer MPs rushed through the Hall each day and instead used a new entrance to St Stephen's built during the extension of a relatively new Palladian-style building outside the Hall's west wall. By 1780, the removal of the Hall's shops and stalls, and repairs to the worn floor, roof and walls, had transformed its reputation from raucous to stately.[6]

However, Hastings's trial excited such keen anticipation that, despite the chilly weather, high society and great crowds packed the Hall. Charles Burney's daughter, Fanny Burney, the writer and a lady-in-waiting to Queen Charlotte, watched from the Deputy Great Chamberlain's box at the north end. To her left were the green benches for MPs. Opposite them sat the peeresses and peers' daughters. 'The bottom [south end] of the hall contained the royal family's box and the lord high steward's'. A gallery above the MPs' benches carried the Duke of Newcastle's box with special accommodation for the queen and 'the four eldest princesses who where there incog., [sic] not choosing to appear in state'. Mrs Fitzherbert, mistress of the Prince of Wales, sat in the royal box. Gibbon, the historian, Joshua Reynolds, the artist, and Mrs Siddons, the actor, also attended. In the middle of the hall 'was placed a large table, and at the head of it the seat for the [Lord] Chancellor, and round it seats for the Judges, the Masters in Chancery, the Clerks, and all who belonged to the Law; the upper end, and the right side to the Bishops and the Archbishops'. The prisoner's seat was located immediately in front of the box occupied by Fanny Burney.

Shortly before noon, Edmund Burke entered and led his fellow prosecutors, including Fox and Richard Brinsley Sheridan, the MP and playwright, to their box, to the left of Hastings's seat. Next, the Commons entered, 'so little like gentlemen and so much like hairdressers', according to Lady Claremont. After the robed peers and bishops came the Lord Chancellor, adopting a solemn expression above his beetled brow. Fox later wondered whether anyone could be as wise as Thurlow looked. Finally, Hastings was summoned and entered behind the Gentleman Usher of the Black Rod. As a lawyer read the charges, Hastings looked round the hall and then up at the box, where Fanny Burney sat. She was distressed that his face seemed 'pale, ill and altered', and felt 'shocked and ashamed to be seen by him in that place'. During the trial, she was worried at what Hastings might think when some of the prosecutors, whom she knew, caught her eye and chatted with her.[7]

Hastings's trial lasted, on and off, for seven years. As time went on, the celebrities and crowds drifted away, occasionally returning to hear Fox or Burke. Yet the oratory of these legendary speech-makers left some spectators cold. Fanny Burney was amused by her brother James's comments when he accompanied her to hear Burke: 'When will he come to the point?' 'These are mere words'. 'This is all sheer distraction'. 'All this is nothing to the purpose'. And so on. When an MP, asked Fanny Burney if she had been entertained, she chastised him for talking as if they were at an opera or comedy. ' "A comedy?" repeated he, contemptuously; "no a farce; 'tis not high enough for comedy. To hear a man rant such stuff. But you should have been here the first day he spoke; this is milk and honey to that'. The trial became a damp squib and eventually ended in Hastings's acquittal.[8]

In the autumn of 1788 Pitt faced a much graver threat when the king became deranged with a 'madness' now thought to have been caused by a genetic disorder. Pitt, having risen to power as the king's man, was extremely vulnerable, especially as the Prince of Wales, whom it was assumed would become Regent, favoured Fox. While Fox began discussing with his colleagues their jobs in his hoped-for future Cabinet, Pitt played for time, hoping that the king might recover.

Fox's presumptuous reaction was his undoing. Infuriated by Pitt's proposal to appoint yet another committee before any final decision on the setting up of a Regency, Fox over-reacted in the Commons; arguing that the Prince of Wales had 'as clear, as express a right to assume the reins of government, and exercise the powers of sovereignty, as in the case of his Majesty's having undergone a natural and perfect demise'. However, Fox's claim that the Prince had the right to assume the powers of monarchy, irrespective of parliament's view, flatly contradicted the Whig view of the constitution.[9]

Pitt could barely contain his delight. As he sat on the front-bench, waiting to reply, he is said to have slapped his thigh and remarked: 'I'll unwhig him for the rest of his life'. When he rose to the despatch box, he played to perfection his role as Fox's nemesis. 'To assert such a right in the Prince of Wales, or anyone else', he told MPs, 'independent of the decision of the two Houses of Parliament, was little less than treason to the constitution of the country'. It was a remarkable political turn-round. Fox's incautious and self-serving demand that the Prince should be allowed to assume the full power of monarchy had allowed Pitt to steal the Whigs' clothes and portray himself as the true defender of the Glorious Revolution.[10]

To Pitt's great relief, the king's health recovered in February 1789. Within five months, the storming of the Bastille heralded the French Revolution, but few shared Burke's prescient, immediate sense of foreboding. Fox welcomed the revolution and Pitt was initially optimistic. By the autumn of 1790, when Burke published his *Reflections on the Revolution in France*, Britain's own, industrial, revolution was boosting not only trade, but also the prime minister's majority in the Commons. With things going his way at last, Pitt succumbed to wishful thinking, much as Fox had done over the Regency question. In February 1792, Pitt confidently predicted that 'there never was a time in the history of this country when, from the situation of Europe, we might more reasonably expect 15 years of peace, than we may at present'. He could not have been more wrong.[11]

30 VILLAGE AT WAR

Only three months after his wildly optimistic prediction of European peace, Pitt, fearing that the French insurrection would spread to Britain, resorted to repression. The 'Pittite terror', as his measures became known, was triggered by a combination of food riots after a bad harvest, and radical agitation encouraged by the publication of Thomas Paine's *The Rights of Man*. Pitt's reactionary response to a scare was part of a pattern that extends from Walpole and the Jacobites, to Asquith and the German scare in the early 1900s, and to Blair and Islamic terrorism after 9/11. The 'Pittite terror' changed the look and feel of Westminster.

Pitt launched his crackdown in May 1792 by issuing a royal proclamation against 'divers wicked and seditious writings'. Anti-French hysteria caused an extraordinary scene in the Commons when MPs debated Pitt's Aliens Bill to control foreigners' travel. Edmund Burke learned that 3,000 daggers were on order from a Birmingham armourer, and flourishing a French prototype of the dagger 'with much vehemence of action threw it on the floor'. Burke accompanied his melodramatic action by declaring his determination 'to keep French infection from this country; their principles from our minds, and their daggers from our hearts!'. Burke's display was met by alarm, but also laughter when Sheridan, the playwright MP, quipped: 'The gentleman has brought us the knife, but where is the fork?'[1]

Within a year of Pitt's prediction, Louis XVI had been beheaded and Britain was at war with France. Pitt largely left strategy to his admirals and generals, concentrating instead on financing the war and keeping the country safe. The war put Britain's financial system under severe strain. Pitt had promised in 1783 to eradicate the national debt of £230 million, but by 1802 the debt more than doubled to £498 million and by 1820 it soared to £840 million. In order to prevent debt spiralling out of control, Pitt launched his own financial revolution in December 1798 by introducing income tax and allowing the taxman to require details of people's income. Income tax was repealed after the war, but was re-introduced in 1842 by Sir Robert Peel. No chancellor since has repealed it.[2]

The most painful step for Pitt came in 1797 when he created a supply of paper money, not fully backed by gold or coinage. His policy breached the Bank's pledge 'to pay the bearer on demand' in gold or coinage. This promise, initially given when issuing receipts in return for deposits, had built confidence in the Bank and made its notes a reliable medium of exchange. In 1759, gold shortages caused by the Seven Years War had forced the Bank to issue a £10 note. In 1793, Pitt boosted the money supply by allowing the bank to print £5 notes, thereby discouraging gold withdrawals and reviving trade. Four years later, reports of a French invasion in Pembrokeshire caused a run on the Bank and threatened a financial crash.

Pitt summoned an emergency Cabinet on Saturday 25 February 1797. Within days cash payments by banks were suspended and legislation was rushed through allowing the issue of the first £1 and £2 notes. The flow of money was maintained and a crash averted, but an anxious Pitt had saved Britain at the risk of creating runaway inflation. For his pains, he was portrayed in one of Gillray's most powerful cartoons, 'Midas Transmuting all into Gold [crossed out] PAPER', standing astride the Bank, with a pot belly full of gold while defecating and spewing banknotes. The restriction on paying out gold lasted until 1821 and prompted Sheridan to decry the Bank as 'an elderly lady in the City'. This image was adapted by Gillray, who showed Pitt's 'political ravishment' of the 'Old Lady of Threadneedle Street', as he tries to take her gold.[3]

The 'Pittite terror' was also intensified. The threat of invasion and a report that radicals planned a national convention prompted Pitt to suspend Habeas Corpus in 1794, in effect introducing imprisonment without trial. Fox condemned the repression, but the Whigs were split and the Duke of Portland led his fellow toffs into coalition with Pitt. The following summer, the soaring price of bread after poor harvests sparked unrest and a mob smashed Number 10's windows. During the state opening of parliament in October 1795, an immense crowd in St James's Park 'hissed and groaned' as the royal procession passed, and many called out: 'No Pitt, no War, Bread, Bread, Peace, Peace'. When the state coach passed along 'the narrow part of St Margaret's Street, between the church and Henry VII's chapel', something was thrown from a nearby house and broke the coach's window.[4]

Pitt responded with new 'gagging bills', restricting public meetings and imposing tough penalties for attacking the constitution or supporting Britain's enemies. Radicals were outraged. Francis Place, a tailor by trade, alleged that ministers had known that 'the king would be assailed by the clamours of ill fed discontented people' and had allowed it to happen. Fox seethed with anger during a mass protest in New Palace Yard. 'Good God Almighty, Sir! Is it possible that the feelings of the people of this country should be thus insulted? ... Good God, Sir, what madness, what frenzy has over taken the authors of this measure?' Fox was in despair and stopped attending Parliament for almost four years.[5]

The violence at the state opening and the mass protest scared the Government. Ministers were determined to control the area surrounding the Houses of Parliament. The heart of Westminster's ancient village was ripped out as Pitt's government and succeeding administrations cleared the medieval warren of lanes and streets on the Palace's doorstep. Between 1799 and 1815, as Sean Sawyer has shown, £250,000 was spent by the Westminster Improvements Commission removing the slums north of the Abbey and the higgledy-piggledy cluster of coffee houses, shops and taverns close by Westminster Hall and St Stephen's. The heart of old Westminster survives only in William Capon's evocative sketches of 1801–15. The new, open space of Parliament Square and an uncluttered St Margaret's Street were much easier to police.[6]

Pitt was a modernizer and also commissioned changes inside Number 10. Although his Cabinet had fewer members than today, he extended the Cabinet room to create a decent-sized meeting room, moving its end wall 12 feet to the east. In place of the old wall, the builders erected two double corinthian columns to support the structure above. At about the same time, another room on the first floor was extended and two ionic columns were installed as supports, creating the Pillared Drawing Room.[7]

Yet, Pitt's biggest impact on Westminster politics was made by his response to the security threat in Ireland. After a series of insurrections and attempted invasions, he decided that only full union would guarantee Britain's hold on Ireland. In 1800, the Act of Union abolished the Irish Parliament from January 1801. However, Pitt failed to persuade George III that Catholic emancipation was also necessary if the Irish were to accept union. The king's intransigence led Pitt to resign and fuelled resentment in Ireland. 'You have swept away our constitution, you have destroyed our Parliament', warned Henry Grattan, the champion of Irish parliamentary independence, 'but we shall have our revenge. We will send into the ranks of your Parliament, and into the very heart of your constitution, a hundred of the greatest scoundrels of the kingdom'.[8]

The addition of 100 Irish seats swelled the total number of MPs at Westminster to 658. The Commons Chamber was already too small to accommodate all MPs at once, but the arrival of the Irish increased the need for more space. The task fell to James Wyatt, who had been controversially preferred to Sir John Soane as Surveyor-General, and who had built a new range of offices alongside Westminster Hall in castellated Gothic style. Wyatt moved the Lords from their old Chamber to the Court of Requests. In the Commons, he added some extra seating by reducing the thickness of the walls between the buttresses. However, he made no attempt to conserve the old chapel's medieval craftsmanship. Among the irreplaceable losses were an attractive wall arcade, painted with figures of angels, and wall paintings behind Sir Christopher Wren's oak panelling.[9]

Fortunately, there is some record of the lost paintings in sketches hurriedly made by J. T. Smith, while 'the workmen very often followed him so close in their operations, as to remove, in the course of the same day on which he had made his drawing, the painting which he had been employed in copying that very morning'. Richard Smirke from the Society of Antiquaries also arrived, but John Carter, a longstanding critic of Wyatt's, was refused entry. Augustus Pugin, designer of today's Houses of Parliament, called Wyatt, 'The Destroyer'.[10]

Wyatt was condemned for reducing the number of seats in the strangers' gallery, having unwisely upset the press by making it harder for reporters to find a seat. Parliamentary reporters already worked long hours in miserable conditions. Although the Commons usually did not sit until 4 p.m., the gallery was open from 12 noon and reporters sometimes queued from 7 a.m. 'I shall give up this newspaper business', wrote the young Samuel Taylor Coleridge, who began reporting parliament for the *Morning Post* in 1799, 'it is too, too fatiguing. I have attended the Debates twice, and the first time I was twenty-five hours in activity, and that of a very unpleasant kind; and the second time from ten in the morning till four o'clock the next morning'. The young poet was adept at improving MPs' speeches for his readers. In February 1800, he told Robert Southey that 'Mr Pitt is much obliged to me. For, by Heaven, he never talked so eloquently in his lifetime. He is a stupid, insipid charlatan, that Pitt. Indeed, except Fox, I, you, or anybody, might learn to speak better than any man in the House'.[11]

Coleridge's labours in the Commons gallery had a less lasting impact than William Wordsworth's fleeting acquaintance with Westminster. Wordsworth and his sister Dorothy took the opportunity of renewed peace in Europe, to visit France. Boarding the Dover coach at Charing Cross on Saturday, 31 July 1802, they headed down Whitehall, along Parliament Street and then turned into Bridge Street. 'The City, St Paul's, with the river & a multitude of little Boats made a most beautiful sight', wrote Dorothy, 'as we crossed Westminster Bridge'. 'Earth has not any thing to show more fair', wrote William, of his view from the roof of the coach, a scene that he immortalised:

> This City now doth, like a garment, wear
> The beauty of the morning; silent, bare,
> Ships, towers, domes, theatres, and temples lie
> Open unto the fields, and to the sky;
> All bright and glittering in the smokeless air.
> Never did sun more beautifully steep
> In his first splendour, valley, rock, or hill;
> Ne'er saw I, never felt, a calm so deep!
> The river glideth at his own sweet will:
> Dear God! the very houses seem asleep;
> And all that mighty heart is lying still![12]

Westminster on a summer's morning may have, as Dorothy wrote, 'something like the purity of one of nature's own grand spectacle', but its human drama is more often tragic-comic. Less than a year after the Wordsworths' journey, Britain was again at war with France under its new leader, Napoleon. On Monday 23

May 1803, Pitt was due to make his first major speech since resigning as prime minister two years earlier. Although he was debilitated by duodenal ulcers, those who heard his speech regarded it as one of his finest. There was no need for a Coleridge to embellish what he said. However, Pitt's rousing come-back speech went unreported. The Speaker, Charles Abbott, had delayed admission to the strangers' gallery and most places were taken by friends of MPs. No reporter could find a seat in the mad scramble when the doors finally opened. After this fiasco, the Speaker decided that the reporter's usual place on the back row of the gallery should be reserved for 'newswriters'. As Andrew Sparrow, the political journalist, observes, it signalled Parliament's begrudging acceptance of the press.[13]

Almost a year after his great, unreported speech, Pitt returned to Number 10, again as both Prime Minister and Chancellor. His vivacious and witty niece, Lady Hester Stanhope, acted as his hostess and became 'a light in his dwelling', but otherwise Pitt's second premiership was more difficult than his first. His health was failing, his administration was less broadly based, and, in April 1805, he was reduced to tears when the Commons impeached his old friend, Viscount Melville, formerly Henry Dundas. Melville was acquitted the following year at the last state trial held in Westminster Hall.

Pitt's second administration lasted less than two years, but it guaranteed Britain's survival in one of the most famous naval victories. In September 1805, six weeks before Trafalgar, Admiral Nelson visited London and called on Pitt at Number 10 to discuss how to defeat the French and Spanish fleets at Cadiz. Nelson's stay in London was also the occasion of his only chance encounter with Wellington (then Major-General Arthur Wellesley and later, Duke), again in Downing Street, when they both called on Lord Castlereagh at the colonial and war office at Number 14, on the site now occupied by Number 12.

Wellington later recalled that he recognized Nelson as they sat in the small waiting room, and engaged him in conversation, 'if I can call it conversation, for it was almost all on his side and all about himself'. However, something that Wellington said made Nelson 'guess that I was somebody'. Nelson stepped briefly outside to find out who Wellington was. On his return, 'he was altogether a different man ... and [he] talked of the state of this country and of the aspect and probability of affairs on the Continent with a good sense ... in fact, he talked like an officer and a statesman'.[14]

Six weeks later, Nelson was killed in his hour of victory. His body was brought to the Admiralty in Whitehall and lay in the old captain's waiting room, now known as Nelson's Room. In the Board Room, a white spot on the wall by the fireplace is known as 'the Nelson spot' because it is at his height of 5 feet 4 inches. Before his earlier triumph at the Nile, Nelson had declared: 'Victory or Westminster Abbey'; but he was buried instead at St Paul's, to the Abbey's annoyance, especially as its canons and vergers depended for part of their income on a share of the admission price charged by the 'shewers of tombs'.

The Abbey retaliated by commissioning a full length effigy of Nelson from Catherine Andras, modeller in wax to the Queen. Andras had previously sketched Nelson for a wax profile while her adoptive father, Robert Bowyer, the artist, was painting his portrait. The Admiral joked that he was not used to being taken 'starboard and larboard at the same time'.[15] Nelson's family supplied a suit of his clothes and the shoe buckles he wore when he fell. A couple of days after the effigy went on show, a woman visitor was moved to tears by its likeness and told an Abbey guide that it would be perfect 'if a certain lock of hair was disposed in the way his lordship always wore it'. When she revealed that she was Emma, Lady Hamilton, the astonished guide allowed her to re-arrange it. Nelson's effigy was the last to be placed in the Abbey and now stands in its Museum.[16]

News of Nelson's victory at Trafalgar reached London two days before Pitt addressed the Lord Mayor's banquet at the Guildhall on 9 November 1805. His carriage was hauled along by cheering crowds and he was greeted as 'the saviour of Europe'. In response, Pitt famously declared: 'England has saved herself by her exertions, and will, as I trust, save Europe by her example'. However, his health was deteriorating. In January he received the shattering news of Napoleon's victory at Austerlitz. On seeing a map of Europe, he remarked sadly: 'roll up that map, it will not be needed these next ten years'.

Pitt died, aged 46, in the early hours of 23 January 1806 at his house near Putney. His habit of drinking the equivalent of a bottle and a half of wine a day probably contributed, but the anxiety of leading his country in war for many years took a heavy toll. 'Oh, my country! how I leave my country', were reportedly his dying words. It was later claimed that he had said: 'I think I could eat one of Bellamy's veal pies', but this suggestion appears to have been spread mischievously by Benjamin Disraeli.[17]

Pitt was given a hero's funeral. His body lay in state in the Painted Chamber of the Palace of Westminster, where tens of thousands filed past. He was buried in the family vault in Westminster Abbey, near the north door. The words on the slab marking the vault have been almost worn away by many thousands of visitors, but Pitt the Younger's monument takes pride of place above the west door. He is shown declaiming, while the muse of history notes his words and a male figure representing the anarchy of the French revolution is shown in chains.

Later the same year, Charles James Fox, died. He is buried near Pitt, and the proximity of their remains inspired Sir Walter Scott's lines in *Marmion*: 'Drop upon Fox's grave the tear, / 'Twill trickle to his rival's bier; / O'er Pitt's the mournful requiem sound, / And Fox's shall the notes rebound'. As Scott concludes, 'But search the land of living men, / Where wilt thou find their like again'.

31 ASSASSINATION

Shortly after 5 p.m. on Monday 11 May 1812, the prime minister, Spencer Perceval, a pale, slight man in his fiftieth year, headed briskly towards the St Stephen's entrance of the old Palace of Westminster, accompanied by Lord Francis Osborne, a younger son of the late Duke of Leeds. Perceval had spent much of the day in Number 10 preparing for a Commons debate authorizing a naval blockade of Napoleonic France. He was late leaving and his friend, William Wilberforce, who was attending another meeting in Downing Street, saw Perceval walk by. On his arrival at St Stephen's, the prime minister left his cloak and stick with an attendant, and was wearing his habitual black, with white waistcoat and shirt, as he dashed up the broad flight of stone steps leading to the lobby of the Commons.[1]

Near the top of the steps, a journalist, William Jerdan, turned to greet Perceval and was met by a benevolent smile from the evangelical premier and loyal keeper of Pitt the Younger's flame. Jerdan opened the part of the double-door by which MPs and visitors entered the lobby and politely allowed Perceval to go first. Moments later a shot rang out.[2]

The gunman had been waiting inside the lobby, by the side of the closed part of the double door. The presence of a stranger would not automatically have aroused any suspicion, since the lobby was frequented by visitors, who were there to meet their MPs or wait for seats in the strangers' gallery. Jerdan, who had not yet entered the lobby, did not hear the shot but saw 'a small curling wreath of smoke' rise above the prime minister's head, 'as if the breath of a cigar'. He then saw Perceval

> reel back against the ledge on the inside of the door; I heard him exclaim, 'Oh God!', or 'Oh, my God!' … and then making an impulsive rush, as it were, to reach the entrance to the house on the opposite side for safety, I saw him totter forward, not half way, and drop dead between the four pillars which stood there in the centre of the space, with a light trace of blood issuing from his lips.[3]

Among the 20 or more MPs and bystanders in the lobby, William Smith, MP for Norwich, had stopped to speak to a visitor when he 'heard the report of a pistol', apparently fired near the lobby's entrance. 'A Babel of a scene', ensued according to Jerdan, as 'no one seemed to know what had been done or by whom'. Smith looked in the direction of where the shot had been fired and 'observed a tumult' as 'a dozen or more persons' gathered round. At almost the same moment, 'a person rushed hastily from among the crowd, and several voices cried out, "shut the door, and let no one escape"'. As Smith recalled,

> The person who came from among the crowd came towards me, looking first one way and then another, and as I thought at the moment rather like one seeking for shelter, than as the person who had received the wound, but taking two or three steps towards me, as he approached he rather reeled by me, and almost instantly fell upon the floor, with his face downwards. Before he fell I heard a cry not very distinctly, what appeared to come from him, in which were the words, murder, or something very much like that.

The next day, the *Morning Chronicle* reported that the victim had uttered: 'Oh, I am murdered', although the last word 'was inarticulate, the sound dying between his lips'.[4]

Smith momentarily thought that the victim might only be slightly wounded, but noticed that he was not stirring. He stooped down to raise him from the ground, with the help of Osborne and several others. Smith realized '[A]s soon as we had turned his face towards us, and not till then', that the prime minister had been shot. They carried Perceval into the office of the Speaker's secretary, through a small passage beyond the fireplace on the left of the lobby, and sat him on a table, supporting him on either side. Perceval was pale, with dribbles of blood from both sides of his mouth. Within a few minutes of the attack 'there were not scarcely any signs of life remaining; his eyes were still open but he did not appear to know anyone, nor take any notice of any person that came about him'.[5]

A surgeon, William Lynn, who lived nearby in Great George Street, had been urgently summoned and arrived to find the prime minister lying on the table in the Speaker's secretary's office. Lynn 'saw some blood upon the white waistcoat and shirt ... found no pulsation and [he] appeared quite dead'. The surgeon's probe into the wound in Perceval's chest 'passed three inches obliquely downwards and inwards; it being immediately over the heart ... I had no doubt that the ball had passed into the heart, if not through it'. Lynn was certain that the prime minister had been killed by a 'large pistol ball'.[6]

News of the prime minister's murder quickly reached the lobby. A clerk in the vote office by the name of Eastaff shouted: 'That is the murderer!' pointing out a slim man in his thirties, with dark hair and a long, thin face, who was dressed in a dark coat and had sat down on a bench by the fire-place at the side of the lobby. A solicitor, Henry Burgess, who happened to be in the lobby, later testified that he went straight to the bench where the gunman 'was sitting in great agitation' and asked 'what could have induced him to do such a thing'. The assassin replied: 'want of redress of grievance', or words to that effect, and according to Jerdan also said, 'I am sorry for it'.[7]

The assassin was recognized as John Bellingham by Lieutenant-General Isaac Gascoyne, the MP for Liverpool, who had heard the shot from a committee room on the floor above and rushed downstairs. Bellingham had set up as an insurance agent in Liverpool, and married after returning from Russia in 1809, but had recently moved to London. The MP suspected that Bellingham might be about to shoot himself, and therefore seized him and 'kept down his arm with all my strength', while Burgess took the pistol from him. As a crowd of MPs and bystanders gathered round him, Bellingham confessed to having another pistol. His pockets were searched and a second, loaded pistol was removed. A bundle of papers tied with red tape was also discovered and helped confirm his identity.[8]

Jerdan, who was holding Bellingham by the collar, had never before seen a man in such distress:

Whilst his language was cool, the agonies which shook his frame were actually terrible. His countenance wore the hue of the grave, blue and cadaverous; huge drops of sweat ran down from his forehead, like rain on the window-pane in a heavy storm, and, coursing his pallid cheeks fell upon the person where their moisture was distinctly visible; and from the bottom of his chest to his gorge, rose and receded, with almost every breath, a spasmodic action, as if a body, as large or larger than a billiard ball, were choking him.[9]

'All the doors had been locked and bolted', Jerdan noted, 'and all the avenues examined and scoured'. Bellingham had not yet been formally arrested, but the MPs who surrounded him in the lobby insisted that he should be brought into the Commons' Chamber. He was escorted to the bar of the House by two messengers. The Speaker proposed that Bellingham 'should be conveyed to the prison-room, and that a magistrate should be sent for to receive the examination of witnesses of the shocking transaction'.[10]

News of the assassination rapidly spread to the streets outside. There were fears that the murder of the prime minister might herald a revolution against an unpopular government's wartime repression. By 6 p.m. the crowd outside the Houses of Parliament 'was so great', reported the *Morning Chronicle*, 'that it was deemed prudent to close the doors of Westminster-Hall as well as to plant Constables at the entrances'.[11] As the multitude grew, the Horse Guards were called out and paraded in Old and New Palace Yards and Parliament Street 'until a late hour'. The *Courier* lamented that 'the mob manifested a most atrocious disposition – that of abetting assassination when the prisoner was attempted to be put into the coach last night, a great bustle was set up, and an attempt to rescue him. In the most detestable spirit they huzzaed and cheered him …'. The mob's cries of

'Burdett forever!' reflected their support for Sir Francis Burdett, the radical MP for Westminster. Curiously, Burdett and Bellingham bore an uncanny resemblance to one another.[12]

Bellingham's trial began at the Old Bailey only two days after Perceval's assassination. It was already clear that he had acted alone and was not part of some wider plot. He had never forgiven the British Ambassador to Russia, Lord Gower, for ignoring his pleas for help during a five-year imprisonment in appalling conditions in Archangel for allegedly failing to pay his debts. After returning to Britain, his failure to achieve redress became an obsession, causing him to leave his family in Liverpool and move to London. He visited Downing Street in 1810 and bombarded the government with demands for redress. After repeated rejections, he became desperate. He claimed that he held no personal grudge against the prime minister and would have shot Lord Gower if he had seen him first.[13]

Bellingham confidently expected the jury to uphold his plea of insanity, but they took less than 15 minutes to return a verdict of guilty. He was sentenced to death by hanging on the following Monday. There was some speculation that he might be executed at Westminster, near the scene of the assassination and where many others had been put to death in earlier times. On the day of the trial, Earl Grey wrote to Lord Grenville, a fellow Whig and former prime minister, reporting that he had expressed concern at 'the impudence of such a measure, to give it no harsher name' to the Lord Chancellor and Lord Ellenborough'. The latter's retort that he would 'recommend it strongly', prompted Grey to note, 'I rejoice that he is not to try Bellingham'.[14]

In the days following Perceval's death, his family rejected the suggestion that he should be buried at Westminster Abbey. At 9 a.m. on Saturday 16 May, a plain hearse drawn by six horses arrived at Number 10, where his body had lain in state in a sealed lead coffin. The coffin was placed inside the hearse, which headed into Whitehall, preceded by the plume bearer, mutes and other attendants. There, it was joined by five mourning coaches, each also drawn by six horses, and they in turn were followed by more than 20 private carriages. The funeral procession moved slowly southwards along Whitehall, before turning left, crossing Westminster Bridge and heading for St Luke's, Charlton, near Greenwich, where Perceval's body was laid in the family vault. Two days after Perceval's funeral and only a week after the assassination, Bellingham was hanged at Newgate.[15]

Four years after Perceval's death, a monument was erected in Westminster Abbey by parliament and the Prince Regent, the future George IV. It can be seen in the north aisle of the nave and shows the dead prime minister on a mattress, with a figure representing Power mourning at his head, and Truth and Temperance at his feet. A relief of the assassination is shown behind Perceval's effigy.

Almost eight years after Perceval's assassination a plot was discovered to murder Lord Liverpool's Cabinet. The would-be assassins in the Cato Street conspiracy, named after their base off the Edgware Road, were revolutionaries who planned to kill ministers as they dined at the home of Lord Harrowby, Lord President of the Council, in Grosvenor Square in February 1820. However, they were betrayed by a Home Office spy and arrested. The ring-leader, Arthur Thistlewood, and four plotters were executed, while five others were transported.[16]

More than 30 years after Perceval's assassination, on 20 January 1843, another would-be assassin tried to kill another prime minister. However, Daniel MacNaghton, a 30-year-old Glaswegian, mistook Sir Robert Peel's 51-year-old secretary, Edward Drummond, for the premier. As the unfortunate Drummond left the Privy Council office and walked up Whitehall towards Charing Cross, he was shot in the back by MacNaghton. Five days later he died. The failed assassination attempt caused a great panic, but it soon became clear that MacNaghton, as with Bellingham, had acted alone, and was also a failed businessman who harboured grievances. However, in MacNaghton's case his counsel's plea of mental illness succeeded. He was acquitted, but spent the rest of his days in a mental asylum. Controversy over the verdict led to the formulation of the MacNaghton Rules, that became the standard legal test for insanity.[17]

Hansard, the official report of parliamentary debates, can be traced back to the time of Perceval's assassination. MPs' shocked reaction to the murder was reported in *Parliamentary Debates* soon after it was taken over by Thomas Curson Hansard. This regular report of debates had been launched in 1803 by William Cobbett and printed by Thomas, son of Luke Hansard, the Commons printer, since 1809. The younger Hansard took full control in early 1812 when Cobbett fell into financial difficulties. By the 1830s, the reports had been re-named *Hansard's Parliamentary Debates* and became known colloquially as 'Hansard'. Although the Hansard family link ended in 1889, the colloquial name stuck. In 1909, 'Hansard' became parliament's official verbatim record, and in 1943 the name of *Hansard* was restored to the title page.[18]

32 ROYAL FARCE

'Our great-grandchildren will see it in operas, tragedies or melodramas, though it would better suit a farce'. Thus the 18-year-old diarist, Henry Edward Fox, in August 1820, on the embarrassing spectacle taking place in the House of Lords, as peers investigated the private life of Queen Caroline, the estranged wife of the new king, George IV. 'One of the queen's lawyers put the trial in a nutshell when he called it a solemn farce', Princess Lieven, the Russian-born political hostess, told one of her lovers, the Austrian diplomat, Metternich.[1]

Yet the 'farce' was anything but 'solemn'. George's tangled love life had fuelled gossip and inspired cartoonists since his days as a young Prince in the 1780s, when he fell for an attractive, young, Catholic widow, Mrs Fitzherbert. Her refusal to become his mistress might have ended a more prudent Prince's interest, but he persisted. The reckless 'Prinny', as he was known, and Maria Fitzherbert were secretly married. Their marriage was recognized by the Anglican and Catholic churches, but by law, George should have obtained the consent of his father, George III. Furthermore, the law excluded a prince or princess married to a Catholic from succeeding to the throne.

The secret marriage was potentially disastrous for the opposition Whigs, who followed tradition by tending to side with the heir to the throne against the king. When 'Prinny' sought extra funds from parliament to meet his debts, Charles James Fox, speaking with the Prince's authority, dismissed rumours of the marriage as a 'miserable calumny'. During George III's 'madness', when the opposition desperately hoped that the Prince might become Regent, the rising Whig star, Charles Grey, knowingly repeated the lie.

Despite his secret marriage, the Prince had later reluctantly agreed to do his royal duty and marry his Protestant cousin, Caroline, daughter of the Duchess of Brunswick. But theirs was the match from hell. His drinking, swearing and whoring were condemned in *The Times*, where he was said to 'prefer a girl and a bottle to politics and a sermon'. She was good natured, but loud, tactless and unbothered about personal cleanliness.

After their first embrace, the Prince asked for a glass of brandy. On their wedding night, he fell drunkenly into the bedroom fireplace, but in the morning managed to clamber into bed. Nine months later, their daughter, Charlotte, was born, but by then they were living apart. The Prince resumed his on-off relationship with Maria Fitzherbert in 1800 and had other affairs. His adultery did not deter him from persuading ministers to investigate rumours of Caroline's affairs. Although the five-man ministerial commission exonerated Caroline of adultery, it condemned her 'levity of conduct'. The Cabinet advised against excluding her from the court, to the Prince's immense annoyance.[2]

Until 1811, the Prince's messy private life had brought royal embarrassment and generally caused public amusement, but in February of the year it risked creating a constitutional crisis. The recurrence of George III's 'madness' required the creation of the Regency. It is difficult to imagine anyone being less fitted for his role as Prince Regent than the louche and insensitive George, especially when the industrial revolution and the Napoleonic war were creating social distress. By keeping the Tory, Lord Liverpool (Spencer Perceval's successor), in Number 10, George snubbed the Whigs, his erstwhile supporters. George's vindictive attempt to deny Queen Caroline access to their daughter meant that when Princess Charlotte tragically died in childbirth, he was blamed by some for her death. In 1819, he was hissed by a mob after publicly backing the magistrates who let troops fire on demonstrators, killing 11 and injuring many more in Manchester's 'Peterloo' massacre.[3]

George's relief at finally becoming king in January 1820 on the death of his father, George III, was marred by the prospect of Caroline returning to Britain and claiming her rights as queen. Attempts to agree to a separation foundered. Armed with lurid reports by private detectives of his wife's adultery with her Italian major-domo, Bartolomeo Bergami, the king demanded a divorce and also that she be tried for treason. Instead, the Cabinet denied Caroline a coronation and excluded her from church prayers said for the royal family. But efforts to find a compromise failed, and ministers introduced a 'bill of pains and penalties': a means of putting Caroline on trial in parliament and, if she were guilty, removing her royal status.[4]

A massive security operation was put in place for the start of Caroline's trial in the House of Lords on 17 August 1820. Ministers feared that popular sympathy for the queen might fuel radical protests, or worse: the Gordon riots were within living memory. Extra troops were summoned to Westminster and hundreds of special constables were sworn in. The riverside was guarded by a 'police-hulk' and gunboats. The army commandeered Westminster Hall. Horse guards lined up at its north door and patrolled Abingdon Street; footguards were stationed in the streets outside parliament and at the House of Lords; and the Surrey horse-patrol paraded the area before drawing up by St Margaret's.

Timber barriers blocked the route between St Margaret's and Parliament Street and also blocked off the area in front of the House of Lords. Only MPs and peers were allowed to enter through a secure passageway. Moments after Thomas

Creevey, a Whig MP, entered the safe area, he heard, 'an uproar, with hissing and shouting'. Turning round, he 'saw it was Wellington on horseback'. As the Duke's horse started, Wellington looked round in surprise and, catching Creevey's eye, 'nodded, but was evidently annoyed'. Inside the Lords' Chamber, Creevey found a vacant spot among his fellow MPs, within two yards of the chair placed for the queen, close to the steps of the throne.[5]

Several minutes after 'the shouts of the populace announced her near approach', Caroline 'popped all at once into the House, made a duck at the throne, another to the peers, and a concluding jump into the chair which was placed for her'. Creevey likened 'this much-injured Princess' to a toy doll with a round bottom, weighted with lead, that always jumps upright from any position. 'Her dress was black figured gauze, with a good deal of trimming, lace, etc: her sleeves white, and perfectly episcopal; a handsome white veil, so thick as to make it very difficult … to see her face'. He suspected that 'a few straggling ringlets of hair on her neck … were not her Majesty's own property'. Behind the queen stood her lady-in-waiting, 'full six feet high, and bearing 'a striking resemblance to one of Lord Derby's great red deer'.[6]

Despite 'great crowds of people about the House, and all the way up Parliament Street', and large numbers of guards, Creevey 'saw nothing but good humour on all sides'. 'Now they are good-humoured', Lady Cowper, the lover, and later wife, of Lord Palmerston, said of the mob, 'but one cannot trust to its lasting, and all the time one thinks what a pity it is to see the country embroiled for a thing that signifies so little'.[7]

Peers packed the Chamber and press reports were read avidly. The queen's shocked cry, 'Oh, Theodore!' at the sight of a witness and her histrionic storming out, excited much comment, especially since the said Theodore revealed details of Caroline's and Bergamo's sleeping arrangements. Yet despite the queen's probable guilt, she won sympathy as the victim of the king's peevish vendetta. Creevey saw the crowds gather along the Thames as she passed on her state barge: 'There was not a single vessel in the river that did not hoist their colours and man their yards for her …'.[8]

The Lords voted narrowly for the bill of pains and penalties, but it stood no chance of getting through the Commons. Yet, its abandonment came only after 'a terrible scene in the Cabinet'. Mrs Arbuthnot, the diarist, quoted her husband Charles, the patronage secretary, on the drama at Cabinet: 'Three fourths of them were for getting rid of the Bill; but Ld Liverpool was in phrenzy, & his rage got so high that for a time it stopped all deliberation. He abused the Chancellor. He complained the ill usage he had received from several in the room, without particularizing them, & ended by crying'.[9]

The queen was the heroine of the hour, and the king the villain, but within a year their roles were reversed. The turning point was George's coronation, delayed until July 1821 because of the queen's trial. It was 60 years since the Abbey had hosted a coronation and George IV's cost a staggering £238,000, about 25 times the amount spent on George III's. The king stage-managed a Tudor-style spectacle that mingled Gothic and modern elements. He wore a robe modelled on Napoleon's and was described by the painter, Benjamin Robert Haydon, as 'a being buried in satin, feathers and diamonds ... [who] looked like some gorgeous bird of the East'. Privy councillors were dressed in white and blue satin, with trunk-hose and mantles, after the fashion of Queen Elizabeth's time.[10]

In the Abbey, some guests were appalled by the king's flirting with Lady Conyngham. According to Lady Cowper, the king 'several times was at the last Gasp, but then came a cheering draught in the shape of a look from L[ad] y C[onyngha]m ... and it revived him like Magic or Ether'. Mrs Arbuthnot saw George 'take a diamond brooch from his breast & looking at her [Lady Conyngham] kissed it, on which she took off her glove and kissed a ring she had on!!! Anybody who could have seen his disgusting figure with a wig the curls of which hung down his back, & quite bending beneath the weight of his robes & his 60 years wd have been quite sick'.[11]

Afterwards, during the feast in Westminster Hall, 'The King behaved very indecently; he was continually nodding & winking at Ly Conyngham & sighing & making eyes at her'. The celebrations in the Hall included the ritual challenge by the monarch's Champion, traditionally a member of the Dymock family. On this occasion, a young member of the family, substituting for his clergyman father, rode a horse hired from Astley's circus. It was the Champion's last appearance at a coronation feast. After the feast, the coronation plate was just saved as spectators rushed from the galleries around the Hall and grabbed anything they could take.[12]

Yet the theatricality of George IV's coronation appealed to some, including Sir Walter Scott, the poet and novelist, who found it 'impossible to conceive a ceremony more august and imposing in all its parts'. He was pleasantly surprised that the 'general tone of solemn circumstance' was sustained, 'considering that it is but one step from the sublime to the ridiculous'. However, the 'ridiculous' occurred when the queen sought to intrude. Caroline had been refused a coronation in her own right and was not invited to George's ceremony. She was strongly advised against trying to attend, but Henry Brougham, her Attorney-General, added that if she persisted, 'she must do it with her wonted firmness', and having given an order, must not flinch.

On the morning of George's coronation, Caroline set out from Mayfair in her coach of state, drawn by six bays, and headed through the parks to Dean's Yard. She expected to be granted entry to the Abbey, but was refused. A witness by the cloister door passed on his account to his grand-daughter, who more than a century later told Lawrence Tanner, Keeper of the Westminster Muniments (1926–66), that the queen, 'wore a black wig, rather crooked, and was crying and much distressed'.[13]

Caroline returned to her carriage and headed round the Abbey towards the Poets' Corner entrance, but on her way made a detour into New Palace Yard in the hope of joining the coronation procession assembling in Westminster Hall. What happened next was recalled by one of the ladies inside: 'we were electrified by a thundering knock at the Hall door, and a voice without loudly said, "The Queen – open!" A hundred red pages ran to the door, which the porter opened a little … She was raging and storming and vociferating, "Let me pass; I am your Queen, I am Queen of Britain."'. The deputy Lord High Chamberlain was dispatched to deal with the crisis, and 'with a voice that made all the Hall ring, cried, "Do your duty, shut the Hall door", and immediately the red pages slapped it in her face'.[14]

Caroline then made for the door at Poets' Corner, tucked away in the south-east corner of the Abbey, but was refused admittance without a ticket. Lord Hood, her aide, suggested that as queen she had no need of a ticket, but the attendant claimed not to know who she was and forbade entry. Finally thwarted, Caroline returned to her carriage and headed through Whitehall and back to Mayfair. According to Brougham, a great crowd 'crammed Cockspur Street and Pall Mall, etc., hooting and cursing the king and his friends, and huzzaing her. A vast multitude followed her home, and then broke windows'.[15]

Yet Lady Cowper claimed that the king 'was very well received everywhere … and had a complete victory over the Queen'. Mustering all the disdain that a society lady felt for Caroline, she added, 'if she could have been lower than she was before she would have made herself so by her miserable attempt of yesterday'. Spectators at the Abbey had hooted her away and she had been jostled by all the lowest rabble. 'Think what a degradation for a Queen, if Queen she can be called'. Within three weeks, Caroline was dead, probably from stomach cancer.[16]

George's popularity faded, but he remained a great patron of the arts. His ambitions were shared by Sir John Soane, who became architect for Westminster and Whitehall in 1813. Soane's work is visible today in the north front of Westminster Hall in New Palace Yard, where he followed Richard II's design when rebuilding the façade after the demolition of coffee houses hard against the Hall. However, this re-construction was untypical of Soane's grandiose plan. He visualized a royal procession route, worthy of a world empire, from Windsor to Westminster, incorporating re-built Houses of Parliament and new public buildings along the western side of Whitehall, complete with triumphal arches at the entrance to Downing Street, in celebration of victory in 1815.[17]

Soane's vision was never realized, but in 1825 he completed the new Law Courts outside Westminster Hall's western wall. No further cases were heard in the Great Hall, but lawyers and their clients were frequently seen scurrying through it on their way to or from the courts. It was in the Court of Chancery that Dickens set some of the hearings for the fictional, long-running Jarndyce and Jarndyce case in *Bleak House*. In 1882, the new Royal Courts of Justice were opened in The Strand and the lawyers finally left Westminster Hall.

The shock of Soane's neo-classical Law Courts adjacent to the Norman Westminster Hall and near Henry VII's Gothic chapel, provoked fierce criticism from Henry Bankes, an MP who owned a five-storey house in Old Palace Yard. Bankes spoke for those who, during the wars with revolutionary France and Napoleon, came to associate neo-classicism with European republicanism and imperialism, and regarded Gothic as reflecting old England in its Tudor heyday. In response, Soane modified his design, adding Gothic battlements. He also built a new royal entrance fronting Old Palace Yard, a staircase (*Scala Regia*), royal gallery, and new committee rooms and libraries.[18]

None of Soane's work at the old Palace of Westminster survives, but there is a glimpse of his neo-classical vision in Whitehall on the north corner of Downing Street, where he built offices for the Board of Trade and Privy Council. Although these offices were later re-modelled by Sir Charles Barry, the four plainer bays fronting Downing Street are Soane's. His interior designs and trademark wood-panelling also survive in Number 10's small dining room and impressive state dining room, and also in Number 11's ground-floor dining room.[19]

George IV's legacy also endures in the majestic settings created by John Nash near the heart of Westminster. Nash re-modelled St James's Park, transformed Buckingham House into a palace and helped to establish the National Gallery in Trafalgar Square, on the site of the old royal mews. George IV's and Charles I's equestrian statues grace the modern site. They were flawed monarchs, but their architectural and artistic legacies are glorious.

The Times obituary of George IV judged that 'there never was an individual less regretted by his fellow-creatures than this deceased King': a fate that would not have surprised the American writer Washington Irving, who expressed, just a year before George's coronation, melancholy thoughts inspired by the tombs of Westminster Abbey: 'how soon that crown which encircles [the brow of living greatness] must pass away; and it must lie down in the dust and disgraces of the tomb, and be trampled upon by the feet of the meanest of the multitude'.[20]

33 REFORM

'The Rotten Parliament, as future historians may know it, must be replaced by one whose ethos is different from those of its predecessors': thus, *The Daily Telegraph* in 2009, following its exposé of the scandal of MPs' expenses. Its epithet 'Rotten Parliament' echoed the much earlier Westminster scandal of 'rotten boroughs': parliamentary seats that were in the gift of the Crown and wealthy landowners during the eighteenth and early nineteenth century. This 'old corruption' was also attacked by journalists of its day. William Cobbett denounced 'The Thing', meaning the borough-mongers, sinecure-holders and tax-eaters, whom he accused of leeching off farm workers. John Wade detailed the full extent of patronage in *The Black Book, or, Corruption Unmasked!*, a best-selling compendium published in 1819 and updated until 1835.[1]

Support for reform had been growing for a quarter of a century before Wade's exposé. The demand for change was taken up by Charles Grey, the scion of an old Northumbrian family, who first arrived at Westminster in 1786, aged 22. He soon fell in with Whig society, became an acolyte of Fox and the lover of Georgiana, Duchess of Devonshire, with whom he fathered a daughter; his later marriage to Mary Ponsonby producing 16 children. In 1793, Grey pressed for the reform of rotten boroughs, because they enabled the Crown and a few magnates to control the Commons. But his timing was wrong. At the height of the revolutionary bloodbath in France, his modest proposals were regarded as dangerously radical and split the Whigs.

After the Napoleonic War, Lord Liverpool's government reacted to economic distress and social unrest by making repression the order of the day. However, Westminster's block on political reform began to crack in 1828 when the Irish reformer, Daniel O' Connell, although victorious in a by-election, was forbidden to take his seat because he was a Catholic. A year later, even the Duke of Wellington, a reactionary prime minister, accepted that civil war in Ireland could only be averted by ending the ban on Catholics entering public life.

However, the Tories were split on further reform. Wellington's military approach to politics did not help. 'An extraordinary affair', he commented after chairing his first Cabinet meeting, 'I gave them their orders and they wanted to stay and discuss them'. Tory liberals declined to join his administration after the death of their leader, William Huskisson: knocked down by Stephenson's Rocket at the opening of the Liverpool and Manchester railway.[2]

A new head of steam for reform was building up in towns such as Liverpool and Manchester, where a proud and wealthy middle class resented having no MPs to call their own. The pressure grew after France's liberal coup in July 1830, followed by menacing rural riots across England. Wellington's authority as prime minister was further weakened by his poor showing in debates. He spoke in 'a bad screeching sort of voice, aggravated by an awkward mode of mouthing the words'. His veto on reform triggered further unrest, forcing King George IV and his ministers to cancel their attendance at the Lord Mayor's banquet. After his government lost a Commons' vote, Wellington resigned.

Charles Grey's long wait for the premiership was finally over. Now aged 66, Grey had led the Whigs since Fox's death 24 years earlier; but had spent 23 frustrating years out of office and, after succeeding to his father's earldom in 1807, out of the Commons. 'What a place to speak in!', Grey lamented to his wife after entering the Lords, 'with just light enough to make darkness visible, it was like speaking in a vault by the glimmering light of a sepulchral lamp to the dead. It is impossible I should ever do anything there worth thinking of'.[3]

While George IV lived, Earl Grey had no hope of holding office, as he had refused to help George over his illegal marriage and sympathized with Queen Caroline and Princess Charlotte. The royal veto ended when William IV succeeded to the throne in July 1830; although Grey was unlikely to have been flattered to be told by 'Silly Billy', or 'the sailor king', that he had his confidence.

Grey's motivation for reform was conservative. Although Grey's Russian mistress, Princess Lieven, told Metternich that the prime minister was a 'true democrat', she can only have meant in contrast to Austrian or Russian standards of the time. Grey was a Whig toff who appointed nine peers to his 13-strong Cabinet. 'I have never thought that Reform should be insisted on as a matter of popular right', he assured the Lords before entering Number 10, 'nor have I ever advocated the principle of universal suffrage'. He wanted to restore parliamentary supremacy; in effect putting the clock back to the Whigs' golden age after the revolution of 1688–89, before the Crown re-asserted its power through patronage.[4]

Yet Grey's modest first Reform Bill, introduced in March 1831, was historic: reform had been talked about for decades, but at long last a government was going to do something about it. The impact was electrifying. The Bill proposed disfranchising 60 of the smallest boroughs and taking seats from 47 others. These seats would be re-distributed to 30 or so newly enfranchised larger towns and elsewhere across the country. Depending on the value of their houses, or the type of tenure, some 300,000 middle-class men were to be enfranchised.

'Reform that you may preserve', Thomas Macaulay, the writer, urged his fellow MPs. Macaulay gives a vivid sketch of the crucial Commons' vote on Grey's bill.

'Such a scene as the division of last Tuesday, I never saw, and never expect to see again', he wrote to a friend. 'If I should live fifty years, the impression will be as fresh and sharp in my mind as if it had just taken place. It was like seeing Caesar stabbed in the Senate House, seeing Oliver taking the mace from the table'. When the votes were counted, the bill passed by one vote, 302 to 301. 'We set up a shout that you might have heard to Charing Cross, waving our hats, stamping on the floor, and clapping hands', Macaulay recalled, 'and went out laughing, crying, and huzzaing into the Lobby'. As MPs left the Chamber:

All the passages and stairs into the waiting rooms were thronged with people who had waited till four o'clock in the morning to know the issue. We passed though a narrow lane between two thick masses of them; and all the way down they were shouting and waving their hats, till we got into the open air. I called a cabriolet, and the first thing the driver asked was, 'Is the bill carried?' 'Yes, by one'. 'Thank God for it, sir!'[5]

Yet the cabbie's relief was premature. Within a month, the government was narrowly defeated during the Bill's committee stage. Grey realized that he was not going to get the Bill through the Commons and asked the king to dissolve parliament. The reformers won the election by a landslide. MPs passed the second Reform Bill by a majority of 136 on its second reading. The Bill then went to the Lords, where, in October 1831, Grey finally presented his creation to parliament. 'His tall, commanding and dignified appearance', observed the diarist, Charles Greville, 'his flow of language, his graceful action, well-rounded periods, and an exhibition of classical taste united with legal knowledge, render him the most finished orator of his day'. However, Greville's view was not shared by a 20-year-old journalist who began reporting parliament the following year and who, in his fifties, could still recall his dislike of Grey. 'The shape of his head (I see it now) was misery to me and weighed down my youth', complained Charles Dickens.[6]

'Do not believe that the desire for Reform will abate', Grey warned his fellow peers, 'the time is past when a smaller measure of Reform would satisfy the people; you must either take this Bill ... or you will have instead of it, a call for something infinitely stronger and more extensive!' Advising the Lords 'to concede freely, generously, and not reluctantly', he described the bill as 'a conservative and not a revolutionary measure'.[7] Yet the show was stolen by a three-hour tour de force from the Lord Chancellor, Henry, Lord Brougham and Vaux. It was described by Grey as a 'miraculous' speech – a felicitous comment, as Brougham was the worse for drink. The Lord Chancellor, unwisely for a tipsy 53-year-old, decided to enact physically his concluding plea: 'I solemnly adjure you – I warn you – I implore you – yea on my bended knees I supplicate you – Reject not the Bill'. But having knelt, Brougham could not get up and only struggled to his feet with great difficulty.[8]

Their lordships, unmoved by Grey's brilliance and Brougham's histrionics, threw out the bill by 199 votes to 158. Outside, people were moved to protest at the peers' defiance. The worst rioting occurred in Bristol, Derby and Nottingham. At Westminster thousands gathered to pelt the Duke of Wellington outside parliament, whack Lord Londonderry with stick and brick-bat in Parliament Street, and smash the panes of Northumberland House. Police prevented the demonstrators marching on St Stephen's. On the night of 12 October 1831, Francis Place and 17 radicals were allowed into Number 10. The prime minister pleaded tiredness and the need for time, but the 'midnight meeting' provoked furious reaction. As Edward Pearce, the writer and historian, observes, Tories regarded it as an outrage; others saw it as proof that the reformers were not going to be stopped.[9]

Grey's third Reform Bill followed two months later. He persuaded the king to agree to create new peers, if necessary, to get the bill through the Lords; following Queen Anne's precedent over the Treaty of Utrecht. The Lords' debate lasted four days and nights before Grey wound up at dawn, as the candles 'blazed on after the sun came fairly in at the high windows, and produced a strange but rather grand effect on the red draperies and furniture and dusky tapestry on the walls'. The government won by nine votes, but on 7 May the Lords passed a wrecking amendment and plunged the country into crisis.[10]

Grey resigned when the king declined to create new peers, hoping to persuade the Tories to carry forward reform. Robert Peel declined to serve, either as prime minister, or in the Cabinet, but Wellington began trying to form a government. This news alarmed radicals and reformers, who threatened to stop paying tax and start a run on the banks by demanding gold instead of banknotes. By 13 May 1832, the capital was plastered with placards proclaiming: 'To Stop the Duke Go For Gold'.

Two days later, Wellington stood down, advising William to recall Grey. The king conceded the demand from Grey's Cabinet to create new peers, if necessary, to get the Reform Bill through. 'The most deafening cheers followed', wrote Brougham's secretary, Denis le Marchant, when the news reached parliament, 'all was now joy and congratulation'. William was spared having to create any new peers by Wellington, who withdrew with his supporters. The opposition benches were empty as one of Britain's greatest reforms was enacted.[11]

At the next election, six months after the Great Reform Act became law, an estimated 813,000 men were entitled to vote compared with 478,000 in 1831. Nonetheless, voting remained a minority activity among a population of 24 million. Grey's supporters won 473 seats and doubled their majority to 288. Many of these MPs are depicted today at the National Portrait Gallery, in the magnificent painting of *The House of Commons, 1833*, by Sir George Hayter. Among the more remarkable characters who can be identified are William Cobbett, elected for the newly represented town of Oldham; William Gladstone, at that time a

23-year-old Tory; Daniel O'Connell, the Irish leader; and Thomas Macaulay. Hayter includes Grey and Wellington: although as they were peers he shows them standing beyond the bar of the House.

Hayter shows MPs packed in their old Chamber, formerly St Stephen's Chapel, as modified by Sir Christopher Wren: the wood panelling along each side; the galleries above with their slender supporting columns; and the three tall windows behind the Speaker's chair at the far, east end, with the riverside trees visible through the panes. However, not all the new members were impressed with their accommodation. 'Why are we squeezed into so small a space that it is absolutely impossible that there should be calm and regular discussion, even from that circumstance alone?' bemoaned Cobbett, whose romanticism was untouched by the old Chamber. 'Why are 658 of us crammed into a space that allows to each of us no more than a foot and a half square, while, at the same time, each of the servants of the King, whom we pay, has a place to live in, and more unoccupied space in that palace than the little hole into which we are all crammed to make laws by which this great kingdom is governed?'[12]

The parliament portrayed by Hayter abolished slavery in the British Empire; but also in the name of reform condemned the unemployed poor to the workhouse. Within a few years, the new workhouses were savaged by Charles Dickens in *Oliver Twist*. Dickens's first literary piece had appeared in the *Monthly Magazine* in December 1833. The budding author bought a copy in the Strand, and 'walked with it into Westminster Hall, and turned in there for half an hour, because his eyes were so dimmed with joy and pride that they could not bear the street, and were not fit to be seen there'. Dickens's talent liberated him from reporting parliament. Thirty years later he recalled the discomfort of working there: 'I have worn my knees by writing on them on the old back row of the old Gallery of the old House of Commons, and I have worn my feet standing to write in a preposterous pen in the old House of Lords, where we used to be huddled together like so many sheep, kept in waiting, say, until the Woolsack might want restuffing'.[13]

34 FIRE!

On the afternoon of Thursday 16 October 1834, two friends, John Snell and Mr Shuter, took the opportunity of parliament's not being in session to visit the House of Lords, then located in the old Court of Requests. At about 4 p.m. they were shown into the Chamber by Mrs Wright, standing in as housekeeper for her daughter-in-law. As they entered, Snell noticed smoke and expressed his surprise, to which Mrs Wright replied: 'Yes, the workmen are below'. The cause of the smell and smoke was the incineration in a stove of the old, wooden tally sticks, on which government accounts had been notched from Norman times until the practice had been discontinued in 1826.[1]

Nobody had thought how to dispose of the accumulated piles of 'worn-out, worm-eaten, rotten old bits of wood', as Charles Dickens described the tally sticks. As he observed, 'it would naturally occur to any intelligent person that nothing could be easier than to allow them to be carried away for firewood by the miserable people who live in that neighbourhood'. Instead of such a practical solution, sticks were thrown onto bonfires on Tothill Fields and in New Palace Yard, or used for kindling in the Palace of Westminster's many fireplaces.[2]

Then came the order to burn more sticks in the stove beneath the House of Lords. At 6.30 a.m. on that fateful Thursday, two workmen, acting on the instructions of the Clerk of Works, Richard Weobley, began stuffing the stove with about two cart-loads of sticks. They carried on all day, but already by 10 a.m., Mrs Wright, upstairs in the Lords, was aware of the smell of burnt wood and smoke. She grew uneasy but took no action, later claiming that a workman had assured her that all was well.[3]

By the afternoon, the smoke in the Lords' Chamber prevented Snell and his companion from viewing the Armada tapestries clearly or seeing the throne from the other end of the Chamber. The heat was so great near the box for the Usher of the Black Rod that Snell felt it through his boots. Bending down and touching the floor, he commented, 'I should almost be afraid this would take fire'. 'Oh no', replied Mrs Wright, 'it is a stone floor'. When Shuter commented on the suffocating heat, she mentioned that the workmen below were burning the tallies, but added, 'I have known when the house was sitting that people who have stood at this spot have fainted'. Later, Snell claimed that her remark took his mind off the heat and smoke, and he and Shuter left.[4]

At 6 p.m. all hell broke loose. A woman's voice cried out: 'Oh, good God, the House of Lords is on fire!' Mrs Mullencamp, a doorkeeper's wife, saw a glittering light under a door and alerted Mrs Wright. At the same time, Weobley was horrified to see a chimney 'very much on fire'. He raised the alarm, but the 'stove, overgorged with these preposterous sticks', as Dickens put it, had overheated and started a fire. Flames were already racing through the passages, lobbies and stair-cases between the Lords and Commons. A brisk wind fanned the fire. As night fell, a great conflagration lit the sky, illuminating the masses of cumulus cloud that floated high and bright across the face of a nearly full moon.[5]

'The whole building in front of Old Palace Yard was in flames, & the fire was gaining ground', noted John Cam Hobhouse, the Minister for Public Works, who had been summoned. He found 'only a few soldiers and policemen [were] present, and three or four engines'. Although more fire-engines arrived, 'the firemen were lamentably deficient in the knowledge of the best way to extinguish the flames'. In *Sketches by Boz*, Dickens tells how an MP and a fireman's dog, Chance, 'both ran up and down, and in and out, getting under people's feet, and into everybody's way, fully impressed with the belief that they were doing a great deal of good, and barking tremendously. The dog went quietly back to his kennel, but the gentleman kept up such an incessant noise for some weeks after the occurrence, that he became a positive nuisance'. The MP was probably William Hughes Hughes, who wrote to the press that he was the only Member present at the start of the blaze.[6]

A vast crowd gathered to watch the conflagration. In Old Palace Yard and nearby streets, foot guards, horse guards and police struggled to prevent the crowd getting too close and impeding the firefighters. Although the *Standard* newspaper reported that people cheered as the Houses of Parliament burned, Hobhouse 'heard nothing of the exclamations' and felt that 'on the whole, it was impossible for any large assemblage of people to behave better'. He noted that 'only one man was taken up for huzzaing when the flames increased', although a weaver reportedly commented that, 'this comes of making the poor girls pay for their children', an allusion to the unpopular new Poor Law; and others also thought that the fire must have been started deliberately. The *Gentleman's Magazine* reported that when the roof of the House of Lords fell in at half past nine, 'bright corusca-tions, as of electric fire, played in the great volume of flames, and so struck were the bystanders with the grandeur of the sight that involuntarily (and from no bad feeling) clapped their hands as though they had been present at the closing scene of some dramatic spectacle'.[7]

As the fire raged, 'the strong glittering of the flames on Henry VII's Chapel and the Abbey Church, on the adjacent buildings, and on the working parties, fire-engines, and soldiers in the open space below, formed a scene of great animation and beauty': thus, the historians of the old palace, Brayley and Britton. On the river, where boats and barges were crammed with spectators, 'the reflections of the wavering flames upon the water, on the neighbouring shores, and on the many thousands thus congregated, composed a spectacle most strikingly picturesque and impressive'. The dramatic scene was captured in a series of nine water-colours by J. M. W. Turner, the artist, who was on the spot,.[8]

'On the first view of it from the water, it appeared as if nothing could save Westminster Hall from the fury of the flames', reported *The Times*:

> There was an immense pillar of bright clear fire springing up behind it, and a cloud of white, yet dazzling smoke, careering above it, through which, as it was parted by the wind, you could occasionally perceive the lantern and pinnacles … At the same time a shower of fiery particles appeared to be falling upon it with such increasing rapidity as to render it miraculous that the roof did not burst out into one general blaze.[9]

Dean Stanley later described the scene as the fire threatened the Great Hall: 'the innumerable faces of that vast multitude, lighted up in the broad glare with more than the light of day, were visibly swayed by the agitations of the devouring breeze, and one voice, one prayer seemed to go up from every upturned countenance: "Oh! Save the Hall!"'. Yet the Dean was economical with the truth. 'Damn the House of Commons, let it blaze away; but save, oh save the Hall', Lord Althorp, the Chancellor of the Exchequer, had bellowed above the noise of firemen yelling, timbers falling, the drums of foot guards beating to arms, the clarions of the horse guards and the bells of St Margaret's. As *The Times* reported, Althorp's cry was 'natural and even praiseworthy'. The Commons was already lost, but the Hall might be saved.[10]

A water colour painting by George B. Campion of the interior of Westminster Hall at the height of the fire shows huge flames blazing beyond the great south window, with more fire and smoke inside. In the foreground, teams frantically man water pumps, while along the side walls, tiny figures clamber up tall ladders and scaffolding trying to douse the wooden beams. These desperate efforts were only possible because restoration work had begun. It seems likely that only the 'zealous exertions' of the contractor, Robert Johnstone, and about 30 masons had saved the Hall.[11]

Lord Melbourne, who had succeeded Grey as prime minister, was credited with directing the efforts to save the Hall, but Hobhouse's account gives a more plausible view of the laconic premier. 'I was with Melbourne, who was as usual very cool, and now and then inclined to the jocose', the diarist recalled. 'He could not help laughing when a man ran up to me and said, "Sir John we have saved King Charles's warrant" – meaning the original death-warrant, as if that document was particularly interesting to me'. [12]

The fire in the rest of the Palace raged for hours, finally dying down in the early hours of the next morning. The Palace had been devastated. All that remained of the old Palace were Westminster Hall, the chapel of St Mary Undercroft, some of the cloisters tucked between the Great Hall and St Stephen's; and the bare walls of St Stephen's, the Court of Requests and the Painted Chamber. Although at least one fireman died and some people suffered burns or fractures from falling rafters, scalding water and hot lead from the roofs, there were few casualties. There were many narrow escapes: firemen, who were dug out after the House of Lords collapsed; and the deputy Serjeant-at-Arms, who rescued the Commons' mace in the nick of time.[13]

The fire was an accident waiting to happen. Only six years earlier, Sir John Soane had warned of the risk in his official report, *Designs for Public Buildings*. Soane noted that when the Lords moved into the Court of Requests in 1800, the old buildings converted into offices and passageways were built of timber covered with plaster. Repairs were often made with highly flammable tar. The use of 'combustible materials' prompted Soane to demand urgent fire precautions:

> what would become of the Painted Chamber, the House of Commons, and Westminster Hall? Where would the progress of the fire be arrested? The want of security from fire, the narrow, gloomy, and unhealthy passages, and the insufficiency of the accommodation in this building, are important objects which call loudly for revision and speedy amendment.[14]

The blame for the fire lies with the political leaders, Tory and Whig, who neglected the very fabric of the Palace, while sparing no effort to hold power. Their negligence verged on the criminal, but they were in no danger of being found guilty. The inquiry was conducted by the Privy Council, thus making the politicians judge and jury. As there was no evidence of criminal intent or revolutionary plot, the inquiry highlighted the carelessness and incompetence shown by officials and workers. Details were extensively leaked in *The Times*. The buck was safely passed.

Not everyone regarded the fire as a disaster. 'I cannot say he was much affected by the calamity, rather the reverse', noted Hobhouse of William IV's reaction. 'He seemed delighted at having an opportunity of getting rid of Buckingham Palace; said he meant it as a permanent gift for Parliament Houses, and that it would be the finest thing in Europe'. After inspecting the gutted ruins, the king 'called the Speaker and me [Hobhouse] to him and said, "Mind, I mean Buckingham Palace as a permanent gift! Mind that!"'[15]

PART FIVE

GLOBAL ICONS

35 VICTORIAN PHOENIX

William IV was not alone in regarding the destruction of the old Houses of Parliament in 1834 as a golden opportunity. Among the crowd at Westminster on that fateful October night, was Augustus Welby Pugin, an ambitious 22-year-old champion of medieval Gothic design, who welcomed the fire as 'a glorious sight'. Pugin rejoiced as Soane's 'mixtures' and Wyatt's 'heresies' went up in flames, and was thrilled as the brick walls and slate roofs 'fell faster than a pack of cards' while the older medieval walls 'stood triumphantly' amid the ruins.[1]

Pugin's excitement was exceptional, but his professional interest was shared by Charles Barry, a 39-year-old architect aboard the Brighton coach on the night of the fire. Barry had been born the son of a stationer in a modest house in Bridge Street, opposite the Houses of Parliament; yet he was the coming man of English architecture and had completed his Italianate-style Travellers' Club in Pall Mall only two years earlier. On seeing the distant red glow of the blazing Palace from his coach, Barry is said to have remarked: 'what a chance for an architect'. He later recalled that people were mesmerized by the 'grandeur and terror' of the fire, but by the next morning, when the scale of destruction was clear, everybody seemed to have an idea for building a new Palace of Westminster. *The Times* advocated 'a noble Parliamentary edifice worthy of a great nation', while the *Westminster Review* wanted a design that allowed the 'legislative functions [to] be best performed'. There was also the vexed question of style: neo-classical or Gothic?[2]

The burnt-out Palace was patched up by Sir Robert Smirke, the architect best known for the neo-classical British Museum. MPs and Peers moved into elegantly restored temporary chambers only three months after the fire: the Commons occupied the Court of Requests, formerly used by the Lords; and the Lords moved to the smaller Painted Chamber. Hobhouse asked Smirke to make plans for the new Houses of Parliament, but a month later the Whig Government fell and was replaced by Sir Robert Peel's first, short-lived Conservative Government. The supporters of the Gothic style seized the opportunity. Leading the charge was Sir Edward Cust, a former soldier and MP in his early forties, who probably first introduced Barry to Pugin.

In an open letter to Peel, Cust attacked the 'poverty' of Smirke's staid neo-classicism and urged Peel to set up a public commission and hold an architectural competition for the new Houses of Parliament. Cust's ideas were taken up. In June 1835, a joint committee of MPs and Peers announced the public competition, with the controversial condition that the design should be either Gothic or Elizabethan. The chosen styles evoked the romantic myth of Tudor England, but were also likely to be more compatible with the nearby Henry VII's Chapel. There was no prospect that Joseph Hume, a radical MP, might persuade his fellow MPs to opt for a semi-circular chamber, modelled on the French assembly.[3]

Ninety-seven designs were submitted by the December deadline. The winner was number 64, submitted by Charles Barry, whose design showed 'evident marks of genius and superiority of talent'. Pugin's evocative drawings of Barry's design played a vital part, although they were later lost. Barry's success lay in presenting his ambitious plans as a coherent whole, extending across eight acres. He had, in effect, designed a small town. When completed, his new Palace contained over 1,100 rooms, 126 staircases, 11 courtyards and two miles of corridors.[4]

Barry's master-stroke was a spine that ran parallel to the line of the Thames. This spine eventually reached 872 feet in length and incorporated the chambers of the Commons and Lords, committee rooms, dining rooms, libraries and an outside terrace. Today, the Palace's long riverfront facade makes an imposing sight. Its apparent classical symmetry is disrupted by the Gothic asymmetry of two awesome but very different towers looming over the palace at opposite ends: the Clock Tower at its north end and Victoria Tower at the south. Pugin is said to have dismissed the exterior of the new Palace as, 'All Grecian, Sir; Tudor details on a classic body'. However, Barry's genius lay in creating a unified design that combined classical grandeur and symmetry with Gothic asymmetry and detail, all cloaked in a Gothic Perpendicular mask.[5]

The politicians were impatient for the building to start and had failed to examine Barry's estimated costs before declaring him the winner. Later, an estimate of £707,104 was produced, based on Barry's measurements and Pugin's drawings, but the final cost rose to nearer £2,500,000. The predicted schedule of six years to completion was even less reliable. After Barry's wife laid the foundation stone in 1840, it took seven more years before the House of Lords was occupied and 12 years before Queen Victoria first used the Royal Entrance at the state opening on 3 February 1852. The Clock Tower was completed in 1858 and the Victoria Tower two years later. Barry's son, Edward, was dismissed in 1870 before he had completed all the remaining work. The mosaic panels in Central Lobby depicting the patron saints of the United Kingdom's four nations, and the history paintings in St Stephen's Hall, were finally completed in the 1920s.[6]

'Westminster New Palace', as it was officially styled in 1846, is part royal palace, part gentlemen's club. Its design was approved by William IV in 1836 and was consciously intended to create an overriding impression of 'Crown-in-Parliament';

not 'people's palace'. At modern state openings of parliament, Her Majesty Queen Elizabeth II arrives in the state coach, with an escort of the Household Cavalry, beneath the 60-foot arch of the Victoria Tower. After alighting at the Royal Entrance, she ascends the Royal Staircase to the vaulted Norman Porch, originally intended to house statues of Norman kings. From there, she enters the Queen's Robing Room, where frescoes by William Dyce evoke the English ideal of monarchy and nationhood in scenes based on the Arthurian legend. In this symbolic setting, the monarch assumes the royal parliamentary robes and Imperial State Crown.[7]

Her Majesty's procession passes through the immense Royal Gallery, dominated by Daniel Maclise's 45 feet by 12 feet paintings of *The Death of Nelson at Trafalgar* and *Wellington Meeting Blucher at Waterloo*. After passing these Victorian portrayals of British military supremacy, the monarch enters the small Prince's Chamber, named after a room in the old Palace. It is packed with Gothic detail in its clocks, fireplaces, fittings, furniture and panelling; and its walls are decorated with portraits of the Tudors and Stuarts. From this exquisite Chamber, Her Majesty enters the Lords' Chamber, steps onto the dais at its far end and occupies the throne, from which she delivers the Queen's Speech.[8]

The climax of Pugin's Gothic interior design is the elevated, ornate, gilded throne and canopy in the Lords' Chamber. His bold masterpiece defines the upper chamber as the monarch's house, designed for the state opening instead of the Lords' daily sittings. Pugin modelled the chairs for the monarch and consort on the Coronation Chair. The central panel above the throne, commissioned later from Dyce, symbolizes the union of Crown and Church by showing the Baptism of King Ethelbert, the first Saxon king to convert to Christianity. The Lords' Chamber itself is an ornamented vision of carved wood, with the benches richly upholstered in red leather, while, high above, the ceiling has decorated and gilded panelling.[9]

During the state opening, the monarch can look directly from the throne and see the Speaker seated in his chair at the far end of the Commons, 450-feet away. The status of the Speaker of the Commons, as the country's highest ranking commoner, reflects a traditionally close relationship with the monarch, and was recognized in Barry's design. The Speaker was given a 60-room house in the north-east corner of the Palace, with a fine drawing room, a state dining room and a state bed. The bed symbolizes political continuity, since it maintains the tradition that a monarch sleeps at Westminster on the eve of his or her coronation.[10]

'The best club in London', was the description given to the House of Commons in Charles Dickens's novel, *Our Mutual Friend*, published in 1864–5. Several years later, an MP suggested that the Commons 'ought to be the best club in the world'. When the new Palace was commissioned, MPs and Peers failed to specify office accommodation, while including cloakrooms, dining rooms, kitchens and libraries. It was assumed that when MPs were not sitting in the Chamber attending a committee, or perhaps briefly perching on a bench in the corridor, they would pass their time in club-time pursuits: dining, drinking, reading or relaxing in the library, or perhaps going to the smoking room – first demanded in 1848 – to chat, or play cards or chess.[11]

Ministers were expected to work in Whitehall offices and were granted only a single office between them in the new Palace. In contrast, parliamentary officials acquired spacious living accommodation and offices to help them run 'the club' smoothly. Gradually, the officials' spacious quarters have been converted into offices for MPs and ministers. The dining room set aside for the Clerk of the Commons became an office for the prime minister and was first used during Balfour's 1902–5 premiership.[12]

Barry ingeniously incorporated Westminster Hall into his design, making it the most historic and imposing entrance hall anyone was ever likely to see. Visitors coming to meet their MPs are then directed through St Stephen's Hall, built on the site of the medieval chapel and Chamber of the old House of Commons, to the Central Hall, now known as Central Lobby. The Central Lobby lies exactly mid-way between the Lords and Commons and was described as 'the political centre of the British Empire', by Erskine May, the Victorian doyen of parliamentary clerks.

The Central Lobby was regarded, by the architect, Sir Hugh Casson, as proof of Barry's 'real genius'. Barry's inclusion of Westminster Hall and St Stephen's in his plans presented an immense challenge, as they are off-line with the north-south axis of his palace's main spine. However, Barry solved the problem by creating an octagonal Central Lobby, thus disguising the fact that his main entrance lies at an odd angle to the rest of the Palace.[13]

Barry's other stroke of genius was to build the Palace's principal floor on the same level, with its main rooms all running from to north to south along its great spine: Robing Room, Royal Gallery, Prince's Chamber, House of Lords, Peers' Corridor, Central Lobby, Commons' Corridor, Commons' Lobby, House of Commons. The Commons and Lords committee rooms, dining rooms and libraries are close by their respective Chambers. Barry achieved this extraordinary feat by extending the New Palace into the Thames, beyond the old shoreline.

Barry's extension into the river required the construction of a huge coffer-dam. It was drained ready for work to start on New Year's Day, 1839. Inside, an enormous, 10 feet thick raft of concrete was built as the foundation for the Palace's great spine. A vast web of cast-iron scaffolding was erected, within which Barry's gigantic new palace gradually took shape. Steam engines hauled up the great mass of stone and wood. Despite the use of the latest technology, on average 1,000 men worked on the building between 1840 and 1860. The stone masons, traditionally Westminster's aristocrats of labour, added to the delays on the building in 1841 by striking for 18 months in protest at a slave-driving foreman, George Allen. Some of the masons carried a Chartist petition to parliament in the same year. The harsh conditions led another mason, Henry Broadhurst, who worked on the

Clock Tower in the 1860s, to become a trade unionist and join the Liberals. He became the first working class MP and, in 1886, minister. Broadhurst's mallet and chisel are displayed in the Palace.[14]

More time was lost because of difficulties with a proposed ventilation system for the new Palace, devised by a Dr David Boswell Reid, who knew about ventilating mines. 'The great ventilator' as Reid became known, convinced MPs that their new Palace required ventilating on a massive scale to remove the smoke from its heating system and the hot air. His network of huge shafts in the towers and long tunnels took up a third of the space in the building. Barry camouflaged the flues in a mass of pinnacles, and disguised the main outlet as the ornate Central Tower, rising 310 feet above the Central Lobby: a tower that survives as a decorative reminder of Reid's folly. Reid was eventually dismissed but the difficulty of heating and ventilating the huge building persisted well into the twentieth century. However, Reid's network of tunnels has been used for cables and pipes.[15]

The disruption caused by the fire, and the need to build a new chamber, led to several breaks with tradition. Barry installed division lobbies on either side of the Chamber, thus ending the practice of 'Ayes' being counted in the Chamber while the 'Noes' were counted in the members' lobby.

In the temporary Chamber, reporters had been given their own gallery; in the new Chamber, Barry continued with this arrangement and built a gallery and offices for the press behind the Speaker's chair. Women had been allocated a few seats in the public gallery of the temporary Chamber from 1842. In the new Chamber, Barry provided a ladies' gallery, with accommodation for about 20 women, above, and set back from, the steeply tiered reporters' gallery. As it was thought necessary to protect the MPs from distractions, the women were hidden from view behind ornate heavy metal grilles. Increasingly, women regarded this arrangement as a symbol of their inferior status.

Unfortunately, the MPs were the most difficult clients and Barry was caused great anguish over disputes about the Commons' Chamber. His design replicated the old Palace's adaptation of St Stephen's Chapel, and was only slightly larger. MPs twice approved Barry's new dimensions, which at 62 feet by 45 feet, were only about 4.5 feet longer and 12 feet wider than the old Chamber's. There were 378 seats in the main body of the Chamber and 191 more in the galleries; but this arrangement provided only 569 seats for 658 members. There were also seats for 100 peers and distinguished visitors; and a public gallery for 128 others.

However, on the Chamber's completion many of the MPs instantly took against its acoustics. Barry had to install a false ceiling, concealing half the height of the windows and requiring more artificial lighting. He also had to scrap a gallery, re-arrange other seats and make changes to the division lobbies. The alterations cut the seating for MPs to 446. Barry hated the false ceiling and refused to enter the Chamber ever again.[16]

The genius of Barry's design for the Palace was complemented by Pugin's Gothic detail. As a Catholic convert and believer in the superiority of medieval design, Pugin pioneered the Gothic revival with fanatical enthusiasm and fantastical flair. His determination to achieve perfection in every tile, fitting and item of furniture created a super-human challenge: in the Lords alone there were 1,100 pieces of furniture, and 325 distinct functional types. Much of his work was later smothered beneath official-issue cream and green paint, but since the 1980s, many of his designs have been restored, using his original printing blocks for the wallpaper and re-creating his medieval-style encaustic tiles.[17]

Pugin's most famous contribution to the Palace is his overhanging clock case with its four faces, high on the Clock Tower known as Big Ben after its great hour bell. The distinctive design of the clock case is now synonymous with Westminster, but Pugin based it on his work for a Catholic aristocrat at Scarisbrick Hall in Lancashire. The 315 feet tall Clock Tower, designed by Barry, leans slightly from the vertical, putting it out of alignment by about 18 inches at its highest point. When viewed from Parliament Square, the Clock Tower's appears to lean marginally to the left (northwards). According to the experts, there is no imminent danger of collapse. The Tower has been moving incredibly slowly since it was first built, as the London clay beneath its foundations dries out. Apparently the leaning Clock Tower should not become a major concern for thousands of years.[18]

Barry was required to include a prison cell in the Tower for anyone whom the Commons might detain. Few other cells boast yellow and silver flock wallpaper by Pugin. Charles Bradlaugh, an atheist, and newly elected MP, was held there briefly in June 1880 during a dispute concerning the oath of allegiance. Despite being repeatedly re-elected to the Commons, Bradlaugh was stopped from taking the oath until the Speaker overruled opposition in 1886. Two years later, he secured an act allowing parliamentary affirmations.[19]

High in the Clock Tower, a giant 5 ton clock, 15 feet across, keeps near-perfect time. Minor variations are regulated by small weights – pre-decimal pennies – on the pendulum. The four clock dials are each 22.5 feet in diameter, with a 14-foot hour hand and 9-foot minute hand, and are illuminated from behind. Above the clock dials, a lantern shines out when either House sits after dark. Known as the Ayrton light after its originator, Acton Ayrton MP, it was first used in 1885. The Tower's roof is a Pugin fantasy, with concave sides that create a tapering effect, topped by a weathervane. The cast-iron structure is combined with gilt Gothic ornamentation.[20]

The tower's hour-bell, 'Big Ben', may have been named after Sir Benjamin Hall, who was the First Commissioner of Works when it was hung; but probably owes its name to Benjamin Caunt, a prize-fighter who fought his last fight in 1857. Pugin did not live to hear Big Ben chime the hours. His explosion of creativity and close attention to detail drove him to madness and, in September 1852, to an early grave, aged 40.[21]

The hourly chimes of Big Ben became a regular feature on BBC domestic radio from February 1924 and on the Empire Broadcasting Service (later the World Service) from December 1932. During the Second World War the chimes became a sound-beacon of liberty round the world. Yet the story of this global symbol is a chapter of accidents. While the huge Big Ben was being cast near Stockton-on-Tees, it was dropped and damaged. Nonetheless, it was shipped to Westminster in August 1856, but while being tested with a huge hammer a four-foot long crack appeared. The bell was broken up, melted down and re-cast in Whitechapel in the East End. In the autumn of 1858, the re-cast Big Ben was brought back to Westminster. It took a team of eight men 36 hours to winch the 13.5-ton monster up the narrow shaft encircled by the Clock Tower's 334-step staircase.[22]

Big Ben began to strike the hours in July 1859, accompanied by the quarter-hour Westminster chimes of four smaller bells ringing out a tune first composed in 1793 at St Mary's the Great, Cambridge and called by students 'Jowett's Jig', after a professor. But by September Big Ben had cracked again. Not everyone regarded the enforced silence as bad news. 'Earl Grey in common with all the inhabitants of that part of London in which he lived', reported *Hansard*, 'rejoiced that the great bell had been cracked'. But their joy was short-lived. Big Ben was turned to present an uncracked surface to the hammer, or clapper, and the 13-hundredweight clapper was replaced by one weighing only 4 hundredweight.

By 1862, hour-bell and quarters were again ringing out across Westminster; although Big Ben never again achieved a perfect 'E'. In the early 1920s, Virginia Woolf's fictional Westminster resident, Clarissa Dalloway, is accompanied while walking through London by Big Ben striking the hours. 'She felt a particular hush, or solemnity; an indescribable pause; a suspense ... before Big Ben strikes. There! Out it boomed'.[23] However, in 1976, the clock was again silent for nine months after pendulum weights fell down the shaft and the clock mechanism broke.[24]

The Clock Tower's clock case and roof rise above the north end of the Palace as Pugin's fantastical epitaph; the Victoria Tower stands at the south end as Barry's majestic memorial. The Victoria Tower was originally designated as the King's Tower until William IV's death in 1837. Barry visualized it as the great keep to a castle, but despite its massive size the tower is beautifully proportioned and is an exquisite exemplar of Gothic Perpendicular. At the top, its pinnacled corner turrets and 75 feet central flagpole rise skywards, each with a gilded crown at its apex. The Union Flag flies on the Victoria Tower when parliament sits but is replaced by the Royal Standard when the monarch visits.[25]

On its completion, the tower became the world's tallest building, but its construction was a nightmare and tested Barry's skills to their limit. Excavation of the foundations encountered the quicksands and springs on a marshy part of Thorney Island. Barry overcame this natural hazard by laying a 10-feet bed of concrete and by building cautiously, adding only 30 feet of wall every six months. He also found that the stone being used, a soft magnesian limestone from Anston, Yorkshire, was susceptible to erosion, especially in Westminster's polluted air.[26]

Barry strengthened the great tower by installing a framework of four cast-iron girders in the roof above the Royal Entrance. Each girder weighed 12 tons and was bedded into six-feet thick walls. These girders were the base for eight, vertical cast-iron columns, each one tapering from 14 inches at the bottom to eight inches at the top. Around these columns, the massive tower was built, using almost 30,000 tons of stone, bricks and iron. Barry had to add an extra 50 feet to his plans when the politicians insisted that the tower should store the growing number of state documents. Finally, the tower stood 323 feet high to the base of its cast-iron flagpole.[27]

By the 1930s, the Victoria Tower was becoming unsafe and was abandoned. Repairs began after the Second World War, and by 1959 the massive structure had been strengthened with new iron girders. Renovation and repairs have been recurrent features of life at the Palace, and have returned much of Barry's and Pugin's work to its original, stunning best. From 1981, the outside of the Palace was given a 12-year facelift, removing filthy soot stains and restoring eroded stonework; but as in any small town, the mending and repairs never stop.[28]

Barry was eventually worn down by all the work and disputes at the new Palace. He died in 1860, aged 65, before he could complete the Victoria Tower, or finish the new Westminster Bridge which was built after the eighteenth-century bridge closed in 1846, and designed in harmony with the new Palace. Barry also designed the Reform Club in Pall Mall and the Privy Council Offices in Whitehall (between Downing Street and Horse Guards); both now elegant reminders of his favoured neo-classical style. His tomb in Westminster Abbey recognizes Barry's role in creating the new Houses of Parliament: engraved on its brass plaque are his plan for the entire building and a depiction of the mighty Victoria Tower.

36 GOLDEN AGE

The period from the early 1830s to the late 1860s was the golden age of parliament, although during much of it the Palace of Westminster was a building site. According to the historian, Robert Blake, 'the period from 1835 to 1868 saw the heyday of the supremacy of the house of commons'. Yet a contemporary sketch by Charles Dickens was less reverential. Dismissing 'all that feeling of awe, which vague ideas of breaches of privilege, Serjeant-at-Arms, heavy denunciations, and still heavier fees are calculated to awaken', he takes us inside the Chamber of the Commons, temporarily housed in the old Court of Requests:

> The body of the House and the side galleries are full of Members; some, with their legs on the back of the opposite seat; some, with theirs stretched out to their utmost length on the floor; some going out, others coming in; all talking, laughing, lounging, coughing, oh-ing, questioning, or groaning; presenting a conglomeration of noise and confusion, to be met with no other place in existence, not even excepting Smithfield on a market-day; or a cock-pit in its glory.

In all this 'noise and confusion', Britain contrived to rule the world's biggest empire.[1]

Behind the 'Crown-in-Parliament' façade being erected by Barry and Pugin, power passed decisively from the monarch to the Commons. In 1841, the young Queen Victoria would have preferred Lord Melbourne to remain prime minister, but when the Conservatives (the name under which the Tories had begun to organize during the reform crisis), won most seats in that year's election she had to accept that only the brusque Sir Robert Peel could command a majority in the Commons.

Peel served as prime minister for almost five years, but like his predecessor never moved into Number 10. Peel preferred instead to use Number 10 as his office while continuing to live in his town house, Number 4 Whitehall Gardens, on the former site of Whitehall Palace. The area around Downing Street was becoming squalid, as the historian Anthony Seldon has noted, with an estimated 170 brothels and 145 gin parlours in the vicinity. In the 1840s conditions became worse, as a trade slump and poor harvests brought unemployment, poverty and starvation; but the misery of Britain's 'hungry 40s' was eclipsed by the horror in Ireland, where potato blight brought the 'great famine'.[2]

Peel's response to the desperate crisis was wholly in character. He had more regard for the facts than for the views of his MPs, who were largely aristocrats or landed gentry. Peel was the proud son of a cotton manufacturer, but many Conservatives resented the rise of businessmen and blamed them for the deep divisions and discontent in the industrial towns. Tory anxieties about laissez-faire capitalism were best expressed by Benjamin Disraeli, a dandified novelist and young MP. Although proud of his Jewish heritage, he would not have been able to sit in the Commons had he not been baptized into the Anglican faith as a child, as Jews were barred from becoming MPs until 1858.

No one who witnessed Disraeli's calamitous maiden speech in 1837 could have foreseen that he would become Peel's nemesis. His foolhardiness as a new MP in daring to challenge Daniel O'Connell, the leader of the Irish MPs, during a debate on Irish elections, ended in disaster. As Disraeli spoke, the cat-calls, groans, hisses, hoots and hubbub from Irish MPs grew louder, and other MPs lost patience until he was forced to stop. 'I sit down now', he cried above the uproar, 'but the time will come when you will hear me'.[3]

Disraeli gradually began to win respect for his sarcastic wit, but was spurned when Peel formed his Government in 1841. Disraeli's failure to gain preferment was mocked by Lord Palmerston, a former Foreign Secretary and veteran of Tory and Whig governments, but Disraeli gave a witty riposte. Thanking the grandee for his 'warm aspirations', Disraeli ventured to suggest; 'if to assist my advancement, he will only impart to me the secret of his own unprecedented rise, and by what means he has continued to enjoy power under seven successive administrations, I shall at least have gained a valuable result by this discussion'.[4]

Sybil or The Two Nations, the novel that brought Disraeli lasting political fame was published in 1845. The book's hero, Egremont, has his eyes opened to the fault-line that ran through Victorian society during a chance meeting:

'Say what you will, our Queen reigns over the greatest nation that ever existed.'
'Which nation?' asked the younger stranger, 'for she reigns over two … two nations between whom there is no intercourse and no sympathy; who are as ignorant of each other's habits, thoughts, and feeling, as if they were dwellers in different zones or inhabitants of different planets; who are formed by different manners, and not governed by the same laws.'
'You speak of —' said Egremont hesitatingly.
'THE RICH AND THE POOR'.

Disraeli had become involved with a group of young Tory aristocrats who adopted a romantic, paternalistic approach to dealing with the problems of the age and were known as Young England. They regarded Peel as unprincipled and not a true Tory. Although the group soon broke up, Disraeli continued to attack Peel for being untrustworthy: a view that was reinforced by Peel's change of mind on the subject of the Corn Laws. The prime minister had come round to the views of Richard Cobden and John Bright of the Anti-Corn Law League, who campaigned to remove the protectionist duties on imported grain that kept the price of bread artificially high.

Repeal of the Corn Laws, as the duties were called, represented a major volte-face for the Conservatives; yet, during the Queen's Speech debate in January 1846, Peel was insistent. 'I have thought it consistent with true Conservative policy', he claimed, 'to promote so much of happiness and contentment among the people that the voice of disaffection should be no longer heard, and thoughts of the dissolution of our institutions should be forgotten in the midst of physical enjoyment'. But Peel's argument was mocked by Disraeli, who made his reputation during the tumultuous debates that followed. As *The Times* reported, Disraeli 'in a strain of sarcasm which elicited the loudest cheers and laughter proceeded to assail the consistency of the Premier'. He goaded Peel mercilessly. 'I remember him making his protection speeches', Disraeli declared:

> They were the best speeches I ever heard. It was a great thing to hear the right hon. Gentleman say, 'I would sooner be the leader of the Gentlemen of England than possess the confidence of Sovereigns'. That was a grand thing. We don't hear much of 'the Gentlemen of England' now.

Only 112 Conservative MPs backed Peel, while 231 supported the 'Gentlemen of England' and protection.[5]

Peel finally managed to repeal the Corn Laws, but had to rely on opposition support. When he resigned as prime minister in June 1846, he told MPs that his name would forever be censured by party loyalists and protectionists, but added, in what stands as his political epitaph: 'it may be that I shall leave a name sometimes remembered with expressions of good will in the abodes of those whose lot it is to labour, and to earn their daily bread by the sweat of their brow, when they shall recruit their exhausted strength with abundant and untaxed food, the sweeter because it is no longer leavened by a sense of injustice'. Four years later, Peel was fatally injured in a riding accident on Constitution Hill, by Green Park. As he lay dying in Whitehall Gardens, many working people joined a great, silent crowd standing vigil outside his home.[6]

After Peel, six prime ministers fell victim to parliamentary revolts in 20 years: Russell in 1852, Aberdeen in 1855, Palmerston in 1858, Derby in 1859, and Russell again in 1866. 'Six parliaments were elected between 1841 and 1868', Blake noted; 'and in all six of them the House of Commons had brought down at least one administration, and sometimes two, before its dissolution'.[7] Ten changes of government occurred within 23 years.

Prime Ministers and their Cabinets had to spend long hours in the Commons trying to win backbench support. The strain was almost unbearable, as Peel had complained privately in 1845: 'I defy the Minister of this country to perform properly the duties of his office ... and also sit in the House of Commons eight hours a day for 118 days'. Mastery of debate became a key political weapon. Press reports of the latest parliamentary cliff-hanger were rushed to breakfast tables across the country by the new railway network. Westminster's star turns – Palmerston, Disraeli, Gladstone – became national celebrities.[8]

Disraeli and Gladstone were both elected as Conservative MPs, but they took different sides when their party split over the Corn Laws. Although Disraeli had never held office, he was leading the Conservatives in the Commons by the time of Peel's death: the party leader, Edward, Lord Stanley, later the Earl of Derby, sat in the lords. Gladstone, despite his greater ministerial experience, was condemned to the backbenches with almost 90 fellow Peelites.

Disraeli was 47-years-old and Gladstone 41 when their personal duel began in early 1852, after the fall of Lord John Russell's Whig Government. The new minority Conservative Government was known as the 'Who? Who?' ministry after Derby, who was attending a debate in the Lords, quietly told Wellington the names of his ministers, only for the deaf Duke to bellow repeatedly, 'Who'? Who?' Disraeli was made Leader of the House of Commons and Chancellor of the Exchequer, despite having doubts about the latter post. 'Don't worry', Derby assured him. 'They give you the figures'.[9]

Yet Disraeli found himself in an impossible position. 'We built up an opposition on Protection and Protestantism', he observed. 'The first the country has positively pissed on'. His options as Chancellor were severely limited. After introducing provisional measures in April 1852, he eventually introduced his budget in December, five weeks after Queen Victoria had officially opened the new Houses of Parliament. No other politician was more at home in Pugin's Gothic setting than Disraeli, who romanticized England's medieval past: a parallel noted by the historian, David Cannadine. As Disraeli rose to introduce his budget shortly after 10 p.m., thunder cracked and rumbled outside and lightning bolts lit up the windows, adding to the sense of Gothic drama in a packed Chamber.[10]

Disraeli's appearance at the dispatch box, was captured by William White, a Commons' door-keeper, who had a ring-side seat for many such parliamentary duels:

When he rises he generally starts bolt-upright, then leans his hands upon the table, and casts his eyes downwards. At first he not infrequently hesitates and stammers a good deal.
He soon warms up to his work. He then takes his hands off the table, thrusts

them it may be into his waistcoat pocket, and turns his face towards the House; or else, if he feels well up, he folds his arms across his breast. Then he hesitates no more, but his sentences come out in stately flow …

White noticed that before bringing wit into his speech, Disraeli 'shifts his position, turning with his face towards the Treasury bench, and heralds the coming witticism with a slight curl of the mouth and twinkle of the eyes'. At such moments, 'it is seen that he still possesses that power of sarcasm and wit which so galled Sir Robert Peel in the Corn Law struggle'.[11]

Pausing for his customary budget night sips of brandy and soda, Disraeli ended by attacking the coalition of opposition MPs – Whigs, Peelites and Radicals – who were hurling abuse, much of it anti-semitic. 'Coalitions have always been brief', he declared. 'This, too, I know, that England does not love coalitions'. His tour de force won praise from all sides. 'This speech was his greatest speech', noted the Radical, John Bright; 'he was in earnest; argument, satire, sarcasm, invective, all were abundant and of the first class'.[12]

No sooner had Disraeli finished than Gladstone, defying the convention that the Chancellor spoke last, rose to his feet. 'His usually calm features were livid and distorted with passion', observed Edward Stanley, 'his voice shook, and those who watched him feared an outbreak incompatible with parliamentary rules. So stormy a scene I never witnessed'.[13] On such occasions, Gladstone's eyes gleamed like a vulture's and he pointed his forefinger straight at his adversary. This sketch of him, crafted on a later occasion by Henry Lucy, the father of parliamentary sketch-writing, depicts Gladstone in full flow:

In the hottest moments he beat the brass-bound Box with clamorous hand that occasionally drowned the point he strove to make. Sometimes with both hands raised above his head; often with left elbow leaning on the box, the right hand with closed fist shaken at the head of an unoffending country gentleman on the back bench opposite … he trampled his way through the argument he assailed as an elephant in an hour of aggravation rages through a jungle.[14]

Gladstone's words as he attacked Disraeli's budget were sometimes lost in the din of Conservative protests, while the Chancellor feigned sleep, stirring only to lift his eyeglass and peer ostentatiously at the clock over the entrance door. When MPs voted at 4 a.m., the government was defeated by 19 votes, but all the talk was of the clash between Disraeli and Gladstone. 'Like two of Sir Walter Scott's champions', The Times reported, 'these redoubtable antagonists gathered up all their force for the final struggle, and encountered each other in mid-career'.[15]

Temperamentally, Disraeli and Gladstone were poles apart. White typified Disraeli as indifferent, polite and superficial; Gladstone as intense, earnest and thorough. Their contrasting characters spiced their contests and focused attention on the ancient job of Chancellor of the Exchequer; but it was Gladstone who made it a major office of state. Previously, the pre-eminence of the Prime Minister in Cabinet derived from his role as First Lord of the Treasury and many premiers, such as Pitt the Younger, had also been Chancellor. Although Peel appointed Henry Goulbourn Chancellor in 1841, Goulbourn was relatively junior and Peel made important financial statements himself.

Gladstone was Peel's disciple, but when he was Chancellor neither of his prime ministers, the Earl of Aberdeen (1852–5) and Palmerston (1859–65), were much interested in public finance. Their indifference enabled Gladstone to turn the Chancellor's office at Number 11 Downing Street into a new power base. Since his day, the Chancellor of the Exchequer has run the Treasury. Gladstone imposed Treasury control on the Civil Service by commissioning the Northcote-Trevelyan Report and replacing patronage with a culture of professional impartiality that became ingrained in Whitehall.

Gladstone's financial rectitude became Treasury orthodoxy:

No Chancellor of the Exchequer is worth his salt who is not ready to save what are meant by candle-ends and cheese-parings in the cause of his country … [T]he Chancellor of the Exchequer is the trusted and confidential steward of the public and lies under a sacred obligation with regard to all that he consents to spend.

Although his rigour made the Chancellor's job more demanding, Gladstone combined it with being prime minister during 1873–4 and 1880–2.[16]

Rivalry between Numbers 10 and 11 existed from the start. Although Palmerston and Gladstone were founding members of the Liberal Party in 1859, they were very different characters. Palmerston was already 70 when he first became prime minister in 1855, but he seemed a lot younger, according to White: 'he is about 5ft 10ins, looks about 55 – albeit he is turned 70 – walks upright as a dart, and steps out like a soldier'. He was a common sight in the streets of St James's and Whitehall as he walked, or rode on his grey, between his town-house, 94 Piccadilly, and Downing Street.[17]

Palmerston's womanizing scandalized the queen but earned him the nickname, 'Lord Cupid', and enhanced his popularity. His love of boxing and horse racing, his gunboat diplomacy as Foreign Secretary and his readiness to court the press by inviting them to society soirees at his Piccadilly home, made him 'the people's darling'. Between the ages of 72 and 84, Palmerston won a hat-trick of general elections. When he was cited in a divorce case as he approached 80, Disraeli suggested that the prime minister was trying to boost his popularity before calling an election.[18]

In the Commons, Palmerston wore 'a surtout coat, buttoned up close, dark trousers, and black necktie'. During debates, 'Pam's witty sallies are evidently suggested by a love of fun, quite as much as by a desire to hit an opponent ... [he] laughs with genuine merriment'. Periodic attacks of gout sometimes obliged him 'to clothe one of his feet in a woollen shoe and hobble upstairs with a stick'. Yet, at the age of 72, and tormented with the gout, Palmerston 'could sit seven hours watching a debate and then get up and make a lively and forcible speech of an hour's length'. Four years later, White attributed Palmerston's ability to spend long hours in the Chamber and leave as fresh as when he arrived to his 'power to sleep at will. When a long-winded orator rises he can fold his arms, and at once, without effort, enter the land of dreams; when another gets up whom he wishes to hear, he can, with equal facility, shake off his sleep'.[19]

In contrast to Palmerston's relaxed calm and Disraeli's inscrutable stillness in the Chamber, Gladstone was a mass of nervous energy. He was a tortured soul, a man torn between devout faith and sexual desire. His Christian conscience alerted him to the plight of the many prostitutes soliciting in Westminster, Whitehall and Soho, but his mission to rescue 'fallen women' condemned him to recurrent temptation. At times of moral anguish, Gladstone scourged himself with a whip. His nocturnal street walks and meetings with prostitutes threatened his career in 1853, when a would-be blackmailer appeared in court. 'It is a very strange affair, and has not yet been satisfactorily explained', noted Charles Greville. The case prompted malicious whispers about Gladstone's night life, but his rescue missions had his wife's active support and, remarkably, he had no further trouble from blackmailers or journalists.[20]

Palmerston knew that his Government's success depended largely on his Chancellor, although they disagreed on re-armament, taxation, reform and religion. During Cabinet meetings, Palmerston managed to control his frustration with Gladstone's verbosity and let his Chancellor air his views, but then he would say, 'right gentlemen, now to business'. When Gladstone rose to deliver his 1860 budget, White, the door-keeper, observed that Palmerston, 'settles himself down into an attitude of the closest attention, and does not lean back as he often does, but sits sideways, with his face turned to the Chancellor, and very happy he looks, as if he were conscious that his Chancellor is about to unfold a scheme of finance that will do credit to the two of them'.[21]

Gladstone's budgets made his reputation. On 10 February 1860, he rose to his feet at 4.50 p.m. in a packed Chamber, having delayed his budget for a week because of ill-health. 'Spoke 5 – 9 without great exhaustion, aided by a large stock of egg and wine', Gladstone noted in his diary. 'Thank God. Home at 11. This was the most arduous operation I have ever had in Parliament'. According to MacDonagh, a press gallery reporter, Gladstone kept his favourite fortifier of egg beaten in sherry, in what looked to observers like a pomatum pot – a small bottle usually used for scented hair dressing – that he placed near the dispatch box before rising to speak. He resorted to his odd little bottle three or four times during his speech: 'for the glow and ardour which his voice, so lubricated, gave to his flowing periods'.[22]

Gladstone's 1860 budget reduced the cost of living by slashing customs duties and food taxes, while raising income tax on the better-off. 'The effect of this speech upon the House was remarkable', noted White:

> There was but little cheering. The House was too deeply absorbed to cheer – too anxious to catch every word. For four hours did the great master hold the house with a spell. During that time the dinner hour and the postal hours came and went, but no one moved, and through all those hours the house was as silent as a desert. Not a whimper nor a rustle was heard – nothing but the clear, musical voice of the speaker'.

When the Chancellor finally sat down, he was greeted by loud cheers.[23]

Before the 'great Budget night' in April 1861, White reported that, 'as early as ten o'clock in the morning St Stephen's gateway was lined with strangers', ready to wait 'seated upon the bare stone benches, for six hours'. By 4 p.m. the House of Commons was full. 'At half-past four Gladstone trooped through the crowd, took his green box from the doorkeeper, and entered the House'. White's reference to the colour of Gladstone's box seems puzzling, since Gladstone's red dispatch box came to symbolize the budget, and has been held aloft by many subsequent chancellors, including George Osborne for his first budget in 2010. However, White's account suggests that in 1861, Gladstone's budget statement was put in one of his civil servants' green boxes.[24]

Gladstone cut tax on higher incomes, and made books and newspapers cheaper. By incorporating all financial changes into a single Finance Bill, he outwitted his opponents in the Lords, since they dared not reject a whole Budget. He also confounded expectations of a government deficit, and instead announced a £2 million surplus: to cheers from the Liberals and dismay from the opposition. 'We do not recollect that any of our Chancellors ever crammed the House as Mr Gladstone does', White noted two years later. 'Men like to see the performer, to hear the ring of his voice, to feel the power of his eloquence, to watch its effect upon the audience'.[25]

A fascinating glimpse of Westminster during the 'golden age of parliament' is given in *The Warden*, the first novel in Anthony Trollope's *Chronicles of Barsetshire*, published in 1855. Septimus Harding, the Warden, visits London for legal advice and kills time by visiting parliament and Westminster Abbey. In the Commons, Harding has to cough up five shillings to an attendant for admission to the strangers' gallery. He watches MPs debate 'the Convent Custody Bill', allowing the searching of nuns by aged clergymen: a satire on the real Recovery of Personal Liberty in Certain Cases Bill, allowing searches of religious houses for females held against their will.

Arriving early at the Abbey, Harding has to pay two pence as a sightseer, and was 'not much edified by the manner of the service' which he later attends in the choir, feeling 'that these things were managed better at Barchester'. Trollope notes, in 1878, the increase in religious zeal that had developed at the Abbey by that date, and the reduction that had occurred in the charges exacted from visitors. However, the better-attended services at the revitalized Abbey of the late nineteenth century were not to everyone's taste. The fastidious novelist, Henry James, writing in 1888, was repelled by the press of people at a Good Friday service in the Abbey: 'I put my nose into the church and promptly withdrew it. The crowd was terribly compact, and beneath the gothic arches the odour was not that of incense'.[26]

Henry James may have been unduly sensitive, but the golden age of political debate was accompanied by social distress on Parliament's doorstep. 'There is no part of the capital that presents a more chequered aspect, both physical and moral, than Westminster', observed *Household Words*, edited by Charles Dickens, in 1850; 'the law-makers of one-seventh of the human race sit, night after night, in deliberation, in the immediate vicinity of the most notorious haunt of law-breakers in the Empire'. This 'notorious haunt' was known as 'The Devil's Acre' and lay to the south-west of the Abbey, between present-day Great Peter Street, Great Smith Street and Strutton Ground. 'There are other parts of the town as filthy, dingy, and forbidding in appearance as this, but these are generally the haunts more of poverty than crime'. Some improvements had been initiated and by 1851, the western quarter of Devil's Acre, towards Tothill Street, had been demolished in an early slum clearance scheme to make way for Victoria Street.[27]

Despite these modest improvements, the politicians endured a much worse stink than Henry James encountered at the Abbey. While MPs sat in the House for long stretches, often till 2 a.m. and sometimes till 4 a.m., their summer debates were frequently accompanied by a foul smell wafting in from the river. London's rapid expansion and its booming population had created an environmental disaster. The Thames was an open cesspit, awash with untreated filth from its 400 factories and raw sewage from three million people. This poisonous and putrid brew festered beneath Barry's glorious riverfront, oozing downstream on the ebb tide and floating back on the flood. Cholera killed 18,000 Londoners in 1849, and 24,000 in 1854; but parliament was slow to act until the long, hot summer of 1858, when MPs found the stench unbearable. Disraeli was seen rushing from the Chamber, clutching a handkerchief to his nose while complaining loudly about, 'a Stygian pool reeking with ineffable and unbearable horror'.[28]

London's foulness had penetrated Westminster's Gothic dream-world and eventually forced the politicians to act. 'What a pity it is that the thermometer fell ten degrees yesterday', *The Times* commented acidly on 18 June 1858:

Parliament was all but compelled to legislate upon the great London nuisance by the force of the sheer stench. The intense heat had driven our legislators from those portions of their buildings which overlook the river. A few members, indeed, bent upon investigating the matter to its very depth, ventured into the library but they were instantaneously driven to retreat, each man with a handkerchief to his nose. We are heartily glad of it.[29]

The construction of an embankment had been recommended as early as 1844 by a Royal Commission. In addition to carrying a new road, an embankment would prevent flooding and increase the tide's flushing effect by narrowing the river. But it soon became clear that sewer pipes were needed to discharge downstream. 'The Great Stink' of 1858 concentrated politician's minds. The plan for an embankment was endorsed in 1860, an Act was passed in 1862, and Sir Joseph Bazalgette, the engineer, began work in 1864.

Work proceeded in sections of huge, one to two hundred feet, caissons, drained and then in-filled. Thirty million cubic feet of earth were excavated. Six million cubic feet of bricks and concrete were used, and in addition the concave riverfront wall required 650,000 cubic feet of granite. Below the new road were massive sewer, gas, water and, eventually, electricity pipes; and a tunnel, added later, for the underground railway. At Westminster, the route of the subterranean pipes, sewer and railway turns away from the river, towards the west in order to avoid the Houses of Parliament.[30]

A site cleared at the corner of Tothill Street and Storey's Gate while building the underground railway was occupied from 1876 by the Royal Aquarium and, a few years later, by a theatre at its west end. The main hall of these winter gardens was 340 feet long and 160 feet, but technical problems prevented fish ever living in its tanks. Instead, visitors were entertained by circus performers and daredevil stunts, or by playing billiards, dancing, dining, listening to music, skating, swimming or watching a play.[31]

The Victoria Embankment runs for more than a mile between Blackfriars and Westminster. It was completed in 1870 and is furnished with distinctive benches, lamp-posts and mooring rings. The total cost was £1.2 million, paid for by dues on coal and wine. Many of the 37¼ acres reclaimed from the river were turned into public gardens, which at Whitehall incorporate the private gardens of the old town-houses. Northumberland Avenue and Whitehall Place were created to give access from Trafalgar Square and Whitehall. The Embankment was extended south, beyond the Houses of Parliament, in the 1880s when Millbank's wharves and jetties were demolished and public gardens laid out.[32]

However, the Thames was not entirely tamed. In January 1928 a flood-swollen high tide poured 'like a waterfall over the parapet into the open space at the foot of the Big Ben', overflowed the terraces of the Houses of Parliament and inundated

Old Palace Yard. Ten people drowned in the Horseferry Road and Millbank area when part of the Embankment wall gave way.[33]

Despite the public access to new gardens and parks at Whitehall and Millbank, public access to the Houses of Parliament was curtailed; reinforcing the idea that it was a politicians' club. Until the late 1860s, New Palace Yard had always been open to the public; providing a space outside Westminster Hall where people drank and ate in its coffee house and taverns, and gathered for public meetings or – in earlier times – executions, the pillory and tournaments. In September 1838, people had congregated there in support of the People's Charter demanding political reform, including votes for all men. In April 1848, special constables were recruited to guard Westminster Bridge and the Houses of Parliament in case of trouble during a mass Chartist march and the delivery of a Chartist petition.

While the finishing touches were being put to the New Palace in July 1866, a demonstration in Hyde Park for further reform turned violent. Within two months Edward Barry was commissioned to erect seven-foot high railings round New Palace Yard. By February 1868, the yard was securely enclosed. Although the public were sometimes admitted to hear Gladstone speak, New Palace Yard's role as an open public space was lost.[34]

The fate of New Palace Yard epitomized Westminster's approach to further reform. The vote, as with public access, was in the gift of politicians, not a basic right. The reward of the gift depended on calculations of party advantage. Disraeli defeated Gladstone's 1866 Reform Bill by siding with Liberal opponents of reform; but a year later, Disraeli shocked his own supporters by accepting an amendment to the Conservatives' bill that almost doubled the numbers eligible to vote.

Disraeli's volte-face came while most MPs were dining. 'Many a snug dinner party was prematurely broken up that night', noted White, as Conservatives rushed back to find out what was happening. 'Think how we've been sold!' exclaimed a Conservative MP, 'we would not have Gladstone's Bill, and, by Jove, we have got one ten thousand times worse!' Yet Disraeli's coup was to end the Conservatives' role as second fiddle to the Liberals and establish them as a party of government, confident of appealing to working-class voters.[35]

By the 1870s, the impact of the Second Reform Act was creating modern parties, with national organizations and greater discipline over their MPs. In 1878, Disraeli, who had been ennobled as the Earl of Beaconsfield, became the first British prime minister to attend an international summit, when the expanding rail networks enabled him to travel to the Congress of Berlin. His skill in curbing Russian ambitions on the Turkish Empire impressed the German chancellor, Prince Otto von Bismarck, who declared: 'Der alte Jude, das ist der Mann!' Beaconsfield's signature to the treaty was accompanied by the term 'prime minister' for the first time.[36]

Beaconsfield returned from Berlin in triumph, having kept the Russian navy out of the Mediterranean, and winning the strategic prize of Cyprus. When his boat train from Dover pulled into Charing Cross, a terminus opened only 13 years earlier, the station was decorated with flags and flowers. The waiting crowds gave him a hero's welcome as he and his foreign secretary, Lord Salisbury, drove down Whitehall in an open barouche. In Downing Street the prime minister, repeating a phrase he had used at Dover, declared that they brought 'peace with honour'. This phrase was to be echoed 60 years later by Neville Chamberlain on his return from appeasing Hitler at Munich.[37]

37 DYNAMITE

The first bomb exploded in Westminster Hall shortly after 2 p.m. on 24 January 1885. As it was a Saturday, the politicians were absent, but the Houses of Parliament were full of visitors. A woman walking through the passage between the chapel of St Mary Undercroft and Westminster Hall, noticed a black bag on the floor, partly covered by a woman's or child's dress. She saw that 'it smoked' and pointed it out to her brother. 'Dynamite!' he warned and hurried her away, calling out for the police. The nearest policeman, PC Cole, picked up the bag and rushed with it to the Great Hall, where he put it down. Within moments, it exploded.

It was fortunate for Cole that he was not holding the bomb when it detonated: the force of the explosion just knocked him out and broke several ribs. The blast was heard in nearby streets and on Westminster Bridge. It left a hole about 3 feet by 5 feet in the stone floor, lifted some of the stone steps leading to St Stephen's, twisted the metal rails round St Mary's Chapel, shattered windows, cracked the roof and filled the great hall with smoke and dust shaken from the overhead beams.

Moments later, a bigger explosion shook the Palace. A second bomb had been planted in the Commons' Chamber below the Peers' Gallery, under the benches on the government side of the house. The Commons' clock had stopped at 2.13 p.m., the time of the blast. The first bomb had been a diversionary tactic. As the policeman on duty at the Commons sprinted to Westminster Hall, the bigger bomb had been planted, undetected. Its blast demolished the partition between the bar of the house and the lobby outside; distorted brass fittings; reduced oak timbers to matchwood; and wrecked nearby benches, hurling some of them into the gallery above.[1]

The bombs at Westminster were planted by Irish republicans, commonly known as Fenians, after the Fenian Brotherhood, founded among New York's Irish diaspora. Their campaign of terror was known as 'the dynamite war', because of their use of the lethal, new explosive. In 1867, they had created a great scare by murdering a policeman in Manchester, and slaughtering 12 people, and maiming many more, in a bomb attack on Clerkenwell gaol. As a result, thousands of special constables were sworn in to guard gas works, search sewers and protect public buildings. However, the police boat moored outside parliament at night to stop attack from the river was shown to have been pointless when terrorists could mingle among visitors and hide bombs in their clothing.[2]

'My mission is to pacify Ireland', Gladstone had remarked in 1868, on learning that he was about to become prime minister. At this stage, he thought that disestablishing the Church of Ireland and land reform would do the trick. 'The attention of the House during these three hours was profound and unflagging', William White, the House of Commons doorkeeper, noted when Gladstone defended his Irish land bill in 1870. MPs missed their dinners to hear the prime minister's speech. As he finally sat down, 'a volley of cheers burst forth'. Yet Gladstone's good intentions were insufficient.[3]

By the 1870s, Irish home rule, in the form of a restored Irish parliament, was widely supported in Ireland. At Westminster, Irish MPs became ingenious at finding ways to disrupt parliament and frustrate the government. In 1874, Conservatives dining at the St Stephen's Club on Bridge Street, only minutes from parliament, missed a vote when the club's division bell failed to ring: an Irish MP had cut its wires. As few of the Irish contingent dined at clubs or dinner parties, their tactics of suddenly forcing votes at dinner time, tabling timetable-wrecking amendments and making endless speeches infuriated British MPs and journalists. Joe Biggar, a Fenian pork butcher from Belfast, was a master at prolonging his speeches by reading out extracts from previous Acts of Parliament, newspapers and government blue books. His four-hour filibuster on 22 April 1875 coincided with the arrival of a new Irish MP, Charles Stewart Parnell, a 29-year-old, Cambridge-educated, Anglo-Irish Protestant, who was briefly to carry the hopes of moderate Irish nationalists.[4]

After an all-night sitting in August 1877, Henry Lucy, the sketch-writer, suggested that it was no longer necessary to wonder what home rule meant. 'After the experience of the last 26 hours', he noted sourly in his diary, 'it is clear enough that home rule means not going home all night yourself, and keeping as many other people as possible out of their beds'. Four years later, Lucy regretted 'the condition to which the House of Commons has now drifted'. It was 'like a gentleman armed with a rapier attacked by a bully with a bludgeon', and was 'perfectly helpless at the feet of Mr Parnell'. Worse still, 'the authority of the Leader of the House is as nothing compared with the influence of Mr Biggar'.[5]

Parliament threatened to descend into farce. British MPs retaliated against the home-rulers with a 'conspiracy of silence', staying silent 'night after night whilst Irishmen have droned forth dreary diatribes'. But when the home-rulers forced the house to sit through two consecutive nights in early 1881, the government had finally had enough. At 8.45 a.m. on the second day of the sitting, Gladstone walked into the Chamber, rose to the despatch box and moved that the debate should end forthwith. 'Never since Cromwell entered the House at the head of his men-at-arms', noted Lucy, 'had regular parliamentary procedure been subject to this swift and arbitrary cutting off by the mandate of one man'. The Commons finally adjourned after having sat continuously for 41 hours.

A few hours later, the Commons resumed, to protests from the home-rulers. 'That the government were aware that something remarkable would happen in the House of Commons tonight is certain', Lucy observed. 'Large bodies of police were distributed throughout the building. Half a hundred stood at ease in the Court Yard and at a signal through the telegraph wires an additional 100 would have marched down from Scotland Yard'. The Chamber was crammed and the galleries packed. Gladstone was repeatedly interrupted as he tried to speak. Eventually, after 3½ hours and the suspension of 37 home-rulers, the prime minister managed to propose changing the rules to prevent business being obstructed.[6]

'The closure' was first used in 1885, when the Speaker refused to allow home-rulers to delay a debate on Egypt. 'Everyone was taken by surprise, the brief silence being broken by a howl of rage and despair from the Parnellites'. But dealing with home-ruler obstructionism came at a price. Today, the closure is routinely used by governments to curtail debate, with the result that ill-considered laws reach the statute book.[7]

Any hopes for a rapprochement between Gladstone and the home-rulers had been shattered in May 1882, when Lord Frederick Cavendish, the Chief Secretary for Ireland, was murdered in Phoenix Park on his first day in Ireland. Within a year, the 'dynamite war' hit Britain. On 15 March 1883, a few minutes after 9 p.m., MPs in the Commons and the staff at Number 10 were shocked by an explosion that was heard up to three miles away. The bomb was planted at the government office block between Parliament Street and St James's Park.

The Italianate government building was the work of Sir George Gilbert Scott, after Palmerston had resolved 'the battle of the styles' in favour of the classicism of his distant youth. It housed the Foreign Office and India Offices on its west side, overlooking the park; the Colonial Office on the north, overlooking Downing Street; the Home and Colonial offices on the east, fronting Parliament Street; and the Local Government Board offices on Charles Street. The bomber probably planned to attack the Home Office, but hid the device by a window of the Local Government Board offices on Charles Street, facing the entrance to King Street. The blast shattered windows along King Street and showered its police station with debris.[8]

The next day, Gladstone was briefed at the scene and policemen were taken off their beats to protect ministers, escort MPs and guard public buildings: 'the Houses of Parliament are searched as if continually on the eve of Guy Fawkes plot'. The Metropolitan Police set up a Special Irish Branch within its Criminal Investigation Department (CID) to tackle the Fenian threat. The Special Branch was housed on the first floor of a building in the middle of Great Scotland Yard, a dingy courtyard off Whitehall, opposite The Rising Sun public house and above a public urinal.[9]

'Scotland Yard' had become the colloquial name of the Metropolitan Police's headquarters after a station was opened there for its Central, or Whitehall (A), Division in 1829, behind the force's main office at 4 Whitehall Place. The Special Branch became a target on 30 May 1884, when one of several bombs planted that evening exploded in the public urinal below its office. Nobody was hurt, but the offices were badly damaged. After 1890, the Metropolitan Police moved into New Scotland Yard: their orange-red brick headquarters built by Norman Shaw on Victoria Embankment.[10]

The bombs at the Commons and Westminster Hall in January 1885 had a lasting impact on political reporting at Westminster. Traditionally, journalists and visitors to parliament had been able to wander into the lobby, immediately outside the Commons Chamber, and chat with or 'lobby' MPs. In 1870 access had been restricted because of overcrowding, and eventually a list was drawn up of those people allowed access; but after the bomb attack in January 1885, this lobby list was scrapped on security grounds. However, as Andrew Sparrow, the political journalist notes, press hostility to the ban forced the Speaker to re-think and a revised list was issued, granting access to a specified number of journalists. The 'lobby' system, in which a limited number of trusted journalists enjoy privileged access to politicians, had begun.[11]

The bombers were soon upstaged by a political drama. Parnell, who had emerged as the leader of the Irish MPs, skillfully played off the Conservatives and Liberals against one another. In June 1885, he had helped the Conservatives defeat Gladstone, who resigned and was replaced by Lord Salisbury at the head of a minority Conservative government. The election later that year was the first held since Gladstone had extended the rural vote in 1884, and begun building the National Liberal Club in Whitehall Place: an imposing campaign headquarters for the new era of mass politics.

Although the Liberals gained some seats in 1885, they fell short of an overall majority. Parnell was the real victor, winning 85 out of Ireland's 103 seats. Gladstone tried to wrest back the initiative when his son leaked the news that his father had converted to home rule. This ploy, known as the 'Hawarden kite' – after the name of Gladstone's Flintshire home – emboldened the Parnellites to desert Salisbury and put Gladstone back in Number 10.

However, Gladstone had failed to consult his colleagues. At the Cabinet on 26 March 1886, Joseph Chamberlain, President of the Local Government Board, announced his opposition to Gladstone's home rule initiative, gathered his papers, left the room and quit the government. In the Commons, 93 Liberals rebelled, the government was defeated and Gladstone resigned.

The split over Irish home rule re-aligned British politics. Conservatives set their face against home rule and, together with the Chamberlainite Liberal Unionists, ruled for 17 of the next 20 years. The Tories and their ex-Liberal partners championed Ulster Protestants, whose fears of majority Catholic rule fuelled talk of mobilization by the Orange Volunteers and civil war. 'Ulster will fight; Ulster will be right', declared Lord Randolph Churchill, shortly before becoming Salisbury's Chancellor and Leader of the Commons at the age of 37. However, as Robert Kee notes, while Churchill hoped that 'the Orange card' would prove the ace of trumps, he acknowledged that it might turn out to be the two.[12]

Salisbury was prepared to go to almost any lengths as prime minister to prevent his government being de-stabilized by the Irish question. Evidence unearthed by Christy Campbell, the investigative historian, for his book, *Fenian Fire*, shows that Salisbury sanctioned an intelligence operation to entrap Fenian suspects in a bogus plot to assassinate Queen Victoria as she made her way to celebrate her Golden Jubilee at Westminster Abbey on 21 June 1887. The would-be bombers were arrested and the Fenian network in Britain was destroyed.[13]

Parnell was brought down when revelations about his private life offended Victorian sensibilities. A moral backlash among Liberals after Parnell was cited in the divorce case of a colleague, Captain O'Shea, led Gladstone to say that his own leadership would be 'almost a nullity' if Parnell continued to lead the home-rulers. Faced with Gladstone's ultimatum, home-rulers gathered in Commons' Committee Room 15, overlooking the Thames, on 1 December 1890. The meeting almost became a fist-fight when Tim Healy, an anti-Parnellite, alluded to Parnell's affair with Kitty O'Shea by calling out, 'who is to be mistress of the party?' Parnell shot back by calling Healy a 'cowardly little scoundrel'. Parnell resigned, but within a year his health gave way. He died aged 45, leaving the home-rulers split by a bitter feud.[14]

'To-night the riot raged midway through the sitting', noted Henry Lucy, the parliamentary sketch-writer, on 27 July 1893. The Commons' fist-fight broke out as the Conservatives obstructed the second Home Rule Bill, introduced by Gladstone during his fourth term as prime minister. Enforcing the new-fangled closure was difficult when the obstructionists consisted of 313 MPs instead of 37. Tempers snapped when Chamberlain met a cry of 'Judas!' from T. P. O'Connor, by declaring, 'Never since the time of Herod have there been such slaves to such a dictator'. A division was called, but a fracas ensued:

> Hats were knocked off in all directions. The House filled with uproar. In the gangway a tumultuous mass of men clutched at each other's throats ... Tim Healy was seen struggling. Colonel Saunderson [leader of the Ulstermen], his coat half torn off his back, struck out right and left. The first blow fell on Mr. Crean – he dealt the Colonel a terrible blow on the face. Hissing, booing, yelling, roared though the House. A mass of fully forty members were still inextricably mingled below the gangway. One member was knocked down and dragged out of the scuffle by the heels.

The uproar lasted 20 minutes. 'All the while', observed Lucy, 'Mr Gladstone sat on the Treasury bench'.[15]

The Commons spent 82 days on the 1893 Home Rule Bill compared with 47 on the 1832 Reform Act. The Home Rule Bill eventually passed its third reading with a majority of 34, but the Lords rejected it by 419 votes to 41. Gladstone dared not risk an election and retired within six months. He had chaired 556 government meetings and kept his composure on the last such occasion, unlike his ministers, whose emotional display caused it to be known as 'the blubbering Cabinet'. The Irish question had occupied much of Gladstone's four administrations, but it remained unresolved. During the next century, it repeatedly came back to haunt Britain and Ireland, with bloody consequences.[16]

38 POMP AND CIRCUMSTANCE

'The Empire had met to celebrate in Imperial fashion the 60th year of a reign unprecedented for its length, its glory, its prosperity, and, let it be added, its goodness.' Thus *The Times*, on 23 June 1897, sustaining the warm-glow of affection and pride that accompanied the pageantry at Queen Victoria's Diamond Jubilee. In many respects little seemed to have changed since the defeat of Napoleon had confirmed Britain as the world's mightiest empire. The prime minister, the third Marquess of Salisbury, descended from Elizabeth I's chief minister, William Cecil, sat in the House of Lords. Salisbury ran foreign policy and delegated running the Treasury and managing the Commons to his nephew, Arthur Balfour, who had the use of Number 10. It almost seemed that the Reform Acts had never happened.

However, Victoria was no Gloriana. Since her beloved Albert's death in 1861, she had become almost an invisible monarch. She stopped attending the state opening of parliament, although the new Palace of Westminster had been designed by Barry and Pugin to emphasize the monarch's pre-eminence. Victoria attended again in 1866, but refused to do so in 1869 when Gladstone was prime minister. Objecting to Gladstone's talking to her as though he were addressing a public meeting, she much preferred Disraeli, who made her Empress of India in 1877. During Disraeli's second premiership, the Queen attended state openings in 1876, 1877 and 1880. She attended her last state opening in 1886. At her Golden Jubilee in 1887, there was a magnificent procession to the thanksgiving service in Westminster Abbey, where a Te Deum composed by Prince Albert was sung; but the celebrations were marred by her anxiety about the bother and expense of entertaining the crowned heads of Europe.

In contrast, Victoria's Diamond Jubilee in 1897 linked ceremonial and empire. The idea had been Joseph Chamberlain's, the assertive Colonial Secretary, whose ill-advised attempt to seize Transvaal in the Jameson Raid two years earlier had sullied the empire's reputation. However, setbacks in the empire were brushed aside in the Diamond Jubilee's imperial extravaganza. As *The Times* reported:

the Queen and Empress of a great kingdom and a huge Empire, preceded first by a procession representing the political and military strength of dominion, colonies and dependencies, and then by a military and Royal procession of unparalleled grandeur, has successfully made an unexampled progress through the greatest city of the world, between enthusiastic crowds of her subjects, and before visitors from all quarters of the earth.

Whitehall was decorated with an avenue of flagstaffs, 'profusely garlanded with wreaths and festoons', but there was a less deferential touch in Parliament Street where one congratulatory message read: '60 not out, well played!'[1]

By 1897, the heart of Westminster was eagerly embracing the stately appearance of an imperial capital and enthusiastically erasing its medieval vestiges. The mood of triumphant imperialism was epitomized in the imposing complex of government offices built during the 1860s and 1870s between Parliament Street and St James's Park. The frontage jutted onto Parliament Street, between Downing Street and Charles Street, and brought the destruction in 1873 of the northern chunk of King Street, the ancient road and royal processional route between Charing Cross and the Abbey.

Pax Britannica was celebrated unashamedly inside the new complex in the Foreign Office and the India Office; the latter department having been created after the 1857 Indian Mutiny. Their glorious interiors were restored in the 1980s. Originally, the Foreign Office occupied the north-west block, overlooking St James's Park and the end of Downing Street near the park. The splendour of its tiled floors and walls, and ceilings stencilled in red, blue and gold, is complemented by the grandeur of the high ceilings, in the style of an Italian palazzo: the Foreign Secretary's first-floor office in the corner tower is 21 feet high. The magnificent marble Grand Staircase makes an awesome impression. The stairs begin as a broad flight that climbs to a landing, where the stairs divide into two flights rising to the floor above. On the upper floor, columns and galleries line three sides of the stair well, with round-arched windows on the fourth side: high above, the ceiling rises to a dome, in which painted figures symbolise the 20 countries that were then represented at the Court of St James's.

The Foreign Office's showpiece is a glorious three-room suite, comprising a Cabinet room (never used as such), conference room and smaller dining room. The magnificent Cabinet room measures 72 feet by 38 feet, and is 40 feet in height and vaulted, with a painted zodiac. The room has windows on both sides: to the east, looking onto the main quadrangle; to the west, an inner courtyard. It later became known as the Locarno Room, after the ill-fated treaty signed there in 1925 that guaranteed the Franco-German border.

The India Office occupied the south-west block, overlooking St James's Park and Charles Street. Along one of its corridors statues of eight muses embody the virtues that policy-makers supposedly follow in their work: Prudence, Justice,

Honour, Wisdom, Charity, Faith, Courage and Truth. The inner courtyard, known since 1902 as the Durbar Courtyard, is the building's jewel in the crown. The courtyard has a patterned marble floor, arcaded walls and polished granite columns. The first floor offices include the Council Chamber, with a towering chimneypiece of 1729 from East India House. Its central relief shows Britannia receiving riches from the Indies, Asia and Africa.[2]

Pax Britannica became Whitehall's leitmotif. The area took on the guise of an imperial and martial capital as imposing state offices were commissioned and built: the architectural and bureaucratic equivalents of the navy's great battle-ships. A major extension to the Admiralty was built along the north side of Horse Guards Parade between 1888 and 1905. This stone and red brick building, with its distinctive green copper roofs, is now known as the Old Admiralty Building. On the opposite side of Whitehall, between Horse Guards Avenue and Whitehall Place, the formidable, stone-clad War Office (now known as the Old War Office) replaced Carrington House. Earlier, the site had housed the kitchens of Whitehall Palace, the offices of the Jewel House and the king's herb house. The War Office's circular turrets and stone domes echo Sir Christopher Wren's 1698 designs for a new Whitehall Palace that was never built.[3]

Departments dealing with matters in Britain assumed the same imperial grandeur. By 1900, the construction of another massive complex, between the Foreign Office and Parliament Square, had swept away the last remnants of ancient King Street. The first phase of the monstrous-sounding 'GOGGS' (Government Offices, Great George Street) was finished in 1908. Two years later, the second phase devoured the eighteenth-century houses on the north side of Great George Street, together with the last of the old alleys, courts and lanes between Parliament Street and St James's Park.[4]

When completed in 1917, 'GOGGS' covered five acres. It is four-storeys high, with an extra attic story in the centre, and faced with Portland stone. Above Great George Street, its end towers rise to turrets, and it is linked to the Foreign Office by a triple-arched bridge across King Charles Street. At its heart, the large, circular court was inspired by Inigo Jones's designs almost 300 years earlier for Whitehall Palace. 'GOGGS' remains an all-devouring monster, as it houses HM Revenue & Customs, and HM Treasury.[5]

The construction of the imposing Admiralty Arch at the junction of the Mall and Trafalgar Square was part of a plan to turn the Mall into a royal, processional route, as a national monument to Victoria. The Arch combined grandiose design and functionality. Its wings and three-storey top-block provided offices for naval back-room staff, and living quarters for the First Lord and First Sea Lord; its three huge arches were furnished with huge wrought-iron and bronze gates, ready just in time for George V's coronation in June 1911.[6]

Westminster became the Empire's ceremonial stage. The same confidence and pride that inspired its architecture and pageantry was evoked by Sir Edward

Elgar in his first four *Pomp and Circumstance* marches, composed between 1901 and 1907. Elgar was a regular visitor to the Westminster home of his friend and patron, Frank Schuster, at 22 Old Queen Street, where dinner parties were held to celebrate the composer's London premieres. From the rear of Old Queen Street, Elgar and his friends enjoyed a fine view across Birdcage Walk to St James's Park and the park-side edifices of imperial Westminster. A century later, Number 22 became home to *The Spectator* magazine.[7]

After Edward VII's accession in 1901, Elgar was invited to compose a Coronation Ode. The king's coronation in August 1902 set the precedent for all four twentieth century coronations to be great musical celebrations, organized by the Abbey's Master of Music assisted by the Master of the King's, or Queen's, Musick. Elgar took a melody from his *Pomp and Circumstance* March No. 1 for the finale of his Ode, to which words were added by A. C. Benson. *Land of Hope and Glory*, albeit with re-written, more imperialistic, words, almost became a second national anthem. Edward VII's coronation inspired Sir Hubert Parry's setting of *I was glad*, a stirring orchestral and choral piece which was played at the wedding of Prince William and the Duchess of Cambridge at Westminster Abbey in April 2011.[8]

Westminster's imperial facades provided an impressive backdrop for Edward VII's revival of the processional state opening of parliament. However, behind the ceremonial pomp, the political circumstance was fragile. Balfour succeeded Salisbury as prime minister in July 1902, but the following year Joseph Chamberlain resigned from a Cabinet for the second time. His campaign for tariff reform (protectionism) divided the Conservatives as deeply as his opposition to Irish home rule had split the Liberals. In December 1905, Henry Campbell-Bannerman, a shrewd, 69-year-old lowland Scot, entered 10 Downing Street: a 'rotten old barrack of a house', as he ungratefully called it. The following month, he led the Liberals to their greatest election victory.[9]

The mainstay of Liberal support, Britain's non-conformists, also made their architectural impact on Westminster. A million Methodists stumped up a guinea each in order to fund their impressive, multi-purpose meeting place opposite the Abbey's west front. The Methodist Central Hall was built on the corner of Tothill Street and Storey's Gate, between 1907 and 1912. It occupies the site of the old Royal Aquarium and the Imperial Theatre; the latter having been owned briefly by Lillie Langtry, one of Edward VII's old flames. As the architectural historians, Bradley and Pevsner note, Central Hall's large, almost square, stone-clad, exterior might have come straight from imperial Vienna; yet its early use of reinforced concrete created a vast meeting hall and large domed roof, without any supporting columns.

The Central Hall obliterated one of Westminster's poorest slums: Lewisham Street, off Storey's Gate. The extent of poverty shocked many Edwardians. Politics was radicalized by the impact of Charles Booth's survey between 1889 and 1903, showing that 30 per cent of Londoners lived in poverty; and also by the poor condition of many volunteers for the Boer War. Gladstone had died in 1898, the year before the war in South Africa began, and was accorded the extraordinary honour for a politician of lying in state in Westminster Hall. After a state funeral at the Abbey his remains were buried there, in like manner to Pitt and Palmerston. But he had realized, after industrial unrest and rioting during the economic slump of the 1880s, that 'retrenchment' was no longer sufficient.[10]

The Liberals remained committed to free trade and temperance, but a younger generation emphasized social reform. The new chancellor in 1905, Herbert Henry Asquith, a brilliant 53-year-old lawyer from a northern, non-conformist background, was the lynch-pin of the new Liberal Government. 'Often called "the last of the Romans"', as Margaret Stansgate, the wife of Liberal MP, William Wedgwood Benn, recalled, 'Asquith had a remarkable gift of speech. Ciceronian periods rolled out of his mouth without any apparent effort. Working with great dispatch he never appeared to be under any strain'.[11]

Asquith had become Home Secretary before he was 40, but when the Liberals lost office he lacked sufficient private funds and had to spend much of his time earning good money at the bar. He combined high living with a rare ability to dominate the Commons, where he was nicknamed 'the sledge-hammer'. When the ailing Campbell-Bannerman resigned as prime minister in April 1908, Asquith was summoned to Biarritz, where Edward VII was holidaying, and kissed hands as prime minister. On his return, Asquith was greeted by cheering crowds at Charing Cross station. He and his wife, Margot, were showered with flowers as they were driven away.[12]

Asquith had married Margot Tennant, the extravagant and snobbish daughter of a wealthy Liberal baronet, after the death of his first wife, Helen. Margot was astonished that Number 10 was so little known: when she failed to give a taxi driver directions, she was taken to Down Street, Piccadilly. 'Liver-coloured and squalid', was her description of Number 10: its outside 'gives little idea to the man in the street of what it is really like'. She blamed its odd lay-out for restricting her party-giving: 'owing to the impossibility of circulation I could only entertain my Liberal friends at dinner or at garden parties'.[13]

Invitations to the Asquiths' dinner parties were highly prized, but the prime minister's fondness for drink caused consternation among colleagues. 'On Thursday night the PM was vy bad: & I squirmed with embarrassment', Winston Churchill, the Home Secretary, wrote to his wife in April 1911, after Asquith appeared on the front-bench drunk: 'He could hardly speak: & many people noticed his condition'. Churchill noted that Asquith entrusted him with every-thing after dinner: 'only the persistent freemasonry of the House of Commons prevents a scandal'. On another occasion, Wedgwood Benn met Asquith 'in a very unsteady state', walking through the Members' Lobby, and asked if he could take him to his room. 'I wish you would', Asquith replied. If Asquith had been drinking, people would sing, with slurred accents, a song from *The Bing Boys*, a popular musical: 'another little drink, another little drink, another little drink wouldn't do us any harm'.[14]

Social reform and votes for women were two of Asquith's greatest challenges during his peacetime years in Number 10, but his approach to them could scarcely have been more different. He had promised social reform as Chancellor and, in his final budget, delivered a month after becoming prime minister, he proposed introducing a state pension, funded from national taxation. His radical plan set him on a collision course with the Lords, where the great majority of peers were Conservatives and had the same power as MPs to make or, more importantly, break new laws. However, Asquith's appointment of David Lloyd George, a radical 45-year-old lawyer of humble Welsh roots, as his chancellor, was a clear declaration of intent on social reform.

Asquith's radicalism on the budget contrasted with his conservatism on votes for women. He did not believe most women were pressing for the vote. He seemed to think that, like the Edwardian ladies he mixed with, their interest in politics went little further than watching the Commons through the grille of the ladies' gallery, enjoying tea on parliament's riverside terrace and gossiping at dinner parties. He enjoyed relaxing with the young women friends of his sons and daughters from his first marriage, and became infatuated with several: 'his harem', as Margot disparagingly called them. He had a reputation as a 'groper', but when one young lady complained to her mother, she was told that it was an honour to be molested by the prime minister. Asquith was in his early 60s when he became infatuated with Venetia Stanley, who was in her mid-twenties. They were probably never lovers, but for three years he sent her playful and indiscreet letters, some written while chairing the Cabinet. Their relationship ended in 1915 when she decided to marry Edwin Montagu, a young Cabinet minister.[15]

Asquith's prejudice against votes for women was reinforced by his political calculation that extending the existing property qualifications for voting to women would mainly enfranchise better-off women, benefiting the Conservatives but harming the Liberals. However, the obduracy of Asquith and many of his fellow politicians encouraged greater militancy among women campaigners; and The Women's Social and Political Union (WSPU) was founded by Emmeline Pankhurst and her daughter, Christabel. In 1906 another daughter, Sylvia Pankhurst, set up the London headquarters.

'The suffragettes took the police by surprise' at the state opening of parliament in October 1906, 'and but for the rush of Members from the inner lobby to the outer [Central Lobby] they would have stormed the Members' Lobby and swarmed in on the floor of the House'. The following February, 58 arrests were made when suffragettes from the WSPU's 'women's parliament' at nearby Caxton Hall tried to lobby MPs. In 1908, suffragettes unfurled a banner in the ladies' gallery inside the Commons' Chamber, demanding the right to vote for women. Two protestors chained themselves to one of the grilles, crying, 'We have listened behind this insulting grille too long!' The eviction of suffragettes from the Houses of Parliament while trying to deliver a petition led them to smash windows in Whitehall and Parliament Street. The grilles were later removed and can now be seen in the windows of Central Lobby.[16]

Asquith and his family also became targets in 1908. After policemen sexually abused suffragettes during a demonstration in Parliament Square, Mary Leigh and Edith New took a cab to Downing Street and hurled two stones through the windows of Number 10. Some suffragettes regarded Margot Asquith as a traitor and sent threatening letters. Her nerves never recovered after she woke one night to the sound of breaking glass as suffragettes threw stones at the windows below the room where her young son, Anthony, slept. 'I nearly vomited with terror that he should wake and scream'.[17]

St Stephen's Hall still bears the mark left by a suffragette protest. On 27 April 1909, four women waiting in St Stephen's Hall, supposedly to meet MPs, 'suddenly left their seats and by means of thick steel chains concealed under their long cloaks attached themselves to statues. At the same time cries of "Votes for women," "We will have the vote, and nothing you can do will stop us," rang through the hall'. Their chains were soon cut by 'powerful shears' and the suffragettes arrested. The two spikes broken off one of the spurs of the statue of Viscount Falkland, to which Margery Humes had chained herself, have never been replaced. On the hundredth anniversary, four climate-change protestors glued themselves around the same statue, 'in a suffragette-inspired protest against the Government's plan for new coal-fired power stations'.[18]

Two days after Margery Humes and her colleagues made their protest, Lloyd George delivered the most famous budget of the twentieth century. Asquith could not have chosen a more passionate warrior against the peers who opposed his plans. Lloyd George's reputation as a great radical was forged by his 'war budget' – a war on 'poverty and squalidness'. Others called it 'the people's budget'. 'I am one of the children of the people, I was brought up amongst them and I know their trials and their trouble', Lloyd George told listeners to a gramophone recording played round the country in a precursor of party political broadcasts. 'I therefore determined in framing the budget', he explained, 'to add nothing to the anxieties of their lot but to do something towards lightening loads they already bear with such patience and fortitude'.[19]

Lloyd George needed extra taxation in order to pay for new Dreadnought battleships and the new state pension, but by proposing to tax land he threw down the gauntlet to the Lords. When it became clear that the peers would oppose his budget, Lloyd George stirred up public resentment against them by brilliantly dismissing the Lords as 'five hundred men chosen at random from amongst the unemployed', on the principle of 'the first of the litter'.[20]

While MPs and peers were locked in an increasingly bitter battle over Lloyd George's budget, the police heard of a plot to shoot Asquith. A suffragette march on parliament in June 1909 had ended in more than 120 arrests and broken windows in Parliament Street and Whitehall. The following month, the Pankhursts' WSPU began a 15-weeks' picket of the carriage entrance to the Commons. In those days, protesters could get close to ministers as they arrived and left. During the picket, two suffragettes were seen practising at a shooting range and the police were sent a letter containing a threat to shoot Asquith. Officials suspected that 'there is something nearly amounting to a conspiracy to murder'; but were concerned about the risk of publicizing their fears. The likely press coverage 'would probably act in the minds of these half insane women, and might suggest effectively the commission of the very act which we wish to prevent'. Officials were also worried that removing the pickets would be seen as violent and unjust, and would make them 'more ready to commit such a crime'. The police took no action, and there was no attempt to shoot Asquith.[21]

After the Lords finally rejected Lloyd George's budget, Asquith turned to the people. The election in January 1910 kept the Liberals in power. Although they won only two more seats than the Conservatives, they could rely on the support of 40 Labour MPs and 82 Irish Nationalists. The Lords conceded defeat over Lloyd George's taxes, but there was deadlock over Asquith's Parliament Bill curbing their power to veto government bills.

After Edward VII's death in May, Asquith sought agreement with the Conservatives on constitutional reform, but their talks failed. Lloyd George floated the idea of a coalition of Liberals and Conservatives, with social reform, or 'national efficiency', and defence as priorities, but it was vetoed. However, the chancellor never abandoned his belief in the benefits of a coalition with a strong leader.

In November 1910, the impasse on Lords' reform prompted Asquith to call a second election. His decision caused the loss of a 'conciliation bill', designed to give women the vote on the same property-owning terms as men. The bill had received all-party support, but the Cabinet was split and the prime minister was stalling. A protest by 300 women in Parliament Square on the day of Asquith's announcement was dealt with violently by the police. More than 100 protestors were arrested and three women later died.[22]

Four days after the riot, Asquith promised to extend the franchise, but was vague about the women's vote, saying only that the bill could be amended. The next morning, Emmeline Pankhurst led 200 suffragettes in 'The Battle of Downing Street'. The window of Asquith's car was smashed and Augustine Birrell, the chief secretary for Ireland, was badly injured in the knee. Churchill arrived to see a suffragette leaning against a wall. She was a friend of his wife's family, but he told a policeman: 'Drive that woman away'.[23]

The December 1910 election produced little change. A few months later, a suffragette devised an ingenious protest that is now honoured at Westminster. On the night of the ten-yearly national census in April 1911, Emily Wilding Davison hid in the Houses of Parliament in order to give it as her place of residence. Her plan was to spend census night in the Chapel of St Mary Undercroft beneath St Stephen's Hall, but she had to hide in a tiny broom cupboard, known as Guy Fawkes' cupboard, when an MP showed two visitors round the chapel. However, before she could return to the crypt, the doors were locked and she had to stay in the cupboard, where she was discovered by a cleaner the next morning. She was taken to Cannon Row Police Station, but was soon released.[24]

The 1911 census return for the Palace of Westminster records Davison (misspelled as Davidson) with the address: 'Found hiding in the Crypt of Westminster Hall, Westminster'. Her protest is commemorated by a plaque inside the cupboard, placed there by Tony Benn, as 'a modest reminder of a great woman with a great cause who never lived to see it prosper but played a significant part in making it possible'. Davison was killed when she tried to bring down the king's horse during the 1913 Epsom Derby. The prospect of female suffrage seemed as distant as ever; and Asquith was privately relieved early in 1913 when the Speaker, James Lowther, vetoed the government's ploy of allowing an amendment on votes for women to be added to its new reform bill. There was no early end in sight to the cycle of violent protests, arrests and forced-feeding.[25]

Lords' reform remained Asquith's priority. Before the December 1910 election, he reached a secret agreement with a reluctant George V that the king would, if necessary, use his prerogative power, as had Anne in 1712 and William IV in 1832, to create the necessary 200 Liberal peers. The final showdown came in the boiling hot summer of 1911, after a Cabinet minute to the king on the creation of peers leaked to the Opposition. The Commons was in uproar on 24 July as Tories shouted down the prime minister. 'In sustained fury', reported *The Times*, 'the scene exceeded the historic disturbance in Committee when the Home Rule Bill was under discussion in 1893'. Although there was no fighting in the Commons in July 1911, Henry Lucy recalled that he had witnessed 'many scenes' over a period of 45 years, 'but never anything comparable with that of yesterday afternoon'. This was 'the first time that I have ever known this or any other Speaker exercise his rights under the Standing Orders, and adjourn the House of his own motion, as a disorderly Assembly'.[26]

The Lords finally succumbed on 10 August. The Parliament Act of 1911 established the supremacy of the elected Commons over the unelected Lords. Peers lost the power to delay a money bill and could only delay other bills for two years. In a further blow against privilege, Lloyd George introduced an annual payment of £400 for MPs (equivalent to about £37,000 today). Birth and class were no longer barriers to becoming an MP.

Only a matter of days after the Lords' surrender, a thinly attended Commons passed, with little debate, another law that was to have a huge impact. The Official

Secrets Bill was rushed through during a war scare caused by German gunboat diplomacy. It was presented as a safeguard against the Kaiser's spies, but its 'catch-all' section 2 forbade a civil servant from disclosing anything about his or her work without explicit authority. As a result, a climate of undue secrecy pervaded Westminster for most of the twentieth century. It never seemed to occur to Asquith, as he gushed to his beloved Venetia about Cabinet meetings and military plans, that he might be flouting his own stringent secrecy regime.[27]

Asquith's final peace-time years as prime minister were anything but peaceful. The bitter clash over home rule between Irish Nationalists and Conservatives threatened civil war. In the Commons, an enraged Tory hurled a bound copy of the standing orders at Winston Churchill, the Home Secretary, and cut open his forehead. A national coal strike, in an age when industry and people's well-being depended almost entirely on coal, put Asquith under immense stress before it was settled. According to Austen Chamberlain, watching from the opposition front-bench, Asquith spoke in the Commons 'under great emotion, his voice breaking and tears in his eyes if not actually running down his cheeks'.[28]

The Strange Death of Liberal England, Thomas Dangerfield's classic study, identified four radical groups who challenged Asquith's reforming government between 1910 and 1914: on the left, the Labour movement and suffragettes; on the right, die-hard Lords and Tories. Only Asquith's battle with the Lords brought him victory. The other conflicts were straining almost to breaking point the disparate coalition of Whigs, Gladstonian Liberals, Radicals, Lib-Lab trade unionists and ex-Conservative free-traders who all clung to the Liberal Party banner. However, these domestic conflicts were about to be submerged in a much greater and bloodier struggle.

39 WAR AND PEACE

'The lamps are going out all over Europe. We shall not see them lit again in our lifetime'. These prophetic words were uttered by Sir Edward Grey, Britain's Foreign Secretary, in his magnificent room overlooking St James's Park and Horse Guards Parade on Monday, 3 August 1914. Germany had declared war against Russia on Saturday 1st and against France earlier that day. During tense Cabinet meetings at Number 10 throughout that early August Bank Holiday weekend, 'hawks' and 'doves' had clashed over Britain's response, but as events unfolded the mood shifted against Lloyd George and his fellow 'doves'.

Outside, crowds gathered in Whitehall. Many of the men wore boaters and the women summer frocks as they joined in singing 'God Save the King' and the 'Marseillaise'. 'We could hear the hum of the surging mass from the Cabinet chamber', Lloyd George, the Chancellor, noted. As people crammed into Downing Street, ministers had to be helped through the dense crowd to the door of Number 10. In Parliament Square, too, the police had to hold back the crowds to enable MPs to reach Parliament. In the Commons, Lloyd George was so sickened by the jubilation as war loomed that he slumped, white-faced, on the government front-bench.[1]

Germany's invasion of Belgium on Tuesday 4th prompted Britain to issue its ultimatum, demanding a response from Berlin by 11 p.m., British time. After 9 p.m., Asquith sent for Lloyd George to join him, Grey and Haldane, the Lord Chancellor, in the Cabinet Room. McKenna, the Home Secretary, and later, Margot Asquith, also arrived. As the minutes ticked by, their silent vigil was broken by the cheering crowds outside. Finally, Big Ben struck eleven. 'We felt it was the strike of doom', Lloyd George later remarked.[2]

War with Germany was the most momentous decision taken by any British prime minister and his cabinet during the nineteenth and twentieth centuries. Had Asquith sent a clearer message to Germany sooner, the catastrophe might have been averted. As it was, the First World War brought mass carnage and shattered European liberalism, the very ideals that Asquith and his colleagues espoused. Britain and its empire lost more than a million people, many the finest of their generation.

The demise of Liberal England was hastened by the personality clash between Asquith and Lloyd George. As the military stalemate in Europe persisted and the death toll soared, Asquith formed a coalition with the Conservatives. However, when he finally agreed to conscription, many Liberals were furious, while Tories regarded his delay as proof that 'Squiffy', as they called him, was ineffectual. Asquith's peacetime attributes – apparent effortlessness, patient chairmanship and disdain for showmanship – were seen as weaknesses when the country needed to be mobilized. By contrast, Lloyd George demonstrated as Munitions Minister that he possessed the dynamic qualities needed in a total war: defiance, energy, inspiration and showmanship.

Asquith was deeply affected by the death of his eldest son, Raymond, on the Somme in September 1916. Raymond was one of 415,000 British casualties in an offensive that advanced only eight miles during five months. By late November, Lloyd George was convinced that only radical change could save Britain. He had always wooed the press, and with the involvement of Max Aitken, later Lord Beaverbrook, he proposed that the war should be run by a small council that excluded the prime minister.

Having won support from Bonar Law, the Tory leader, and Sir Edward Carson, the Irish Unionist, Lloyd George agreed a compromise plan in which Asquith would remain prime minister. However, *The Times* leaked the plan and strongly criticized Asquith, who then tried to re-assert his authority. At this, Lloyd George and Bonar Law resigned. With the coalition dead and the Liberals split, Asquith resigned. His premiership had lasted more than eight and a half years, the longest continuous premiership in the twentieth century until Margaret Thatcher's. George V turned first to Bonar Law, but he declined. On 7 December 1916 Lloyd George kissed hands as prime minister.[3]

Lloyd George was a rank outsider. He had left his village school aged 15, and became Britain's first and, to date, only Welsh prime minister. When he and his family moved into Number 10, their cook and maids were Welsh, and Welsh was always spoken below stairs and often above. Lloyd George rose early and gave breakfast to ministers and other advisers in Soane's small dining room, where top secret matters were freely discussed in his family's presence.[4]

Although Lloyd George and his wife, Margaret, shared a first floor bedroom, she spent much of her time at their home in Wales. Down a flight of stairs from their room, and next to the Cabinet room, was the office of Lloyd George's personal secretary, Frances Stevenson, who had been his mistress since 1913 and later became his second wife. 'With an attractive woman he was as much to be trusted as a Bengali tiger with a gazelle', his eldest son, Richard, remarked.[5]

Frances had been a school-friend of Mair, Lloyd George's eldest daughter, who had died aged only 17. When Frances first met Lloyd George in 1911 after becoming governess to his youngest daughter, Megan, she said she felt 'a magnetism which made my heart leap and swept aside my judgment, producing an excitement which seemed to permeate my entire being'. She was struck by his 'sensitive face, with deep furrows between the eyes – the broad brow, the beautiful profile – straight nose, neat insolent chin', with a complexion 'as young and fresh as a child's'.[6]

However, Lloyd George was as ruthless in personal life as in politics. His affair with Frances was arranged 'on his own terms', like a 'business deal', according to the author, Ffion Hague. 'It was very carefully spelled out to Frances that Lloyd George would not leave his wife, there would be no divorce, no scandal, his career came first'. It seems remarkable that political journalists who knew of Lloyd George's affair never spilled the beans; but the Westminster village remained a male club.[7]

Lloyd George's premiership was a presidency in all but name. He revolutionized the office of prime minister and the Cabinet. 'I had for some time come to the conclusion', he told BBC listeners in 1939, when Britain again faced war, 'that to entrust the direction of the war to a Sanhedrin of some 20 ministers, chosen largely for party reasons, and all engaged in the administration of departments which demanded their whole attention, was worse than worthless'. A five-man war Cabinet was set up and included the Conservative and Labour Party leaders, Bonar Law and Arthur Henderson. New departments were created to tackle the problems of war – Air, Food, Labour, National Service, Shipping – and businessmen such as Sir Eric Geddes took charge.

A Cabinet secretariat was created under Sir Maurice Hankey, who began taking the first ever formal note of a Cabinet meeting at 11:30 a.m. on Saturday 9 September 1916: the moment at which 'modern, bureaucratized Cabinet Government' began, according to the historian, Peter Hennessy. The presidential tendency of modern prime ministers to stuff Number 10 full of personal, or 'special', advisers began with Lloyd George, who created his own secretariat, separate from the Cabinet and civil service. It had to be housed in temporary huts in Number 10's garden and became known as 'the garden suburb'.[8]

Yet Winston Churchill, a colleague of Lloyd George's, remained in denial about the presidential nature of a war-time government in which maps were laid out on the Cabinet table while the prime minister and military chiefs thrashed out strategy. In March 1917, at the end of a day's sitting in the Commons, Churchill called a fellow Liberal MP, McCallum Scott, into the dimly-lit, empty chamber. 'Look at it', he said. 'This little place is what makes the difference between us and Germany. It is in virtue of this that we shall muddle through to success and for lack of this Germany's brilliant efficiency leads her to final destruction. This little room is the shrine of the world's liberties'.[9]

Within weeks of Churchill's romantic eulogy, Russia's abandonment of the war after its revolution was more than compensated by America's decision to fight Germany. In July 1917, the inclusion of the South African General, Jan Smuts, in the War Cabinet emphasized the huge contribution and great sacrifices made by the Commonwealth and Empire. At Number 10, Lloyd George struggled to convince the Admiralty that the convoy system should be adopted as a counter to the growing threat from German U-boats. Army resistance to his call for a unified Allied command was an even tougher nut to crack. General Haig, the Commander-in-Chief, was allowed another attempt to defeat the Germans by sheer force of numbers at Passchendaele, but the British suffered 260,000 casualties without success. In April 1918, Lloyd George finally achieved unity of Allied command under the French General Foch. Today, an equestrian statue of Haig, who earned the distrust of Britain's Welsh prime minister, stands opposite Gwydyr House, the Welsh Office's Whitehall base.[10]

The war made little lasting impact on the fabric of Westminster, although Number 41 Whitehall was damaged. Searchlights were set up on Admiralty Arch; gun batteries positioned in open spaces. At Westminster School, warning of Zeppelin raids was given by the Head Master's bell, at which masters and boys sprinted across Little Dean's Yard to shelter in the Abbey's Norman Undercroft. At the top of Whitehall, Charles I's equestrian statue was protected from bombs by sand-bags, wood and corrugated iron. The War Office was extended and temporary huts erected on its roof – nicknamed 'Zeppelin Terrace'. Temporary huts were also set up on Horse Guards Parade for extra staff at the Paymaster General's Office dealing with new recruits, and the National Liberal Club was requisitioned.[11]

By November 1918, less than two years after entering Number 10, Lloyd George was no longer simply 'The Welsh Wizard', or 'The Goat', but 'The Man Who Won the War'. News of the Armistice was rushed to Number 10 early on the morning of the 11th. The messenger hurried up the stairs to the first-floor corner bedroom, overlooking St James's Park, and the prime minister was woken. As word quickly spread, crowds began to gather outside. Downing Street was soon crammed solid, and many spilled into the Foreign Office's quadrangle. The crowd's calls for 'L. G.' were met when the prime minister appeared at a window. His face flushed with emotion, he was for once barely able to speak as he announced the Armistice.[12]

The Armistice came into effect at the eleventh hour of the eleventh day of the eleventh month. 'Thus at eleven o'clock this morning', Lloyd George told MPs, 'came to an end the cruellest and most terrible war that has ever scourged mankind. I hope we may say that thus, this fateful morning, came to an end all wars'. The peace negotiations lay ahead, but before they began Lloyd George confirmed his leadership by calling a snap 'coupon' election: so called because of the written endorsement issued to *bona fide* coalition candidates.[13]

Yet the election presented a paradox. It was a tribute to Lloyd George's radicalism, in that he almost trebled the size of the electorate to 21 million in a dramatic double first: universal male suffrage and the enfranchisement of women aged 30 and over (depending on their, or their husband's, qualification as local council electors). The coalition won a landslide victory. Lloyd George became the most powerful prime minister since Pitt the Younger, ruling as a *de facto* President. However, the result was ultimately to make him a prisoner of the Conservatives, who had 335 seats compared with 133 Liberals who backed him.[14]

The war made its greatest physical impact on Westminster after it ended. In the spring of 1919, the Government decided to mark the forthcoming signing of the peace treaty with national celebrations, including a victory parade through London. The gesture had a political motive, as the historian, Eric Homberger, has suggested: a Peace Day with religious services, pageants and other celebrations offered a calming influence when union militancy and strikes were sweeping post-war Britain and ministers were talking of Bolshevik subversion.[15]

After the signing of the Treaty of Versailles in June, Clemenceau, the French prime minister, told Lloyd George that allied troops would honour the dead as they marched through Paris on Bastille Day by saluting a great catafalque. Lloyd George wanted a similar focus in Britain. He invited Sir Edwin Landseer Lutyens, the architect of British war memorials, to Number 10 and asked him to design a catafalque, of non-denominational character. However, Lutyens suggested instead building a cenotaph, a monument traditionally dedicated to the honour of a person whose body is buried elsewhere; 'cenotaph' meaning 'empty tomb' in classical Greek. The prime minister agreed. 'With other things on their mind', as Homberger noted, 'Lloyd George and his ministers created the most potent symbol of the inter-war years – almost by accident'.[16]

The first Cenotaph was built of timber and plaster. Within an hour of being unveiled in the middle of Whitehall on the morning of the Peace Day parade, 19 July 1919, wreaths were piled high around its base. Nearly 15,000 Allied troops marched past in silence and saluted the memorial to the dead. For several days, long lines of people waited patiently to pay their respects. Merchant sailors carried their trade union banners among the flags and regimental colours. Photographs of the Allied commanders – Pershing, Foch, Haig and Beatty – saluting to dead comrades appeared in newspapers throughout the country. For weeks afterwards, there were queues of people waiting to place wreaths at the Cenotaph.[17]

'The Cenotaph', declared *The Times*, 'is only a temporary structure made to look like stone; but Sir Edwin Landseer Lutyens's design is so grave, severe and beautiful that one might well wish it were indeed of stone and permanent'. This sentiment captured the public mood. The Cabinet agreed that the Cenotaph should be rebuilt permanently and designated it Britain's official war memorial. *The Times* wanted it moved elsewhere because it might slow the traffic and cause accidents in Whitehall, but Lutyens lobbied against any move and ministers decided that 'the Cenotaph in its present position had memories which could not be uprooted'. The temporary Cenotaph still stood on Armistice Day in 1919, when thousands walked past and added floral tributes to the wreath from the king and queen. For the first time, a two-minute silence falling at the striking of 11:00 a.m. by Big Ben was observed.[18]

Yet stately ceremonial could not entirely erase raw politics, as the economy slumped and unemployment soared. Only a fortnight before the unveiling of Lutyens's permanent Cenotaph in November 1920, the headlines read, 'RIOTING AT DOWNING-ST: DISORDERLY MOB OF UNEMPLOYED: POLICE OBLIGED TO CHARGE'. The trouble began when marchers tried to demonstrate outside Number 10, where a group of London mayors, including George Lansbury, Poplar's Labour Mayor, were lobbying Lloyd George. The police, some mounted, used their batons to break up the crowd. Between 30 and 40 people were injured and ten policemen hurt. The marchers had been joined by 'many hundreds of irresponsible young hooligans, who took a leading part in the afternoon's disorders'. Afterwards, 'a great mob remained massed in Whitehall' periodically trying to break the police cordon by sheer weight and throwing stones, brickbats and bottles. Newsreel shows a man mounted on the bare back of a white horse attempting to ride up Downing Street; but he was seized by the police and led away. During a police charge to clear the crowd, the stone balustrade outside the Privy Council Office collapsed. All ground floor windows at the War Office and some at the Treasury were smashed. On Armistice Day, two weeks later, the Government took no chances. Downing Street and King Charles Street were protected by 'substantial wooden barricades'. [19]

Large crowds were expected at Westminster for the unveiling of the Cenotaph and the funeral of the Unknown Warrior in Westminster Abbey. The idea of bringing back the body of an unknown soldier from the battlefield for burial, as a symbol of all those who died, seems to have been first made in 1916 by the Reverend David Railton, an army padre on the western front. Nothing was done, but in August 1920 he put the idea to the Dean of Westminster, Dr Herbert Ryle, suggesting that only the Abbey would be suitable for the burial as it was the 'Parish Church of the Empire'. [20]

The lead was again given by the French, as their plan to bury a dead soldier in the Pantheon rather shamed the British Government into action. The Dean of Westminster won Lloyd George's support and, only a month before Armistice Day, the Cabinet backed the idea. Every precaution was taken to ensure that the identity of the 'unknown warrior' could never be known. The train bearing his coffin arrived at Victoria Station on 10 November 1920 and remained there overnight. The next morning a Union Jack was draped over the coffin and a steel helmet and side arms put on top. The coffin was placed on a gun carriage and drawn by six black horses along the Mall, through Admiralty Arch and along Whitehall, accompanied by Britain's highest ranking officers and followed by ex-servicemen. Thousands of silent mourners lined the route. [21]

The procession paused at the Cenotaph, where George V, wearing a Field Marshal's uniform, placed a wreath of red roses and bay leaves on the coffin. When Big Ben chimed the last note of eleven o'clock, the king pressed a button to release the flags and unveil the Cenotaph. Two minutes' silence were observed, the start and finish marked by artillery fire from Hyde Park a mile or two away. The Cenotaph was visited by 400,000 people in three days, and during the 1920s and 1930s men would doff their hats when passing.[22]

After the Cenotaph's unveiling, the king and other dignitaries joined the Unknown Warrior's funeral procession. At the Abbey, the coffin was carried from the north door through the quire and up the length of the nave. As the Choir sang the hymn, 'Lead Kindly Light', the coffin was lowered into the grave. The king sprinkled earth from the Flanders battlefield on the coffin as the Dean said 'Earth to earth, ashes to ashes'. After the service, the public filed past the grave, the queue stretching as far back as the Cenotaph. Thousands of people paid their respects over the coming days, casting their poppies onto it until it became a mass of red poppies. A week after the burial, the grave was filled with earth from France and covered with a slab of Tournai marble.[23]

The present gravestone of black Belgium marble was installed in 1921 and bears these words:

BENEATH THIS STONE RESTS THE BODY OF A BRITISH WARRIOR UNKNOWN BY NAME OR RANK BROUGHT FROM FRANCE TO LIE AMONG THE MOST ILLUSTRIOUS OF THE LAND ... THEY BURIED HIM AMONG THE KINGS BECAUSE HE HAD DONE GOOD TOWARD GOD AND TOWARD HIS HOUSE ...

The Tomb of the Unknown Warrior receives unique respect. Even coronation processions avoid walking on it. Every autumn since 1928, the grass lawns along the northern side of the Abbey have become a place of pilgrimage, where people can plant a small cross and poppy in the Field of Poppies, or Field of Remembrance.

In 1945, Armistice Day fell on a Sunday and became officially known as Remembrance Day, when the dead of both world wars were honoured: since 1946, Remembrance Day has been held on a Sunday near 11 November. The Cenotaph's accessibility in the middle of the street and its elegant simplicity enable people to express their sense of loss and respect for the fallen. Lutyens's use of proportion and slightly convex horizontal and vertical lines are touches of genius, drawing the viewer's eye upwards to the stone coffin resting on top. The contrast between the Cenotaph's modest scale and Whitehall's stately edifices creates an evocative memorial to every individual who gave his or her life.[24]

Little more than two weeks after the Cenotaph's unveiling in November 1920, the barricades went up again in Whitehall. 'Much comment was aroused during the weekend', reported *The Times*, 'by the erection of substantial wooden barricades at both ends of King Charles-street and at the Whitehall entrance to Downing-street'. According to the *New York Times*, the barriers were eight-feet high, and 'of a substantial character, foundations having been dug to receive them'.

The suspension of the customary Saturday tours of the Houses of Parliament and the arrest of a man, said to be Irish, in Central Lobby 'led people to think that acts of violence by Sinn Feiners were feared'.[25]

The Government's attempt to play down the return of Downing Street's barriers was dutifully echoed by *The Times*: 'we understand that no exaggerated importance need be attached to this precaution ... the doors of the barricades were open yesterday afternoon, and people were allowed to walk past the prime minister's official residence without question or interference'. The wooden barriers came down in February 1921 only to be put back up again. Plans were announced 'to set up iron gates in Downing-street in place of the wooden barrier standing there at present'. The present black steel gates finally materialized in 1989.[26]

40 BITTER FRUIT

'Their demolition most people will interpret as an act of common sense', opined *The Times* when Downing Street's wooden barriers were taken down in January 1924, 'but some minds will doubtless prefer to regard it as what the jargon of the day calls a "gesture"'. The removal of Downing Street's barriers was one of the first decisions made by Britain's first-ever Labour prime minister, James Ramsay MacDonald, and sent a clear political message: Labour represented people who had previously been locked out of power. However, MacDonald unwittingly came to epitomize Britain's inter-war descent from high hopes to bitter disappointment. It is a poignant tale.[1]

MacDonald's rise to power was astonishing for the illegitimate son of a ploughman, John MacDonald, and a seamstress, Anne Ramsay, who brought him up. As a bright boy and good speaker, MacDonald became a pupil-teacher in his school at Lossiemouth, a fishing village in Morayshire. He grew into a handsome man of above average height, with thick, wavy dark brown hair. After finding work as a clerk in Bristol, he became active in left-wing politics and by the age of 21 was secretary to Thomas Hough, a Liberal Radical politician in London. Hough was elected to the Commons in 1892, when the first working class men standing as Labour candidates were also elected.

One of these new Labour MPs, James Keir Hardie, went on to found the Independent Labour Party. At the Opening of Parliament, as Henry Lucy reported, Hardie 'drove up to Westminster in a break, accompanied by a brass band', but the police refused to allow the musicians into New Palace Yard. Hardie's appearance in the Chamber shocked many MPs, as instead of wearing the conventional top hat and frock coat, he wore a 'somewhat dingy, weather-worn' cap, a short jacket, trousers 'frayed at the heel', a flannel shirt, and sported 'a shock of uncombed hair'. On Hardie's initiative, and with the backing of the trade unions, the Labour Representation Committee was set up in 1900. Ramsay MacDonald became its secretary, and did more than anyone to establish Labour as a parliamentary party; forming a tacit electoral pact with the Liberals. He became an MP in 1906, aged almost 40, and five years later was elected chairman of Labour's 42-man parliamentary party (the PLP).[2]

Yet it took the cataclysm of the First World War to transform Labour into a major party. Although MacDonald's criticism of the war cost him the PLP chairmanship, the Labour movement's importance in the war was recognized when MacDonald's successor, Arthur Henderson, was appointed to Lloyd George's War Cabinet. When peace came, Labour, profiting from the Liberal split and the extension of the vote to all men, trebled its share of the vote to 22 per cent and won 62 seats.

None of their MPs was a woman, although most women of 30 or over had won the right to vote in 1918. The first woman to be elected to the Commons was Constance, Countess Markiewicz (née Gore-Booth), but the 50-year-old Sinn Feiner did not take her seat because of her party's boycott of parliament. A year later, Nancy, Lady Astor, became the first woman to sit as an MP when she was elected for the Conservatives in the by-election caused by her husband's reluctant succession to a viscountcy.

Fourteen of the 22 by-elections held during the three years from July 1919 were won by Labour as Lloyd George's promise of making Britain 'a fit country for heroes' rang hollow. Labour's emergence alarmed many Tories, who felt increasingly trapped in a coalition led by a quasi-presidential prime minister who shamelessly sold honours (£12,000 for a knighthood, £30,000 for a baronetcy, £100,000 for a peerage) to raise funds for his own political ambitions, and who also negotiated Irish independence.[3]

Lloyd George's nemesis was the unlikely figure of Stanley Baldwin, a sandy-haired scion of Worcestershire iron-masters in his mid-fifties. Together with MacDonald, he dominated British politics from the early 1920s to the mid-1930s. Baldwin was an old Harrovian and classical scholar with a close interest in Westminster Abbey. 'I want to think of it [the Abbey] here as it was when it stood in its first fairness', he once remarked, 'when Henry III, in 1262, ordered pear trees to be planted "in the herbiary between the King's Chamber and the Church," evidently so that he might see it over a bank of blossom'. Baldwin's fondness for the English countryside, pig-rearing and pipe-smoking helped him portray himself as the authentic voice of England.[4]

Baldwin rose to sudden prominence in October 1922 with a devastating attack on Lloyd George, whom he portrayed as 'that dynamic force', at a meeting of Conservative MPs at the Carlton Club, located, in those days, in Pall Mall. His speech captured the mood of Tory MPs who voted to fight the next election as an independent party. Such was the suddenness of Lloyd George's resignation that the new prime minister, Bonar Law, held his first Cabinet at his South Kensington home. The Carlton Club meeting is often wrongly described as the origin of the '1922 committee': the curiously named official forum of the Conservative parliamentary party. In fact, the name derives from meetings organized by the new intake of Tory MPs after Bonar Law's snap election in November 1922.

Although MacDonald became Leader of His Majesty's Opposition when Labour won 142 seats in 1922, many of his MPs were disinclined to play by Westminster rules. 'Gusts of passion had swept the House from time to time', reported *The Times* on 12 April 1923, 'and disorder rose in crescendo until a temporary suspension had to be ordered'. The row was sparked by the Government's failure to make a statement after its defeat on the treatment of ex-servicemen. Labour MPs called for the House to be adjourned and began singing. 'Gradually this swelled into a *fortissimo* rendering of the "Red Flag" by the whole of the numbers of the Labour Party, except the occupants of the Front Opposition Bench'.

In the pandemonium when the Speaker tried to continue with the day's business, 'Mr Ramsay MacDonald, who was watching the activities of his followers with frowning face', consulted his colleague Sidney Webb, the Fabian socialist, who in turn approached the Speaker. A Tory shouted: 'Is Labour fit to govern?' Amid renewed uproar, the Speaker suspended the sitting. As insults were hurled across the Chamber, a scuffle broke out before the Mace, where MacDonald and Baldwin, the Chancellor, struggled to separate their followers. This incident was a portent: MacDonald and Baldwin were to spend the rest of their careers trying to keep people calm during difficult times.[5]

A month after the fracas, Bonar Law stepped down as prime minister because of throat cancer. At his funeral in Westminster Abbey, Asquith supposedly said: 'it is fitting that we should have buried The Unknown Prime Minister next to the Unknown Soldier'. The succession was settled by the king, who opted for Baldwin instead of Lord Curzon, the pompous Foreign Secretary who had expected the job. George V's decision set the precedent that a prime minister should sit in the Commons. The last prime minister in the Lords, Salisbury, had retired in 1902.[6]

It seemed that Baldwin might become a second 'Unknown Prime Minister' when he took up the old Tory cause of protectionism and honoured Bonar Law's promise to hold an election before any return to tariffs. Baldwin's reward was the loss of power; but he resisted all entreaties to form another coalition with the Liberals, despite Tory fears that a Labour government would lead to Bolshevism.

MacDonald accepted the king's invitation to form a government and became Britain's first Labour prime minister on 22 January 1924. George V complained about the singing of the 'The Red Flag' and the 'Marseillaise' at a Labour victory celebration at the Albert Hall, but MacDonald replied that had he tried to stop it there would have been a riot; and he had managed to prevent 'The Red Flag' being sung in the Commons when Baldwin fell. The king told him and several other new ministers that, 'the immediate future of my people is in your hands, gentlemen. They depend on your prudence and sagacity'. J. R. Clynes, who accepted the ancient post of Lord Privy Seal, later recalled that he 'couldn't help marvelling at the strange turn of fortune's wheel which had brought MacDonald, the starving clerk, Thomas, the engine driver, Henderson, the foundry labourer, and Clynes, the mill-hand, to this pinnacle beside the man whose forebears had been kings for generations'.[7]

At Number 10, MacDonald's elder daughter, Ishbel, who took on the duties that her late mother would have fulfilled, was surprised to find no linen, crockery or cutlery for private living or official hospitality. 'The January sales are on', MacDonald told her, 'get hold of your aunt Bessie, get yourselves to the Co-op and buy whatever you think is needed in the way of crockery, linen and so on. But don't go mad!'[8]

Despite removing the Downing Street barricades within days of becoming prime minister, MacDonald remained under mental siege. His ministers were suspected of being Soviet agents and, as working men, not up to the job. 'Because of their two detriments', as Roy Hattersley, the former Labour Deputy Leader, observed, 'they felt they had to be more part of the Establishment than the Establishment'. MacDonald's enthusiasm for wearing full court dress on ceremonial occasions caused some amusement, and prompted one of his successors at Number 10, Harold Macmillan, to remark: 'He was very vain and he liked being in uniform very much … Had good legs, liked showing them off'.[9]

The eagerness with which MacDonald sought to establish Labour's respectability began to sow suspicions that deep down he craved to be part of the Establishment. These suspicions were apparently confirmed when, to MacDonald's evident delight, he was taken up socially by the Marquess and Marchioness of Londonderry. His intense fondness for Lady Londonderry, although platonic, fuelled speculation. According to Margaret Stansgate, George V was said to have told Lord Londonderry, 'I hear that my Prime Minister is in love with your wife'. Londonderry, assuming that such a relationship made socialism less likely, replied enthusiastically, 'Oh yes, but don't you think it's a good thing?'[10]

MacDonald's 1924 minority administration survived for only nine months, but he had established Labour as a party of government. While there had been no Soviet-style revolution; a very different revolution was about to change Westminster's relationship with the rest of the country. Newsreels were already bringing silent film of political leaders to the local cinema, but the wireless brought their voices into people's homes. Radio transmissions had begun in 1922, with only 30,000 wireless sets registered in the first year, but by the end of Baldwin's second spell as prime minister in 1929 there were three million sets, and by the end of the 1930s, nine million. For the first time, a prime minister at Westminster could speak directly to people at home.

Baldwin mastered the art of the 'fireside chat'. Although his broadcasts sound almost comically formal to a modern ear, Baldwin realized that despite the huge size of his total audience, he was talking to each family in its own living-room. He gave hours of thought to each broadcast and met the challenge of Labour's idealistic appeal by presenting himself as a reasonable country gentleman. When the unions called a General Strike in 1926 in protest at pay cuts for a million mineworkers, Fleet Street's printers took newspapers off the streets. Baldwin went on the radio. 'I am a man of peace', he reassured listeners. 'I am longing and working and praying for peace but I will not surrender the safety and security of the British constitution'.[11]

The General Strike brought the first of many confrontations between ministers and broadcasters. The Chancellor, Winston Churchill, who was in charge of government propaganda, urged the Cabinet to commandeer the British Broadcasting Company, the present BBC's forerunner. The BBC's first boss, Sir John, later Lord, Reith, would have none of it and insisted on impartial news. However, as Michael Cockerell, the BBC film-maker, has observed, Reith saw nothing wrong in helping Baldwin make his broadcast and refusing to allow MacDonald or the unions on the air.[12]

Baldwin's insipid election slogan, 'Safety First', in 1929 could not prevent Labour becoming the largest party. Although MacDonald lacked an overall majority, he chalked up an impressive series of prime ministerial firsts. His Minister of Labour, Margaret Bondfield, a trade unionist in her mid-50s, became the first woman to sit in the Cabinet. When Labour's privy councillors were sworn in, George V broke the traditional silence, telling Bondfield that, 'I am pleased to be the one to whom has come the opportunity to receive the first woman privy councillor'.[13]

Bondfield's appointment was appropriate after the first election at which women aged 21 and over had voted on equal terms with men: a right conceded casually in the Commons one Friday afternoon by the unlikely figure of William Joynson-Hicks, the Tory Home Secretary. Baldwin, who had been prime minister at the time, unveiled a statue of Emmeline Pankhurst in Victoria Tower Gardens, by the Houses of Parliament. The ceremony, in March 1930, was broadcast live on radio and included a performance by the Metropolitan Police Band of 'The March of the Women', conducted by the composer, Dame Ethel Smyth. In his speech, Baldwin acknowledged that although he had opposed Mrs Pankhurst, she 'had set the heather alight' and it had fallen to him, while prime minister, 'to put the coping-stone upon her labours'.[14]

In September 1929, MacDonald became the first British prime minister to visit the United States, for talks with the President on Anglo-American naval rivalry. The impact of subsequent bilateral summits has been amplified by television's insatiable demand for images. Again, MacDonald was something of a pioneer, as he installed Number 10's first television set in the pillared room in early 1930, courtesy of the inventor, James Logie Baird. However, MacDonald's fascination with this 'miracle' was mild compared with modern prime ministers who live and die by television.[15]

Within two weeks of MacDonald's ticker-tape welcome on Broadway, the Wall Street crash signalled the onset of the Great Depression. By 1931, Britain's jobless had more than doubled to 2.5 million and the Government faced a massive budget deficit. The Bank of England's reserves were almost exhausted after the collapse of an Austrian bank triggered a run on sterling. At Westminster, a cross-party committee urged cuts in public spending, including a 20 per cent cut in unemployment benefit: but Labour was split. The Chancellor, Philip Snowden, preached Gladstonian rigour; the unions resisted cuts; and others, including a young minister, Oswald Mosley, demanded job creation through public works.

During late August 1931, the Cabinet grappled with a desperate financial crisis on a daily basis. At a traumatic meeting on the evening of Sunday 23rd it became clear that the division within the Cabinet was unbridgeable. When the prime minister asked his colleagues for their views, one by one, only 11 backed him and nine were against.

After the fateful Cabinet meeting, MacDonald phoned his son, Malcolm, also an MP, to tell him that he was about to resign. He initially resisted pleas from the Tory and Liberal leaders for him to carry on as prime minister, because he feared that a Conservative-Liberal coalition would lack sufficient public support to make the necessary cuts. However, MacDonald's mind was changed by George V, who persuaded him of his duty to put country before party. A day after agreeing to form a national government, MacDonald went on the radio to explain why he had teamed up with his old enemies: 'Public opinion abroad was concerned about our budget position. They saw a big deficit in trust. They fear that we are living beyond our means and may continue to do so'.[16]

MacDonald stood condemned by the Labour Party as a traitor, whose betrayal confirmed that all along he wanted to be part of the Establishment. However, Roy Hattersley believes that although MacDonald acted partly from vanity, he also thought that 'it was his duty to do his best by the country, whatever party happened to be in power'. This belief explains MacDonald's slogan at the October 1931 election: 'The Captain Who Stuck by the Ship'. When Labour expelled him, MacDonald's contempt for his old party exploded across the airwaves during an election broadcast: 'every opposition Labour candidate and every opposition Labour elector will remember this: he is fighting for no principle'.[17]

MacDonald's tragedy was that having done more than anyone to build up Labour, he almost annihilated it. In the 1931 election, Labour plummeted from 287 seats to 52. MacDonald fielded only 20 'National Labour' candidates and won 13 seats. The National Government won 554 seats; 473 of them represented by Conservatives. MacDonald continued as prime minister for almost four years and devoted himself to the principled but fruitless task of disarmament. He sat in the Cabinet until 1937 and died five months later. It took more than 30 years before a memorial plaque was unveiled in Westminster Abbey. In the Commons, Jacob Epstein's bust of MacDonald was eventually allowed to join likenesses of other former premiers in the members' lobby.

Baldwin returned to Number 10 for the third time in 1935, having survived a fierce press campaign against him in the mass-circulation papers, the *Daily Express* and *Daily Mail*, by their respective owners, Lord Beaverbrook and Lord Rothermere. A by-election in Westminster St George's in March 1931 became a test of Baldwin's leadership. During the campaign, Baldwin fought back by accusing the press barons of seeking 'power without responsibility – the prerogative of the harlot throughout the ages'. His brilliant phrase – suggested by his cousin, Rudyard Kipling – and the victory of the Tory candidate, Duff Cooper, great grand-uncle and look-a-like of David Cameron, quelled Baldwin's critics.[18]

Radio remained Baldwin's preferred medium. 'We are now weathering world recession better than any other country in the world, but much remains to be done', he re-assured his audience in 1932. A year later, his relaxed broadcast from Number 10 extolling the English character veered into self-parody. 'No people grumble more than we do, I do myself every day. But though I grumble I do not worry and I keep cheerful, and the more difficult times are, the more cheerful we become'.[19]

It took all Baldwin's conciliatory skills to prevent the monarchy self-destructing after the death of George V in 1936. The new king, Edward VIII, seemed a breath of fresh air, with his dashing good looks, easy manner and his readiness to champion ordinary people; although this latter trait made him unpopular with pro-government MPs, except for mavericks such as Churchill. However, disapproval among those in the know of his affairs with married women deprived him of much support when he decided to marry an American divorcee, Wallis Simpson. Baldwin counselled that marrying Mrs Simpson would not be popular and rejected the king's suggestion of a morganatic marriage, whereby his wife would not be queen. Edward's request to broadcast to the nation was also vetoed by Baldwin, who understood the power of the medium better than anyone, and feared that the country would be polarized. Lacking any significant support, Edward abdicated. Only then was he allowed on the radio.

Baldwin had defeated a king and saved the monarchy. The task of reviving people's special affection for the monarchy began in earnest with the coronation of Edward's brother George VI and Queen Elizabeth, in May 1937. The ceremony inside Westminster Abbey was brought into people's living-rooms and local cinemas for the first time. Millions listened to the live radio broadcast from inside the Abbey, as 'words of immemorial solemnity that have never yet been heard outside the walls of Westminster' were transmitted across Britain, the empire and the world. At the previous two coronations, in 1901 and 1911, only the procession had been filmed, but in 1937 film cameras were allowed inside the Abbey.[20]

Less than three weeks after the coronation, Baldwin retired from Number 10 aged almost 70. His replacement, Neville Chamberlain, was only a couple of years younger but had long been regarded as the natural successor, having been a reforming Health Minister in the 1920s and Chancellor since 1931. Chamberlain had also created a power base in 1929 by founding the Conservative Research Department at Number 24 Old Queen Street. However, he never quite shook off the feeling that his father, Joseph, or his brother, Austen, should have become prime minister rather than him. Neville Chamberlain's business background could make him seem brusque. Baldwin advised him to stop giving the impression that he 'looked on the Labour Party as dirt'. Chamberlain's experience as a reforming Lord Mayor of Birmingham counted for little, and he was unfairly mocked for viewing politics 'through the wrong end of the municipal drainpipe'. His lean frame, Victorian garb, winged-collar shirts, lugubrious delivery, and the pince-nez he wore while speaking at the dispatch box, earned him his nicknames as 'The Coroner' and 'The Undertaker'.[21]

Yet, Chamberlain dominated Westminster. James Margach, an astute political commentator, reckoned that he was the 'first Prime Minister to employ news management on a large scale'. Chamberlain regularly lunched with lobby journalists at the St Stephen's Club, opposite the Houses of Parliament in Bridge Street. He assiduously courted editors and press barons. Joseph Ball, his Director of the Conservative Research Department, was well-versed in media manipulation. The BBC was leaned on to censor its broadcast talks and the decision of which politicians should give talks from the BBC's Westminster studios was decided by the whips. Churchill, the most senior critic on the government backbenches, was effectively banned from the BBC during Chamberlain's first two years at Number 10.

However, as with Lord North, Neville Chamberlain was in the wrong place at the wrong time. He wholeheartedly supported Baldwin's policy of appeasing Europe's fascist dictators, Hitler and Mussolini. The death of Chamberlain's young cousin, Norman, in the First World War, underpinned his overwhelming desire to avoid any repeat of the slaughter of 1914–18. He continued to believe that negotiation with the German leader was the right course, despite the occupation of the Rhineland, the bombing of Guernica and the annexation of Austria. The prime minister could not imagine that Hitler would plunge his people into another European war.

However, war suddenly seemed imminent in the late summer of 1938 as Hitler threatened to invade Czechoslovakia. Air Raid Precautions (ARP) began in earnest. As loudspeaker vans toured Westminster urging people to be fitted with gas masks, Duff Cooper's wife, Lady Diana, and Asquith's old flame, Venetia Montagu, 'sat in Tothill Street workrooms clamping snouts and schnozzles on to rubber masks, parcelling them and distributing them to queues of men and women'. Lady Diana 'felt sick all the time, like many others, no doubt. It was a grisly job for a neurotic but better than inaction'. At nearby Caxton Hall, a couple went straight from their wedding in the registry office to another part of the building to be fitted for masks. Trenches were dug as temporary shelters in St James's Park and other central parks.

During the panic, Chamberlain launched a desperate bout of shuttle-diplomacy, flying to Germany three times in the space of a fortnight. 'If at first you don't concede, fly, fly, fly again', quipped Foreign Office wags. Chamberlain had never trusted the Foreign Office and preferred instead to rely on his aide, Sir Horace

Wilson, nominally the government's chief industrial adviser, whose office was located next to the Cabinet room. The late Sir Frank Roberts, a young diplomat in 1938, told the present author of an incident when he delivered new intelligence reports to Number 10 and overheard Chamberlain remark: 'Oh, the Foreign Office will keep sending me this stuff to try to make me change my mind!'

After returning from his second flight, the gulf between Hitler's demands and the British and French positions seemed unbridgeable. On the evening of Tuesday 27 September, Chamberlain spoke live on radio to the country and the empire from Number 10. Shortly before the broadcast's scheduled start at 8 p.m., he made his way from Wilson's office into the Cabinet room, where the microphone was set up and commented: 'I'm wobbling all over the place'. His broadcast revealed his view of the entire crisis: 'How horrible, how fantastic, incredible, it is that we should be digging trenches and trying on gas masks here because of a quarrel in a faraway country between people of whom we know nothing'. He claimed that if he 'were convinced that any nation had made up its mind to dominate the world by fear of its force', he would resist. Apparently, the prime minister did not yet believe that Hitler intended to do any such thing.

Next day, the crowds gathered around the Houses of Parliament were eerily quiet as MPs arrived to hear Chamberlain update them. The Commons was packed and among those watching from the gallery were Chamberlain's wife, Anne; George V's widow, Queen Mary; and the Duke and Duchess of Kent. Also present was one of the American Ambassador's sons, John F. Kennedy, then in his early twenties. The prime minister entered the Chamber to ecstatic cheers from his supporters. 'Today we are faced with a situation which has had no parallel since 1914', he warned. Having spoken for about an hour, he was handed a message. 'His whole face, his whole body, seemed to change', observed Harold Nicolson, an anti-appeaser MP. 'All the lines of anxiety and weariness seemed suddenly to have been smoothed out; he appeared ten years younger and triumphant'. Chamberlain then broke the news that Hitler had invited him to further talks in Munich. Government loyalists rose and cheered, but anti-appeasers sat still. 'Get up! Get up!' many MPs yelled at Winston Churchill.

Chamberlain's last-ditch talks with Hitler culminated in the Munich Agreement. The price of peace was the brutal abandonment of the Czechs; but in Britain there was huge relief that war had been averted. The prime minister received an ecstatic welcome when he alighted at Heston aerodrome on Friday 30 September. Jubilant crowds lined the streets all the way to London. At Buckingham Palace, the King and the prime minister emerged onto the balcony at about 7 p.m., accompanied by the queen and Mrs Chamberlain, as the crowd sang: 'For he's a jolly good fellow'.

Crowds had packed Whitehall and Downing Street from early afternoon. The Chamberlains had difficulty struggling from their car and onto the doorstep of Number 10. Inside, they were greeted by a crush of people in the entrance hall, among them members of the Cabinet who were due to meet. Outside, the chanting grew louder. Lord Home, who was Chamberlain's Parliamentary Private Secretary, later recalled that as the prime minister made his way upstairs to wave to the crowd from a first-floor window, somebody called out: 'Tell them it's "Peace with Honour"!' Chamberlain stopped, turned round sharply and replied: 'I don't do that kind of thing'.

Opposite Number 10, Jock Colville, a young official, was watching from a first floor balcony, when he was joined by Sir Orme Sargent, a senior diplomat. Surveying the hysterical scene below with disdain, Sargent remarked: 'You might think that we had won a major victory instead of betraying a minor country'. As the window opposite opened and the crowd shouted for Chamberlain to speak, Sargent added, 'I can bear almost anything, provided he doesn't say "Peace with Honour"', before turning on his heels and leaving Colville alone on the balcony.

Moments later, Neville and Anne Chamberlain appeared at the first-floor window above Number 10's front-door. The prime minister held up his hand, and as the crowd quietened, he began to speak. 'My good friends', he declared, 'this is the second time in our history that there has come back from Germany to Downing Street "Peace with Honour"'. As the renewed cheering subsided, he added, 'I believe it is peace for our time'.

Chamberlain had been unable to resist the temptation to repeat the words that Benjamin Disraeli, the Earl of Beaconsfield, had uttered from the same window 60 years earlier on his triumphant return from the Congress of Berlin. However, he told Anne shortly afterwards: 'I should never have said that'.[22]

Despite intense relief that war had been averted, many felt deep shame. Churchill's wife, Clementine, and Lord Robert Cecil, a former minister, discussed marching to Downing Street and hurling a brick through Number 10's window. Duff Cooper resigned as First Lord of the Admiralty and received private support from a naval officer, Lord Louis Mountbatten. 'I have ruined, perhaps, my political career', Duff Cooper told MPs, 'but that is a little matter; I have retained something which is of great value – I can walk about the world with head erect'.[23] Duff Cooper's resignation statement was chosen, by his relative, David Cameron, when Leader of the Opposition in 2009, as the greatest parliamentary speech of the last 100 years.[24]

MPs debated Munich for four days. Thirty to 40 government backbenchers abstained, including three future prime ministers: Churchill, Anthony Eden and Macmillan. Munich cast a long shadow over Westminster. The debate was wound up by 'Rab' Butler, a young Foreign Office minister and convinced appeaser. Although Macmillan and Butler became Tory modernisers after the Second World War, they remained bitter rivals.

41 FINEST HOUR

Winston Churchill's statue in Parliament Square, showing him defiant and great-coated, honours the man who became prime minister in May 1940 and led the country when Britain and her empire stood alone against Hitler. During World War II, radio broadcasts of Westminster's chimes, and of Big Ben striking the hour, inspired hope round the world during the struggle against fascism and tyranny. In Europe, members of the Resistance risked their lives tuning in to the BBC broadcasts, and survivors who visited Westminster after the war were reduced to tears by the familiar chimes and the sound of the hour being struck.

Today, the most accessible and evocative links with Britain's desperate struggle for survival are the Churchill War Rooms. The entrance to this wartime warren lies at the end of King Charles Street near St James's Park, at the foot of the 'Clive Steps': named after the nearby statue of Sir Robert Clive ('Clive of India'). The War Rooms' corridors and rooms have been restored to their appearance in the Blitz, when the prime minister was forced to move from Number 10. Although Churchill found the War Rooms' cramped conditions claustrophobic, they became a second headquarters for him, the Cabinet, the chiefs of staff and their back-up teams; and were equipped with secure communications, a map room, meeting room, facilities for eating, and sleeping quarters.

Planning for the War Rooms had begun in March 1938. They became operational on 27 August 1939, a week before Hitler's invasion of Poland and Britain's declaration of war. The War Rooms were built in the basement of the north-west corner of the strong, steel-framed Government Offices in Great George Street, relatively close to Number 10. A machine-gun post guarded their entrance. They were linked to other departments and shelters by a network of tunnels and shafts beneath Westminster that provided access, mail, heating, and telephone and telegraph lines. A visible remnant of this network is the Citadel, now a creeper-covered block that was built as a vast fortress-cum-air raid shelter next to the Old Admiralty Building, at the north-west corner of Horse Guards Parade.[1]

Britain's first municipal air raid shelters were built at Westminster's Caxton Hall in 1938. During the Munich crisis, the Abbey's keeper of the muniments,

Lawrence Tanner, drove to Oxford with the most valuable items, depositing some in the Radcliffe Camera's cellars and others at Chiselhampton House, a few miles away. After Munich, Tanner brought back the treasures, but as war became inevitable the Coronation Chair was sent for safety to Gloucester Cathedral: the only time, except for Cromwell's installation as Lord Protector in Westminster Hall, that the Chair has left the Abbey since it was made in about 1300. The Stone of Scone was buried in a secret place beneath the Abbey's Islip Chapel. Later, when invasion threatened, a plan showing its precise location was entrusted to Canada's prime minister. Bronze effigies from royal tombs; contemporary portraits of Richard II; statues of saints; and historic documents and books, were evacuated from London for safe keeping.[2]

In parliament, MPs despaired at Neville Chamberlain's failure to declare war immediately after Hitler's invasion of Poland on 1 September 1939. 'Speak for England, Arthur!' was the cry the next day from the Tory benches – attributed variously to Bob Boothby and Leo Amery – when Labour's Arthur Greenwood rose to speak. Finally, at 11.15 am on Sunday 3 September, Chamberlain spoke into the microphone in the Cabinet room and told the world: 'You can imagine what a bitter blow it is to me that all my long struggle to win peace has failed'.

Churchill, the prime minister's old adversary, was appointed to the War Cabinet as First Lord of the Admiralty, and was filled with emotion as he took the First Lord's chair in the boardroom that he had occupied during World War I. Although there was heavy loss of life when the battle ship *Royal Oak* was sunk at Scapa Flow, the expected German offensive failed to materialize. However, no sooner had Chamberlain said that Hitler had 'missed the bus' than the Nazis invaded Norway. Britain's military response was a fiasco and brought to a head growing criticism of the prime minister. In the Commons, on 7 May 1940, Leo Amery turned on his leader, and repeated Cromwell's savage injunction to the Long Parliament in 1653: 'You have been here too long for any good you have been doing. Depart, I say, and let us have done with you! In the name of God, go!'[3]

As MPs voted at the end of the Norway debate, 'Chips' Channon and other Tory Chamberlainites, 'watched the insurgents [rebels] file out of the Opposition lobby. "Quislings", we shouted at them, "Rats". "Yes-men" they replied'. The Government's majority was cut from over 200 to 81 as more than 40 government supporters voted with the opposition, while a further 60 abstained. 'The final scene in the House was very distasteful', Rab Butler, the young Foreign Office minister, later wrote of the bitter recriminations among Tories. 'It reminded me of certain scenes in the history of Peel. The singing of *Rule Britannia* by Harold Macmillan was much resented by Neville who rose looking old and white-haired, as he had become, and marched out realizing, as he did, that he could not go on'.[4]

In a final bid to cling onto power, Chamberlain tried to bring Labour into coalition. In the Cabinet room on 9 May he explained his plan to his two potential successors: the Foreign Secretary, Lord Halifax, and Churchill. However, when

Attlee and Greenwood joined them, Attlee was characteristically blunt. 'Our party won't have you', he told Chamberlain, 'and I think I am right in saying that the country won't have you either'. After they left, Halifax ruled himself out as the country could not be led from the Lords in wartime. Churchill did not demur. The next day, the British people awoke to the news that Germany had invaded the Low Countries. The Labour Party backed Attlee in his refusal to serve Chamberlain and readiness to enter coalition under somebody else. At 6 p.m. on Friday 10 May 1940, the king invited Churchill to form a government.[5]

Others harboured doubts about Churchill. Across Horse Guards Parade at the Foreign Office, Rab Butler, Channon, Alec Dunglass (the future prime minister, Sir Alec Douglas-Home) and civil servant Jock Colville, expressed their loyalty to Chamberlain by drinking: 'To the King over the water'. Tory MPs cheered Chamberlain to the rafters when he next appeared in the Commons, whereas Churchill was met by silence on his first appearance, and for months had to rely on Labour and Liberal MPs for his cheers. The new prime minister was already 65 years old, and, as he put it: 'qualified to draw the Old Age Pension'. He was almost totally bald, and with age had come a stoop that made him seem shorter than his five feet and a half frame. Yet he came to embody the bull-dog spirit; his mastery of the English language and power of expression were to make him Britain's most inspirational war leader.

'I have nothing to offer but blood, toil, tears and sweat', Churchill told MPs. In his first radio broadcast from the Cabinet room on 19 May, he declared: 'I speak to you for the first time as prime minister in a solemn hour in the life of our country, of our Empire, of our Allies and, above all, of the cause of Freedom'. He finished with both a warning and an exhortation: 'the long night of barbarism will descend … unless we conquer, as conquer we must; as conquer we shall'. In parliament after the fall of France a month later, he urged people to prepare for 'the Battle of Britain', declaring that, 'if the British Empire and its Commonwealth last for a thousand years, men will still say, "*This* was their finest hour"'.[6]

Churchill's prime ministerial broadcasts, and the sound of Big Ben, became symbols of wartime defiance. Big Ben had been silenced in World War I for fear of helping Zeppelin crews, but during World War II the bells were of no help to enemy aircraft and were allowed to sound: although the lights behind the clock faces, and the 'Ayrton light', signalling parliament's sittings, were extinguished. However, listeners to the BBC's Home Service, the main domestic network, at the start of the war heard only the Greenwich Time Signal before the main news at 9 p.m. During 1940, MPs, churchmen and others lobbied the BBC to replace the pips with Big Ben's 9 p.m. strike. From November, the 'Big Ben minute' was inaugurated and lasted till 1960. Big Ben was also heard many times a day on overseas programmes: its distinctive sound raised morale at home and abroad.[7]

The Churchills moved into Number 10 Downing Street in June 1940 and settled into the second-floor flat. As Churchill's routine involved dictating speeches until 3 a.m. or later, his secretaries were on constant call and slept at Number 10. He usually woke at about 8 a.m., and, after eating breakfast and reading the papers, began dictating letters, memos and speeches, propped up in bed, cigar in hand. The dictating done, Churchill took a bath and by the time he emerged the typescript of his latest speech was ready.[8]

The London Blitz first hit Whitehall on 11 September 1940, but Churchill was determined to remain at Number 10. One reason for staying put was his anger that the War Rooms were not bomb-proof in the event of a direct hit. However, his claim that he had been 'sold a pup' was indignantly rejected by the head of the Office of Works, Patrick Duff, who had made it clear that the War Rooms were not, 'and cannot be made bomb-proof in any sense'. None the less, the War Rooms afforded better protection than the old, poorly-built and somewhat shaky Number 10. Churchill improved safety by taking over the offices in the rooms at garden level, under the Cabinet Room, and reinforcing them. These 'garden rooms' provided a meeting area, a bedroom for Churchill's use, and a small room alongside the kitchens, where he sometimes dined with George VI.[9]

The early raids also took their toll on the Palace of Westminster and the Abbey. On 16 September, the blast from a high explosive bomb in Old Palace Yard severely damaged the south wall of St Stephen's Porch and its great window, and lifted the statue of Richard Coeur de Lion from its pedestal, leaving its sword bent. At the Abbey the remaining fragments of original stained glass in the east windows of Henry VII's Chapel were shattered, and a small hole was made in the Abbey's eastern-most chapel. After the war, this chapel was dedicated to the memory of the men in the RAF killed in the Battle of Britain. The wartime hole was glazed and remains part of the memorial.[10]

On 14 October 1940, Churchill was dining with colleagues in the room under the Cabinet Room when an air raid began. After a bomb fell, with a great bang, on Horse Guards Parade, Churchill sent the kitchen staff to the shelter under Number 10's garden. A few minutes later, a high explosive bomb that fell in Treasury Green, about 20 yards to the east of Number 10, shook the house. The kitchens, the Soane dining rooms and state drawing rooms were all damaged; windows were smashed, doors were blown off hinges and curtains and furniture was tossed about. The underground Treasury shelter across the court was blown to pieces by a direct hit, killing an official and wounding two others.[11] Three nights later, Jock Colville, Churchill's private secretary, was woken from his bed at Number 10 by the almighty crash of a bomb: 'The air was thick with smoke and the choking smell of sulphur and gunpowder'. Part of the Treasury was totally destroyed, revealing some of the original Tudor palace.[12]

As the damage sustained by Number 10 left only the Cabinet Room and the private secretaries' room next door operational, on 20 October 1940 Churchill began moving out. He authorized the reinforcement of the War Rooms by enlarging and extending a large concrete slab above the ceiling. Churchill and his wife, Clementine, had a flat above the War Rooms and, in addition, small bedrooms underground in the War Rooms for use during heavy air raids; but Churchill always preferred to remain in the flat. The prime minister held evening meetings in the War Rooms with his Cabinet and chiefs of staff, or broadcast on the BBC from there; but he preferred to work at Number 10 during the day and held cabinets and other meetings there.[13]

Churchill hated staying indoors. He insisted on his evening walk in St James's Park, even though in the black-out he and his bodyguard, Walter Thompson, almost bumped into the trees; and if there was an air raid, he loved to walk from Number 10 to the War Rooms. On one such occasion, he and Thompson had just entered the War Rooms, when there was a huge explosion behind them. 'The pavement where we had been walking twenty seconds earlier was now a crater', Thompson recalled. 'As we went to the edge, the water main burst and we were drenched'.[14]

Most dangerous of all, Churchill watched air raids from the high, exposed roof above the War Rooms. Wearing his thick blue siren suit, air force overcoat, and sometimes a tin helmet, he would insist on going up. During an air raid in March 1941, Churchill insisted that his dinner guests, Averell Harriman, Roosevelt's envoy, and an American ambassador, together with his private office, should accompany him 'up to the roof of the Air Ministry to watch the fun'.[15]

Westminster suffered its heaviest damage on the clear, moonlit night of 10 May 1941, Churchill's first anniversary as prime minister. More than 500 German aircraft dropped hundreds of high explosives and over 100,000 incendiaries on London, killing more than 1,400 people and destroying 11,000 houses. Shortly before midnight, Colonel Walter Elliot, a Conservative MP and head of public relations at the War Office, was woken by the sound of sirens. Leaving his house in Lord North Street, situated between the Abbey and St John's, Smith Square, he was soon fire-fighting around Lord North Street and Great George Street.[16]

As incendiaries showered down on Westminster, Elliot noticed a great blaze near the Abbey. The roof of the Abbey's Lantern, the low square tower at the centre of the building, was destroyed. 'It is distressing to look up at a great square of sky over the Lantern', Lawrence Tanner, later recalled, 'but it was the *only* place where the roof could fall in without doing much harm. The whole burning mass fell in a heap in the central space between the Choir and the Altar steps and burnt itself out'. The choir stalls were only 'a bit singed' and the seventeenth-century pulpit slightly damaged. In the adjoining Chapter House, the windows, part of the mid-Victorian restoration, had been shattered, but the remaining glass was enough to re-glaze three windows, and the other three were filled with modern stained glass.[17]

Although most of the Abbey's fabric was saved, the precincts were severely damaged, as was Westminster School. The school's 'great hall ('School'), with its fine roof, the seventeenth-century Busby Library, and the College dormitory were gutted, only the walls remaining'. In the precincts, 'the Deanery and the lovely houses round the Little Cloister are just heaps of bricks', noted Tanner. 'The curious thing is that the monastic buildings have been laid bare. The medieval stone walls stand out everywhere in the ruins ...' Although the Jerusalem Chamber and the Jericho Parlour escaped damage, much of the Deanery's long gallery and other rooms were completely destroyed, including the Langham Room's late seventeenth-century panelling and the secret chamber, reached by a ladder, where Dean Atterbury was said to have plotted against George I. During the post-war restoration, the medieval custom of embellishing a cornice with carved bosses was revived in the Lytlington Room: among the heads depicted are Tanner's and those of the post-war dean and chapter.[18]

Across Old Palace Yard, the Houses of Parliament took a heavy pounding. At about 3 a.m., a policeman told Elliot, the fire-fighting MP, that the House of Commons was on fire. As Elliot rushed to parliament, he saw flames leaping from the scaffolding round the Victoria Tower, where a high explosive bomb had killed two policemen. At St Stephens' entrance, Elliot found hose-pipes running up the steps and into the Palace. Inside, Westminster Hall's ancient timber roof was alight. Although the fire brigade had 50 pumps trying to subdue the blaze, the flames spreading from the south end of the Hall threatened to engulf the great, medieval hammer-beam roof. The heat was turning the gutters to molten lead and the huge oak beams were beginning to smoulder.[19]

The immediate threat was heightened by the fire raging nearby, in the Chamber of the House of Commons. The Chamber was separated from the Hall only by the width of a courtyard. Suddenly, an explosion intensified the blaze. Flames engulfed the Chamber in an inferno that consumed the benches, panelling and ceiling. As there were not enough pumps to save both buildings, Elliot urged the firemen to save the ancient Hall and suggested running hoses through the doors from New Palace Yard, nearer the water pumps, where they could spray the roof with stronger jets of water.[20]

Elliot led the firemen outside from St Stephen's, past Cromwell's statue and into New Palace Yard, where he used a fireman's double-handed axe to smash through the great locked doors. As the heavy jets of water played on the blazing roof and doused the oak beams, the flames began to subside. Before long the fire was subdued. As Churchill later reported, on a night when 'the enemy lit more than two thousand fires', the vast Norman hall and its great, medieval hammer-beam were saved.[21]

Early the next day, as Colville walked from Number 10 to the Abbey for the morning service, he saw 'flames still leaping' from the roof of Westminster Hall. A fireman showed him Big Ben, 'the face of which was pocked and scarred'. The clock tower had suffered a direct hit, but the clock and bells had kept going. The sounds of the air raid had been picked up by the microphones in the belfry and broadcast with the bells. Later, while standing on Westminster Bridge, Colville 'thought ironically of Wordsworth in 1802. St Thomas's Hospital was ablaze ... flames were visible all along the Embankment, there was smoke rising thickly as far as the eye could see'.[22]

At the Palace of Westminster, the Member's lobby and the Commons Chamber were charred ruins, with smoke rising and steam hissing as firemen doused the embers. Elliot found that the place was open to the sky, and from the floor of the Chamber, his wife, who had accompanied him, could see a barrage balloon hanging over parliament. Harold Nicolson, another MP, made his way to the Ladies Gallery, 'when suddenly, I turned the corridor, there was the open air, and a sort of Tintern Abbey gaping before me'. Churchill was reduced to tears by the sight of the wreckage, but he remarked, 'This chamber must be re-built – just as it was. Meanwhile, we shall not miss a single day's debate through this!'[23]

The Commons took over the Lords' Chamber and the Peers moved to the King's Robing Room. This arrangement lasted until the re-built Commons' Chamber was ready in 1952, except for brief spells in war-time, when Hitler's bombing raids and unmanned V-1 flying-bombs, or 'doodlebugs', forced MPs and peers to retreat to Church House in Dean's Yard. Live broadcasts of Big Ben were replaced by a recording from 16 June 1944, to avoid the sound of explosions helping the enemy to locate targets. Live transmissions were restored within three months.[24]

Churchill's fascination with the doodle-bug encouraged his habitual disregard for his own safety. His detective, Walter Thompson had difficulty persuading him to take shelter. Whenever Churchill tried to go to the roof of the War Rooms' building to watch a doodle-bug, Thompson would delay the progress upstairs. Eventually, Churchill, suspecting a ruse, confronted Thompson, who retorted that his duty was to prevent him being killed. Churchill agreed not to go up again.[25]

By early April 1945, Churchill was able to spend most of his time at Number 10. On the 24th, the Speaker re-lit the 'Ayrton light', near the top of the Clock Tower, and six days later switched on the lights on the clock faces. On 8 May, 'Victory in Europe Day', Churchill broadcast at 3 p.m., British Double Summer Time, from the Cabinet room and announced Germany's unconditional surrender. His final words were: 'Advance Britannia! Long live the cause of freedom! God save the King!' The crowds in Parliament Square heard the broadcast over loudspeakers and all joined in singing 'God Save the King' at the end, 'and then cheer upon cheer'.[26]

Later, in the Commons, some MPs wept as Churchill repeated Lloyd George's words in 1918, proposing that MPs attend St Margaret's to offer thanks to Almighty God. The Speaker, followed by Churchill and Labour's Arthur Greenwood, headed the 500-strong procession. 'Through the Central Lobby we streamed, through St Stephens Chapel, and out into the sunshine of Parliament Square', Nicolson reported. They entered St Margaret's by the furthest, west door, creating a 'long sinuous procession through a lane kept for us through the crowd'. At the end of the short service, the Chaplain read out the names of those MPs who had laid down their lives. 'Tears came into my eyes', Nicolson noted, prompting Nancy Astor's dismissive aside, 'men are so emotional'.[27]

Later, after seeing the king, Churchill joined his ministers on the balcony of the Government Offices complex, overlooking the packed crowds stretching far up Whitehall and down to Parliament Square. ' "God Bless you all", Churchill told them, "This is your victory!" at which the crowd roared back, "No – it is yours" '. In the evening, Big Ben was floodlit and Churchill ventured out again. As the crowd rushed round him, he managed to climb onto a car for his safety. 'Then after a while, he climbed along the car roof on all fours until he could sit with his legs dangling over the windscreen', Thompson recalled. 'The crowd cheered their heads off'.[28]

Within months, however, the crowd who had cheered Churchill booted him out of Number 10 and elected Britain's first majority Labour government. 'Never again' were the voters prepared to tolerate the unemployment and poverty of pre-war Britain. As Big Ben struck midnight on 14 August 1945, marking the start of Victory in Japan Day, the clipped tones of Clement Attlee, the prime minister, announced that, 'at last and on every front war was over'. Although his new government oversaw many radical changes to Britain's economy and society, Attlee was no radical when it came to the House of Commons. At the laying of the new Chamber's foundation stone in May 1948, he declared that the Commons 'is not a building. It is a living fellowship, renewed though the centuries, changing in its membership but always in essence the same'.[29]

The basic design of the re-built Chamber remained the same as Barry's 'little room', with an identical floor area (68 feet by 45 feet 6 inches). Its architect, Sir Gilbert Scott, made its neo-Gothic style less ornate and the woodwork less dark by using bleached oak. The stone archway of the entrance from the Members' Lobby was left damaged, at Churchill's wish, as a reminder of the bombing, and as a memorial to those who fought in the war. On one side of the entrance stands a statue of Lloyd George, Britain's leader during the First World War, and on the other a bronze statue of Churchill: its foot polished brightly by the touch of passing MPs hoping for inspiration. Although Churchill served a second term as prime minister, between 1951 and 1955, his own 'finest hour' was his wartime premiership, and it was in recognition of this, that not only did he have a state funeral at St Paul's Cathedral, in January 1965, but also a lying-in-state at Westminster Hall: an exceptional honour given to only one other prime minister – Gladstone.

42 MASTERS AND MODERNISERS

'When at last, after decades in which the miners had suffered every kind of danger and low pay and deprivation, they got their nationalization, I can remember the miners streaming through the lobby singing Cwm Rhondda'. This emotional scene, as Labour MPs voted to take the coal industry into public ownership in 1946, was recalled almost 50 years later by Barbara Castle. She had been among the 1945 Labour in-take when its commanding 146-seat majority gave it a mandate for the most socialist measures ever introduced in Britain.[1]

Bizarrely, Labour stormed the economy's 'commanding heights', as Lenin had described them, in the ornate, neo-Gothic surroundings of Barry's and Pugin's House of Lords, because the blitzed Commons' Chamber was being re-built. The state take-over of coal-mining was totemic, as it supplied 90 per cent of British energy and employed 700,000 people. Labour's great nationalizations, the creation of the National Health Service and the granting of independence to India were all debated and voted through in the Lords' Chamber by 'young majors from the army', 'intellectuals' and 'working people from traditional Labour areas'.[2]

Labour's proselytizing mood was epitomized in a famous, but often misquoted phrase, by Sir Hartley Shawcross, a somewhat unlikely socialist hero who, as he displayed more conservative sympathies, was later dubbed 'Sir Shortly Floorcross' by the columnist, Bernard Levin. 'We are the masters at the moment and not only for the moment', Shawcross proclaimed, 'but for a very long time to come'. Another much-quoted phrase that evokes this period, 'the gentleman in Whitehall knows best', is also misquoted. Douglas Jay, a post-war adviser in Number 10 had actually written in his book, *The Socialist Case*, published in 1937 and updated ten years later, that, 'in the case of nutrition and health, just as in the case of education, the gentleman in Whitehall really does know better what is good for people than the people know themselves'. His words appear patronizing, but Jay was arguing against full state control and wanted to limit intervention to areas such as education, health, inequality and nutrition.[3]

Attlee, Labour's post-war prime minister, was too steeped in the virtues of Christianity, fair play and modesty to have allowed control of the 'commanding heights' to turn him into a British Lenin. 'He had none of the flash arts or the dark arts of politics', as Peter Hennessy, the historian, has observed, plus 'all the charisma of a gerbil'. Attlee was bald, be-spectacled and small in stature. He left handling the media entirely to his press secretary, Francis Williams, who persuaded him to have the Press Association news wire service installed in Number 10 on the pretext that Attlee could see how Middlesex were faring at Lords. On the first day, Williams was suddenly confronted by a shocked prime minister rushing into his office, complaining that his 'cricket machine' was printing out the Cabinet minutes. Attlee had no idea that Williams routinely let the press know which subjects were dealt with by the Cabinet.[4]

Attlee demonstrated that a prime minister does not need to mimic a president in order to achieve massive change. He was virtually 'monosyllabic', according to Shirley Williams, who met him when she was a young Labour activist, a trait that discouraged other members of the Cabinet from being prolix and aided the efficient dispatch of business. Attlee relied on Whitehall's war-time workhorses, the Cabinet committees, to push through Labour's reforms. He also had the benefit of a strong Cabinet containing big political beasts who had served in the war-time coalition: Ernest Bevin, the Foreign Secretary, a working class union boss built like a tank; Herbert Morrison, Lord President of the Council, a formidable organizer and old London party boss; and Sir Stafford Cripps, President of the Board of Trade and later Chancellor, an austere, moralistic socialist. Attlee's position was bolstered by the rivalries between them and by Bevin's blunt loyalty when dismissing talk that he might replace Attlee: 'I'm sticking to Little Clem'.[5]

Attlee and Bevin acted as one when deciding that Britain should make its own atomic bomb, probably the most fateful decision taken by any post-war British government. Attlee kept the subject in a Cabinet sub-committee, reducing the risk of such a sensitive matter leaking. The key meeting was held at Number 10 on 25 October 1946. Bevin turned up late and realized that the economic ministers were winning the argument. 'We've got to have this thing over here whatever its costs', he declared. 'We've got to have a bloody Union Jack on top of it'. Thanks to Bevin's sheer force of personality, and his simple logic that without the Bomb the country would not be treated as a major power, Britain went nuclear: it little mattered that World War II had left Britain crippled by debt.[6]

Britain's post-war, military over-reach is epitomized by the gigantic, wedge-shaped Ministry of Defence building that dominates the eastern side of Whitehall and dwarfs the Banqueting House. Prime ministers relish the world stage and have put Britain's military clout before its economic strength, even though punching above one's weight risks being knocked out. The Ministry of Defence's huge pile extends for 550 feet between Horse Guards Avenue and Richmond Terrace. Its construction between 1939 and 1959, originally for the Board of Trade and the

Air Ministry, removed almost all trace of Whitehall Palace: only the wine cellar, Queen Mary's Steps and the Banqueting House survive. The eighteenth-century town houses that replaced the Palace after the 1698 fire were destroyed, except for Gwydyr House, adjoining the Banqueting House and dating from the 1770s. However, remnants salvaged from several town houses were installed inside the new building.[7]

In the deepening chill of the Cold War in 1950, an echo of a 650-year-old conflict shattered the peace at the Abbey. In an early signal of profound political change, Ian Hamilton, a student at Glasgow University, and three fellow members of Scotland's Covenant home rule movement plotted to remove the Stone of Destiny, looted from Scone by Edward I, and return it to Scotland. Hamilton hid in the Abbey overnight on Christmas Eve, but was disturbed by a nightwatchman. However, he bluffed that he had been locked in by mistake and was set free. In the early hours of Christmas morning, Hamilton returned and with two accomplices broke into the Abbey through the door by Poets' Corner. As they prised the three hundred-weight Stone from under the Coronation Chair, about a quarter of it broke away. Hamilton lugged the smaller lump to a getaway car, where Kay Matheson, another student, was waiting. Hamilton and Matheson fooled a passing policeman by canoodling, and then drove off. By the time Hamilton returned to the Abbey, his accomplices had abandoned the rest of the Stone and fled, having been unable to find the keys to their getaway car. However, Hamilton eventually found the keys and dragged the Stone to the car. By chance, he later found his accomplices and they finally hid the Stone in Kent.[8]

The theft of the Stone Destiny from Westminster Abbey caused a sensation. Roadblocks were put on the main routes to Scotland and the Dean of Westminster, Alan Don, a Scot, made an emotional radio appeal for the Stone's return. After the brou-haha subsided, Hamilton and his accomplices brought the Stone to Scotland, where it was professionally repaired. The four were arrested a couple of months later, but the question of their prosecution was highly political. As many Scots felt that the Stone's rightful place was in Scotland, prosecution might raise a storm of protest and result in the Stone's permanent disappearance. After it became clear that no prosecution would be made, the Stone reappeared on the high altar of the ruined Abbey of Arbroath.[9]

The Stone of Destiny was brought back to Westminster Abbey in April 1951 and put in the vault beneath Abbey Islip's Chapel, where it had been hidden during World War II. However, its installation in the Coronation Chair in February 1952, following the death of George VI, created a row in parliament. Scottish MPs pressed the prime minister, Winston Churchill, to say whether any Scots had been consulted. A Scottish Conservative MP, Colonel Gomme-Duncan, asked if Churchill was aware that many 'loyal Scottish subjects' would feel 'profound disappointment at this decision', as many thought that the Stone should be kept in Edinburgh between coronations.[10]

However, John Major's decision to return the Stone to Scotland in 1996, the 700th anniversary of its removal by Edward I, was too little, too late. At the 1997 election, the Conservatives failed to win a single Scottish seat. Two years later, the queen opened a devolved Scottish Parliament. Although the Stone and the Coronation Chair are due to be re-united at future coronations, the Stone's removal has left the ancient chair in the Abbey, as Alan Bennett observed, 'looking like an empty commode'. The chair has suffered worse indignities. In 1914, it was battered by an abortive bomb attack, presumed to have been perpetrated by a suffragette, and it is scarred by the carved initials of visitors, and boys from Westminster School.[11]

The crowning and anointing of Elizabeth II in the Coronation Chair on 2 June 1953 followed a tradition that had begun 1,100 years earlier when the Vikings introduced a throne, high seat, or stone, into such ceremonies. The Coronation Chair itself dates back to about 1300, when Walter of Durham, a painter and carpenter at the Palace, was commissioned to make an oak chair that incorporated the Stone of Destiny. Since at least 1399, every English monarch has been crowned in the same chair, with a few exceptions: Edward V and Lady Jane Grey, who were deposed; Edward VIII who abdicated; Mary I who used a different chair; and Mary II, who used a duplicate chair for her joint coronation with her husband, William III.[12]

Elizabeth II's coronation reinvented an ancient ceremony, traditionally witnessed by a select few, and made it a shared, national experience. King George VI's coronation in 1937 had set a precedent, as it was broadcast on radio, partly to help restore popular support for the monarchy after Edward VIII's Abdication. By 1953, television broadcasting was becoming popular, but although about half a million people held television licences, Churchill and the Archbishop of Canterbury advised against allowing intrusive cameras to film the ceremony. However, the press reacted with such fury that the decision was quickly reversed. Overnight, according to Roy Strong, the number of television licence holders doubled to three million.[13]

On the day of the coronation, despite the cold and rain, the streets around Westminster were packed with people; but many more crammed into the homes of neighbours and relations with television sets. An estimated 20 million people in the United Kingdom saw the queen crowned in Westminster Abbey on live television. In addition to the usual monochrome newsreels, two colour films of the coronation were released in cinemas only six days after the event. Fears that after the privations of austerity and rationing, people might turn against a display of rich pageantry and ancient tradition were confounded. Television and film re-affirmed Westminster's status as Britain's royal, ceremonial capital and gave the monarchy a new medium through which to strengthen its bond with the people.[14]

Yet optimistic talk of a new Elizabethan age was soon dispelled by the Suez debacle in 1956. During the months of crisis in Number 10, Lady Eden, wife of the prime minister, Sir Anthony Eden, felt as if 'the Suez canal was flowing throughout the drawing-room'. In a sense, the canal flowed though everyone's living-room. Abandonment by Britain's closest ally, the United States, and the humiliating Anglo-French withdrawal from Suez, was a rude awakening to the chilling reality of the country's relative decline and triggered a loss of confidence in Westminster and Whitehall.[15]

'He will be the worst Prime Minister since Lord North', Lord Swinton, one of Churchill's senior ministers, had said of Eden. Eden's decline in power was cruelly exposed on his return to the Commons after a break to restore his health, when only one Tory MP leapt up to cheer while others sat in awkward silence. The Salisbury family briefly resumed their role as Westminster power-brokers following Eden's resignation through ill-health, when the fifth Marquess, 'Bobbety', met each of the Cabinet in turn in his room in the Privy Council Offices off Whitehall and asked which of the two favourites, Rab Butler or Harold Macmillan, each minister preferred: 'Well, which is it to be, Wab or Hawold?'[16]

Although Macmillan told the queen that he 'could not answer for the government lasting more than six weeks', he affected a relaxed, urbane image at Number 10. Instead of his predecessor's fraught and interfering regime, Macmillan delegated work to ministers, kept a sense of proportion by reading Jane Austen and Anthony Trollope, and pinned a quotation from Gilbert and Sullivan, written in his own hand, on the Cabinet door: 'Quiet, calm deliberation disentangles every knot'. His wife, Lady Dorothy, whose long affair with a raffish Tory, Lord (Bob) Boothby, had caused Macmillan much anguish, nonetheless helped her husband feel relaxed at Number 10, by making it a family home with grand-children and toys about the place.[17]

Macmillan was aged almost 63 when he became prime minister, old by current standards, and was a cartoonists' dream with his moustache, hooded eye-lids, swept back hair and old-fashioned clothes. He was the last prime minister to have fought in World War I and never forgot the working men from the north-east who served with him, and whom he later represented as MP for Stockton-on-Tees. Yet there was a ruthless streak behind Macmillan's languid pose and paternalist politics. When all three Treasury ministers resigned over the Cabinet's refusal to accept their spending cuts in early 1958, Macmillan dismissed their resignations as 'little local difficulties' and flew off on a lengthy Commonwealth tour. Several years later, he sacked a third of his Cabinet in what became known as 'the Night of the Long Knives', prompting a gibe from the Liberal MP, Jeremy Thorpe: 'Greater love hath no man than that he lay down his friends for his life'.

Macmillan master-minded an astonishing political turnaround. 'Supermac' began as a satirical caricature but soon became a flattering nickname. His orches-tration of a consumer boom and his gift for appearing statesmanlike on television won the Conservatives a third successive election victory with a 100-seat majority. No wonder that Enoch Powell dubbed him an 'actor-manager'. Macmillan, for his part, ironically nicknamed Powell 'Aristides', after the Athenian statesman who was called 'The Just' and was never wrong. Macmillan replaced the Cabinet's old, rectangular table with a boat-shaped one in order to improve eye contact with ministers; but the change proved to be a mixed blessing after Powell joined the Cabinet in 1962. On one occasion, the Foreign Secretary, the Earl of Home, arrived to find a new seating plan. 'Has one of us died in the night?' he asked. 'Oh no', replied the Cabinet Secretary, 'the PM can't have Enoch's accusing eye looking at him straight across the table anymore'. As Home recalled, 'poor Enoch was put away down the left where Harold couldn't see him'. Powell later reflected that sitting in Macmillan's Cabinet was 'like having a debate with Henry VIII … I was conscious that he [the Prime Minister] had the axe down by his chair'.[18]

Behind the scenes, Macmillan was much less sanguine than his public persona suggested and commissioned secret Whitehall studies of Britain's likely position by 1970. One report made such depressing reading that, as Peter Hennessy found, the prime minister never put it to the Cabinet. Macmillan became a man in a rush, an Edwardian 'gent' turned desperate modernizer. Britain's withdrawal from empire was accelerated and its application to join the European Economic Community hastened. Motorways were built, railways pruned (courtesy of Dr Beeching), towns made traffic-free and universities commissioned. The economy's performance was supposed to be improved by getting businessmen, politicians and union bosses together at a new National Economic Development Council (Neddy). However, the lift broke after Neddy's first meeting at the St Stephen's Club, a Victorian pile on the corner of Bridge Street and the Victoria Embankment. A year later, Neddy moved to the new Millbank Tower, a 32-storey symbol of 1960s' modernism.[19]

Where better than ancient Westminster for modernizers to realize their dream? Massive rebuilding was first envisaged in 1959, but previous schemes were overtaken during 1964–5 in a master-plan drawn up by the architect, Sir Leslie Martin, and the traffic planner, Sir Colin Buchanan. Their megalomaniac scheme involved demolishing 'and rebuilding as a comprehensive layout' the entire southern half of Whitehall, from Parliament Square to Downing Street, and from the river to St James's Park, including the Foreign Office, the Government Offices Great George Street complex, Richmond Terrace and all the buildings along Parliament Street, Bridge Street, Cannon Row and Derby Gate. They also suggested building flats across Victoria Tower Gardens, and planned extensive rebuilding around the Methodist Central Hall and Smith Square, involving the likely loss of many Georgian gems.[20]

Martin and Buchanan sought to give re-assurance by saying that they had no plans to demolish the Houses of Parliament, Westminster Abbey, St Margaret's Church and the Cenotaph, although the latter would be engulfed by their massive office complex and might be moved to the entrance of Parliament Square. Instead, they claimed, the setting of Westminster's ancient buildings would be improved by constructing a riverside tunnel, thus creating a traffic-free Parliament Square:

except, of course, for ministerial and official cars. Martin's report blithely stated that his replacements for Great George Street and the Foreign Office 'need be no more than eight or nine storeys', adding airily that 'massiveness and scale could be broken down'.[21]

Plans based on Martin's utopian scheme were killed off by a public inquiry in 1970. After the reprieve of Richmond Terrace and the north block of New Scotland Yard (now the Norman Shaw North building), two later schemes were dropped because of budget cuts. In the 1980s, a further reprieve saved the buildings between Cannon Row and Parliament Street. However, the St Stephen's Club was demolished to make way for Portcullis House, a five storey building with a great sloping roof and stacks. It houses parliamentary offices, meeting rooms and an atrium with restaurant, cafeteria and coffee shop, and is linked by a tunnel beneath Bridge Street to the Houses of Parliament.

Luckily, central Westminster largely escaped the horrors visited on other British cities as post-war planners purged them of their history and humanity; but it was a close run thing. It was also fortunate that when Number 10 was found to be unsafe, the inquiry into what should be done was headed not by a planner, but by the Earl of Crawford and Balcarres, an eminent figure in the world of art and chairman of the National Trust. Renovation rather than demolition was recommended.

The Macmillans left Number 10 in August 1960 and moved across Horse Guards Parade to Admiralty House while the work was done. It was at Admiralty House in October 1962, as the world teetered on the edge of nuclear oblivion during the Cuba missile crisis that Macmillan talked, on the 'hot line', with President Kennedy. It was also there in 1963 that Macmillan had to contend with General de Gaulle's veto of British entry into the European Common Market and the Profumo scandal, after the War Minister had lied to MPs about his affair with Christine Keeler.

The architect at Number 10, Raymond Erith, replaced the building's shallow, shrunken foundations, stabilized it with concrete floors, and updated the water supply, sanitation, heating, lifts and wiring. He also gave Number 10 the entire basement, including Number 11's; and extended Number 10's top-floor living accommodation above Numbers 10, 11 and 12 Downing Street. Inside Number 10, Erith left the appearance of the Cabinet Room unchanged, and preserved the atmosphere and look of all the main rooms, while letting in more light. His biggest change was the addition of more rooms on the east side: his two extra bays can be discerned on Number 10's frontage, adjoining his new, bow-windowed office on the corner by Treasury Green. Erith also completely rebuilt the tall, red-brick Number 12, replacing the two-storey remnant that had survived a fire in 1879.[22]

Macmillan had little opportunity to savour the new comforts of Number 10, as he resigned through ill-health in October 1963. The choice of Number 10's next occupant provoked one of Westminster's bitterest leadership crises. The trouble stemmed from Macmillan's determination to block the favourite, 'Rab' Butler, his rival for the job six years earlier. Instead, Macmillan preferred either Viscount Hailsham or the Earl of Home. They were both contenders as a result of the success of a long campaign by the Labour MP Anthony Wedgwood Benn, whose father had been ennobled on Attlee's recommendation, to allow reluctant hereditary peers to renounce their titles and seek election to the Commons. Home had never seemed a reluctant Earl, but he became the new prime minister as plain Sir Alec Douglas-Home after renouncing his earldom. Butler's acolytes – Iain Macleod, a rising star in the Cabinet and Party Chairman, and Enoch Powell – were furious and refused to serve Home.

Macleod, Powell and their colleague, Reginald Maudling, had been recruited in the late 1940s in Butler's drive to modernize the Tories. They had cut their political teeth in the Conservative Research Department (CRD), based in the late-seventeenth century house at 24 Old Queen Street and an annexe (number 34), dating from the 1770s. Later alumni included Andrew Neil, Chris Patten and Michael Portillo. The CRD's blend of eccentricity, intellectualism and raffishness is glimpsed in Matthew Parris's memoir, *Chance Witness*; its intoxicating proximity to power inspired Michael Dobbs's novel, *House of Cards*.

Macleod's excoriating portrayal of the Tories' secretive leadership process as 'The Magic Circle', published only three months after Home's victory, was devastating. The procedure was changed, and 18 months later, Edward Heath, an abrasive modernizer, was elected Conservative leader in a secret ballot of Conservative MPs held in Commons Committee Room 14.[23]

Heath's victory was a tribute to Harold Wilson, the Labour prime minister, who had stolen the Macmillan government's modernizing clothes. Wilson won the 1964 election by promising to harness 'the white heat' of a 'scientific revolution'. However, a chance encounter at Number 11 between the new Chancellor of the Exchequer, Jim Callaghan, and his Tory predecessor, Maudling, revealed that the economy was worse than Labour feared. Maudling had returned to Number 11 for his personal possessions, and as he left put his head round Callaghan's study door and remarked: 'Sorry, old cock, to leave it in this shape', before ambling out across the garden.[24]

Within hours of entering Number 10, Wilson, together with his deputy, George Brown, and Callaghan, took the fateful decision not to devalue the pound from its $2.80 parity, despite a huge balance of payments deficit. Devaluation became the great 'unmentionable' in Whitehall, but Wilson ultimately paid a high political price for his doomed attempt to avoid being the third Labour prime minister, after MacDonald and Attlee, to devalue. When a devaluation of 14 per cent was eventually made in 1967, Wilson tarnished his reputation by claiming in his televised broadcast: 'It does not mean, of course, that the pound here in Britain, in your pocket or purse or in your bank, has been devalued'.[25]

The modernizers' dream of boosting Britain's rate of economic growth repeatedly ended in higher and higher inflation in every upturn, followed by higher and higher unemployment in every downturn. The uproar in the Commons in early 1972, when the jobless total exceeded a million for the first time since the war, forced the Speaker to suspend the sitting. The governments of Wilson, Heath and Callaghan, in their search for the economic holy grail of rapid, non-inflationary growth, all resorted to prices and incomes policies. Ministers and officials ended up struggling to keep tabs on wage rates, salaries and the price of everything. Strikes against pay controls, by the miners in 1973–4, and public sector unions during the 'Winter of Discontent' in 1978–9, led to the fall of Heath and Callaghan, and raised the question: 'Who governs?'

British entry into the European Economic Community (EEC, or 'Common Market') became the modernizers' mantra. The debate on British entry cut across party and personal allegiances at Westminster. At first sight, the most surprising unholy alliance was between Michael Foot, a radical socialist, and Enoch Powell, an opponent of mass immigration and a free-market Tory; but their passionate opposition to European integration sprang from a shared commitment to parliament. They had successfully scuppered House of Lords reform in 1968–9, although for diametrically opposed reasons: Powell wanted the upper Chamber to remain hereditary; Foot wanted the Lords abolished and replaced with a one-chamber parliament.

Powell was a romantic about parliament. While completing his history of the medieval parliament, he was shocked when Heath proposed that the Conservatives should support the abolition of a custom whereby Black Rod, acting as messenger from the House of Lords, could interrupt the Commons in mid-debate and summon MPs to the Lords to hear the Royal Assent to Bills. 'Ted, we can't do this', Powell exclaimed, 'the formula … is that which was used in 1306 when Edward I was ill at the time of a parliament in Carlisle … You simply cannot destroy a thing like that'.[26]

At the end of the historic Commons debate on the principle of British entry into the EEC in October 1971, Heath acted on the advice of his chief whip, Francis Pym, to allow a free vote for Conservative MPs. This shrewd tactic encouraged Labour's 69 pro-European MPs to defy their party's three line whip and vote for entry, cancelling out the 39 anti-EEC Tories. In scenes reminiscent of the bitter debate over Munich in 1938, Jenkins was called a 'fascist bastard' by a fellow Labour MP, while Powell was provoked to call out to a minister leaving the Chamber after the division: 'It won't do! It won't do!'[27]

Before the second reading of the Bill for British entry in February 1972, the government's whips identified three groups on the backbenches: 'the robusts' were staunchly pro-EEC and received a blue tick against their name; 'the wets' were less certain in their views; and 'the shits' were anti-EEC and received a brown tick. 'Wets' and pliable 'shits' were threatened with de-selection as Conservative candidates at the next election if they rebelled. In a remarkable move on a government Bill, the vote was made one of confidence: if the vote was lost, the government would resign and call an election. Powell was regarded as too much of 'shit' on the EEC to be approached. In his speech, he expressed his belief in the Commons as the embodiment of the nation, its history and traditions:

> For this House, lacking the necessary authority either out-of-doors or indoors, legislatively to give away the independence and sovereignty of this House now and for the future is an unthinkable act. Even if there were not those outside to whom we have to render account, the very stones of this place would cry out against such a thing.

Fifteen Conservatives (including Powell) rebelled, the first occasion since World War II that a group of Tory MPs had voted against their government on a motion of confidence.[28]

While the EEC divided the main British parties, the conflict over national identity in Ireland returned to haunt Westminster. In 1969, Jim Callaghan, the then Home Secretary, sent British troops to Northern Ireland to protect the Catholic minority; but as the violence escalated the troops were seen as an occupying force. In July 1970, a canister of tear gas was thrown into the Commons' Chamber in protest at conditions in Northern Ireland. After 'Bloody Sunday' in January 1972, when British soldiers killed 13 people during a civil rights march in Derry, the Home Secretary, Maudling, claimed that the soldiers had returned fire and alleged that those who died had been armed. His claims were later shown to be untrue by Lord Saville's judicial inquiry into 'Bloody Sunday'. In the Commons a furious Bernadette Devlin (later McAliskey), the MP for Mid-Ulster, rushed across the floor of the House and began pummelling and punching Maudling, and pulling his hair, while shouting that he was a 'murdering hypocrite'.[29]

Parliament was targetted by the Provisional IRA in June 1974, when a 20 lb bomb exploded in Westminster Hall and injured 11 people. The bomb fractured a gas main and fire spread rapidly from a corner of the ancient Hall, causing extensive damage and threatening to set the ancient timber roof alight: outside, smoke could be seen billowing from the roof. Although security was tightened, terrorists managed to exploit an oversight to dreadful effect five years later.

On Friday 30 March 1979, Airey Neave, the Shadow Northern Ireland Secretary and a close adviser of Margaret Thatcher, was assassinated by a bomb as he drove from the Commons car park. MPs and others at the Commons that afternoon, including the present author, heard a dull thud. Within minutes, MPs rushed into the building saying that a bomb had exploded outside and someone was grievously injured. Neave died shortly afterwards. His assassins belonged to the Irish National Liberation Army, who had attached a bomb beneath his car, primed to go off as he drove up the ramp into New Palace Yard. Neave's shield was later placed in the Commons' Chamber, above the main doorway, joining the 42 shields on the Chamber's walls in memory of MPs who died in two World Wars.[30]

On the morning of his murder, Neave had attended a meeting of Margaret Thatcher's Shadow Cabinet to finalize the Conservative 1979 manifesto. He was one of Thatcher's closest advisers, having master-minded her surprise election as Tory leader in 1975, telling MPs that, 'Margaret is doing very well, but not quite well enough'. The implication was that MPs could vote for Thatcher as a protest against Heath, but she probably wouldn't win. Thatcher won 130 votes to Heath's 119. Her victory was dubbed 'the peasant's revolt', but it was to make a greater impact on Britain than the 1381 uprising after which it was named.

43 NEW WINE IN OLD BOTTLES

The heart of Westminster has become a curious combination of a tribal reservation for those who want political power, and a tourist attraction. Ancient buildings and memorials provide a seemingly timeless setting in which politics and pomp, prayer and protest constantly jostle for attention. The global icons of the Abbey, Big Ben and the Houses of Parliament, Downing Street and Horse Guards all bear testimony to earlier battles for power that have shaped the present.

Britain's first woman prime minister, Margaret Thatcher, demonstrated how to use power to maximum effect. She became Britain's longest serving twentieth-century prime minister and re-shaped its economy. Her 11 years at Number 10 (1979–90) was the longest uninterrupted premiership since Tory Lord Liverpool's 15 years (1812–27). Among Conservative prime ministers, only Lord Salisbury, who totted up more than 13 years in separate spells during 1885–1902, spent longer in the top job. However, unlike the third Marquess, Thatcher was not born to rule, and it was perhaps a sense of uncertainty about the daunting task ahead in May 1979 as she was about to enter Number 10, that led her to utter the uncharacteristic words: 'Where there is discord, may we bring harmony'.

Thatcher did not do harmony. It was not in her nature, and as a woman, she could not adopt the easy manner of a Baldwin or Macmillan with her ministers and swap small talk about fishing or shooting. Yet, Thatcher's sex also worked to her advantage. Her male contemporaries were disarmed: unused to arguing politics with a woman, they did not know how to deal with her. Their discomfort was exacerbated by her combative approach, learned, as she acknowledged, in the 1960s, from Iain Macleod, when she was in his Shadow Treasury team and saw him master a brief by testing other people's ideas to destruction.[1]

As a woman in an essentially male government, Thatcher could portray herself as something of an outsider. Her only woman Cabinet minister, Lady Young, lasted less than three years. Thatcher distanced herself from her Cabinet to become 'Battling Maggie', heroically taking on a self-serving, male establishment.

In reality she was a domineering prime minister, but it was a spell-binding act as she made the political weather with a combination of 'conviction politics' and 'Victorian values'. She was more an old-style Liberal than a Tory. Her Methodist father, Alfred Roberts, had been a grocer, and a National Liberal councillor, in inter-war Grantham. In the 1980s it sometimes seemed that Britain was governed by the ghost of Alderman Roberts, whose guiding star had been Gladstonian rigour. As Thatcher proudly boasted, while her father was in charge of the town's finances it never went into debt.

Whereas Attlee achieved change by developing the Cabinet committee system, Thatcher packed the Treasury and other economic departments with allies who wanted to purge Britain of its post-war, state intervention. Her critics were on the back-foot, as the Callaghan government in 1976 had abandoned the post-war priority of maintaining full employment at almost any cost, and instead tried to keep inflation down by controlling the supply of money and credit, a policy known as 'monetarism'. Thatcher berated senior civil servants, an unnerving experience that prompted the sexist barb of being 'hand-bagged', but did not create an alternative power-base on the lines of Lloyd George's 'garden suburb'. Instead, she relied on a few personal advisers, such as the economist, Alan Walters, who made a powerful impact in 1981 by persuading her to defy the views of many other economists and cut government borrowing during a deep recession.

However, Thatcher casually broke Westminster's convention of Cabinet collective responsibility in spirit, if not in letter, by allowing her aides and allies to snipe at Cabinet ministers and encourage MPs to revolt against policies that she personally disliked. Although Jim Prior won Cabinet approval for his policy on trade union reform and later on restoring devolution to Northern Ireland, he faced backbench revolts encouraged by prime ministerial aides. After her 1983 landslide victory, Thatcher entrenched her dominance over the Cabinet, replacing the centrist Francis Pym with Sir Geoffrey Howe at the Foreign Office, and promoting Nigel Lawson as Chancellor and Leon Brittan as home secretary.

Such was the extent of Thatcher's dominance by the mid-1980s that she became the only British prime minister whose name is commonly transmuted into an '-ism'. Thatcherism transformed Britain by reducing unions' power, tolerating previously unacceptable levels of unemployment and de-regulating the City. She and John Major, who followed her at Number 10, delivered the biggest state sell-off since Henry VIII dissolved the monasteries.

After Thatcher had rid her Cabinet of critical voices, there were few ministers left who might have saved her from herself. Thatcher's animus against domestic rates led her to impose the Community Charge: a local tax that was in essence a poll tax. Thatcher's 'poll tax' was likened by Chris Patten, who had the impossible task of trying to make it work, to a heat-seeking missile that homed in on marginal seats as some households, who had paid £150 to £200 in rates, suddenly faced bills of £750 to £800. A rally against the 'poll tax', on 31 March 1990, attracted huge crowds that packed Trafalgar Square, Whitehall and Parliament Square. Clashes between the police and protesters became a riot, ending in 339 arrests and leaving 113 people injured. In April's Gallup poll, Tory support fell to 28 per cent, while Labour's soared to 52 per cent.[2]

There was a certain irony in Thatcher's downfall after imposing a 'poll tax', as it had often been said at Westminster that she had won the leadership 15 years earlier in a 'peasant's revolt' by Tory MPs, an allusion to the 1381 uprising against a poll tax. Her dramatic fall became the stuff of Westminster legend. She had faced a potential challenge to her leadership since January 1986, when Michael Heseltine walked out of the Cabinet room in the style of Joseph Chamberlain 100 years earlier. Heseltine's dramatic gesture revived memories of his seizing the Commons' Mace ten years earlier and brandishing it at Labour MPs in protest at what he felt had been sharp practice in forcing through nationalization. In the pandemonium, Labour MPs had sung 'The Red Flag', and although Heseltine apologized, he was depicted in cartoons as a club-wielding Tarzan.

Although Thatcher chalked up a remarkable third successive election victory in 1987, the resignation in 1989 of Nigel Lawson, her chancellor and former close ally, could not be dismissed merely as 'little local difficulties'. A year later, Sir Geoffrey Howe, the Deputy Prime Minister and former Chancellor and Foreign Secretary, also quit. He had been humiliated by Thatcher's 'rolling her eyes and looking at the ceiling' when he spoke in Cabinet, but the final straw for the pro-European Howe was her outburst in the Commons against a proposed single European currency, when she shouted: 'No, No, No'. In his resignation statement, Howe told a packed Commons: 'The time has come for others to consider their own response to the tragic conflict of loyalties with which I myself have wrestled for perhaps too long'. These dramatic exchanges were seen by millions, as the Commons had been televised since 1989.

The pressure on Heseltine to challenge Thatcher was irresistible. While he and his team lobbied the electoral college of Tory MPs and ministers, Thatcher remained grandly above the fray. On the day of the first ballot, she left for Paris to attend a major summit on European security after the Cold War. Shortly after 6 p.m. on Tuesday 20 November, the result was declared to Conservative MPs who had crammed into Commons Committee Room 10: 'Michael Heseltine 152 votes, Margaret Thatcher 204 votes'. Thatcher had fallen four votes short of the total required for an outright win on the first ballot.

Within minutes, the prime minister announced her intention to put her name forward for the second ballot, but that night, knots of MPs and ministers mingled around Westminster anxiously debating what would happen next. Almost half of Tory MPs had voted against Thatcher and some who had voted for her were saying they would not do so again. The analogy was drawn with Neville Chamberlain's plight in May 1940, when his majority fell from 200 to 81 in the Norway debate. He had not been defeated, but had lost his authority and resigned.

By the time that Thatcher returned to Number 10 the next morning, John Wakeham, her former chief whip and new campaign manager, realized that her position was hopeless. He wanted to prevent the Cabinet being corralled into a collective show of loyalty and instead persuaded her to see ministers, one by one, at the Commons. However, the proximity of ministers' rooms at parliament meant that they chatted to each other and most felt that she was finished. During their awkward one-to-one meetings with the prime minister, most ministers told her that she risked being defeated. Later, Thatcher talked things over with her husband, Denis, at Number 10. His advice, that he did not want to see her humiliated, confirmed what she had heard from her Cabinet.

The next morning's Cabinet was one of the most emotional since Gladstone's 'blubbering Cabinet', almost a century earlier. Shortly before 9 a.m., ministers gathered outside the Cabinet Room. Usually when the prime minister appeared, they would continue chatting and follow her into the room, but on this occasion they fell quiet and gazed at her as she walked past. She began the meeting by reading out her resignation statement, and briefly broke down; although she seemed better once the Cabinet turned to the deployment of troops in response to Saddam Hussein's invasion of Kuwait.

Thatcher's tearful farewell from Downing Street showed that, in exceptional circumstances, a dominant prime minister can be brought down if he or she loses the confidence of the parliamentary party and the Cabinet. As for Heseltine, he had long suspected that 'he who wields the dagger never wears the crown'. Thatcher's resignation freed Douglas Hurd, the Foreign Secretary, and John Major, the Chancellor, from their obligations to her. Hurd's Etonian schooling was held against him on the grounds that the Tories needed to show that they had moved on; although 15 years later, David Cameron, another old Etonian, became leader largely because he was thought to be more in touch with contemporary Britain than his rivals.

Major became prime minister principally because he was not Thatcher or Heseltine. Within his first 100 days, the Allied Forces' liberation of Kuwait gave his premiership a perfect start, but while the Gulf War was in progress he came under fire from a much older enemy. Just after 10 o'clock on the snowy morning of 7 February 1991, Major was chairing the War Cabinet in the Cabinet Room, when there was a deafening explosion. Some of the Ministers ducked for cover. Charles Powell, Major's private secretary on foreign affairs, pushed the prime minister by the shoulders underneath the Cabinet table. 'There was a very loud bang, two plops, and a cold draught', recalled an official who was present.[3]

The bomb had exploded in the garden behind Numbers 10 and 11. Other bombs landed on a patch of grass at the back of Downing Street, but failed to explode. They had all been launched from the back of a white Ford transit van that had pulled up in Horse Guards Avenue, near its junction with Whitehall by the Banqueting House and had been parked at an angle. The back of the van had been converted into a crude mortar unit. After the driver made his getaway and police approached the van, three bombs were fired through the roof, flying over Whitehall and the Cabinet Office towards Downing Street. The bomb that exploded in the back garden blasted a cherry tree out of the ground only about 40 yards away from the Cabinet room. The explosion could be heard about 12 miles away.[4]

The attack was the work of the IRA and came close to succeeding. Their original target had been Lady Thatcher, whom they almost assassinated at Brighton in 1984. The IRA's use of mortars was an ingenious attempt to overcome the installation in 1989 of large, steel security gates at the end of Downing Street to prevent a car-bomb attack. Their attack led to a further review of security, and among the new measures were the installation of blast-proof windows and the replacement of Number 10's historic, shiny, black oak front door with a bombproof, steel replica, complete with brass letter-box bearing the title of First Lord of the Treasury.[5]

The need for repairs and improved security at Number 10 forced Major to move across Horse Guards to Admiralty House, where Macmillan had moved to in the early 1960s. It was there that John Major; Douglas Hurd; Norman Lamont, the Chancellor of the Exchequer; Ken Clarke, the Home Secretary; Michael Heseltine, the President of the Board of Trade; and Richard Ryder, the Chief Whip, met on 16 September 1992 – 'Black Wednesday' – as the pound came under intense pressure on the markets, and finally sanctioned the pound's exit from the European Exchange Rate Mechanism (ERM), that Britain had entered in October 1990. That evening, Lamont made a statement at the Treasury, accompanied by his special adviser, David Cameron. 'Black Wednesday' shattered the Tories' reputation for economic competence, but by summoning senior ministers to Admiralty House the prime minister had shrewdly dipped their hands in the blood and made them share responsibility.

'Black Wednesday' tarnished the Major government's image. Despite an economic recovery, the Conservatives did not benefit from any 'feel good factor' and tore into each other, day after day, on the question of Europe. After the early death of John Smith, the Labour leader, in May 1994, his successor, Tony Blair, re-branded his party as 'New Labour' and personified change. Three years later, New Labour won an election landslide comparable with Labour's in 1945 and the Liberals' in 1906.

The notion that Britain was changing went much wider than politics. The outpouring of affection and grief for Princess Diana after her death in August 1997 was widely held to epitomize this change. The Princess's emotionally charged funeral at Westminster Abbey was neither a full state funeral, nor a ceremonial royal family funeral. Instead, it became 'a unique funeral for a unique person' in the ancient setting of the royal church. Many people in the congregation of 2,000 were associated with charities that Princess Diana had helped. Earl Spencer's tribute to his sister and Elton John's performance of 'Candle in the Wind' were deeply personal moments. The occasion was watched by an estimated 2.5 billion people worldwide Afterwards thousands lined the streets and cascaded the hearse with flowers as it took the Princess's body on its final journey.

Yet there was nothing new in people showing their grief for a young princess whose life had been tragically cut short. In November 1817, the death in childbirth of Princess Charlotte, the 21-year-old daughter of the Prince Regent and future George IV, and a likely future Queen, prompted widespread mourning. And in December 1694, Queen Mary's sudden death at age of 32 caused heartfelt anguish and was marked by 'the saddest and most august' funeral that Westminster 'had ever seen'.

A different but deeply resonant chord was struck by the death of Queen Elizabeth, the Queen Mother, in March 2002. She and her late husband, King George VI, had won a place in people's hearts during the Second World War by remaining in Britain and enduring the horrors of the Blitz. Londoners never forgot the royal family's morale-boosting visits to the bomb-ravaged East End. In a show of people's special affection for the Queen Mother, more than 200,000 people paid their last respects as her coffin lay in state for three days in Westminster Hall; some mourners waiting up to 12 hours in a queue that stretched as much as four miles from Westminster, over the Thames and along the South Bank to London Bridge.

The Queen Mother's funeral was the first one for a king or queen held at Westminster Abbey for almost two and half centuries. The Abbey had played a special role in the Queen Mother's life. It was there, in 1923, that the young Elizabeth Bowes-Lyon, as she then was, married the future King George VI, and spontaneously placed her wedding bouquet on the Tomb of the Unknown Warrior to honour her brother Fergus who had been killed in the First World War. Fourteen years later she and her husband were crowned at the Abbey after Edward VIII's abdication.

The Queen Mother's wedding had helped revive a tradition of royal weddings at Westminster Abbey. Henry I had married Princess Matilda of Scotland there in 1100 and five royal weddings were held in Henry III's new Gothic Abbey between 1269 and 1382.[6] The next royal wedding at the Abbey was not until 1919 when Princess Patricia, Queen Victoria's granddaughter, was married there. Three years later, the wedding of Princess Mary, George V's daughter, at the Abbey, was such a success that it became known as the 'people's wedding'. Ten royal weddings have been held in the Abbey since 1919, including that of Her Majesty Queen Elizabeth II (Princess Elizabeth as she then was) in 1947.

The wedding of Prince William, Duke of Cambridge, and Catherine Middleton on 29 April 2011 was a popular re-assertion of royal ceremonial and spirituality at Westminster. A global audience of two billion people watched as Prince William and his bride took their wedding vows at the High Altar, standing on the Abbey's ancient Cosmati pavement: no longer hidden beneath a carpet after being restored to its full, mystical glory. The couple signed the register in the chapel containing Edward's the Confessor's shrine, a symbolic moment that linked the future heir to the throne with the king who had founded the royal church almost a millennium before. Six months before the royal wedding, Pope Benedict XVI, had prayed at the shrine with the Archbishop of Canterbury, Dr Rowan Williams, during the first papal visit to the Abbey.

Probably no other event better symbolizes Westminster's exceptional continuity of a thousand years than the presentation of Loyal Addresses by both Houses of Parliament to Her Majesty Queen Elizabeth II in Westminster Hall in March 2012 on the occasion of her Diamond Jubilee. The Queen's remarkable achievement of 60 years as head of state was given lasting recognition by the gift from Members of both Houses of Parliament of a stained-glass window, in keeping with the ancient Westminster tradition of celebrating monarchs with artistic imagery. The window, depicting the royal arms, above the Hall's north door, complements the south window's memorial to Members and staff killed in the Second World War, set around the royal arms of the Queen's father, King George VI.

In the early years of the new millennium, the monarchy adapted to change better than Westminster's political class. The Blair government was essentially a duumvirate that reflected the close relationship and rivalry between the prime minister and Chancellor as New Labour's joint architects. Tony Blair controlled foreign policy, home affairs, the constitution and Northern Ireland; while ceding the economy to Gordon Brown. The Chancellor thus exerted enormous influence over domestic policy through the Treasury's control of spending. As the years passed, the mutual recriminations between Numbers 10 and 11 were amplified by their bag-carriers, to the glee of Westminster journalists. Brown finally moved into Number 10 in 2007, but never recovered his authority after allowing the idea of an autumn election to grow but then failing to call one.

Shortly after the banking crisis and credit crunch in 2008, Professor Anthony King, the political and constitutional expert, warned that 'the deepest divide in British politics' was not between Labour and the Tories: 'It is between Britain's whole political class and the great majority of the British people'. King reported that almost three-quarters of people did not trust MPs and ministers to tell the truth and thought that politicians 'constantly make promises that they know they can't keep'. Scepticism about politicians 'had morphed into cynicism, even contempt'.[7]

Then came the scandal of MPs' expenses. In May 2009, the *Daily Telegraph* splashed details of expenses' claims made by Cabinet ministers across its front page. The impact was sensational, but it was only the start. The paper's revelations about MPs' expenses continued every day for six weeks. MPs' claims for the cost of cleaning a moat, a floating duck house (the Commons' authorities rejected this one), and a bath plug captured the headlines; but the investigation showed that MPs were using an array of scams to play the system. The most notorious scam was 'flipping', when MPs nominated one property as a second home, charging the taxpayer for refurbishment, and then 'flipped' the designation to another property so that they could do-up that one too.[8]

The abuse of MPs' allowances developed over 30 years with the connivance of party managers. Although MPs appeared to have set an example by limiting their pay, privately they were encouraged to claim extra on their allowances. Martin Bell, the former broadcaster who sat as an MP during 1997–2001, reckoned that if he had 'pushed every allowance to the limit' he could have made an extra £62,000 tax-free over the four years. Elizabeth Filkin, the Parliamentary Commissioner of Standards (1998–2002), tried to change things, but her zeal annoyed MPs. Dr Tony Wright MP, chairman of the Commons select committee on Public Administration, warned in 2002 that MPs' expenses would be the next scandal, but nothing was done. Requests from Heather Brooke, a journalist, for details of MPs' records under the Freedom of Information Act, were resisted; but attempts to outlaw the release of MPs' records failed in 2007 and 2009. The *Daily Telegraph*'s exposé followed the leak of a computer disk with details of MPs' expenses. After the scandal, Michael Martin resigned as Speaker, the first time since Speaker Trevor, in 1695, that a Speaker was, in effect, forced from office.[9]

'Old corruption' in eighteenth century Westminster had allowed politicians to enrich themselves and helped prime ministers retain power. The 'new corruption' seemed to have a similar effect. 'The highest claimants of the Alternative Costs Allowance [for second homes] were also the MPs most obedient to the bidding of the whips', Martin Bell has argued. 'There was nothing they wouldn't claim for or, when the division bell sounded, vote for'.[10]

Westminster's first hung parliament for more than three decades triggered a five-day marathon of negotiations in May 2010, as Conservatives, Liberal Democrats and Labour desperados, criss-crossed the Westminster village in search of a deal that would bring them power. The Conservatives had won 306 seats, leaving them 20 seats short of an overall majority. However, Labour's 258 seats and the Liberal Democrats' 57 also left a possible Lib-Lab pact 11 seats short.

If Cameron, as Leader of the largest party, had tried to form a minority government, as many expected, he would have needed an assurance from the Liberal Democrats that, in return for some concessions, they would not oppose a Queen's Speech and Budget. But this approach was fraught with risk. The incoming government faced a massive budget deficit, while the danger of political uncertainty was highlighted by scenes of riots in Greece and fears that the Greek debt crisis might spread across Europe. The Bank of England and the Treasury were worried that if the country lacked a stable government and the EU failed to agree a Greek bail-out, the markets would panic and sell British debt, thus exacerbating the financial crisis.

Nick Clegg's pre-election comment that the party which won the most votes and seats would have a 'mandate' to try to form a government had handed

Cameron the initiative. Cameron, for his part, had been aware that winning an overall majority might be beyond the Tories. As Nick Robinson, the BBC's Political Editor, reported, Cameron had planned for such a contingency by commissioning a detailed comparison of the Conservative and Liberal Democrat manifestos.[11] Yet Cameron caused great surprise on the morning after the election when, instead of trying to form a minority government, he announced a 'big, open and comprehensive' offer to the Liberal Democrats.

Cameron's move was in character. A year earlier on BBC Radio 4's *The Prime Ministers*, he had praised Disraeli's audacity in the 1867 Reform Act by taking a Liberal plan to increase the franchise and making 'a hugely bold move' to go further with 'a leap in the dark'. In the same interview, Cameron also praised Sir Robert Peel's decision to put country before party by repealing the Corn Laws.[12]

A key figure during the negotiations between Cameron and Clegg was the Cabinet Secretary, Sir Gus O'Donnell, who had prepared for a hung parliament. The main talks between Tories and Liberal Democrats were held at the Cabinet Office, where Sir Gus left them in no doubt what 'the gentleman in Whitehall' thought was best by impressing on them that 'the more comprehensive the deal the better'. TV crews mounted a vigil in Whitehall, door-stepping the negotiators every time they emerged. Clegg was smuggled into Admiralty House for a secret meeting with Cameron; and Brown and Lord Mandelson dodged the cameras by squeezing along one of Whitehall's war-time tunnels.[13]

On the Tuesday evening after the election, Brown finally forced the issue by resigning. The Queen invited Cameron, as leader of the largest party, to try to form a government. Even at this stage he had to say that he was not sure what sort of government it would be, but his entry into Number 10 was hugely symbolic and enabled him to form Westminster's first Coalition government for 65 years with a majority of 76 seats.

Whoever is in office, presidential-style government has steadily grown at the expense of Cabinet and Parliament. This trend has been encouraged by the triumph of image over the word, as television became the dominant means of political communication. Prime ministerial photo-opportunities, statements in Downing Street and televised press conferences ape the White House. Lloyd George's Garden Suburb has been revived and transformed into a Prime Minister's Department in all but name, equivalent to the White House's West Wing. In 1994, Major employed six special advisers inside Number 10. Blair trebled the number in 1997 and was employing 28 by 2004. Brown ended his tenure with 25. Coalition government has not reversed the trend. By the end of 2011 Cameron employed 31, including those serving Clegg. The number of prime ministerial and deputy prime ministerial special advisers multiplied five-fold in only 17 years (1994–2011), but the number across the rest of Whitehall has not quite doubled.[14]

Blair preferred making decisions informally from a sofa in his 'den' by the Cabinet Room with his close aides, instead of doing so in the Cabinet Room with Ministers. Brown moved his special advisers to Number 12 Downing Street (linked by a corridor to Numbers 10 and 11) and set up a 'hub and spokes' command centre. Media interest in Cameron's Number 10 aides reflects their influence and the subordinate role of most Cabinet Ministers.

Prime ministers have also increased their power by putting more MPs on the government's payroll. The comparison between 1900 and 2000 is 'startling', as Geoffrey Wheatcroft, the journalist and writer, has shown. In 1900, 'the entire salaried ministry' numbered 60, of whom 33 sat in the Commons, together with nine Parliamentary Private Secretaries (PPSs), who are unpaid but count as part of the payroll vote. The Commons payroll vote thus comprised 42 MPs; only 6 per cent of all 670 MPs. By 2000, the salaried ministry had increased to 106, of whom 82 were in the Commons, plus 47 PPSs. The Commons payroll vote had thus risen to 129 MPs; almost 20 per cent of all 650 MPs. And by 2010, the entire ministry had risen to 122, with 97 ministers in the Commons, plus 46 PPSs. The Coalition's Commons payroll vote had increased to 143 MPs; 22 per cent of all 650 MPs.[15]

Yet the government's hold is already stronger than these 'startling' figures imply. Prime ministers have to take notice of parliament when their own MPs threaten to rebel. Although the number of backbench revolts has increased in recent decades, there has been a huge shift in power in the executive's favour on the government's side of the House. In 1900, the payroll vote amounted to less than 10 per cent of Lord Salisbury's 402 MPs; by 2000, it had leapt and accounted for 31 per cent of Blair's 419 MPs; and by 2010 it had climbed again, to represent almost 40 per cent of the Coalition's 363 MPs. The Government's admission in February 2012 that it loses £31 billion a year through fraud and error suggests that parliament has become a feeble watchdog.

The Coalition's plan to reduce the number of MPs threatens to boost the government's power in the Commons further, unless the number of ministers and PPSs is also slashed. The experience of attempts to reform the Lords is not encouraging. Blair's abolition of the automatic right of hereditary peers to sit in the Lords was presented as a democratic step, but the Lords, despite the presence of some independent-minded experts, became swollen with political appointees. While governments persist in forcing masses of ill-considered bills through the Commons, the Lords has a vital role in revising and sometimes making the Commons think again. However, it seems unlikely that an elected second Chamber could resist letting its ambitions roam far beyond merely delaying and revising.

Parliament began as a creature of the King's Council but gradually took on a life of its own. Power has ebbed and flowed between Crown and Parliament since the seventeenth century. By the eighteenth century, parliament was susceptible to Crown patronage; in the mid-nineteenth century, parliament enjoyed its golden age; by the twentieth century, parliament was ruled by party discipline. Today, parliament is threatened by the rise of presidential-style government and the executive's increased grip.

This threat to democracy is exacerbated by an insidious danger. Terror in its various guises – holy, state, political – is ingrained in Westminster's history. But since 9/11 in America and 7/7 in London, the menace of terrorism has taken on a new dimension. The thorough security measures that are necessary to protect elected politicians exact a heavy price on democracy. It is no longer possible to turn up and lobby one's MP in Central Lobby, attend a meeting, or watch the Commons without all the palaver of a security scan and search, and wearing an identity pass. Similarly, the days when prime ministers were seen walking in the street, or travelling on public transport, without armed protection, have long since gone.

Echoes of ancient Westminster persist. The old nickname of 'the Westminster village' implied a vibrant if somewhat gossipy and self-regarding community. Nowadays talk of 'the Westminster bubble' suggests the emergence of a political class insulated from others, self-regarding and self-obsessed, in the manner of medieval monarchs and their courts.

The court feared the mob. Westminster, as the centre of national government, remains the focus of protest, most of it, in modern times, peaceful. The inexcusable desecration of the Cenotaph has no part in any protest and it should be better protected during demonstrations. However all protesters, such as the late anti-war activist, Brian Haw, who camped in Parliament Square for ten years; the opponents of Heathrow Airport's expansion who occupied the roof of the Houses of Parliament; the climate change campaigners who scaled the roof of Westminster Hall; and those who marched against changes to public sector pensions and increased tuition fees, want to make their presence felt and their voices heard, where power resides.

Westminster's long experience of violent protest shows that people's anger at being ruled by a closed elite – monarch and court, landowning magnates, a male establishment – encourages violence. The contempt for politicians expressed after the banking crisis and the scandal over MPs' expenses is a stark warning. Parliament must regain its place as the forum of national debate; as the place where people's anger and grievances can be forcefully and freely expressed; and the means by which the executive is held fully to account.

Ever since the early monarchs settled on the Isle of Thorney, the place has been concerned with power – political and religious – and with its use and abuse. Shelley famously questioned the ultimate purpose of power: ' "My name is Ozymandias, king of kings: / Look on my works, ye Mighty, and despair!" / Nothing beside remains ...' In 1819, he also foresaw Westminster's distant demise in words that bring a sense of humility to the pursuit of power. In his vision of the once-mighty, but long since deserted, capital, Shelley evokes a return to conditions long before the Isle of Thorney was settled: 'When London shall be an habitation of bitterns; when St Paul's and Westminster Abbey shall stand, shapeless and nameless ruins, in the midst of an unpeopled marsh'.[16]

NOTES

Notes to Chapter 1

1 Stanley, 1869, pp.9–10.
2 *A History of Middlesex*, vol. xiii, part 1, 2009, pp.2–3.
3 Ibid., p.3.
4 Stow, 1908, p.105; Stanley, 1869, pp.9–10.
5 Thomas, Cowie and Siddell, 2006, pp.10–11.
6 Lethaby, 1925, p.2.
7 Wheatley, 1891, vol. iii, p.301. Merrifield, 1983, pp.15–16, 31; Hunting, 1981, p.3.
8 Thomas, Cowie and Sidell, 2006, p.138; Hunting, 1981, pp.14, 16; Neale and Brayley, 1818, p.5; Carpenter, 1972, p.5.
9 Thomas, Cowie and Sidell, 2006, p.41; Rosser, 1989, pp.9–11, 97; Mason, 1996, p.5.
10 Harvey, 1977, pp.22–3; *A History of Middlesex*, vol. xiii, part 1, 2009, p.9.
11 Henry of Huntingdon, 2002, pp.17–18.
12 Ibid., 2002, Introduction.
13 Stanley, 1869, p.7; Brayley and Britton, 1836.
14 Thomas, Cowie and Siddell, 2006, p.169; Inwood, 2000, p.49.
15 Brayley and Britton, 1836, p.8; Widmore, 1751, pp.8–9.
16 Mason, 1996, pp.11–12.

Notes to Chapter 2

1 Barlow, 1962, p.44.
2 Barlow, 1970, pp.162–3.
3 Stanley, 1869, pp.14–15.
4 Flete, 1909, p.83; Barlow, 1970, p.166; Mason, 1996, p.148.
5 Barlow, 1962, pp.44–5.
6 Mason, 1996, p.289

7   Gem, 1980, p.39.

8   Luard, 1858, vol. iii, pp.90, 244.

9   *Guardian*, 5 August 2005.

10 Luard, 1858, vol. iii, pp.90, 244.

11 Gem, 1980. pp.55–60.

12 Mason, 1996, p.17; Rosser, 1989, p.252.

13 *St Margaret's Church*, Dean and Chapter of Westminster, p.2; Hunting, 1981, p.41; Rosser, 1989, p.251, fn.

14 Stanley, 1869, p.30; Barlow, 1970, p.244.

15 Barlow, 1970, p.247; Stanley, 1869, pp.30–1.

16 Harmer, 1952, pp.559–60; Barlow, 1970, pp.249–54; Stanley, 1869, pp.32–3.

17 Barlow, 1970, pp.253–4, 264; *Daily Telegraph*, 2 December 2005.

Notes to Chapter 3

1   Brayley and Britton, 1836, p.15.

2   Stanley, 1869, p.45.

3   Strong, 2005, p.40; Douglas, 1964, p.256.

4   Strong, 2005, p.42.

5   Ibid.

6   Stanley, 1869, p.46, fn.

7   Stanley, 1869, p.36, citing Knyghton; Robinson, 1909, pp.4–6.

8   Neale and Brayley, 1818, p.5.

9   Ibid., pp.5–6.

10 Ibid., p.6.

11 Stanley, 1869, pp.21–2.

12 Neale and Brayley, 1818, p.6, fn.; Stanley, 1869, p.23.

Notes to Chapter 4

1   Bates, 1989, p.112.

2   Hennessy, 1989, pp.18–19.

3   Henry of Huntingdon, 2002, pp.47–8.

4   Brayley and Britton, 1836, p.17, quoting Matthew Paris.

5   Enoch Powell likened Westminster Hall to a broadcasting station in the BBC television series, *The Great Palace*, November 1983.

6   Gerhold, 1999, pp.9–12.

7   Barlow, 1983, pp.399–401.

8   Henry of Huntingdon, 2002, p.49.

9   Barlow, 1983, pp.109–10 and 401–2; Henry of Huntingdon, 2002, pp.48–9.

10 Barlow, 1983, pp.105–6, pp.113–4; Brayley and Britton, 1836, pp.22, 416, 445–6; Robinson, 1911a, p.35.

11 See, for example, Mason, 2005.

12 Strong, 2005, pp.43, 51, 62.

13 Hollister, 2001, p.108.

14 Ibid., p.164.

15 Ibid., p.217.

16 Wheatley, 1891, vol. ii, p.22; Hennessy, 1989, p.19.

17 Knowles, 1963, pp.101–2.

18 Widmore, 1743, p.11; Robinson, 1909, p.14; quoted in Harmer, 1952, p.338.

19 Chaplais, 1962, pp.92–7.

20 Harmer, 1952, pp.313–14; Mason, 1996, p.121; Sawyer, 1968, no.774.

21 Flete, 1909, p.24.

22 Chaplais, 1962, p.95.

Notes to Chapter 5

1   Weir, 2000, pp.1, 18, 107–8.

2   Walcott, 1851, pp.5–6, quoting Fitzstephen.

3   Warren, pp.446–67.

4   Stanley, 1869, pp.450–1, quoting Gervase, 1433, and Fuller's Church History, 1176.

5   Thomas, Cowie and Siddell, 2006, pp.56–68.

6   Rosser, 1989, pp.15–16.

7   Legg, 1901, pp.51–3, quoting Roger of Howden, AD 1189.

8   Brayley and Britton, 1836, p.23, citing Roger of Howden; Gillingham, 1999, p.108; Weir, 2000, pp.260–1.

9   Weir, 2000, p.306; Brayley and Britton, 1836, p.23.

10 Hay and Riding, 1996, p.85.

11 Hunting, 1981, p.187; Stanley, 1869, p.57, citing Matthew Paris.

12 Brayley and Britton, 1836, pp.25–6.

13 Carpenter, 1972, p.24.

Notes to Chapter 6

1   Brayley and Britton, 1836, pp.29–32.
2   Ibid., p.45.
3   Ibid., p.37, quoting Matthew Paris.
4   Powicke, vol. i, 1947, pp.85–121.
5   Peter Hennessy, Lecture, Queen Mary College, University of London, 1 February 1994.
6   Brayley and Britton, 1836, pp.38–9, quoting Matthew Paris.
7   Wickham Legg, 1901, pp.61–3; Strong, 2005, p.102.
8   Giles, 1852, p.9.
9   Brayley and Britton, 1836, pp.41–3, quoting Matthew Paris.
10 Powicke, vol. ii, 1947, pp.740–9.
11 Brayley and Britton, 1836, pp.50–1; Carpenter, 1996, p.209.
12 Goodall, in Riding and Riding, 2000, p.56.

Notes to Chapter 7

1   Bradley and Pevsner, 2003, pp.111–12, 116–17, 124.
2   Legg, 1901, p.56; Brayley and Britton, 1836, pp.27–8; Binski, 1995, p.10; Jenkyns, 2004, p.36.
3   Brayley and Britton, 1836, p.52; Oxford DNB; Binski, 1995, pp.1–5.
4   Binski, 1995, p.33; Rosser 1989, p.151; Powicke, vol. II, p.572; Field, 2002, pp.47–8.
5   Rosser, 1989, p.152; Oxford DNB.
6   Oxford DNB; Binski, 1995; pp.15, 29; Jenkyns, 2004, p.12; Brayley and Britton, 1836, p.68.
7   Brayley and Britton, 1836, pp.53, 61–2; Rosser, 1989, p.98.
8   Stanley, 1869, p.136; Paris, 1854, vol. ii, p.241
9   Brayley and Britton, 1836, pp.54–5; Paris, vol. ii, p.735; Oxford DNB, entry on Henry III.
10 Rosser, 1989, pp.97–8; Liber de Antiquis Legibus, s.a. 1248, in H. T. Riley, 1863; Brayley and Britton, 1836, pp.56–7.
11 Brayley and Britton, 1836, p.58, quoting Paris.
12 Field, 2002, p.50; Stanley, 1869, pp.135–6.
13 Brayley and Britton, 1836, pp.73–4.
14 Carpenter, in Grant and Mortimer, 2002, p.46; Brayley and Britton, 1836, p.74.
15 Powicke, 1947, p.589–92; Stanley, 1869, p.137; Oxford DNB.
16 Stanley, 1869, p.133,
17 Malcolm, 'Londinium', 1803–7, quoted by Norton in Grant and Mortimer (eds), 2002, p.7.

18 Bradley and Pevsner, 2003, pp.124, 134.

19 Brayley and Britton, 1836, pp.73–4; Stanley, 1869, pp.133–4.

20 Bradley and Pevsner, 2003, p.155; Field, 2002, p.30; *The Spectator*, Number 329.

21 Foster, 1991, pp.70–1; Scott, 1861, p.46; Stanley, 1869, p.134; Hunting, 1981, p.50.

22 Bradley and Pevsner, 2003, pp.156–7; *Daily Telegraph*, 25 April 2005; Field, 2002, p.30.

23 Scott, 1861, pp.47–8.

24 Binski, 1995, p.10; Foster, 1991, p.2.

25 Binski, 1995, p.97; Oxford DNB.

26 Carpenter, in Grant and Mortimer (eds), 2002, p.44.

27 Jenkyns, 2004, p.38; Foster, 1991, pp.3, 21.

28 Jenkyns, 2004, p.38; Carpenter, in Grant and Mortimer (eds), 2002, p.44; Foster, 1991, pp.3, 164.

29 Strong, 2005, p.98; Icons UK website;

30 Rodwell, 2002, pp.3, 11.

31 Oxford DNB; *Westminster Abbey Guide*, 2005, p.109; Stanley, 1869, pp.434–5.

32 Stanley, 1869, pp.435–6; *The Westminster Abbey Guide*, 2005, p.109.

33 Scott, 1861, pp.32–3; Rodwell, 2002, p.8; Thornbury, 878, vol. iii, chapter liv; Bradley and Pevsner, 2003, p.190.

34 Rodwell, 2002, pp.8–9; Bradley and Pevsner, 2003, pp.190–1.

35 Scott, 1861, pp.36–7; Bradley and Pevsner, 2003, pp.191–2; Rodwell, 2002, pp.4–5, 11.

36 *Guardian*, 1 June 2005; Rodwell, 2002, p.8.

37 Bradley and Pevsner, 2003, p.192; Rodwell, 2002, pp.14–15.

Notes to Chapter 8

1   Carpenter, 1996, pp.382–3; Oxford DNB; Powicke, 1947, vol. i, p.298.

2   Paris, 1853, vol. ii, p.36.

3   Paris, 1853, vol. ii, p.36; Brayley and Britton, 1836, p.62.

4   Paris, 1852, vol. i, p.117.

5   Paris, 1852, vol. i, p.194; Oxford DNB.

6   Paris, 1854, vol. iii, p.225; Oxford DNB.

7   Paris, 1854, vol. iii, p.225; Oxford DNB.

8   Powicke, 1947, p.377; Brayley and Britton, 1836, pp.65–6; Oxford DNB.

9   Paris, 1854, vol. iii, pp.294–5.

10 Powicke, 1947, pp.399–400; Brayley and Britton, 1836, p.67,

11 Brayley and Britton, 1836, pp.68–70.

12 Oxford DNB; Brayley and Britton, 1836, pp.70; Carpenter, 1996, p.393.

13 Carpenter, 1996, p.393; Brayley and Britton, 1836, pp.70–1; Oxford DNB.

14 Brayley and Britton, 1836, p.71; Oxford DNB.

15 Oxford DNB; Brayley and Britton, 1836, pp.72–3.

16 Carpenter, 1996, pp.393–5.

17 Carpenter, in Grant and Mortimer, 2002, pp.38–41; Stanley, 1869, p.139.

18 Cormack, 1981, p.13; Oxford Companion to British History, 1997, p.978.

19 Cormack, 1981, p.13.

20 Thornbury, 1878, vol. iii, p.330; Cormack, 1981, pp.45–6.

21 Prestwich, 1988, pp.134–43, 156–7.

22 Field, 2006, pp.49–50; Oxford DNB.

23 Oxford DNB.

24 Prestwich, 1988, pp.454–7; Oxford DNB.

25 Prestwich, 1988, p.443; Oxford DNB.

Notes to Chapter 9

1 Mason, 1996, pp.56–7; Thornbury, 1878, vol. iii, p.330; Oxford DNB.

2 Stow, 1908, ii, p.101; Thornbury, 1878, vol. iii, p.330.

3 Brayley and Britton, 1836, p.79.

4 Stanley, 1869, p.292; Brayley and Britton, 1836, p.79.

5 Oxford DNB.

6 Stanley, 1869, pp.594–6; Strong, 2005, p.75; Wilkinson, 2006, p.8.

7 Wilkinson, 2006, pp.6, 16–17.

8 Wilkinson, 2006, pp,11, 16–17; *Westminster Abbey Official Guide*, 2005, p.65; Field, 2002, pp.40–1.

9 Wilkinson, 2006, pp.11–13; *Westminster Abbey Official Guide*, 2005, p.65; Field, 2002, pp.40–1.

10 Oxford DNB; Edwards, 1948, pp.296–309; Gerhold, 1999, p.53.

11 Brayley and Britton, 1836, p.9; Oxford DNB; Doherty, 2005, pp.40, 145–6.

12 Joseph Burt in G. G. Scott, 1861, Appendix iii, pp.40–1; *Westminster Abbey Official Guide*, p.109; Doherty, 2005, pp.21, 54.

13 Brayley and Britton, 1836, pp.94–5; Field, 2002, p.41; G. G. Scott, 1861, Appendix iii, p.40.

14 Doherty, 2005, pp.120–8; G. G. Scott, 1861, Appendix iii, pp.41–2; Field, 2002, p.38.

15 Doherty, 2005, p.181; Field, 2002, p.41; Brayley and Britton, 1836, pp.94–5.

16 Field, 2002, p.41; *Guardian*, 5 August 2005; Doherty, 2005, pp.181, 191.

17 Gerhold, 1999, p.53; Oxford DNB.

18 Brayley and Britton, 1836, p.97.

19 Ibid., p.100, quoting 'Froissart's Chronicles', i, p.xxv.

20 Stanley, 1869, pp.144, 275.

21 *Westminster Abbey Official Guide*, 2005, p.46; Ayloffe, 1775, pp.376–413; Prestwich, 1988, p.567; Rowlandson and Combe, 1815.

22 Ackroyd, 1999, p.47–8.

23 Prestwich, 1988, p.566; Oxford DNB; Field, 2006, p.53.

24 Brayley and Britton, 1836, pp.138–9; Oxford DNB; Field, 2006, p.53.

25 Rosser, 1989, p.121.

26 Field, 2006, pp.54–5; Rosser, 1989, p.36; Brayley and Britton, 1836, pp.241–4.

Notes to Chapter 10

1 Thornbury, 1841, vol. iii, pp.123–4; Wheatley, 1891, p.353; Bradley and Pevsner, 2003, p.284.

2 Wheatley, 1891, vol. iii, p.4.

3 Binski, 1986, pp.2–3; Brayley and Britton, 1836, p.420; Field, 2006, p.11.

4 Brayley and Britton, 1836, pp.46, 71–2.

5 Goodall in Riding and Riding, 2000, p.200; Hunting, 1981, p.144; Field, 2006, p.11.

6 Goodall in Riding and Riding, 2000, p.55; Binski, 1986, p.84; Field, 2006, p.11; Hunting, 1981, p.144.

7 Binski, 1986, pp.11, 37, 83, 84, 144; Wheatley, 1891, vol. iii, p.4; Field, 2006, p.11; Brayley and Britton, 1836, pp.418–19; Goodall in Riding and Riding, 2000, p.55.

8 Smith, 1807, p.72.

9 Walcott, 1851, p.226; Smith, 1807, pp.147, 152–63; Bradley and Pevsner, 2003, pp.228–9; Goodall, in Riding and Riding, 2000, pp.56–7; Brayley and Britton, 1836, pp.419–20.

10 Smith, 1807, p.81; Walcott, 1851, Appendix, p.34; Field, 2002, p.29.

11 Wheatley, vol. iii, 1891, p.324; Bradley and Pevsner, 2003, p.229.

12 Jay, 2000, p.149.

13 Smith, 1807, p.175; Brayley and Britton, 1836, pp.181–5.

14 Brayley and Britton, 1836, pp.185–6.

15 Brayley and Britton, 1836, pp.170–1; Field, 2003, p.14; Smith, 1807, pp.82, 164.

16 Smith, 1807, pp.152–63.

Notes to Chapter 11

1 Wheatley, 1891, vol. iii, pp.532–3; Hunting, 1981, p.78; Stow, 1908, p.104.

2 Brayley and Britton, 1836, p.196; Taylor, 1996, p.8.

3 Taylor, 1996, pp.5, 7–8; Goodall, in Riding and Riding, 2000, p.58; Field, 2002, p.60; Rosser, 1989, p.58.

4 Taylor, 1996, pp.24–6; Bradley and Pevsner, 2003, p.232.

5 Wheatley, 1891, vol. iii, p.6; Field, 2002, p.17.

6 Field, 2002, pp.41–2; *Westminster Abbey Official Guide*, 2005, p.101; Bradley and Pevsner, 2002, pp.114, 188–9.

7 Field, 2002, pp.42–4; *Westminster Abbey Official Guide*, 2005, p.84.

8 Thornbury, 1897, p.458; Lethaby, 1925, cited in Bradley and Pevsner, 2002, p.196.

9 Armitage Robinson, 1911, p.9; Rosser, 1989, pp.66–9. Harvey, 2002, p.33.

10 Armitage Robinson, 1911, p.9; Rosser, 1989, pp.66–9; Walcott, 1897, p.273; Thornbury, 1841, pp.488–9; Wheatley, 1891, vol. ii, pp.88–90,

11 Geoffrey Chaucer, *The Canterbury Tales*, The Prologue, lines 200–6; Philippa Patrick, 'In Search of Friar Tuck', in *Current Archaeology*, No. 198, July/August 2005, p.307.

12 Harvey, 1993, pp.56–61; Field, 2002, p.64.

13 Harvey, 1993, pp.156–61; Walcott, 1851, p.320; Stanley, 1869, pp.396–7; Field, 2002, p.56–8.

14 Stanley, 1869, pp.396–8; Watson, 1993, p.37; Tanner, 1969, p.19; Hunting, 1981, pp.64–5; Walcott, 1851, p.89.

15 Hunting, 1981, p.63; Mason, 1996, p.343; Rosser, 1989, pp.44–7, 60–1.

16 Harvey, 2002, p.xxvi, p.2; Stanley, 1869, p.398; Pearce, 1916, p.ix.

17 Ormrod, 1990, p.164; Field, 2006, pp.52–3.

18 House of Commons website; Brayley and Britton, pp.219–20, 241–4; Field, 2006, p.55; Rosser, 1989, p.39.

19 Myers, 1969, vol. iv, pp.453–4, no.266, Passus IV, extracts from lines 24–93.

20 Brayley and Britton, 1836, pp.232–4; Oxford DNB.

21 Ormrod, 1990, p.35; Field, 2006, pp.57.–8.

22 Brayley and Britton, 1836, p.240.

23 Saul, 1997, pp.22–3; Litten, in Harvey and Mortimer, 1994, pp.4–5, 31

Notes to Chapter 12

1 *Westminster Abbey Official Guide*, 2005, pp.14–15; Saul, 1997, pp.238–9.

2 *Westminster Abbey Official Guide*, 2005, p.111; Hunting, 1981, p.189; Legg, 1901, pp.81–130.

3 Strong, 2005, pp.91–3; Legg, 1901, pp.147, 166; Saul, 1997, p.25.

4 Strong, 2005, p.93; Saul, 1997, p.25.

5 Legg, 1901, pp.141–2, 160–1; Stanley, 1869, p.70; Strong, 2005, pp.103–4.

6 Legg, 1901, pp.141–61; Stanley, 1869, p.70; Strong, 2005, pp.103–4.

7 Stanley, 1869, pp.150–1.

8 Litten, in Harvey and Mortimer, 1994, pp.5, 37; *Westminster Abbey Official Guide*, 2005, pp.47–8; Bradley and Pevsner, 2003, p.159.

9 Gerhold, 1999, pp.17–18; Bradley and Pevsner, 2003, p.159.

10 Gerhold, 1999, pp.15, 36.

11 Gerhold, 1999, pp.17–18; Rosser, 1989, p.36; Bradley and Pevsner, 2003, p.159; Read in Riding and Riding, 2000, p.65.

12 Brayley and Britton, 1836, pp.437–8; Gerhold, 1999, pp.19, 25; Bradley and Pevsner, 2003, p.230.

13 Gerhold, 1999, pp.19–20; Bradley and Pevsner, 2003, p.230.

14 Gerhold, 1999, pp.17–18, 21–3; Bradley and Pevsner, 2003, p.159.

15 Saul, 1997, p.422; Stow, 1908, vol. ii, p.117.

16 Stow, 1908, vol. ii, p.116.

17 Brayley and Britton, 1836, p.288.

18 Stanley, 1869, pp.416–17; Act V, Scene VI, line 19.

19 Scott, 1861, pp.82–3; *Henry IV, Part II*, Act V, Scene V, lines 232–40.

Notes to Chapter 13

1 Westlake, 1914, p.19.

2 Stanley, 1869, pp.446–7.

3 Stow, quoted in Clay, 1914, p.153; Tanner, 1969, p.93; Oxford DNB.

4 Clay, 1914, p.154.

5 Besant, 1895, pp.102–8.

6 Tanner, 1969, p.93.

7 *Westminster Abbey Official Guide*, 2005, p.85.

8 Rosser 1989, pp.218–19.

9 Walcott, 1851, p.81; Thornbury, 1841, vol. iii, p.488; Rosser, 1989, p.66; Bradley and Pevsner, 2003, p.272.

10 Stanley, 1869, pp.404–5; Loades, in Knighton and Mortimer, 2003, p.75.

11 Rosser, 1989, pp.218–20; Thornbury, 1841, vol. iii, p.483–6; Walcott, 1851, pp.70–1; J. T. Smith, 1807, p.27.

12 Stanley, 1869, pp.407–9; *Westminster Abbey Official Guide*, 2005, p.91.

13 Field, 2002, p.48.

14 Thornbury, 1841, vol. iii, p.484.

15 Jones et al., 2003, pp.286–9.

16 Ibid., passim.

17 Stanley, 1869, p.410; Baldwin, 1938, p.47; Okerlund, 2005, p.119.

18 Okerlund, 2005, p.122; Baldwin, 2002, p.47; *Westminster Abbey Official Guide*, 2005, p.60.

19 Stanley, 1869, pp.410–11; Baldwin, 2002, p.105–7.

20 Stanley, 1869, p.411; Baldwin, 2002, p.103.

21 Stanley, 1869, pp.411–12; Baldwin, 2002, pp.103–6.

22 Okerlund, 2005, pp.224–6; Stanley, 1869, p.412; Baldwin, 2002, pp.103–6.

23 Stanley, 1869, p.412.

24 Okerlund, 2005, p.245.

25 Tanner, 1969, p.153; *Westminster Abbey Official Guide*, 2005, p.69.

26 Tanner, 1969, pp.153–65.

27 Baldwin, 2007, reported in *Daily Telegraph*, 27 May 2007.

28 Stanley, 1869, p.412; Thornbury, 1841, vol. iii, p.484; Loades, in Knighton and Mortimer, 2003, pp.79–81.

29 Loades, in Knighton and Mortimer, 2003, pp.76, 89.

Notes to Chapter 14

1   Rosser, 1989, p.214; Jay, 2000, p.151.

2   Painter, 1976, p.101.

3   Tanner, 1969, p.171; Painter, 1976, pp.82–3.

4   Rosser, 1989, p.213; Painter, 1976, pp.121–2.

5   Painter, 1976, pp.141–4.

6   Rosser, 1989, p.273; Holland, 1993, p.28.

7   Rosser, 1989, pp.157–8, 163–73; pp.214–15; *St Margaret's*, Dean and Chapter of Westminster Abbey, p.8.

8   Oxford DNB.

9   Strong, 2005, p.120, citing Froissart.

10 Stanley, 1869, p.74.

11 Stanley, 1869, p.74.

12 Oxford DNB.

13 Thornbury, 1891, vol. iii, p.538.

14 Thurley, 1992, p.36; Loades, 1989, p.91; Channel 4, www.channel4.com, 'The Worst Jobs in History'.

15 Colvin, vol. iv, p.287.

16 Strong, 2005, p.121.

17 Tanner, 1969, pp.110–11; Stanley, 1869, pp.160–1; Lindley, in Tatton-Brown and Mortimer, 2003, p.259.

18 Stow in Field, 2002, p.69; Tanner, 1969, pp.191–2.

19 Condon, in Tatton-Brown and Mortimer, 2003, p.64.

20 Bradley and Pevsner, 2003, p.123.

21 Lindley, in Tatton-Brown and Mortimer, 2003, pp.94, 276; Bradley and Pevsner, 2003, pp.123, 137.

22 Wilkinson, 2007, pp.21–3, 38–9; Lindley, in Tatton-Brown and Mortimer, 2003, pp.266, 280; Tracy, in Tatton-Brown and Mortimer, 2003, p.227.

23 *Westminster Abbey Official Guide*, 1997, p.72.
24 Little, in Tatton-Brown and Mortimer, 2003, p.46; Pepys, vol. ix, p.457.

Notes to Chapter 15

1 Stow, vol. ii, 1908, p.117.
2 Scarisbrick, 1997, p.502.
3 Sheppard, 1902, pp.185–6.
4 Ibid.
5 Oxford DNB.
6 Bradley and Pevsner, 2003, p.243.
7 Thurley, 1999, pp.19, 25–7, 1996, p.36.
8 Scarisbrick, 1997, p.154.
9 Thurley, 1999, p.33.
10 Ibid., pp.29–36.
11 Thurley, 1999, p.37; Ives, 2004, p.128; Oxford DNB.
12 Scarisbrick, 1997, p.502; Thurley, 1999, p.33.
13 Act IV, Scene I.
14 Colvin, vol. iv, pp.287–8.
15 Sheppard, 1902, p.2.
16 Merritt, 2005, p.25; Rosser, 1989, p.151; Thurley, 1993, p.39.
17 Ives, 2004, p.165.
18 Thurley, 1998, p.12; Ives, 2004, pp.162, 168; Starkey, 2003, p.475.
19 Oxford DNB.
20 Pollard, vol. 6, 1903, pp.11–18; Ives, 2004, p.176–8; Colvin, vol. iv, pp.290–1.
21 Pollard, vol. 6, 1903, pp.11–18; Ives, 2004, p.176–8.
22 Pollard, vol. 6, 1903, p.18; Strong, 2005, p.162; Ives, 2004, p.178.
23 Ives, 2004, pp.178–80; Strong, 2005, p.174; Pollard, vol. 6, 1903, p.19.
24 Thurley, 1993, pp.39, 1999, p.45.
25 Colvin, vol. iv, p.301; Foreman, 1995, pp.8–9; Strong, 2005, p.122.
26 Foreman, 1995, pp.11, 170–1.
27 Colvin, vol. iv, p.303; Bradley and Pevsner, 2003, pp.259–60; Thurley, 1998, p.12; Foreman, 1995, pp.11, 170–1.
28 Colvin, vol. iv, pp.303–4; Foreman, 1995, p.11; Thurley, 1998, p.12; Young, 1987, p.119; Pollard, vol 6, 1903, p.19.
29 Foreman, 1995, p.6.; Thurley, 1993, p.54; Brayley and Britton, 1836, p.356.

Notes to Chapter 16

1   Gerhold, 1999, pp.53–4; Ackroyd, 1999, p.388.

2   Ackroyd, 1999, p.390.

3   Ives, 2004, pp.309–10; Loades, 2004, p.19.

4   Ives, 2004, pp.339–40.

5   Wriothesely, 1857–77, vol. i, pp.99–100.

6   Strype, quoted in Oxford DNB.

7   Hume, 1889, pp.97–9.

8   Ibid., pp.98–9.

9   Oxford DNB.

10 Merritt, 2005, p.28.

11 Knighton, in Knighton and Mortimer, 2003, p.19; Hunting, 1981, p.70; Merritt, 2005, pp.9, 25; Field, 2002, p.79; Stanley, 1886, p.397.

12 Knighton, in Knighton and Mortimer, 2003, pp.7–8, 17; Merritt, 2005, pp.27–8.

13 Stanley, 1886, p.395; Field, 2002, p.81; Rosser, 1989, p.208; Lehmberg, in Knighton and Mortimer, 2003, pp.94–5. Merritt, 2005, p.28.

14 Thurley, 1999, pp.54–7, 173; 1998, p.13.

15 Thurley, 1999, pp.59, 61, 67, 1993, pp.60, 200; Colvin, vol. iv, 1982, plate 23A.

16 Thurley, 1998, p.13, 1999, p.60; Colvin, vol. iv, 1982, pp.301–2.

17 Thurley, 1993, pp.113–22 *passim*.

18 Ibid., pp.197–8.

19 Waterhouse, 1994, plates 5 and 6, pp.20–1.

20 Hutchinson, 2005, pp.152–5; Thurley, 1993, pp.176–7, 1999, p.139.

21 Thurley, 1993, p.212.

22 Southworth, 1998, p.74; Hutchinson, 2005, p.147; Colvin, vol. iv, pp.314–15.

23 Thurley, 1993, pp.212–40 *passim*.

24 Ibid., p.150.

25 Rosser, 1989, p.41; David Starkey, *Sunday Telegraph*, 19 December 2004; Hutchinson, 2005, pp.142, 149–50; Thurley, 1999, p.139.

26 Hutchinson, 2005, pp.13–14, 205–10, 218–21; Anglo, 1969, p.281; Scarisbrick, 1997, p.496.

Notes to Chapter 17

1   *Hansard*, 28 October 1943, col.403.

2   Hutchinson, 2005, pp.13–14, 221.

3   Jordan, 1968, pp.68, 409, 534; Hoak, in Knighton and Mortimer, 2003, pp.130, 148–9; Strong, 2005, pp.199–200.

4   Rosser, 1989, p.275; Merritt, 2005, p.44.

5   Stanley, 1886, pp.397–8; Robertson, 1849, pp.72–3.

6   Strype, quoted in Thornbury, 1841, vol. iii, p.459.

7   Hastings, 1955, p.2; Clare Wilkinson, 2002, pp.141–65.

8   Jones, 1983, p.49.

9   Colvin, vol. iv, pp.61n, 291–2; Hawkyard, 2002, pp.76–7.

10 Loades, 2004, pp.107–10; Jordan, 1970, pp.45, 96, 240, 468.

11 Thomas, 1971, p.1; Field, 2002, pp.76–7.

12 Hastings, 1950, p.81, quoting Neale, J. E., 1950, p.364.

13 Field, 2002, p.77; Jones, 1983, p.56.

Notes to Chapter 18

1   Stanley, 1886, pp.396–7; Knighton, in Knighton and Mortimer, 2003, p.6; Carpenter, 1971, p.118; Widmore, quoted in Thornbury, 1841, vol. iii, p.459.

2   Jordan, 1968, p.512; *Westminster Abbey Official Guide*, 1997, p.71.

3   Oxford DNB.

4   Loades, 2004, p.139.

5   Ibid. pp.166–7.

6   Underhill, 1553, in Pollard, 1903, pp.186–7.

7   Ibid.

8   Underhill, 1553, in Pollard, 1903, pp.190–1.

9   Westlake, 1914, p.42.

10 Machyn, 1848, pp.76, 84.

11 Machyn, 1848, pp.56, 72–4, 86; Merritt, 2005, pp.56–7.

12 Strype, quoted in Brayley and Britton, 1836, fn, 363–4.

13 Stanley, 1886, p.400.

14 Machyn, 1848, p.85; Thornbury, 1841, vol. iii, p.489; Merritt, 2005, p.42; Hunting, 1981, p.46.

15 Stanley, 1886, p.399; Machyn, 1848, pp.140–1; Merritt, 2005, pp.57–9.

16 Machyn, 1848, pp.118–19; Stanley, 1886, pp.401–2.

17 Machyn, 1848, p.178; Field, 2002, p.83

18 *Calendar of State Papers.*

19 Young, 1987, pp.84–6, 107, 121; Merritt, 2005, p.161.

20 Sheppard, 1902, p.73; Stow, 1608, vol. ii, p.102; Young, 1987, pp.118, 121–2.

21 Oxford DNB.

22 Ridley, 1987, p.78; Strong, 2005, p.209; *Calendar of State Papers.*

23 Stanley, 1886, p.405; Brayley and Britton, 1836, p.365.

24 Tanner, 1969, pp.110–12; Carpenter, 1972, pp.451–6.

25 *St Margaret's*, Dean and Chapter of Westminster Abbey, p.3; Carpenter, 1972, p.265; Merritt, 2005, pp.128, 326.

26 Field, 2002, p.86.

27 Merritt, 2005, pp.75–8; 129.

28 Oxford DNB; Journal of the House of Commons, 1566; Ridley, 1987, pp.146–7, 301.

29 Ridley, 1987, p.210; Oxford DNB.

Notes to Chapter 19

1 *Calendar of State Papers.*

2 Cobbett's *State Trials*; Williams, 1964, pp.233–4.

3 Oxford DNB.

4 *State Trials*; Oxford DNB.

5 Oxford DNB; wikipedia.

6 Dan Jones, *Spectator*, 9 May 2009.

7 Ridley, 1987, p.332; Goodman quoted in Thornbury, 1841, vol. iii, p.345.

8 *Westminster Abbey Official Guide*, 2005, p.68.

9 Lecture, Oxford, 24 March 2003.

10 Fraser, 2005, pp.50–1; Oxford DNB.

11 Fraser, 2005, p.107.

12 Oxford DNB; Fraser, 2005, p.117.

13 Oxford DNB; Fraser, 2005, pp.122–3.

14 Fraser, 2005, pp.143–5, 159; Field, 2006, p.98; Oxford DNB.

15 *Timewatch*, BBC2, 2005; 'The Gunpowder Plot: Exploding the Legend', ITV, 2005.

16 Oxford DNB; Fraser, 2005, pp.180–8 *passim*.

17 Fraser, 2005, pp.189–99 *passim*; Oxford DNB.

18 Oxford DNB.

19 Merritt, 2005, p.334; Fraser, 2005, pp.201–3.

20 Fraser, 2005, pp.202–3; Brayley and Britton, 1836, p.378.

21 Hunting, 1981, p.149; House of Commons Journal, 5 November 1605.

22 House of Lords Journal, 9 November 1605.

23 Saunders, 1951, p.139; Fraser, 2005, pp.211–15, 264.

24 Saunders, 1951, p.144.

25 Stanley, 1869, pp.74–5; Jones, 1983, pp.56–7.

Notes to Chapter 20

1   Lee, 1990, pp.109, 149; Saunders, 1951, pp,145–6.
2   Peck, 1991, p.141; Field, 2006, p.94.
3   Lee, 1990, pp.155, 252.
4   Field, 2006, pp.94–5; Lee, 1990, p.93, quoting Gardiner, 1887–91.
5   Lee, 1990, p.242.
6   Saunders, 1951, pp.151–2.
7   Oxford DNB.
8   Trevelyan, 2002, pp.541–3.
9   Ibid, pp.545–6.
10 Ibid., pp.551–3.
11 Thurley, 2008, pp.48–50.
12 Ibid., p.50.
13 Lee, 1990, p.131; Trevelyan, 2002, pp.460–1.
14 Bradley and Pevsner, 2003, p.239; Thurley, 2008, p.51.
15 Thurley, 2008, p.52, 1999, pp.84, 94.
16 Bradley and Pevsner, 2003, p.241; Thurley, 2008, p.52.
17 Bradley and Pevsner, 2003, p.240; Thurley, 2008, p.54.
18 Thurley, 2008, pp.60–1.
19 Ibid., pp.56–9.

Notes to Chapter 21

1   Lee, 1990, p.247; Whitelocke, 1732, quoted in Merritt, 2005, p.293.
2   Hunting, 1981, pp.185–90.
3   Clarendon, quoted in Brayley and Britton, 1836, p.383, fn.
4   Donne, Satire 4, lines 75–7.
5   Merritt, 2005, pp.167–8.
6   Ibid., pp.154–9, 187, 236.
7   Thurley, 1999, pp.91–8; Brotton, 2006, pp.85–107, 227.
8   Sargeaunt, 1898, pp.65–8; Saunders, 1951, pp.158–60.
9   Quoted in Silvester, 1996, p.299.
10 Field, 2006, pp.94, 104–5.
11 Jennings, 1899, p.89
12 Field, 2006, p.106; Lee, 1990, p.258; Oxford DNB; quoted in Rushworth, 1721.
13 Quoted in Brayley and Britton, 1836, pp.385–6.
14 Ibid; Field, 2006, p.106.

15 Oxford DNB; Field, 2006, p.106; quoted in Brayley and Britton, 1836, pp.385–6.

16 Thurley, 1999, p.97; Merritt, 2005, p.178.

17 Brotton, 2006, pp.203–5 Thornbury, 1841, vol. iii, p.124; Westlake, 1914, pp.53–4; Thurley, 1999, p.98; Field, 2006, p.97; Stanley, 1868, pp.482–3.

18 Brotton, 2006, p.205; Stanley, 1868, p.483; Field, 2006, p.97.

19 Sir Philip Warwick, 1701, quoted in Silvester, 1996, p.299.

20 Wedgwood, 1964, pp.38–44.

21 Ibid, pp.82–92.

22 Gerhold, 1999, p.55.

23 Gerhold, 1999, p.55; Wedgwood, 1964, pp.108–10, 123–6; Brayley and Britton, 1836, pp.386–7.

24 This account of Charles I's trial and execution draws primarily on Brayley and Britton, 1836, pp.386ff; Sheppard, 1902, pp.205ff; Wedgwood, 1964, pp.120ff; and the Oxford DNB.

25 *The Death Warrant of King Charles I*, Historic Parliamentary Documents Reproduction No. 7.

26 Thurley, 2008, p.76; Thornbury, 1841, vol. iii, p.128; Wedgwood, 1964, pp.209–10.

Notes to Chapter 22

1 Hay and Riding, 1996, p.45; Field, 2006, p.226; Foot, 1981, passim.

2 Oxford DNB.

3 Ibid.; Fraser, 1973, p.418.

4 Ludlow, quoted in Silvester, 1996, pp.146–8; Oxford DNB; Fraser, 1973, pp.419–22.

5 Sheppard, 1902, p.239.

6 Ibid., pp.239–44; Alan Marshall, *History Today*, February 2003, pp.20–5; Oxford DNB.

7 Sheppard, 1902, p.388, quoting Prestwich, 1787.

8 Little, in Harvey and Mortimer, 1994, p.12.

9 Pepys, 7 February 1660, vol. i, p.45.

10 McMains, 2000, pp.131–75 passim; Cormack, 1981, p.58.

11 Evelyn, 29 May 1660, vol. iii, p.246; Sheppard, 1902, p.318.

12 Wilson, 2003, p.159; Pepys, 23 April 1661, vol. i, pp.84–6.

13 Pepys, vol. x, p.15; Tomalin, 2002, p.67.

14 Pepys, vol. i, p.cxxvii.

15 Oxford DNB; Hennessy, 1989, pp.24–5.

16 Hennessy, 1989, p.24; Simon Hurst, email to author, October 2008.

17 Hunting, 1981, p.171; Pepys, 11–14 October 1660, vol. i, pp.263–6.

18 Wilson, 2003, p.144; Pepys, vol. x, p.308; Oxford DNB.

19 Harvey and Mortimer, 1994, p.95, quoting Pepys, 13 July 1663, vol. iv, p.95.

20 Evelyn, 1 March 1671, vol. iii, p.573.

21 Thurley, 1999, p.125; Wilson, 2003, pp.277, 334.

22 Pepys, November 1663–September 1665, vols. iii–v *passim*; Wilson, 2003, pp.171–2; Oxford DNB.

23 Wilson, 2003, pp.171–2; Oxford DNB.

24 Mackintosh, 1968, p.37.

25 Ibid., 1968, pp.37–8.

26 Ibid.

27 Oxford DNB.

28 Quoted in the Oxford English Dictionary.

29 Ibid.

Notes to Chapter 23

1   Evelyn, 1955, vol. iv, pp.416, 418.

2   Shepherd, 1990, p.18; Thurley, 2008, p.98.

3   Shepherd, 1990, pp.18–23.

4   Thurley, 2008, p.100; Shepherd, 1990, pp.23–4.

5   Shepherd, 1990, pp.24–34.

6   Shepherd, 1990, p.35; Beddard, 1988, pp.25–7.

7   Shepherd, 1990, p.36.

8   Sheppard, 1902, pp.260–1.

9   Shepherd, 1990, pp.36–7; Beddard, 1988, pp.32–4.

10 Shepherd, 1990, p.37.

11 Beddard, 1988, pp.44–50.

12 Shepherd, 1990, p.38; Thurley, 2008, p.102; Beddard, 1988, pp.59–60; Oxford DNB; Miller, 1977, p.208 .

13 Shepherd, 1990, p.38.

14 Stanley, 1886, p.94.

15 Harris, 2006b, pp.276–7, 347–8.

16 Quoted in Sheppard, 1902, pp.263–4.

17 Luttrell, quoted in Thurley, 1999, p.142; Evelyn, vol. v, p.47; Thurley, 2008, p.103.

18 Shepherd, 1990, pp.79–80.

19 Harris, 2006b, p.491.

20 Ibid., p.492.

21 Mackintosh, 1968, pp.43–6.

22 Van der Zee, 1988, p.388; Oxford DNB.

23   Macaulay, quoted in Stanley, 1886, pp.165–6; Evelyn, vol. v, p.204.

24   Macaulay, ibid; Oxford DNB; Harvey and Mortimer, 1994, pp.116–17.

25   Thurley, 2008, p.105; Fiennes, 1982, p.224; Ned Ward, 1955, p.154.

Notes to Chapter 24

1   Thurley, 1999, p.144; 2004, p.38.

2   Celia Fiennes, www.visionofbritain.org.uk, London, Part 2, Westminster.

3   Hay and Riding, 1996, p.36; Thomas, 1971, p.2.

4   Saunders, 1951, pp.259–61; Oxford DNB.

5   Ross, 1982, pp.34–6; Oxford DNB.

6   Ross, 1982, p.210.

7   Ibid., pp.199, 201–5.

8   *Spectator*, 30 March 1711

9   Ross, 1982, p.50, Oxford DNB.

10   Bradley and Pevsner, 2003, pp.710, 713; Hague, 2004, pp.224–5.

11   St John's Church website, history; Watson, 1993, p.87; Bradley and Pevsner, 2003, pp.679–81.

12   Oxford DNB; Bradley and Pevsner, 2003, pp.699–700; deadpubs.co.uk

13   Jay, 2000, pp.201–8.

14   Pearce, 2007, pp.218–22.

15   Strong, 2005, p.407.

16   Ibid., pp.4–5.

17   Trowles and Reynolds, in Sagovsky and Trowles, 2006; *The Spectator*, letter, Robert Davies, 2 July 2005.

18   Voltaire, 1722–34, Letter xxiii, google.books.com; Trowles and Reynolds, in Sagovsky and Trowles, 2006.

Notes to Chapter 25

1   *Parliamentary History*, 13 February 1741, cols. 1232, 1385.

2   Minney, 1963, pp.25–33.

3   *The Prime Ministers*, BBC Radio 4, 24 February 2009.

4   Bradley and Pevsner, 2003, pp.262–4.

5   Minney, 1963, pp.25–33, 51–2.

6   Wheatley, 1891, vol. iii, section on Craig's Court.

7   Simon Thurley, Simon Hurst, emails to author, October 2008.

8   Hennessy, 1989, p.26; Foreman, 1995, pp.46–7.

9   Foreman, 1995, pp.46–7; Bradley and Pevsner, 2003, pp.261–2.

10 Baker, 1995, pp.24–5.

11 *The Prime Ministers*, BBC Radio 4, 24 February 2009; Gay, Fables II, 13, lines 99–100.

12 Gay, Fables II, 14, lines 63–6; *Parliamentary History*, 3 February 1741, col. 1387.

13 *Parliamentary History*, 13 March 1734, col. 475; *The Prime Ministers*, BBC Radio 4, 24 February 2009.

14 *The Prime Ministers*, BBC Radio 4, 24 February 2009.

Notes to Chapter 26

1   Bradley and Pevsner, 2003, pp.122–3, 207; Jenkyns, 2004, pp.135–6; Carpenter and Gentleman, 1987, p.31.

2   Bradley and Pevsner, 2003, pp.250–7; Foreman, 1995, pp.45–57; Oxford DNB.

3   Walker, 1979, pp.14, 27–43 passim.

4   Oxford DNB; Walker, 1979, pp.44–5, 50–2, 245.

5   Walker, 1979, pp.55–73; Saunders, 1951, p.252.

6   Walker, 1979. pp.75, 82–7, 225–6.

7   Pearce, 2008, pp.394–5; Walker, 1979, pp.105–44.

8   Links, 1994, pp.162–88.

9   Links, 1994, pp.162–88; Walpole, 1840, ii, p.324

10 Walker, 1979, pp.169–208.

11 Foreman, 1995, pp.40–2, 51; Bradley and Pevsner, 2003, pp.275–6.

12 Thurley, 2004, p.38.

13 Boswell, 1951, 26 November 1763.

14 Ibid., 22 March – 26 November 1763.

15 Walpole, 1840, i, pp.108–9; Little in Harvey and Mortimer, 1994, pp.16, 130, 143.

16 Boswell, 1951, 13 November 1760.

17 Cocke in Harvey and Mortimer, 1994, p.324; Trowles, 1997, p.71; Stanley, 1886, p.183.

18 Grant Duff, 1901, vol. i, p.235.

19 Walpole, 1840, vol. iv, p.172.

20 Ibid., p.176; Gray, 1853, pp.269–77.

21 Stanley, 1886, p.101.

Notes to Chapter 27

1   Speck, 1977, p.16.

2   Jarrett, 1965, p.40; Gilmour, 1992, pp.147–9.

3   MacDonagh, 1920, pp.90–2.

4   Sparrow, 2003, pp.10–12.

5   *Parliamentary History*, vol. 10, 13 April 1738, cols. 809–10.

6   MacDonagh, 1920, pp.135–40, 162; Life of Johnson, 1791.

7   Gilmour, 1992, pp.85–9.

8   Gilmour, 1992. p.73; Saunders, 1951, p.265.

9   MacDonagh, 1920, pp.164–2.

10 Gilmour, 1992, p.303; Oxford DNB; Pottle, J. ed., 1951, 6 May 1763.

11 Whiteley, 1996, p.80, King to North, 23 Jan 1770.

12 BBC Radio 4, *The Prime Ministers*, 3 March 2009.

13 MacDonagh, 1920, pp.186–226, Sparrow, 2003, p.22.

14 MacDonagh, 1920, pp.242–8.

15 Ibid., pp.246–52; 257.

16 MacDonagh, 1920, pp.258–82; Sparrow, 2003, p.23.

17 MacDonagh, 1920, pp.282–3, 308–9.

18 Baker, 1995, p.49.

19 *Parliamentary History*, 14 March 1774.

20 A contemporary quoted in de Castro, 1926, p.14.

21 Eye-witnesses quoted in de Castro, 1926, pp.34–5.

22 de Castro, 1926, pp.34–7.

23 Dickens, *Barnaby Rudge*, Penguin, 2003, pp.408–12; de Castro, 1926, pp.37–8.

24 de Castro, 1926, pp.39–46.

25 de Castro, 1926, pp.79–80; Hibbert, pp.67–8.

26 de Castro, 1926, pp.103–10.

27 Wheatley, 1884; Minney, 1963, pp.110–11.

28 Hibbert, 1958, pp.97–102.

29 Minney, 1963, pp.110–11; Hibbert, 1958, p.102.

30 Hibbert, 1958, pp.112, 134; Gilmour, 1992, p.370.

31 Wheatley, 1884, vol. ii, p.138.

Notes to Chapter 28

1   Englefield, 1995, p.78.

2   J. S. Harford, 1864, quoted in Silvester, 1996, p.498.

3   C. P. Moritz, 13 June 1782; Joseph Pearson, 1793, quoted in Silvester, 1996, pp.549, 586–7.

4   P. D. G. Thomas, 1971, p.148; Bentley, 1836, vol. iii, p.48; MacDonagh, 1902, p.10.

5 Jennings, 1899, pp.147–8; Grant, 1836, quoted in Silvester, 1996, pp.471–2.

6 Englefield, 1995, p.80.

7 Ibid., p.81.

8 C. P. Moritz, Letter to a friend, 13 June 1783, in Silvester, 1996, p.498.

9 Hague, 2004, pp.102–3; Seldon, 1999, pp.16–17.

10 Hague, 2004, pp.162–4; Bentley, 1836, vol. iii, p.281.

11 Hague, 2004, pp.171–3.

12 Ayling, 1991, p.134; Hague, 2004, p.173; Corfield, Green and Harvey, 2001, pp.163–8.

13 Ayling, 1991, p.135; Foreman, 1998, pp.144–51; Hague, 2004, p.172.

14 Charles Burney, 1785, *An Account of the Musical Performances in Westminster Abbey and the Pantheon, May 26th, 27th, 29th & June the 3rd & 5th 1784 in Commemoration of Handel.*

15 William Weber, 1989, pp.43–69.

Notes to Chapter 29

1 Mathias, 1983, p.39.

2 Hennessy, 2000, p.46.

3 Hague, 2004, p.219.

4 *The Rolliad*, 1784–5; Hague, 2004, pp.388–94.

5 Hague, 2004, pp.230–4.

6 Gerhold, 1999, pp.61–2, 64; Bradley and Pevsner, 2003, pp.213–14.

7 d'Arblay, 1904–5, vol. iii, pp.408ff; Saunders, 1951, pp.267–8.

8 d'Arblay, 1904–5, vol. iii, p.448.

9 Quoted in Hague, 2004, p.258.

10 Hague, 2004, pp.258–9.

11 Ibid., p.306.

Notes to Chapter 30

1 *Parliamentary History*, 28 December 1792, col. 189.

2 Hague, 2004, pp.433–4.

3 The original cartoons can be seen at The Bank of England Museum.

4 Hague, 2004, p.370; Place, 1972, pp.145–6

5 Hague, 2004, p.378; Corfield, Green and Harvey, 2001, pp.177, 182.

6 Sawyer, 2003; Dale, 1956, p.121.

7 Seldon, 1999, p.18.

8   Quoted in Hastings, 1950, p.110.

9   Sawyer, 2003; Dale, 1956, pp.121–3.

10 Smith, 1807, p.vi; Dale, 1956, pp.121–2.

11 Sparrow, 2003, pp.29–30; quoted in MacDonagh, 1920, pp.299, 307.

12 Quoted on the official Wordsworth website.

13 MacDonagh, 1920, pp.309–10; Sparrow, 2003, p.31.

14 *Croker Papers*, vol. ii, 1984.

15 Andrew Graham-Dixon, *Sunday Telegraph*, 9 January 2005.

16 Hill, 1836, pp.13–14.

17 Hague, 2004, pp.565, 578; Silvester, 1996, p.469.

Notes to Chapter 31

1   Jerdan, 1852, vol. i, pp.133–4; *Morning Chronicle*, 12 May 1812; *The Times*, 12 May 1812.

2   Ibid.

3   Jerdan, 1852, vol. i, p.134.

4   *Proceedings of the Old Bailey*, 13 May 1812; *Morning Chronicle*, 12 May 1812.

5   *Old Bailey*, 13 May 1812; Jerdan, 1852, vol. i, p.135.

6   *Old Bailey*, 13 May 1812.

7   Jerdan, 1852, vol. i, pp.135–6; *Old Bailey*, 13 May 1812.

8   Jerdan, 1852, vol. i, pp.135; *Old Bailey*, 13 May 1812.

9   Jerdan, 1852, vol. i, pp.136–7.

10 Jerdan, 1852, vol. i, p.137; *Hansard*, 11 May 1812, col. 167.

11 *Morning Chronicle*, 12 May 1812.

12 *Morning Chronicle*, 12 May 1812; The *Courier*, 12 May 1812.

13 *Old Bailey*, 13 May 1812.

14 Quoted in Gillen, 1972. p.122.

15 Gillen, 1972. pp.113–14.

16 *Oxford Companion to British History*; Wikipedia.

17 Gash, 1972, p.364; Hurd, 2007, pp.298–300.

18 Macdonagh, 1920, pp.425–35; Sparrow, 2003, pp.70–1.

Notes to Chapter 32

1   21 August 1820, quoted in E. A. Smith, 1993, p.80; Letter, 23 August 1820, Maxwell ed, 1904.

2   Oxford DNB; Mellikan, 2001, pp.311–22.

3   Oxford DNB.

4   Ibid.; Mellikan, 2001, pp.313–14.

5   Letter to Elizabeth Ord, 17 August 1820, Maxwell ed, 1904, i, pp.306–7; Smith, 1993, pp.67–8.

6   Ibid., 1904, i, pp.307–9.

7   Ibid, 1904, i, pp.307–9; Letter to Frederick Lamb, 19 August 1820, in Smith, 1993, pp.74–5.

8   8 September 1820, Maxwell ed., 1904, i, p.318.

9   Smith, 1993, p.141.

10 Strong, 2005, pp.372–4, 392–4; Lockhart, 1902, vol. vi, p.323.

11 Lady Cowper to Frederick Lamb, 20 July 1821, in Smith, 1993, p.185; Mrs Arbuthnot's Journal, 19 July 1821, in Smith, 1993, p.141.

12 Strong, 2005, p.414.

13 Smith, 1993, pp.179, 183–4; Tanner, 1969, p.49.

14 Fraser, 1996, p.7, quoting Richardson, *Disastrous Marriage*, pp.207–8.

15 The *Traveller*, July 1821, and Henry Brougham, in Smith, 1993, pp.183–4, 179.

16 Lady Cowper to Frederick Lamb, 20 July 1821, in Smith, 1993, p.185.

17 Sawyer, 2003, pp.245–6; Gerhold, 1999, p.62; Bradley and Pevsner, 2003, p.214; DNB.

18 Bradley and Pevsner, 2003, p.214.

19 Bradley and Pevsner, 2003, pp.258, 264; Hastings, 1950, p.165.

20 Irving, 1821, i, p.295.

Notes to Chapter 33

1   Tristram Hunt, *Guardian*, 9 December 2009; Oxford DNB.

2   Number 10 official website.

3   Oxford DNB.

4   Amanda Foreman, *The Prime Ministers*, BBC Radio 4, 19 April 2011; House of Lords, 2 November 1830.

5   Letter to Thomas Flower, 30 March 1831, quoted in Silvester, 1996, p.153.

6   December 1830, quoted in J. R. M. Butler, 1914, p.286; MacDonagh, 1920, p.350.

7   Earl Grey, House of Lords *Hansard*, 3 and 7 October 1831.

8   Lord Brougham, House of Lords *Hansard*, 7 October 1831, cols. 274–5.

9   Butler, 1914, p.287; Pearce, 2003, p.201.

10 Lord Cockburn, quoted in Brock, 1973, pp.281–2.

11 Brock, 1973, p.304.

12 Cobbett, quoted in Jones, 1983, p.62.

13 Thornbury, 1891, vol. iii, p.557; MacDonagh, 1920, p.361; Dickens, May 1865, quoted in MacDonagh, 1920, p.345.

Notes to Chapter 34

1 *The Times*, 17 November 1834, pp.1–2.

2 Quoted in Saunders, 1951, p.297.

3 *The Times*, ibid; Brayley and Britton, 1836, pp.413–15.

4 *The Times*, ibid.

5 Brayley and Britton, 1836, pp.408–9.

6 Broughton, 1911, vol. v, 16 October 1834; Dickens, 'A Parliamentary Sketch' (chapter 18), 1995; Jones, 1983, p.71.

7 Broughton, 1911, vol. v, pp.21–2; The *Gentlemen's Magazine*, cited by Andrew Graham-Dixon on his website.

8 Brayley and Britton, 1836, pp.410–11.

9 *The Times*, 17 October 1834, p.3.

10 Jones, 1983, p.70; The *Gentlemen's Magazine*, cited by Andrew Graham-Dixon on his website.

11 Gerhold, 1999, pp.63–4.

12 Broughton, 1911, vol. v, pp.21–2.

13 Brayley and Britton, 1836, pp.410–11; Dan Cruickshank, *The Best of British Buildings*, BBC2 Television, 25 October 2004; Jones, 1983, p.71.

14 Brayley and Britton, 1836, fn, pp.409–10.

15 Broughton, 1911, vol. v, pp.22–3.

Notes to Chapter 35

1 Hill, 2007, p.129.

2 Cocks, 1977, p.23; Hill, 2007, pp.128, 130.

3 Quinault, 1992, pp.79–80; Hill, 2007, pp.141–2.

4 Jones, 1983. p.79. Cormack, 1981, p.111.

5 *The Great Palace*, BBC Television, November 1983; Jones, 1983. p.80; Bradley and Pevsner, 2003, pp.215–16.

6 Jones, 1983, p.80; Bradley and Pevsner, 2003, p.216; Fell and Mackenzie, 1977, pp.18–19, 43–4.

7 Quinault, 1992, pp.79–80; Hill, 2007, p.80.

8 Bradley and Pevsner, 2003, p.220–2

9 Quinault, 1992, pp.79–80; Hill, 2007, p.100; *The Great Palace*, BBC Television, November 1983.

10 Quinault, 1992, p.92; Dan Cruickshank, *The Best of British Buildings*, BBC2, 25 October 2004.

11 Port, 2002, p.166; Hansard, 3rd ser., CXCV, 30 (1869).

12 *The Great Palace*, BBC Television, November 1983.

13 Ibid.; Cruikshank, BBC 2, 25 October 2004.

14 Port, 1976. p.98; *The Great Palace*, BBC Television, November 1983; Quinault, 1992, pp.99–100.

15 *The Great Palace*, BBC Television, November 1983; Port, 2002, p.169.

16 Port, 2002, pp.175–7; Cruickshank, BBC2, 25 October 2004.

17 *The Great Palace*, BBC Television, November 1983.

18 Quinault, 1992, p.95; BBC News online, 11 October 2010, 23 January 2012.

19 Jones, 1981, pp.112–13; Oxford DNB.

20 Cruickshank, BBC2, 25 October 2004; MacDonald, 2004, pp.49–50; Bradley and Pevsner, 2003, p.218.

21 Fell and Mackenzie, 1977, p.28.

22 The number of steps was given by Cruickshank, BBC2, 25 October 2004.

23 *Mrs Dalloway*, Virginia Woolf, 1925.

24 McKay, 2010, p.89; Quinault, 1992, p.95; Cruickshank, BBC2, 25 October 2004; BBC News online, 23 January 2012.

25 Jones, 1983, pp.113–14; Cormack, 1981, p.113.

26 Cocks, 1977, p.72; Bradley and Pevsner, 2003, p.218.

27 Jones, 1983, pp.113–14.

28 Ibid., p.114–15; Bradley and Pevsner, 2003, p.218.

Notes to Chapter 36

1 Blake, 1975, p.36; Charles Dickens, 1995, Chapter 18, 'A Parliamentary Sketch'.

2 Seldon, 1999, p.21.

3 Quoted in Kuhn, 2006, p.178.

4 Ibid. p.183.

5 Quoted in Gash, 1972, p.568.

6 Quoted in Gash, 1972, pp.603–4; Hurd, 2007, p.384.

7 Blake, 1975, pp.36, 41.

8 Quoted in Hurd, 2007, p.347.

9 Blake, 1985, p.63 fn; Hibbert, 2004, p.203.

10 Riding and Riding, 2000, pp.15–20; Richard Aldous, 2007, p.65.

11 White, 1897, vol. i, pp.6–8.

12 MacDonagh, 1920, p.140; Aldous, 2007, p.70; Weintraub, 1993, p.323.

13 Aldous, 2007, pp.70–1.

14   Sir Henry Lucy, 1921, pp.123–4.

15   *The Times*, December 1852, quoted in Aldous, 2007, p.72.

16   Speech, 29 November 1879; Englefield, 1995, p.198.

17   White, 1897, vol. i, p.2.

18   Chambers, 2004, pp.475–6.

19   White, 1897, vol. i, pp.2, 3, 16, 151–4.

20   Aldous, 2007, p.85.

21   David Brown, *The Prime Ministers*, BBC Radio 4, 17 March 2009; White, 1897, vol. i, p.124.

22   Quoted in MacDonagh, 1921, p.140.

23   White, 1897, vol. i, p.128.

24   Ibid. pp.156–7.

25   White, 1897, vol. ii, p.5.

26   Trollope, 1981, p.220; James, 1905, p.134.

27   *Household Words*, 22 June 1850, article by Alexander Mackay; Bradley and Pevsner, 2003, p.271.

28   Halliday, 1999, preface.

29   Quoted in Halliday, 1999, preface.

30   Bradley and Pevsner, 2003, pp.376–7.

31   Watson, 2002, pp.117–18; Wikipedia.

32   Bradley and Pevsner, 2003, pp.377–8, 706–7.

33   *The Times*, 7–9 January 1928.

34   *The Times* and *Illustrated London News*.

35   White, 1897, vol. ii. p.67.

36   Aldous, 2007, p.285.

37   Bradley and Pevsner, 2003, p.299; *The Times*, 17 July 1878.

Notes to Chapter 37

1   *The Times*, 26, 27, 28 January 1885.

2   Kee, 1976, vol. ii, pp.45–51; Short, 1979, pp.11–12, 200–10.

3   Aldous, 2007, p.202; White, 1897, vol. ii. p.163.

4   White, 1897, vol. ii. p.163; Silvester, 1996, p.263; Lucy, 1885, pp.76–7.

5   Lucy, 1886, p.113.

6   Ibid., pp.116–38.

7   Ibid., pp.139–42.

8   *The Times*, 16 March 1883; Short, 1979, pp.105–6.

9   Short, 1979, pp.102–8.

10   Short, 1979, pp.53, 110; Browne, 1956, p.80; Bradley and Pevsner, 2003, pp.248–50.

11   Sparrow, 3, pp.58–61.

12   Kee, 1976, vol. ii, p.106.

13   Andrew Roberts, *Daily Telegraph*, 18 May 2002.

14   Oxford DNB; Kee, 1976, vol. ii, pp.114–5.

15   Lucy, 1896, pp.201, 198–9.

16   Aldous, 2007, p.323.

Notes to Chapter 38

1   *The Times*, 23 June 1897.

2   The present author was granted extensive access to the Foreign Office while filming *All the Presidency Men*, for 'Dispatches', Channel 4 Television, in 1992.

3   Foreman, 1995, p.140; Bradley and Pevsner, 2003, pp.238–9.

4   Bradley and Pevsner, 2003, p.270–1.

5   Foreman, 1995, pp.121–3.

6   Bradley and Pevsner, 2003, pp.375–6.

7   Michael Kennedy, *Spectator*, 3 February 2007.

8   Strong, 2005, p.467.

9   Englefield, 1995, p.228.

10   Watson, 2002, pp.117–18; 134; Bradley and Pevsner, 2003, p.211.

11   Stansgate, 1992, p.31.

12   Oxford DNB; Englefield, 1995, p.228; Clifford, 2003, p.137.

13   Minney, 1963, pp.343–4.

14   Alan Watkins, *Independent*, 28 March 2004; Stansgate, 1992, p.60.

15   Alan Watkins, *Independent*, 28 March 2004; Oxford DNB.

16   *Manchester Guardian*, 24 October 1906; Phillips, 2003, p.187.

17   Clifford, 2003, p.145; Phillips, 2003, pp.189–94.

18   *Manchester Guardian*, 28 April 1909; *The Times*, 27 April 2009.

19   Gramophone recording, 1909.

20   Speech, Newcastle, 9 October 1909, quoted in Oxford DNB.

21   Phillips, 2003, p.226; *BBC News online*, 8 September 2010.

22   Phillips, 2003, pp.231–2.

23   Rosen, 1974, pp.143–4; Phillips, 2003, p.232.

24   Ian White, in *Population Trends*, no. 142, 2010, p.14.

25   Ibid, p.16; Clifford, 2003, pp.254–5.

26   *The Times*, 25 July 1911.

27   BBC Radio 4, *One Hundred Years of Secrecy*, 18 August 2011.

28   Minney, 1963, p.348; Oxford DNB.

Notes to Chapter 39

1   Minney, 1963, p.350; Seldon, 1999, p.64; Rowland, 1975, p.284.

2   Rowland, ibid.

3   Oxford DNB.

4   Minney, 1963, pp.355–8.

5   Englefield, 1995, p.242.

6   Oxford DNB.

7   BBC Radio 4, *The Prime Ministers*, 31 March 2009.

8   Hennessy, 1989, p.64; *The Prime Ministers*, BBC Radio 4, 31 March 2009.

9   Hennessy, 1995, p.142.

10 Bradley and Pevsner, 2003, p.242.

11 Tanner, 1969, p.70; Foreman, 1995, passim.

12 Minney, 1963, p.358.

13 *Hansard*, 11 November 1918

14 Butler and Butler, 2005, p.234.

15 Allan Greenberg, 1989, p.6.

16 Greenberg, 1989, pp.6–8; Homberger, 1976, pp.1429–30.

17 Greenberg, 1989, p.5, 9; Homberger, 1976, pp.1429–30.

18 Homberger, 1976, pp.1429–30; *The Times*, 31 July 1919.

19 *The Times*, 29 October 1920.

20 James Wilkinson, 2006, pp.3–5.

21 Homberger, 1976, pp.1429–30; Wilkinson, 2006, pp.10–14.

22 Greenberg, 1989, pp.11, 13.

23 Wilkinson, 2006, p.15.

24 Wilkinson 2006, pp.17–21; Greenberg, 1989, pp.5, 13–14.

25 *The Times*, 29 November 1920; *New York Times*, 27 November 1920.

26 *The Times*, 29 November, 2 December, 2 1920; 22 February 1921; 24 May 1922.

Notes to Chapter 40

1   *The Times*, 28 January 1924.

2   Silvester, 1996, p.33.

3   *Oxford Companion to British History*, 1997, pp, 30–1, 585–6.

4   Tanner, 1969, p.109.

5   *The Times*, 12 April 1923.

6   Blake 1955, p.13; Shepherd, 1991, p.127.

7   *The Prime Ministers*, BBC Radio 4, 10 May 2011.

8   Feely, 1982, pp.193–5.
9   *The Prime Ministers*, BBC Radio 4, 10 May 2011.
10 Stansgate, 1992, p.114.
11 Baldwin's broadcast, May 1926, quoted in *The Prime Ministers*, BBC Radio 4, 7 April 2009.
12 Cockerell, 1988, p.3.
13 BBC Radio 4, *The Prime Ministers*, 10 May 2011.
14 Cooke, 2008, p.20; *The Times*, 7 March 1930.
15 Number 10 website; Cockerell, 1988, pp.1–2.
16 BBC sound archive, in Radio 4's *The Prime Ministers*, 10 May 2011.
17 *The Prime Ministers*, BBC Radio 4, 10 May 2011.
18 *The Times*, 17 March 1931.
19 BBC sound archive in Radio 4's *The Prime Ministers*, 7 April 2009.
20 *The Times*, 13 May 1937.
21 Shepherd, 1988, pp.2, 136.
22 Ibid., *passim*.
23 Hansard, 3 October 1938, col. 40.
24 Church, 2009, Duff Cooper's resignation speech over Munich, 3 October 1938,

Notes to Chapter 41

1   Foreman, 1995, p.155; Bradley and Pevsner, 2003, pp.84, 253–4.
2   Tanner, 1969, p.103.
3   *Hansard*, 7 May 1940, col. 1150.
4   Quoted in Shepherd, 1988, p.292.
5   Shepherd, 1988, pp.292–3.
6   Broadcast, 19 May 1940; *Hansard*, 18 June 1940.
7   MacDonald, 2004, pp.123–4.
8   Seldon, 1999, pp.78–9.
9   *Daily Telegraph*, 20 July 2009.
10 Tanner, 1969, pp.103–4.
11 Churchill, 1949, in Foreman, 1995, p.153; Seldon, 1999, p.81.
12 Colville, 1985, p.267; Bradley and Pevsner, 2003, p.85.
13 Foreman, 1995, p.156; Colville, 1985, pp.240–2; Hickman, 2005, pp.103–4.
14 Hickman, 2005, p.106.
15 Ibid., pp.101–8; Gilbert, 1983, pp.103–8.
16 *Daily Telegraph*, 12 May 1941.
17 Saunders, 1951, pp.13–14; Tanner, 1969, pp.104, 188.

18 Tanner, 1969, pp.104, 189–90.

19 Saunders, 1951, pp.14–15.

20 Ibid., pp.141–6.

21 Ibid., p.17.

22 Colville, 1985, p.386 MacDonald, 2004, p.125.

23 Jones, 1983, p.166; Nicolson, 1967, p.166; J. B. Seatrobe, in *Total Politics*, October 2010, p.97.

24 MacDonald, 2004, pp.128–9.

25 Hickman, 2005, p.193–6.

26 J. B. Seatrobe, in *Total Politics*, October 2010, p.97; Nicolson, 1967, pp.456–7.

27 Nicolson, 1967, pp.457–8.

28 Gilbert, 1986, pp.134–7; Hickman, 2005, pp.235–6.

29 MacDonald, 2004, p.131; Kelsey, 2002, p.20.

Notes to Chapter 42

1 *What Has Become Of Us*, presented by Peter Hennessy, Wide Vision Productions for Channel 4, 1994.

2 Hennessy, 1992, p.204.

3 Butler and Butler, 2005, p.289; Douglas Jay, *The Socialist Case*, 1947, p.258.

4 *The Prime Ministers*, BBC Radio 4, 14 April 2009.

5 Ibid.

6 National Archives, CAB 130/2, GEN 75; Hennessy, 1992, p.268.

7 Bradley and Pevsner, 2003, pp.242–4.

8 Hamilton, 1952, *passim*; 1990, pp.35–63 *passim*.

9 Hamilton, 1952, pp.129–91.

10 Parliamentary report, *Guardian*, 27 February 1952.

11 *Spectator*, 22 October 2005.

12 James Wilkinson, 2006, p.17.

13 Strong, 2005, p.435.

14 Strong, 2005, p.435.

15 Hennessy, 2000, p.209.

16 Cross, 1982, p.284; Shepherd, 1991, p.145; Kilmuir, 1964, p.285.

17 Hennessy, 2000, pp.251, 253–4.

18 *All the Prime Minister's Men*, Brook Productions for Channel 4, 1986.

19 Hennessy, 2000, p.258.

20 *The Times*, 20 July 1965.

21 Ibid.

22 Seldon, 1999, pp.31–4.

23 *The Spectator*, 17 January 1964.

24 Callaghan, 1987, p.162.

25 Television broadcast, 20 November 1967.

26 Whitehead, 1985, pp.32–3.

27 Shepherd, 1996, pp.415–16.

28 *Hansard*, 17 February 1972, col.698–707; Shepherd, 1996, pp.417–18.

29 Baston, 2004, pp.384–5; *Hansard*, 31 January 1972, cols. 31–3; Flackes, 1980, p.135.

30 *Sunday Times*, 19 February 2006.

Notes to Chapter 43

1   Author's interview with Lady Thatcher, Number 10, 14 April 1989.

2   Shepherd, 1991, p.10; Butler and Butler, 2005, p.277.

3   *The Times*, 8 February, 1991.

4   Ibid.

5   *BBC News Online*, 12 May 2010.

6   www.westminster-abbey.org/our-history

7   *Daily Telegraph*, 3 December 2008.

8   Winett and Rayner, 2009, pp.101–3.

9   Bell, 2009, pp.32–4.

10 Ibid., p.18.

11 *Five Days That Changed Britain*, BBC2, 29 July 2010

12 *The Prime Ministers*, BBC Radio 4, 17 and 24 March 2009.

13 Nick Robinson, *Daily Telegraph*, 29 July 2010.

14 Based on parliamentary answers and Government data releases, House of Commons Library, December 2011

15 *The Spectator*, 17/24 December 2011.

16 Shelley, 1839.

BIBLIOGRAPHY

Details of those books cited in abbreviated form in the Notes; a full bibliography is impracticable for reasons of space. The place of publication is London unless otherwise stated.

Ackroyd, Peter (1999), *Blake*.
—(1999), *The Life of Thomas More*.
—(2001), *London: The Biography*.
Aldous, Richard (2007), *The Lion and the Unicorn*.
Anglo, S. (1969), *Spectacle, Pageantry, and Early Tudor Policy*. Oxford.
Ayling, Stanley (1991), *Fox: The Life of Charles James Fox*.
Ayloffe, Joseph (1775), *Archaeologica*, vol. iii, pp.317–413.
Baker, Kenneth (1995), *The Prime Ministers: An Irreverent Political History in Cartoons*.
Baldwin, David (2002), *Elizabeth Woodville*. Stroud.
Barlow, Frank (ed. and transl.) (1962), *Vita AEdwardi Regis*.
—(1970), *Edward the Confessor*.
—(1983), *William Rufus*.
Baston, Lewis (2004), *Reggie: The Life of Reginald Maudling*. Stroud.
Bates, David (1989), *William the Conqueror*.
Beddard, John (1988), *A Kingdom Without a King*. Oxford.
Bell, Martin (2009), *A Very British Revolution*.
Besant, Walter (1895), *Westminster*.
Binski, Paul (1986), *The Painted Chamber at Westminster*, The Society of Antiquaries of London.
—(1995), *Westminster Abbey and the Plantagenets*. New Haven.
Blake, Robert (1966), *Disraeli*.
—(1975), *The Office of Prime Minister*. Oxford.
—(1985), *The Conservative Party from Peel to Thatcher*.
Bradley, Simon and Pevsner, Nikolaus (2003), *The Buildings of England: London 6, Westminster*.
Brayley, Edward W. and Britton, John (1836), *The History of the Ancient Palace and Late Houses of Parliament at Westminster*.
Brock, Michael (1973), *The Great Reform Act*.
Brotton, Jerry (2006), *The Sale of the Late King's Goods: Charles I and His Art Collection*.
Broughton, Lord, (John Cam Hobhouse) (1909–11), *Recollections of a Long Life*.
Brown, Colin (2009), *Whitehall*.
Brown, Dan (2003), *The Da Vinci Code*.

Burney, Charles (1785), *An Account of the Musical Performances in Westminster Abbey ... In Commemoration of Handel.*

Butler, David and Butler, Gareth (2005), *Twentieth Century British Political Facts, 1900–2000.* Basingstoke.

Butler, J. R. M. (1914), *The Passing of the Great Reform Act.*

Callaghan, James (1987), *Time and Chance.*

Campbell, Christy (2002), *Fenian Fire.*

Carpenter, D. A. (1996), *The Reign of Henry III.*

Carpenter, Edward, ed. (1972), *A House of Kings.*

Chambers, James (2004), *Palmerston, The People's Darling.*

Chaplais, Pierre (1962), in *A Medieval Miscellany for D. M. Stenton*, (eds) P. M. Barnes and C. F. Slade. London.

Church, Ian (2009), *Great Speeches from 100 Years*, Official Report (Hansard) House of Commons: Centenary Volume 1909–2009.

Clay, R. M. (1914), *The Hermits and Anchorites of England.*

Clifford, Colin (2002), *The Asquiths.*

Cobbett, William, *Parliamentary History of England*, 36 vols, to 1803.

—*State Trials*, 33 vols, to 1820.

Cockerell, Michael (1988), *Live From Number 10.*

Cocks, Barnett (1977), *Mid-Victorian Masterpiece.*

Colville, Jock (1985), *The Fringes of Power, Downing Street Diaries, 1939–55.*

Colvin, H. M., ed. (1971), *Building Accounts of Henry III.* Oxford.

—ed.,*The History of the King's Works*, 6 vols, 1963–82.

Cooke, Alistair (2008), *Tory Heroine: Dorothy Brant and the Rise of Conservative Women.* Eastbourne.

—(2009), *Tory Policy-Making: The Conservative Research Department, 1929–2009.* Eastbourne.

Corfield, Penelope, Green, Edmund and Harvey, Charles (2001), 'Westminster Man: Charles James Fox and his Electorate, 1780–1806' in *Parliamentary History.*

Cormack, Patrick (1981), *Westminster, Palace and Parliament.*

Creevey, Thomas (1904), *The Creevey Papers*, ed. Sir Herbert Maxwell.

Croker, John Wilson (1884), *The Croker Papers*, ed. Louis J. Jennings.

Cross, J. A. (1982), *Lord Swinton.* Oxford.

Dale, Anthony (1956), *James Wyatt.*

Dangerfield, George (1936), *The Strange Death of Liberal England.*

D'Arblay (1904–5), *Diary and Letters of Madame D'Arblay*, ed. A. Dobson.

De Castro, John Paul (1926), *The Gordon Riots.* Oxford.

Dickens, Charles (2003), *Barnaby Rudge*, Oxford.

—(1996), *Bleak House.*

—(1995), *Sketches by Boz.*

Dobbs, Michael (1989), *House of Cards.*

Doherty, Paul (2005), *The Great Crown Jewels Robbery of 1303.*

Douglas, David C. (1964), *William the Conqueror.*

Edwards, J. G. (1948), 'The Treason of Thomas Turberville, 1295', in *Studies in Medieval History Presented to Frederick Maurice Powicke.* Oxford.

Englefield, Dermot (1995), *Facts about the British Prime Ministers.*

Evelyn, John (1959), *The Diary of John Evelyn*, ed. E. S. de Beer.

Feely, Terence (1982), *Number 10, The Private Lives of Six Prime Ministers.*

Fell, Sir Bryan and Mackenzie, K. R. (1977), *The Houses of Parliament.*

Field, John (2002), *Kingdom, Power and Glory*.

—(2006), *The Story of Parliament*.

Flete, John (1909), *The History of Westminster Abbey*, ed. J. Armitage Robinson. Cambridge.

Foot, Michael (1973), *Debts of Honour*.

Foreman, Amanda (1998), *Georgiana, Duchess of Devonshire*.

Foreman, Susan (1995), *From Palace to Power: an Illustrated History of Whitehall*. Brighton.

Foster, Richard (1991), *Patterns of Thought: The Hidden Meanings of the Great Pavement of Westminster Abbey*.

Fraser, Antonia (1973), *Our Chief of Men*.

—(2002), *The Gunpowder Plot: Terror and Faith in 1605*.

Fraser, Flora (1996), *The Unruly Queen: The Life of Queen Caroline*.

Gardiner, Samuel R. (1895–1900), *History of England, 1603–42*.

Gash, Norman (1961), *Mr Secretary Peel*.

—(1972), *Sir Robert Peel*.

Gem, R. D. H. (1980), 'The Romanesque Rebuilding of Westminster Abbey', in *Proceedings of the Battle Conference of Anglo-Norman Studies III*, ed. R. A. Brown. Woodbridge.

Gerhold, Dorian (1999), *Westminster Hall*.

Gilbert, Martin (1983), *Finest Hour, 1939–41, Winston S. Churchill*.

—(1986), *Road To Victory, 1941–45, Winston S. Churchill*.

Gillen, Mollie (1972), *Assassination of the Prime Minister*.

Gillingham, John (1999), *Richard I*. New Haven.

Gilmour, Ian (1992), *Riot, Risings and Revolution*.

Grant, Lindy, and Mortimer, Richard (eds) (2002), *Westminster Abbey – the Cosmati Pavement*. Aldershot.

Grant Duff, Sir M. E. (1901), *Notes from a Diary, 1889–91*, 2 vols.

Gray, Thomas (1853), *The Correspondence of Thomas Gray*, ed., Rev. John Mitford.

Greenberg, Allan (1989), 'Lutyens's Cenotaph', in *Journal of the Society of Architectural Historians*.

Hague, Ffion (2008), *The Pain and the Privilege*.

Hague, William (2005), *William Pitt the Younger*.

Halliday, Stephen (1999), *The Great Stink of London*. Stroud.

Hamilton, Ian R. (1952), *No Stone Unturned: The Story of the Stone of Destiny*.

—(1990), *A Touch of Treason*. Moffat.

Harmer, Florence (1952), *Anglo-Saxon Writs*. Manchester.

Harris, Tim (2006a), *Restoration: Charles II and his Kingdoms, 1660–85*.

—(2006b), *Revolution: the Great Crisis of the British Monarchy, 1685–1720*.

Harvey, Barbara F. (1977), *Westminster Abbey and its Estates in the Middle Ages*. Oxford.

—(1993), *Living and Dying in England, 1100–1540*. Oxford.

—(2002), *The Obedientiaries of Westminster Abbey and their financial records, c.1275–1540*. Oxford.

Harvey, Anthony and Mortimer, Richard (eds) (1994), *The Funeral Effigies of Westminster Abbey*. Woodbridge.

Hastings, Maurice (1950), *Parliament House: the Chambers of the House of Commons*.

—(1955), *St Stephen's Chapel and its Place in the Development of the Perpendicular Style in England*. Cambridge.

Hawkyard, Alasdair (2002), 'From the Painted Chamber to St Stephen's Chapel', in *Parliamentary History*.

Hay, Malcolm and Riding, Jacqueline (1996), *Art in Parliament*. Westminster and Norwich.

Hennessy, Peter (1989), *Whitehall*.

—(1995), *The Hidden Wiring: Unearthing the British Constitution*.

—(2000), *The Prime Minister*.

Henry of Huntingdon (2002), *The History of the English People, 1000–1154*, (introduction and transl.) Diana Greenway. Oxford.

Heylyn, P (1849), *Ecclesia Restaurata: The History of the Reformation of the Church of England*, ed. Robertson, James Craigie. Cambridge.

Hibbert, Christopher (1958), *King Mob*.

—(2004), *Disraeli, A Personal History*.

Hickman, Tom (2006), *Churchill's Bodyguard*.

Hill, Benson E. (1836), *Reflections of an Artillery Officer*.

Hill, Rosemary (2007), *God's Architect: Pugin and the Building of Romantic Britain*.

Hoak, Dale (2003), *The Coronations of Edward VI, Mary I, and Elizabeth I, and the Transformation of the Tudor Monarchy*, in Knighton and Mortimer (2003).

Holland, Philip (1993), *St Margaret's Westminster*. Nuffield.

Hollister, C. Warren (2001), *Henry I*. New Haven.

Homberger, Eric (12 November 1976), 'The Story of the Cenotaph', in *The Times Literary Supplement*.

Hume, Martin, A. (1889), *Chronicle of King Henry VIII of England* (translation from an anonymous account in Spanish).

Hunting, Penelope (1981), *Royal Westminster*.

Hurd, Douglas (2007), *Robert Peel*.

Hutchinson, Robert (2005), *The Last Days of Henry VIII*.

Inwood, Stephen (1998), *A History of London*.

Irving, Washington (1821), *The Sketch Book of Geoffrey Crayon, Gent*.

Ives, Eric (2004), *The Life and Death of Anne Boleyn*.

James, Henry (1905), *English Hours*. Cambridge.

Jarrett, Derek (1965), *Britain, 1688–1815*.

Jay, Douglas (1947), *The Socialist Case*, 2nd edn.

Jay, Peter (2000), *Road to Riches*.

Jenkyns, Richard (2004), *Westminster Abbey*.

Jennings, George Henry (1899), *An Anecdotal History of the British Parliament*.

Jerdan, William (1852), *The Autobiography*, vol. I.

Jones, Christopher (1983), *The Great Palace*.

Jones, Terry, et al. (2003), *Who Murdered Chaucer?*

Jordan, W. K. (1968), *Edward VI, The Young King*.

—(1970), *Edward VI, The Threshold of Power*.

Kee, Robert (1976), *The Green Flag*, 3 vols.

Kelsey, Sean (2003), 'Housing Parliament', in *Parliamentary History*.

Kilmuir, Earl of (1964), *Political Adventure*.

Knighton, C. S. and Mortimer, Richard (2003), *Westminster Abbey Reformed, 1540–1640*.

Knowles, D. (1963), *The Monastic Order in England*. Cambridge.

Kuhn, William (2006), *The Politics of Pleasure*.

Lee, Maurice, Jnr (1990), *Great Britain's Solomon: James VI and I in His Three Kingdoms*. Urbana.

Lethaby, W. R. (1925), *Westminster Abbey Re-examined*.

Links, J. G. (1994), *Canaletto*.

Loades, David (1989), *Mary Tudor*. Oxford.

—(2003), 'The Sanctuary', in Knighton and Mortimer.

—(2004), *Intrigue and Treason: The Tudor Court, 1547–58*.

Lockhart, J. G. (1902), *The Life of Sir Walter Scott*, vol. vi. Edinburgh.

Loyn, H. R. (1991), *The Making of the English Nation*.

Low, Sir Sidney (1904), *The Governance of England*.

Luard, H. R. (1858), *Lives of Edward the Confessor*.

Lucy, Sir Henry (1885), *A Diary of Two Parliaments: The Disraeli Parliament, 1874–80*.

—(1886), *A Diary of Two Parliaments: The Gladstone Parliament, 1880–5*.

—(1896), *A Diary of the Home Rule Parliament*.

—(1920) (1922), *The Diary of a Journalist*, 2 vols.

—(1921), *Lords and Commons*.

MacDonagh, Michael (1921), *The Pageant of Parliament*, 2 vols.

MacDonald, Peter (2004), *Big Ben: The Bell, The Clock and The Tower*. Stroud.

Machyn, Henry (1848), *The Diary of Henry Machyn*, ed. J. G. Nichols.

Mackintosh, John (1968), *The British Cabinet*.

Mason, Emma (1996), *Westminster Abbey and its People c.1050–1216*. Woodbridge.

—(2005), *William II: Rufus, the Red King*. Stroud.

Matthew, H. C. G. (1986), *Gladstone, 1809–1874*. Oxford.

—(1986), *Gladstone, 1875–1898*. Oxford.

Matthias, Peter (1983), *The First Industrial Nation*.

McKay, Chris (2010), *Big Ben: The Great Clock and the Bells at the Palace of Westminster,* Oxford.

McMains, H. F. (2000), *The Death of Oliver Cromwell*. Lexington.

Mellikan, R. A. (2001), 'Pains and Penalties Procedure' in *Parliamentary History*.

Merrifield, Ralph (1983), *London, City of the Romans*.

Merritt, Julia (2005), *The Social World of Early Modern Westminster Abbey, Court and Community, 1525–1640*. Manchester.

Miller, John (1978), *James II: A Study In Kingship*. Hove.

Minney, R. J. (1963), *Number 10 Downing Street*.

Morris, Christopher ed. (1982), *The Illustrated Journeys of Celia Fiennes*. Exeter.

Myers, A. R. ed. (1969), *English Historical Documents*, vol. iv, no.266.

Neale, Sir J. E. (1950), *The Elizabethan House of Commons*.

Neale, J. P. and Brayley, E. W. (1818 and 1823), *The History and Antiquities of Westminster Abbey and Henry VII's Chapel*, 2 vols.

Nicolson, Harold (1967), *Diaries and Letters, 1939–45*, ed. Nigel Nicolson.

Oborne, Peter (2007), *The Triumph of the Political Class*.

Okerlund, Arlene (2005), *Elizabeth Wydeville: The Slandered Queen*. Stroud.

Ormrod (1990), *The Reign of Edward III*, New Haven.

Old Bailey, Proceedings (13 May 1812), John Bellingham, www.oldbaileyonline.org

Oxford Companion to British History (1997) ed. John Cannon. Oxford.

Oxford Dictionary of National Biography (2004) with online updates, Oxford.

Painter, George D. (1976), *William Caxton*.

Paris, Matthew (1852–4) (ed. J. A. Giles), *English History: From the year 1253 to 1273*, 3 vols.

—*Chronicles* (1984) (transl. Richard Vaughan). Gloucester.

Parris, Matthew (2002), *Chance Witness*.

Pasquet, D. (1925) (transl. R. G. D. Laffan), *An Essay on the Origins of Parliament*. Cambridge.

Patrick, Philippa (2005), 'In Search of Friar Tuck', in *Current Archaeology*, no. 198.

Pearce, Edward (2003), *Reform! The Fight for the 1832 Reform Act.*

—(2008), *The Great Man, Sir Robert Walpole.*

Pearce, E. H. (1916), *The Monks of Westminster.* Cambridge.

Peck, Linda Levy (1991), *The Mental World of the Jacobean Court.* Cambridge.

Pepys, Samuel (1970–83), *The Diary of Samuel Pepys* (eds) Robert Latham and William Matthews, 11 vols.

Phillips, Melanie (2003), *The Ascent of Women.*

Place, Francis (1972), *The Autobiography of Francis Place,* ed. Mary Thrale.

Pollard, A. W. ed. (1903–4), *An English Garner.* Westminster.

Port, M. H. ed. (1976), *The Houses of Parliament.* New Haven.

—(February 2002), ' "The Best Club in the World," The House of Commons, *c*.1860–1915', in *Parliamentary History*, vol. 21, issue 1, pp.166–99.

Pottle, Frederick A. ed. (1951), *Boswell's London Journal, 1762–3.*

Powicke, F. M. (1947), *King Henry III and the Lord Edward*, 2 vols. Oxford.

Prestwich, M. (1972), *War, Politics and Finance under Edward I.*

—(1988), *Edward I.*

Quinault, Roland (1992), 'Westminster and the Victorian Constitution', in *Transactions of the Royal Historical Society.*

Riding, Christine and Riding, Jacqueline (2000), *The Houses of Parliament, History, Art and Architecture.*

Ridley, Jasper (1987), *Elizabeth I.*

Riley, H. T. (ed and transl.) (1863), *Chronicles of the Mayors and Sheriffs of London* AD *1188 to 1274 (attributed to A. Fitz-Thedmar).*

Robinson, J. Armitage (1911a), *Gilbert Crispin, Abbot of Westminster.* Cambridge.

—(1911b), *The Abbot's House at Westminster.* Cambridge.

Rodwell, Warwick (2002), *Chapter House and Pyx Chamber,* English Heritage.

Rosen, Andrew (1974), *'Rise Up, Women'.*

Ross, Angus (1982), *Selections from The Tatler and The Spectator.* Harmondsworth.

Rosser, Gervase (1989), *Medieval Westminster 1200–1540.* Oxford.

Rowland, Peter (1975), *Lloyd George.*

Rowlandson, Thomas and Combe, William (1815), *The English Dance of Death.*

Rushworth, John (1721), *Historical Collections of Private Passages of State, 1618–38.*

Rushworth, John and Herbert, Thomas (1959), *The Trial of Charles I*, ed. Roger Lockyer.

Sagovsky, Nicholas and Trowles, Nicholas (2006), *Booklet on the Da Vinci Code and Westminster Abbey.*

St Margaret's Westminster Abbey, Dean and Chapter of Westminster Abbey.

Sargeaunt, John (1898), *Annals of Westminster School.*

Saul, Nigel (1997), *Richard II.* New Haven.

Saunders, Hilary St. George (1951), *Westminster Hall.*

Sawyer, Sean (2003), 'Delusions of National Grandeur', in *Transactions of the Royal Historical Society.*

Scarisbrick, J. J. (1997), *Henry VIII.* New Haven.

Scott, G. C. (1861), *Gleanings from Westminster Abbey.*

Sebba, Anne (2004), *The Exiled Collector, William Bankes.*

Seldon, Anthony (1999), *10 Downing Street: An Illustrated History.*

Shelly, Percy Bysshe (1839), *Peter Bell the Third.*

Shepherd, Robert (1988), *A Class Divided: Appeasement and the Road to Munich 1938.*

—(1990), *Ireland's Fate: The Boyne and After.*

—(1991), *The Power Brokers: The Tory Party and Its Leaders*.

—(1994), *Iain Macleod: A Biography*.

—(1996), *Enoch Powell: A Biography*.

Sheppard, J. Edgar (1902), *The Old Royal Palace of Whitehall*.

Short, K. R. M. (1979), *The Dynamite War*. Dublin.

Silvester, Christopher (1996), *The Literary Companion to Parliament*.

Smith, J. T. (1807), *The Antiquities of Westminster, &c.*, 2 vols.

Smith, E. A. (1993), *A Queen on Trial: the Affair of Queen Caroline*. Stroud.

Southworth, John (1998), Fools and Jesters at the English Court. Stroud.

Sparrow, Andrew (2003), *Obscure Scribblers, A History of Parliamentary Journalism*.

Speck, W. A. (1977), *Stability and Strife: England 1714–60*.

Stanley, Arthur Penrhyn (1868) (1886), *Historical Memorials of Westminster Abbey*, 5th edn.

Stansgate, Margaret (1992), *My Exit Visa*.

Starkey, David (2003), *Six Wives: The Queens of Henry VIII*.

—(2004), *The Monarchy of England*, vol. 1.

Stow, John Stow (1908), *A Survey of London*, introduction and notes by C. L. Kingsford, 2 vols. Oxford.

Strong, Roy (2005), *Coronation: A History of Kingship and the British Monarchy*.

Strype, John (1720), *A Survey of the Cities of London and Westminster*, 2 vols.

Survey of London (1926–31), vols, 10, 13 and 14, London County Council.

Tanner, Laurence E. (1969), *Recollections of a Westminster Antiquary*.

Tatton-Brown, Tim and Mortimer, Richard (eds) (2003), *Westminster Abbey: the Lady Chapel of Henry VII*. Woodbridge.

Taylor, A. J. (1996), *The Jewel Tower*, English Heritage.

Thomas, P. D. G. (1971), *The House of Commons in the Eighteenth Century*. Oxford.

Thomas, Christopher, Cowie, Robert and Siddell, Jane (2006), *The royal palace, abbey and town of Westminster on Thorney Island, Museum of London*.

Thornbury, G. W. (1878), *Old and New London*, 3 vols, ed. Edward Walford.

Thurley, Simon (1993), *The Royal Palaces of Tudor England*. New Haven.

—(1998), *The Whitehall Palace Plan of 1670*, London Topographical Society.

—(1998), *The Lost Palace of Whitehall*.

—(1999), *Whitehall Palace: an Archaeological History of the Royal Apartments, 1240–1698*. New Haven and London.

—(2004), *Lost Buildings of Britain*.

—(2008), *Whitehall Palace: The Official Illustrated History*.

Tomalin, Claire (2002), *Pepys: The Unequalled Self*.

Trevelyan, Raleigh (2002), *Sir Walter Raleigh*.

Trollope, Anthony (1981), *The Warden*. Oxford.

Van der Zee, Henri and Barbara (1988), *William and Mary*.

Victoria History of the Counties of England (1909), ed. William Page, *London*, vol. I.

—(2009), ed. Patricia Croot, *A History of the County of Middlesex*, vol. XIII: City of Westminster, Part 1. Oxford.

Vincent, Nicholas (2001), *The Holy Blood: the King Henry III and the Westminster Blood Relic*. Cambridge.

Voltaire, François-Marie Arouet, *Letters on England, 1722–34*, www.google.books.com

Walcott, Rev. Mackenzie E. C. (1851), *Westminster: Memorials of the City, Saint Peter's College, the Parish Churches, Palaces, Streets and Worthies*, 2nd edn. Westminster.

Walker, R. J. B. (1979), *Old Westminster Bridge: the Bridge of Fools*. Newton Abbot.

Walpole, Horace (1840), *The Letters of Horace Walpole, Earl of Orford*, 6 vols.

Ward, Ned (1951), *The London Spy*, ed. Kenneth Fenwick, Folio Society.

Warren, W. L. (1973), *Henry II*.

Waterhouse, Ellis Kirkham (1994), *Painting in Britain, 1530–1790*.

Watson, Isobel (1993), *Westminster and Pimlico Past*.

Weber, William (1989), 'The 1784 Handel Commemoration as Political Ritual', in *Journal of British Studies*.

Wedgwood, C. V. (1964), *The Trial of Charles I*.

Weintraub, Stanley (1993), *Disraeli: A Biography*.

Weir, Alison (2000), *Eleanor of Aquitaine*.

Westlake, H. F. (1914), *St. Margaret's Westminster: The Church of the House of Commons*.

—(1919), *Westminster, A Historical Sketch*.

—(1923), *Westminster Abbey: The Church, Convent, Cathedral and College of St. Peter's, Westminster*, 2 vols.

Westminster Abbey: Official Guide, Dean and Chapter of Westminster Abbey, 2005.

Wheatley, Henry, B. (1891), *London Past and Present*, 3 vols.

White, William (1897), *The Inner Life of the House of Commons*, 2 vols.

Whitehead, Phillip (1985), *The Writing on the Wall: Britain in the Seventies*.

Whiteley, Peter (1996), *Lord North: the Prime Minister Who Lost America*. London.

Wickham Legg, Leopold G. (1901), *English Coronation Records*.

Widmore, Richard (1743), *An Enquiry into the Time of the First Foundation of Westminster Abbey*.

—(1751), *An History of the Church of St Peter Westminster*.

Wilkinson, B. W (1969), *The Later Middle Ages in England, 1216–1485*.

Wilkinson, Clare (2002), 'Politics and Topography in the Old House of Commons, 1783–1834', in *Parliamentary History*.

Wilkinson, James (2006), *The Coronation Chair and the Stone of Destiny*.

—(2006), *The Unknown Warrior and the Field of Remembrance*.

—(2007), *Henry VII's Lady Chapel in Westminster Abbey*.

Williams, Neville (1964), *Thomas Howard, Fourth Duke of Norfolk*.

Wilson, Derek (2003), *All the King's Women*.

Winnett, Robert and Rayner, Gordon (2009), *No Expenses Spared*.

Woolf, Virginia (1925), *Mrs Dalloway*.

Wriothesley, Charles (1875–7), *A Chronicle of England during the Reigns of the Tudors*, ed. William Douglas Hamilton, 2 vols.

Young, Alan (1987), *Tudor and Jacobean Tournaments*.

Young, Hugo (1989), *One of Us*.

INDEX

Abbot's House
  sanctuary 101–2
  scope 85, 95
Abbott, Charles 241
Abingdon Street 212
Absalom and Achitophel 178
Ackroyd, Peter 74–5
Act in Restraint of Appeals 119
Act of Settlement 192
Act of Supremacy 123
Act of Union (Ireland) 239
Act of Union (Scotland) 192–3
Adam of Warfield 72–3
Adam, Robert 209
Addington, Henry, Viscount Sidmouth
  196
Addison, Joseph 56, 193–5
  burial 195
  partisanship 194, 195
Addled Parliament 152
Admiralty 295
Admiralty Arch 295
Admiralty House 209, 335, 345
Admiralty Screen 209
Air Raid Precautions (ARPs) 318
air raids 324–7
Albert, Prince Consort 145
America
  warfare 221, 224–5
    expenditure 233
anchorites 97
  confession to 97
  consecration 98
  death 98
  location 98
  penalties 97

Anglo-Saxon Britain 6, 29 *see also*
  individual terms
Anne, Queen 192, 193, 195–6
  expenditure 191
  family and 192
Anne of Bohemia 92–3
  burial 92
Anne of Cleves 125
Anne of Denmark 154–5
Anselm, Archbishop of Canterbury 29
  rivalry 29
anti-Semitism 41
Apollo, Temple of 6
apology for economy 336
appeasement 318–20
Arbuthnot, Charles 251
Arbuthnot, Harriet 252
Archer, Thomas 196
Armada tapestries 145
armadas 145, 181
Armistice 306
Armistice Day 307–9
army 162–3, 165–7
  disparities 165, 172
ARPs (Air Raid Precautions) 318
Arthur of Brittany 42
Asquith, Herbert Henry, Earl of Oxford
  297, 298, 300, 301, 303
  downfall 304
  enfranchisement 298, 300
  family and 297, 304
    enfranchisement 299
  laxity 297–8
  pensions 298
  power struggles 302
  rivalry 304

Asquith, Margot 297
  enfranchisement 299
Astor, Nancy, Lady 312
atomic bomb 330
Atterbury, Dean Francis 198
Attlee, Clement, Earl 328, 330
  coalition 322–3
Axe Yard 173
Ayrton light 272

Babington Plot 144
Bad Parliament 88
Baker, Kenneth, Lord 205
Baldwin, Archbishop of Canterbury 40
Baldwin, Stanley 312, 313, 315, 316–17
  radio broadcasts 314–15, 317
Bank of England 185
  run 237–8
banking crisis 347
banqueting 27, 48, 120, 252
Banqueting House
  ceiling 155–6
  coronations 184
  disparities 156
  rebuilding 154–5
  scope 151, 155
Barebones Parliament 171
barons' revolt 43
baroque style 155–6, 196
Barry, Charles 267, 268, 270, 271–2,
    273–4
  death 274
Barton Street 197
Bastwick, John 159
Battle of Britain Chapel 324
Battle of Downing Street, The 300
Bayeux tapestry 14, 17
  disparities 12
  scope 22
BBC 321, 323, 327
  impartiality and 315, 318
Becket, Thomas, Archbishop of
    Canterbury 37–8
Bede 24
Beggar's Opera, The 205
Bell, Martin 348
Bellamy, John 220
Bellingham, John 244–6
  trial 246

bells 84, 272, 273
Benedictine monks 7, 15–16, 86–7, 138
  laxity 86
Benn, Anthony Wedgwood 301, 336
Benn, William Wedgwood 197, 297
Bevin, Ernest 330
bibles 85, 151
Big Ben 272, 273, 321, 323, 327
  bomb 326
Biggar, Joe 288
Black Death 80–1
Black Rod 337
Black Wednesday 345
blackmail 281
Blair, Tony 203, 237, 345, 349, 350
  rivalry 347
Blake, William 74–5
Blitz 324–5
blood relic 53
Bloody Sunday 338
Board of Trade building 254
Boleyn, Anne 117, 118
  coronation 119–20
  expenditure 124
  legitimacy 119
  treason and 124
bombs 287, 289, 290, 306, 324–7, 330,
    338, 344–5
  death 338–9
Bonar Law, Andrew 304, 312
  death 313
Bondfield, Margaret 315
Book of Martyrs 127
boom and bust 197–8, 205, 315–16, 347
Booth, Barton 197
Boston, Abbot 126
Boston Tea Party 221
Boswell, James 212, 217
  prostitutes 212
Bourchier, Thomas, Archbishop of
    Canterbury 102
Boyer, Abel 216
Bradlaugh, Charles 272
Bradshaw, John 164
Bradshaw, Lawrence 133
Brayley, Edward W. 41, 66
bribery 205–6
Bridge Street 211–12
Brittan, Leon, Lord 342

Britton, John 41, 66
Broadhurst, Henry 270–1
Brooks's club 230
Brougham, Henry, Lord 257
Brown, Gordon 203
    rivalry 347
Buchanan, Sir Colin 334–5
Buckingham, Duchess of (Katherine
        Darnley) 212–13
Buckingham, Duke of (George Villiers) 209
Buckingham Palace 213, 264
budgets 281–2, 299–300
bureaucracy 305
Burgess, Henry 244–5
Burke, Edmund 235, 236, 237
Burnet, Bishop Gilbert 180
Burney, Charles 231
Burney, Fanny 235
Burton, Henry 159
business 87, 107–8, 129, 276
Butler, Richard Austen (Rab), Lord 184,
        196, 320, 322–3, 333, 336
butlers 47–8
Byron, George Gordon, Lord 208–9

cabals 176
Cabinet 233, 315
    bureaucracy 305
    coalition 305
    collective responsibility 345
    constraint on 342
    power and 344
    schism 251, 316
    scope 175–6, 185, 330
    seating 334
    security 246–7
Cabinet room (Downing St) 202–3
Cabinet room (Foreign Office) 294
Callaghan, James, Lord 336
Cameron, David 320, 348–9
Campbell, Christy 291
Campbell-Bannerman, Henry 296
Campion, Edward 144
Campion, George B. 263
Canaletto 207, 211
Canon Row 80
Canterbury Tales, The 83, 86
Canute, King (Cnut) 7, 8
    family and 8–9

    tide turning and 7–8
caricatures 204–5, 218–19, 220–1, 238
Carlton Club 312
Caroline of Ansbach 213
Caroline of Brunswick 249–50
    downfall 253
    exclusion 250, 252–3
    trial 249, 251
        protests 251
        security 250–1
cartoons 204–5, 218–19, 220–1, 238
cash for honours 152, 312
Castle, Barbara 329
Castlemaine, Countess of (Barbara
        Palmer) 174, 175
Castlemaine, Earl of (Roger Palmer) 174
Catesby, Robert 147
Catherine of Aragon 116–17
Catherine of Valois 113
Catholic Relief Act 221, 222
Cato Street conspiracy 246–7
Catuvellauni 5
Cave, Edward 216, 217
Caxton, William 107–9
Cecil, John 171
Cecil, Robert, Earl of Salisbury 146
    expenditure 152
    power and 141
    spies 148
Cecil, William, Lord Burghley 139–40, 141
    power and 141
Celtic Britain 5
Cenotaphs 307, 308–9
census 300–1
Central Lobby 270
Chamberlain, Anne 320
Chamberlain, Joseph 296
Chamberlain, Neville 317–18, 322, 323
    appeasement 318–20
    coalition 322–3
    downfall 343
    family and 320
    power struggles 322
    radio broadcast 319
Champart, Robert, Archbishop of
        Canterbury 12
Champions 92, 252
Chancellor of the Exchequer 46, 280 see
        also individual names

Chancery 49, 115–16
Chapter House 59
  crypt 60–1
  filming 60
  scope 58–60
  tile pavement 60
Character of a Trimmer, The 184
charity 49–50
Charles I 154, 157, 169
  arts patronage 158–9
  burial 167
  coronation 157
  death 165–7
  downfall 162–3
  expenditure 159
  family and 152, 157
  power struggles 157–8, 159, 160–1
  protests 161
  trial 163–7
Charles II 102–3, 172, 174, 175, 176, 208
  cliques 176
  coronation 172–3
    crown jewels 172
  court 175
  exclusion and 177, 178
  family and 175–7, 178, 179
  legitimacy 174
  mistresses 174–5
Charlotte, Princess 346
Charlotte of Mecklenburg-Strelitz 214
Chaucer, Geoffrey 83–4, 86
  murder and 100–1
  sanctuary and 100
Cheltham, John 138
Churchill, Lord Randolph 291
Churchill, Sir Winston 297, 305, 315, 321,
    323–5, 331
  downfall 328
  lying-in-state 328
  oratory 323
  power and 323
  security 325, 327
  victory 328
    radio broadcasts 327
  walks 325
Churchill War Rooms 321, 324–5, 327
Civil List Act 185
civil service 25
civil wars 65, 66, 290–1

allegiances 31
pillage 162
protests 31
scope 162–3
Clarendon, Earl of (Edward Hyde) 175
  downfall 175
Clarendon Code 175
Clarke, Kenneth 345
Clegg, Nicholas 348–9
Clement, Henry 48
Clerk of the Pells 229–30
cliques 176
clock towers 84, 272, 273
cloisters 15, 28, 80
closure 289
Cnut, King (Canute) 7, 8
  family and 8–9
  tide turning and 7–8
coalitions 300, 304, 305, 306–7, 312, 316,
    322–3, 348–9
Cobbett, William 259
Cockpit 191
Cockpit Passage 121
Cockpit Steps 196
coffee houses 173
Colchester, Abbot 100
Coldstream Guards 172
Coleridge, Samuel Taylor 240
College Hall 85
Colville, John (Jock) 320, 323, 324, 326–7
common market 337–8
Commons Journal 149, 161
Commonwealth 169, 170–2
  downfall 172
concerts 231–2
Congress of Berlin 285–6
Conservative Research Department
    (CRD) 336
Conservatives 275, 312
  business 276
  coalitions 304, 306–7, 312, 316, 322–3,
    348–9
  collective responsibility 345
  common market entry 337–8
  deprivation 276–7
  enfranchisement 285
  expenditure 277
  power struggles 290
  schism 322

secrecy on leadership 336
Constituto domus Regis 30
Convention Parliament 184
Conyngham, Elizabeth, Lady 252
Cooper, Alfred Duff, Lord 316–17, 320
Cooper, Diana, Lady 318
Corn Laws 277
Coronation Chair 69, 71, 331, 332
   safeguards 322
Cosmati pavement 57–8
   uncertainty 58
counter-reformation 135–6
   penalties 138
   revolt 136–7, 138
   scope 137–8
Court Gate 120
Cowley Street 197
Cowper, Lady (Emily Lamb) 253
Cox, Dean Richard 132
Crabbe, George 223
Cranmer, Thomas, Archbishop of
      Canterbury 119, 120, 131–2
Crawford and Balcarres, Earl of 335
CRD (Conservative Research
      Department) 336
credit crunch 347
Creevey, Thomas 250–1
Crispin, Abbot Gilbert 31–2, 33
Cromwell, Oliver 159, 160, 162–3, 164,
      169
   burials 172
   defilement 172
   family and 172
   investiture 171–2
   power and 170–2
   security 171
Cromwell, Richard 172
Cromwell, Thomas 119
   expenditure 124
   power and 123, 124
   treason and 125
Crosby, Brass 219, 220
crown jewels 172
Crusades 41
crypts 60–1, 116
Cust, Sir Edward 267–8

Da Vinci Code, The 60, 199
Daily Telegraph 255, 347

dandyism 27–8
Danegeld 13
Dangerfield, Thomas 302
Dartmouth, Baron (George Legge) 181–2
Davison, Emily Wilding 301
de Burgh, Hubert 39
de Glanvil, Ranulf 39
de Kéroualle, Louise, Duchess of
      Portsmouth 174–5
de la Mare, Sir Peter 88
de Montfort, Simon, Earl of Leicester
      64–5, 66
   death 66
   expenditure 64
   family and 64, 66
   power struggles 65–6
de Rivallis, Peter 46
de Turberville, Sir Thomas 71
Deanery
   sanctuary 101–2
   scope 85, 95
Declaration of Indulgence 176
department of the wardrobe 67
Depression 315–16
deprivation 259, 275–6, 277, 281, 283,
      296–7
Derby, Earl of (Edward Smith-Stanley)
      278, 279
Derby Day 301
des Roches, Peter 46
devaluation 336
Devil's Acre, The 283
Devlin, Bernadette 338
Devonshire, Duchess of (Georgiana
      Cavendish) 231
Dialogus de Scaccario 38
Diana, Princess of Wales 345–6
Dickens, Charles 196, 222, 257, 259, 261,
      262, 275, 283
Disraeli, Benjamin (Earl of Beaconsfield)
      276, 278–9, 293, 320
   debating skills 277, 279
   deprivation 276, 277
   enfranchisement 285
   power and 285–6
   rivalry 277, 278, 279–80
dissolution of the monasteries 124, 126, 140
division lobbies 271
Dobbs, Michael, Lord 336

Domesday Book 25
doodle-bugs 327
Douglas-Home, Sir Alec, Earl of Home,
    Lord Home of the Hirsel 320, 323,
    334, 336
Dover House 208–9
Downing, Sir George 173
Downing Street 121, 173, 203, 212, 254
  laxity 275
  protests 299, 300, 308
  rebuilding 335
  security 309, 310, 311
  special advisers 349–50
  see also 10 Downing Street
drinking 228, 249–50, 257, 297–8
Drummond, Edward 247
Dryden, John 178
Dudley, Robert, Earl of Leicester 141
Dunstan, Archbishop 6–7
Durbar Courtyard 295
Dyer, John 216
Dymoke, Sir John 92
dynamite war 287–8, 289, 290

Ealdred, Archbishop of York 20, 21
earthquakes 211
Ecclesiastical History of the English People
    24
Eden, Eleanor 234
Eden, Sir Anthony, Earl of Avon 320, 333
Edgar, King 7
  coronation 198
education 126, 141
Edward I 66–7, 68, 70, 71–2, 79
  burial 74
  coronation 70
  death 74
  expenditure 68
  family and 70, 73–4, 75, 77–8, 79
  warfare 70–1
Edward II
  downfall 75
  family and 75
  warfare 73–4
Edward III 75, 79, 80, 84
  burial 89
  coronation 91–2
  court 88
  expenditure 87

family and 88, 91–2
forced labour 81
power struggles 88
warfare 75
Edward IV 108
Edward V 101
  murder and 102–3
Edward VI
  coronation 131–2
  Crown and Church 131–2
  death 135
  family and 131, 135
Edward VII 296
Edward VIII 317
Edward the Confessor 9, 11–14, 51, 54,
    55–6, 347
  burials 17, 33, 38, 54–5
  canonization 33–4
  cult 33–4
  death 12, 16–17
  decline 16
  expenditure 13
  family and 11, 12, 16, 17, 19–20
  miracles 21–2, 33, 56
  retinue 12–13, 16–17
EEC (European Economic Community)
    337–8
Eleanor of Aquitaine 40, 41
  coronation 37
Eleanor of Castile 70, 78
  coronation 70
  death 77
Eleanor Crosses 77
Eleanor of Leicester 64
Eleanor of Provence, coronation
  butlers 47–8
  rivalry 47
  scope 48
elections 300, 312
  constraint on 215
  engineering 218
  laxity 215
  power play 290
  rivalry 230–1
  scope 230
Elgar, Sir Edward William 295–6
Eliot, Harriot 234
Elizabeth, Queen (Elizabeth Bowes-Lyon)
    317, 346

family and 346
   lying-in-state 346
Elizabeth I 138, 140, 141, 145
   burial 146
   coronation 138–9
   excommunication 143
   expenditure 142
   family and 139, 144–5, 146
      legitimacy 143–4
   free speech and 142
   military displays 139
   personal touch 139
   security 145
Elizabeth II 269
   coronation 332
   jubilee 347
Elizabeth of York 110, 112
   burial 113
Elliot, Colonel Walter 325, 326
Emma of Normandy 11
empire 293–4, 295–6
employment 129
enfranchisement 255, 285
   constraint on 298, 300, 301
   protests 258, 298–9, 300–1
   schism 256–7, 258, 285
   scope 256, 257, 258–9, 306, 315
English Civil War Society 167
English language 87–8
Englishman 195
Erith, Raymond 335
ERM (European Exchange Rate
   Mechanism) exit 345
Essay on Woman 218
Ethelgoda, Queen 24
European Economic Community (EEC)
   337–8
European Exchange Rate Mechanism
   (ERM) exit 345
Evelyn, John 174, 179, 184
Ewens, Ralph 149
Exchequer 30, 38, 46
   rebuilding 46
exclusion crisis 176–8
Exclusion Parliaments 177–8
expenses scandals 255, 347–8

Fabyan, Robert 8, 95
Fairfax, Sir Thomas 164, 165

fairs 52–3
   expenditure 53
   location 53
Family of Henry VIII, The 128
Fawkes, Guy 145, 147, 148, 149
   death 150
ferries 5–6, 22, 209
festivals 108
Fifty Churches Act 196
film 60, 317, 332
fire 20, 71–2, 115, 184, 186–7, 261–4, 267,
   325–7, 338
First World War see World War I
fist-fight 291
FitzAlan, Richard, Earl of Arundel 92
Fitzherbert, Maria 249
FitzNigel, Richard 38
Fitzstephen 37
Flambard, Ranulf 28
Flete, John 6, 13, 23
flipping 347–8
flooding 48, 284–5
Flower, William 138
fools 128
Foot, Michael 337
forced labour 81
Foreign Office 229
   constraint on 318–19
   scope 294
Fox, Charles James 227, 229, 238
   burial 242
   downfall 232, 236
   laxity 229
   rivalry 229, 230–1, 234, 236
Foxe, John 127
France
   coronation attendance 214
   invasion from 43
   lost claims in 65
   style 52, 55
   warfare 75, 80
      expenditure 237
Fraser, Lady Antonia 148
Frederick, Duke of York 208
Frederick II, Holy Roman Emperor 47
free speech 181
   constraint on 152, 215–16, 217, 220
   disparities 142, 218
   penalties 142, 159

protests 219–20
scope 193, 216–17, 218–19, 220–1
French language 87–8
French Revolution 236
fear 237
Froude, James 213

Gaimark, Geffrie 7–8
gas masks 318
Gascoyne, Lieutenant-General Isaac 245
gatehouse 85–6
Gatehouse Prison 153–4
Gay, John 205
Gazetteer 219
General Strike 314–15
Gentleman's Magazine 216, 262
Geoffrey, Bishop of Coutances 20
George I 195, 198
George II 201
burial 213
coronation 198
family and 198, 213
George III 218, 229
coronation 213–14
omens 214
decline 236
power and 231–2
George IV (Regent) 236, 253, 254
coronation 251–2
death 254
family and 249–50
exclusion 250
laxity 249–50, 252
legitimacy 249
George V 301, 313
George VI 317
Georgian Britain 196–7 *see also individual terms*
Gerald, Archbishop of York 29
Germany
appeasement and 318–20
surrender 327
warfare 303, 322
Gervase of Blois, Abbot 33
Gibbon, Edward 225
Gillray, James 238
Gilmour, Sir Ian, Lord 215
Gladstone, William Ewart 280, 281, 291, 292, 293

budgets 281–2
hours 281
death 297
debating skills 282
deprivation 281
power and 288–9
power struggles 290
rivalry 278, 279–80
Glorious Revolution 179, 180–5
Gloucester Cathedral 43
gluttony 86
GOGGS (Government Offices, Great George Street) 295
gold 237–8
Good Parliament 88
Goodman, Dean Gabriel 141
Gordon, Lord George 221, 222–3, 224
Gordon riots 221–4`
gossip 173, 249
Gothic style 51, 55, 207, 267, 268, 269, 272
Government Offices, Great George Street (GOGGS) 295
Great Chamber 127
Great Contract 152
Great Council 63
Great George Street 295
Great Hall *see* Westminster Hall; Whitehall Palace
Great Palace *see* Westminster Hall
Great Reform Act 258
Great Scotland Yard 69
Great Tom of Westminster 84
Greece 348
green boxes 282
Grenville, George 227
Greville, Charles 257
Grey, Charles, Earl 246, 255, 256, 258
Grey, Lady Jane 135
downfall 135
Grey, Sir Edward 303
Groom of the Stool 110–11, 128
Guardian 195
Gulf War, First 344
Gundulf, Bishop of Rochester 33
Gunpowder Plot 146–50
Gwyn, Nell 174

Hague, Ffion 305
Hague, William 234

Haig, Douglas, Earl 306
Hales, John 142
Halifax, Marquess of (George Savile) 184
Halley's Comet 22
Hamilton, Emma, Lady 242
Hamilton, Ian 331
Hampden, Elizabeth 173
Hampden, John 157, 160
Handel, George Frideric 198, 231–2
Hansard 247
Hansard, Thomas Curson 247
Hardie, Keir 311
    attire 311
Harley, Robert, Earl of Oxford 193, 194
Harold I 8
    burials 8–9
    family and 9, 29
Harold II 19
    omens 22
Harris, Tim 185
Harthacnut 8, 9
Harvey, Barbara 86
Hastings, Warren 234
    trial 234, 235
Hattersley, Roy 314, 316
Hawksmoor, Nicholas 207
Hawley, Robert 99
Hay, James 152
Hayter, Sir George 258–9
Healy, Tim 291
Heath, Sir Edward 336, 337
Heinrich V (Henry), Holy Roman
        Emperor 30
Hennessy, Peter, Lord, 25, 204, 305, 330,
        334
Henrietta Maria of France 157
Henry I 28, 29–30
    coronation 29
    death 30
    expenditure 30
    family and 30–1
    retinue 30
Henry II 37, 38–9
    coronation 37
    Crown and Church 37–8
    expenditure 46, 48–9
    family and 39–40
Henry III 17, 45–7, 49–50, 51, 52–3, 54,
        55, 58, 63, 78, 85

burials 51–2, 54–5, 77
coronations 43
court 47
death 54
expenditure 45, 52, 53
    protests 53–4
    schism 63, 64
family and 47, 54, 64
fear 64–5
lost claims 65
power struggles 65, 65, 66
protests 65
rivalry 53
Henry IV
    coronation 109
    legitimacy 95
    rivalry 94
Henry IV Part II 95
Henry V 97
Henry VI 111
Henry VII 108, 111, 112
    accessibility 110
    burial 113
    coronation 109–10
    court 110
    family and 109, 111, 113
        legitimacy 109–10
    legitimacy 109, 111
    pretenders 110
    security 110–11
Henry VII Chapel 111–13
    bomb 324
    fan-vaulted roof 112
    mausoleums 113
    scope 109, 112
Henry VIII 115, 117–18, 121, 128–9
    accessibility 127–8
    Crown and Church 117, 118–19, 123,
        124–5, 126
    death 129
    decline 129
    dissolution 126
    expenditure 126–7
    family and 116–17, 118, 119, 120, 125,
        127–8
        legitimacy 123
        power and 124
    power and 118
    tennis 121

Henry VIII 117
Henry of Huntingdon 7–8, 28
Henry of Reyns 52, 60
Herbert, Abbot 32
hereditary peers 336
Herland, Hugh 83–4, 93
Heseltine, Michael, Lord 343, 344, 345
　resignation 343
High Table 49
Hitler, Adolf 318
Hobhouse, John Cam 262, 263, 264
Holbein, Hans 127–8
Holbein Gate 118, 120, 127
Homberger, Eric 307
Home Rule Bills 291–2
Horse Guards building 207, 208, 209
House of Commons 66, 67, 282, 337–8
　appeasement 319
　attire 227–8
　benches 134
　bombs 287, 326, 327
　debating skills 278
　defiance 170
　disparities 271, 275
　enfranchisement 255, 256–7, 258–9,
　　285
　exclusion 255
　　protests 256
　expenditure 133, 347–8
　　disparities 87
　　expenses scandals 255, 347–8
　　scope 185
　fear 237
　fire 326
　free speech and 216–17, 218, 219–20
　hours 278, 282
　laxity 228
　lobby system 290
　location 87, 327, 329
　maces 170, 343
　MP numbers 350
　MP payroll 350
　power and 162, 165
　power struggles 157–8, 161
　prime minister in 313
　protests 221, 222–3, 291
　rebuilding 131, 134, 192–3, 328
　　constraint on 239–40, 259
　　galleries 271

　lobbies 271
　renounced peers 336
　revolt 312–13
　scope 88, 133–4, 157, 269–70
　security 163, 351
　Serjeants at Arms 170
　Speakers 88–9, 110, 133, 161, 241, 269,
　　313
　spoiling tactics 288–9
　strangers' gallery 217, 220, 228, 240
House of Commons, 1833, The 258–9
House of Lords 145
　enfranchisement 257–8
　expenditure 87
　location 87, 327, 329
　reform 301, 337, 350
　scope 269
　trial 249, 251
　　protests 251
　　security 250–1
　woolsack 67
Household Words 283
Howard, Henry, Earl of Northampton 153
Howard, Thomas, Duke of Norfolk 143–4
Howe, Geoffrey, Lord 343
Howman, Abbot John 138
Hughes Hughes, William 262
Hugo the Illuminator 79
Hugolin 12–13
Hume, David 214
Humphrey of Lambhythe 98
Hundred Years' War 75
Hungerford, Sir Thomas 88
Hunter, John 233–4

I Was Glad 296
Immortal Seven 180
impeachment 88
impositions 152
Imworth, Richard 99–100
income tax 237
India Office 294–5
industrial revolution 236
inflation 336–7
Innocent II, Pope 33
insanity test 247
international summits 285–6, 315
IRA 338, 344–5
Ireland 181, 255

laxity 178
national identity 292
  civil war 290–1
  downfall 291
  power play 290
  protests 291
  spoiling tactics 288–9
  terror campaigns 287–8, 289, 290,
    338–9, 344–5
  union and 239
  warfare 160
Irish National Liberation Army 338–9
Irving, Washington 254
Isabella, Empress 47

Jacobitism 192
James, Henry 283
James II 176, 180
  downfall 176, 181–3
  exclusion 176–7
  family and 176–7, 179, 180, 181–2, 183
  laxity 175
  power and 179–80
  power struggles 181
  protests 182
James VI and I 146, 154, 155, 156
  court 152–3
  expenditure 152
  family and 151, 152, 154–5, 156
  free speech and 152
  legitimacy 146
  retinue 151–2
  security 146–7, 149
  union and 146, 151–2
Janyns, Robert 112
Jay, Douglas 329
Jay, Peter 197
Jerdan, William 243, 245
Jerusalem Chamber 85, 95
Jewel Tower 84
Jewish community 41
John, King 22, 42, 43
  coronation 42
  expenditure 42–3
John of Droxford 72
John of Gaunt 88
Johnson, Samuel 216–17
joint sovereignty 183
Jones, Inigo 154–5

Jones et al., Terry 100
jousting 121, 139
jubilees 293–4, 347

Kent, William 199, 202, 204, 208
King, Anthony 347
King James Bible 151
King Street Gate 127
King's Bench 49
King's Body Guard, The 150
King's Chamber
  rebuilding 78
  scope 78, 79
  state bed 78–9
King's Champions 92
King's Council 46–7, 125
King's Ditch 4
Kirby, Christopher 177
Kit-Cat Club 192
Knyghton, Henry 8

La Estoire de Seint Aedward le Rei 14, 15
Labelye, Charles 210
Labour 311, 313, 329, 330
  coalition 322–3, 348, 316
  disparities 314
  downfall 316
  revolt 312–13
  scope 312
  see also New Labour
Lady Chapel 51 see also Henry VII Chapel
Lamb, Lady Caroline 208–9
Lambeth Palace 115
Lamont, Norman, Lord 345
Land of Hope and Glory 296
Lanfranc, Archbishop of Canterbury 21
Langham, Abbot Simon 84–5
Lantern 325
Latimer, William 88
Latin language 87–8
Laud, William 159
Laudes Regiae 19
law 39, 116 see also individual terms
Law Courts 253, 254
Lawson, Nigel, Lord 342, 343
Lee, Sir Henry 139
Lenthall, William 157, 161
Lesser Hall 12
Liber Regalis 91

Liberal Democrats 348–9
Liberals 297
    coalitions 304, 306–7, 312, 316
    disparities 281
    enfranchisement 285
    power and 296
    power struggles 290
Licensing Act 215–16
Lilburne, John 159
Lilliburlero 181, 205
Litlyngton, Abbot Nicholas 85, 99
Litlyngton Missal 85
Little Sanctuary 98–9
    belfry tower 98
Liverpool, Lord (Robert Jenkinson) 251
Lloyd George, David, Earl 303, 304
    advisers 305
    budget 299–300
    coalitions 300, 305, 306–7
    downfall 312
    enfranchisement 306
    family and 304
    laxity 304–5, 312
    power struggles 306–7
    presidency and 305
    rivalry 304
Lloyd George, Frances, Countess (*nee*
    Stevenson) 304–5
Llywelyn ap Gruffud 64, 67
lobbies
    murder 243–5
    scope 270, 271
lobby system 290
London 6 *see also individual terms*
London, John 97
    death 98
London Evening Post 219
London Gazette 193–4
London Magazine 216, 220–1
London Spy, The 186
Londonderry, Lady (Edith Vane-Tempest-
    Stewart) 314
Londonderry, Lord (Charles
    Vane-Tempest-Stewart) 314
Long Parliament 159
Longditch 4
Lord North Street 197
Lord Protector 171–2
lotteries 210

Louis, Dauphin 43
Louis IX (France) 65
    rivalry 53
Louis XIV (France) 176, 179–80
Lovelace, Richard 161–2
Lovell, Thomas 110
Lucius, 'King' 6
Lucy, Henry 279, 288–9, 291, 301
Luttrell, Colonel Henry 218
Lutyens, Sir Edwin Landseer 307
Lynn, William 244

Macaulay, Thomas 256–7
MacDonald, James Ramsay 312–13, 314,
    315
    coalition 316
    downfall 316
    family and 314
    power and 311
    TV 315
maces
    authority and 170
    protests 343
Mackreth, John 196–7
Macleod, Iain 336
Macmillan, Harold, Earl of Stockton 184,
    314, 320, 322, 333–4, 335–6, 341,
    345
    family and 333
    power and 333
MacNaghton, Daniel 247
MacNaghton Rules 247
Macpherson, Sir John 223, 224
Mad Parliament 64
Magna Carta 43
Major, Sir John 344
Malcolm, James Peller 55
Margaret, Queen of Scots 69–70
Markiewicz, Constance, Countess 312
Marochetti, Baron Carlo 41–2
Marshal, Richard, Earl of Pembroke 48
Martin, Rector of Rotherhithe 23
Martin, Sir Leslie 334–5
Mary, Queen of Scots
    burials 151
    legitimacy 143–4
    treason and 144–5
Mary I (Tudor) 128, 135, 138
    coronation 135–6

Crown and Church 135
  family and 135, 137–8
    legitimacy 136
    revolt 136, 137
Mary II 179
  burial 186
  coronations 183, 184
  death 185–6, 346
  family and 183, 184
  legitimacy 183
Mary of France 118
Mary of Modena 180, 181–2
Masque of Blackness, The 154
Matilda, Empress 30–1
  civil war 31
Matilda, Queen 29
Maudling, Reginald 336, 338
mausoleums 77–8, 113
Melbourne, Lord (William Lamb) 263
Melbourne House 208–9
Mellitus, Bishop of London 23
'Messiah' 231–2
Methodist Central Hall 296
Metropolitan Police 69
Middlesex Journal 219
Middleton, Catherine, Duchess of
    Cambridge 346–7
migration 39
military coup 163
military displays 121, 124–5, 137, 139
Miller, John 219
Milton, John 170
miners 329
Ministry of Defence 330–1
missals 85, 108–9
mistrust in politicians 347
mobs *see* protests and mobs
Model Parliament 68
Monck, George, Duke of Albemarle 172
monetarism 342
Monthly Magazine 259
More, Sir Thomas 98
  trial 123–4
Moritz, Carl P. 228
Morning Chronicle 220
Morning Post 240
mortar bombs 344–5
Mortimer, Roger, Earl of March 75
mosaic pavement 57–8

Mosley, Oswald 196–7
Mowbray, Anne 111
Mrs Dalloway 273
Munich crisis 318–20
murder 48, 146–50, 152–3, 243–5, 247,
    289
  protests and 245–6
  trial 246
  uncertainty 100–1, 102–3
Murymouth, John 97

Nash, John 254
national debt 185, 233, 237
  crash and 197–8, 205
National Economic Development Council
    (Neddy) 334
National Government 316
nationalization 329
navy
  expenditure 185
  press gangs 210
  victory 241, 242
Neave, Airey 338–9
Neddy (National Economic Development
    Council) 334
Neil, Andrew 336
Nelson, Admiral Horatio 241
  death 241–2
neo-classical style 254
Netherlands 181
New Labour 345
New Palace Yard 25
  etymology 25
  exclusion 285
Newcastle, Duke of (Thomas Pelham-
    Holles) 213, 214
Newton, Sir Isaac 197
  burial 198–9
Nicolson, Sir Harold 327
1922 committee 312
Norden, John 8
Norman Britain 11, 19, 29 *see also*
    individual terms
Norman style 13–15, 26–7
Norris, Henry 124
North, Frederick, Lord 221, 229
  free speech and 218–19, 220–1
  protests 222–3, 224
  warfare 224–5

North Briton 218
Norway 322

Oates, Titus 177
O'Connell, Daniel 276
O'Donnell, Sir Gus 349
Offa, King 32
Official Secrets Bill 301–2
Old Admiralty 209, 295
Old Bailey 246
Old Palace Yard 154
Old Queen Street 196, 296
Oliver, Richard 219
Oliver Twist 259
Onslow, Colonel George 219
operations 233–4
Order of the Bath 112
Ordo 7
Osbert of Clare, Prior 3, 13, 32, 33, 34
O'Shea, Kitty 291
Overbury, Sir Thomas 152–3
overcrowding 146, 158, 209
    easing 211–12, 238–9, 283
    laxity 158

Page, William 142
pageant 211
Painted Chamber
    rebuilding 78
    scope 78, 79
    state bed 78–9
Palace of Westminster 8, 42–3
    expenditure 45
    location 12
        disparities 12
    rebuilding 11, 12, 38–9
        expenditure 45, 48–9
    scope 80
    see also individual terms
Palladian style 154–5
Palmerston, Lord (Henry John Temple)
    280–1
    hours 281
pamphlets 194
    free speech and 142, 193
    partisanship 195
Pankhurst, Emmeline 315
    family and 298
papal power 20, 22, 24, 33, 57, 137

consecration 22–3
Crown and 117, 118–19, 124–5
    schism 123
rivalry 38
schism 140, 143
tithe of salmon 23–4
Paris, Matthew 47–8, 53–4, 63
Parkside 120–1
parliament 63, 64, 66–7, 94–5, 171, 184,
    192, 293
    accessibility 210
    accommodation 183–4
    Black Rod 337
    bombs 326, 327
    budgets 299–300
    Cabinet 175–6, 185, 233
    constraint on 133, 177–8, 179, 239, 259
    deprivation 259
    disparities 159, 315–16, 350
    elections 215, 218, 230–1, 290, 300, 312
    enfranchisement 298–9, 300–1
    exclusion 285
    expenditure 184–5
        disparities 63, 64, 68, 142, 152, 159
        scope 185
    fire 261–4, 267
    free speech and 152
        disparities 142
    language 87–8
    laxity 215
    limitations 88, 172
    lobbies 243–4
    location 94
        uncertainty 68
    nepotism 215
    official reports 247
    patronage 215, 255
    penal code 215
    petitions 68
    pollution and 283–4
    power struggles 129, 159–61
    primacy 351
    protests 75, 238
    rebuilding
        cell 272
        competition 268
        disparities 270
        expenditure 268
        extension at river 270

lobbies 270
longevity 268, 270
scope 267, 268–9, 270–1, 272
towers 268, 272, 273–4
ventilation 271
redress 65
revolt 160, 277–8
schism 64
scope 67, 68, 75, 132, 164, 176–7, 191, 269
security 146, 147–9, 150, 160
Speakers 88
summonses 65–6
treason and 94
trials 88
see also individual Houses, parties and names
Parliament Act 301
parliamentary rolls 68
Parnell, Charles Stewart 288
downfall 291
power play 290
Parris, Matthew 336
Parry, Sir Hubert 296
Parry, William 144
Patrick, Philippa 86
Patten, Chris, Lord 336, 342
Paving Acts 204
Pax Britannica 294–5
Pearce, Edward 258
Peasants' Revolt 97, 99–100
Peel, Sir Robert 275, 276, 277, 278
deprivation 277
downfall 277
rivalry 277
security 247
penal code 215
pensions 298
Pepys, Samuel 113, 172–3, 174
gossip 173
wigs 175
Perceval, Spencer 243, 246
burial 246
murder 243–6
Percy, Thomas 147, 148–9
Perry, James 220
Philip II (France) 41
Philip II (Spain) 136, 137–8
attire 137

military displays 137
pilgrimage of grace 124
pilgrimages 13
Pitt the Elder, William, Earl of Chatham 212, 227
Pitt the Younger, William 227, 230, 236, 237–8, 239, 240–1, 242
burial 242
death 242
duel 196
expenditure 229–30, 233, 237
family and 227, 234
fear 237, 238
laxity 228
operation 233–4
power and 228–30
rivalry 229, 230, 234, 236
protests 230
sexual orientation 234
Pittite terror 237, 238
plague 80–1, 157
Plantagenet, Geoffrey 31
Pole, Cardinal Reginald 137–8
police 69, 287–8, 289–90
inaction and 300
protests and 308
Political State of Britain, The 216
poll tax 97, 99–100, 342–3
pollution 283–4
Pomp and Circumstance 295–6
Portcullis House 335
Portillo, Michael 336
Powell, John Enoch 333–4, 336, 337, 338
praemunire 117
Presence Chamber 127
presidency 305, 349
press 193–4, 255, 257, 262, 267, 283–4, 293–4, 307, 309–10
constraint on 240
expenses and 255, 347–8
free speech and 193, 216–17, 218–19
galleries for 271
lobby system 290
partisanship 194
power and 316–17, 347, 348
scope 194–5, 215, 240, 241, 304, 318, 330
press gangs 210
press secretary 330

Princes in the Tower
  murder 102–3
  pretender 110
  survival 103
printing 107–9
  free speech and 142
Prior, James, Lord 342
Privy Chamber 110–11
  scope 127–8
Privy Council 46–7, 176
  scope 125–6
Privy Council building 254
privy gardens 127
Privy Wardrobes 84
prostitutes 212, 281
Protestant reformation 144
  accommodation 140
  constraint from 132–4
  scope 131–3, 135
  security 146–50
Protestant wind 181
protests and mobs 53–4, 65, 75, 97,
    99–100, 161, 182, 210, 217,
    219–20, 230, 238, 251, 256, 258,
    291, 298–9, 342–3
  death and 224, 245–6, 301
  inaction and 300
  penalties 45–6
  race and 41
  scope 31, 215, 221–4, 300–1, 308, 351
Provisional IRA 338, 344–5
Prynne, William 159
public relations 111, 203, 349
publishing 107–9
pubs and inns 158
Pugin, Augustus Welby 267, 268, 269,
    272–3
Pulteney, William, Earl of Bath 74
Puritans 159
  power and 162
Pym, Francis, Lord 337, 342
Pym, John 157, 160
Pyx Chamber 15

Queen Anne's Footstool 196
Queen Anne's Gate 196
Queen Mary's Steps 179
Queen's Bench 49
Queen's Body Guard, The 150

race riots 41
radio 319
  impartiality and 315
  scope 314–15, 317, 321, 323, 327
Railton, Rev David 308
Raleigh, Sir Walter 153–4
  burial 154
  death 154
  trial 153
Ramsey, William 80
re-enactment society 167
recession 316, 317
red boxes 282
'Red Flag, The' 313
Reform Bills 256, 257, 258
Regency 236, 250 see also George IV
Reid, Dr David Boswell 271
Reith, John, Lord 315
Remembrance Day 307–9
Restoration 172–4, 175–6
  exclusion 176–8
  laxity 174–5
  reversal and 176
revolt 43, 136, 138, 160, 277–8, 312–13
  mobs see protests and mobs
  penalties 137
  pillage 162
  revolution 179, 180–5, 236
Reynolds, Frederick 222
Richard, Archbishop of Canterbury 38
Richard, Duke of York 101, 102
  murder 102–3
  pretender 110
  survival 103
Richard I (the Lionheart) 39–40, 41–2
  coronation 40
    omens 40–1
Richard II 92–3, 94, 100
  confession 97
  coronation
    legitimacy 91–2
    safeguards 91
    scope 91
  downfall 94–5
  family and 92
  rivalry 94
Richard III 101, 102, 108
  coronation 102
    legitimacy 109

Richard of Pudlicote 72
    death 73
Richard of Ware, Abbot 57, 59
Ridolfi Plot 143–4
riots *see* protests and mobs
robberies 72–3
    penalties 73
Roberts, Alfred 342
Roberts, Sir Frank 319
Robinson, Nick 203, 349
Roger, Archbishop of York 38
Roger of Howden 40
Roman Britain 5, 6
Romanesque style 13–15, 26–7
Rosebery, Lord (Archibald Primrose) 169
Rosser, Gervase 99
Rotheram, Thomas 101
rotten boroughs 255
Rotten Parliament 255
roundheads 160
Royal Aquarium 284
royal household 67–8
Royal Peculiar status 140–1
royalists 161–2
    downfall 169–70
Rubens, Peter Paul 155–6
Rump Parliament 163, 170, 172
Ryder, Richard, Lord 345
Ryder, Dudley, Earl of Harrowby 196
Rye House Plot 178
Ryle, Dean Herbert 308

Sacheverell, Dr Henry 193
St Augustine 22
St Benedict's Chapel 98
St Catherine's Chapel 38
St James's Palace 165
St James's Park 174
St John's Church 196
St Margaret's Church 16, 108, 327–8
    anchorites 97
    burials 154
    constraint on 126
    defiance 132
    rebuilding 16
    revolt 138
St Peter 24
    miracles 22–3
St Peter's Church *see* Westminster Abbey

St Stephen's Chapel
    deconsecration 132–4
    forced labour 81
    rebuilding 79
    scope 79–80, 81
St Stephen's Cloister 80
St Stephen's Hall 270
    enfranchisement 299
Salisbury, fifth Marquess of, ('Bobbety')
    33
Salisbury, third Marquess of, (Robert
    Gascoyne-Cecil) 291, 293
salmon, tithe 23–4
sanctuary 98–9, 101–2
    desecration 99–100
    disparities 103
    limitations 100, 103
    scope 99, 100
    uncertainty 100
Sandys, Sir Samuel 201
Sargent, Sir Orme 320
Sarum Missal 108–9
satire 178, 181, 204–5, 218–19, 220–1,
    230, 238, 282, 318, 333
scaremongering 237, 238
school 85
Scotland 69, 70, 146, 178, 331–2
    union and 146, 151–2, 192–3
    warfare 70–1, 73–4, 75, 221
        expenditure 159
Scotland Yard 69–70
Scotland Yard (police) 289–90
Scott, Sir Gilbert 328
Scott, Sir Walter 242, 252
scriptoria 31
scrofula 56
Sebert of the East Saxons 23, 24
Second Reform Act 285
Second World War *see* World War II
secrecy 301–2, 336
Septennial Act 215
Serjeants at Arms 170
sewerage 283–4
Sexby, Edward 171
Seymour, Jane 124
Shaftesbury, Earl of (Anthony Ashley-
    Cooper) 176–7
    downfall 178
Shakell, John 99

Shakespeare, William 95, 117
shaven heads 28
Shawcross, Sir Hartley 329
Shelley, Percy Bysshe 351
Short Parliament 159
shuttle diplomacy 318–19
Sidney, Henry 180–1
Simeon, Simon 79
Simpson, Wallis 317
Sindercombe, Miles 171
single currency 343
Sketches by Boz 262
Smith, John 345
Smith, J. T. 239
Smith, William 243–4
Smith Square 196–7
Snell, John 261
Soane, Sir John 253–4, 264
Somerset, Countess of (Frances Carr) 152, 153
Somerset, Duke of (Edward Seymour)
    downfall 133
    power and 131, 132
Somerset, Earl of (Robert Carr) 152–3
Somme, battle 304
South Sea Bubble crisis 197–8, 205
Southwell, Sir Richard 136
Spain
    revolt 136–7
    warfare 145
Spanish Armada 145
Speakers 88, 110, 133, 241, 269, 313
    personal responsibility and 88–9, 161
special advisers 305, 342, 349–50
Special Branch 289, 290
Spectator, The 194–5
spies 144, 148
spin 3, 34, 7, 124–5, 127–8, 146, 170, 181, 192, 194, 198, 231, 318, 349
    forgeries and 3, 32, 33
    longevity 3, 7
spoiling tactics 288–9
springs 4
stage 215–16
Stangate 6
Stanley, Dean Arthur Penrhyn 3, 4, 8, 16, 23–4, 55, 59, 213, 263
Stanley, Sir William 110
Stanley, Venetia 298, 318

Stansgate, Margaret, Lady (Margaret Wedgwood Benn) 297
Star Chamber 116
Steele, Richard 194
    downfall 195
    partisanship 194, 195
Stephen, King 31
Stigand, Archbishop of Canterbury 17, 20–1
stock market crashes 197–8, 205, 315–16
Stone of Destiny
    chair 69, 71
        removal 331–2
    removal 70–1
    safeguards 322
Stow, John 4
Strafford, Earl of (Thomas Wentworth) 160
Strange Death of Liberal England 302
strangers' gallery 217, 220
    constraint on 228, 240
streams 4
Strong, Roy 20, 131, 198, 332
Strype, John 137
Stuart, Charles (Bonnie Prince Charlie) 214
Stuart, Frances 174
Stuart, James (Old Pretender) 192
Stubbe, John 142
Suez crisis 332–3
Suffolk, Earl of (Thomas Howard) 148–9
suffragettes 298–9, 300–1
Sulcard 13
Swalwe, John 93
Swift, Jonathan 194, 195
Sybil or The Two Nations 276
synods 21

tally sticks 261
Tanner, Lawrence 98, 103, 107, 252, 321–2, 325–6
Tatler 194
tax and duty 30, 185, 221, 233
    Corn Laws 277
    Danegeld 13
    disparities 87
    expenses and 347–8
    impositions 152
    income tax 237

poll tax 97, 99–100, 342–3
  protests 217
tea 221, 233
10 Downing Street 201, 323–4, 325
  appeasement 319–20
  bombs 324, 344–5
  door 203
  limitations 297, 314
  numbering 204
  protests 223, 224
  rebuilding 239, 335
  scope 202–3, 229
  security 345
tennis 121
terrorism 287–8, 289, 290, 338–9, 344–5,
  351
Terry, Quinlan 203
Test Act 176
Thames, River 3–4, 145, 182, 270
  embankment 284
  ferries 5–6, 22, 209
  fire 263
  flooding 48, 284–5
  fording 5–6
  frozen 211
  military display 124–5
  pageant 211
  pollution 283–4
  tide turning and 7–8
Thatcher, Margaret, Lady 339, 341, 342
  advisers 342
  downfall 343, 344
  family and 342
  poll tax 342–3
  power and 341–2
Thatcherism 342
Thirlby, Bishop Thomas 135
Thompson, Roger 219
Thompson, Walter 325, 327
Thorney Island 4, 5, 6, 351
  etymology 4
  location 4–5
  scope 5
  staging point 5
  see also individual terms
Thurley, Simon 117, 118, 126, 128, 135
Thurloe, John 171
Tierney, George 196
tile pavement 60

Tillemans, Peter 192
tiltyard 121, 139
Times, The 263, 283–4, 293–4, 307, 310
Torel, William 78
Tories 178, 193, 194, 195
  etymology 178
  schism 255–6
  see also Conservatives
Torrigiano, Pietro 112
Tothill 5
Tothill Fields 5
Tothill Street 5
tourism 158, 341
Tower of London 102–3
Townshend, Charles, Viscount 198
trade 5, 6
  business 87, 107–8, 129, 276
  wool 83
Trafalgar, battle 241, 242
treason 94, 123, 125, 143–4, 149–50, 153,
  163–4
  disparities 164
  penalties 100, 110, 123–4, 125, 144–5,
    150, 154, 165–7
  safeguards 165
Treasury
  bombs 324
  rebuilding 204
  scope 204
treasury 72–3
Treatise on the Laws and Customs of
  England 39
Treaty of Dover 176
Tresham, Francis 148
Tresilian, Sir Robert 100
Triennial Act 185
Trollope, Anthony 282–3
Tudor, Margaret 146
Turner, J. M. W. 263
TV 315, 332, 349
Twelfth Night festivities 154
Tyburn, River 4

undercrofts 60–1, 116
underground railway 284
Underhill, Edward 136
unemployment 336–7
Union of the Crowns 146
  imbalances 146, 151–2

limitations 151
Union Jack 151
United States 315
   warfare 221, 224–5
      expenditure 233
Unknown Warrior 308, 309
Unreported Parliament 217
Ushborne, William 97
utility works 284

Van Dyck, Anthony 158–9
Vardy, John 208
Victoria, Queen 275, 293
   jubilees 293–4
Victoria Embankment 284
Victoria Tower 273–4
Viking Britain 6
Vita Aedwardi Regis 11, 33
Voltaire 198–9

Wall Street crash 315–16
Wallace, Sir William 73
Walpole, Horace, Earl of Orford 211,
   213–14
Walpole, Sir Robert, Earl of Orford 191–2,
   193, 197–8, 199, 201, 203, 204–5
   bribery 205–6
   downfall 217
   expenditure 217
   family and 205
   free speech and 193, 215–16
   patronage 205, 206
   power and 198, 201–2
Walsingham, Sir Francis 144
Walter, Hubert, Archbishop of Canterbury
   42
Walter of Durham 71
Walters, Alan 342
Walton, Watkin 93
War Office 295
Warbeck, Perkin 110
Ward, Ned 186
Warden, The 282–3
Washbourne, Richard 93
Watling Street 5
wealth 31, 158
Weir, Alison 37
Wellington, Duke of (Arthur Wellesley)
   241, 255–6, 258

downfall 256
Wentworth, Peter 142
Westminster 187, 240, 341
   abandonment 72, 75, 351
   disparities 158
   etymology 6, 24
   image 3, 351
   location 3, 11, 37
   power and 351
   rebuilding 11–12
   royalty in residence 67
   see also individual terms
Westminster Abbey 6–7, 8, 19, 63, 66,
   73–4, 241–2, 312, 345–6
   Abbot's House 85, 95, 101–2
   anchorites 97–8
   bombs 326
   burials 8–9, 13, 17, 24, 33, 38, 51–2,
      54–5, 74, 89, 92, 102–3, 111, 113,
      146, 151, 172, 186, 195, 198–9,
      213, 242, 308, 309
   business 87, 107–8
   canonization 33–4
   Chapter House 58–61
   cloisters 15, 28
   concerts 231–2
   consecration 16, 22–3, 54
   constraint on 21, 135
   coronations 19–20, 25–6, 37, 40, 42,
      70, 102, 120, 139, 157, 172–3, 183,
      198, 213–14
      broadcasts 317, 332
      crown jewels 172
      exclusion 252–3
      fire 20
      haste 29, 31
      High Table 49
      legitimacy 91–2, 109–10
      manifestos 29
      oak chair 69, 71, 322, 331, 332
      omens 40–1
      safeguards 91
      scope 91, 251–2, 296
      tension 19, 20
      visibility 20
   decline 32
   disparities 24, 283
   dissolution and 126, 140
   education 126

etymology 24
exclusion 16, 22–3
expenditure 283
forgeries 32
free speech and 159
gatehouse 85–6
Henry VII Chapel 109, 111–13, 324
Lantern 325
laxity 72, 86
limitations 11
location 12
longevity 3
mausoleums 77–8
miracles 21–2
missal 85
mosaic pavement 57–8
museum 15
nave 85
oak door 15
pillage 162
precedence 54
Pyx Chamber 15
re-founding 126, 138
rebuilding 11, 13, 15, 16, 51, 84, 85
    disparities 55, 56
    expenditure 13, 52, 53–4
    scope 13–14, 52, 55–6
    uncertainty 14
relic 53
retable 56–7
rivalry 3, 159
Royal Peculiar status 140–1
safeguards 321–2
St Benedict's Chapel 98
St Catherine's Chapel 38
sanctuary 98–100, 103
scope 14, 15–16, 26, 31–2, 51, 74–5, 85,
    87, 346
scriptoria 31
self-sufficiency 86–7
tithe of salmon 23–4
towers 14–15, 207–8
treasury 72–3
wealth 31
weddings 346–7 *see also individual
    names*
Westminster Bridge 207, 209, 210, 211
    constraint on 210–11
    expenditure 210

location 210
protests 210
warfare 210
Westminster bubble 351
Westminster Hall 26–7, 39, 49, 94, 253,
    270
    bombs 287, 326, 338
    coronations
        banqueting 27, 48, 120, 252
        Champions 252
        exclusion 253
        legitimacy 92
    explosion 210
    fire 263, 326
    flooding 48
    investiture 171–2
    location 26
    lying-in-state 328, 346
    rebuilding 93, 111, 253
        hammer-beam roof 93–4
    scope 26, 49, 93, 119, 234–5
    shaven heads 28
    stained glass window 347
    trials 71, 73, 152–3, 193, 234, 235
        security 163
        treason and 123–4, 143, 144, 149–50,
            163–4
Westminster Retable 56–7
Westminster School 85, 141
    bombs 325–6
Westminster village 351
Wheatcroft, Geoffrey 350
Wheble, John 219
Whigs 178, 192, 193, 195
    constraint on 249
    etymology 178
    power and 215
    rivalry 218
    see also Liberal Democrats; Liberals
White, William 278–9, 281, 282
White Hall 12
Whitehall Palace 118, 121, 165–6, 174,
    183, 184, 191
    Banqueting House 151, 154–6, 184
    business 129
    Cockpit Passage 121
    Court Gate 120
    decline 162
    employment 129

etymology 117–18
fire 115, 184, 186–7
Great Chamber 127
Great Hall 127
Holbein Gate 118, 120, 127
King Street Gate 127
overcrowding and 158
Parkside 120–1
Presence Chamber 127
Privy Chamber 127–8
privy gardens 127
Queen Mary's Steps 179
revolt 136
scope 120, 121–2, 126–7, 128–9, 139
security 171
tennis 121
tiltyard 121, 139
wind vane 179, 181
Whitehall and the Privy Garden 212
Who? Who? ministry 278
Widmore, Richard 8, 31
wigs 175, 228
Wilberforce, William 227–8
Wilkes, John 217–18
free speech and 218, 219
William, Prince, Duke of Cambridge 346–7
William I (the Conqueror) 21, 22
coronation 19–20
fire 20
tension 19, 20
visibility 20
family and 25–6
power and 19
crown-wearing 25
William II (Rufus) 26, 27, 28
boorish dandyism 27
coronation 25–6
court
laxity 27–8
shaven heads 28
death 28
family and 28–9
laxity 28
power and 26
retinue 28
sexual orientation 28
William III (Orange) 180–1, 182–3, 184–5
coronations 183, 184
expenditure 184–5, 191

family and 185–6
William IV 256, 258, 264
William of Malmesbury 30
William of the Palace 72, 73
Williams, Dean John 159
Williams, Francis 330
Wilson, Harold, Baron Rievaulx 197, 336
devaluation 336
Wilson, Sir Horace 318–19
wind vane 179, 181
Winter, Thomas 147
death 150
Wolsey, Cardinal Thomas 115–16
downfall 117
women
anchorites 97
Cabinet 315
elections 312
enfranchisement 298–9, 300–1, 315
galleries and 228, 271
see also individual terms
Women's Social and Political Union
(WSPU) 298, 300
Woodfall, William 220
Woodville, Elizabeth 102
family and 101–2
sanctuary 101–2
wool trade 83
Woolf, Virginia 273
woolsack 67
Worcester, battle 169–70
Wordsworth, Dorothy 240
Wordsworth, William 240
workhouses 259
World War I 303, 304, 305–6, 312
Armistice 306
remembrance 307–9
Zeppelins 306
World War II 322, 346
air raids 324–7
Big Ben 321, 323
radio 321, 323
safeguards 321–2
victory 327–8
war rooms 321, 324–5, 327
Wraxall, Sir Nathaniel 224, 228–9
Wray, Sir Cecil 230–1
Wren, Sir Christopher 191, 192–3
Wright, John 147

WSPU (Women's Social and Political Union) 298, 300
Wulfstan, Bishop of Worcester 21–2
Wulnoth, Abbot 8
Wyatt, James 239–40
Wyatt, Sir Thomas 136–7

Yevele, Henry 83–4, 93
York Place 39, 115, 117

crypt 116
rebuilding 116
see also Whitehall Palace
Yorktown 224–5
Young England 276–7

'Zadok the Priest' 198, 231
Zeppelins 306